Management Science

An Introduction

David G. Dannenbring
Martin K. Starr

Graduate School of Business
Columbia University

McGraw-Hill Book Company

New York   St. Louis   San Francisco   Auckland   Bogotá   Hamburg
Johannesburg   London   Madrid   Mexico   Montreal   New Delhi   Panama   Paris
São Paulo   Singapore   Sydney   Tokyo   Toronto

MANAGEMENT SCIENCE: An Introduction

1234567890DODO8987654321

This book was set in Times Roman by Better Graphics. The editors were Donald G. Mason, Ellen R. Friedman, and Laura D. Warner; the design was done by Caliber Design Planning; the production supervisor was Charles Hess. New drawings were done by J & R Services, Inc.
R. R. Donnelley & Sons Company was printer and binder.

Library of Congress Cataloging in Publication Data

Dannenbring, David G
    Management science.

    (McGraw-Hill series in quantitative methods for management)
    Includes index.
    1. Management—Mathematical models. 2. Operations research. I. Starr, Martin Kenneth,
date   joint author. II. Title.
HD30.25.D36   658.4'034   80-22874
ISBN 0-07-015352-3

About the Authors

DAVID G. DANNENBRING is Associate Professor of Management Science at the Graduate School of Business, Columbia University. He received a B.S. in accounting at California State Polytechnic College–Pomona and a Ph.D. in business at Columbia. Professor Dannenbring taught at the University of North Carolina before accepting his present teaching appointment. He was previously employed as a financial accountant for Pacific Finance Company and served as a supply officer in the U.S. Navy. He has contributed articles to such professional journals as *Management Science, Decision Science, AIIE Transactions,* and the *Naval Logistics Review Quarterly.* At present he is the departmental editor for production and operations management for *Management Science* and an associate editor for *The Operations Management Newsletter.* He has been a consultant for several private and public organizations and has taught in various executive programs.

MARTIN K. STARR is Professor of Management Science at the Graduate School of Business, Columbia University. He received his B.S. at M.I.T. and his Ph.D. at Columbia. Professor Starr is editor-in-chief of the journal *Management Science* and a past president of The Institute of Management Sciences. He is consulting editor for the McGraw-Hill Series in Quantitative Methods for Management. In addition, he serves on the editorial board of *Behavioral Science,* the advisory board of the *Nijenrode Studies in Business,* and the academic advisory board of the *Journal of Management Studies,* and he is an editorial adviser to the *Operational Research Quarterly.* Professor Starr has written a number of well-known texts in operations management and management science and has contributed numerous papers in a variety of journals. He is a member of TIMS, ORSA, and the Academy of Management, the Design Methods Group, and the Society of Manufacturing Engineers Management Council, and has served as chairman of professional meetings for IFORS, TIMS, ORSA, and the Society for General Systems Research.

To Our Families

Contents

Part Two
Using Linear Programming to Solve Resource Allocation Problems

Part Three
Network Flow Problems

Part Five
Inventory Models

Part Six
Predictive Models

Preface

We begin this Preface by stating the obvious: There are numerous introductory management science texts. Yet many of our colleagues express dissatisfaction that there is no one *adequate* text. We set ourselves the goal of determining what is wanted—by most instructors—and then writing that book. Simply stated, what we believe is wanted is breadth of coverage, achieved at a relatively high and uniform level, but always accessible to beginners (no linear algebra or calculus prerequisites) by means of patient and detailed explanation which uses examples.

Design of the Book

The main differences in teaching approaches are by level and by division of materials. By level, our book occupies a unique position. It is designed to eliminate the effect of variability in student capabilities and motivation. Starting at the simplest level, it then stretches idea development and application to near the top of what is available in the text market. It does this for the broadest range of topics (as the Table of Contents indicates). The instructor can control the level, for any particular topic, by assigning a continuous sequence of pages with a cutoff when the level exceeds the course objectives. In other words, as development moves from simple to complete, there are no discontinuities requiring page-jumping.

For example, decision trees are first introduced at the conclusion of Chapter 2, for simple, single-stage problems. Sequential, multiple-stage decision trees are not treated until Chapter 3. Those instructors who require only a brief introduction to the use of decision trees can assign Chapter 2, omitting Chapter 3; those who wish to provide a more thorough treatment can assign both chapters; and those who prefer to skip coverage of decision trees can omit the last section of Chapter 2 and all of Chapter 3. No matter which choice is taken, the flow of the rest of the book is not disturbed.

Similar nondependent modularity is provided for many other topics in the book. Where possible, major topics have been subdivided into several chapters. For example, linear programming is covered in four chapters, decision analysis in three chapters, forecasting in two chapters, and inventory in two chapters. Where single chapters are used, we have attempted to organize the material with the more complex topics at the end so that they may be omitted, if the instructor so desires, without loss of continuity.

The division of materials differs among various schools. The typical breakdown is:

One-third programming, especially linear programming
One-third decision analysis
One-third miscellaneous topics (queuing, inventory, simulation, etc.)

Our book is structured to match the usual breakdown but, because of its breadth and attention to the patient development of all topics, the percentage of these divisions can be changed more easily than with other books. This meets the often expressed desire of our colleagues to have topical flexibility for matching course content with course objectives and student profiles. Thus, with this text, programming can readily be increased to about two-thirds of the course coverage. Similarly, decision analysis or miscellaneous topics can be accorded greater attention. In addition, miscellaneous topics can include separate chapters on heuristic programming, goal programming, forecasting methods (two chapters), simulation, and management information systems (MIS).

Chapters can be included and excluded as modules to satisfy different course plans. We believe that the extent to which our chapters are modularly structured is a unique feature of this text, as is the ease with which topical sequence can be altered. For example, decision making may follow or precede mathematical programming, without the awkward disruptions that can accompany chapter assignments made out of order.

Special Features

One of the most crucial goals we addressed was text readability for beginning students. We accomplish this by carefully explaining the nature of the problems that are tackled and resolved by each method. Using illustrative problems, we develop a conceptual basis for understanding each different topic. In the three categories of programming, decision analysis, and miscellaneous topics, we provide a great variety of problems. All of them deal, in one way or another, with utilization of resources. But the specific kinds of application (e.g., blending, inventory levels, service capacities) must be understood by students if they are to be motivated to read and understand the text material. We explore each of the diverse problem areas in detail, concentrating on relating problem solving to the realities of the appropriate managerial situation. With an understanding of why a problem exists, and how it relates to real management situations, students are motivated to study a new method that can resolve the problem.

We assiduously avoid viewing our world as techniques in search of a problem. Nor do we wish to enter competition for achieving mathematical elegance, by which we mean providing brief and terse explanations of ideas. We have instead tried to close every gap of understanding with patient, detailed explanation. The use (throughout the text) of examples to explain methods makes it difficult indeed to fall into the math language trap. Yet even difficult topics, such as integer and goal programming, are fully comprehensible to the students.

Throughout the text, particularly where the going may be tough for the students, Instant Replays are introduced. These are problem variants requiring new calculations of what was just explained. With answers provided, the Instant Replays generate self-checking feedback to the students about their comprehension of the material.

Numerous problems at the end of each chapter cover all areas of management, including both the profit and not-for-profit sectors. There are manufacturing-, service-, and government-focused problems. To assist students who are concentrating in various functional areas, the problems treat issues in finance, marketing, production, accounting, personnel, and so forth. (The Instructor's Manual provides information helpful in selecting problems for assignment, including an assessment of each problem's difficulty.)

The in-text examples are worked out in detail. Six case studies are presented as end-of-chapter supplements, providing application descriptions of material covered in the text. Computer applications are attached whenever feasible. Instructors can include these, or not, depending upon course objectives. Key words are listed at the end of each chapter, and a glossary is provided inside the front and back covers. Each chapter concludes with an overview of the material covered. Each overview takes a managerial perspective rather than simply recounting the text material.

Organization of the Book

The book is divided into six parts and 21 chapters. Although most of the topics covered will be quite familiar to instructors, there are several features that we feel deserve specific mention. Chapter 1 provides the framework for the management science process and walks the student through a simple example. By discussing the relationship of management science to the manager, with specific examples of successful applications, we attempt to build the students' motivation. Part One (Chapters 2 through 4) provides a comprehensive presentation of the use of management science in decision making. Of particular note is the inclusion of multiple-objective decision problems in Chapter 4.

Part Two, which includes Chapters 5 through 8, addresses linear programming problems and methods. From the beginning, students are shown how to use the computer to solve linear programming problems, including how to interpret output. Chapter 8 focuses on the use of goal programming to handle problems with multiple objectives.

Part Three (Chapters 9 and 10), provides a comprehensive review of general network flow problems, including transportation, transshipment, assignment, and minimal spanning tree problems. Part Four surveys other programming methods, such as integer programming (Chapter 11), dynamic programming (Chapter 12), and heuristics (Chapter 13). We feel that students will particularly enjoy the coverage of heuristics because it presents an opportunity for them to be creative in designing their own heuristic methods.

Inventory models are covered in Part Five, where Chapters 14 and 15 treat the traditional EOQ models and safety stock concepts, as well as considering computerized applications. A thorough discussion of material requirements planning is provided, including a review and comparison of heuristic ordering rules. Part Six (Chapters 16 through 20) concentrates on a broad variety of models used for making predictions. Chapter 16 covers the use of PERT/CPM for project planning and control. Chapter 17 reviews the use of waiting line, or queuing, models. Chapters 18 and 19, which examine the use of forecasting models, are certain to be of practical interest to almost all students. Chapter 18 treats extrapolation forecasting models, including moving average and exponential smoothing models. Chapter 19 reviews the use of explanatory models and includes regression and Markovian models. Chapter 20 covers simulation and contains three examples as well as a discussion of validation, experimental design, and analysis of results. The final chapter addresses MIS (management information systems), the organized data files that feed the management science models from inception to resolution. Often, the first part of the management science study is to define data needs.

Because of the previously described modular structure of this book, it can be used effectively for a one- or two-term sequence. In business schools, the level can be adjusted to be uniform for undergraduates above the freshman level, for graduate students at the basic introductory level, and also for an advanced elective. Industrial engineering courses span the same undergraduate and graduate levels. This text has been designed for repeat usage. It is our expectation and hope that experience with our text will provide much information about how to employ it more effectively the next time.

Text Supplements

We have taken special care to provide supplemental tools that will assist the instructor in using this text. The Instructor's Manual contains a number of features worth highlighting. Fully worked-out solutions, rather than just the final answers, are given for all problems. As mentioned above, we also provide helpful hints in selecting problems for student assignments. These include a brief description of the problems, an assessment of their level of difficulty, opportunity to modify problems, and connections between problems within a chapter or between chapters. In addition, we provide a bank of potential examination problems complete with solutions.

Sample course outlines are also included in the Instructor's Manual, and we have provided, on a chapter-by-chapter basis, suggestions and ideas for teaching the material based on our own experience. Where appropriate, we recommend supplemental readings. For those who wish to use case materials, we have identified a number of cases for potential student assignment, including those available in published case books as well as those from other sources such as the Intercollegiate Case Clearing House.

Another important supplement accompanying this text is a Study Guide designed to help students measure their progress by immediate feedback. The Study Guide contains an outline of important points for each chapter of the text, plus a variety of objective questions and short problems. Answers to the questions and problems are provided to help students in a prompt self-evaluation of their understanding of significant subject matter in each chapter.

Acknowledgments

We want to thank our reviewers. They were positive about our book, given that we address the weaknesses. We have tried our best to do this. Our appreciation goes to Milton Chen, San Diego State University; John J. Dinkel, Penn State University; John Fisk, SUNY at Albany; Janet C. Goulet, Wittenberg University; Edgar Hickman, University of South Carolina; Gene B. Iverson, University of South Dakota; Fred R. McFadden, University of Colorado; Grover Rodich, Portland State University; and George Schneller, Bernard Baruch College. Special acknowledgment is due Don Chatham of McGraw-Hill, who got us started; Don Mason, who helped us finish; and Ellen Friedman, who kept us on track throughout. Ellen's encouragement and many useful suggestions have had a measureable impact on the final product. We also wish to thank Laura Warner, Gail Hughes, and Celeste Thompson for their help and bright spirits.

David G. Dannenbring
Martin K. Starr

Management Science

An Introduction

1

The Nature of Management Science

The past three decades have seen a steady and at times spectacular growth in the development and application of management science. This has placed continually increasing demands on managers who may be called upon to participate in the design of, provide data for, or use the output from management science models. Of particular importance to these developments has been the phenomenal impact of the electronic computer on the traditional tasks of management.

What Is Management Science?

The term "management science" is not always clearly understood. We shall define it simply as the *application of scientific methodology, or principles, to management decisions*. One difficulty with this definition is the varied interpretations that can be applied to the term "scientific methodology." Methodology has a special meaning and is not to be confused with technology. Technology generally takes the form of machinery and equipment often extending or increasing an individual's physical abilities. An electric drill, for instance, allows a person to drill a hole more quickly, with less physical effort, and more accurately than would otherwise be possible.

Scientific methodology, on the other hand, is essentially a process or logical approach to developing models that explain and predict real-world behavior. The scientific method can operate *inductively* by recognizing and observing a pattern of behavior in the real world, developing a model or theory as

1

to what causes this behavior, testing this model and refining it where necessary, and then generalizing, where possible, by finding similar real-world behavior patterns that the model also explains and predicts.

The scientific method can also be applied *deductively* by formulating hypotheses concerning some real-world behavior, developing a model or theory based on these hypotheses, deducing new truths about the real world through analysis of the model, and testing or verifying the model and its predictions through real-world observation, again refining the model or hypotheses where necessary. The history of science reflects the development of both approaches and includes the rise and fall of various models, where new models replace old ones as better explanations are found.

Management science is concerned with the application of this process to managerial decision problems. In order to make more effective decisions, we develop models that attempt to explain and predict the impact that these decisions have on organizational performance. These explanations and predictions can then be used to aid or assist the manager in carrying out tasks.

For example, to assist marketing personnel in best allocating their advertising budget among the products produced and sold, we can develop a model that explains and predicts the relationship between product sales and advertising expenditures. The model can then be used to test the effects of alternative advertising plans on total sales, or analysis using the model might produce an optimal or most effective allocation of advertising dollars among the products sold.

The important point for us is that management science deals with methodology that is intended to augment or assist the traditional managerial decision-making functions. Just as importantly, we should recognize that much of this methodology would be of little practical use without the electronic computer, the technology used to carry out the methodology.

The focus of management science is on managerial decisions. These decisions involve the acquisition and allocation of scarce resources in carrying out organizational objectives. The purpose of this text is to provide current and future managers with an understanding of some of the more important ways in which management science can be used to help make these decisions on a more rational and scientific basis.

What we are calling management science is sometimes referred to by other names, such as operations research, decision science, policy analysis, and systems analysis. While each of these terms implies a slightly different focus, they are often used interchangeably. We prefer to use the term management science since it emphasizes the application of scientific principles to management problems.

A Brief History

Some of the tools and concepts of modeling and analysis used by management scientists date back several centuries. Probability theory can trace its origins to the seventeenth century and the work of Blaise Pascal and Pierre de Fermat. The development of differential and integral calculus by Sir Isaac Newton and Gottfried von Liebnitz, working independently, dates from about the same time. The early part of this century brought the development of economic

inventory control models by Ford Harris of the Westinghouse Corporation and
R. H. Wilson of Bell Telephone Labs, classic work on dynamic models by
A. A. Markov, and the foundations of the economic analysis of waiting lines by
A. K. Erlang of the Copenhagen Telephone Company.

It is generally acknowledged, however, that management science as a
field of study had its early beginnings during World War II. In 1940 the British
military organized a group of scientists headed by Professor P. M. S. Blackett,
a Nobel Prize-winning physicist, to investigate a number of complex operational decision problems. This group, which included physicists, mathematicians, physiologists, surveyors, mathematical physicists, astrophysicists,
army officers, and others, was officially known as the Army Operational Research Group, and unofficially as Blackett's Circus. The diversity of backgrounds of the group members produced a synergistic effect, since the collec-
tive skills of the group enabled them to deal with problems too complex for any
single member. The group was highly successful in finding solutions to a variety
of problems, such as convoy routing, logistical planning, strategies for searching for submarines, and so on.

The group was so successful that similar groups were established in each
of the other British armed services by the time the war was 2 years old. The
United States followed suit by establishing similar mixed groups of scientists in
all branches of the military. The problems successfully solved were many and
varied, including explaining large unexpected losses of bombers on mass raids,
developing submarine search strategies, planning defense tactics against
Kamikaze attacks, and deciding whether antiaircraft weapons should be placed
on merchant vessels.

After the war, some of the scientists who had gained experience in using
operations research carried that experience into other areas. Think tanks were
developed, building a relationship with the military through research grants and
consulting projects. Other scientists began to demonstrate that the application
of management science was much broader than military problems by applying
similar methodology in business situations.

It is important to recognize that the commercial availability of computers
in the 1950s was a key development in the field. The practical solution of managerial problems frequently required the ability to perform numerous calculations and keep track of large quantities of data. Since the computer provided
such a capability, the early use of management science was often restricted to
firms large enough to have computing facilities. Even then, it should be noted
that the speed and accuracy of computers during these early years was anemic
when compared with those available today.

The individuals involved in the immediate postwar years were not trained
as management scientists, but, instead, came from a variety of fields including
mathematics, physics, economics, and so on. It was not until the 1960s that
academic programs were established to train individuals specifically for management science positions. Growth in such programs was spurred by favorable
recommendations by the Ford and Carnegie Foundations.

The late 1960s and early 1970s saw another development of interest, the
application of management science methods to government. A notable example
of this was the establishment of a New York City branch of the RAND Corporation which worked closely with such areas of city government as the fire,
police, and sanitation departments.

Although the tools used in the application of management science are quite varied in specifics, there are certain key aspects of the process that are generally common to all. Figure 1-1 presents a simplified view of these general components and their relationships.

The problem must first be recognized or identified. A model or abstract representation of the problem is then formulated. The model is then analyzed and a solution to the problem is selected. The solution is then implemented or applied to the problem. Experience gained from the application of the solution may lead to further refinements or improvements in any of the earlier stages as shown by the feedback loop at the right of Figure 1-1. In the sections below we will examine in more detail each of these components to provide you with a better understanding of the management science process.

Problem Identification

The process of management science begins with the recognition or identification of a managerial decision problem. This step is often more complex than might be imagined. There is a temptation to confuse the discovery of a symptom with the identification of the problem. The fact that a firm is experiencing declining profit margins is an example of a symptom. The specification of the underlying problem requires a much greater depth of analysis. Do the declining profit margins result from rising costs, increased price competition in the marketplace, or some other contributory cause?

FIGURE 1-1 Key aspects of the management science process and their relationships.

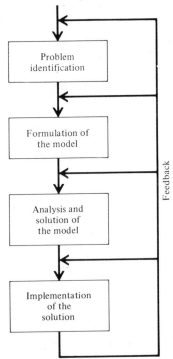

There is also a tendency to define a problem either too broadly, creating confusion and overcomplicating the analysis and solution of the problem, or too narrowly, limiting the impact or likelihood of success of the problem solution. For example, if the source of declining profit margins is primarily attributable to one specific product, a detailed study of a company's entire product line is too broadly focused. On the other hand, if corporationwide pricing policies are the real source of the problem, an in-depth study of a single product may be too narrow in scope.

Formulation of the Model

Once the problem has been properly identified and defined, a *model* of the problem can usually be developed. A management science model is an abstract representation of the actual decision problem, usually expressed mathematically or symbolically. The model is frequently a convenient simplification of the problem it attempts to represent. A model airplane purports to represent, at least visually, the real airplane on which it is based. A major simplification, in this case, is the vast reduction in size that the model embodies. The purpose of simplification is to strip away any complexity that is not essential to understanding or solving the problem.

An Example: Break-even Analysis To illustrate what "model" means, we will develop a *break-even model. Break-even analysis* measures the relationship between revenues and costs. The objective is to determine the break-even point: *the point at which revenues equal costs and profit is zero.* As we will see later, break-even analysis is an important tool in situations concerning plant expansion and new product decisions.

For our purposes here, suppose that Westminster Inc. is planning to launch a new type of spark plug and is therefore concerned about the sales volume (sales revenue) that will be necessary before the product will break even. Thus, the firm has *identified* the problem. Westminster now needs to *specify* a model that answers the question: What sales volume will achieve break-even? In order to develop the model, the problem has first to be restated in quantitative terms—*break-even volume is defined as the sales volume at which revenue and total costs are equal and net profit is zero.* Clearly, the model must contain a means of relating sales volume to profitability. But note that sales volume has a two-pronged effect on profits: As sales volume increases, both the revenue received and the cost of manufacturing the units sold will increase.

Thus, our initial version of the model might simply be an equation of the form

$$\text{Net profit} = (\text{sales revenue}) - (\text{total costs})$$

Although this version does not explicitly incorporate sales volume, it does include the two elements—sales revenue and total costs—that determine net profit and that are affected by sales volume. Now we need to extend the model by defining *how* sales revenue and total costs are related to sales volume.

First, we can recognize that sales revenue is equal to the per-unit sales price multiplied by the number of units sold (sales volume), or

$$\text{Sales revenue} = \left(\begin{array}{c} \text{per-unit} \\ \text{sales price} \end{array} \right) \times \left(\begin{array}{c} \text{sales volume} \\ \text{in units} \end{array} \right)$$

To define a relationship for total costs, we have to consider the two types of costs—*variable costs* and *fixed costs*—that account for total costs. Variable costs are *direct* costs that can be charged directly and specifically to the product (labor, materials, packaging, and so on). These costs vary with the volume of goods produced. Fixed costs are *indirect* costs (rent, property taxes, supervision, and so on) and do not vary with the volume of goods produced. Variable costs are, therefore, affected by sales volume; fixed costs are not. Thus, assuming a specific variable cost per unit, we can now state the total cost relationship to sales volume in equation form as

$$\text{Total cost} = \left(\begin{array}{c}\text{per-unit}\\\text{variable cost}\end{array}\right) \times \left(\begin{array}{c}\text{sales volume}\\\text{in units}\end{array}\right) + \left(\begin{array}{c}\text{fixed}\\\text{costs}\end{array}\right)$$

At this point we have defined the two elements (sales revenue and total costs) that will determine profitability in terms related to the volume of sales. Substituting these more specific definitions of revenue and cost into our original profit equation, we can now define a relationship of profit to sales volume:

$$\text{Net profit} = \left(\begin{array}{c}\text{per-unit}\\\text{sales price}\end{array}\right) \times \left(\begin{array}{c}\text{sales volume}\\\text{in units}\end{array}\right)$$

$$- \left(\begin{array}{c}\text{per-unit}\\\text{variable costs}\end{array}\right) \times \left(\begin{array}{c}\text{sales volume}\\\text{in units}\end{array}\right) - \left(\begin{array}{c}\text{fixed}\\\text{costs}\end{array}\right)$$

In order to achieve our goal of finding a solution to the model (what sales volume will achieve break-even), we normally express the model in terms more convenient for analysis than the verbal description we just developed. In the next sections we will discuss two ways of doing this, a graphic and a symbolic representation.

Graphic Model   Figure 1-2 presents a graphic view of how the various elements of Westminster's break-even problem are related to sales volume. Fixed costs are represented by a horizontal line because changes in the sales volume level are assumed to have no effects on fixed costs. Variable costs are zero if there is no sales volume and increase at a constant rate as sales volume grows; the constant rate of increase is equivalent to the per-unit variable cost. Total costs are found by adding together the variable and fixed costs at each level of sales volume. The total cost line lies parallel to the variable cost line, and the distance between these lines at any specific volume level equals the fixed cost.

The revenue line is similar to the variable cost line in that revenue is zero when nothing is sold and increases at a constant rate—equivalent to the per-unit sales price—as sales volume increases. The revenue line increases more steeply than the variable cost line, since otherwise Westminster would be selling its new spark plugs at a price less than the variable costs, thereby losing money on every sale.

Finally, the net profit for any specific sales volume is equivalent to the difference between the revenue and total cost lines. Positive profits are only generated when revenue exceeds costs, which occurs only at specific higher sales volumes.

The break-even point can be seen by inspection as the point at which the revenue and total cost lines intersect, since profit would be zero at that point. To the left of the break-even point the difference between revenue and total

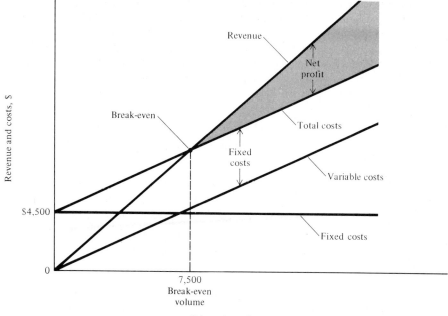

FIGURE 1-2 Graphic representation of Westminster's break-even problem.

cost represents the net loss, since costs there exceed revenue. To the right of the break-even point the difference between revenue and total cost represents the net profit.

The major advantage of the graphic model is the ease with which the problem can be conceptualized and communicated. The major disadvantage is the lack of flexibility embodied in this type of model and the difficulty in manipulating the model's elements to determine the solution to the problem. For example, our graphic approach to Westminster's break-even problem would be difficult if not impossible to use if several product lines were included or if costs and price were to vary over time rather than remain constant.

Symbolic Model Most of the disadvantages of the graphic approach can be overcome by using a symbolic, or mathematical, model in which the various elements of the model are represented by symbols. Thus, suppose for the Westminster break-even model we let

$$p = \text{per-unit sales price}$$

$$v = \text{sales volume in units}$$

$$c = \text{per-unit variable costs}$$

$$f = \text{fixed costs}$$

$$n = \text{net profit}$$

We can then write the total profit equation symbolically as

$$n = pv - cv - f$$

The model is dimensionally correct because the dimensions or the ways in which the variables are measured are consistent with the equation, as shown below:

$$n = p \times v - c \times v - f$$
$$\$ = (\$/\text{unit}) \times (\text{units}) - (\$/\text{unit}) \times (\text{units}) - \$$$

which after canceling leaves

$$\$ = \$$$

One of the advantages of symbolic representation is the ease with which we can manipulate the model. For instance, noting that v (sales volume) appears twice in the equation, we can, by factoring, simplify it by writing

$$n = (p - c)v - f$$

In fact, the expression in parentheses—price minus variable cost per unit—can be redefined even further. It represents what is generally referred to as *contribution margin per unit*. The amount of revenue that is left over after variable costs have been paid is the *contribution* toward payment of the fixed costs. Clearly, once the accumulated contributions equal the fixed costs, the break-even point is reached. Thus, if we let

$$m = \text{contribution margin per unit}$$

we now have
$$n = mv - f$$

which is a much simpler equation than we began with.

Assumptions and Simplifications in Modeling The process of building or designing a model is not always as straightforward as it was in the break-even case. Generally, the model will invoke certain simplifications and assumptions that make the problem easier to model or easier to solve. These approximations may also permit us to recognize that the problem we are dealing with is analogous to some other situation for which there is a ready-made model and solution.

This *application by analogy* is an important concept that deserves further comment. Since the models and methodology described in this text are of a general nature, they can be applied to widely diverse situations. In other words, when we present the break-even model in its general form, as implied by the equation $n = mv - f$, we do not restrict its application to Westminster Inc. or even a specific product within one firm. The model is applicable to all types of organizations whether they are manufacturing or service firms, profit-making or non-profit-making. It may seem at first glance to be incorrect to include non-profit organizations as appropriate for the break-even model, since such firms do not strive to make a profit. Nonetheless, we could redefine the term n (which we previously called *profit*) to represent *budget surplus* or *budget deficit* for a governmental unit.

It is also important to note that the assumptions and simplifications are frequently overlooked because they are not explicitly spelled out but are implicit in the model's structure. For instance, in the break-even model we developed, we implicitly made several assumptions. We assumed that those costs not directly affected by production volume (fixed costs) were truly fixed and not subject to change. We also assumed that both the variable cost and sales price per unit were constant.

Assumptions such as these require explicit specification and analysis. This is because such assumptions may or may not be good approximations of reality. It needs to be acknowledged that the usefulness of a management science model can be severely limited if the simplifying assumptions produce a model that grossly distorts the important and relevant characteristics of the problem being modeled. Distortion of reality so that a problem will "fit" some ready-made model should be avoided.

To illustrate, recall that our model classifies all costs as either fixed or variable, where variable costs are assumed to be constant per unit of sales volume. Certain types of cost are what might be described as semifixed in that they will not be affected by sales volume, as long as sales volume stays within a certain range. Outside of that range, different levels of fixed cost are appropriate. For example, supervisory costs are often related to the number of shifts that a manufacturing facility operates. As long as the sales volume stays within the capacity of a single shift, these supervisory costs may indeed be fixed. As soon as a second shift is put into operation, the fixed costs related to supervision will rise to some new semifixed level. If the situation being modeled is more appropriately described using semifixed costs, it makes little sense to use a model that does not incorporate them.

For these reasons it is extremely important that management be involved in the model formulation phase (see Figure 1-1) to ensure that the model is a valid representation of the decision problem. As we noted earlier, many assumptions and simplifications can be embodied in a model without ever being made explicit. The wise manager will probe for these assumptions and question their validity and reasonableness.

Analysis and Solution of the Model

Once a model has been developed and validated, the analysis phase can begin. The objective of this step is to develop a solution to the decision problem. This is usually done by applying scientific methods and techniques, ranging from the very simple to the quite complex. Management scientists use a variety of analytical tools—some of recent origin, such as linear programming, and others of much earlier origin, such as differential calculus. One of the purposes of this text is to examine the most important tools and methods of analysis. We will be concerned, not with their theoretical development, but with their application. We will study how they are used, why they work, and how they can be applied and the results interpreted.

It is important to understand that the term "solution" can have many meanings. In some cases the solution will simply state *which of several alternative actions should be undertaken.* For example, we may be faced with the problem of selecting a site for a new warehouse from among a set of competing geographical locations. The solution to the problem would designate the preferred site.

In other cases, the solution may be a *rule or procedure to be applied in repetitive situations.* For example, the problem may be to assign specific customer deliveries from a warehouse to a set of drivers so as to minimize transportation or delivery costs. Although it would be useful to have a solution to today's delivery problem, it would be considerably more useful to identify a set of rules or procedures that could be used every day to determine the least-cost assignment of that day's customer shipments to drivers. Thus, we can speak of a solution as a general procedure that can be used repetitively to solve similar problems; such procedures are often called *algorithms*.

Finally, in still other cases, the solution may be a *description of what is likely to happen if certain actions are followed*. Thus we might build a model that allows us to forecast future shipment volume from our warehouse, based on assumptions concerning economic conditions, our own marketing actions, and so on.

Normative vs. Descriptive Solutions   It is useful to distinguish between two general types of solutions that may result from the application of our methodologies. A *descriptive solution* describes the outcomes likely to occur for some set of specific actions. A *normative solution* identifies the set of actions that will result in the best outcome. To illustrate, we could use the equation developed earlier ($n = mv - f$) to determine the net profit that would result for a specific level of spark plug sales. This would be a *descriptive* solution since it answers the question: What if we do the following? Alternatively, we could use this same model to derive an equation identifying the specific volume necessary to achieve a target profit. This is a normative solution since the question: What should be done? is answered by: Ensure that sales volume is at least such and such.

Analysis for the Break-even Problem   We can obtain the normative solution of the break-even problem by using either the graphic model of Figure 1-2 or the net profit equation. Recall that we defined the condition of break-even as the volume at which no profits or losses are earned and total costs just equal revenues. In fact, we earlier identified the break-even point in Figure 1-2 as the point at which the revenue line intersects the total cost line. A vertical line drawn from that point of intersection to the horizontal axis will permit us to identify the specific sales volume level necessary to break even.

Suppose for the Westminster situation that the fixed costs for spark plugs are $4,500 per year, selling price is to be $1.60 per unit, and variable costs are $1 per unit; the graphic model of Figure 1-2 reflects these values. As shown in the figure, the break-even volume is read as 7,500 units since that volume corresponds to the point at which revenue and total costs are equal.

Alternatively, the net profit equation could be manipulated to determine that same point. Recall that this equation had been simplified to

$$n = mv - f$$

where n = net profit
  m = per-unit contribution margin
  v = sales volume
  f = fixed costs

This equation can easily be rewritten so as to state sales volume v in terms of the other elements. Thus

$$mv = n + f$$

$$v = \frac{n + f}{m}$$

This last equation says that sales volume is equal to net profit plus fixed costs divided by per-unit contribution margin. Of course, break-even implies a net profit of zero. Therefore, letting BEV correspond to *break-even sales volume*,

$$\text{BEV} = \frac{0 + f}{m} = \frac{f}{m}$$

In other words, break-even volume is equivalent to the fixed costs divided by the per-unit contribution margin.

Using the data for Westminster, we note that

$$f = \$4,500$$

$$m = p - c = \$1.60 - \$1 = \$.60$$

and therefore $\quad \text{BEV} = \frac{f}{m} = \frac{4,500}{.60} = 7,500 \text{ spark plugs}$

It is worth pointing out that this equation is much more general than the graphic solution of Figure 1-2. The analysis of Figure 1-2 is appropriate only for the particular product for which it was drawn. Other products are likely to have different fixed or variable costs or sales revenues. A new chart will have to be drawn for each situation. The equation, however, is a general model and can be used for any product whose fixed costs and per-unit contribution are known and fit the model's assumptions.

Using the Break-even Model for Decision Making As illustrated above, the break-even model is useful in estimating the sales volume necessary to reach break-even. Thus, for example, Westminster might use the 7,500 spark plug break-even volume as a check against anticipated sales volume. If the marketing department forecasts a sales volume of only 5,000 spark plugs at the $1.60 price, management might consider abandoning the new product, changing the price to increase demand or lower the break-even, or modifying the production process to change the fixed and variable costs. Each of these alternatives can then be evaluated by comparing the new break-even volume with the new demand forecast. As an example, consider the following *Instant Replay*.[1]

INSTANT REPLAY Compare the break-even volumes for two alternative production processes for Westminster's new spark plug—process *A* (fixed costs of $5,000 and contribution margin of $.80 per unit) and process *B* (fixed costs of $2,500 and contribution margin of $.50). What would be the profits for these two alternatives if actual sales volume were forecast at 10,000 units?

CHECK Process *A*'s BEV is 6,250 units and process *B*'s BEV is 5,000 units. Process A would have a $3,000 profit, while process B would have a $2,500 profit, at a sales volume level of 10,000 units.

---

[1]Instant Replays are provided as self-tests of prior material. If your answer is incorrect, review the previous section before continuing.

The instant replay illustrates the difficulties of decision making, even with a well-defined model. Process *B* has a lower break-even volume, while process *A* yields higher profits for large sales volumes. Which process should be chosen? The best choice is impossible to make without more information. There are really two objectives, since we desire a low break-even volume, in case the eventual sales volume is low, and a high profit potential, in case the sales volume is high. In Chapter 4 we will reconsider this multiple objective problem where we see that additional information, in the form of sales volume expectations or likelihoods, can be used to select the best process.

Throughout the text we will frequently use both graphic and symbolic models in our dealings with management science modeling. The graphic models are often a better means of conceptualizing a problem, while the symbolic models are easier to manipulate analytically and provide a more general description of a problem situation. Thus these two forms complement each other.

FIGURE 1-3 Computer program for break-even analysis. (*a*) Program listing. (*b*) Sample output (next page).

```
10 REM THIS PROGRAM CALCULATES BREAKEVEN VOLUME, VOLUME
20 REM NECESSARY TO ACHIEVE TARGET PROFIT, OR PROFIT EARNED
30 REM FROM PROJECTED VOLUME
40 PRINT "ENTER THE NUMBER CORRESPONDING TO THE TYPE OF"
50 PRINT "ANALYSIS DESIRED:"
60 PRINT "1 - CALCULATE BREAKEVEN VOLUME"
70 PRINT "2 - VOLUME NECESSARY TO EARN TARGET PROFIT"
80 PRINT "3 - PROFIT EARNED WITH STATED VOLUME"
90 PRINT "0 - END PROGRAM"
100 INPUT K
110 IF K = 0 THEN 350
120 IF K > 1 THEN 190
130 PRINT "ENTER THE VALUES FOR FIXED COST, SALES PRICE"
140 PRINT "PER UNIT, AND PER UNIT VARIABLE COST"
150 INPUT F,P,C
160 LET B=F/(P-C)
170 PRINT "BREAKEVEN VOLUME IS " B
180 GO TO 40
190 IF K > 2 THEN 260
200 PRINT "ENTER THE VALUES FOR FIXED COST, SALES PRICE"
210 PRINT "PER UNIT, PER UNIT VARIABLE COST, AND TARGET PROFIT"
220 INPUT F,P,C,T
230 LET B=(F+T)/(P-C)
240 PRINT "VOLUME TO ACHIEVE TARGET PROFIT OF" T "IS" B
250 GO TO 40
260 IF K > 3 THEN 330
270 PRINT "ENTER THE VALUES FOR PROJECTED VOLUME, FIXED COST,"
280 PRINT "SALES PRICE PER UNIT, AND PER UNIT VARIABLE COST"
290 INPUT V,F,P,C
300 LET N=(P-C)*V-F
310 PRINT "PROJECTED PROFIT IS" N
320 GO TO 40
330 PRINT "INVALID TYPE CODE.  TRY AGAIN."
340 GO TO 100
350 END
```

(*a*)

Implementation of the Solution

Once a solution has been found for a decision model, the solution needs to be implemented or applied to the actual problem. Frequently the form of implementation requires the development or use of a computer program. This was not really necessary for the break-even model, since any required calculations can be accomplished by hand. In many other situations treated in this text, however, particularly those whose solution is a set of rules, procedures, or equations to be followed, a computer is necessary for implementation.

Figure 1-3 illustrates the use of the computer to implement our break-even

```
RUN
BREAKE  12:51            29-FEB-80
ENTER THE NUMBER CORRESPONDING TO THE TYPE OF
ANALYSIS DESIRED:
1 - CALCULATE BREAKEVEN VOLUME
2 - VOLUME NECESSARY TO EARN TARGET PROFIT
3 - PROFIT EARNED WITH STATED VOLUME
0 - END PROGRAM
? 1
ENTER THE VALUES FOR FIXED COST, SALES PRICE
PER UNIT, AND PER UNIT VARIABLE COST
? 900,2,1
BREAKEVEN VOLUME IS  900
ENTER THE NUMBER CORRESPONDING TO THE TYPE OF
ANALYSIS DESIRED:
1 - CALCULATE BREAKEVEN VOLUME
2 - VOLUME NECESSARY TO EARN TARGET PROFIT
3 - PROFIT EARNED WITH STATED VOLUME
0 - END PROGRAM
? 2
ENTER THE VALUES FOR FIXED COST, SALES PRICE
PER UNIT, PER UNIT VARIABLE COST, AND TARGET PROFIT
? 900,2,1,1000
VOLUME TO ACHIEVE TARGET PROFIT OF 1000 IS 1900
ENTER THE NUMBER CORRESPONDING TO THE TYPE OF
ANALYSIS DESIRED:
1 - CALCULATE BREAKEVEN VOLUME
2 - VOLUME NECESSARY TO EARN TARGET PROFIT
3 - PROFIT EARNED WITH STATED VOLUME
0 - END PROGRAM
? 3
ENTER THE VALUES FOR PROJECTED VOLUME, FIXED COST,
SALES PRICE PER UNIT, AND PER UNIT VARIABLE COST
? 2000,800,2,1
PROJECTED PROFIT IS 1200
ENTER THE NUMBER CORRESPONDING TO THE TYPE OF
ANALYSIS DESIRED:
1 - CALCULATE BREAKEVEN VOLUME
2 - VOLUME NECESSARY TO EARN TARGET PROFIT
3 - PROFIT EARNED WITH STATED VOLUME
0 - END PROGRAM
? 5
INVALID TYPE CODE   TRY AGAIN.
? 0
```

(*b*)

model and solution. The computer program shown is written in BASIC and offers the user the option of determining (1) the break-even volume, (2) the sales volume necessary to achieve a user-specified target net profit level, and (3) the net profit achievable for a projected sales volume level. The program is general in that it allows the user to select which option is appropriate for the decision situation and permits the user to supply the data related to cost, revenue, target profit, and so on.

Thus, we have seen three ways in which the break-even model can be implemented: (1) the graphic model, with its obvious communication advantages; (2) the symbolic model, with its analytic advantages; and (3) a computer model, with its advantages of speed and accuracy.

In other situations the solution to a problem, instead of requiring a simple equation, may require a series of complex logical and mathematical operations that again can best be done by computer. An example is the simplex method for solving linear programming problems. Simplex, which we will discuss in Chapter 6, is a step-by-step procedure that begins with an initial solution to the problem and at each step finds a closely related but better solution, stopping when no better solution can be found. Even a relatively unsophisticated, computer-implemented version of the simplex procedure will often contain several hundred programming operations. Since many of these operations are performed at each step in the solution of an actual problem, the number of mathematical and logical operations to be executed to solve even moderate-size problems will easily number in the hundreds of thousands. Clearly the computer offers a distinct advantage over manual, or hand, calculation.

Even for the case of our simple break-even model, it may be desirable to build the break-even volume calculation into a larger product-analysis computer program, which, in addition to the break-even calculations, might provide detailed marketing and production plans and an analysis of their impact on financial planning.

Because of the importance of the computer in the implementation of management science models, we will frequently discuss implementation requirements when presenting the models in this text. It is important to note that we do not intend, nor do we feel it important, to teach computer programming. Our discussion of computer implementation is focused on the managerial issues related to the use of computerized models, including the formulation of problems and the analysis and interpretation of solutions. In addition, the last chapter of the text will examine the relationship between management science and management information systems.

Accuracy and Timeliness of Input Data   Another implementation problem is the development of accurate and timely *input data*. The solution to any management science problem requires the identification and measurement of specific data before the solution can be properly implemented.

Consider the Westminster break-even problem. In order to calculate a break-even volume using the formula we derived, two pieces of data are necessary: the fixed expenses f and the contribution margin per unit m. The contribution margin, in turn, is based on the per-unit sales price p and variable costs c. Without this information we could not find the break-even volume. Furthermore, if the data used in the formula are not accurate, the solution we find will be erroneous and could lead to an improper decision with costly implications.

Data problems posed by other situations can be even more complex. In some situations the volume of input data may be substantial. Rather than deal with a few pieces of data, we may need to use thousands of data items. For instance, in Chapters 14 and 15 we will consider inventory control models. Although these models require only a small amount of data for any given inventory item, many firms will have inventories containing thousands of items. Since the relevant costs used in determining an economic inventory policy for each of these items may be different, the data-gathering problem becomes significant and cannot be ignored when we consider the cost of implementation.

Observe that the data to be used in implementing solutions for these management science models must be both *accurate* and *timely*. We have already touched on the issues of accuracy, and the importance of timeliness should not be overlooked. It is not uncommon to find firms that have implemented, say, an inventory model, such as that described above, where the data were timely and accurate when implemented, only to find that no system was developed to keep the data up to date. Consequently the relevant costs used with the model may be several years out of date. In times when inflation and escalating interest rates are the rule rather than the exception, the use of outdated information can easily defeat the purposes of any scientific problem solution.

It is becoming more common to find that companies are able to tie their problem solution into already available information systems so that the input data can be obtained from records maintained for other purposes. For instance, cost accounting systems may already be generating unit cost data, which can be used in the break-even equation.

Other Issues Related to Input Data   In any event, the manager should be careful that the evaluation of a potential management science solution to a real problem includes some consideration of the data requirements. Does it call for data readily available? If not, how much will it cost to make these data available? How accurate must the data be? Fortunately, many management science models can help provide answers to these questions. It turns out that the inventory model, for instance, is not very sensitive to errors in the data. How often does the data need to be revised and who is responsible for updating? Although no general guidelines are available, analysis using the management science model may be able to provide answers to this question. For example, tests can be run using the model in which data are revised at, say, 3-, 6-, and 12-month intervals. The total costs for these three update frequencies can be compared, account being taken of the cost of the update as well as the cost of using outdated information.

Improvement through Feedback

Applying management science tools should not end with implementing the solution. Although we may have an estimate of the benefits of using the model, it is always wise to insist that a follow-up evaluation be conducted, probably on a regular basis.

For instance, a comparison of current inventory practices with a proposed new system may suggest that total inventory-related costs can be reduced by, say, $100,000 annually if the new system is implemented. These savings may have been used to justify the expenditures needed to implement the new system. All too often, this may be the last formal evaluation of the new system, at least until something starts to go wrong. It would be better if a formal ongoing review process were established with target goals that the system is to achieve, a means of measuring performance against these goals, and a formal follow-up review to take corrective action if necessary. Thus, at the end of the first year under the new system, we would check to see if the expected $100,000 savings has actually been achieved.

Guidelines for Keeping the Process on Track   The description of the process of applying management science techniques may have implied that the right steps are always followed and that the result is a perfect system. This is not the case. There are a number of ways in which the process can get off track, such as (1) picking the wrong problem, (2) defining it too narrowly or too broadly, (3) excluding relevant factors, (4) choosing the wrong model, (5) solving the model incorrectly, (6) selecting the wrong form for implementing the model, (7) using inaccurate data, and (8) not keeping the data or model up to date.

This list of pitfalls is not intended to scare you away from using management science techniques. In fact, many of these same problems would apply to decision problems whether or not management science models are used. Rather, the list is intended to point out that the application process should be viewed, not as a once-around-and-forget-it process, but as an ongoing, adaptive, and corrective process.

The key is the *feedback loop* shown in Figure 1-1. It implies that the entire formulation/analysis/implementation process should be repeated as often as necessary. This does not mean that the entire process needs to be redone from scratch. The feedback process attempts to refine the original solution to the problem, either in responses to errors made in previous run-throughs or to changes in the nature of the problem itself.

Improving the Break-even Model   Suppose, for example, that the break-even formula was found by Westminster's management to be adequate as far as it went, but that some managers felt that omitting the effects of multiple manufacturing shifts lessened the usefulness of the model. Instead of being abandoned altogether, the model could be redefined to include the missing elements.

In particular, suppose Westminster's management wanted to know if the new spark plug should be manufactured on either a one-shift or a two-shift basis. Moving to a second shift causes the fixed costs to increase by some constant and causes the variable costs to also increase because of a second-shift labor-cost premium. This is shown graphically in Figure 1-4.

The problem as now defined has two break-even points, one that applies if the product is manufactured on a one-shift basis and the other if two shifts are used. From the standpoint of symbolic (mathematical) representation, we must derive separate equations for each of the two shift options. We can define the two models if we let

$$f_1 = \text{fixed costs for a one-shift operation}$$

$$f_2 = \text{fixed costs for a two-shift operation}$$

$$m_1 = \text{per-unit contribution margin for a one-shift operation}$$

$$m_2 = \text{per-unit contribution margin for a two-shift operation}$$

$$\text{BEV}_1 = \text{break-even volume for a one-shift operation}$$

$$\text{BEV}_2 = \text{break-even volume for a two-shift operation}$$

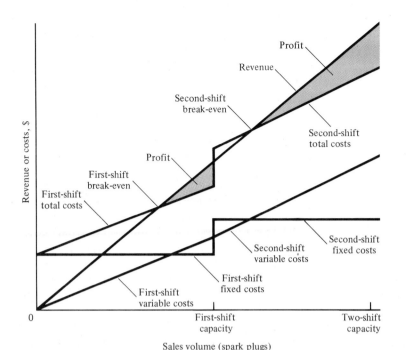

FIGURE 1-4 Westminster's break-even problem with two manufacturing shifts.

The first-shift break-even formula is identical to that derived earlier, namely

$$\text{BEV}_1 = \frac{f_1}{m_1}$$

The break-even formula for the two-shift option is somewhat more complex. We must first define the net profit for this situation as

$$\begin{array}{l} \text{Two-shift} \\ \text{net profit} \end{array} = (\text{revenue}) - \left(\begin{array}{c} \text{total variable costs} \\ \text{for units produced} \\ \text{on first shift} \end{array} \right) - \left(\begin{array}{c} \text{total variable costs} \\ \text{for units produced} \\ \text{on second shift} \end{array} \right)$$

$$- (\text{fixed costs for two shifts})$$

The total variable cost for units produced on the first shift is derived by multiplying the first-shift variable cost per unit c_1 by the first-shift capacity in units v_1 or

$$\text{Variable costs for units produced on first shift} = c_1 v_1$$

The total variable cost for units produced on the second shift is derived by multiplying the second-shift variable cost per unit c_2 by the total units produced minus those produced on the first shift $(v_2 - v_1)$ or

$$\text{Variable costs for units produced on second shift} = c_2(v_2 - v_1)$$

Combining these definitions with those for revenue and fixed costs, we find

$$\text{Two-shift net profit} = pv_2 - c_1v_1 - c_2(v_2 - v_1) - f_2$$
$$= (p - c_2)v_2 + (c_2 - c_1)v_1 - f_2$$
$$= m_2v_2 + (c_2 - c_1)v_1 - f_2$$

Setting the net profit to zero (break-even implies a zero net profit), we can now solve for the second-shift break-even volume:

$$0 = m_2(\text{BEV}_2) + (c_2 - c_1)v_1 - f_2$$

$$\text{BEV}_2 = \frac{f_2 - (c_2 - c_1)v_1}{m_2}$$

INSTANT REPLAY   What would be the first- and second-shift break-even volume if the product sells for $2, costs $1 to produce on the first shift, $1.10 on the second shift, single-shift capacity is 1,000 units, and fixed costs are $800 for the first shift and $1,200 for two shifts?

CHECK $\text{BEV}_1 = 800$; $\text{BEV}_2 = 1,222.2$.

Thus, the single break-even formula we derived earlier has been replaced with two equations, one more complex than the other. Developing the previous model proved quite useful in helping with the more complex situation. These new models and their solutions can now be implemented in the same fashion as before. Note, however, that the data requirements for the two-shift situation are more demanding than previously.

We should point out that although our two-shift break-even model is mathematically correct, it may produce results that are misleading. The situations presented graphically in Figure 1-4 and in the instant replay above reflect cases in which separate break-evens exist for both single- and double-shift operations. It is not unusual, however, to encounter situations in which a break-even volume cannot be defined that is feasible with respect to the production volume capacities of the shifts.

Four possible break-even situations are represented graphically in Figure 1-5. The first situation depicted (part a) corresponds to the situation described above in which separate break-even volumes can be defined for both single- and double-shift operations. Situation b represents the case in which fixed costs are so high that even at full first-shift capacity, the contribution received is not sufficient to cover costs and break-even cannot be achieved. This can also be demonstrated numerically. If fixed costs for the first shift, f_1, are $6,000, the contribution margin m_1 is $.60, and first-shift capacity v_1 is 8,000 units, we find the first-shift break-even value to be:

$$\text{BEV}_1 = \frac{f_1}{m_1} = \frac{6,000}{.6} = 10,000 \text{ units}$$

Since the first-shift capacity is less than the calculated break-even volume, it is not feasible to break even with a single-shift operation.

Consider next part c of Figure 1-5. The situation depicted there corresponds to the case in which fixed costs are relatively low and break-even volume can only be defined for a single-shift operation. Break-even cannot be defined for the second shift, since net profit exceeds zero for all feasible sec-

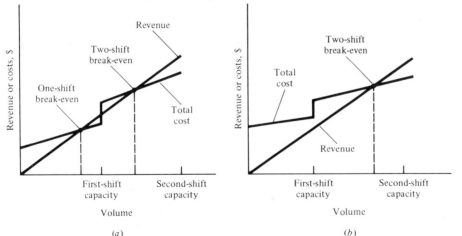

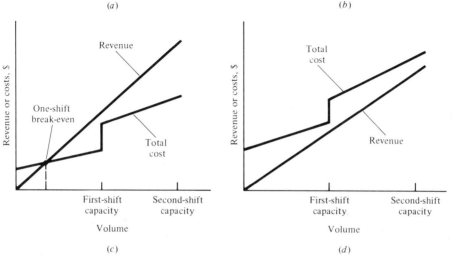

FIGURE 1-5 Feasibility of break-even with a two-shift operaton. (*a*) Break-even levels can be defined for both single- and double-shift operations. (*b*) Break-even is feasible only with two shifts. (*c*) Break-even is achieved for a single-shift operation, but is not defined for two shifts. (*d*) Break-even cannot be achieved for either one- or two-shift operations.

ond-shift production levels. This will always occur when the net profit earned at first-shift capacity exceeds the additional fixed costs incurred by moving to a two-shift operation.

INSTANT REPLAY Identify the break-even point(s) if $f_1 = \$2,400$, $f_2 = \$4,500$, $m_1 = \$.60$, $m_2 = \$.50$, $v_1 = 8,000$, and $c_2 - c_1 = \$.10$.

CHECK $BEV_1 = f_1/m_1 = 4,000$ units. $BEV_2 = [4,500 - (.1)(8,000)]/.5 = 7,400$ units. However, since BEV_2 is less than the first-shift capacity (8,000), there is no break-even point for the second shift. Observe that the profit earned at first-shift capacity is $m_1 v_1 - f_1 = \$.60(8,000) - \$2,400 = \$2,400$, which exceeds the fixed-cost differential for the second shift ($f_2 - f_1$) of $\$4,500 - \$2,400 = \$2,100$.

The fourth situation is illustrated in part d of Figure 1-5. In this case the only break-even point that can be found lies beyond the achievable capacity of even a full, two-shift operation. For example, suppose $f_1 = \$6,000$, $m_1 = \$.60$, $f_2 = \$9,000$, $m_2 = \$.50$, $c_2 - c_1 = \$.10$, and the capacity of either shift is 8,000 units (16,000 in total).

The first-shift break-even volume is calculated as

$$BEV_1 = \frac{f_1}{m_1} = \frac{6,000}{.6} = 10,000 \text{ units}$$

This break-even volume is not feasible with a single-shift operation, since the required volume of 10,000 units exceeds the first-shift capacity of 8,000.

Consider next the two-shift break-even volume. Substitution of the values given above into our two-shift break-even formula yields

$$BEV_2 = \frac{f_2 - (c_2 - c_1)v_1}{m_2} = \frac{9,000 - (.1)(8,000)}{.50} = 16,400 \text{ units}$$

This volume is also infeasible since the full two-shift capacity is only 16,000 units.

The problems discussed above in using our two-shift break-even model can be overcome if care is taken in the application and use of the model. If the model is implemented in a computer program, as shown in Figure 1-3 for the single-shift model, the program can be designed to include checks and balances to prevent erroneous interpretation of the output. Figure 1-6 shows such a self-checking program for the two-shift break-even model. Tests are included to

FIGURE 1-6 Computer program for two-shift Break-even analysis. (a) Program listing. (b) Sample output (next page).

```
10 REM THIS PROGRAM CALCULATES BREAKEVEN VOLUMES FOR A TWO-SHIFT
20 REM OPERATION
30 PRINT "ENTER 0 TO STOP OR 1 TO CALCULATE BREAKEVEN"
40 INPUT N
50 IF N = 0 THEN 270
60 PRINT "ENTER FIRST SHIFT VARIABLE COST, SECOND SHIFT"
70 PRINT "VARIABLE COST, SALES PRICE PER UNIT, FIRST SHIFT"
80 PRINT "FIXED COST, SECOND SHIFT FIXED COST, FIRST SHIFT"
90 PRINT "CAPACITY, AND SECOND SHIFT CAPACITY"
100 INPUT C1,C2,S,F1,F2,V1,V2
110 LET B1=F1/(S-C1)
120 IF B1 > V1 THEN 150
130 PRINT "FIRST SHIFT BREAKEVEN VOLUME IS" B1
140 GO TO 160
150 PRINT "BREAKEVEN NOT POSSIBLE ON FIRST SHIFT"
160 LET B2=(F2-(C2-C1)*V1)/(S-C2)
170 IF B2 < V1 THEN 210
180 IF B2 > V2 THEN 240
190 PRINT "SECOND SHIFT BREAKEVEN VOLUME IS " B2
200 GO TO 30
210 PRINT "SECOND SHIFT BREAKEVEN VOLUME IS"
220 PRINT "LESS THAN FIRST SHIFT CAPACITY"
230 GO TO 30
240 PRINT "SECOND SHIFT BREAKEVEN VOLUME IS" B2
250 PRINT "WHICH EXCEEDS SECOND SHIFT CAPACITY"
260 GO TO 30
270 END
```

(a)

```
RUN
BREAK2   13:11              29-FEB-90
ENTER 0 TO STOP OR 1 TO CALCULATE BREAKEVEN
? 1
ENTER FIRST SHIFT VARIABLE COST, SECOND SHIFT
VARIABLE COST, SALES PRICE PER UNIT, FIRST SHIFT
FIXED COST, SECOND SHIFT FIXED COST, FIRST SHIFT
CAPACITY, AND SECOND SHIFT CAPACITY
? 1,1,1,2,900,1200,1000,2000
FIRST SHIFT BREAKEVEN VOLUME IS 900
SECOND SHIFT BREAKEVEN VOLUME IS  1222.22
ENTER 0 TO STOP OR 1 TO CALCULATE BREAKEVEN
? 1
ENTER FIRST SHIFT VARIABLE COST, SECOND SHIFT
VARIABLE COST, SALES PRICE PER UNIT, FIRST SHIFT
FIXED COST, SECOND SHIFT FIXED COST, FIRST SHIFT
CAPACITY, AND SECOND SHIFT CAPACITY
? 1.4,1.5,2,6000,9000,8000,8000
BREAKEVEN NOT POSSIBLE ON FIRST SHIFT
SECOND SHIFT BREAKEVEN VOLUME IS 16400
WHICH EXCEEDS SECOND SHIFT CAPACITY
ENTER 0 TO STOP OR 1 TO CALCULATE BREAKEVEN
? 1
ENTER FIRST SHIFT VARIABLE COST, SECOND SHIFT
VARIABLE COST, SALES PRICE PER UNIT, FIRST SHIFT
FIXED COST, SECOND SHIFT FIXED COST, FIRST SHIFT
CAPACITY, AND SECOND SHIFT CAPACITY
? 1.4,1.5,2,6000,9000,8000,16000
BREAKEVEN NOT POSSIBLE ON FIRST SHIFT
SECOND SHIFT BREAKEVEN VOLUME IS 16400
WHICH EXCEEDS SECOND SHIFT CAPACITY
ENTER 0 TO STOP OR 1 TO CALCULATE BREAKEVEN
? 1
ENTER FIRST SHIFT VARIABLE COST, SECOND SHIFT
VARIABLE COST, SALES PRICE PER UNIT, FIRST SHIFT
FIXED COST, SECOND SHIFT FIXED COST, FIRST SHIFT
CAPACITY, AND SECOND SHIFT CAPACITY
? 1.4,1.5,2,2400,4500,8000,16000
FIRST SHIFT BREAKEVEN VOLUME IS 4000
SECOND SHIFT BREAKEVEN VOLUME IS
LESS THAN FIRST SHIFT CAPACITY
ENTER 0 TO STOP OR 1 TO CALCULATE BREAKEVEN
? 1
ENTER FIRST SHIFT VARIABLE COST, SECOND SHIFT
VARIABLE COST, SALES PRICE PER UNIT, FIRST SHIFT
FIXED COST, SECOND SHIFT FIXED COST, FIRST SHIFT
CAPACITY, AND SECOND SHIFT CAPACITY
? 1.4,1.5,2,6000,9000,8000,16000
BREAKEVEN NOT POSSIBLE ON FIRST SHIFT
SECOND SHIFT BREAKEVEN VOLUME IS 16400
WHICH EXCEEDS SECOND SHIFT CAPACITY
ENTER 0 TO STOP OR 1 TO CALCULATE BREAKEVEN
? 0
```

(b)

identify each of the four cases pictured in Figure 1-5. The sample output shown in Figure 1-6*b* repeats some of the example situations presented in our discussion above.

The Impact of Management Science

There is no question that management science models and techniques have had a major impact on managerial functions. Unfortunately, it is not always possible to find firms willing to report successful management science applications. (Why let competitors know?) Despite this reticence, there is sufficient direct evidence in the form of written descriptions and indirect evidence in the demand for management scientists to conclude that the impact has been significant.

Arthur M. Geoffrion and Richard F. Powers[1] recently reported a number of very successful management applications and the benefits that the using firms received. Table 1-1 presents a summary of their findings. It is worthwhile examining the table to see the breadth of the applications, the range of companies included, and the size of benefits earned. The applications include financial, production, marketing, personnel, logistics, resource allocation, and project selection, as well as models that integrate these various functions. The firms include national and international manufacturing and service-oriented companies. The magnitude of the benefits is generally in millions of dollars. Dollar figures are not always used; in some cases, percentage improvement in the relevant performance measures are given instead. This table shows just a small fraction of the past, current, and future applications of management science techniques and is intended to give you some idea about their breadth and power.

As we discussed earlier, applying management science techniques to the public sector is of more recent origin, although no less impressive. The Urban Institute in Washington, D.C., and the New York City RAND Institute, both formed in the late 1960s, represent the intense management science efforts brought to bear on national, regional, and local governmental problems. The breadth of applications and the extensive changes that have occurred in public management attest to the efforts of those organizations as well as many others in bringing management science to the public sector.

Their applications include political redistricting; developing school desegregation plans; determining the number, location, and response plans for urban emergency units, such as ambulances and fire-fighting units; locating hospitals; analyzing police patrol plans; analyzing alternative policies for improving the criminal justice system; and scheduling hospital operating rooms.

More recently the area of public application has spread to the management of nongovernmental not-for-profit organizations such as museums, ballet companies, university athletic departments, etc.

Why Management Science Is Important to You

As described above, management science has played a major role in a broad variety of organizations. Your response may be: "So what? I'm not going to be

[1]Arthur M. Geoffrion and Richard F. Powers, "Management Support Systems," Western Management Science Institute Working Paper No. 287, University of California, Los Angeles, March 1979.

TABLE 1-1
Illustrative Management Science Applications

Company	Application	Benefits
British Airways European Division	Integrated profit planning and analysis	Profits up more than 10,000,000 pounds per year
Booth Fisheries	Integrated materials management	Finished inventories down 55%, transport costs down 9%, production costs down 8%, order fill rate up 8%
Cerro de Pasco	Production planning	Multi-million-dollar profit improvement
Flying Tiger Line	Flight crew scheduling	$300,000 per year savings
Getty Oil Company	Financial planning and analysis	Benefits in the millions
Hertz Rent-a-Car	Fleet management	Fleet productivity up 10%
Market Compilation Europe	Project selection	Major turnaround in profitability
National Airlines	Fuel management and allocation	Multi-million-dollar fuel savings
Scott Paper Company Packaged Products Division	Resource utilization and allocation	Productivity of 2,000,000 cases per year above previous "maximum"
Union Carbide	Production and distribution planning	Multi-million-dollar savings
United Airlines	Sales force management	Salespeople's productivity up 8%
Whirlpool Corporation	Distribution operations planning and management	Annual savings in the millions

a management scientist. Why do I need to know anything about the subject?'' This is a fair question and one that deserves an answer.

There are several reasons why knowledge of management science should be important to you regardless of the managerial position you now or soon will hold. For one thing, the nature of the environment in which a manager operates has become considerably more complex. Since 1973 managers have had to cope with rising interest rates, material shortages, energy crises, escalating inflation, and environmental regulations, to name but a few of the growing complexities.

The traditional methods of analyzing problems and making decisions have often been found incapable of effectively handling this increased complexity. This has tended to strengthen the reliance of managers on management scientists to assist them in dealing with these issues. For example, the increased cost of carrying inventories (a result of both inflation and higher interest rates) as well as the shortage of materials has placed greater importance on the efficient management and control of inventories. Management science offered needed help because inventory control theories and models had long since been developed. More recently, the increased cost of fuel has placed greater importance on the management of distribution systems. Again management science has played an active role (see Table 1-1, for instance) in helping managers make better decisions.

A study conducted in 1975 by Stanley J. PoKempner for the Conference Board analyzed, among other things, the areas in which management science was being used by major business organizations. Table 1-2 reports some of the results from this study, based on responses from 296 of the 1,000 largest industrial concerns. The table lists those application areas that were most frequently mentioned as being actively engaged in then by management science personnel or as making the greatest contribution to the firm. The breadth of application is illustrated by the distribution among the major functional areas including finance, general management, logistics, manufacturing, and marketing.

Thus, no matter what managerial position you are likely to hold, there is a strong possibility that you will be involved with management science.

TABLE 1-2
Management Science Projects Ranked by Popularity and Greatest Contribution

Application	Major functional area*	Actively engaged in (1975)	Making the greatest contribution to the firm
Corporate planning models	GM	1	2
Cash-flow analysis	FIN	2	17†
Long-range financial forecasting	FIN	3	19†
Inventory management	LOG	4	3†
Long-range economic forecasting	GM	5	9†
Production planning	MFR	6	1
Investment analysis	FIN	7	14
Capital budgeting	FIN	8	
Financial information systems	FIN	9	9†
Generating strategy alternatives	GM	10	
Facilities planning	GM	11	3†
Administrative information systems	GM	12	
Budgeting and control	FIN	13†	9†
Production scheduling	MFR	13†	15
Marketing research	SM	15	5
Developing plans	GM	16	
Pricing studies	SM	17	9†
Strategy evaluation	GM	18	
Marketing strategy analysis	SM	19†	12†
Marketing information systems	SM	19†	
Production methods research	MFR		6
Risk/venture analysis	FIN		9†
Physical distribution	LOG		12†
Portfolio analysis	FIN		17†
Logistics facilities planning	LOG		17†
New product analysis	SM		19†

*FIN = finance and accounting, GM = general management, LOG = logistics or distribution, MFR = manufacturing or production, and SM = sales or marketing.
†Indicates tie in rank in same column.
Note: Blank indicates that application is not in the top 20.

Source: Stanley J. PoKempner, *Management Science in Business,* The Conference Board, New York, 1977, table 2, p. 18.

Some of you may even hold a position as a management scientist. Several companies make it a policy to assign its brighter new managers to management science positions for several years before rotating them to higher staff or line positions. These are not necessarily individuals with mathematics or management science backgrounds, but they can come from a variety of areas, such as accounting, finance, personnel, or marketing. There is also some evidence that people with management science backgrounds can advance to high-level line managerial positions. For example, top management at Standard Oil of California includes a number of individuals who at one time filled management science roles. These included, in the mid-1970s, three of the sixteen corporate vice presidents, two of the three executives comprising the office of the chief executive, and the manager of corporate planning and three of his staff members as well.[1]

Others of you may work for management consulting organizations. Some of these organizations specialize in management science activities, while others, such as the major public accounting firms, contain major divisions that offer management science services. In some cases, corporate management science groups, such as that at Westinghouse Electric Corporation, perform outside consulting work for other corporate clients in addition to their internal work.

Thus, the knowledge you gain from this text can be valuable either in launching your career in management science or in building your ability to work with management scientists to help you do your job more effectively.

What Is to Come

As stated earlier, the focus of this text is to provide an understanding of the management science process. Since management science models and techniques are used to aid and advise the manager in making decisions, the first major section of the book (Chapters 2 to 4) contains a general study of decision making. In these chapters we will examine the basic elements of a decision and consider the various criteria that might be used to select the "best" decision alternative. We will also discuss the value of experimentation as it improves the manager's ability to determine the best decision.

In the next major section of the text (Chapters 5 to 13), we will focus primarily on a collection of general-purpose management science models. By "general purpose" we mean that the models can and have been applied to a wide variety of managerial decision problems. Although our focus in these chapters will be on the models—how they work and why they work—we attempt to provide a feel for the type of problem situations to which they might apply through the use of in-text examples as well as end-of-chapter problems.

Four chapters (5 to 8) are devoted to the linear programming model. This model is applicable to a general class of resource allocation problems in which strict constraints are placed on such things as the amount of resources available, the pattern in which they can be allocated, and so on. Linear programming is one of the earliest management science models and as such has developed a long history of successful application.

In Chapters 9 and 10 we will deal with a special category of linear pro-

---

[1] Stanley J. PoKempner, *Management Science in Business,* The Conference Board, New York, 1977, appendix C.

gramming problems, sometimes referred to as network models. An example would be a distribution problem, in which we seek the cheapest way of shipping product from factories with limited capacities to demand points with specific quantities demanded. The network analogy results from the weblike network that one obtains from a geographic view of the supply and demand points and the shipment routes that connect them.

We will consider another special class of linear programming problems, called integer programming, in Chapter 11. Integer programming problems differ from regular linear programming problems in that at least some of the decision variables are restricted to being whole numbers, or integers. An example would be the problem of deciding which research and development projects should be undertaken by a firm, given various kinds of resource limitations.

Dynamic programming, which we will treat in Chapter 12, is concerned with decision problems containing a set of interrelated decisions, the individual decisions representing, for example, resource allocations for different time periods.

We will examine heuristic programming, a relatively new technique, in Chapter 13. Heuristic programming, unlike the methods treated in the previous chapters, generates problem solutions that while normally good are not guaranteed to be the "best," or optimal decisions. Heuristic techniques are appropriate to a large class of problems for which it is not practical to find the optimal solution, because of excessive computational requirements.

Beginning with Chapter 14, the focus of the text changes somewhat in that the models we will consider are appropriate for dealing with more specific types of problems. Chapters 14 and 15 are devoted to an extensive treatment of models related to the management of inventorics. This topic has been the subject of considerable management science work, as is evident from the number of inventory-related applications in Table 1-1.

In Chapter 16 we will consider a special type of applied network model called the critical path model. This model has been frequently applied to the management of large-scale projects, particularly construction projects.

We will examine the management of service systems in Chapter 17. A variety of what are called waiting-line, or queueing, models are examined, which describe the impact of various system design options on the performance of the system.

We will treat models for use in forecasting in Chapters 18 and 19. This is another area in which extensive applications have occurred. Although forecasting is a relatively old topic, certainly predating management science as a field, there have been a number of improvements generated in recent years as a result of management science studies.

In Chapter 20 we will be concerned again with a broad topic, simulation, which has many applications to nearly any management decision one can name. Because of its flexibility, simulation can be used to model rather large and complex decision situations. For instance, the recent growth in the area of corporate planning models could not have been possible without simulation. We have chosen to position this topic toward the end of the book because of its ability to deal with complex, integrated decision problems.

In the final chapter we will examine the relationship of management science models to computerized management information systems. The role of the computer is central to the ability of management science to provide effective support for managerial decision making. Although we will emphasize this role throughout the text, we will examine it more closely in Chapter 21.

Special Features

Throughout the text you will observe that we have included certain features designed to facilitate your understanding of the material and provide a foundation for being able to apply the models to real-world problems. Some of these features have already been mentioned, but are worth repeating.

You will already have noticed the periodic use of review questions, which are called *instant replays*. These will be used both as a self-test of your understanding of material just presented and also to present extensions or alternative viewpoints. In each case we provide check figures, brief answers, or, in some cases, more detailed explanations. We strongly recommend that you use these instant replays to measure your understanding of the material presented. If you are unable to arrive at the same answer provided, you should reread the preceding section before continuing further.

We have attempted to include in this text models that have the most general applicability. At the same time we have made liberal use of specific examples because understanding the problem concepts is often easier for a concrete example than for a more general or abstract situation. Do not be misled into thinking that a particular model is limited to the specific example described. This book will be of greater use to you if you attempt to visualize the broader application potential. To help in this, we have tried to include a broad range of problems both as in-text examples as well as end-of-chapter exercises. This breadth includes problems from the various functional areas such as marketing, finance, operations, accounting, and personnel and for different types of organizations ranging from manufacturing to service and including both public and private organizations.

We also wish to point out that, as emphasized in this chapter, successful implementation of many of the models presented will require the use of a computer. Thus throughout the text we frequently consider the role of the computer in the application of the models. This has led us to focus heavily on the formulation and implementation aspects of management science. In addition, when discussing problem solution we focus on an understanding of "why," rather than simply list a step-by-step cookbook description of "how." We feel that a good conceptualization of the models is essential to developing the skills and confidence for formulation and implementation.

Final Comments

At this point you probably have a rough understanding of the basic nature of management science and its role in the modern organization. The remaining chapters in the text will help to refine and expand your understanding by providing more details as to what management science consists of, how you can use it, and why it works.

As a manager it is highly likely that you will be involved with one or more of the steps in the management science process that we have identified: problem identification, model formulation, analysis and solution, implementation, and evaluation and improvement through feedback. Although this text will provide insight and help in understanding each of these steps, you will find it particularly helpful in the formulation, analysis, and implementation areas.

No one can anticipate the nature of managerial decision problems that will be encountered in the future. For this reason it is important for you to recognize the types of problems and situations to which the models and solution methods discussed in this book can be applied.

The objective is not to train you to be a management science technician but to show you how you can become a more effective manager by using management science to augment your other managerial skills. Already, management science has had an impact on the strategic and tactical operations of a variety of private and public organizations. The future promises an even greater role for management science.

Key Words

Algorithm **10**	Graphic model **6**
Analysis **9**	Implementation **13**
Application by analogy **8**	Inductive **1**
Assumption **8**	Input data **14**
Break-even **5**	Management science **1**
Break-even analysis **5**	Managerial decision problem **2**
Break-even model **5**	Methodology **1**
Computer **2**	Model **5**
Computer model **14**	Model formulation **5**
Contribution margin **8**	Normative **10**
Deductive **2**	Descriptive **10**
Descriptive **10**	Problem identification **4**
Feedback **15**	Solution **9**
Feedback loop **16**	Symbolic model **7**
Fixed cost **6**	Technology **1**
	Variable cost **6**

A Case Study of a Management Science Project*

Most of the work of a typical management science project is person to person. Some mathematics and some computer skills may enter in, but common sense is the most important tool. The progress of a specific consulting effort will be described to illustrate the varieties of communicating tasks which we encountered. But first, consider the broad problems that a consultant, either internal or external, can expect to encounter.

The stages of a project that generally occur are:

1. Recognizing that a problem exists
2. Defining the problem
3. Obtaining the data
4. Obtaining results
5. Presenting the results
6. Effecting implementation

*Adapted from L. Ted Moore and Jack Byrd, Jr., "For Practitioners Only: A Case Study in Selling an OR/MS Project to a Nameless Company," *Interfaces*, vol. 8, no. 1 (November 1977), pp. 96–104.

Initially, someone in a position of authority must be convinced that a problem exists which can be successfully addressed by an organized approach. Once a management science consultant is contacted, his communicating job begins. He must first find those in the organization who understand the problem and convince them that the problem requires some thought. Problems are rarely straightforward, and the reason for this is obvious: few people have difficulty formulating and working on clear-cut, straightforward problems.

Complicating the problem-definition stage of the work (and all later stages) is the fact that there is a significant variation of viewpoints among individuals in a business concern. Everyone perceives things differently, and everyone has an individualized herd of sacred cows and ungored oxen.

Typically divergent viewpoints are those held by management personnel in the marketing and production areas. Marketing people are interested in moving product and making a profit. Production people are faced with accomplishing production goals and overcoming obstacles to doing so. While the marketing and production viewpoints occasionally dovetail, they more often conflict; so the consultant must be sensitive to varieties of opinion and understand their objective and subjective origins.

The problem was initially posed as a linear programming (LP) problem. Such a specific model request is rare, but the manager who wanted the work done believed that an LP approach was indicated.

What was the problem? Since it had already been established that an LP approach was to be used, one might expect that the problem statement would be succinct and clear. Here is the initial form of the problem statement:

• Define maximum manufacturing capabilities and capacity
• Define maximum physical volume and profit contribution
• Determine ways and costs to round out production capacity in existing plants and optimize product mix
• Perform design and cost studies of the low-cost production facility that achieves maximum machine-rate contribution
• Perform plant location cost studies
• Perform analysis of overall return on investment (ROI) and cash flow on capacity expansion designs
• Establish standard costs of products
• Examine margins, capacity cost, and total contribution by product of possible product mixes

It added up to a "modest" request. The consultant's first communicating job consisted of convincing the manager who wanted the work done that the first step was to establish a workable problem statement—in particular, one which the consultant could understand. A meeting with the manager solidified the problem statement into:

Develop for a single plant a linear programming model which is capable of analyzing profit, product mix, and machine loadings under the assumption that there will be no capital expansion.

To prove that such a model could be prepared to specifications and to generate an understanding of the data required, the consultant proposed a prototype model of a generalized plant. This proved to be a fortunate suggestion as we will show.

Almost a month expired during devising, revising, punching, running, and debugging the computer model, but at the end of that time the consultant could show the company personnel in both marketing and production departments the following:

1. Flow diagrams of plant production
2. A description of the model's capabilities
3. Types of results obtainable from such a model
4. Sample runs of the model
5. Descriptions of the type of data needed to apply such a model to a specific plant

The prototype model showed that product mix could be optimized; weekly plant production plans could be studied prior to actual scheduling of production; the effects of future expansion and changes in market demand could be studied. Marketing and production were both enthusiastic, and by general agreement the consultant was sent to a plant with the object of developing a model for that plant.

Upon reaching the plant the prototype model again proved useful. Immediately the plant people lopped off a large part of the model, saying, "That doesn't really concern us."

A significant piece of information obtained was that the plant people felt that they were constrained by orders from above which dictated that so many tons of a specific line of products were to be produced each week. This was the first time the consultant had heard this piece of information.

After the plant tour, the consultant knew the kinds of data needed to prepare a model of that plant. Data sheets were prepared and submitted to the company to be filled in by people the company had already assigned to work on the data. However, when the data arrived, they were not in the *form* requested, nor was it *what* was requested. Rather than harangue people with little likelihood of getting better results, the consultant constructed the plant model as implicitly dictated by the data.

Model design, punching, running, and debugging continued until—about 4 months after the initial problem statement—the model, a preliminary write-up, and early computer runs were ready to show at a meeting.

The model results were presented in an easy-to-read form, and they immediately provoked controversy. Packaging was found by the model to be the primary constraint on plant capacity. None of the production people believed this. After reviewing the data base, they found the area of difficulty. No one had told the consultant that there were three packaging lines. However, the way that the model responded in a predictable manner to incorrect data was a convincing display of its capabilities. As a result the plant manager was contacted, and in 2 days he was on hand to help repair the data base. During the next week cases to be analyzed were decided upon and run. A "case" is a set of assumptions which depict a specific situation. For instance, a base case imitating 1976 was run to show what was happening in 1976 and to provide a benchmark for the other cases to be compared with. One case allowed the model to pick an optimal 1976 product mix (different from the actual 1976 mix). The optimal mix showed a profit increase of 81 percent over actual 1976 profits. The implication was that, if marketing had been able to move the required mix of product volumes, a lot more money could have been made.

A report detailing the cases run, major conclusions, and the model data base was prepared and presented to the management group involved in the project. The report centered on five illustrative cases:

1. What do the model results look like when run under 1976 conditions? (Answer: reasonable.)
2. Could the 1976 product mix have been more profitable if marketing could have sold more of individual products? (Yes.)
3. What will happen to present capacity constraints under the expanded plant configuration in 1978? (They will disappear.)
4. Can production be increased far above expected demand with the new configuration? (Yes.)
5. Can the plant be changed from a make-to-customer-order policy to one of building inventories in advance of actual orders? (Yes, and very quickly.)

The philosophies espoused by the model results were those of long-range planning, an aggressive marketing strategy, and avoidance of capital investment by improved use of facilities.

Even though the project is not completed, implementation of the results to date is underway. The potential product line has been reduced from more than 200 products to 85. Orders will be accepted for products not in the list of 85 but only on a delayed basis (which generally leads to loss of the order). This move was made because the model had provided numerical evidence backing the prevailing suspicion that product proliferation was eating into profits.

Plans are underway for new storage facilities that will house the inventory that the new plant will build. Plans for expanding at the other plants have been shelved at least until the next plant is modeled and analyzed. Data collection for the next plant is already underway.

Discussion Questions

1. Figure 1-1 outlined the basic steps in the management science process. On the right of that figure are shown a number of feedback loops. The application description above discussed several examples of such feedback. Identify each feedback example mentioned and determine which step in the management science process is involved.
2. Assume the role of a manager for the nameless company described. How would you assess the impact (major or minor) of this management science project on the organization? What evidence can you provide to support your assessment? How would you suggest that the success or failure of the management science efforts be appraised?
3. Would you claim that the application described above has general applicability and could be used by other organizations, or is it too specific and focused to be used anywhere else?

Part One

Management Science Models in Decision Making

In the next three chapters we will examine the general problem of *decision making*. Decision problems are faced by managers every day. These decisions range from the trivial to the important and from the simple to the complex. Our objective in these chapters is to develop a structure or framework, that is, a *decision model,* within which we can conceptualize these problems and to suggest rational ways in which to approach and solve them.

In Chapter 2 we will show how decision problems can be viewed in the general structure of a decision model. We will consider various ways in which these problems can be solved. We refer to rules used in making decisions as *decision criteria*. We will show that the choice of a decision criterion is dependent on the amount of information we have concerning the future. We will demonstrate two important ways in which decision problems can be modeled: a tabular approach and a graphical, *decision-tree* approach.

In Chapter 3 we will explore ways in which the risk of decision making can be reduced. These include examining the sensitivity of both the choice of an optimal decision and the anticipated return achievable to changes in the decision problem parameters. We will also show how additional information obtained by experimentation can be evaluated with respect to the effect on our decision and how this value can be used to determine whether such information should be obtained. We will then consider a more complex type of decision problem called a sequential decision problem. This type of problem involves several related or dependent decisions.

We will expand our concept of a decision model in Chapter 4 by considering several extensions. First, we will measure the outcome from decisions in terms of the *utility* or perceived value to the decision maker. The use of utilities helps explain some otherwise irrational decision-making behavior. Second, we will cover how decisions can be made for problems with multiple, conflicting objectives.

2

Using Decision Models

The primary purpose of this chapter is to show how to use a general decision model. We will use this model to describe decision-making situations. To do this we will first consider the various elements that are common to decision problems. We will examine two ways in which the decision model can be formulated. A tabular approach will be used initially. Later in this chapter we will also use a graphical model. There are a variety of procedures called decision criteria that can be used to make a decision. We will examine these and show that the choice of a method depends on the amount of knowledge that we have about the future. We now begin by developing a general decision model.

Components of a Decision Model

In order to develop a general decision-making model, we first need to identify and categorize the various elements that are a part of a decision problem and its solution. The first element to consider is the *objective* to be met in making the decision. For instance, if you are about to purchase a new car, you might establish as an objective obtaining the car which is the most economical to operate. Having chosen an objective, you next need to identify the *decision alternatives*. This would amount to making a list of the various makes and models available to choose from. The effectiveness with which each of the decision alternatives meets the objective is dependent upon future events that are beyond the control   **35** of the decision maker. These are usually referred to as *uncontrollable events*. For our car purchase decision, the future cost of gasoline will certainly affect the operating economy for any of the cars being considered. Furthermore, this cost is beyond our control. Thus, you can identify potential future gasoline price increases as the uncontrollable events for your purchase decision.

Now that the decision alternatives and the uncontrollable events have been specified, we need to select a means of measuring the *outcome* or payoff that we expect to result from each possible combination of decision alternative and uncontrollable event. Thus, if we had 3 alternatives and 4 uncontrollable events, we would need to determine 12 outcomes, since each of the 3 alternatives can result in 1 of the 4 outcomes corresponding to the 4 possible uncontrollable events.

The outcome measure selected must be relevant to the decision objective. In our car purchase example, recall that the objective was to select the most economical car to operate. Suppose we decide that operating cost should include fuel costs, maintenance costs, and depreciation (difference between initial purchase price and subsequent resale value) over a 5-year period, assuming that the car is to be driven an average of 15,000 miles per year. This requires estimating what these costs will be for each of the decision alternatives. Note that the uncontrollable events (future gasoline prices) will have an effect on the outcomes because they will impact on the fuel cost to operate each of the cars.

At this point all of the elements of our decision model have been identified except one. We need to select a *decision criterion* for choosing one of the alternatives. A decision criterion is a logical or rational method of choosing the decision alternative that best meets the objective. As we will see, the choice of decision criterion depends on the degree to which we can predict the actual uncontrollable event that will occur in the future. If we can identify with certainty which uncontrollable event will apply, we would classify our decision problem as one of *decision making under certainty*. This would be the case if, say, you have signed a contract to purchase gasoline at a predetermined price for the 5-year period that you will operate the new car.

If we do not know with certainty which of the uncontrollable events will result, but we can attach likelihoods or probabilities of occurrence to each event, we can classify our decision problem as *decision making under risk*.

In some cases we may not be able to provide such probabilities. Although we can identify the uncontrollable events, the future may be so uncertain that we are unable to estimate with any confidence the likelihood of the uncontrollable events. Such decision situations are referred to as *decision making under uncertainty*.

Each of the situations described above calls for a different decision criterion. In this and the next two chapters we will examine each of these decision-making categories and the appropriate decision criteria. More attention will be devoted to problems of decision making under risk, since the majority of managerial decisions fall in this category.

Clearly, given the choice, we would prefer to face a problem under certainty than one under risk. Chapter 3 shows that it may be advantageous to obtain additional information to reduce the risk involved. The chapter shows how a manager can weigh the cost of gathering the information against the potential benefits from using it. In this way the manager can decide whether the information should be obtained.

Applying the Decision Model Concepts

With this brief overview of decision models and their components, let us now consider a simple example problem to illustrate how these concepts can be applied. The example shows first how the decision objective, decision alternatives, uncontrollable events, and outcome values can be obtained. The chapter then covers how the various decision criteria might be applied to this problem. It concludes with a discussion of how decision problems can be modeled graphically by what are called decision trees.

Defining the Problem and the Objective

The Astro Games Corporation manufactures a computer game console, Astrosport, which can be attached to an ordinary television set and allows users to play a set of simulated games, including checkers, baseball, and basketball. Recent sales volume has grown considerably, and orders are outstripping the factory's capacity to produce Astrosport consoles. The amount of back orders (unfilled orders) has led management to consider expanding factory capacity. The problem is unfilled orders and the solution is increased capacity, for which three options have been proposed.

In choosing from among these alternatives, Astro Games management wishes to select the expansion option which provides the highest profit. Thus, the decision objective—maximize profits—has been identified.

We have assumed for this problem that a *single* decision objective exists. In practice many decision problems deal with *multiple*, often conflicting, objectives. For example, Astro Games might have chosen maximum market share as a second objective in the expansion decision. We will consider the treatment of multiple objectives in Chapter 4. For the moment we will stick to the simpler case of a single objective.

Identifying the Alternatives

One alternative identified by management involves building an extension onto the factory. However, the increase in capacity that could be obtained is constrained by space limitations of the current location. A more ambitious expansion plan calls for constructing a second plant in a different geographic location. This option, although more costly, would permit a greater increase in capacity than is possible through expanding the current plant. There is no guarantee that the rise in demand will continue. Thus, there is a third option, which is to leave things as they are and not increase capacity at all.

Enumerating the Uncontrollable Events

To determine which of these three alternatives to select, the Astro Games management must assess the long-term level of demand for Astrosport consoles. Some managers feel that the current increase in demand is only temporary and that demand will eventually return to the previous levels. Others feel that the new rate of demand is likely to continue into the future with no foreseeable return to earlier levels. A third option, admittedly more optimistic, is that the product is entering a period of rapid growth in demand and that future sales will be at a level even higher than that now being experienced. These three possible levels of demand are the uncontrollable events, or states of nature, that will determine the outcome or payoff received from each of the three decision alternatives.

Measuring Decision Outcomes

In order to select the best expansion alternative, an outcome will have to be estimated for each combination of expansion alternative and possible demand level. The decision outcomes must be measured in terms of the decision objective. Astro Games management, as we mentioned earlier, wishes to choose the expansion alternative that generates the most profit. Two factors are identified as affecting profit: the cost of the expansion and the profit achievable for a given level of demand and a given plant capacity.

First consider the cost of expansion. The no-expansion option obviously requires no expansion costs. The other two alternatives require an investment in facilities that will generate an additional annual charge against profits. Expanding the current factory will require $50,000 per year and constructing a new plant $100,000.

Next consider the effect that the capacity and demand levels will have on profit. The capacity of the existing plant has been sufficient to sustain a production rate that yields an annual profit of $300,000. This profit level will be sustainable for each of the three possible future demand levels.

Expansion of the current plant will increase capacity enough to satisfy demand at current levels, which will yield an additional profit of $150,000, or a total profit of $450,000. This level of profit can be achieved as long as demand remains at current levels or increases to higher levels. If demand falls to previous levels, no additional profit can be earned over that achievable with the current plant ($300,000).

A new plant will increase capacity to meet even the most optimistic demand forecast and will yield, at that demand level, an additional $240,000 in profits over that capable with the current plant or a total profit of $540,000. If demand remains at current levels, the new plant will earn a profit equivalent to that obtained by expanding the current plant, or $450,000. If demand returns to previous levels, the profit earned will be $300,000.

The outcomes for each combination of expansion alternative and demand level can now be found by subtracting the expansion costs, if any, from the achievable net profit. The outcomes for the no-expansion option under all three levels of demand will be $300,000. This is because the current factory capacity is limited to earning $300,000 no matter what the level of demand is, and there are no expansion costs to be incurred.

Expanding the current capacity results in a differential outcome, depending on the demand level. If demand returns to previous levels, a net profit of $250,000 will be earned ($300,000 profit from sales less $50,000 in expansion costs). If demand continues at current levels, the expanded capacity would yield $400,000 in profit ($300,000 + $150,000 in profit from sales less $50,000 expansion cost). If demand reaches the higher level, no additional profit can be earned, over that at current levels, because the expanded capacity is limited and cannot produce enough Astrosport consoles to pick up the additional demand. Thus profit will be $400,000 even at the optimistic demand level.

Constructing a new plant also results in differential returns, depending on the demand level. At previous levels of demand, a new plant would yield a

TABLE 2-1
Decision Outcomes, Events, and Alternatives for
Astro Games Expansion Problem

	Uncontrollable events		
Alternatives	*Demand at previous level*	*Demand at current level*	*Demand at higher levels*
Expand current plant	250*	400	400
Build new plant	200	350	440
Don't expand	300	300	300

*Outcome values represent annual profits in thousands of dollars.

profit of $200,000 ($300,000 profit from sales less $100,000 construction costs). At current demand levels, profit will be $350,000 ($300,000 + $150,000 less $100,000). At higher demand levels, profit will be $440,000 ($300,000 + $240,000 less $100,000).

The various decision alternatives, events, and outcomes can be conveniently summarized in tabular form as shown in Table 2-1.

Choosing a Decision Criterion

How the actual decision is to be made is more involved than the previous steps and is dependent on the degree of information known about the *likelihood* of the various uncontrollable events or states of nature. In the sections below we will distinguish the several ways of classifying problems on the basis of event likelihood information. One particular class, decision making under risk, will be dealt with in some detail. Other classes will be considered in detail later. In order to carefully consider the effect that knowledge of event likelihoods has on the choice of the best alternative, we will postpone for the moment solution of the Astro Games problem. Solution of this problem will be concluded later in this chapter.

With most decision problems, the way in which the uncontrollable events are defined precludes any two (or more) events from occurring simultaneously. These events are therefore *mutually exclusive* since the occurrence of one event precludes or excludes all of the other events. The degree of likelihood of any one state or event occurring is usually represented as a *probability*. For example, in the Astro Games situation, if there is a 20 percent possibility that demand will return to previous levels, we would attach a probability of .20 to that particular event.

It is also normal to define the events such that all possible future situations are included. If three future events, *A, B,* or *C,* are possible, then we need to include all three in our analysis. Ignoring one may lead us to take the wrong decision alternative. More formally, we would say that the set of events is *collectively exhaustive*, meaning that they include all possible future events. This, in turn, implies that the *sum of the probabilities is 1.* For example, Astro Games management has assumed that the future demand level will either return to previous levels, remain at current levels, or increase to higher levels. These three cases represent the *only* future courses for demand. If management assumes a .20 probability of demand returning to previous levels and a .45 probability of demand remaining at current levels, it follows that there must be a .35 probability of demand increasing to higher levels, since the sum of these probabilities for three possible events must equal 1 (.20 + .45 + .35 = 1.00).

Decision Making under Certainty

An obvious extreme case in reference to the likelihood of events is that in which one specific event or state is certain to happen. In other words, the probability of that event is 1 while all other events have probabilities of 0. We refer to this category of decision problems as *decision making under certainty* (DMUC).

At first glance it may appear that such problems are quite simple, even trivial, to solve. For instance, if all Astroport consoles are sold to a single buyer (such as a large retail chain) and that buyer has contracted to purchase the consoles at a rate consistent with current demand levels over the near future, the future demand state would be known with certainty. A probability of 1 would be assigned to the current demand event, and 0 would be assigned as the probability of demand at previous or higher levels.

Looking at Table 2-1, we can see that for demand at current levels the best decision alternative—the one with the highest annual profit—is to expand the current plant. The annual profit of $400,000 for that alternative is greater than the $350,000 achievable by building a new plant or the $300,000 that could be earned by not expanding at all. (Actually, this last alternative is probably not feasible because the contract signed with the buyer calls for some sort of expansion.)

INSTANT REPLAY   If a new contract with the purchaser of Astrosport consoles called for production volume sufficient to meet the higher demand level, which alternative should Astro Games choose and what will be their annual profits?

CHECK   They should build a new plant, and the annual profits will be $440,000.

If there is some possibility of larger contract amounts in the future, the probability of demand remaining at current levels would be less than 1, and the problem would not be one of certainty, but would be one of risk, a situation to be treated later in this chapter.

Difficulties in Solving DMUC Problems   In general, for problems in which the future state is known with certainty, the decision criterion used to determine the best alternative is simply to select that alternative yielding the best outcome for the designated state of nature. Although this was trivially easy to accomplish for the Astro Games problem, in practice, solving such problems is often quite difficult.

The difficulty in solving DMUC problems results from the large number of alternatives that the decision maker may have to consider. For example, suppose that the supplier of one of the key circuits used in the manufacture of the

Astrosport console announces a price increase effective in 30 days. The purchasing manager for Astro Games is faced with the decision of how many of these circuits should be purchased prior to the price increase, given the current, fixed level of demand. Assuming that the objective is to minimize the costs of purchasing and carrying this item in inventory, the purchasing manager will have to consider the cost tradeoffs resulting from such an anticipatory purchase. The more circuits purchased now, the cheaper will be the cost for the circuits. But, because these items will have to be carried in inventory in advance of their actual use in manufacturing, inventory costs will increase in relation to the size of the advance purchase. Such costs would include the cost of storage, risk of obsolesence, and funds tied up in inventory, to name a few.

These costs will have to be examined in relation to the number of circuits ordered in advance of the price increase. Suppose that company policy prohibits, in any situation, stocking more than 1 year's supply. Furthermore, assume that (because of the contract for a fixed output of Astrosport consoles) next year's purchase requirements are known with certainty to be 10,000 circuits.

The decision problem faced by the Astro Games purchasing manager is one under certainty because the demand is fixed and known. Nonetheless, solving this problem is not trivial because the purchasing manager can order anywhere from 0 to 10,000 items. In effect the manager has 10,001 alternatives to choose from. It may be possible to determine, with the aid of a computer, the total relevant purchase and inventory costs for each of the 10,001 alternatives in order to find the best alternative. But, it is not likely that anyone would really wish to spend this much effort.

As later chapters will show, management science models can be of particular value in quickly solving this type of DMUC problem. We can, for example, develop a model relating the effects of order size on total costs, and this model can then be solved mathematically. The solution to this model will usually be in the form of a single equation, which when combined with specific cost information (size of price increase, cost of placing an order, cost of holding inventory) yields an easily computed optimal order size. Thus, instead of evaluating 10,001 alternatives, the purchasing manager could simply solve a single equation to find the best alternative directly. A large portion of this text will be taken up with management science models applicable to decision making under certainty problems. For example, beginning in Chapter 5 we consider what are called linear programming problems, which relate to the optimal use of scarce resources. Such problems are characterized as decision making under certainty and have an infinite number of possible solutions. Nevertheless, we will examine a management science approach that reduces the number of solutions that need be explicitly considered to a small, finite number.

Why DMUC Problems Are Important You may also question the frequency with which one finds decision problems in practice that have such perfect knowledge as to which uncontrollable event is going to occur with certainty. In fact, you would be perfectly correct to assume that such certainty problems would be rare.

Nevertheless, there are several reasons why decision problems under certainty are important to decision makers. For one thing, as already demonstrated with the purchasing example, many problems may have a very large number of alternatives to consider. Since the solution of such problems under certainty is often quite difficult to accomplish, the consideration of more than one uncontrollable event adds another level of complexity to the problem that may put its solution beyond the realm of possibility.

In other cases the likelihood of one particular event occurring may be so high that we can disregard the other events. In such cases we assume that the designated event occurs and then find the best alternative conditioned on that event. Furthermore, we could also examine whether the best alternative for the most likely event changes significantly when some other event is assumed to occur. Such analysis of alternative events is one form of what is often called *sensitivity analysis*.

It should be noted that the most likely event is not always the one assumed to occur for a decision making under certainty problem. In other cases, we may choose some alternate event, as, for instance, when we wish to restrict the risk of being wrong. For example, in cash planning we may wish to base our projection of cash needs on a lower estimate of demand than is expected to occur to avoid the risk of not having enough cash on hand. On the other hand, for production planning, we may wish to plan production levels to meet a higher estimate of demand than is expected to occur so as to minimize the risk of running out of inventory and losing sales.

Decision Making under Risk

A second major category of decision problems results when the uncontrollable events can be assigned credible fractional probabilities or likelihoods of occurring. In this case, none of the events j has a likelihood of 1 (certainty) or 0 (can be excluded), but each has some probability p_j of occurring, where p_j is greater than 0 but less than 1 and the sum of the probabilities is $1 (\Sigma p_j = 1)$.

As you can see, since any one of several uncontrollable events can possibly occur, the criterion used to solve problems under risk must in some way take account of the outcomes associated with a particular strategy for each of the states of nature. The criterion usually suggested for solving problems under risk is called the *expected value criterion*. For each alternative a weighted average outcome is calculated, and the alternative with the best weighted average (the maximum average if outcomes are profits or the minimum average if outcomes represent costs) is selected as the best alternative. The weights used for the outcomes are simply the probabilities that those outcomes will occur, which are equivalent to the likelihoods that the events associated with these outcomes will occur. These weighted averages of the outcomes are thus the expected value of choosing a particular decision alternative.

Calculating Expected Values We will shortly calculate expected values for the Astro Games decision problem. First, however, we will consider a smaller example. Consider a simple game of chance in which a coin is flipped and you must call out heads or tails while it is in the air. If you call heads, you win $10 if the coin actually shows heads when it comes to rest, and you lose $5 if it shows tails. Alternatively, if you call tails, you win $5 if the coin shows tails and you lose $1 if it shows heads. Provided that you are not able to foretell the future and that the coin is a fair coin, whatever you call, approximately one-half the time you will be correct and one-half the time wrong. If you were to play this game, you would likely be interested in knowing the expected return for the two call options (heads or tails).

TABLE 2-2
Decision Problem Formulation for Coin-Flipping Example

	Uncontrollable events		
	Coin shows heads	Coin shows tails	
Alternatives	*heads*	*tails*	*Expected value*
Call heads	$10	−$5	2.50
Call tails	−$1	$5	2.00
Event probabilities	.5	.5	

This problem can be viewed in the general decision-making framework introduced earlier in this chapter. The two decision alternatives are whether to call heads or tails, the uncontrollable events or states of nature are the results of the flip (coin actually comes up heads or tails), and the outcomes are the monetary gains or losses resulting from the call alternative and the flip result. In addition, since the probabilities of the states of nature are known in advance to be .50 for heads and .50 for tails, we have a problem of *decision making under risk*. The standard tabular format for this problem is shown in Table 2-2. Note that the event probabilities are shown below the column corresponding to each event.

Suppose you were to play this game repeatedly and in every case you called heads while the coin was in the air. How much money would you win or lose on average with this strategy? It is apparent that, on average, you would make the correct call 50 percent of the time, winning $10 each time that happened, while 50 percent of the time you would be wrong and lose $5 as a result.

Suppose, for example, you did this 100 times and 50 times the coin showed heads and 50 times tails. Your net gain or loss in this instance would be

$$\text{Net gain} = (50)(10) + (50)(-5) = \$250$$

which is equivalent to an average gain of $2.50 ($250/100) per flip. This expected value per flip could have been calculated directly by multiplying the outcome associated with each event by the probability of occurrence for that event and then adding together the results thus

$$\begin{pmatrix} \text{Expected value} \\ \text{``call heads''} \end{pmatrix} = \begin{pmatrix} \text{probability of} \\ \text{head} \end{pmatrix} \times \begin{pmatrix} \text{outcome for heads} \\ \text{when heads called} \end{pmatrix}$$

$$+ \begin{pmatrix} \text{probability of} \\ \text{tail} \end{pmatrix} \times \begin{pmatrix} \text{outcome for tails} \\ \text{when heads called} \end{pmatrix}$$

$$= (.5)(\$10) + (.5)(-\$5)$$

$$= 5 - 2.50 = \$2.50 \text{ per flip}$$

In a similar manner we could calculate the expected value per flip for calling tails. This is given by

$$\text{Expected value ``call tails''} = (.5)(-\$1) + (.5)(\$5)$$

$$= -.50 + 2.50 = \$2.00 \text{ per flip}$$

We can thus conclude that, in the long run, we will be better off to call heads each time since we can average $2.50 per flip under that strategy as compared to the $2.00 per flip that could be earned by calling tails.

It is important to note that the outcome from any single flip will not be a $2.50 gain if heads are called nor a $2.00 gain if tails are called. We will either win $10 or lose $5 if heads are called and win $5 or lose $1 if tails are called. The $2.50 and $2.00 figures are *average returns* that are expected to result if identical calls are made for a large number of flips.

Mixed Strategies You may wonder whether some strategy by which you call heads on some proportion of the flips and tails on the remaining proportion would not better your chances. It can easily be shown that no matter how intuitively appealing such a *mixed strategy* sounds, it always results in a worse expected return than does sticking with the best single alternative.

Suppose you decide to call heads on a certain proportion k of the flips ($0 \leq k \leq 1$), calling tails on the remaining $1 - k$ of the flips. As determined earlier, the expected value per flip of calling heads is $2.50 and of calling tails is $2.00. Thus, the expected return ER per flip is

$$ER = 2.50k + 2.00(1 - k)$$
$$= 2.50k + 2.00 - 2.00k$$
$$= 2.00 + .5k$$

Note that this expected return is dependent on the value of k. If k is 0, representing a call of tails on all flips, the expected return is $2.00 per flip, the same as found for the pure alternative of calling tails on each flip. As k increases, representing fewer calls of tails and more calls of heads, the expected return increases. The largest return is obtained when $k = 1.0$, corresponding to the pure strategy of calling heads on every flip. Thus, a mixed strategy in this case can only lead to a lower expected return than that achievable with the best pure strategy.

Expected Values for Astro Games Problem Let us next return to the Astro Games example problem as first formulated in Table 2-1. We will now assume that the future level of demand for Astrosport consoles is not known with certainty but that Astro Games management has attached specific probabilities to the three possible demand levels. For illustration, suppose these probabilities were 20 percent for demand to decline to previous levels, 45 percent for demand to remain at current levels, and 35 percent for demand to increase to the higher levels. These probabilities are shown in Table 2-3, which repeats the information originally shown in Table 2-1 without the probabilities and expected values. The expected value for each decision alternative is shown to the right of the corresponding row in the table.

These expected values were calculated in a manner identical to that for the coin-tossing illustration. For example, the expected value for the "expand current plant" alternative is equal to the weighted average profit earned, where the weights are the probability that each potential outcome occurs, or:

$$\text{Expected value "expand current plant"} = (.2)(250) + (.45)(400) + (.35)(400)$$
$$= 50 + 180 + 140 = 370$$

TABLE 2-3
Expected Values for Astro Games Decision Alternatives*

Alternatives	Uncontrollable events			Expected value
	Demand at previous level	Demand at current level	Demand at higher level	
Expand current plant	250	400	400	370.00
Build new plant	200	350	440	351.50
Don't expand	300	300	300	300.00
Event probabilities	.20	.45	.35	

*Annual profits in thousands of dollars.

Table 2-3 shows that the highest profit, or best expected value, results from the "expand current plant" alternative and promises an expected return of $370,000, which is $18,500 greater than that for the "build new plant" alternative and $70,000 more than for the "don't expand" alternative. Based on the expected value criterion, the decision maker should select the "expand current plant" option.

Observe, however, that if this option is indeed chosen, the decision maker should not expect to receive a $370,000 annual profit. From Table 2-3 we note that the actual profits will either be $250,000 or $400,000 per year, depending upon what level of demand actually occurs. Furthermore, the actual differential return of this strategy when compared to the nonselected options will also depend on the demand level.

We encountered this same disparity between expected value and actual outcome values when discussing the coin-flipping decision problem. Then it was possible to point out that the expected value corresponded to the average return resulting from a large number of flips. In the Astro Games example, however, we do not have the opportunity to make a large number of repeated plant expansion decisions. Of what use, then, is the expected value criterion in making decisions for one-shot (i.e., one-flip) decision problems?

Despite the difficulties mentioned above, the expected value criterion is appropriate and valuable for one-shot decision problems. Although any single one-shot decision, as illustrated here for Astro Games, will not occur repeatedly, it is certainly true that many other decision problems under risk will occur. If the chosen decision alternative is consistently based on the expected value criterion, in the long run the *expected* return from this set of problems will be better than for any other decision criterion.

This is not to say that in practice apparently rational people will always base their decisions on the expected value criterion. This is particularly true if one or more of the outcomes for the decision chosen by the expected value criterion have catastrophic monetary results. In Chapter 4 we will consider several situations under risk in which the apparently rational choice is not consistent with the expected value criterion when applied to monetary outcome values. This problem is overcome by restating the outcome values in terms of their utility to the decision maker. The expected value criterion can then be correctly applied to the utilities. Chapter 4 will show how this is done.

INSTANT REPLAY What decision should Astro Games management make with respect to expansion (using the expected value criterion) if the demand probabilities are .60 for past demand, .30 for current demand, and .10 for higher future demand?

CHECK Expanding the current plant will yield $310,000 per year compared to $300,000 for no expansion and $269,000 for building a new plant.

Consideration of Opportunity Loss

One criticism sometimes raised by those first exposed to the expected value criterion is the apparent failure to consider the costs of lost opportunity. For example, referring again to the Astro Games example in Table 2-3, note that the outcome received from choosing to expand the current plant is the same whether demand stays at the current level or increases to the more optimistic level. It can be argued that a loss of $40,000 is incurred if the demand does grow to higher levels because Astro Games could have earned $440,000 by building a new plant rather than the $400,000 earned by expanding the current plant. Although, on the surface, it may appear that this lost opportunity was not acknowledged when we applied the expected value criterion to this problem, it will become apparent shortly that it was considered.

To see this, suppose that Astro Games management redefines the decision objective to be to minimize the *expected opportunity losses*. Then they must redefine the decision outcomes in terms of opportunity losses, calculate the expected opportunity loss for each decision alternative, and apply the expected value criterion by selecting the strategy that minimizes the expected opportunity loss.

Determining Opportunity Losses An *opportunity loss* is defined to be the difference between the outcome earned for a particular alternative and that which could have been earned had the best outcome been chosen for each specific uncontrollable event. For instance, if demand returns to the previous level, the best outcome can be achieved by not expanding ($300,000 profit earned). The opportunity loss for the strategy of not expanding would be zero for that event, since no better outcome could have been earned. However, the opportunity loss associated with the decision alternative of expanding the current plant would be $50,000 for the "previous demand level" event because the outcome of $250,000 is $50,000 less than the best outcome. Similarly, the opportunity loss for the option of building a new plant would be $100,000, which is the difference between the $200,000 achievable if a new plant is built and the $300,000 that could have been earned if the company did not expand.

The opportunity losses associated with the other uncontrollable events are calculated in the same manner and are summarized in Table 2-4.

Expected Opportunity Loss Since we are dealing with a decision making under risk problem, we can then use the event probabilities to calculate an expected opportunity loss for each decision alternative. For instance, the calculation for

the option of expanding the current plant would consist of

$$\left(\begin{array}{l}\text{Expected opportunity loss} \\ \text{for ``expand current plant''}\end{array}\right) = .2(50) + .45(0) + .35(40)$$
$$= 10 + 0 + 14 = 24$$

Relationship between Expected Profit and Expected Opportunity Loss As shown in Table 2-4, the lowest expected opportunity loss was that associated with expanding the current plant. Recall that this alternative also had the highest expected annual profit as calculated earlier (see Table 2-3). It is not coincidental that the strategy that minimized expected opportunity loss also maximized expected profit. In fact, as we shall shortly show, there is a very good reason why *the strategy with the highest expected profit will always be the one with lowest expected opportunity loss*.

First of all, observe that the sum of the expected profit and expected opportunity loss for every decision alternative equals a constant:

Strategy	Expected profit (EP)		Expected opportunity loss (EOL)		EP + EOL
Expand current plant	370.0	+	24.0	=	394.0
Build new plant	351.5	+	42.5	=	394.0
Don't expand	300.0	+	94.0	=	394.0

If you accept for the moment that for any strategy the sum of the expected profit and expected opportunity cost is the same constant, it should be obvious that whichever strategy has the highest expected profit *must* have the lowest opportunity cost.

Next let us see why this sum will be a constant and provide an interpretation of the constant's meaning. Recall that the expected opportunity loss for the "expand current plant" strategy was calculated as:

$$\left(\begin{array}{l}\text{Expected opportunity loss} \\ \text{for ``expanding current plant''}\end{array}\right) = .2(50) + .45(0) + .35(40)$$

The amounts shown in parentheses represent the opportunity losses for each of the events and were found by subtracting the profit outcome achievable

TABLE 2-4
Opportunity Losses for Astro Games Decision Alternatives*

Alternatives	Uncontrollable events			Expected opportunity loss
	Demand at previous level	Demand at current level	Demand at higher level	
Expand current plant	50	0	40	24
Build new plant	100	50	0	42.5
Don't expand	0	100	140	94
Event probability	.20	.45	.35	

*Opportunity losses in thousands of dollars.

for that strategy from the best outcome achievable for each event. Suppose we replace each of these opportunity losses by the profit outcome values. Thus

$$\left(\begin{array}{c}\text{Expected opportunity loss} \\ \text{for "expand current plant"}\end{array}\right) = .2(300 - 250) + .45(400 - 400)$$
$$+ .35(440 - 400)$$

This expression can then be arranged as

$$\left(\begin{array}{c}\text{Expected opportunity loss} \\ \text{for "expand current plant"}\end{array}\right) = .2(300) + .45(400) + .35(440)$$
$$-[.2(250) + .45(400) + .35(400)]$$

Note that the expression in the brackets is identical to the calculations performed in finding the expected profit for this strategy. Thus, we could redefine the expected opportunity loss as

$$\left(\begin{array}{c}\text{Expected opportunity} \\ \text{loss for "expand} \\ \text{current plant"}\end{array}\right) = .2(300) + .45(400) + .35(440)$$
$$- (\text{expected profit for "expand current plant"})$$

If the same steps were performed for both of the other strategies, the same general relationship would result. Namely,

$$\left(\begin{array}{c}\text{Expected opportunity} \\ \text{loss for any strategy}\end{array}\right) = .2(300) + .45(400) + .35(440)$$
$$- (\text{expected profit for that strategy})$$

Rewriting this expression leads to the result found earlier, that the sum of the expected profit and expected opportunity loss is a constant ($394,000):

$$\left(\begin{array}{c}\text{Expected} \\ \text{profit}\end{array}\right) + \left(\begin{array}{c}\text{expected} \\ \text{opportunity loss}\end{array}\right) = .2(300) + .45(400) + .35(440) = 394$$

What can be said about the constant that appears on the right-hand side of this expression? Observe that the calculations that led to the constant could be stated as

$$\left(\begin{array}{c}\text{Probability} \\ \text{of previous} \\ \text{demand}\end{array}\right) \times \left(\begin{array}{c}\text{best outcome} \\ \text{given previous} \\ \text{demand}\end{array}\right) + \left(\begin{array}{c}\text{probability} \\ \text{of current} \\ \text{demand}\end{array}\right) \times \left(\begin{array}{c}\text{best outcome} \\ \text{given current} \\ \text{demand}\end{array}\right)$$
$$+ \left(\begin{array}{c}\text{probability of} \\ \text{higher demand}\end{array}\right) \times \left(\begin{array}{c}\text{best outcome given} \\ \text{higher demand}\end{array}\right) = 394$$

Perfect Information

For each event, the probability of that event occurring was multiplied by the best outcome achievable. To understand this, suppose management was given *perfect information* about what demand level will exist for the Astrosport console. If the managers find that the previous demand level will result, they will choose the option of not expanding and earn an annual profit of $300,000. If they find that the current demand level will occur, they would expand the current plant and earn a profit of $400,000. Finally, if the higher demand level is to exist, a new plant should be built and a profit of $440,000 will be obtained. Each of these "perfect outcomes" must be weighted by the likelihood that the corresponding event will occur. This weighted sum represents the expected profit, or return, that could be obtained from this decision if managers were to receive perfect information concerning the future demand level.

Thus, we see that the constant obtained by adding the expected profit to the expected opportunity loss represents the *expected return with perfect information*:

$$\begin{pmatrix} \text{Expected} \\ \text{profit} \end{pmatrix} + \begin{pmatrix} \text{expected} \\ \text{opportunity loss} \end{pmatrix} = \begin{pmatrix} \text{expected return} \\ \text{with perfect information} \end{pmatrix}$$

Another way of looking at this relationship is to view the expected opportunity loss as the price paid for not having perfect information. Recall that the expected profit for the best strategy ("expand current plant") was $370,000 and that the expected opportunity loss for this same strategy was $24,000. The $24,000 represents the loss in expected return because of the absence of perfect information. With perfect information we expect to earn $394,000; without it we expect to earn $370,000. Therefore, the *value of perfect information* must be equal to the difference between those two amounts, or $24,000. In other words,

$$\begin{pmatrix} \text{Value of} \\ \text{perfect} \\ \text{information} \end{pmatrix} = \begin{pmatrix} \text{return with} \\ \text{perfect} \\ \text{information} \end{pmatrix} - \begin{pmatrix} \text{expected profit} \\ \text{without perfect} \\ \text{information} \end{pmatrix}$$

Assume, for the sake of illustration, that Astro Games is negotiating with a single purchaser to sign a long-range contract to buy all the Astrosport consoles that it can produce. Although negotiations are proceeding in an orderly fashion, it is not likely that the number of consoles to be contracted for will be determined or the final contract signed early enough to permit plant expansion. How much would it be worth to Astro Games to be able to find out now the size of the demand to be contracted for?

The value of this information would be $24,000, which is equivalent to the value of perfect information. Without it the company expects to earn $370,000, and with it they expect to earn $394,000.

Of course, in reality it is not very frequent that one is able to obtain perfect information in a decision making with risk situation. Nonetheless, the ability to calculate the value of perfect information in a risk situation can be quite important. Although perfect information may not be available, frequently it is possible to obtain additional information that will increase our confidence in the probability measures associated with the various uncontrollable events. Since this information is likely to cost something to obtain, we can use the value of perfect information as an upper bound on how much we would be willing to spend. Since we know that

$$\begin{pmatrix} \text{Value of perfect} \\ \text{information} \end{pmatrix} > \begin{pmatrix} \text{value of imperfect} \\ \text{information} \end{pmatrix}$$

it follows that the value of perfect information represents an upper limit on the amount that can be beneficially spent on less than perfect information. The concept of an upper (or lower) bound is of general usefulness, and we will encounter it again in later chapters.

For example, suppose Astro Games is considering conducting a market survey (of current and potential consumers) to better refine its estimates of the likelihood of the three potential demand levels. If, say, the cost of the market survey is estimated to be $25,000, it should be clear that Astro Games would be foolish to undertake such a survey. Without the survey they expect to earn $370,000 per year from sales of the Astrosport console. Although the market survey is not likely to yield perfect information, let us assume for the moment that it does. If this were the case, as we saw earlier, the return (with perfect information) would increase to $394,000. However, the cost of this survey would have to be subtracted from the return, leaving a net return of $369,000 (394,000 − 25,000). Since this is less than could be obtained without the survey and since the survey would not yield perfect information anyway, Astro Games would be better off without the survey.

In Chapter 3 we will look more closely at the value of information obtained through experimentation, such as through market surveys. Before we leave this point, it is important to recognize why additional information is of value. The information is of value because it sharpens and refines our estimates of the probabilities of the uncontrollable events. With perfect information we learn precisely which event will actually occur. This allows us to select the best strategy appropriate to each potential event. The outcomes that could be earned by matching the perfect strategy to each potential event must then be weighted by the probability or likelihood that each of these events will be the one that occurs.

This point is often confusing, so it is worth restating. The information received does not let us know with greater certainty that the probabilities of the three states are .20, .45, and .35. Rather, it changes the probabilities so that one of them moves toward unity and the others toward zero. But, because we don't know in advance which probability will move toward unity, our best estimate is the original probability (.20, .45, and .35).

Decision Making under Uncertainty

We next consider decision problems where the uncontrollable events can be identified but no probabilities or likelihoods of occurrence can be established for them. Such problems result from situations in which there may be no basis in fact on which event probabilities can be anchored. They are more likely to occur in innovative situations such as might exist with a new product decision, especially one dealing with new technology. Because of the frontier nature of such decision problems, they are likely to be of major importance and involve high risk, but provide little information on which to base event probability estimates.

The determination of the best decision criterion to use for problems of this class is not as easy as for the categories discussed previously. For one thing, a number of criteria have been suggested. The choice of any one of these criteria can be defended in a logical and rational manner. In fact, this area of decision making has prompted an extensive philosophical, and occasionally heated, debate. Since no one particular criterion can be shown to be universally best, we shall examine some of the major criteria that might be used. These criteria will be illustrated by means of a common example.

Defining the Problem   The president of Bradley Scientific has just learned of an opportunity to bid on a small but potentially profitable research contract. He estimates that to obtain detailed estimates and prepare a proposal will cost the firm approximately $100,000.

The profitability of the contract depends on the bid price that Bradley

TABLE 2-5
Bidding Decision Problem for Bradley Scientific Company[*]

Decision alternatives	Uncontrollable events			
	No other bids lower than $800	No other bids lower than $575	No other bids lower than $500	At least one bid lower than $500
Bid $800	400	−100	−100	−100
Bid $575	175	175	−100	−100
Bid $500	100	100	100	−100
Don't bid	0	0	0	0

[*]Values in thousands of dollars.

places on its proposal. In this regard the president has sought the counsel of the three members of his management team. The operations manager recommends the lowest bid price, $500,000, since he prefers to expand the volume of business the company handles. The chief accountant recommends a bid price of $575,000, based on his analysis of costs and desire for a minimum rate of return. The chief financial officer suggests the highest bid price of $800,000, as she desires to increase the overall rate of return for the firm.

On the assumption that the costs associated with the project are $300,000, in addition to the cost of preparing the proposal, the various profit or loss outcomes for these bidding strategies are shown in Table 2-5. Note that the outcomes depend on whether the company's bid is accepted and that the firm can choose not to prepare and submit a bid.

Unfortunately, because of a lack of information concerning whether Bradley's competitors will bid or, if they do, what price they will bid (all bids are to be sealed), the president and other management people do not feel they can even guess as to what the event probabilities should be.

Choosing a Decision Criterion under Uncertainty   Thus, the problem, as described, represents a decision making under uncertainty situation. All elements of the problem can be determined except for the event probabilities. Next we shall examine how some of the criteria suggested for problems of this type can be applied.

Pessimistic Criterion   The first criterion to be examined can be referred to as the *pessimistic criterion* since it follows an extremely conservative approach.[1] Each decision alternative is evaluated by considering only the worst possible outcome that could occur with that strategy. It should be noted that the pessimistic criterion is often used in military or defense decision situations.

To illustrate the application of this criterion to the Bradley Scientific problem, note that the "bid $800,000" alternative has only two possible outcomes: a profit of $400,000 (if Bradley's is the lowest bid) or a loss of $100,000 (if a competitor bids below $800,000). Clearly the worst outcome for this

[1]A. Wald, "Statistical Decision Functions which Minimize the Maximum Risk," *Annals of Mathematics,* vol. 46, no. 2, 1945, pp. 265–280.

TABLE 2-6
Application of the Pessimistic Criterion to Bradley Scientific

Decision alternative*	Worst outcome profit*	
Bid $800	−100	
Bid $575	−100	
Bid $500	−100	
Don't bid	0	← *Best*

*Amounts in thousands of dollars.

TABLE 2-7
Application of the Optimistic Criterion to the Bradley Scientific Decision Problem

Decision alternative*	Best outcome profit*	
Bid $800	400	← *Best*
Bid $575	175	
Bid $500	100	
Don't bid	0	

*Amounts in thousands of dollars.

strategy is a $100,000 loss. Both of the other strategies involving bids have a $100,000 loss as their worst outcomes. The last alternative, not bidding, always has the same outcome of 0 profit. So 0 is the worst outcome for this strategy.

These worst outcomes for each decision alternative are summarized in Table 2-6. If the pessimistic criterion were to be applied, the "don't bid" alternative should be chosen because it leads to the best pessimistic outcome, or the best of the worsts.

Optimistic Criterion   If one can base decisions on the conservative or pessimistic approach, we can also argue that an *optimistic criterion* is appropriate for a risk-seeking individual. This criterion assumes that whatever strategy is chosen, the best outcome will result. The criterion then calls for selection of the decision alternative that has the most favorable of these best outcomes, or the best of the bests.

Table 2-7 summarizes the best outcomes for each decision alternative taken from Table 2-5. As you might expect, the optimistic criterion selects the option with the highest bid price, since the profit earned from that price is the highest if Bradley gets the contract. If this criterion were logically extended, one could argue that Bradley should consider ever higher bid prices since this criterion assumes that no matter how high the bid price, Bradley will win the contract. This is, of course, ignoring the competitive aspects.

Coefficient of Optimism Criterion   These first two criteria considered, pessimistic and optimistic, have been criticized on the grounds that in practice most decision makers are not pure pessimists or perfect optimists; the truth lies somewhere in between. This led to a compromise proposal which we shall call the *coefficient of optimism criterion*.[1]

This criterion suggests that the best and worst outcomes should be weighted by coefficients representing the degree of optimism or pessimism appropriate for the decision maker. Suppose we define r as the coefficient of optimism and $1 - r$ as the coefficient of pessimism, where $0 \leq r \leq 1$.

A weighted outcome for each strategy could then be calculated as

$$\begin{matrix} \text{Weighted} \\ \text{outcome} \end{matrix} = r\left(\begin{matrix} \text{best} \\ \text{outcome} \end{matrix}\right) + (1 - r)\left(\begin{matrix} \text{worst} \\ \text{outcome} \end{matrix}\right)$$

[1] L. Hurwicz, "Optimality Criteria for Decision Making under Ignorance," *Cowles Commission discussion paper, Statistics,* no. 370, 1951.

TABLE 2-8
Application of the Coefficient of Optimism Criterion to
the Bradley Scientific Decision Problem ($r = .5$)*

Decision alternative	Best outcome	Worst outcome	Weighted average	
Bid $800	400	−100	150.0	← *Best*
Bid $575	175	−100	37.5	
Bid $500	100	−100	0	
Don't bid	0	0	0	

*Amounts in thousands of dollars.

Clearly, if $r = 1$, all the weight would be given to the best outcome and the criterion would select the same decision alternative as did the optimistic criterion. Alternatively, if $r = 0$, all the weight would be assigned to the worst outcome and the decision made would be identical to that for the pessimistic criterion.

To illustrate, suppose the decision maker feels he is about 50:50 with regard to optimism and pessimism. Therefore, we assume his coefficient of optimism r to be .5. The calculations necessary to apply this decision criterion are reported in Table 2-8. The best weighted average belongs, in this case, to the "bid $800,000" strategy, and this alternative would be selected.

Although this criterion on the surface appears to resemble the expected value criterion, recall that only the best and worst outcomes are considered here, any intermediate outcomes being ignored. The expected value criterion, on the other hand, must consider all outcomes.

How should the decision maker estimate his coefficient of optimism? One method suggested is based on what is called the *standard gamble*. The standard gamble is an artificial decision problem in which the decision maker is offered a choice of two alternatives. One, called the gamble option, has two outcomes equal to the best and the worst outcomes for any of the strategies in the original decision problem. The other, called the certainty option, has two identical outcomes of some unspecified value k. Suppose, to illustrate, we pick the best and worst outcomes for the "bid $800,000" strategy and offer these in competition with a certain outcome k, as shown in Table 2-9.

The decision maker is now asked to determine the value for k that will leave him indifferent between the two alternatives, assuming that the probability of receiving the best and the worst outcomes for this standard gamble are the same as those for the original decision problem. Suppose that the decision

TABLE 2-9
Use of Standard Gamble to Determine Coefficient of Optimism

Alternatives	Events	
	E_1	E_2
Gamble	400,000	−100,000
Certainty	k	k
Event probabilities	r	$1 - r$

maker picks $100,000 as the value of k that will leave him indifferent between the gamble and certainty options. Although no probability information was provided to the decision maker, he must have made use of subjective estimates of the likelihood of receiving the two outcomes. As will now be shown, the subjective estimate of the likelihood of receiving the higher of the two outcomes is equivalent to the decision maker's coefficient of optimism r.

In other words, the decision maker was indifferent between the two options because their expected values were identical. Thus,

$$\text{EV (gamble option)} = \text{EV (certainty option)}$$

$$400,000r + (-100,000)(1 - r) = k$$

$$500,000r = 100,000 + k$$

$$r = \frac{100,000 + k}{500,000}$$

As stated before, the decision maker was indifferent if k was $100,000. This now allows us to find the coefficient of optimism r:

$$r = \frac{100,000 + k}{500,000} = \frac{100,000 + 100,000}{500,000} = .4$$

This newly found coefficient of optimism can now be used to determine the best strategy. The coefficient r is therefore a means by which the largest and smallest outcomes can be weighted in accordance with the decision maker's own feeling of optimism.

INSTANT REPLAY   Using a coefficient of optimism of .4, determine the weighted averages for the four strategies of the Bradley Scientific problem, and select the best using the coefficient of optimism.

CHECK   The weighted averages for the four alternatives are 100, 10, -20, and 0. The best option is therefore to bid $800,000.

Regret Criterion   Another criterion recommended for decision making under uncertainty problems is the *regret criterion*.[1] The rationale for this criterion is based on the assumption that the true evaluation of decision-making performance is the amount of regret expressed, once the actual event is known, for having selected one strategy when a better strategy could have been chosen.

For example, if the president of Bradley Scientific submits a bid of $500,000 and obtains the contract because no other bids were received, he clearly will regret not having made the highest bid of $800,000 (or even higher). The decision chosen earns a profit of $100,000 but misses the opportunity to have earned $400,000, a difference in profit of $300,000.

Measuring Regret   The regret criterion requires that the outcome values be restated in terms of regret. *Regret* is measured as the difference between the actual outcome received and that which would have been received had the best

---

[1]L. J. Savage, "The Theory of Statistical Decisions," *Journal of the American Statistical Association,* vol. 46, 1951, pp. 55–67.

strategy been chosen. Consider the outcomes that will result if no other bids lower than $800,000 are received (column 1 of Table 2-5). Clearly, if the firm had put in a bid price of $800,000, it would have no regret because that alternative would earn it the most profit ($400,000). If, however, Bradley had bid at $575,000, the profit earned of $175,000 would be $225,000 less than the company could have earned with the higher bid. Thus, it would incur regret of $225,000.

If the firm had chosen to bid $500,000, only $100,000 would have been earned instead of the maximum profit of $400,000 and regret would be $300,000. If management had chosen not to bid, regret would be $400,000, the difference between what could have been earned ($400,000) and what was earned by not bidding (zero).

Considering the outcomes for each event separately, a regret table can be prepared as shown in Table 2-10. The one question remaining is what criterion to use to select the best strategy on the basis of regret measures. The usual approach suggested is to select the strategy which minimizes the maximum regret. Since this is equivalent to selecting the best of the worsts, this criterion is just like the pessimistic criterion, although applied to regret rather than losses.

The maximum regret for each decision alternative is shown in the right margin of Table 2-10. The strategy of bidding $575,000 is the best alternative as chosen by this criterion. If the $575,000 alternative is chosen, the decision maker is assured of not having to incur regret of more than $225,000.

Similarity of Regret Criterion to Hedging   It should be noted that this criterion is similar to a hedging strategy. *Hedging* is the process by which a decision maker settles for some intermediate outcome to avoid the penalties and forgo the benefits of more extreme outcomes. Hedging is frequently used in commodity markets to purchase a specific quantity of the given commodity for future delivery, avoiding the risk of potential future price increases, but giving up the potential gains from future price declines.

Suppose, for example, a firm producing an instant-coffee product knows on July 1 that it needs to receive on September 1 a delivery of 100,000 pounds of coffee. The firm could wait until the end of August to actually purchase the

TABLE 2-10
Regret Table for Bradley Scientific Decision Problem*

Decision alternatives	Uncontrollable events				Maximum regret
	No other bids lower than $800	No other bids lower than $575	No other bids lower than $500	At least one bid lower than $500	
Bid $800	0	275	200	100	275
Bid $575	225	0	200	100	225 ← *Best*
Bid $500	300	75	0	100	300
Don't bid	400	175	100	0	400

*All values in thousands of dollars.

TABLE 2-11
Use of Regret Criterion to Justify Hedging*

| | Uncontrollable events | | |
Decision *alternatives*	*Market price of* *$3 per pound*	*Market price of* *$4 per pound*	*Maximum* *regret*
Hedge by purchasing *futures contract* *at $3.25 per pound*	325,000 Regret = 25,000	325,000 Regret = 0	25,000 ← *Best*
Wait and purchase *at actual* *market price*	300,000 Regret = 0	400,000 Regret = 75,000	75,000

*Outcomes reflect total dollar cost of purchasing 100,000 pounds of coffee as well as regret.

coffee but if the firm does wait, it is uncertain as to what the price per pound will be. The price in effect at that time will reflect the supply of and demand for the harvest. Thus, if the firm waits, the price might be, say, as high as $4 or as low as $3 per pound. Alternatively, through the commodity market the firm can purchase a futures contract calling for delivery of the 100,000 pounds on September 1 at a price of, say, $3.25 per pound.

Table 2-11 shows the costs and regrets for the two decision options (purchase a futures contract at $3.25 per pound or wait and purchase at market price) and two hypothetical market prices of $3 and $4. If the market price is actually $3, no regret will be incurred by waiting and regret of $25,000 will be incurred by hedging since the firm paid $325,000 for the coffee that could have been obtained for $300,000 by waiting. On the other hand, if the price rose to $4, the firm would have no regret if the futures contract had been purchased and regret of $75,000 by waiting. The maximum regret by hedging is $25,000, while waiting yields a maximum regret of $75,000. To minimize this maximum regret, the firm should hedge by purchasing the futures contract.

Difficulty with the Regret Criterion   The use of the regret criterion does pose one technical problem. Altering the set of decision alternatives can sometimes cause an optimal alternative to become nonoptimal. For example, suppose we drop the "bid $800,000" alternative from the Bradley Scientific problem. Because that alternative was not optimal (the "bid $575,000" strategy was), its inclusion or exclusion from the set of alternatives *should have no effect* on the optimality of the "bid $575,000" option. Unfortunately, as shown in Table 2-12, dropping the "bid $800,000" option and then applying the regret criterion causes the "bid $500,000" strategy to now be preferred to the "bid $575,000" alternative.

The reason for this change relates to the manner in which the regret values are calculated. The outcome for a given strategy is compared with the best outcome for all available alternatives to determine the size of the regret. Thus, if the set of available alternatives is changed (as it was by dropping the "bid $800,000" alternative), the regret values can also change, possibly leading to a revision in the ranking of the alternatives (as such a change did here by making the "bid $500,000" option preferred to the previous best "bid $575,000" alternative).

TABLE 2-12
Regret Table for Bradley Scientific Decision Problem
with ''Bid $800,000'' Alternative Excluded

Decision alternatives	*Uncontrollable events*				Maximum regret
	No other bids lower than $800	*No other bids lower than $575*	*No other bids lower than $500*	*At least one bid lower than $500*	
Bid $575	0	0	200	100	200
Bid $500	75	75	0	100	100 ← *Best*
Don't bid	175	175	100	0	175

*All values in thousands of dollars.

Rationality Criterion   The *rationality criterion* differs from the other criteria considered so far in that all the outcomes for each particular alternative are considered. It resembles the expected value criterion, since event probabilities are used to weight the potential outcomes to arrive at an expected outcome. The decision alternative with the highest expected outcome is then chosen as the best decision.

Recall that in the situations categorized as decision making under uncertainty problems, it is impossible to specify event probabilities. The rationality criterion is based on the principle[1] that if we have no basis on which to claim that one event has a higher probability than another, we should assume that all events have equal probabilities.

Thus, for our example, since there are four possible events, each should be assigned a probability of $\frac{1}{4}$ if the rationality criterion is to be used. In general, if there are n events, each should be assigned a probability of $1/n$.

Table 2-13 shows the application of the rationality criterion to the Bradley

[1]This principle, often called the *principle of insufficient reason*, was first proposed by Jacob Bernoulli and is sometimes associated with Pierre Simon, Marquis de Laplace, and Thomas Bayes.

TABLE 2-13
Application of the Rationality Criterion to the Bradley Scientific Decision Problem*

Decision alternatives	*Uncontrollable events*				Expected profit
	No other bids lower than $800	*No other bids lower than $575*	*No other bids lower than $500*	*At least one bid lower than $500*	
Bid $800	400	−100	−100	−100	25.0
Bid $575	175	175	−100	−100	37.5
Bid $500	100	100	100	−100	50.0 ← *Best*
Don't bid	0	0	0	0	0
Event probabilities	.25	.25	.25	.25	

*All values in thousands of dollars.

Scientific problem. Equal probabilities of .25 were assigned to each of the four events and the expected value for each alternative calculated. The decision alternative with the highest expected profit is to bid $500,000, and this decision would be chosen in accordance with the rationality criterion.

Unfortunately, this criterion suffers from one major problem. The decision called for by the criterion is quite sensitive to the way in which the problem is stated. Suppose, for example, we expand the list of uncontrollable events to include the possibility that no other bids less than $900,000 are submitted. Table 2-14 is the revised decision table for this situation.

Note that with 5 events, rather than the 4 previously, the rationality criterion assigns each event a probability of $\frac{1}{5}$, instead of the $\frac{1}{4}$ used before. The somewhat surprising result of these changes is that the "bid $800,000" strategy has now become best. In Table 2-13, observe that this same strategy not only was not the best alternative, but had a lower expected value than both the "bid $575,000" and "bid $500,000" alternatives. The addition of the fifth event (which was previously subsumed in the "no other bids lower than $800,000" event) should not have affected the relative ordering of the other alternatives, yet that is precisely what happened. In fact, the relative ordering of the three bidding strategies ($800,000, $575,000, and $500,000) is completely *reversed* from what it was before.

If the other criteria (pessimist, optimist, coefficient of optimism, and regret) had been used with the modified problem of Table 2-14, the decision selections would not have changed. Thus, use of the rationality criterion must be accompanied by caution.

Comparison of Criteria   It is informative to summarize the results found from application of the various decision criteria to the Bradley Scientific decision problem. Each of the four alternatives was chosen as the best decision by one of the criteria:

1. The pessimist criterion selected the "don't bid" option.
2. The optimist criterion chose the "bid $800,000" alternative.
3. The regret criterion selected the "bid $575,000" strategy.

TABLE 2-14
Bradley Scientific Decision Problem Expanded to Include a Fifth Event*

Decision alternatives	Uncontrollable events					Expected profit
	No other bids lower than $900	No other bids lower than $800	No other bids lower than $575	No other bids lower than $500	At least one bid lower than $500	
Bid $800	400	400	−100	−100	−100	100 ← *Best*
Bid $575	175	175	175	−100	−100	65
Bid $500	100	100	100	100	−100	60
Don't bid	0	0	0	0	0	0
Event probabilities	.2	.2	.2	.2	.2	

*All values in thousands of dollars.

4. The rationality criterion selected the ''bid $500,000'' strategy (for the four-event situation).

Thus, even for this simple decision problem, there is a complete lack of agreement among the criteria as to which alternative should be chosen. The reason for this disagreement is that each criterion assumes different likelihoods for the various events based on differential treatment of the underlying risks. Thus, in effect, the solution to the problem and hence a choice of criterion must depend on the decision maker's general assessment of the outcomes and risks involved.

Using Decision Trees

We can now expand our understanding of decision analysis through the use of *decision trees*. They are a strong graphical means of organizing the various elements of a decision making under risk problem, as an alternative to the tabular format used, for example, in Table 2-3. Decision trees enable us to analyze sequences of different decisions and uncontrollable events along a time continuum. In this chapter we will restrict our attention to relatively simple problems. In Chapter 3 we will examine more complex decision problems wherein the tabular approach is not nearly as useful as the decision tree method.

A decision tree is a pictorial way of organizing the three elements of a decision problem (the decision alternatives, the uncontrollable events, and the outcome values) as well as permitting the calculation of expected returns and choosing the best alternative.

A Simple Example: A Coin-Toss Problem

Consider again the coin-tossing example we treated earlier. A decision tree corresponding to this problem is shown in Figure 2-1. At the top of the figure we have labeled the various elements corresponding to our problem. As we move from left to right, branches are added to the tree corresponding to either decision alternatives or event possibilities. To help distinguish between decision alternatives and event possibilities, we will represent decision alternatives as boxes and uncontrollable events as circles.

The first pair of branches corresponds to the decision alternatives of calling heads or tails. Another pair of branches follows each decision alternative to correspond to the result of the coin toss. To the right of these events are shown the respective outcomes or payoffs. Observe that the event ''heads'' appears twice, once for each decision alternative, and that the outcome payoff shown is dependent on the decision alternative to which it corresponds.

Along each branch representing an event we record the probability of that event occurring. Note that probabilities are not shown along branches for decision alternatives, since they do not apply to them.

Finding the Optimal Decision with Decision Trees

To determine the optimal decision using a decision tree, we work backwards, starting at the right. We know the outcomes farthest to the right (the future), but we must make a decision now (to the left of the tree). In order to know the

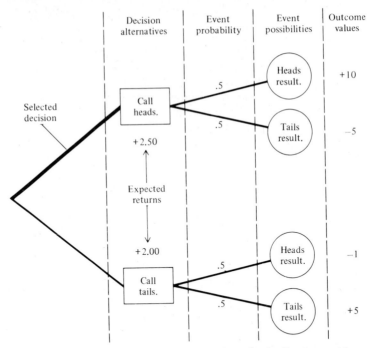

Decision alternatives	Event probability	Event possibilities	Outcome values

FIGURE 2-1 Decision tree representation of coin-flipping problem.

consequences of the decision alternatives we must work from right to left. For this simple example, we first compute the expected value for each decision alternative, by multiplying the event probabilities by their respective outcome values and then summing the results. Thus for the decision alternative "call heads" we calculate:

$$.5(+10) + .5(-.5) = +2.50$$

This expected return is then recorded next to the decision alternative to which it corresponds. A similar calculation for the decision alternative "call tails" yields a +2.00 result as shown in Figure 2-1. You may recall that these expected return values are identical to those found in Table 2-2.

Since maximum payoff is the objective, the optimal decision is determined by selecting the alternative or branch with the higher expected value, in this case the "call heads" option. This choice is shown in Figure 2-1 by a thicker line for the chosen branch.

Using a Decision Tree for the Astro Games Problem

The decision tree for the Astro Games problem, shown originally in tabular form as Table 2-3, is displayed graphically in Figure 2-2. We form the tree by first listing each of the decision alternatives and then the demand events for each alternative (with event probabilities and outcome values as shown). Next, working backward, we calculate the expected values for each decision alternative by multiplying event outcomes by their probabilities. Since the objective is to maximize profits, we select the alternative ("expand current plant") with the highest expected profit ($370,000).

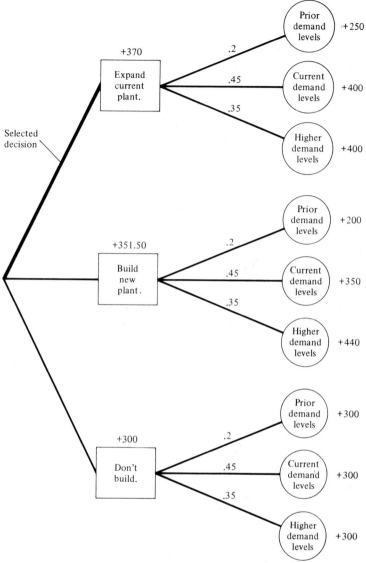

FIGURE 2-2   Decision tree representation of Astro Games problem.

Final Comments

This is the first of three chapters concerned with the process of decision making and how management science can be used to improve that process. The primary objective of this chapter was to present a general model of decision making so that we can examine the components of this model. We identified five major components or steps required for decision making:

1. Define the problem and the objective.
2. Identify the decision alternatives.

3. Enumerate the uncontrollable events.
4. Measure the outcomes.
5. Select a decision criterion and make a decision.

You should recognize that management science offers the most help in carrying out the last two steps in this process—measuring outcomes and selecting a criterion for making decisions. This chapter focused more on the fifth step; in Chapter 4 we will consider how management science can help with the fourth step. The first three steps are important managerial functions, and we should emphasize that if the problem is incorrectly defined, or the wrong objective selected, or the decision alternatives haphazardly chosen, or important uncontrollable events ignored, no amount of scientific sophistication in carrying out the last two steps will yield effective decisions.

You should at this point be able to recognize that the appropriate choice of a decision criterion depends on your knowledge of the likelihoods of the potential uncontrollable events. We categorized decision problems on this basis and examined three of those categories in this chapter: decision making under certainty (if one event is known with certainty to occur), decision making under risk (if each potential event has an estimated probability of occurrence), and decision making under uncertainty (if each potential event can be identified but probabilities of occurrence cannot be specified).

We also examined briefly the impact that additional information can have on the decision-making process. We saw that perfect information converts a problem under risk to one under certainty and that we can place a value on that information. In Chapter 3 we will consider the impact of less-than-perfect information on decision-making problems. You will learn there that we can determine a value for such information which allows us to decide whether or not the cost of obtaining it is justified.

Two methods of organizing decision problem data were presented in this chapter—a tabular approach and the graphic, decision tree approach. You should be able to use both of these, since each has distinct advantages and will be used in Chapters 3 and 4.

Key Words

Coefficient of optimism criterion 52
Collectively exhaustive 39
Decision alternative 35
Decision criterion 36
Decision making 35
Decision making under certainty 36
Decision making under risk 36
Decision making under uncertainty 36
Decision tree 59
Expected return with perfect information 49
Expected value 42
Expected value criterion 42
Hedging 55
Likelihood 39

Mixed strategy 44
Mutually exclusive 39
Objective 35
Opportunity loss 46
Optimistic criterion 52
Outcome 36
Perfect information 48
Pessimistic criterion 51
Probability 39
Rationality criterion 57
Regret 54
Regret criterion 54
Sensitivity analysis 42
Standard gamble 53
Uncontrollable event 36
Value of perfect information 49

Problems

2-1. The foreman of the Drill Press Work Center for the ABC Corporation is attempting to prepare a schedule of the order in which jobs are to be processed by an expensive numerically controlled press. Five jobs are available for scheduling as shown below:

	Hours	
Job number	Machine setup time	Job run time
1	2	12
2	3	18
3	1	4
4	5	20
5	3	12

a. What might the objective(s) be for this decision problem?

b. What kind of decision alternatives are available to the foreman and how many alternatives are there?

c. What type of decision problem is this (i.e., certainty, risk, or uncertainty)?

d. Suggest some outcome measures that would relate to the objective(s) outlined in part *a*.

2-2. The Battle Creek Breakfast Food Company has developed a new breakfast cereal called Rainbo's which it is considering for full-scale production. Test market results have provided the following demand estimates:

Demand in cases per year	Probability
500,000	.15
1,000,000	.25
2,000,000	.45
5,000,000	.15

Development costs have totaled $1,200,000. If the new cereal goes into production, the company expects to receive $12 per case sold, variable production costs are estimated to be $5 per case, and annual fixed costs are estimated at $5,000,000.

Despite the high development costs already invested, the company does not intend to introduce this new product unless it is expected to earn a minimum of $500,000 per year.

a. What decision alternatives does the company have?

b. What are the relevant uncontrollable events?

c. What type of decision problem is this?

d. What is the objective of this decision problem?

e. What outcome measure would you use to reflect the objective accurately?

f. How many outcomes does this problem have?

2-3. Set up the Battle Creek decision problem (see problem 2-2) in tabular form and find the optimal decision.

2-4. Set up the Battle Creek decision problem (see problem 2-2) in decision tree form and find the optimal decision.

2-5. Set up the Battle Creek decision problem (see problem 2-2) in tabular form using opportunity-loss outcome values. Find the decision that minimizes the opportunity loss.

2-6. What is the value of perfect information in the Battle Creek decision problem (see problem 2-2)? What information might the company obtain, and what limit would you place on the cost of obtaining it?

2-7. Treat the Battle Creek decision problem (see problem 2-2) as a decision making under uncertainty situation. That is, the probabilities of the demand levels cannot be estimated. Determine the strategy that would be chosen by each of the following criteria: (*a*) Pessimistic, (*b*) Optimistic, (*c*) Coefficient of optimism (assuming a coefficient of .3), (*d*) Regret, (*e*) Rationality.

2-8. The U.S. Navy is negotiating with the supplier of a new sonar system for the provision of key spare parts. Typical of the problem faced in these negotiations is that concerning the power-supply circuit board for the sonar. If replacement circuit boards are manufactured along with those to be used in the sonar units, they can be supplied at a cost of $50 apiece. If sufficient spares are not available to meet replacement demand over the expected life of the sonar units, they can be obtained from the supplier on a special order basis at a cost of $100 each. If too many replacement circuit boards are ordered now, those not needed will be discarded as scrap at the end of the sonar's useful life.

On the basis of engineering analysis and tests, the demand for replacement circuit boards over the life of the sonar is expected to be:

Replacement boards needed	Probability
0	.10
1	.25
2	.40
3	.15
4	.07
5	.03

If the objective is to minimize the total supply costs for circuit boards over the useful life of the sonar units, determine the number of spares that the navy should order now.

2-9. The manager of the Main Street branch of the Shopping Basket supermarket chain is concerned about improving the purchase decision process for bakery supplies. Ordering the right number of doughnuts has been a particular problem. Doughnuts can be ordered daily from the bakery for delivery fresh early in the morning. They are ordered by the case and can be sold fresh for approximately $30 per case. Each case costs the supermarket $10. If not sold on the day they were delivered, they can be sold the following day for approximately $15 per case.

An analysis of past demand for fresh doughnuts has provided the following demand distribution:

Demand for fresh doughnuts in cases	Probability
1	.15
2	.25
3	.40
4	.20

Set up this problem in the decision table format and determine the number of cases of fresh doughnuts that the Shopping Basket manager should order each day. (Assume that all day-old doughnuts can be sold at the reduced price without affecting demand for fresh doughnuts.)

2-10. Set up the Shopping Basket doughnut decision problem (see problem 2–9) using decision trees and determine an optimal ordering rule for the manager.

2-11. The director of the M.B.A. program at Metropolis University has been asked by the dean of the Graduate School of Business to prepare an analysis of expansion possibilities for the school's M.B.A. program. Each new class of students is divided into sections of 30 students. These sections commonly take all their required first-year courses together. Presently the program admits two sections of students per year, but with an increase in faculty size and an expected reduction in the size of the undergraduate program it is generally acknowledged that the M.B.A. program could expand to as many as five sections per year.

After extensive discussions with employers and analysis of the market for M.B.A.s, the director has prepared the following estimate of demand by employers for graduates from the Metropolis M.B.A. program:

Number of Metropolis M.B.A.s demanded by employers	Probability
50	.05
75	.15
90	.20
100	.30
110	.20
120	.10

Revenue to the school for each student admitted is estimated at $5,000. However, those students admitted to the program in excess of those demanded by employers are estimated to cost the school $10,000 each in additional placement costs and damage to the reputation of the school.

How many *sections* of students should the school admit so as to maximize net revenue (revenue less additional costs to place excess graduates)?

2-12. What would be the value of perfect information for the director of the Metropolis M.B.A. program (see problem 2-11).

2-13. Set up the Metropolis M.B.A. program decision problem (problem 2-11) so as to minimize opportunity loss. Determine the class size that accomplishes this objective.

2-14. The manager of the Boardwalk Casino at Atlantic City is considering the introduction of a new gambling game at the casino. In this game, called *pairs*, the player rolls a pair of dice and wins or loses according to what is rolled as shown below.

Probability of outcome	Outcome of role	Gain or loss, $
$\frac{1}{12}$	Pair of odd numbers (1s, 3s, or 5s)	+4
$\frac{1}{12}$	Pair of even numbers (2s, 4s, or 6s)	+4
$\frac{5}{6}$	No pair	−1

a. What is the casino's expected gain or loss per role?

b. Set up this problem in decision tree format from the standpoint of a potential gambler. Should the gambler play the game?

c. How high would the payoff for rolling pairs (both odd and even) have to be in order to make this a "fair" game (net expected value of zero)?

2-15. Another game being considered by the management of the Boardwalk Casino (see problem 2-14) involves random draws of colored balls from a large bin. Players bet on the outcome of the draw, losing $4 if they bet incorrectly, winning the amount shown below for a correct guess:

Draw outcomes	Probability	Payoff, $
Red ball	.15	22
Blue ball	.55	3
White ball	.30	8

Assume for the moment that you are a compulsive gambler. What is your best strategy to play this game so as to minimize your losses?

2-16. The Thornbread Company has received an offer from an electrical supply firm to provide Thornbread with an electrical motor at a cost of $12 per motor. The motor is currently assembled by Thornbread, in house, with fixed costs of $2,000 per year and variable costs of $10 per motor. The motor is used in one of Thornbread's major products which has steady demand of 400 units per year. There is some likelihood, estimated at 50 percent, that the motor will be used in a redesigned version of another Thornbread product which has an estimated annual demand of 1,000 units. It is assumed that if the motor were purchased from outside, the entire $2,000 in fixed costs now incurred could be avoided.

a. Draw the decision tree for the Thornbread problem.

b. Should Thornbread continue to produce the motor in house or should they take the supplier's offer?

c. Suppose management at Thornbread is uncertain about the probability that the motor will be used in the redesigned product. How high would this probability have to be to leave the managers indifferent between making the motor themselves or purchasing it from the outside supplier?

2-17. The World Petroleum Company is interested in acquiring a piece of land thought to possibly contain oil. The company is considering three alternatives: (1) purchase the land outright; (2) obtain an option to buy, drill for oil, and if found exercise the option; and (3) don't buy the land or obtain an option.

For land of this type, there are three events likely to happen: (1) large deposits are found, (2) small deposits are found, or (3) no oil is found at all.

Alternatives	Events		
	Large deposits	*Small deposits*	*No oil*
Buy land	3,000,000	1,000,000	−2,000,000
Take option	2,000,000	500,000	−100,000
Do nothing	0	0	0

a. What strategies would be chosen by the following criteria, if it is assumed that the problem is one of decision making under uncertainty: pessimistic, optimistic, coefficient of optimism (.7), regret, and rationality?

b. Suppose that past experience and preliminary geological tests have been used to provide event probability estimates of .1 for large deposits, .5 for small deposits, and .4 for no deposits. Which strategy should be chosen?

3

Reducing Risk in Decision Making through Experimentation

We continue our examination of decision making in this chapter by considering more complex decision problems. The major emphasis will be on the evaluation of options for obtaining additional information to improve the decision-making process by reducing risk. Although there is a tendency to believe that more information is better, the issue is not quite as simple as that. In each case a tradeoff must be made between the benefits obtained from using the additional information and the costs incurred to obtain it.

We will begin this chapter by analyzing the sensitivity of our choice of the best decision to our knowledge of the probabilities or likelihoods of the uncontrollable events. We will demonstrate that the expected return achievable by the best decision is also affected by these probabilities. We will show that the more we know about the future, the higher will be the expected return obtainable. Since our knowledge of the future can be improved by gathering additional information, we can use the change in the expected return as a means of valuing this information. In Chapter 2 we showed how this could be done with perfect information; in this chapter we show how a value can be assigned to less than perfect information.

The availability of information increases the complexity of any decision problem. This is because the problem now contains at least two decisions: *a decision as to whether the benefits of obtaining new information exceed the costs* and *the original decision problem itself*. The original decision problem becomes a dependent decision problem because the choice of the best decision now depends upon whether new information is obtained and, if it is, what it tells us about the likelihoods of the uncontrollable events.

In the last section of the chapter we show that sequential dependent decision problems can arise in other contexts (where additional information is not an issue).

Sensitivity Analysis

We shall begin by examining methods by which *sensitivity analysis* can be applied to decision making under risk problems. We will focus on measuring the sensitivity of both the choice of an optimal decision and the achievable expected return to changes in the probabilities of the uncontrollable events.

Sensitivity analysis is useful for several reasons. First of all, you should recognize that the event probabilities are likely to be estimates or educated guesses, and, as such, subject to estimation errors. Sensitivity analysis is used to determine how large these estimation errors must be in order that the decision we think is optimal (based on the erroneous probability estimates) is not the best decision (based on the correct probability estimates). If we find that very large errors would be necessary to change the optimal decision, our confidence would be high that the decision chosen is the correct one. If, however, we find from the sensitivity analysis that small changes in the event probabilities will cause the optimal alternative to change, our degree of confidence in the selected decision will be low. In such a case, we may be willing to spend additional effort in refining these probability estimates to ensure that the wrong decision is not made. One means of doing this is to gather additional information. We will have more to say about this possibility later.

Problem Description

An explanation of sensitivity analysis is aided by consideration of the following problem situation. The Battle Creek Breakfast Food Company is concerned that one of their major brands, Rainbo's, uses an ingredient which has come under suspicion of being carcinogenic, that is, a cancer-causing substance. Although this substance has not yet been placed on the FDA prohibited list, the FDA is shortly expected to begin tests on it.

The Battle Creek Research and Development group has developed a substitute for this ingredient, and management is now exploring possible actions they might take with respect to Rainbo's formulation.

One possibility being considered is the immediate decision to substitute the new ingredient for the suspected carcinogenic substance. Although this avoids the potentially damaging effects of having to make the substitution in haste if the FDA bans the ingredient to be tested, the conversion would be expensive, costing the company approximately $1,000,000.

Another possible option would be to tough it out and hope for a favorable FDA test result. If the FDA reports favorably, the company would experience no additional charges. On the other hand, an unfavorable report would be extremely damaging, costing the company approximately $3,000,000 in lost sales, ill will, and rapid conversion costs, not to mention possible legal action.

Discussions with Battle Creek scientists concerning their own tests of this substance have estimated a .70 probability that the FDA will rule favorably, i.e., that the ingredient is *not* carcinogenic. The cost and probability data for this decision problem are summarized in Table 3-1.

TABLE 3-1
Battle Creek Decision Problem

Decision alternatives	Uncontrollable events		Expected cost
	FDA favorable ruling	FDA unfavorable ruling	
Substitute new ingredient	1,000,000	1,000,000	1,000,000
Tough it out	0	3,000,000	900,000
Event probabilities	.7	.3	

Initial Solution

Observe that the optimal decision, based on expected costs, is to tough it out, saving approximately $100,000 over the cost of definitely substituting the new ingredient in the near future. The severity of the consequences to the company of an unfavorable FDA ruling and a lack of confidence in the probability estimate for a favorable ruling leave Battle Creek management unwilling to accept the risk of the "tough it out" alternative without further reassurance. As a first step let us analyze the risks involved through the use of sensitivity analysis.

Solution Sensitivity to Changes in Event Probabilities

Clearly if we know that the FDA will rule favorably (probability of a favorable ruling equals 1 and probability of an unfavorable ruling equals 0), the optimal strategy is to tough it out and the expected cost to the company is 0. At the other extreme, if the probabilities are reversed such that we know that the FDA will rule unfavorably, the outcomes dictate that the new ingredient should be substituted as soon as possible, with an expected cost to the firm of $1,000,000. Observe that as the probability of a favorable FDA ruling changes from 1 to 0, the optimal decision switches from "tough it out" to "substitute new ingredient." This is because the expected cost from following the "tough it out" alternative increases as the probability of a favorable ruling decreases, while the expected cost of the "substitute new ingredient" alternative remains constant. At some point the cost of the "tough it out" alternative becomes higher than the cost of the other alternative. This can be seen pictorially in Figure 3-1.

As you can see from Figure 3-1, the "substitute new ingredient" alternative yields a lower expected cost for a low probability of a favorable FDA ruling, while the "tough it out" alternative has the smaller expected cost when the probability of a favorable ruling is high. The two alternatives have the same expected cost at some intermediate probability value. This intermediate point is referred to as the *indifference point*. We would be indifferent between choosing either of the alternatives at this point, because both have the same expected cost.

It is useful to calculate the probability associated with the indifference point. This is done by letting p represent the *indifference probability* for a favorable FDA ruling, equating the expected costs for that probability, and

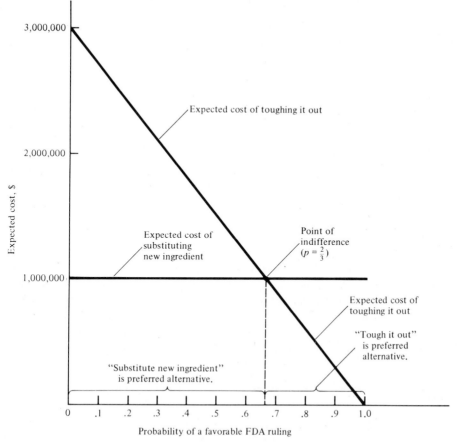

FIGURE 3-1 Sensitivity of expected costs and optimal decision to changes in the probability of a favorable FDA ruling for the Battle Creek decision problem.

solving for p. To illustrate, the expected cost EC for the "tough it out" alternative is

$$\text{EC (tough it out)} = 0p + 3,000,000(1 - p)$$

and for the "substitute new ingredient" alternative is

$$\text{EC (substitute new ingredient)} = 1,000,000p + 1,000,000(1 - p)$$
$$= 1,000,000$$

These equations were in fact used to plot the cost lines shown in Figure 3-1.

Since these two costs are equal to each other at the indifference point, the indifference probability p is found by equating these costs and solving for p:

$$0p + 3,000,000(1 - p) = 1,000,000$$
$$3,000,000 - 3,000,000p = 1,000,000$$
$$3,000,000p = 2,000,000$$
$$p = \tfrac{2}{3}$$

That this in indeed the probability at which we are indifferent between the two alternatives can be easily seen by calculating the expected cost for both alternatives using $\frac{2}{3}$ as the probability of a favorable FDA ruling:

$$EC \text{ (tough it out)} = 0p + 3,000,000(1 - p)$$

$$= 3,000,000(1 - \tfrac{2}{3}) = 1,000,000$$

which is the same as the expected cost for the "substitute new ingredient" alternative, which has a constant expected cost of $1,000,000.

Thus, if the probability of a favorable ruling is $\frac{2}{3}$, we could choose either alternative and obtain the same expected cost of $1,000,000. It is interesting to note that this is the worst possible probability from the standpoint of expected cost. Referring again to Figure 3-1, note that as the probability of a favorable ruling increases from 0, we can slide along the "substitute new ingredient" line, receiving a constant expected cost of $1,000,000 until we reach the indifference point. From that point on we can slide down the expected cost line for the "tough it out" alternative, with the result that expected cost declines as the probability increases above the indifference point.

INSTANT REPLAY Suppose that the cost to Battle Creek of an unfavorable FDA ruling with the "tough it out" alternative is $2,000,000 instead of $3,000,000. What would be the indifference probability, assuming all other outcomes remain the same? What is the expected cost at that point?

CHECK Indifference probability is $\frac{1}{2}$ with the expected cost for either alternative $1,000,000.

Solution Sensitivity to Changes in Outcome Values

Other types of sensitivity analysis could be performed, for instance, by determining the change in outcome values necessary to cause a change in the optimal decision. Suppose we assume that the true probability of a favorable ruling is .7. Consider the $1,000,000 it is estimated to cost Battle Creek to substitute the new ingredient. By how much would that cost have to change, and in what direction, before we would be indifferent between the two alternatives?

This can be answered by letting x represent the questioned outcome value and finding the value of x that will leave the alternatives with the same expected cost. Thus,

$$0(.7) + 3,000,000(1 - .7) = .7x + (1 - .7)x$$

$$900,000 = .7x + .3x$$

$$x = \$900,000$$

This shows that an outcome value of $900,000 rather than $1,000,000 for the cost of substituting the new ingredient will leave Battle Creek indifferent between the two decision alternatives.

INSTANT REPLAY What would be the new point of indifference with this change? What alternative is preferred when the cost of substituting the new ingredient is less than $900,000?

CHECK $p = .7$ is the new indifference point. For costs below $900,000, the substitution alternative yields the lower expected cost.

Using Sensitivity Information

At this point what have we learned about the sensitivity of the Battle Creek decision problem? First of all, we found that the two alternatives will yield the same expected cost if the probability of a favorable FDA ruling is $\frac{2}{3}$. If the probability is higher than $\frac{2}{3}$, the "tough it out" alternative has the lower expected cost and is the preferred decision. If the probability is less than $\frac{2}{3}$, the substitution alternative is preferred because it then has the lower expected cost.

Observe that the indifference probability ($\frac{2}{3}$) is very close to our original estimate of the probability of a favorable ruling (.7). The closeness of these two values indicates the risk of making a decision without further information. A small error in our probability estimate could lead us to select the wrong decision.

We also found that even if the probability estimate is accurate, if the true cost of substituting the new ingredient is more than 10 percent less than our estimate, choosing the "tough it out" alternative would be the wrong decision.

Given the high degree of sensitivity in the Battle Creek problem, we now turn our attention to methods of reducing the risk by gathering additional information. This will be discussed at length in the next major section of this chapter.

Evaluating Information for Decision Making

There are many real-world business problems that include decisions concerning the value of additional information. If a decision is to be made about whether to introduce a new product, it may be desirable to refine estimates of demand potential by trying the product in a test market. A decision regarding a new production process may be made more confidently if the economic and technological feasibility are first tested by means of a pilot plant that is smaller in scale than the planned-for process. If a new computerized accounting system were being considered for installation in a multidivisional company, it may be wise to test the new system while continuing to operate the old system, before implementing the new system on a company-wide basis.

In each of these examples, the additional decision-aiding information could be obtained only by means of costly experiments (test market, pilot plant, duplicate accounting records). Although the benefits obtained from such additional information may be obvious from these brief examples, the decision as to whether the information should be collected must take into account these benefits in comparison with the cost of obtaining the information.

Reflecting Information in the Decision Model

Next we will consider how the benefits and costs of additional information can be reflected in our decision model. We will refer to the Battle Creek decision problem first presented in Table 3-1. It is convenient for our present purpose to   **73** recast this problem in the decision tree format first described in Chapter 2. Figure 3-2 shows the Battle Creek decision problem in decision tree form. The figure shows that the "tough it out" alternative has the lowest expected cost ($900,000), as we found earlier with the tabular approach of Table 3-1.

As you will recall, the sensitivity analysis showed that the indifference probability ($\frac{2}{3}$) was very close to the estimated probability of a favorable FDA ruling (.7), leaving considerable doubt as to the best alternative to be chosen. Although the "tough it out" alternative has the lowest expected cost, it is also the riskiest alternative because of the severe penalty incurred if the FDA rules unfavorably. For these reasons, Battle Creek management has decided to consider whether additional information can help resolve the dilemma.

The director of research and development has suggested that the company undertake a more intensive study of the carcinogenic properties of the suspect ingredient. She feels that such a study could be accomplished fairly quickly for an expenditure of $140,000 and should be an accurate prediction of the eventual FDA recommendation.

Pressed further to describe the nature and reliability of the tests, she indicated that if the substance being tested is carcinogenic, the tests will yield a positive (meaning evidence of cancer) result with a .95 probability. Thus, the chance of not detecting carcinogenic properties if they in fact exist is only 5 percent. The director also indicated that if the tested substance is *not* in fact carcinogenic, there is a .98 probability that the test results will be negative (meaning no evidence of cancer) and only a 2 percent chance that the tests will incorrectly yield a positive result.

Thus the proposed study represents a way in which Battle Creek can gain additional information for the decision. The information is *not* perfect because there is only a .95 probability of detecting carcinogenic properties if they exist

FIGURE 3-2 Decision tree for Battle Creek decision problem.

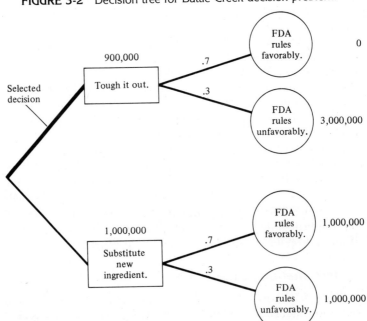

and a .98 probability of confirming the lack of carcinogenic properties if they do not exist.

Valuing Information

It is important to recognize that an evaluation of the usefulness of the information that could be obtained from this study must be accomplished *before* the information is actually obtained. This may seem strange, because it may be difficult to see how we can place a value on information until we know what that information is. Nevertheless, that is what must be done. We can accomplish the valuation by identifying what the information can potentially tell us.

Our purpose here is to estimate in advance the potential value of the information so that this potential value can be compared with the cost of obtaining it. Recall that the proposed study in the Battle Creek situation will cost $140,000 if it is carried out. Unless this study can be shown to save potentially at least that amount, the study should not be conducted.

Modifying the Decision Tree

In effect our original decision problem ("tough it out" or "substitute new ingredient") is now really several related and dependent decision problems. Consider the decision tree shown in Figure 3-3, which incorporates the decision on whether the test proposed by the director of research and development should be conducted. (For the sake of clarity we have temporarily omitted the uncontrollable events and their probabilities; these will be added later.)

Note first that the decision concerning the test appears as the beginning of the tree before the decision concerning the breakfast food ingredient. This is logical since it would make no sense to consider the test after the "tough it out" or substitution alternative has been chosen.

Second, observe that the tough-it-out/substitution decision appears in three different places in the tree. This is because the decision related to conducting the test could result in one of three situations: the test is conducted and a *positive* test result found (top of tree), the test is conducted and a *negative* test result found (middle of tree), and a decision is made not to conduct the test (bottom of tree).

There is another very important reason that the tough-it-out/substitution decision is shown in three separate places in the tree. That is, the probabilities of the uncontrollable events (not shown in Figure 3-3) are different for each of the three possible decisions. They are different because the information obtained from the test, if it is conducted, will cause us to revise the probabilities to reflect the test results.

Our original estimate of the probability of a favorable FDA ruling was .7. If, however, Battle Creek decides to conduct the test and the test result is positive (indicating the likely presence of carcinogenic properties), we would expect that the probability of a favorable FDA ruling would be somewhat less than .7. If the test result turns out negative, on the other hand, we would expect the probability of a favorable FDA ruling to increase.

Reflecting the Effect of Information on Event Probabilities

Since we already know the event probabilities for the tough-it-out/substitution decision at the bottom of the tree (.7 for favorable ruling and .3 for unfavor-

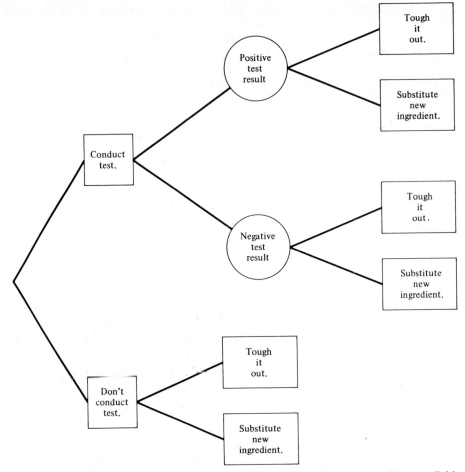

FIGURE 3-3 Battle Creek decision tree with decision on conducting test. (Uncontrollable events have been omitted for clarity.)

able), let us turn our attention to the portion of the tree corresponding to the decision to conduct the test. This portion of the decision tree, including each of the uncontrollable events, is shown in Figure 3-4.

Careful examination of this partial decision tree will disclose that there are six distinct probabilities needed to complete the tree. We need to know the probability that the test result will be positive, $p(+)$, and that the test will be negative, $p(-)$.

The four other probabilities needed to complete Figure 3-4 are called *dependent probabilities*, since the likelihood of each event (FDA ruling) is dependent upon the outcome of the test. It is convenient to use notational shorthand to represent dependent probabilities; the notation $p(A|B)$ is used to represent the probability that event A will happen given that event B happened. Thus, the probability of a favorable FDA ruling given that the test result is positive could be written as

$$p(\text{favorable FDA ruling} \mid \text{test result is positive})$$

or more conveniently as simply $p(F|+)$. In a similar manner we can define

$p(U\,|+)$ to represent the probability of an unfavorable ruling given a positive test result. The other two probabilities shown in Figure 3-4, $p(F\,|-)$ and $p(U\,|-)$, are the respective probabilities of favorable and unfavorable rulings given a negative test result.

How do we find these missing probabilities so that our decision tree can be completed? Suppose we assume that the FDA ruling is based on an extremely accurate test and that if the substance is carcinogenic the FDA will determine this and therefore rule unfavorably. Alternatively, if the substance is

FIGURE 3-4 Partial decision tree for Battle Creek decision problem (showing the "conduct test" option only).

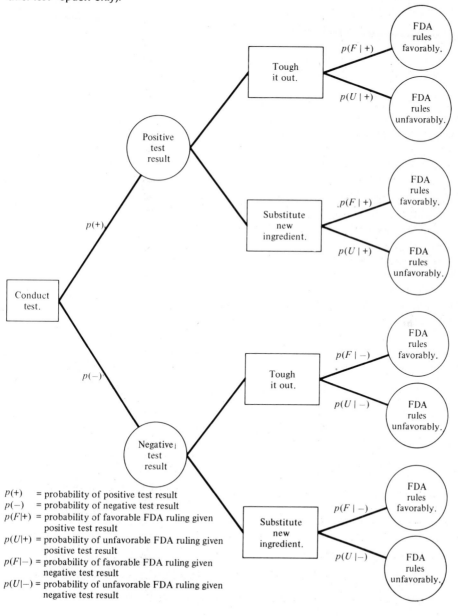

$p(+)$ = probability of positive test result
$p(-)$ = probability of negative test result
$p(F|+)$ = probability of favorable FDA ruling given
positive test result
$p(U|+)$ = probability of unfavorable FDA ruling given
positive test result
$p(F|-)$ = probability of favorable FDA ruling given
negative test result
$p(U|-)$ = probability of unfavorable FDA ruling given
negative test result

noncarcinogenic, the FDA will also determine that and therefore rule favorably.

Probability Trees Consider next the probabilities shown in Figure 3-5, arranged in what we call a *probability tree*. A probability tree is a convenient means of organizing probability data in order to calculate the likelihood of certain experimental results. A probability tree differs from a decision tree in that no decision alternatives are involved. Instead, all branches represent probabilistic events. To avoid unnecessary confusion, we distinguish a probability tree from a decision tree by arranging the branches from top to bottom rather than left to right. Of course, if you prefer you may draw the trees with either orientation.

At the top of the tree we indicate that the questionable substance is either carcinogenic (and the FDA will rule unfavorably) or noncarcinogenic (and the FDA will rule favorably). These two branches reflect our initial estimates of the probabilities of favorable (.7) and unfavorable rulings (.3).

As the director of research and development indicated, the proposed detailed test is not infallible and both positive and negative test results can be obtained whether or not the substance is truly carcinogenic. As the probability tree shows, if the substance is carcinogenic, a positive test result will be obtained with probability .95 and a negative test result with probability .05. A positive test result is one in which some evidence of cancer-causing properties is found, while a negative test result reflects the absence of such evidence. If, on the other hand, the substance is noncarcinogenic, the test result branches in Figure 3-5 show a .02 probability of a positive test result and a .98 probability of a negative result.

Observe that there are four possible combinations of actual carcinogenicity and test results as shown by the four distinct paths from the top to the bottom of the tree. The product of the probabilities along the branches of any of these paths is equivalent to the probability of the joint occurrence of the events on that path. For example, the left-hand path corresponds to the events that the substance is carcinogenic and that the test result is positive. Since there is a .3 probability that the substance is carcinogenic and a .95 probability that a carcinogenic substance will yield positive test results, there is a .3(.95) = .285 probability that both events will occur. Similar calculations are shown under each of the four paths. Observe that the sum of the branch probabilities (.285 + .015 + .014 + .686) is 1.0, reflecting the fact that one of these four event combinations must occur.

Using Probability Trees With this brief introduction to probability trees, we are now ready to use the tree to determine the six probabilities needed for our decision tree (Figure 3-4). First we need to know the probabilities that the test result will be positive, $p(+)$, and negative, $p(-)$. This information can be obtained directly from the probability tree. Note that of the four possible paths in Figure 3-5, two end with a positive test result, and two end with a negative test result. To determine the overall probability of a positive test result, we simply add the probabilities for the two paths that end with positive test results:

Probability of positive test result = $p(+)$ = .285 + .014 = .299

Similarly, we add the remaining probabilities to find the likelihood of a negative test result:

Thus, we find that there is a .299 probability that the test result will be positive and a .701 probability it will be negative.

The remaining four probabilities needed to complete the decision tree were identified previously as dependent probabilities. These were $p(F\,|+)$, $p(U\,|+), p(F\,|-)$, and $p(U\,|-)$. Note that the probability tree of Figure 3-5 also contains dependent probabilities. That is, the lower branches of the tree reflect the probability of a positive or negative test result given the substance's carcinogenic properties or type of FDA ruling. These could have been written in our notational shorthand, from left to right, as $p(+\,|U), p(-\,|U), p(+\,|F)$, and $p(-\,|F)$.

A careful comparison of the probabilities given in the probability tree and those we need for the decision tree will show that the order of the dependencies for the probabilities needed are just the reverse of those for the probabilities that we know. That is, we need to find the probabilility of a favorable ruling given a positive test result, $p(\mathrm{F}\,|+)$, but what we know is the probability of a positive test result given a favorable FDA ruling, $p(+\,|F)$. How do we find the probabilities when the dependency is reversed?

Actually a few simple calculations are all that is required. Observe that positive test results are expected to occur with probability

$$p(+) = p(+\,|U)p(U) + p(+\,|F)p(F) = .285 + .014 = .299$$

as determined earlier. Referring to the probability tree (Figure 3-5), note that the .299 probability was a combination of a .285 probability representing posi-

FIGURE 3-5 Probability tree for carcinogenic tests of suspected substance.

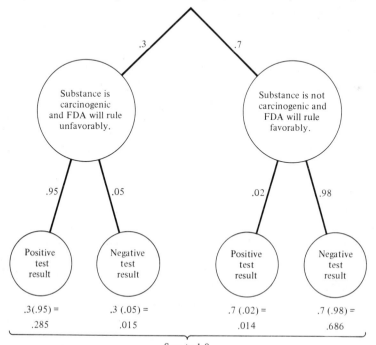

tive test results where the ruling will be unfavorable and a .014 probability for positive results where the ruling will be favorable. Therefore, if a positive test result is obtained, it is much more likely to occur if the FDA is to rule unfavorably. In fact, the probability that the FDA will rule unfavorably is equivalent to the proportion of positive test results when the FDA will rule unfavorably relative to the proportion of positive test results regardless of the FDA ruling, $p(+)$, or

$$p(U\,|+) = \frac{.285}{.299} = .953$$

Similarly, the probability that the FDA will rule favorably if the test result is positive is equivalent to the ratio of that branch's probability to the probability of a positive test result, or

$$p(F\,|+) = \frac{.014}{.299} = .047$$

We can calculate this last probability more easily if we recognize that the FDA will rule either favorably or unfavorably. Since .953 of all positive test results correspond to situations in which the FDA will rule unfavorably, the remaining $1 - .953$ or .047 proportion must correspond to situations in which the FDA will rule favorably. Thus,

$$p(F\,|+) = 1 - p(U\,|+)$$

$$= 1 - .953 = .047$$

Bayes' Formula A general equation exists for calculating dependent probabilities, as above, developed by Reverend Thomas Bayes, an eighteenth-century British clergyman. The equation, commonly referred to as Bayes' formula, relates the probability dependencies of two events A and B as

$$p(A|B) = \frac{p(A \text{ and } B)}{p(B)}$$

In our situation, event A could correspond to the FDA ruling unfavorably, and event B could represent a positive test result. Thus,

$$p(U\,|+) = \frac{p(U \text{ and } +)}{p(+)}$$

The probability $p(U \text{ and } +)$ is shorthand notation for what is normally called a *joint probability*, corresponding, in this case, to the probability that the FDA will rule unfavorably *and* that a positive test result is obtained. This was calculated at the leftmost path in the probability tree corresponding to the two events (U and $+$) by taking the product of the two probabilities of the branches of that path.

The final two probabilities needed to complete the decision tree of Figure 3-4 refer to the FDA ruling given negative test results and are calculated as above. Thus, the probability that the FDA will rule unfavorably if the test result is negative can be found from

$$p(U\,|-) = \frac{p(U \text{ and } -)}{p(-)}$$

$$= \frac{.015}{.701} = .021$$

Similarly, the probability that the FDA will rule favorably if the test result
is negative is given by either

$$p(F\,|-) = \frac{p(F \text{ and } -)}{p(-)}$$

$$= \frac{.686}{.701} = .979$$

or
$$p(F\,|-) = 1 - p(U\,|-)$$

$$= 1 - .021 = .979$$

INSTANT REPLAY Suppose that our initial estimate of the probability of a
favorable ruling had been .5 (rather than .7). What would be the revised values
for the six probabilities we need to complete the decision tree—$p(+)$, $p(-)$,
$p(F\,|+)$, $p(U\,|+)$, $p(F\,|-)$, and $p(U\,|-)$?

CHECK The probability tree would now appear as

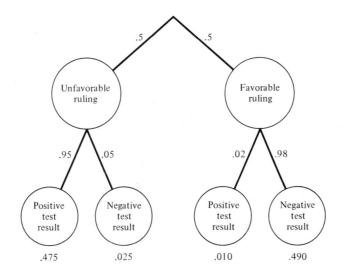

The probabilities would be calculated thus:

$$p(+) = .475 + .010 = .485$$

$$p(-) = .025 + .490 = .515$$

$$p(U\,|+) = \frac{p(U \text{ and } +)}{p(+)} = \frac{.475}{.485} = .979$$

$$p(F\,|+) = 1 - p(U\,|+) = 1 - .979 = .021$$

$$p(U\,|-) = \frac{p(U \text{ and } -)}{p(-)} = \frac{.025}{.515} = .049$$

$$p(F\,|-) = 1 - .049 = .951$$

Now that the missing probabilities have been determined, we can complete the decision tree for the Battle Creek problem. The full tree is shown in Figure 3-6. As stated earlier, all three tough-it-out/substitution decision problems have different probabilities for the uncontrollable events. The top problem, based on conducting the test and obtaining a positive result, shows a .047 probability of a favorable ruling, considerably lower than our original estimate. This low probability is the result of the high likelihood that the substance is carcinogenic if the test result turns out to be positive.

However, the decision problem in the middle of the tree shows a very high probability, .979, for a favorable ruling. This reflects the high likelihood that the substance is noncarcinogenic if the test result is negative. The decision problem at the bottom of the tree reflects our original probability estimates because the problem assumes that the test is not conducted and no new information is available to change these estimates.

Solving the Dependent Decision Problems   Each of the three decision problems is solved in the standard manner by calculating expected costs and then selecting the alternative with the lowest expected cost. Thus, if the test is conducted and the test result is positive, the new ingredient should be substituted because the $1,000,000 expected cost for that alternative is considerably less than that for the "tough it out" alternative ($2,859,00).

If the test is conducted and the test result is negative, the "tough it out" alternative should be selected because its expected cost of $63,000 is substantially less than the $1,000,000 cost of the substitution alternative. Finally, if the test is not conducted, the "tough it out" alternative should be chosen because its $900,000 expected cost is slightly less than the $1,000,000 cost of the substitution alternative. The selected decision for each problem is indicated by the thicker branch.

Observe that the probability changes for the uncontrollable events, based on the test results, cause a change in the optimal decision to the tough-it-out/substitute decision if the test result is positive. Without any additional information, the "tough it out" decision is best. If the test is conducted and a positive test result is obtained, the optimal decision is now to make the substitution. If the test result is negative, the optimal decision ("tough it out") remains the same as it would be without conducting the test.

Deciding Whether the Information Should be Collected   We should note that the information obtained from conducting the test has value only if at least one of the test outcomes (in this case a positive test result) results in a change in the tough-it-out/substitute decision. If the same decision is called for with or without the test (i.e., regardless of the test outcome), it should be obvious that the test has little or no value. The value of additional information is derived from the ability to predict better which uncontrollable event is likely to occur and to adjust the decision strategy accordingly. If no adjustment can take place, no matter what information is gathered, the test has no value for decision making.

In our case, however, a positive test result would cause our decision to change. Therefore, we need to determine whether the benefits of the information justify the cost of obtaining it. To do this, we need first to calculate the

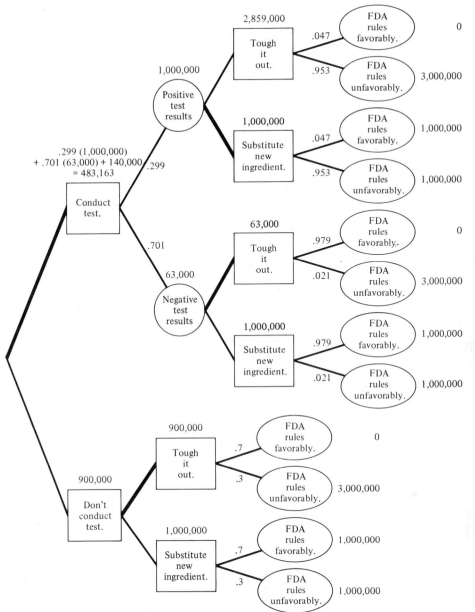

FIGURE 3-6 Completed decision tree for Battle Creek decision problem with an information option.

expected cost for the "conduct test" alternative. Obviously, the expected cost, if the test is conducted, is dependent on the probabilities of the test results and the expected costs of the decisions based on those results. Because the test itself is expected to cost $140,000, we must also add this cost.

Therefore, we can calculate the expected cost of the conduct-test option as:

$$\begin{pmatrix} \text{Expected cost} \\ \text{of ``conduct''} \\ \text{test'' option} \end{pmatrix} = \begin{pmatrix} \text{probability} \\ \text{of positive} \\ \text{test result} \end{pmatrix} \times \begin{pmatrix} \text{expected cost of} \\ \text{best decision for} \\ \text{positive test result} \end{pmatrix}$$

$$+ \begin{pmatrix} \text{probability} \\ \text{of negative} \\ \text{test results} \end{pmatrix} \times \begin{pmatrix} \text{expected cost of} \\ \text{best decision for} \\ \text{negative test result} \end{pmatrix} + \begin{pmatrix} \text{cost of} \\ \text{conducting} \\ \text{test} \end{pmatrix}$$

$$= .299(1,000,000) + .701(63,000) + 140,000 = \$483,163$$

The expected cost of the "don't conduct test" option was calculated previously to be \$900,000. (This was the original decision problem.) Since the expected cost of the "conduct test" option (\$483,163) is less than expected with the "don't conduct test" option (\$900,000), we can conclude that the test should be conducted.

Finding the Value of the Information   The *value of the information* provided by the test is the difference between the expected cost of the no-test option, \$900,000, and that expected if the test is conducted *ignoring the cost of the test*. The expected cost of the "conduct test" option is \$483,163. This, however, includes the \$140,000 cost of the test. Deducting this cost leaves a net cost of \$483,163 − 140,000 = \$343,163. Subtracting this net cost from the expected cost of the "don't conduct test" option yields a value of \$900,000 − 343,163 = \$556,837 for the information provided by the test. Thus, since the test provides expected benefits of \$556,837 and costs only \$140,000, the test should be conducted and will leave a net expected savings of \$416,837.

Thus, the optimal decision strategy for the company to follow is to conduct the test, and if the test gives a positive result, the new ingredient should be substituted as soon as possible without waiting for the FDA to take action. If, on the other hand, the test result is negative, the company should tough it out and wait for the FDA ruling.

Reduction of Risk   Observe that without the test information the best decision is to tough it out. The risk of having to make a crash substitution in response to an unfavorable ruling is 30 percent, the probability that the FDA will so rule. Under the revised decision plan, which calls for additional information to be obtained through testing, this risk has been reduced because the company will tough it out only if the test results are negative. From Figure 3-6 we note that the probability of a negative test result is .701 and that the probability of an unfavorable FDA ruling given a negative test result, $p(U\,|-)$, is .021. The joint probability of obtaining a negative test result and an unfavorable ruling by the FDA is therefore

$$p(-)p(U\,|-) = .701(.021) = .015$$

Thus, the risk of a crash substitution has been reduced from 30 to 1.5 percent.

INSTANT REPLAY   Suppose that our initial estimate of the probability of a favorable FDA ruling had been .5 (rather than .7). As we saw in the previous Instant Replay, this led to probabilities of $p(+) = .485$, $p(-) = .515$, $p(U\,|+) = .979$, $p(F\,|+) = .021$, $p(U\,|-) = .049$, and $p(F\,|-) = .951$. If the test costs

$140,000, what would be the optimal set of decisions, the net expected cost, the value of the test, and the risk of making a crash substitution?

CHECK   If the test is conducted and the result is positive, the best decision is to substitute with an expected cost of $1,000,000. If the test result is negative, the best decision is to tough it out with an expected cost of $147,000. If the test is not conducted, the best decision is to substitute with an expected cost of $1,000,000. The expected cost if the test is conducted is equal to

$$.485(1,000,000) + .515(147,000) + 140,000 = \$700,705$$

which is less than the expected cost if the test is not conducted.

   Thus the optimal set of decisions is to conduct the test and, if the test result is positive, to substitute, but if the test is negative to tough it out. The net expected cost of this decision plan is $700,705.

   The value of the test is the difference between the expected cost if the test is conducted and that if the test is not conducted, adjusted for the cost of the test, or

$$1,000,000 - 700,705 + 140,000 = \$439,295$$

   The risk of making a crash substitution is 50 percent if the test is not conducted. With the test, a decision to tough it out is made if the test is negative $[p(-) = .515]$ and the probability of an unfavorable ruling given a negative test result, $p(U|-)$, is, .049. Thus, the risk of a crash substitution is

$$p(U) = p(U|-)p(-) = .049(.515) = .025$$

or 2.5 percent.

Review of Decision Making with Information Options

As you now must realize, the incorporation of information options in decision problems complicates the analysis considerably. Nevertheless, as we saw in the case of the Battle Creek decision problem, the rewards of performing that analysis can be quite high. Therefore, you may find it useful to review the steps required so that you will be able to apply the concepts to other similar problems.

   To simplify this review, we will use the term *information decision* to refer to the decision concerning whether or not the information should be obtained, the term *original decision* to refer to the original decision problem without the information option, and the term *information-dependent decision* to refer to the decision problems whose probabilities are dependent on the information received, given that the information is obtained.

   The following steps summarize the solution process:

1. Prepare a decision tree including the information decision as the first decision in the tree, the original decision options for each possible result of the information decision, possible uncontrollable events, and decision outcomes for each branch in the tree.

2. Use a probability tree to find the event probabilities for each information-dependent decision problem as well as the probabilities of the possible information options.

3. Calculate expected values for each of the information-dependent decision problems and select the best decision for each.

4. Calculate the expected value for the "don't test" option by solving the original decision problem.

5. Determine the expected values for the "conduct test" option using the best decision for the resulting information-dependent decision problem weighted by the probability of the information options.

6. Make a decision concerning whether the information should be obtained, based on the expected values.

7. Determine the value of the information by comparing the expected value if the information is obtained (omitting the cost of obtaining it) with that if the information is not obtained.

Observe that the procedure summarized can be used for problems with objectives to be maximized (such as profit) as well as objectives to be minimized (such as costs). Furthermore, no limitations are placed on the size of the problem, as measured by the number of original decision options or the number of information options, other than your ability to draw decision or probability trees.

Sequential Decision Problems

Many decision problems in practice are not of the simpler single-stage type so far considered. Such *multistage*, or *sequential, decision problems* are characterized by a series of related but separate decisions. Frequently these decisions are separated by time, such as quarterly production volume decisions, or by some natural precedence order, such as when the product design decision precedes the processing design decision.

In this section we will illustrate how these sequential decision problems can be conveniently treated by means of a decision tree. This is best illustrated with an example.

Problem Situation

The Pandora Toy Company is faced with a complicated series of operating decisions. They have developed a new novelty toy for which they have high expectations. Unfortunately, their existing production capacity is almost fully utilized by the requirements of existing products. In order to introduce this new toy in time for the coming selling season, the company would have to expand their production facilities now or subcontract much of the production requirements with another firm.

The toy is expected to be priced at $10 each. If Pandora makes the toy itself, the variable production costs will be $5 per unit and the fixed production costs (including expansion costs) will run approximately $50,000 per year. If the item is subcontracted, no fixed costs will be incurred but the variable costs will be higher, since Pandora will have to pay the subcontractor $7.50 per unit.

Because of the newness of the proposed product, there is a great deal of uncertainty regarding anticipated sales volume. Past experience has shown that demand for similar items follows a boom or bust pattern. Either the toy is a big winner or it is only a moderate seller. For this reason, the company has narrowed the number of demand states to two. If the toy is successful, it is likely to sell about 50,000 units the first year. If, on the other hand, the reception in the marketplace is moderate, demand is expected to be approximately 10,000 units.

Products of this nature have traditionally had a short lifespan. This has led Pandora management to limit their planning horizon for this product to 2 years. Demand forecasts have been prepared which assume a .2 probability that first-year demand will reach the higher level (50,000 units) and thus a .8 probability at the lower level (10,000 units). Second-year demand estimates are dependent on those achieved in the first year. If first-year demand is at the high level, there is assumed to be a .8 probability of continued high demand in the second year and a .2 chance that demand will fall to the lower level (10,000). Alternatively, if demand during the first year was at the lower level, the assumption is that there will be a .1 probability in the second year for demand to be at the high level and a .9 probability for low demand.

Some individuals on the management team at Pandora feel that the production facility should be expanded now so that the new product can be produced by Pandora to meet any anticipated demand. Others promote a wait-and-see approach, calling for subcontracting the first year, the decision on subcontracting or expanding for the second year to be made after 1 year's demand experience.

Preparing the Decision Tree

These decision alternatives and demand possibilities are summarized in the decision tree of Figure 3-7. (For simplification the outcome values are omitted; these will be added later.) Note that a decision to expand for the first year (lower portion of the tree) precludes any further subcontracting/expansion decision. On the other hand, if a decision is made to subcontract for the first year (wait and see) a new decision is required for the second year. The second-year decision is a dependent decision because the probabilities of demand for the second year are dependent on the level of first-year demand.

You should recognize that a decision to wait and see by subcontracting for the first year is equivalent to a decision to obtain additional information (the level of the first year's demand) before making the subcontract/expand decision for year 2. Two problems remain: calculating the outcome values and determining the optimal decision. Let us consider each of these in turn.

Calculation of Outcome Values

Note that the annual profit for either year is a function of both the demand level for that year and whether or not that demand is met by subcontracting or by expansion of Pandora's own capacity.

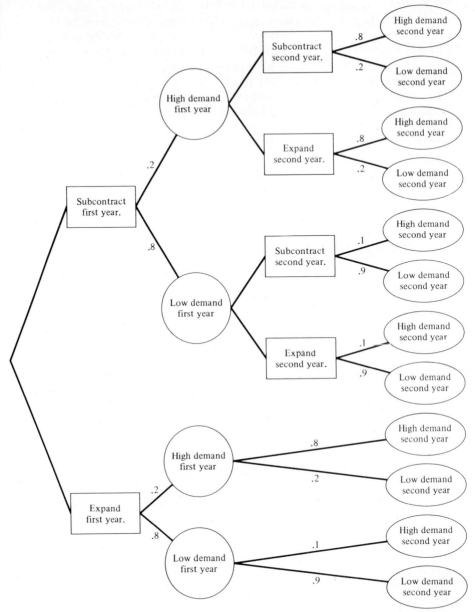

FIGURE 3-7 Partial decision tree for Pandora Toy Company problem (omitting outcome values).

Let us consider the subcontracting alternative first. If Pandora subcontracts, the company will earn a net profit of $10 − 7.50 = $2.50 for each unit sold. With high demand, sales will be 50,000 units or

$$\begin{array}{l}\text{Annual profit with} \\ \text{subcontracting and high demand}\end{array} = \$2.50(50{,}000) = \$125{,}000$$

With low demand, sales will be only 10,000 units or

$$\text{Annual profit with subcontracting and low demand} = \$2.50(10,000) = \$25,000$$

Next consider the expansion alternative. The gross margin is equal to $10.00 − 5.00 = $5.00 per unit sold, but from this must be subtracted the $50,000 fixed costs. Thus, for high demand

$$\text{Annual profit with expansion and high demand} = \$5.00(50,000) − 50,000 = \$200,000$$

and for low demand

$$\text{Annual profit with expansion and low demand} = \$5.00(10,000) − 50,000 = 0$$

These outcome values are shown at the right of the complete decision tree of Figure 3-8.

Finding the Solution

Determining the optimal set of decisions requires starting with the second year and working backward, because the first-year decision is dependent on the profit achievable in the second year. Observe that the demand probabilities for the second year reflect their dependencies on first-year demand. Assuming high

FIGURE 3-8   Decision tree for Pandora Toy Company problem.

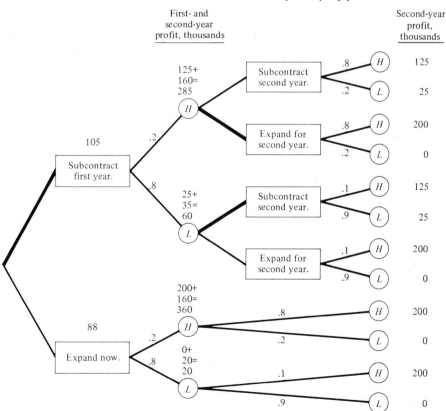

demand and subcontracting for the first year, subcontracting for the second year yields an expected profit of $105,000 [.8(125,000) + .2(25,000)] and expansion yields an expected profit of $160,000. Therefore, *the optimal decision for the second year, for high demand and subcontracting for the first year, is to expand and produce the item in house for the second year.*

If the subcontracting option is followed the first year but low demand results, the expected profit for the second year is $35,000 ($12,500 + 22,500) for continued subcontracting and $20,000 for expansion. Therefore, *the optimal second-year decision, for low demand and subcontracting for the first year, is to continue subcontracting for the second year.*

Next a word about the profit figures shown for the two demand possibilities in the first year with subcontracting. With high first-year demand (and subcontracting) Pandora will earn $125,000 as calculated earlier. To this must be added the expected second-year profit of $160,000 (based on the previously determined optimal decision of expansion), leaving an expected two-year profit of $285,000. With low first-year demand the first-year profit of $25,000 is added to the expected second-year profit of $35,000, yielding a two-year profit of $60,000.

When these two-year profits are then weighted by the probability of the two first-year demand possibilities, we find an expected 2-year profit of $105,000 [.2(285) + .8(60)] for the decision to subcontract the first year.

The expected profit for the other major branch in the decision tree, "expand now," is easier to compute since a decision to expand precludes a second-year expansion/subcontracting decision. If the first year demand was high, the expected profit for the second year is $160,000. This is added to the first-year profit for high demand of $200,000, yielding a 2-year profit estimate of $360,000. If the first-year demand is low, the expected profit for the second year is $20,000, which when added to the zero profit for the first year leaves an expected 2-year profit of $20,000.

These two profits are then weighted by the respective probabilities for the first-year demand to arrive at the expected 2-year profit for the "expand now" option of $88,000 ($16,000 + 72,000).

Since the expected profit for the first-year subcontract option exceeds that for expansion, the optimal decision is now to: (1) subcontract for the first year, and (2) expand the second year if the first-year demand is high, or (3) continue subcontracting if the first-year demand is low. This decision plan, marked with heavy lines on Figure 3-8, will yield an expected 2-year profit of $105,000.

INSTANT REPLAY   Suppose that the second-year demand probabilities were .5 for each level if low demand is experienced in the first year. Does this change the optimal decisions? What is the expected 2-year profit?

CHECK   The only decision affected is the second-year decision when demand was low in the first year. Expansion rather than subcontracting is now called for. This revised decision set yields an expected 2-year profit of $157,000.

This example illustrates one advantage of decision trees relative to decision tables. The Pandora Toy Company problem would be difficult to state compactly as a decision table because of the sequential nature of the decisions.

The decision for the second year is conditional on both the decision for the first year and the demand outcome for the first year. Thus, the decision tree approach is particularly well suited to sequential or multiple-stage decision problems.

Final Comments

In Chapter 2 we developed the basic decision-making framework. In this chapter we saw how this framework can be used to improve the decision maker's ability to deal with risky situations through experimentation.

We began by analyzing the sensitivity of the best decision to changes in the various decision model elements. In particular, we considered changes in either the probabilities of the uncontrollable events or in the decision outcomes. We showed how to calculate indifference points as a means of quantifying the decision sensitivity.

Next we examined how to include the potential benefits and costs of gathering additional information through experimentation. The potential benefits of this information were determined by solving a set of information-dependent decision problems. The dependencies were a result of the fact that the event probabilities for these problems (and thus the choice of a best decision) were dependent upon the information that might be received from experimentation. We used probability trees to determine the dependent event probabilities as well as the probability of the potential experimental results.

We calculated the value of information by comparing the expected return if the information is collected with the expected return if the information is not obtained. This value is then compared with the cost of obtaining the information to determine whether the information is worth obtaining.

In the final section of the chapter we used decision trees to solve sequential decision problems and those with several separate but related decisions.

Key Words

Bayes' formula **80**
Decision alternatives **69**
Decision making under risk **69**
Decision model **68**
Decision tree **74**
Dependent probability **76**
Event probabilities **68**
Indifference point **70**
Indifference probability **70**
Information decision **85**
Information-dependent decision **85**

Joint probability **80**
Less-than-perfect information **68**
Original decision **85**
Outcomes **72**
Perfect information **68**
Probability tree **78**
Sensitivity analysis **69**
Sequential decision problem **86**
Uncontrollable events **75**
Value of information **73**

Problems

3-1. The McHill Publishing Company specializes in publishing a series of self-help books, most of which achieve only a moderate sales volume. Occasionally, however, a book in this field will catch on and become a major best seller. Past history indicates that a moderate seller in this category will cause McHill to lose, on the average, $80,000. A best seller should return $1,000,000. An editor for McHill is currently reviewing a manuscript in this field and must soon decide whether or not the company will publish it.

a. Suppose the editor estimates that the book has a .1 probability of being a best seller. Should the book be published? What is the expected profit for the alternative selected?

b. How much would the editor be willing to pay if it were possible to know in advance whether the book will be a best seller?

c. The editor frequently asks publishing advice from a reviewer with a good track record in predicting a manuscript's degree of success. In the past, for books of this type, 50 percent of books that he has predicted to be best sellers actually became best sellers while 94 percent of the books that he predicted only moderate success for did, in fact, achieve only moderate sales. The reviewer has in the past predicted that 9 percent of the books he reviewed were destined to be best sellers. If the reviewer charges $5,000 to review a book of this type, determine whether the editor should pay for a review of the current manuscript and what actions he should take with respect to publication.

d. What is the expected profit from the decision in part c?

e. What is the value of the reviewer's opinion?

3-2. Refer again to the McHill Publishing Company problem (see problem 3–1). Prepare a graph showing the expected returns for the alternatives as a function of the probability of the book becoming a best seller.

a. What probability corresponds to the point of indifference between the two alternatives? What is the expected return at that point?

b. Suppose that the editor has a third alternative. That is, the book could be produced more elaborately (fancy dust cover, two colors, etc.) and sold at a higher price. For this alternative assume a $150,000 loss if the book is only a moderate success and a $1,300,000 profit if the book is a best seller. Add this third alternative to your graph. How many indifference points now exist, and what are they?

c. If the probability that the book is a best seller is .1, what would the profit have to be if the book is a best seller and the more elaborate version of the book produced in order for the editor to be indifferent between the elaborate version and the less expensive version? Between the elaborate version and not publishing the book?

3-3. The principal partner for Angel Investors, a limited partnership that invests in Broadway shows, is faced with a decision concerning a new musical, based on a government scandal ("Watergate Follies"), that the partnership is backing. A decision needs to be made whether the show should open in a large theater or a small theater or be closed immediately. Shows of this type are subject to the whims of the public, and three receptions are possible: smashing success, moderate success, or disaster. The anticipated profits and losses in thousands for these options are:

	Smashing success	Moderate success	Disaster
Open in large theater	3,000	− 400	−2,000
Open in small theater	1,000	200	−1,500
Close now	−1,000	−1,000	−1,000

Although past history indicates that no one is much good at estimating success, the principal partner feels that the show has a .2 probability of being a smashing success, a .5 probability of being a moderate success, and a .3 chance of ending in disaster.

a. What decision should the principal partner make with respect to this show? What is the expected profit of the chosen option?

b. How much would the principal partner be willing to pay to know in advance the degree of success the show can receive?

c. The ultimate success achieved by such a show often depends to a great extent on the reaction of the critics in the major metropolitan newspapers. One such recently retired critic now earns a nice living as a consultant to Broadway producers. He is willing to evaluate "Watergate Follies" for a set fee of $50,000. Analysis of his past record indicates that the following probabilities reflect his prediction accuracy:

$$p \text{ (predicts hit } | \text{ smashing success)} = .7$$

$$p \text{ (predicts hit } | \text{ moderate success)} = .5$$

$$p \text{ (predicts flop } | \text{ disaster)} = .9$$

How much is the critic's prediction worth to Angel Investors?

d. What is the optimal strategy both in terms of hiring the critic and in terms of opening or closing the show?

3–4. To help finance his education, Rich Sammond earns money as a concessionaire for one of the professional soccer teams. Rich has invested funds in a large insulated vat with a tap for dispensing hot or cold liquids. The day before a home game, Rich brews either coffee or iced tea with which he fills the vat for sale at the game. Since he has a single vat, Rich must decide ahead of time whether he wishes to sell coffee or iced tea. His actual sales volume depends to a large extent on the weather, which in this locality tends to extremes, either hot or cold. On cold days, if he brings coffee he will earn $400. On the other hand, if he brings iced tea on cold days he only breaks even. On hot days he can earn $300 by bringing iced tea, but if he brings coffee he earns only $100. Unfortunately, Rich has found the weather forecast to be unreliable, and he frequently has guessed wrong and brought the wrong drink to sell.

a. What probability of hot weather would be necessary for Rich to be indifferent between bringing coffee and iced tea?

b. Rich has kept track of past weather results on game days and has found that cold weather occurs 40 percent of the time and hot weather 60 percent. What type of drink should Rich bring to the next game and how much is his expected profit?

c. How much would it be worth to Rich to be able to know exactly what type of weather will exist at the next day's game?

d. One of Rich's neighbors is a meteorologist who has offered to help Rich forecast the weather. They decide to run a test to determine the meteorologist's forecasting accuracy. He provides Rich with a forecast for 20 randomly selected days with the following results.

Meteorologist predicts	*Actual weather*	
	Cold	*Hot*
Cold	6	2
Hot	2	10

What is the maximum amount that Rich would be willing to pay his neighbor to provide weather forecasts?

e. What decision should Rich make with respect to hiring his neighbor, if he charges $20 per forecast, and with respect to brewing coffee or iced tea? What will Rich's expected profit be for the optimal decisions?

f. Suppose that rather than invest his money in weather forecasts, Rich decides he can avoid the forecasting problem altogether by renting a second insulated vat so that he can bring both coffee and iced tea. What is the maximum amount Rich would be willing to pay per game to rent a second vat? Assume that coffee and iced tea sales are independent of each other.

3-5. The treasurer of the Baldcore Company is faced with a decision as to how best to invest $1,000,000 in funds for the next year. These funds were obtained through a stock issue in anticipation of a company expansion. Because of legal problems that developed in connection with a building permit, the expansion had to be postponed for a year, hence the need to invest the excess money on a short-term basis. The treasurer has identified the investment options shown below. The total return received from each is dependent on general economic and financial conditions for the year, as shown in the table.

Investment options	Anticipated total return, %		
	Economy rises	Economy stabilizes	Economy declines
Bonds	7	9	12
Commercial paper	8	10	14
Stocks	25	6	2

a. Suppose the treasurer estimates that there is a .1 probability that the economy will fall, .2 probability that it will rise, and a .7 probability that it will stabilize. What investment decision should the treasurer make and what is his expected rate of return?

b. How much would it be worth to the treasurer to know the economic conditions for the coming year?

c. An investment service has approached Baldcore's treasurer with an offer to provide help in forecasting economic conditions. He offers these services for $5,000. He has provided a prospectus which indicates the following record of accuracy over the past 40 years:

Predicted economy	Actual economy		
	Increased	Stabilized	Declined
Economic increase	7	3	2
Economic stability	3	14	2
Economic decline	1	3	5

Would it be worthwhile for Baldcore's treasurer to purchase the advice of the investment service?

d. What action with respect to advice buying and investment selection should the treasurer take and what will be the expected rate of return?

3-6. Wings Airlines has just been awarded a new route between New York and Cairo. In order to offer service on this route, the company will have to obtain additional aircraft. Given the uncertainties concerning the demand for seats on this route, the company is considering several ways in which to provide capacity.

One option is to purchase a used aircraft at a cost of $1,000,000. This aircraft can be resold for $900,000 at the end of 1 year or $800,000 after 2 years. Another option is to lease a larger airplane from a competitor for an annual fee of $150,000.

The company already has ordered a new airplane from the manufacturer for delivery in 2 years. The manufacturer has indicated that this aircraft could be delivered 1 year early, if Wings wished, for an added cost of $200,000.

Capacities and operating costs for the three types of aircraft are sufficiently different to yield varying operating margins as shown below under relevant demand assumptions. Operating margins represent the difference between revenue and operating costs. They have not been adjusted for leasing or other fixed costs described earlier.

| Type of aircraft | Annual operating margin, thousands of dollars | | |
	High demand	*Moderate demand*	*Low demand*
Purchased used	250	250	220
Leased	290	260	200
New	325	290	210

Probability estimates of demand for the 2-year period are shown below. Note that the second year demand estimates are dependent on demand achieved in the first year.

| Demand | First year | Second year if first-year demand was | | |
		High	*Moderate*	*Low*
High	.1	.5	.3	.2
Moderate	.5	.3	.5	.6
Low	.4	.2	.2	.2

a. Prepare a decision tree for the Wings capacity decision with the following options:

First year
   Purchase used plane
   Lease plane
Second year, used plane purchased in first year
   Continue operating used plane
   Sell off used plane and lease instead
   Sell off used plane and take early delivery on new plane
Second year, plane leased in first year
   Continue leasing
   Stop leasing and purchase used plane (same price, $1,000,000, and resale value, $900,000, as now)
   Stop leasing and take early delivery on new plane

b. What is the optimal set of decisions for the company to follow?

3-7. The Witherspoon Garage operates a highly successful forklift overhaul service. The cost of the overhaul to Witherspoon depends on whether major or minor overhaul work is required. A major overhaul has an average cost of $200 and a minor overhaul a cost of $60. A major overhaul will find and correct any defects in the forklift. If a minor overhaul is performed when a major overhaul is needed, the cost of the minor overhaul is wasted since an additional $200 would have to be spent to complete the necessary work. If a major overhaul is performed when only a minor one was necessary, the costs are the same as if the forklift had needed a major overhaul to begin with. Approximately 20 percent of all forklifts received for overhaul eventually require a major overhaul.

a. Prepare a decision tree for this problem and determine whether it is better to subject all forklifts to a major overhaul or to first send them through a minor overhaul.

b. What is the expected overhaul cost for the best strategy in part *a*?

c. It has been suggested that one of the senior mechanics could inspect each forklift prior to making the overhaul decision. The cost of this inspection is estimated to be $25. On the basis of his inspection, the forklifts would be subdivided into those that he thought needed a minor overhaul and those that needed a major overhaul. It is further estimated that if a forklift needs a major overhaul, there is a .8 probability that the inspector would correctly place it in that category. If, on the other hand, the forklift needs only minor overhaul, he would correctly identify this 90 percent of the time. Draw a decision tree incorporating the possibility of using the inspector to prescreen all forklifts.

d. Based on the decision tree of part *c*, what decisions should the company make with respect to using the inspector and processing forklifts? What would be the expected overhaul cost per forklift?

e. Suppose that the company quotes a firm price to the customer of $300 for a major overhaul and $100 for a minor overhaul based on the inspector's recommendation as to what is needed. If the customer agrees to a minor overhaul and a major overhaul is needed, the Witherspoon Garage absorbs the additional cost with no increase in revenue. If the customer agrees to a major overhaul and only a minor overhaul was actually needed, they refund $50 of the purchase price. Do these conditions change the optimal decisions from part (d)? What will be the expected profit per forklift overhauled? (*Note:* This is a general type of problem that could also be applied to auto repair, television servicing, surgery, etc.)

3-8. Refer to the Astro Games problem discussed in Chapter 2 (see pages 37 to 50). Suppose that Astro Games is considering the possibility of doing market research on the Astrosport console to obtain additional information with which to make their expansion decision. The estimated cost of this study is $5,000.

The research firm that will undertake the market study if Astro Games decides to conduct it provides either a "green" recommendation, meaning that demand prospects appear to be good, or a "red" recommendation, meaning that demand is likely to stabilize or decline.

The past reliability of the research firm is indicated by the following data:

Research firm forecast	Actual demand, %		
	Fell	Stabilized	Grew
Green	12.5	33.3	92.9
Red	87.5	66.7	7.1

These data show that for those products whose demand actually fell, the research firm had given a green recommendation 12.5 percent of the time and a red recommendation in the other 87.5 percent of the cases. For those products whose demand eventually grew, the research firm accurately provided a green recommendation 92.9 percent of the time, missing with a red recommendation on only 7.1 percent of the cases.

a. Prepare a decision tree for this problem incorporating the decision on whether or not the research firm should be hired.

b. What is the optimal set of decision for this problem? What would be the expected profit?

c. What is the value of the information provided by the research firm?

d. What cost for the research firm's information would leave Astro Games indifferent as to whether the market research study should be conducted?

Application:
Using Decision Trees in Financial Analysis*

Investments totaling billions of dollars annually are now required of the nation's energy companies in order to keep up with the nation's needs. Getty Oil Company itself is now investing $200,000,000 to $300,000,000 annually. This requires many significant investment decisions each year, and the fortunes of the company are tied to the wisdom of the choices. The incentive to excel is a strong one—avoiding even a few bad investments can save millions of dollars.

This incentive has fostered a dynamic evolution in Getty's financial analysis. Decisions once necessarily based on limited information and shortcut discounted cash flow calculations are now supported by much more thorough and rapid analysis. Financial analysts who seldom used computers are now directly and effectively exploiting this resource to extend their capabilities. A key factor in this progress is PAMS, the Plan Analysis and Modeling System.

To illustrate how PAMS can be effectively used, we consider an example involving a major investment proposal which top management had under consideration. A special corporate study group was assigned to review the project and to make a recommendation. There were some serious problems. The investment was to be in a completely new business area. There would be a great deal of uncertainty with all the attendant risk. Most of the income from the project was to occur after 1985. The total of capital expenditures and preproduction expenses could exceed $80,000,000. However, sales could exceed a billion dollars for the life of the project.

The authors provided the PAMS modeling and developed the results for the study group. Data were different for each year as the project expanded during 28 years. Over 30 alternatives were developed and analyzed. The entire part of this analysis from initial definition of the problem to final report took less than 5 working days.

Midway through the project (the third day) a number of questions developed when some of the alternatives showed large losses during sensitivity testing. The mixture of high and low returns proved unsettling. The project leader inquired if there was anything that could be done to provide a more conclusive result. The next afternoon the major possibilities were diagrammed in a decision tree. This resulted in a new set of alternatives and major changes in the model. The work was promptly completed with PAMS, and a computer report that summarized results from all the cases was delivered the next morning. This was a significant accomplishment, considering that the company had never used decision tree analysis before. Proceeding from the idea stage to management report took 1 day!

A simplified version of the "1-day" decision tree analysis is shown in Figure 3-9. About half the branches have been removed and the data have been disguised. However, the figure does show the key aspects of the uncertainties that were considered.

Management was very pleased with the results, particularly the decision tree analysis. The expected present worth of the investment proposal was positive. But more important, they had much more insight into the risks involved. The decision tree analysis showed that there were many ways to alleviate the most bothersome adverse circumstances and to reduce potential losses. This was valuable information that had not been provided by the conventional sensitivity analysis. With this insight management concluded that the remaining risks were within acceptable limits. There was another significant result. The decision tree had a branch representing delay of the project at a critical phase. A 1-year delay at this

*Adapted from D. O. Cooper, L. B. Davidson, and W. K. Denison, "A Tool for More Effective Financial Analysis," *Interfaces*, vol. 5, no. 2, part 2 (February 1975), pp. 91–93.   **97**

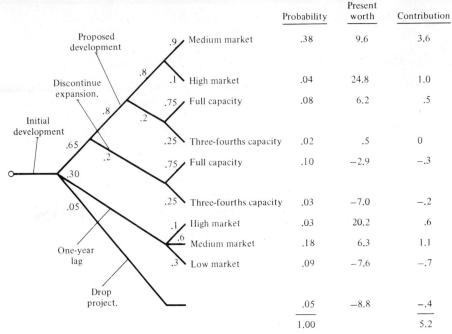

	Probability	Present worth	Contribution
Medium market	.38	9.6	3.6
High market	.04	24.8	1.0
Full capacity	.08	6.2	.5
Three-fourths capacity	.02	.5	0
Full capacity	.10	−2.9	−.3
Three-fourths capacity	.03	−7.0	−.2
High market	.03	20.2	.6
Medium market	.18	6.3	1.1
Low market	.09	−7.6	−.7
	.05	−8.8	−.4
	1.00		5.2

FIGURE 3-9 Decision tree analysis at Getty Oil.

point cost one-third of the entire present worth of the project. Needless to say, having a quantitative value for this cost helps management to determine how much effort should be spent to avoid it.

Discussion Questions

1. Why was it necessary to use a computer to augment the financial decision tree which is essentially a graphic model? Why do you suppose that management was so pleased with the decision tree analysis?
2. Although the details provided in the tree are purposely rather sketchy, some interesting observations can be made. Why are there no decision branches shown in the tree (observe that each branch has a probability)? What kind of tree is this? Has something been omitted from the tree? If so, what should be added?
3. If a decision is made to proceed with initial development of this major investment proposal, what is the risk that the proejct will result in a negative return to the company?

4

Extensions to Decision-Making Models

In the previous two chapters we have developed the fundamental concepts of decision making, focusing primarily on decision making under risk problems. In this chapter we extend our treatment of decision models to consider situations in which monetary value is not an appropriate outcome measure and those in which more than one objective apply.

In the first section we examine several decision making under risk situations in which monetary value fails as a decision outcome measure because it does not measure the proper objective. Therein we will consider the concept of *utility* which is a more accurate way of measuring the true value of decision outcomes. Since each decision maker has a unique way of measuring the utility of decision outcomes, we will see how, for the same decision problem, different decisions can be rationally obtained. In this regard we identify three classes of decision makers as to their decision-making behavior: *risk-seeking, risk-neutral,* and *risk-averse.*

In the second section we treat those problems for which a *single* objective is not adequate. These *multiple-objective decision-making* problems require specialized treatment as will be discussed.

Expected Utility as a Decision Criterion

The decision problems considered in the previous chapters have all used monetary values as outcomes. For those problems under risk we calculated an expected value for each alternative and selected the alternative with the best   **99** expected value as the best decision. As we will soon see, there are some instances in which the use of expected monetary value is inappropriate. Instead we must transform these monetary outcomes into what are called utilities which reflect the perceived value of these outcomes to the decision maker. Before we do this, let us consider a few examples where monetary outcomes fail us.

Examples where Expected Monetary Value Fails

There are many practical, real-life decision situations in which apparently rational individuals select a decision alternative that does *not* yield the best expected monetary value. A few simple examples can best show this.

Car Owner's Insurance Example Consider Table 4-1 which represents a car owner's decision on whether or not to purchase a comprehensive automobile insurance policy for a $6,000 car insuring against theft and other hazards. A decision not to purchase such a policy can be viewed as *self-insuring*. The car owner retains the money that would have been spent on insurance but also takes on the risk of loss. To simplify, suppose we assume that the uncontrollable events are whether the car is stolen or is not stolen during the period considered.

If the car is not insured, the owner will incur a cost only if the car is stolen. Suppose that the probability of a theft is .01 per year. The expected cost of self-insuring is thus $60, or .01($6,000) + .99(0). Since insurance companies have profit-making objectives and can accurately predict the likelihood of losses due to theft, we would expect them to price an insurance policy higher than the actual risk. The price of the policy will thus cover the actual risk, the company's operating costs, as well as some profit margin. Therefore to reflect these elements we have assessed a $200 cost to the car owner's policy.

Clearly the lowest expected cost can be obtained by self-insuring, saving $140. Nonetheless, millions of apparently rational people ignore this conclusion and willingly take out comprehensive automobile insurance. Of course, if the car was financed by borrowing from a financial institution, the lenders will require that such insurance be obtained. However, even those car owners who have paid cash for their automobile almost invariably purchase comprehensive insurance. We will soon examine why the expected monetary value criterion is

TABLE 4-1
Car Owner's Insurance Decision Problem

Decision alternatives	Uncontrollable events		Expected cost per year
	Theft occurs	No theft occurs	
Car is insured	200	200	200
Car is not insured	6,000	0	60
Event probabilities (for 1 year)	.01	.99	

not the correct objective for this problem. First we will consider other related

examples.

Coin-Toss Example Consider a second example of apparently irrational behavior. Suppose you were offered the chance to play the following game. A coin is to be flipped, and if it comes up heads, you win $1, otherwise you lose $.50. If it is assumed that the coin being flipped is a fair coin (equal probability of heads and tails), the expected value per flip can be easily calculated:

$$\text{Expected value per flip} = .5(1.00) + .5(-.50) = \$.25$$

In other words, anyone playing this game would expect to gain an average of $.25 per flip. Most rational people if offered a chance to play this game would accept the opportunity and would generally play as long as they were allowed.

Suppose, however, we make a slight adjustment to the game by increasing the positive reward from $1 to $10 and the negative result from $.50 to $5. The expected value per flip remains positive and has actually increased tenfold:

$$\text{Expected value per flip} = .5(\$10) + .5(-\$5) = \$2.50$$

If this modified game were to be offered to those people willing to play the $1/$.50 version, we would find some individuals who do not choose to play the new game, even though the *same relative relationship* between the two outcomes and the expected return has been maintained. The reason for this will soon be evident.

Consider one final version of this game in which the payoff for a head is changed to $1,000,000 and the loss from a tail is $500,000. Again the same relative relationship between payoffs and expected value has been maintained:

$$\text{Expected value per flip} = .5(1,000,000) + .5(-500,000) = \$250,000$$

The expected return is positive and considerably higher than that for either of the other two versions of this game. Yet it would be extremely rare to find an individual who is willing to play this last game, although some large companies would be willing to take similar risks. The risk of the high negative payoff offsets the high positive expected value.

Since the expected return is positive in all three versions of the game, if people actually use the expected value criterion they should be willing to play any of the three versions. This would not happen in practice. In fact the last game would have the fewest takers despite offering the highest expected value.

Entrepreneur's Sellout Example As yet another example of apparent irrationality, consider a decision faced by a young entrepreneur whose new, but growing, firm is the subject of an attractive sellout offer. If the entrepreneur agrees to sell her interest in the firm, she stands to earn a profit on her investment of $3,000,000. If, however, she decides to retain her interest, the ultimate outcome depends on what happens competitively in the market that her firm competes in.

Assume that her firm, unlike some others, has already survived one period of intense price competition. The current situation is described as one of volatile stability; although price has stabilized in recent periods, there is some indication that another round of competitive price cutting may soon begin.

The entrepreneur has estimated that in 5 years her interest in the firm will be worth $10,000,000 if competition remains stable, but will only be worth

TABLE 4-2
Entrepreneur's Sellout Problem

Decision alternatives	Uncontrollable events		Expected profit
	Competition intensifies	Competition stabilizes	
Hold for 5 years	1,000,000	10,000,000	3,700,000
Sell out now	3,000,000	3,000,000	3,000,000
Event probabilities	.7	.3	

$1,000,000 if competitive tensions set off another round of price slashing.[1] Her best estimate is that there is a .3 probability of a 5-year period of competitive stability, or a .7 probability of renewed price cutting. The decision situation for the entrepreneur is summarized in Table 4-2.

On the basis of expected values, it would appear that the best decision alternative is to hold on to the firm and not sell out at this time. Yet it would not be too difficult to find individuals who, faced with this hypothetical decision, would choose to sell out now. In fact we would find that, regardless of the decision, the decision maker would argue that it was made rationally.

Utility

Each of the examples described above resulted in selection of a decision that was apparently inconsistent with the expected value criterion. This would seem to imply either that many people act irrationally or that the expected value criterion is not a rational criterion for making decisions.

Actually neither of these conclusions is correct. The decision tables presented for the three examples were incorrect because we have been confusing monetary outcomes with their actual value or utility to the decision maker. The *utility* or *disutility* associated with a particular monetary outcome reflects the perceived value or penalty of these outcomes from the standpoint of the individual decision maker. That a specific monetary outcome will be valued differently by individual decision makers is easily seen by considering the differential impact of a $100 loss on, say, a multimillionaire as opposed to a struggling owner of a small shop. Clearly the $100 loss would be viewed considerably more seriously by the small-shop owner than the millionaire.

In short, if the monetary outcomes for the decision examples described earlier in the chapter were converted to a measure of utility, the apparent irrationality would disappear. In other words, the expected value criterion is rational in every case described if the criterion is modified slightly to require *selection of the decision alternative that maximizes expected utility* rather than expected monetary value.

Measuring Utility   The difficulty presented by redefining the criteria in terms of utility is the problem of measuring utility. Most dictionaries define "utility" as

---

[1] Assume that the value of the firm in 5 years has been discounted to the present to adjust for inflation or any money that might be earned by selling out now and investing those funds for 5 years.

usefulness. As used in decision making we consider utility to be a measure of the relative value or usefulness of decision outcomes whether they are described in monetary terms or otherwise. Since most business decisions involve monetary outcomes, we are most interested in the relationship between dollar outcomes and their relative utility. Such a relationship is sometimes referred to as a *utility function*.

The concept of utility and attempts to define a utility function date back to the eighteenth century.[1] Daniel Bernoulli and Gabriel Cramer, both Swiss mathematicians, were early examiners of these questions. In 1730 Bernoulli argued that utility was related to the logarithm of monetary outcomes. Cramer argued that utility was a function of the square root of the monetary outcomes. Neither of these approaches provided an adequate definition of utility, and neither gained general acceptance.

Much attention has been devoted to the question of utility measurement in the field of economics. The focus of this discussion concerns the effect of various economic policies on the utilities of various members of society. As an example, Vilfredo Pareto in 1927 raised the notion of what is now called Pareto optimality.[2] A decision alternative affecting several individuals is *Pareto-optimal* if no other alternative exists that increases the utility of one person without decreasing another person's utility.

An interesting and enterprising approach to measuring the utility of a specific decision maker was suggested in 1947 by John Von Neumann and Oscar Morgenstern.[3] Their approach does not require that utility be measured on some universal or absolute scale but that a specific set of utility transformations can be inferred from the observed decision behavior of an individual.

The underlying concept of their method is that if a decision maker is indifferent between two decision alternatives, those two alternatives must have identical utilities regardless of any monetary differences.

The Standard Gamble Using the Von Neumann/Morgenstern approach, we can infer the proper utility values to be used from the answers to a series of questions asked the decision maker. The best monetary outcome is arbitrarily assigned a "utility" value of 1 and the worst outcome a utility of 0. Since all intermediate outcomes are both better than the worst outcome but not as good as the best outcome, they must have utility values that fall somewhere between zero and one.

The actual utility value for an intermediate outcome is deduced by what is referred to as the *standard gamble* method. We used the standard gamble in Chapter 2 as a means of identifying a decision maker's coefficient of optimism when dealing with decision problems under uncertainty. Here we use the standard gamble to determine utility values. Gambling is a convenient model for examining risk-taking behavior and the term "standard" refers to the fact that the utilities obtained are standardized, since in every case the utilities will range from 0 (worst outcome) to 1 (best outcome). In order to demonstrate the use of the standard gamble approach, we refer again to the Astro Games decision problem of Chapter 2. The outcome values are repeated here in Table 4-3.

[1]W. Fellner, *Probability and Profit*, Irwin, Homewood, Ill., 1965.
[2]V. Pareto, *Manuel d'economie politique*, Girard, Paris, 1927.
[3]J. Von Neumann and O. Morgenstern, *Theory of Games and Economic Behavior*, Princeton University Press, Princeton, N.J., 1947.

TABLE 4-3
Monetary Outcome Values for Astro Games Decision Problem*

	Uncontrollable events		
Decision *alternatives*	*Demand* *returns to* *previous level*	*Demand* *remains at* *current level*	*Demand* *increases to* *higher level*
Expand current plant	250	400	400
Build new plant	200	350	440
Don't expand	300	300	300

*Outcome values in thousands of dollars.

The best monetary outcome is the $440,000 received if a new plant is built and demand increases to higher levels. This outcome is assigned a utility of 1. The worst outcome is the $200,000 received if a new plant is built and demand returns to previous levels. This outcome is assigned a utility of zero.

Determining the Utility Value of Intermediate Outcomes   The utility values of intermediate returns are found as follows. The decision maker is offered a hypothetical decision problem in which one alternative offers *with certainty* one of the intermediate outcomes and the other alternative offers a chance *p* of receiving the best outcome and a chance of $1 - p$ of receiving the worst outcome. This standard gamble is shown for the general case in Table 4-4.

The decision maker is then asked to determine the value of *p* (the probability of receiving the best outcome) that will create indifference between the two alternatives. The particular value of *p* chosen can be determined by trial and error. That is, if for some value of *p* the certainty option is preferred to the gamble option, the value of *p* should be increased to make the gamble option more attractive. If the gamble option is preferred to the certainty option, the value of *p* should be decreased to make the certainty option more attractive. This adjustment process continues until a value of *p* is found that leaves neither option preferred.

Whatever value of *p* is finally chosen will fall somewhere between 0 and 1, since probabilities must be so constrained. Of major interest, however, is the

TABLE 4-4
The Standard Gamble

Decision *alternatives*	Uncontrollable events	
	Win gamble	*Lose gamble*
Gamble option	Best monetary outcome	Worst monetary outcome
Certainty option	Intermediate monetary outcome	Intermediate monetary outcome
Event probabilities	p	$1 - p$

soon-to-be-demonstrated fact that *the selected value of p is equivalent to the utility value for the intermediate monetary outcome* that was offered with certainty as part of the standard gamble.

To see why this is so, observe that if the decision maker is indifferent between any two decision options in the standard gamble, the expected utility of these two options must be identical, or if EU represents expected utility,

$$EU(\text{certainty option}) = EU(\text{gamble option})$$

As the name implies, the certainty option always offers the intermediate outcome, and the expected utility of this option is therefore the utility of that intermediate outcome. If U represents utility, it is possible to define

$$EU\left(\begin{array}{c}\text{certainty}\\\text{option}\end{array}\right) = U\left(\begin{array}{c}\text{intermediate}\\\text{monetary outcome}\end{array}\right) \tag{4-1}$$

The expected utility of the gamble option is a weighted average of the utilities of the best and worst outcomes, the weights equivalent to p and $1 - p$. Thus,

$$EU\left(\begin{array}{c}\text{gamble}\\\text{option}\end{array}\right) = p\left[U\left(\begin{array}{c}\text{best}\\\text{monetary}\\\text{outcome}\end{array}\right)\right] + (1 - p)\left[U\left(\begin{array}{c}\text{worst}\\\text{monetary}\\\text{outcome}\end{array}\right)\right]$$

Recall that we have already defined the utilities for the best and worst outcomes as 1 and 0, respectively. Substituting these utility values, we find

$$EU(\text{gamble option}) = p(1) + (1 - p)(0) = p \tag{4-2}$$

If the decision maker is indifferent between the certainty and the gamble options, their respective utilities must be equal. Therefore,

$$EU(\text{certainty option}) = EU(\text{gamble option})$$

Using the definitions of expected utility for these two options from equations (4-1) and (4-2), we find

$$U(\text{intermediate monetary outcome}) = p$$

Therefore, as stated earlier, the value of p that leaves the decision maker indifferent between the options in a standard gamble is equivalent to the utility value of the intermediate monetary outcome value offered with certainty.

To determine the appropriate utility equivalents for each of the intermediate monetary outcomes requires a separate standard gamble for each such outcome. In every case, the appropriate intermediate value is offered with certainty, and the alternative is the best outcome with probability p or the worst outcome with probability $1 - p$. The value of p selected by the decision maker will change with each intermediate outcome.

To illustrate, note that there are four intermediate monetary outcomes for the Astro Games problem. These are $250,000, $300,000, $350,000, and $400,000. The best outcome of $440,000 is assigned a utility value of 1 and the worst outcome of $200,000 a utility of 0.

The first standard gamble, to determine the utility of the $250,000 outcome, is shown in Table 4-5. The decision maker must decide what probability p will leave him indifferent between the certainty alternative ($250,000 outcome) and the gamble alternative (chance p of receiving $440,000 and $1 - p$ of

TABLE 4-5
Standard Gamble to Determine Utility Equivalent for
·Astro Games Decision $250,000 Outcome Value

Decision	Uncontrollable events	
alternatives	Win gamble	Lose gamble
Gamble	440,000	200,000
Certainty	250,000	250,000
Event probabilities	p	$1 - p$

receiving $200,000). Suppose that probability turns out to be .4. The utility of a $250,000 return is now known to be .4 for that decision maker.

Each of the remaining three intermediate values is assigned a utility equivalent between 0 and 1 in a manner similar to that above. For example, the standard gamble used to determine the utility of a $300,000 monetary outcome will be identical to that shown in Table 4-5 except that $300,000 will appear as the outcome values for the certainty alternative in place of the $250,000.

Determining Expected Utility   Assume that after completing the standard gambles for all the intermediate values, the appropriate utility equivalents shown in Table 4-6 were found. These values are hypothetical and are given for the sake of discussion. Ordinarily these would be obtained through the standard gamble process for a specific individual. Now that utility values have been determined, the decision that yields the highest expected utility can be found by substituting the utility equivalents for each monetary outcome value and calculating the expected utility for each alternative.

Table 4-7 shows the substitution of utility values equivalent to the original monetary outcomes. The monetary outcomes are shown in parentheses, and the corresponding utility is shown above the monetary outcome. For instance, the monetary value of $400,000 is shown in Table 4-6 to be equivalent to a utility of .95. Therefore, wherever the value $400,000 appears in the decision table (Table 4-7), it is replaced by the utility value of .95. This occurs twice in Table 4-7, corresponding to the second and third columns in the first row. Similar substitutions of utility values for dollar outcomes are made for other entries in Table 4-7, in each case based on the utility equivalents of Table 4-6.

TABLE 4-6
Utility Equivalents to Monetary Outcomes for
the Astro Games Decision Problem for a Specific Decision Maker

Monetary outcome values	Equivalent utility values
$200,000	.00
250,000	.40
300,000	.85
350,000	.90
400,000	.95
440,000	1.00

TABLE 4-7
Determination of Expected Utilities for the Decision
Alternatives of the Astro Games Decision Problem

| Decision alternatives | Uncontrollable events | | | Expected utility |
	Demand returns to previous level	Demand remains at current level	Demand increases to higher level	
Expand current plant	.4 (250)	.95 (400)	.95 (400)	.840
Build new plant	.0 (200)	.9 (350)	1.0 (440)	.755
Don't expand plant	.85 (300)	.85 (300)	.85 (300)	.850
Event probabilities	.2	.45	.35	

The expected utilities are calculated in the same way in which expected monetary values are found; the utility appropriate for each uncontrollable event is weighted by the probability of that event's occurrence, and the sum of these weighted utilities determines the expected utility. For example, the expected utility for the strategy of building a new plant was found by:

$$EU(\text{build new plant}) = .2(0) + .45(.9) + .35(1.0) = .755$$

Observe that the highest expected utility is achieved by not expanding the plant. Thus, the optimal decision based on utility is not the same as was found on the basis of monetary outcomes. (The optimal decision based on monetary outcomes was to expand the current plant.) It should not be surprising that the expected utilities and the optimal decision depend entirely on the decision maker's subjective assessment of the indifference probabilities or utility values of the various monetary outcomes.

INSTANT REPLAY   Suppose that equivalent utility values for the monetary outcomes had, instead, been found to be (utilities shown in parentheses) $200,000 (0), $250,000 (.1), $300,000 (.2), $350,000 (.3), $400,000 (.5), and $440,000 (1.0). What would be the optimal decision based on utility values for this decision maker? What would be the expected utility for the optimal decision?

CHECK   The three strategies have expected utilities of .420 ("expand"), .485 ("build"), and .200 ("no change"). Thus, the optimal decision would be to build the new plant with an expected utility of .485.

Interpersonal Comparisons   It is informative to note that although the expected utility found in the instant replay above is less than that found in Table 4-7, we cannot conclude that this decision maker is worse off. Interpersonal comparisons such as this cannot be made because of the way in which these utility equivalents were formed. We arbitrarily started by assigning values of one and zero to the best and worst monetary outcomes, respectively. Even though the absolute utility of the best and worst outcomes differs for each decision maker, we assign standard utility values of 1 and 0. Therefore, any interpersonal utility comparisons between the two decision makers would be valid only if in fact the real utility of the best and worst outcomes (intermediate ones as well) are the same for both decision makers. Thus the utility values obtained are appropriate only to the decision maker from which they were obtained.

Behavior toward Risk

Table 4-8 summarizes three possible sets of utility values which might have been obtained. For reasons which will soon be apparent, these three decision makers are referred to as *risk-seeking, risk-neutral,* and *risk-averse*. Note that a different optimal decision is identified for each of the three decision makers. Two of these utility assessments were treated earlier. The one now called risk-averse was considered in Table 4-7. The one referred to as risk-seeking was initially discussed in the instant replay above.

The utility values assigned to the risk-neutral decision maker are those that would result if there was a straight line or linear relationship between utility and monetary outcome. This can be seen in Figure 4-1, where the utility values are plotted relative to the monetary outcomes for each of the three decision makers. Points plotted in Figure 4-1 represent each combination of monetary outcome and utility value shown in Table 4-8. The points appropriate to each decision maker are connected to provide separate pictorial relationships between utility and outcomes for each.

TABLE 4-8
**Utility Assessments and Expected Utilities for the Astro Games Problem
for Three Hypothetical Decision Makers**

	Decision maker		
	Risk-seeking*	Risk-neutral†	Risk-averse‡
Utility equivalents for monetary outcomes:			
$200,000	.00	.0000	.00
250,000	.10	.2083	.40
300,000	.20	.4167	.85
350,000	.30	.6250	.90
400,000	.50	.8333	.95
440,000	1.00	1.0000	1.00
Expected utility for decision alternative:			
Expand	.420	.7083	.840
Build	.485	.6313	.755
Don't	.200	.4167	.850
Optimal decision	Build	Expand	Don't

*As in Instant Replay.
†As in Figure 4-1.
‡As in Table 4-7.

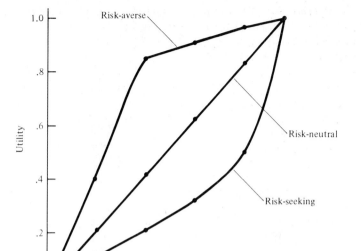

FIGURE 4-1   Relationship between utility and monetary outcomes for three hypothetical decision makers (Astro Games example).

As stated before, the points for the so-called risk-neutral decision maker fall on a straight line. This implies that there is a constant relationship between utility and outcomes for that decision maker equivalent to the equation for that straight line, given by

$$\text{Utility} = \frac{(\text{monetary outcome}) - 200{,}000}{240{,}000} \qquad (4\text{-}3)$$

Thus, for example, the utility associated with a monetary outcome of $350,000 would be calculated as

$$\text{Utility }(350{,}000) = \frac{350{,}000 - 200{,}000}{240{,}000} = \frac{150{,}000}{240{,}000} = .625$$

which is precisely the value shown in Table 4-8 as the utility of $350,000 for the risk-neutral decision maker.

Whenever the relationship between utility and monetary outcome is linear, it can be shown that whatever decision alternative yields the highest expected monetary value will also yield the highest expected utility. This means that utility values can be successfully ignored in such cases, since monetary values serve just as well as utility in finding the decision alternative that maximizes expected utility.

Recall that the expected monetary values for the three strategies as calculated in Chapter 2 were $370,000 (expand), $351,500 (build), and $300,000 (don't). If these expected monetary values are converted to utilities using the linear relationship of equation (4-3) we will obtain utility values identical to those found as the expected utility for each strategy in Table 4-8. Thus,

$$U(370{,}000) = \frac{370{,}000 - 200{,}000}{240{,}000} = .7083$$

$$U(351,500) = \frac{351,500 - 200,000}{240,000} = .6313$$

$$U(300,000) = \frac{300,000 - 200,000}{240,000} = .4167$$

Comparison of these values with the expected utilities for the risk-neutral decision maker in Table 4-8 will show them to be identical.

INSTANT REPLAY What are the expected utilities for the two decision alternatives shown below if the decision maker's utility is risk-neutral (linear) with respect to monetary values?

		Event	
Alternative	E_1	E_2	E_3
A_1	100	125	150
A_2	150	150	130
Event probabilities	.1	.5	.4

CHECK By definition $U(100) = 0$ and $U(150) = 1$. An increase of $50 caused an increase of 1 in utility. Therefore, each dollar above $100 will increase utility $1/50 = .02$. The utility for 125 is thus $25(.02) = .5$ and for 130 is $30(.02) = .6$. Substituting these values for the monetary outcomes yields EU = .65 for alternative A_1 and EU = 0.84 for alternative A_2.

Relationship between Utility and Monetary Outcomes

The distinction "risk-averse" implies that the decision maker's utility is enhanced by avoiding risk. Recall that the utilities assigned to monetary outcomes were equal to the probability p of obtaining the best monetary outcome with the standard gamble. Thus, as shown in Figure 4-1, the risk-averse person needs a higher probability p than the risk-neutral person of obtaining the best outcome to make the decision maker indifferent between the standard gamble and the certain intermediate monetary outcome.

The risk seeker, on the other hand, requires a smaller probability of obtaining the best outcome in order to be indifferent between the gamble and certainty options.

You may wish to approximate your own utility function by experimenting with the standard gamble, as was done hypothetically for the Astro Games example. (See problem 4-1.)

Car Owner's Insurance Example Revisited Note that reference to utility rather than monetary outcome values can easily explain the apparently irrational behavior of the decision makers in the situations described earlier in the chapter (automobile insurance, coin flip, entrepreneur's sellout). To illustrate, consider the car owner's insurance problem of Table 4-1.

Three monetary outcomes are possible for this problem, all of which are *costs* rather than profits. Thus, we would assign the utility value of 1 to the best

cost outcome, which is the cost incurred if no theft occurs and the car is not
insured ($0). The utility value of 0 is assigned to the worst cost, which is the
loss of $6,000 resulting from an uninsured theft.

The standard gamble can be used to find an appropriate utility value for
the $200 insurance cost. Note that, in this case, the decision maker is asked to
choose between a sure loss of $200, on the one hand, or a chance of losing zero,
with probability p, or $6,000 with probability $1 - p$, on the other hand. It is
likely that the probability of receiving zero would have to be very high in order
for the decision maker to be indifferent between the gamble and certainty
outcomes.

Suppose the standard gamble results in a probability of .995, this being
equivalent to the utility of a $200 loss. The expected utility of the two insurance
strategies would therefore be:

$$U(\text{insure}) = .01(.995) + .99(.995) = .995$$
$$U(\text{don't insure}) = .01(0) + .99(1) = .990$$

Thus, by using utility rather than monetary outcomes, we have shown
that the decision to insure is rational, since a higher expected utility results.

When to Use Utility Measures As a final note, consider the hypothetical relationship between utility and monetary value shown in Figure 4-2. Observe
that the relationship is approximately linear for a limited range of monetary
values on either side of zero. This implies that for moderate positive or negative
monetary values, this decision maker's utility relationship is linear. Therefore
any decision problems faced by this decision maker, if their monetary outcomes all lie within the range of linearity, can be solved directly with monetary
values, and the problem of conversion to utility is avoided.

Outside of this range, however, larger and larger positive monetary outcomes contribute ever smaller amounts of utility. This implies that beyond
some upper limit, the gain in utility of an extra dollar is approximately zero. As
an example, the difference in utility between $1,000,000 and $1,000,100 is likely
to be a lot less than the difference between $100 and $200, even though in
monetary terms the difference in both cases is $100.

FIGURE 4-2 Hypothetical relationship between monetary value and utility—risk-complex
behavior.

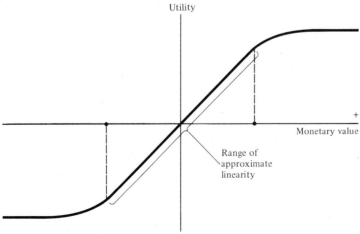

The utility relationship for large negative monetary values in Figure 4-2 shows a similar bending corresponding to some lower limit on utility associated with such monetary values. In other words, once the monetary loss is big enough, any increase in the size of the loss has little if any impact on utility. Such asymptotic behavior might describe a deductible insurance situation where the insured person pays all losses up to the deductible amount and the insurance company pays all losses beyond that amount. Alternatively, if we assume that there is some negative monetary value equivalent to bankruptcy or ruin for our hypothetical person, the utility function would curve downward approaching negative infinite utility as the negative monetary value approaches the point of financial ruin.

The situation described by Figure 4-2 is probably representative of the utility pattern for many decision makers. It does not fit precisely into one of the three risk-behavior patterns (risk-seeking, -neutral, or -averse) described earlier and might be called *risk-complex*. Such behavior has some interesting conclusions with respect to the application of the decision-making approaches described in Chapters 2 through 4. For most decision problems, those whose monetary values fall within the approximately linear range, the decision can be based on expected monetary values rather than on utilities, with little risk of making an incorrect decision. For those problems containing monetary values outside the linear range, in either a positive or negative direction, the decision maker would be wise to consider the utility outcomes rather than rely on monetary values. In the next section we consider another situation in which utilities are important.

Multiple-Objective Decision Making

Until now all the decision problems we have considered have had a single objective, usually expressed in monetary terms. Frequently, however, a decision maker is faced with a problem for which more than one objective needs to be considered.

Examine, for instance, the inventory problem faced by a typical retailer. The retailer desires to have enough inventory available to avoid running out of stock and losing sales, on the one hand, and to keep inventories low to reduce the costs of carrying those inventories, on the other hand. Thus, in deciding on the best level of inventory to maintain for any given item, the decision maker wishes to *maximize service* and to *minimize costs*.

This two-objective problem could be reduced to a single objective by translating the risk of running out of stock into a "stockout" cost. In practice this may be difficult to accomplish because of the inability to determine an appropriate cost for running out of stock.

Difficulties Raised by Multiple Objectives

For many decision problems the list of objectives can be rather extensive. For example, someone searching for a house in which to live may list as objectives: low cost, short commute, good schools, friendly neighbors, lots of space, close to shopping, etc.

As the number of objectives increases, the difficulties in finding the "best" solution are compounded. Each potential solution will now have a set of outcome measures associated with it rather than a single outcome. For example, a specific inventory level for the retailer described above will have two outcomes or attributes—a level of service provided and a cost for carrying that level of inventory. Although in this case it is possible to provide quantitative measures of these two attributes, in other situations it may be impossible to do so. In the home-buying example, while such attributes as cost of the house, commuting distance, size of house, and distance to shopping areas can be quantified, other intangible attributes such as quality of schools and friendliness of neighbors are much more difficult to attach quantitative measures to.

Methods for Dealing with Multiple Objectives

The concept of utility is important in comparing the attributes of potential solutions to the problem when multiple objectives exist. However, the ability to measure utility in multiple-objective situations is difficult to accomplish. Because of this, a number of different methods have been suggested for solving these problems. These include transformation of several objectives into a single objective, optimizing on one objective while meeting target levels for the others, using a weighted average of objectives, establishing priorities for the objectives, analyzing the tradeoffs that result among the objectives, and assigning utilities. In the sections below we will examine several of these.

Transformation to Single Objective One method mentioned above is the conversion or transformation of all objectives into a single objective. The goal with this approach is to find a single substitute objective that in some way reflects the impact that the decision alternatives have on the objectives being replaced.

To illustrate how such a transformation might be accomplished, we return to an earlier problem. In Chapter 1 we considered the break-even problem as an example of the management science modeling process. At that time we examined the problem of choosing between two manufacturing alternatives with different cost structures and break-even points. We pointed out that ideally we would like to find an alternative with a low break-even point and high profit potential. In practice, however, we are much more likely to find that one alternative has the lowest break-even point while another alternative has the highest profit potential.

You have probably recognized that this is a multiple-objective decision problem since the goal is both a low break-even point and a high profit potential. As with many multiple-objective problems, these two objectives are frequently not compatible.

Consider the Westminster break-even example introduced in Chapter 1. Two manufacturing options were being considered. Process A had a fixed cost of \$5,000 and a contribution margin of \$.80 per unit. Process B had a lower fixed cost of \$2,500 but also a lower contribution margin of \$.50 per unit. The break-even volumes were calculated as

$$\text{BEV(process } A\,) = \frac{f}{m} = \frac{5,000}{.80} = 6,250 \text{ units}$$

$$\text{BEV(process } B\,) = \frac{f}{m} = \frac{2,500}{.50} = 5,000 \text{ units}$$

In addition we considered the profit potential for the two alternatives by calculating the profit that would be earned for a sales volume of 10,000 units:

$$\text{Profit}(\text{process } A) = 10,000(\$.80) - \$5,000 = \$3,000$$

$$\text{Profit}(\text{process } B) = 10,000(\$.50) - \$2,500 = \$2,500$$

Thus, we saw that process B had the lower break-even point but process A had the higher profit potential for a sales volume of 10,000 units. In fact, we can define a *process break-even volume* at which the profit from the two manufacturing alternatives would be equal. Letting PV represent this break-even volume, we equate the profit for the two processes in terms of PV and then solve for PV. Thus,

$$\text{Profit}(\text{process } A) = \text{profit }(\text{process } B)$$

$$\$.80\text{PV} - \$5,000 = \$.50\text{PV} - \$2,500$$

$$(.8 - .5)\text{PV} = 5,000 - 2,500$$

$$.3\text{PV} = 2,500$$

$$\text{PV} = \frac{2,500}{.3} = 8,333\tfrac{1}{3} \text{ units}$$

Thus, we find that if the actual sales were $8,333\tfrac{1}{3}$ units we would be indifferent between alternatives A and B since they would both earn the same profit of $1,666.67:

$$\text{Profit} = \$.80(8,333\tfrac{1}{3}) - 5,000 = \$.50(8,333\tfrac{1}{3}) - 2,500 - \$1,666.67$$

Furthermore, note that since process A has the higher contribution margin ($.80), if the sales volume exceeds $8,333\tfrac{1}{3}$ units each additional unit will increase the profit from process A by $.80 while that for process B will only increase by $.50. Therefore, the profit from process A will exceed that for process B for *all* sales volume levels above $8,333\tfrac{1}{3}$ units. On the other hand, if the sales volume is less than $8,333\tfrac{1}{3}$ units, the profit for process A will decrease (from the $1,666.67 earned at a volume of $8,333\tfrac{1}{3}$ units) by $.80 for each unit below $8,333\tfrac{1}{3}$ while that for process B will decrease only $.50 per unit. Thus, at *all* sales volume levels below $8,333\tfrac{1}{3}$ units, process B will be preferred to process A.

To answer the question of which process alternative should be chosen, we need additional information concerning the sales volume expectations. A low break-even volume is a desirable attribute for a decision alternative only if there is some high likelihood that actual sales volume will be relatively low. If we know for certain that demand will be relatively high, we can disregard the break-even volume attribute and use the profit potential as our objective. Alternatively, if we know that demand will be relatively low, the profit potential for high volumes becomes irrelevant and the break-even attribute takes on prime importance.

Since expected profit reflects the consequences of both high and low volumes in proportion to their probabilities, it serves as an appropriate single objective in place of the two original objectives. In other words, the two objectives, low break-even volume and high profit potential, are transformed into a single objective, expected profit.

To illustrate, suppose we feel that there are four distinct demand possibilities and that we can estimate the probability of each of these demand possibilities. Table 4-9 identifies these demand possibilities as sales volumes of

TABLE 4-9
Manufacturing-Process Decision Problem

Decision alternatives	Uncontrollable events (sales volume)				Expected profits
	5,000	*7,000*	*9,000*	*12,000*	
Process A	−1,000	600	2,200	4,600	2,280
Process B	0	1,000	2,000	3,500	2,050
Event probabilities	.1	.2	.4	.3	

5,000, 7,000, 9,000, and 12,000 units with probabilities of .1, .2, .4, and .3, respectively. Observe that we have organized our manufacturing-process decision problem in the standard decision table format. The uncontrollable events are the four demand possibilities, the decision alternatives are process options A and B, and the decision outcomes have been stated in terms of profit. Thus, if we choose option A and demand is 9,000 units, we will earn a profit of 9,000 ($.80) − $5,000 = $2,200 as shown in the table.

At the right of Table 4-9 are the expected profits for the two options, weighted by the demand probabilities for the various profit outcomes. Process alternative A is the preferred option since it has the higher expected profit of $2,280.

Thus, we see that the use of expected profit to make our manufacturing process decision allowed us to substitute a single objective, expected profit, for the two objectives we started with, low break-even volume and high profit potential. The sales volume likelihoods or demand probabilities were the means by which we were able to make such a substitution.

The identification of some aggregate single objective is usually not this simple. There are many problems for which a single objective cannot be defined. The home buying illustration is a good example of a situation without such an easy transformation.

Constrained Optimization   Another approach commonly suggested for solving multiple-objective problems is to treat all objectives but one as *constraints* and then choose the solution, from among those that satisfy all the constraints, that optimizes the remaining objective. This approach is referred to as *constrained optimization*. As an example, the retailer could specify a target level of service (i.e., a maximum risk of running out of stock) and then select the lowest-cost inventory level that achieves that stated target level of service.

As another illustration, consider the home buyers who have narrowed their choice of homes to the four shown in Table 4-10. As the table shows, they have identified four attributes—cost, size, commuting distance, and property taxes—as important in this decision. Observe that house A is the largest, house B has the lowest property taxes, house C is the least expensive, and house D has the shortest commuting distance.

As described above, one way to handle a multiple-attribute problem such as this is to select one of these attributes as the primary objective and set acceptable levels or constraints on the other objectives. For instance, suppose our home buyers decide that cost is most important but that they need a house with at least 2,200 square feet, a commuting distance of no more than 15 miles,

TABLE 4-10
Hypothetical Home-Buying Problem: Alternatives and Attributes

Decision alternatives	Cost	Attributes		
		Size, square feet	Commuting distance, miles	Annual property taxes
House A	$110,000	2,800	15	$3,400
House B	98,000	2,000	12	2,400
House C	95,000	2,600	30	2,500
House D	104,000	2,200	8	3,000

and property taxes of no more than $3,500. Their decision problem is thus to buy the least-expensive house that also meets the constraints imposed on the other objectives (size, commuting distance, and property taxes).

For the situation described in Table 4-10, houses A, C, and D satisfy the constraint on size, houses A, B, and D satisfy the constraint on commuting distance, and houses A, B, C, and D satisfy the constraint on property taxes. In this instance, only houses A and D satisfy all three constraints. Since house D is less expensive than house A, D is chosen as the best alternative.

One of the difficulties with this approach is the possibility that no decision alternative can be found that satisfies all the constraints. For instance, the home buyers may find that none of the houses on the market satisfy all the standards specified. Suppose, for instance, they have set constraints of 2,500 or more square feet on size, no more than 10 miles commuting distance, and no more than $3,000 in property taxes. A review of the four alternatives in Table 4-10 will show that none of the four houses meets all three constraints.

To resolve this problem, the home buyers will need to change either the alternatives, the constraints, or the objective. For example, they can wait until new homes enter the market (adding alternatives), be more flexible in setting the minimum standards (relaxing the constraints), or make the cost of a home a constraint and optimize on some other attribute such as commuting distance (switch objectives).

Using Weighted Averages of Attributes One approach often suggested for solving multiple objective problems is to calculate a *weighted average* of the various attributes for each alternative and then select the alternative with the best weighted average. One difficulty with this approach is that the resulting average is difficult to interpret or give meaning to—calculating such an average is equivalent to adding apples and bananas. Another problem is that a simple change in the unit of measure may result in a shift in the relative ranking of the alternatives.

For illustration, consider again the home buyers' decision problem of Table 4-10. This problem has four objectives, of which three (cost, commuting distance, and property taxes) are to be minimized and one (size) is to be maximized. Suppose our home buyers indicate that cost is twice as important as the other three objectives. This suggests that we can calculate a weighted average of these four objectives where cost is given twice as big a weight as the others. Thus, cost can be given a weight of $+2$ while commuting distance and property taxes are given a weight of $+1$ and house size a weight of -1. (A minus weight is used because the objective for house size is to be maximized

while the other objectives are to be minimized.)

Thus, the weighted outcome for house A would be:

$$2(\text{cost}) - 1(\text{size}) + 1(\text{commuting distance}) + 1(\text{property taxes})$$

$$= 2(110,000) - (2,800) + 15 + 3,400 = 220,615$$

Similar calculations for the other three houses would yield values of 196,412 for house B, 189,930 for C, and 208,808 for D. Thus, C has the lowest weighted average, B the next lowest, then D, and A has the highest. But what do these numbers mean? They are weighted averages made up partly of costs, partly of miles, and partly of square feet. As such they are impossible to interpret and, as we will next show, subject to distortion by nothing more than a change of measurement scale for one or more of the objectives.

To illustrate, suppose cost was measured in thousands of dollars rather than in dollars. What effect would that have on the weighted averages? For house A we would calculate

$$2(110) - 2,800 + 15 + 3,400 = 835$$

For house B, we would find 608; for house C, 120; and for house D, 1,016.

With the original calculations (cost in dollars) we saw that house A had the highest weighted average. A simple change in the cost measurement scale to thousands of dollars caused a change in the relative ordering of the weighted averages. House D now has a higher average than A.

It is for these reasons that such arithmetic weighted averages are to be avoided. In fact, there is a better approach that avoids both the "apples and bananas" problem (interpreting the weighted averages) and the "change in measurement scale" problem. This approach is sometimes referred to as *dimensionless analysis* because the objectives are combined in a way that eliminates any units of measure (or dimensions) such as cost, size, etc.[1]

In general, we compare one alternative with another by multiplying a set of ratios, one for each objective, each ratio raised to a power equivalent to its relative weight. For example, if we are comparing two alternatives, say A and B, and we let a_1, a_2, and a_3 be the three outcomes for alternative A, b_1, b_2, and b_3 be the corresponding outcomes for alternative B, and w_1, w_2, and w_3 be the weights to be applied to the three objectives, the ratio comparing A and B, $R(A/B)$, would be calculated as

$$R\left(\frac{A}{B}\right) = \left(\frac{a_1}{b_1}\right)^{w_1} \left(\frac{a_2}{b_2}\right)^{w_2} \left(\frac{a_3}{b_3}\right)^{w_3}$$

As we have defined them, each ratio of one outcome value to another has no dimensions or unit of measure. This is because whatever unit of measure is used in the numerator of the ratio will also be used in the denominator and the units will cancel themselves out. This eliminates the problem we observed earlier with a change in the unit of measure. For example, the ratio of the cost of house A to that for house B would be the same whether these costs were in dollars or thousands of dollars:

$$\frac{\text{Cost of } A}{\text{Cost of } B} = \frac{110,000}{98,000} = \frac{110}{98} = 1.122$$

[1]See P. W. Bridgman, *Dimensional Analysis*, Yale University Press, New Haven, 1922.

Note that a ratio greater than 1 implies that the cost of house A is greater than that for B. If the reverse were true, the ratio would be less than 1. If the two were equal in cost, the ratio would equal 1.

Next observe the effect of weights on these ratios. The larger the weight applied, the farther from 1 will be the resulting weighted ratio. For example, compare the effect of a weight of 2 on the cost ratio for houses A and B:

$$\left(\frac{\text{Cost of } A}{\text{Cost of } B}\right)^2 = \left(\frac{110,000}{98,000}\right)^2 = (1.122)^2 = 1.259$$

which is larger than found for a weight of 1 (1.122).

If the ratio had been less than 1, the resulting weighted ratio is also farther from 1. Suppose we reverse the order of the house costs so that B is the numerator and A is in the denominator. For a weight of 1 this yields

$$\left(\frac{\text{Cost of } B}{\text{Cost of } A}\right)^1 = \left(\frac{98,000}{110,000}\right)^1 = (.891)^1 = .891$$

A weight of 2 yields

$$\left(\frac{\text{Cost of } B}{\text{Cost of } A}\right)^2 = (.891)^2 = .794$$

which is clearly further from 1 than .891 is.

A combined comparison, incorporating all the objectives, is achieved by multiplying these weighted ratios (one for each objective) by each other. Suppose we were to do this in order to compare houses A and B, and we wish to assign a weight of 2 to cost and a weight of 1 to each of the other measures. The ratio of A to B, $R(A/B)$ is thus

$$R\left(\frac{A}{B}\right) = \left(\frac{\text{cost of } A}{\text{cost of } B}\right)^2 \left(\frac{\text{size of } A}{\text{size of } B}\right)^{-1} \left(\frac{\text{distance of } A}{\text{distance of } B}\right)^1 \left(\frac{\text{taxes of } A}{\text{taxes of } B}\right)^1$$

$$= \left(\frac{110,000}{98,000}\right)^2 \left(\frac{2,800}{2,000}\right)^{-1} \left(\frac{15}{12}\right)^1 \left(\frac{3,400}{2,400}\right)^1$$

$$= (1.122)^2(.714)(1.25)(1.417) = 1.592$$

It is important to note that we used a weight of -1 for the ratio of the size of house A to the size of house B. The negative sign was used to ensure that the size ratio is consistent with the other three. In the case of cost, commuting distance, and taxes, low values are preferred to higher numbers and A would be preferred to B if the ratios were less than 1. On the other hand, high values for house size are preferred to low values. Assigning a negative weight to the ratio for house size corrects for this by, in effect, using the reciprocal of the weighted ratio. Thus, a ratio of less than 1 will indicate a preference for house A as do the other ratios for cost, distance, and taxes.

What does the combined ratio 1.592 imply? Because the individual ratios of less than 1 imply A is preferred to B, the product of these individual ratios represent an averaging of the individual ratios, and the combined result is subject to the same interpretation. That is, if the combined ratio is less than 1, house A is preferred to B. If the ratio is exactly 1, we would be indifferent. If the ratio exceeds 1, house B would be preferred.

In our case, house B is preferred to A. We next compare house B with C. Thus,

$$R\left(\frac{B}{C}\right) = \left(\frac{\text{cost of } B}{\text{cost of } C}\right)^2 \left(\frac{\text{size of } B}{\text{size of } C}\right)^{-1} \left(\frac{\text{distance of } B}{\text{distance of } C}\right)^1 \left(\frac{\text{taxes of } B}{\text{taxes of } C}\right)^1$$

$$= (1.032)^2(1.3)(.4)(.96) = .532$$

Because the ratio is less than 1, house B is also preferred to house C. Finally, we need to compare house B with house D:

$$R\left(\frac{B}{D}\right) = \left(\frac{\text{cost of } B}{\text{cost of } D}\right)^2 \left(\frac{\text{size of } B}{\text{size of } D}\right)^{-1} \left(\frac{\text{distance of } B}{\text{distance of } D}\right)^1 \left(\frac{\text{taxes of } B}{\text{taxes of } D}\right)^1$$

$$= (.942)^2(1.1)(1.5)(.8) = 1.171$$

This shows that house D is preferred to B. In fact, since B is preferred to A and C and D is preferred to B, we can conclude that D is preferred to the other three alternatives.

The difficulty in using this method is the proper selection of weights to be used for the individual ratios. A change in the weights can lead to a different set of preferences as shown in the following instant replay.

INSTANT REPLAY   Suppose we had used a weight of 2 for taxes as well as cost and a weight of 1 for distance and -1 for size. What would be the preferred house?

CHECK $R(A/B) = 2.256$, so B is preferred to A. $R(B/C) = .511$, so B is preferred to C. $R(B/D) = .937$, so B is preferred to D. Therefore, in this case, B is the preferred choice.

Prioritized Objectives   Another approach suggested for multiple-objective problems is to establish a priority ranking for the objectives and then rate solutions on the degree to which they meet these *prioritized objectives*. For instance, if cost is the most important objective for the home buyer, whichever house has the lowest cost would be selected for purchase without regard to the other objectives. If two or more houses have the same cost, the next objective, say size of house, would be considered, and the largest of these minimum cost houses would be selected. Each lower-priority objective would only be considered if several decision alternatives remained that met all higher level objectives. In Chapter 8 we will consider one version of this approach, called goal programming, in more detail.

Tradeoff Analysis   Another approach to multiple-objective problems that is frequently used in practice is to prepare an analysis of the tradeoffs of one objective for another. Consider again the retailer's inventory problem, described above. For a given level of investment in inventory it is possible to calculate the cost of carrying that inventory and the level of stockout risk provided.

For instance, consider Figure 4-3 which shows the relationship between expected stockouts and inventory carrying costs for a hypothetical item. Note that reduced stockouts can be obtained only at the expense of higher carrying costs and that the incremental drop in stockouts diminishes as carrying costs increase.

The curve shown in Figure 4-3 can be used to measure specific tradeoff

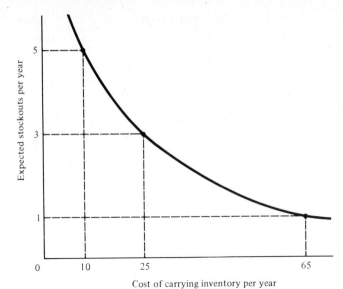

FIGURE 4-3 Tradeoff analysis of annual stockout risk and cost of carrying inventory for a hypothetical item.

options. For instance, note that five stockouts are expected per year for a $10 inventory carrying-cost expense. This stockout risk could be lowered to three stockouts per year for an additional $15 expenditure or to one stockout per year for an additional $40 increase in carrying costs.

Using this curve, the decision maker can then determine which of the points on the curve provide the highest utility. This can only be done subjectively, not explicitly, since measuring utility for each possible stocking decision (note that there are an infinite number of points on the curve) would be difficult analytically.

The Standard Gamble Approach for Multiple-Attribute Outcomes In some situations it may be possible to use the Von Neumann/Morgenstern standard gamble to estimate the utility of multiple-attribute decision outcomes so that the expected utility can be calculated to determine the best decision alternative.

To illustrate this, we return once again to the Astro Games decision problem. Suppose that top management at Astro Games is concerned with the impact that the expansion decision will have on *market share*. Market share can be measured in several ways, but generally represents the proportion of total sales among competing products achieved by one specific product. Market share is considered important because of the long-run effects that it has on product marketability, production costs, and, ultimately, success of the firm.

The expansion alternatives, reexamined in this light, result in the multiple-attribute outcomes shown in Table 4-11. Each outcome is now characterized by two attributes, the annual profit and the expected market share. Observe that previously identical outcomes, such as the three outcomes for the "don't expand" option, are now differentiated by the expected market share. Although profits remain at $300,000 for the "don't expand" option, the higher demand events lead to lower market shares since the lower Astro Games capacity restricts the portion of total demand that can be captured.

TABLE 4-11
Astro Games Decision With Multiple Objectives

Decision alternative	Uncontrollable events		
	Demand returns to previous level	Demand remains at current level	Demand increases to higher level
Expand current plant	Profit = 250 Share = 25%	Profit = 400 Share = 30%	Profit = 400 Share = 23%
⸱ Build new plant	Profit = 200 Share = 25%	Profit = 350 Share = 30%	Profit = 440 Share = 40%
Don't expand plant	Profit = 300 Share = 25%	Profit = 300 Share = 20%	Profit = 300 Share = 15%
Event probabilities	.20	.45	.35

Assigning Utility Values to Multiple-Attribute Outcomes The assignment of utility values to these multiple-attribute outcomes using the standard gamble approach requires more caution than when a single objective was used. Recall that the first step was to assign a utility of 1 to the best outcome and a utility of 0 to the worst. One difficulty presented by multiple attributes is determining which are the best and worst outcomes.

An analysis of Table 4-11 will show that there is clearly a single best outcome—that obtained if the new plant is built and higher demand levels result. This outcome is obviously the best, since it has the highest profit level possible ($440,000) and the highest market share (40 percent). Identification of the worst outcome is more difficult, however. The lowest profit is $200,000, which occurs when a new plant is built and demand returns to previous levels. The smallest market share (15 percent), however, is associated with a different outcome, that resulting from not expanding and increased demand levels. Which of these two outcomes is worse than the other? The answer depends on whether, in the view of the decision maker, the 10 percent gain in market share is worth the $100,000 loss in profit.

One way of finding the answer is simply to ask the decision maker which of the two pairs of outcomes is preferable. Another approach, the one followed here, is to create an artificial worst outcome by combining the worst market share, 15 percent, with the worst profit, $200,000. Thus the standard gamble would use a best outcome of $440,000 profit and 40 percent market share, and a worst outcome of $200,000 and 15 percent. These two outcomes would be assigned utilities of 1 and 0, respectively.

The utility values for the other outcomes would be determined by asking the decision maker to state what probability of receiving the best outcome is necessary to make him indifferent between the gamble alternative and receiving one of the other outcomes with certainty. The standard gamble decision table to determine the utility of a $300,000 profit and 15 percent market share is shown in Table 4-12.

Thus, the decision maker would estimate the value of p, the probability of

TABLE 4-12
Standard Gamble Decision Table to Determine Utility of Outcome Resulting
from Not Expanding when Higher Demand Occurs

	Events	
Alternatives	*Win gamble*	*Lose gamble*
Gamble	Profit = 440 Share = 40%	Profit = 200 Share = 15%
Certainty	Profit = 300 Share = 15%	Profit = 300 Share = 15%
Event probabilities	p	$1 - p$

winning the gamble, that results in an indifference between the gamble and certainty outcomes. In other words,

$$pU(440, 40\%) + (1 - p) \times U(200, 15\%) = U(300, 15\%)$$

Since we have previously defined

$$U(440, 40\%) = 1 \quad \text{and} \quad U(200, 15\%) = 0$$

we have now defined

$$U(300, 15\%) = p(1) + (1 - p)(0) = p$$

This process is repeated for each of the intermediate outcomes.

Determining Expected Utility Assuming that a series of these standard gambles are offered to the decision maker, a set of utility values associated with each profit and share outcome would be determined, such as that shown in Table 4-13. From these utility values, used in place of the profit and share outcomes, a utility outcome table such as shown in Table 4-14 could be developed. The expected utility for each decision alternative would be calculated in the usual manner, resulting in the values shown in Table 4-14.

TABLE 4-13
Utility Values Determined for Astro
Games Multiple-Objective Problem

Profit	*Market share*	*Utility*
$200,000	.15	.00
300,000	.15	.10
200,000	.25	.12
300,000	.20	.18
250,000	.25	.24
300,000	.25	.30
400,000	.23	.50
350,000	.30	.65
400,000	.30	.80
440,000	.40	1.00

TABLE 4-14
Expected Utility Calculation for Multiple-Objective
Astro Games Decision Problem

	Uncontrollable events			
Decision alternatives	*Demand returns to previous level*	*Demand remains at current level*	*Demand increases to higher level*	*Expected utility*
Expand current plant	.24	.80	.50	.583
Build new plant	.12	.65	1.00	.667
Don't expand	.30	.18	.10	.176
Event probabilities	.20	.45	.35	

Note that the "build new plant" option has the highest utility. When only the expected monetary profits are considered, as in Chapter 2, the best decision alternative is to expand the current plant. The consideration of market share has caused the best decision alternative to change.

INSTANT REPLAY   Suppose that the utility values shown in Table 4-13 were .0, .2, .25, .3, .33, .5, .7, .72, .95, and 1.00, top to bottom. What would be the expected utilities of the three decision alternatives?

CHECK   Expand, .7385; build, .724; don't, .305. Note that the expand alternative is now preferred to the build option.

Transitivity and Consistency of Utility   We should comment here that we have been assuming throughout our discussion of utility that the decision maker is logical in the assessment of utility values and that the decision maker's preferences are both consistent and transitive. By *consistency* we mean that we would not expect to find a lower utility value assigned to a higher profit figure. For example, if a profit of $1,000 was assigned a utility value of .5, we would expect to find the same decision maker assign a utility value greater than .5 to a profit of $2,000.

Similarly, we expect to find *transitivity* with respect to outcome preferences. That is, if alternative *A* is preferred to *B* and *B* is preferred to *C*, we would expect the decision maker to also prefer *A* to *C*.

Occasionally, however, we do find situations in which there is an *apparent* inconsistency or lack of transitivity. Suppose, for example, we are considering a decision problem for a bettor at a horserace, and we find to our surprise that he assigns a higher utility to an $800 winning ticket than to a $1,100 winning ticket. At first glance this assessment would appear peculiar to say the least. However, in discussing the matter with the bettor, we may find that the racetrack is required to report the names and social security numbers of all bettors holding winning tickets in excess of $1,000 to the Internal Revenue Service. If our bettor is unethical, he may desire not to report his gambling winnings for income tax purposes. Thus, to him the $800 winning bet has a higher utility than the $1,100 ticket, because the income taxes paid on the latter will actually leave him with less net profit than the $800 ticket (which would not be taxed since he would not report these winnings).

Thus, apparent inconsistencies such as this are not real inconsistencies. The decision maker viewed these two outcomes as multiple-attribute (profit and IRS notification) and was able to synthesize the effects of the attribute combinations in order to assess a single utility measure.

Final Comments

We considered three extensions to our general decision-making model in this chapter. The first of these involved transforming or converting monetary outcomes into utility values. The utility appropriate for a specific monetary outcome was defined as the true value of that outcome *as perceived by the decision maker*. This allows us to reflect the decision maker's behavior toward risk in making decisions.

Two decision alternatives can have identical expected monetary value and yet we will find that most individuals will not be indifferent between those alternatives. For instance, would you prefer $50 with certainty or a 50:50 chance of winning $200 or losing $100? Both of these alternatives have an expected monetary value of $50. Which one you selected depends upon your behavior toward risk. If you are a gambler at heart, you likely selected the 50:50 option. Such behavior was referred to as risk-seeking. If you are conservative when it comes to risk, you probably accepted the certainty option. We have described such behavior as risk-averse. If you are neither a gambler nor a financial conservative, you may have found yourself indifferent between the two options. We referred to such individuals as risk-neutral.

We saw how the standard gamble approach could be used to determine the correct transformation of monetary outcomes into utilities. You should now recognize that the resulting utilities are dependent on the decision maker's own internal perceptions of values and risks. We also pointed out that the major requirement in assigning utilities is that they be consistent (larger monetary values yield higher utility values for maximizing problems) and transitive (if A is preferred to B and B is preferred to C, then A is also preferred to C).

An important concept to be remembered is that it is not necessary to express decision outcomes as utilities in all situations. We mentioned that most individuals exhibit behavior that is risk-complex, behaving in some instances as risk-neutral, in others as risk-averse, and in still others as risk-seeking. As long as the monetary outcomes are in the risk-neutral area, we can use monetary outcomes without converting them to utilities. Most moderate monetary values fall in the risk-neutral region. Therefore, it is only when the decision problems involve large (positive or negative) monetary values that utilities need be obtained.

In the second major section of this chapter we examined decision problems with more than one objective. We discussed a variety of methods that could be used to solve such problems. In general, each of these methods involved condensing the multiple objectives into a single objective and then solving this single-objective problem using the normal decision-making criteria.

The various methods considered differ in the manner in which the many objectives are converted to one. In one case we saw how objectives of a low break-even point and a high profit potential could be converted to a single objective of expected profit by using event probabilities. We used the home-buying situation to demonstrate two other methods. In one case we converted all but one objective into constraints. In the other we showed how a weighted average of the ratios of attributes could be used to compare alternatives.

We also mentioned that a strict priority order could be assigned to the objectives and a method such as goal programming (to be considered in Chapter 8) used. We also showed how the tradeoffs between two objectives could be considered. Finally, we extended our treatment of utility analysis by demonstrating how utility values could be assigned to multiple-attribute outcomes.

Although this chapter concludes our formal treatment of decision making as a separate subject, the remainder of this text will, nonetheless, be concerned with decision making. Only the focus will change; future chapters will deal with specific types of decision problems rather than decision making in general.

Key Words

Problems

4-1. Assume the role of the decision maker for the Astro Games problem discussed in this chapter.

a. Using the standard gamble approach, determine your own subjective utilities corresponding to the monetary outcomes.

b. Calculate the expected utilities based on your assessment in part a.

c. Which decision would you chose?

d. Would you characterize your decision behavior for this problem as risk-seeking, risk-neutral, or risk-averse?

4-2. Suppose you were offered the following game, with three decision options: bet heads, bet tails, or don't bet.

	Event	
Options	*Heads*	*Tails*
Bet heads	$10	−$8
Bet tails	−$2	$3
Don't bet	0	0

a. If the payoffs shown above are determined by the flip of a fair coin, what are the expected values of the three strategies? Which one would the expected value criterion designate as best? _____

b. Use the standard gamble approach to estimate the utilities that *you* attach to the outcomes shown above. Which betting strategy should be followed, to maximize your expected utility?

c. Suppose the standard gamble approach was applied to another individual whose utilities were found to be:

Outcome	Utility
10	1.0
3	.8
0	.7
−2	.5
−8	0

Determine which betting strategy this individual should follow to maximize utility. Is this person risk-averse, risk-seeking, or risk-neutral?

d. Multiply each of the outcome values shown in the table above by 100. Then reassess your utility values for these new outcomes and redetermine the alternative that maximizes utility. Did you notice any difference?

4-3. The World Petroleum Company is interested in acquiring a piece of land thought to possibly contain oil. The company is considering three alternatives: (1) purchase the land outright; (2) obtain an option to buy, drill for oil, and if found exercise the option; and (3) don't buy the land or obtain an option.

For land of this type, there are three events likely to happen: (1) large deposits are found, (2) small deposits are found, or (3) no oil is found at all.

The monetary profits for these alternatives and events are shown in the table below:

	Events		
Alternatives	*Large deposits*	*Small deposits*	*No oil*
Buy land	3,000,000	1,000,000	−2,000,000
Take option	2,000,000	500,000	− 100,000
Do nothing	0	0	0

a. Suppose that past experience and preliminary geological tests have been used to provide event probability estimates of .1 for large deposits, .5 for small deposits, and .4 for no deposits. Which strategy should be chosen?

b. The president of World Petroleum has provided the following utility assessments for the outcomes shown above, based on the standard gamble.

Outcome	Utility
3,000,000	1.0
2,000,000	.7
1,000,000	.6
500,000	.4
0	.3
-100,000	.2
-2,000,000	0

Would you say the president is risk-averse, risk-seeking, or risk-neutral? What decision should be taken to maximize the president's utility if the event probabilities are as given in part *a*? Why does the -2,000,000 outcome have a zero utility rather than a negative utility?

4-4. Consider again the two-objective treatment of the Astro Games decision problem as shown in Table 4-11.

    a. Suppose you know that demand will remain at current levels. Which alternative should be chosen so as to maximize both profit and market share?

    b. Using the event probabilities shown in Table 4-11, which strategy will yield the maximum expected profit? Which will yield the maximum expected market share?

    c. Suppose you establish a target expected market share of at least 25 percent. Which of the strategies that meet this constraint provides the greatest profit?

    d. Suppose you establish a target expected profit of at least $350,000. Which of the strategies that meet this constraint provides the greatest expected market share?

4-5. Pete Macleod is trying to decide which of three pieces of equipment to purchase as part of an expansion of his manufacturing operation. Pete has identified two objectives of concern: productivity in terms of units per hour and operating costs. The operating costs incurred depend to some extent on whether energy prices are decontrolled. He has identified the following set of outcomes for his decision problem:

	Uncontrollable events	
Decision alternatives	Energy prices decontrolled	Energy prices not decontrolled
Equipment A	Hourly output = 1,000 Cost = $14,000	Hourly output = 1,000 Cost = $9,000
Equipment B	Hourly output = 800 Cost = $12,000	Hourly output = 800 Cost = $7,000
Equipment C	Hourly output = 750 Cost = $10,000	Hourly output = 750 Cost = $8,000

Pete estimates that there is a .3 chance that energy prices will be decontrolled.

    a. If Pete ignores the operating cost issues, which machine should he buy?

    b. If Pete ignores the output characteristics, which machine should he buy?

    c. Pete used the standard gamble approach to arrive at the following utility equivalents of the various options:

Output	Cost	Utility
750	14,000	.00
800	12,000	.05
750	10,000	.20
1,000	14,000	.25
750	8,000	.40
800	7,000	.65
1,000	9,000	.90
1,000	7,000	1.00

What decision should Pete make so as to maximize his utility?

4-6. Refer again to the equipment purchase decision of Pete Macleod (problem 4-5). Transform the two attributes (output and cost) into a single attribute and find the equipment selection that optimizes this new objective. (*Hint:* Consider a ratio of cost to benefits.)

4-7. Consider Pete Macleod's equipment purchase decision of problem 4-5.

a. Assuming that energy prices are to be decontrolled and that weights of 2 for output and 3 for cost are appropriate, use dimensionless analysis to choose the best machine.

b. Assuming that energy prices will not be decontrolled and that weights of 2 for output and 1 for cost are appropriate, use dimensionless analysis to choose the best machine.

c. Can you suggest a way in which the probability of energy price decontrol can be incorporated directly in the dimensionless analysis?

Part Two

Using Linear Programming to Solve Resource Allocation Problems

In this section we will examine a general-purpose class of problems called linear programming problems. These problems involve determining the best allocation of scarce resources. Such problems are characterized by an objective (a way of measuring how good a particular allocation is), a set of decision variables (the way in which the scarce resources are to be allocated), and a set of resource constraints (limitations placed on the decision variables to reflect the resource scarcity). The relationships between the decision variables and the objective and the constraints must be linear or of constant proportionality. That is, the per-unit increase in the objective or the per-unit decrease in scarce resources is assumed to be constant for each decision variable.

We will consider two fundamental ways of solving linear programming problems: a graphical approach and an algebraic method called simplex. The graphical approach provides an excellent conceptual view of linear programming problems and will be presented in Chapter 5. The simplex method is a more efficient approach and the basis for most commercially available linear-programming computer programs. We will explore the simplex method in detail in Chapter 6.

The importance of sensitivity analysis will be considered in Chapter 7. There we will see that many important questions—with managerial significance—can be answered by examining the simplex solution to the problem.

In Chapter 8 we will deal with linear programming problems with multiple objectives. There we will consider a modified version of the simplex method which can be used to solve such problems when the objectives can be ranked in priority order. These problems are usually called *goal programming problems*.

Linear programming is an important management science topic. The simplex method has been used to solve many different resource allocation problems in the more than 30 years since it was developed. It remains today one of the most widely used management science procedures.

5

Introduction to Linear Programming: Problem Formulation and Graphical Solution

The resource allocation problem is one that affects every human being. As a student you face such decisions all the time. For instance, you must determine how to allocate your time among studying, sleeping, eating, and other recreations. Most of you are on a limited financial budget and must make difficult (often painful) decisions as to how these funds can best be used.

This resource allocation problem is also important for managers of all types of organizations. Decisions must be made concerning how to allocate productive capacity to the various products that could be produced, how to allocate an advertising budget among the various media or advertising alternatives, or how to select a set of capital investment projects given budget and personnel limitations.

When we examine these allocation problems in more detail, we find they have several common elements. There is, first of all, an objective to meet. This might be to maximize profits or to minimize costs. The amount of profit earned or the level of costs incurred are often constrained by limitations imposed on the resources needed to meet the objectives. For instance, the amount of profit that can be earned will be limited by the available productive capacity. The number of people who will see our ads is limited by the size of the advertising budget.

The allocation problem results from the need to decide how to apportion or allocate these limited resources among the available alternatives. If we can produce a thousand cars per day, how many of each model should we make? If we have an advertising budget of $250,000, how much of this do we spend on television ads? The number of cars produced of a specific model or the amount of money spent on television ads are examples of what are called *decision variables*. These are known as decision variables because the manager must decide on the best value for each.

Thus there are three key elements to the resource allocation problem that a manager must determine; the *objective* must be stated, the *decision variables* must be isolated, and the *resource constraints* must be identified.

In order to make an effective decision, we also need to specify the relationships that show the effect of the size of the decision variables on both the objective and the resources. For instance, we need to know both the profit achieved for a car model (effect on the objective) and the amount of available production capacity required to produce that car (effect on resources). For the advertising example, we need to know how many people will see a television ad (effect on objective) and how much each ad will cost (effect on resources).

This chapter will analyze a special subset of resource allocation problems known as *linear programming problems*. Each of the elements mentioned above is a necessary ingredient for a linear programming problem. Defining these elements and stating them mathematically is usually called *formulating the problem*. We will see how this can be done. Then we will see how such problems can be solved graphically.

It is convenient to classify linear programming problems on the basis of the type of objective. If the objective, such as profit, is to be maximized, we refer to the problem as a *maximization problem*. If the object, such as cost, is to be minimized, we call the problem a *minimization problem*. We will consider both types of problem in this chapter. We will begin with a maximization problem. A second example will illustrate minimization problems.

Other examples of linear programming problems will be discussed briefly to provide a view of the breadth of applications that exist. These examples will help you develop your ability to recognize and formulate linear programming problems.

The final sections of this chapter will provide a short guide to the use of the computer in solving linear programming problems, and will examine, in more general terms, the nature of linear programming problems and their assumptions.

Maximization Problems

The first type of linear programming problem to be discussed is the maximization problem. The only conceptual difference between maximization and minimization problems is that we maximize the objective of the former and we minimize the objective of the latter. To begin with, an example of a maximization problem will be described.

Problem Description

The Nevada Instruments Company produces pocket calculators and recently introduced two new low-priced models—the Computron and the Approxymate—both of which have been experiencing rapid sales growth. In fact, the present demand for these new calculators far outstrips the plant manufacturing capacity. Additional facilities are being constructed nearby to increase the manufacturing capacity, but the expansion won't be completed for another several months. At present these two models represent roughly 5 percent of the total sales volume for Nevada Instruments, although they are expected to reach 20 percent in 2 years if sales continue to grow at the present rate.

In the meantime, the plant manager faces the problem of determining production quantities for the two calculators given the capacity restrictions. Production decisions are stated in cases of calculators rather than individual units, each case containing 10 calculators. The plant manager has identified three basic capacity problems. First, although the majority of the components used in manufacturing the calculators are purchased from other companies, Nevada Instruments does fabricate the plastic case and a number of other parts. As shown in Table 5-1, a case of 10 Computron calculators requires 3 hours of work in the fabrication department, and a case of 10 Approxymate calculators uses 2 hours of fabrication time. The fabrication department expects to have 36 hours of capacity available for the coming week.

The second major constraint exists in the assembly department, where the calculators are put together and packaged. The department has 40 hours available in the week ahead. A case of Computrons requires 2 hours of assembly time, and a case of Approxymates needs 4 hours.

Third, the process is further constrained by the fact that the company has been experiencing delivery problems on the integrated circuit (IC) chip used in the Computron. The supplier of the chip has experienced production problems and has been able to supply only 100 chips per week. Because of the specialized nature of the chip, an alternative supplier is not available. The chip used in the Approxymate is in plentiful supply from several suppliers, so that it represents no capacity restriction for Approxymate production.

Finally, there is one more fact the plant manager will consider: The Approxymate generates a higher contribution to profit than does the Computron. Specifically, each case of 10 Approxymates generates $10 contribution to profits and each case of Computrons generates $7. This information is summarized in Table 5-1.

Formulating the Problem

The steps necessary in solving the plant manager's production allocation decision are to determine the decision variables, the objectives, the constraints, and how all these relate. This process has been referred to as *problem formulation*. Table 5-2 illustrates the steps necessary to formulate the Nevada Instruments problem. We will now examine each of these steps.

TABLE 5-1
Nevada Instruments Production Problem*

| | *Contribution to profit* | *Capacity utilization* | | |
		Fabrication hours	*Assembly hours*	*Number of IC chips*
Computron	7	3	2	10
Approxymate	10	2	4	0
Available capacity		36 hours	40 hours	100 chips

*Figures shown are per case. (Each case contains 10 calculators.)

TABLE 5-2
Problem Formulation Summary

General procedure for problem formulation	Formulation of the Nevada Instruments problem
1. Specify the objective(s)	*Maximize* the *total contribution* to profits earned by next week's production
2. Identify the decision variables	Contribution is determined solely by the *number of cases of Computrons and Approxymates* to be produced
3. Determine the resource constraints	Production volume is limited by (1) *fabrication hours*, (2) *assembly hours*, (3) *number of IC chips for computrons*
4. Specify the relationships between the decision variables and (*a*) objective function, (*b*) constraints	Maximize: $TC = 7C + 10A$ Subject to: $3C + 2A \leq 36$ $2C + 4A \leq 40$ $1C \quad\quad \leq 10$ $C \quad\quad \geq 0$ $A \quad\quad \geq 0$ where C = number of cases of Computrons A = number of cases of Approxymates TC = total contribution

Specify the Objective   The first step is to identify the objective to be used in evaluating the decision alternatives. The plant manager's performance is evaluated by top management, at least in part, by the profit earned on the plant's operations. His objective, therefore, is to determine the most profitable production schedule for Approxymates and Computrons that is consistent with the three capacity restrictions. In other words, the objective is to *maximize the total contribution to profits*. The difference between price and variable production costs represents the contribution to profits that each case of calculators provides. These contributions were identified earlier as $10 per case of Approxymates and $7 per case of Computrons.

Identify the Decision Variables   The second step consists of identifying the decision variables or alternatives. The plant manager can affect the total contribution to profit by his choice of the number of cases of each calculator to be produced. Hence the decision variables are *the number of cases of each type of calculator that he chooses to produce*.

Determine the Resource Constraints   Determining the relevant resource constraints that limit the size of the decision variables is the third step in the problem formulation. As described earlier, the number of cases of the two types of calculator that can be produced is restricted by *the fabrication capacity, the assembly capacity, and the number of Computron IC chips available*. Thus, there are three relevant constraints for the plant manager's decision, one for each limited resource.

Specify the Relationships The fourth formulation step consists of setting up equations to relate the decision variables to the resource constraints and the desired objective. For our example, let C represent the number of cases of Computrons and A the number of cases of Approxymates. The use of the number of cases rather than the actual number of calculators simplifies the calculations.

Stating the Objective Function Since the objective is to maximize the total contribution to profits, we need to identify the contribution that each variable makes to the total. An equation that defines the objective in terms of the decision variables is called the *objective function*. Hence the objective function can be written as

$$\frac{\text{Total}}{\text{contribution}} = \left(\begin{array}{c} \text{contribution from} \\ \text{Computrons} \end{array} \right) + \left(\begin{array}{c} \text{contribution from} \\ \text{Approxymates} \end{array} \right)$$

The total contribution (TC) for each type of calculator is equal to the profit contribution of each unit multiplied by the number of units. Since each case of Computrons contributes \$7 to profit and we are going to produce C cases, the total contribution from Computrons is $7C$; the total contribution from Approxymates ($10A$) is determined in the same manner. The objective function is thus

$$TC = \$7C + \$10A$$

Another way to say that is that the company seeks to

$$\text{Maximize } 7C + 10A$$

Stating the Constraints Next we need to express the constraints mathematically. In each case we need to relate the use of scarce resources (labor, materials, etc.) to their availability. The first constraint concerns fabrication capacity, and we need to ensure that the total fabrication time required in producing the Computrons and Approxymates is not more than the capacity available. Hence

$$\left(\begin{array}{c} \text{Fabrication} \\ \text{capacity utilized} \\ \text{in producing} \\ \text{Computrons} \end{array} \right) + \left(\begin{array}{c} \text{fabrication} \\ \text{capacity utilized} \\ \text{in producing} \\ \text{Approxymates} \end{array} \right) \leq \left(\begin{array}{c} \text{available} \\ \text{fabrication} \\ \text{capacity} \end{array} \right)$$

Note the use of the symbol $\leq$ to denote a less than or equal to inequality. The expression $x \leq y$ would be read as x is less than or equal to y. At a later point the symbol $\geq$ will also be used to represent a greater than or equal to inequality.

We know that fabrication capacity is expressed in hours (36 hours), and we also know the fabrication utilization rates for both products: 3 hours required to make each case of Computrons and 2 hours for each case of Approxymates. Thus we can represent the second constraint (fabrication) mathematically as

$$3C + 2A \leq 36$$

In a similar manner we can relate the utilization of assembly capacity to the available capacity.

$$\begin{pmatrix} \text{Assembly} \\ \text{capacity utilized} \\ \text{in producing} \\ \text{Computrons} \end{pmatrix} + \begin{pmatrix} \text{assembly} \\ \text{capacity utilized} \\ \text{in producing} \\ \text{Approxymates} \end{pmatrix} \leq \begin{pmatrix} \text{available} \\ \text{assembly} \\ \text{capacity} \end{pmatrix}$$

or
$$2C + 4A \leq 40$$

The third constraint concerns the limitation on the number of IC chips available for the Computron. Note that this constraint is not affected at all by the number of Approxymates produced. This leads to

Chips required to produce Computrons $\leq$ available chip capacity

Since only one chip is used in each calculator, a case of calculators will require 10 chips, and our constraint becomes

$$10C \leq 100$$

Alternatively, we could have noted that there are enough IC chips to make 10 cases of Computrons. This leads to the following constraint:

$$1C \leq 10$$

which is equivalent to the one above.

Obviously, production is limited to positive amounts of either product. This leads to the final pair of constraints which restrict both decision variables to nonnegative quantities. These constraints are, appropriately enough, referred to as the *nonnegativity constraints*. In this case, we require

$$C \geq 0 \qquad A \geq 0$$

At this point the necessity for the nonnegativity constraints may not be readily apparent. From a logical viewpoint we realize that negative quantities cannot be "produced." Since "positive production" uses up capacity, it should not be surprising that "negative production" has the *mathematical effect* of creating capacity. To prevent this illogical development, the decision variables are restricted to nonnegative values.

Summary of Formulation To summarize, we can now list the objective function and constraints for the problem as we have formulated it. This is usually done in the form

$$\text{Maximize:} \quad TC = 7C + 10A$$

$$\begin{aligned} \text{Subject to:} \quad 3C + 2A &\leq 36 \\ 2C + 4A &\leq 40 \\ C \quad\;\; &\leq 10 \\ C \quad\;\; &\geq 0 \\ A &\geq 0 \end{aligned}$$

INSTANT REPLAY Formulate the Nevada Instruments problem letting C and A represent the number of *calculators* of each type produced, instead of the number of *cases*.

CHECK The problem would now appear as

$$\text{Maximize:} \quad TC = .70C + 1.00A$$

$$
\begin{aligned}
\text{Subject to:} \quad .3\,C + .2\,A &\leq 36 \\
.2\,C + .4\,A &\leq 40 \\
.1\,C \quad\;\; &\leq 10 \\
C \quad\quad &\geq 0 \\
A &\geq 0
\end{aligned}
$$

Solving the Problem

The preceding section analyzed the resource allocation problem to find the decision variables, the objective, the resource constraints, and their mathematical relationship. This process was referred to as problem formulation. At this point we will turn our attention to the *problem solution*. The plant manager must decide what values should be assigned to the decision variables to arrive at a solution. This is equivalent to determining the number of cases of Approxymates and Computrons that should be produced.

We will now see how this problem can be solved graphically. Many possible values could be chosen for the decision variables. Not all of these are feasible, however, because they may violate one or more of the resource constraints. The solution procedure to be described first identifies the complete set of feasible solutions and then selects the feasible solution that provides the most profit. This solution is the *optimal solution*.

Identifying the Feasible Solutions Once the problem is formulated, the next step is to identify those solutions that are potentially optimal. Since any optimal solution must satisfy all the constraints, we need only search among the constraint-satisfying solutions to find the optimal. Every solution that satisfies all the constraints is called a *feasible solution*; the feasible solution with the best objective function value is the *optimal solution*.

For a problem with two decision variables like the Nevada Instruments example, we can easily isolate the set of feasible solutions from those that are infeasible. This is accomplished by graphically eliminating those solutions that do not satisfy each constraint. When all constraints have been considered, only those solutions that have passed each constraint test constitute the set of feasible solutions.

Figure 5-1a illustrates the set of all possible solutions corresponding to various combinations of Computrons and Approxymates. On our graph, the horizontal axis represents the number of cases of Computrons produced and the vertical axis represents the number of cases of Approxymates. We will plot a line on this graph for each of the five constraints (three resource constraints and two nonnegativity constraints). All the points that lie on one side of each line will be infeasible. These points can therefore be eliminated. After all five lines have been added, the set of points that have not been eliminated by one or more of the lines must satisfy all the constraints. This set constitutes the set of feasible solutions.

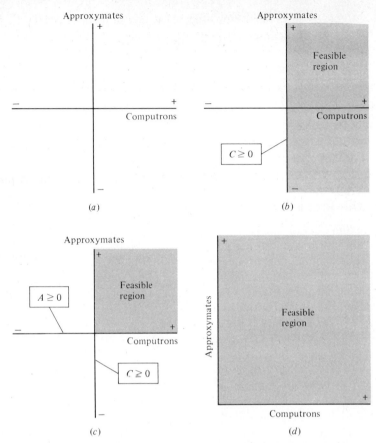

FIGURE 5-1 (*a*) Set of all possible solutions for Nevada Instruments problem. (*b*) Eliminating negative values for Computrons. (*c*) Eliminating negative values for Approximates. (*d*) Set of feasible solutions for Nevada Instruments problem after eliminating negative values for decision variables and changing scale.

Eliminating Solutions with Negative Values for the Decision Variables We shall begin by plotting the lines corresponding to the nonnegativity constraints. Since we are limited to nonzero values for the number of cases of Computrons C, we can eliminate all solutions that fall to the left of the vertical axis because any such solution will have a negative value for C. This is illustrated in Figure 5-1*b*. Similarly, we can restrict our attention to those solutions that lie on or above the horizontal axis, since they are the only solutions that have nonnegative values for A. Figure 5-1*c* shows this division. Note that the number of solutions was halved by the first constraint and then halved again by the second constraint so that only one-fourth of the original number remain. This is shown in Figure 5-1*d*, where all but the upper right-hand quadrant of the original graph has been omitted.

Next consider the fabrication constraint. It specifies that only certain combinations of the decision variables are feasible. Note that the constraint is an inequality ("less than or equal to" rather than "equal to"), and an inequality cannot be plotted directly on our graph. However, we can plot a line corresponding to the limits of the inequality and then determine which side of the line represents feasible solutions and which side infeasible ones.

In the case of the fabrication constraint, the limits are reached when the left-hand side of the inequality exactly equals the right-hand side. This requires that $3C + 2A = 36$, which is an equation that can be plotted.

Hints on Plotting

A straight line is completely specified by knowing any two points that fall on that line. Therefore, to plot any constraint limit equation, we need only specify two points on that line and then draw the line that connects them. A point can easily be found by choosing a value for one of the variables and then solving for the necessary value of the other variable. This can be repeated with different values to obtain the second point. The work involved can be considerably simplified by choosing values of zero for each variable in turn.

To illustrate, let $C = 0$ in the fabrication equation and solve for A. This yields $A = 18$. Then let $A = 0$; C must be 12. We now have two points—(1) $C = 0, A = 18$; and (2) $C = 12, A = 0$—which can be connected by a straight line to obtain the appropriate constraint limit equation, as shown in Figure 5-2.

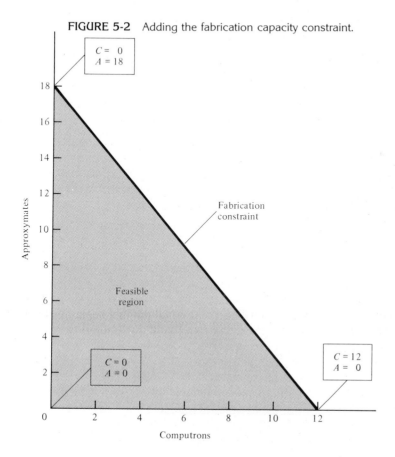

FIGURE 5-2 Adding the fabrication capacity constraint.

$C = 0$
$A = 18$

Approxymates

Fabrication
constraint

Feasible
region

$C = 0$
$A = 0$

$C = 12$
$A = 0$

Computrons

139

Eliminating Solutions Exceeding the Fabrication Capacity The fabrication constraint limit equation is graphed in Figure 5-2, using the two points found above. The next step is to identify the feasible side of the limit equation. This is simple to do, since we need examine only one point on either side of the constraint line. If that point is feasible, all points on that side of the line are also feasible. If it is infeasible, all the points on the opposite side of the line are the feasible points. Although any point not on the line can be chosen for testing, it is usually convenient to use the point where both variables are zero, the origin. Thus, if $C = 0$ and $A = 0$, our constraint would be $3(0) + 2(0) \le 36$ or $0 \le 36$.

Since zero is indeed less than 36, our constraint is satisfied and the point with $C = 0$ and $A = 0$ is feasible. Hence all points on that side of the line are feasible, and all points above and to the right can be eliminated.

With experience you will learn that the feasible area for the standard "less than or equal to" constraint will be down and to the left and that the upper area can be eliminated without actually checking a point for feasibility. For the moment, you may wish to continue making that check.

Eliminating Solutions Exceeding the Assembly Capacity In a manner similar to that for the fabrication constraint, we can add the assembly capacity constraint.

INSTANT REPLAY Determine two points for purposes of plotting the assembly capacity constraint.

CHECK Figure 5-3 shows the correct constraint. Ensure that the points you chose actually fall on that line.

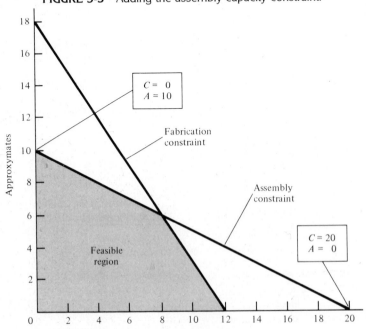

FIGURE 5-3 Adding the assembly capacity constraint.

141

INTRODUCTION TO
LINEAR
PROGRAMMING:
PROBLEM
FORMULATION
AND GRAPHICAL
SOLUTION

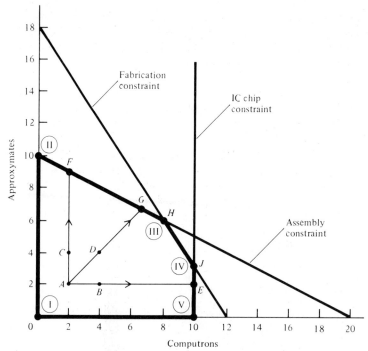

FIGURE 5-4   Set of feasible solutions.

Figure 5-3 illustrates the assembly capacity constraint as well as the reduced feasible region.

Eliminating Solutions Exceeding the IC Chip Capacity   The final constraint, that on IC chips for Computrons, is quite simple to add to the graph. The constraint requires that no more than 10 cases of Computrons be produced, $10C \leq 100$ or $C \leq 10$.

This constraint is represented as a vertical line, which at the limit corresponds to solutions in which exactly 10 cases of Computrons are produced. Obviously, points that fall to the left are feasible, since they represent fewer than 10 cases of Computrons. Figure 5-4 shows the complete set of feasible solutions with the addition of this last constraint. The feasible region is bordered by the heavy line as shown.

Identifying the Optimal Solution   Now that the set of feasible solutions has been identified, we turn our attention to the problem of determining which of these feasible solutions is optimal. Although there are an infinite number of feasible solutions, we need examine only a small number of these. As we shall see, the set of solutions called the extreme points will always contain the optimal solution. The *extreme point solutions* correspond to the corners of the feasible region. These are labeled with Roman numerals in Figure 5-4.

Extreme Points and the Optimal Solution   In order to show that the optimal solution must be one of the extreme point solutions, we will next examine the relative value of the various feasible solutions. We will begin with the interior points and show that these are always inferior to one or more of the points lying on the border of the feasible region. Next we will see that the extreme points (those at the corners) are always at least as good as the noncorner points that lie on the borders. In this way we see that the optimal solution must be one of the extreme point solutions.

Relative Value of Interior Points   Consider point A in Figure 5-4, which represents two Approxymates and two Computrons. This point is feasible—it satisfies all constraints—since it falls within the feasible region. Using the objective function, we find that the point has an objective function value of $7(2) + 10(2) = 34$.

Next note point B. What can be said about the relative value of this point compared with point A? Since point B represents the same number of Approxymates as point A but two more Computrons than A, it must be preferred to point A, because B's objective function value is bound to be higher. In fact we find that the total contribution for point B is $7(4) + 10(2) = 48$, which is \$14 higher than for point A.

Suppose we consider the line on which both points A and B lie. It should be obvious that as we move to the right, from A to B, the objective function value increases: We are holding the number of Approxymates constant while increasing the number of Computrons. Of course, if we move to the left, the objective function value falls, as the number of Computrons decreases with no change in the number of Approxymates.

In a similar manner if we compare points A and C and the line on which they lie, it is clear that C is preferred to A, since C corresponds to the same number of Computrons as A but more Approxymates. C has a total contribution of $7(2) + 10(4) = 54$. Likewise, as we move up the line connecting A and C, we find larger and larger objective function values, which decline as we move in the opposite direction.

Consider also point D, which lies diagonally above and to the right of point A. D is also preferred to point A because it represents more of both types of calculator. Specifically D corresponds to an objective function value of $7(4) + 10(4) = 68$.

Relative Value of Border Points   At this point you may have observed that along any line successive points in one direction lead to better and better solutions while in the other direction they decline in value. This is true for any lines drawn through the set of feasible points, with one major exception that we shall examine shortly.

If we proceed along any of these lines in the direction of increasing objective function value, we eventually reach a border of the feasible region. The border, you recall, was formed from the limiting values of the problem constraints. Reaching the border, therefore, means that the solution at that point is limited by the corresponding constraint.

Note that the border point solution is preferred to all solutions that lie on the line leading to that border point. Thus point E, the border point for the line connecting points A, B, and E, is preferred to any of the other points that lie on that line. This is true because all points to the left have a lower objective function value while all points to the right are infeasible.

Similarly point F is preferred to all other points on the line connecting A, C, and F, and point G dominates the other points on the $A\,D\,G$ line. This leads to the following conclusion:

Only points on the border of the feasible region can be optimal.

This conclusion recognizes that all internal points (those not on the border) are always dominated by at least one border point.

INSTANT REPLAY Take a few moments to convince yourself of this conclusion. Try to select an internal point that is not dominated by a border point.

NOTE It can't be done.

The significance of this conclusion is important. It allows us to ignore all internal points and focus our attention on the border points. Although we still have a large, in fact infinite, number of points to consider, we have made a quantum reduction in the size of the search area. Furthermore, as we will see next, we can now reduce the search even further—to a small, finite number of points.

Relative Value of Extreme Points Consider the border, or constraint, line that contains points F and G in Figure 5-4. This line corresponds to the assembly constraint or $2C + 4A \leq 40$. Point F represents two cases of Computrons and nine cases of Approxymates, which exactly uses up the 40 hours in the assembly department:

$$2(2) + 4(9) \leq 40$$
$$40 = 40$$

Point F has an objective function value of

$$7(2) + 10(9) = 104$$

Point G corresponds to equal quantities of Computrons and Approxymates and also exactly uses up all the assembly hours. Thus, if $C = A$ and

$$2C + 4A = 40$$

we can substitute C for A:

$$2C + 4C = 40$$
$$6C = 40$$
$$A = C = 6\tfrac{2}{3}$$

The objective function value for point G is

$$7(6\tfrac{2}{3}) + 10(6\tfrac{2}{3}) = 113\tfrac{1}{3}$$

Point G has a higher objective function value than point F. Why did this occur? Point G represents fewer Approxymates and more Computrons than point F. In other words, as we slide down the constraint that connects point F to point G, we are giving up Approxymates to gain Computrons. Since the objective function value of point G is greater than that for point F, it must be profitable to make such an exchange. Note that this occurs in spite of the greater contribution per unit of A ($10 vs. $7) because for each unit of A given up we gain 2 Cs.

143

In moving from point F to point G, we gave up $2\frac{1}{3}$ cases of Approxymates $(9 - 6\frac{2}{3} = 2\frac{1}{3})$ but gained $4\frac{2}{3}$ cases of Computrons $(6\frac{2}{3} - 2 = 4\frac{2}{3})$. Since $4\frac{2}{3} \div 2\frac{1}{3} = 2$, we gained 2 Computrons for each Approxymate lost. The source of this relationship can be found in the assembly constraint, which indicates that each Computron requires 2 hours of assembly time and each Approxymate 4 hours. Thus, if we reduce the number of cases of Approxymates produced by 1, we gain 4 hours of assembly time. This 4 hours can be used to produce 2 cases of Computrons.

This exchange is profitable since we gain \$14 ($2 \times \$7$) in contribution for the two cases of Computrons and lose only \$10 for the one case of Approxymates, leaving a net gain of \$4. In moving from point F to point G, we exchanged $2\frac{1}{3}$ cases of Approxymates for $4\frac{2}{3}$ cases of Computrons. The net increase in contribution is $\$4 \times 2\frac{1}{3} = \$9\frac{1}{3}$, which is the change in contribution we observed ($\$113\frac{1}{3} - 104 = 9\frac{1}{3}$).

It should be clear from the above analysis that as we move along the assembly constraint line in the direction from F to G, we are increasing our objective function value because of the substitution of two Computrons for each Approxymate. There is no need to stop at point G; we can continue to substitute profitably as we move past G until we reach point H. At that point we note two things. First, H is preferred to, or dominates, all other points along the line extending through F, G, and H. Second, a new constraint takes over at point H that applies to fabrication time. Point H may or may not dominate all other points on the fabrication line depending upon the relative profitability of trading off Approxymates for Computrons while maintaining fabrication feasibility. Note that the fabrication constraint requires $3C + 2A \le 36$. In this case, for each Approxymate given up we gain 2 hours of fabrication time, but since each Computron takes 3 hours of fabrication time, we gain only two-thirds of a case of Computrons for each case of Approxymates given up. This causes the objective function to decrease because we gain $\frac{2}{3}(7)$ but we lose $1(10)$: $\frac{2}{3}(7) - 1(10) = -5\frac{1}{3}$.

Thus point J, corresponding to 10 cases of Computrons and 3 of Approxymates, yields an objective function value of $7(10) + 10(3) = 100$.

This is a loss of 16 from the total contribution at point H, representing 8 cases of Computrons and 6 cases of Approxymates. Losing 3 cases of Approxymates costs $3 \times 5\frac{1}{3} = 16$, as occurred. Therefore, point H dominates all other feasible points along the fabrication constraint line.

We observe that each of the border lines has one point that dominates all others. What is quite important to note is that the dominating point always occurs at the *corners*, that is, where the constraints intersect. These points were earlier called *extreme points*, and their importance follows from the conclusion that:

> The optimal solution to a linear programming problem must occur at an extreme point.

This conclusion is important because our search for the optimum solution can be limited to the extreme points. In the Nevada Instruments problem, there are only five extreme points, each of which is labeled by a Roman numeral in Figure 5-4. With this knowledge we next explore procedures for examining these extreme points in order to find an optimum solution.

Enumerating Extreme Points   When the number of extreme points is small, one of the simplest methods of solving the problem is to list each extreme point, solve for the values of the decision variables at each point, calculate the value of the objective function corresponding to these decision variable values, and select the point that yields the best objective function value as the optimal solution.

As we saw for two variables, the extreme points are identified by constructing the graphical set of feasible solutions. Figure 5-5 illustrates the solution space for the Nevada Instruments problem.

Determining the Values of the Decision Variables at Extreme Points   The next step in enumerating the extreme points is to determine the value of the decision variables at each point. The way we do this is to solve the pair of constraint equations that intersect at each extreme point for the values of the decision variables that satisfy both constraints simultaneously. Point I of Figure 5-5 is quite simple because it corresponds to the origin where $C = A = 0$, or the point where the constraint limits $C = 0$ and $A = 0$ intersect. In fact, each and every extreme point is the result of the intersection of two or more constraints.

Point II is the intersection of the lines $C = 0$ and $2C + 4A = 40$. The values of C and A at the point of intersection must satisfy both equations simultaneously. Because $C = 0$ in one equation, it must also be zero in the other. Thus:

FIGURE 5-5   Feasible region for Nevada Instruments problem.

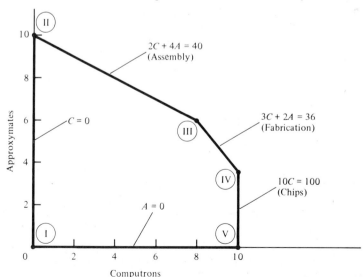

$$2(0) + 4A = 40$$

$$4A = 40$$

$$A = 10$$

Point II, then, has values of $C = 0$ and $A = 10$. Of course, we could have read these values directly off our graph, provided we had drawn it accurately. The ability to be precise in reading the graph is sometimes more difficult, especially when fractional values occur.

Point III corresponds to the intersection of the constraint lines $2C + 4A = 40$ and $3C + 2A = 36$. An easy way to find the values for C and A that solve the pair of equations at point III is to multiply one of the two equations by a factor chosen so that when one equation is subtracted from the other, one of the two variables is eliminated. To illustrate, if we multiply the second constraint by 2 and then subtract the first from it, we will eliminate variable A. Thus:

Multiply by 2:

$$2C + 4A = 40$$
$$3C + 2A = 36$$
$$6C + 4A = 72$$
$$-(2C + 4A = 40$$
$$4C \qquad = 32$$
$$C = 8$$

Then we can substitute the value of C in either of the two constraints to find the value of A,

$$2C + 4A = 40$$

$$2(8) + 4A = 40$$

$$4A = 40 - 16$$

$$A = \tfrac{24}{4} = 6$$

Thus $A = 6$ and $C = 8$ at point III.

Point IV is simpler in that the chip constraint has $C = 10$. Thus we can substitute the value of C into the other constraint to obtain the value of A:

$$3C + 2A = 36$$

$$C \qquad = 10$$

$$3(10) + 2A = 36$$

$$2A = 36 - 30$$

$$A = 3$$

Hence, point IV has $C = 10$ and $A = 3$.

Point V is similar to point II in that one of the variables, in this case A, is equal to zero. The IC chip constraint is the other constraint intersecting at point V. This has $C = 10$; so point V represents values of $A = 0$ and $C = 10$.

Determining the Value of the Objective Function at Extreme Points   The next step in the enumeration process is to determine the value of the objective function for each extreme point. We do this by substituting the values for the decision

147

INTRODUCTION TO
LINEAR
PROGRAMMING:
PROBLEM
FORMULATION
AND GRAPHICAL
SOLUTION

TABLE 5-3
Summary of Decision Variable and Objective Function Values
for Extreme Points of Nevada Instruments Problem

Extreme point	Values for variable		Objective function value
	C	A	
I	0	0	0
II	0	10	100
III	8	6	116
IV	10	3	100
V	10	0	70

variables we found in the previous step into the objective function. These values are summarized in Table 5-3.

We can find that optimum solution by inspecting Table 5-3. Extreme point III has an objective function value of 116, which is greater than that for any other point. Thus, extreme point III represents the optimal solution. The solution calls for 8 cases of Computrons and 6 cases of Approxymates to be produced. This results in a total contribution to profit of $116.

Extreme point III is, of course, the same point as point *H* in Figure 5-4. It is instructive to note that when we examined point *H*, we found that it dominated all the points on the two constraints intersecting at that point. It was not by chance that this happened: Such dominance is characteristic of an optimal solution to a linear programming problem. More remarkable, perhaps, is that *if any extreme point dominates, or is preferred to, all neighboring extreme points, that dominating extreme point is optimal.* This principle will be of great value when we consider the simplex solution procedure in the next chapter.

INSTANT REPLAY   Referring to the previous instant replay, evaluate the extreme points and determine the optimal solution to the Nevada Instruments problem without the fabrication constraint.

CHECK   The optimal solution is $C = 10$ and $A = 5$, with total contribution to profit of $120.

Isoprofit Line Approach   Another way we can solve graphical (two-variable) linear programming problems is to analyze the relative profitability of the feasible solutions. Earlier we examined solution points on lines drawn through the feasible region, and we found that the objective function increased as we moved in one direction on the line and decreased in the other direction.

There are some lines, a whole family in fact, for which the objective function remains constant as we slide along these lines. All points on these lines have the same objective function value. For this reason they are called *equal profit*, or *isoprofit, lines*.

Several other facts about isoprofit lines are worth noting. For one thing, all such lines are parallel to each other. For another, as we move from one line to the next, the profit increases as we move away from the origin and decreases as we move toward the origin.

We can use this knowledge together with the principle that only extreme points are potentially optimal to solve linear programming problems. We begin by drawing any isoprofit line on the diagram of feasible solutions. Since all other isoprofit lines are parallel to the one we have just drawn, we can slide a ruler parallel to our isoprofit line in the direction toward increasing profits, or away from the origin, until we reach the optimal solution. This is found by noting the point at which our ruler leaves the feasible region. Since we have been sliding our ruler in the direction of increasing profits, the last feasible point that our ruler touches must be the feasible point with the highest objective function value, which is optimal.

Choosing an Isoprofit Line   To illustrate, consider Figure 5-6. Note that we have simply added several isoprofit lines to Figure 5-5. Although there are an infinite number of such lines, it matters little which one we choose to start with. However, it is helpful if we choose one somewhere near, if not in, the feasible region; this makes it easier to slide the ruler to the optimal point. It also helps if we choose an initial profit value that is evenly divisible by both objective function coefficients, because this makes it easier to plot the line accurately.

Accordingly, we shall choose a profit of 70 for our initial isoprofit line. Note that 70 is evenly divisible by 7 and by 10, the objective function coefficients for Computrons and Approxymates, and the number of Computrons and Approxymates needed to generate an objective function value of 70 is in the neighborhood of the feasible region.

To draw the line, we select two points, as before. First we restrict one of the decision variables to zero and solve for the other. Then we reverse the process. With $C = 0$, A must equal 7 to achieve a profit of 70; and if $A = 0$,

FIGURE 5-6   Using isoprofit lines to solve the Nevada Instruments problem.

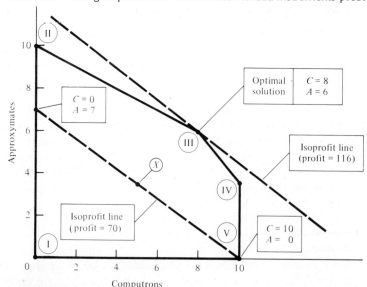

C must equal 10, so that profit will again be 70. The isoprofit line based on these points is shown in Figure 5-6.

At this point you may question whether or not all points on that line yield objective function values of 70. One way to convince yourself would be to sample some of the other points on the line and test the objective function value of each. For instance, consider point X in Figure 5-6, where $C = 5$ and $A = 3.5$. If we plug these values into the objective function, we find $7(5) + 10(3.5) = 70$.

Perhaps a more convincing substantiation is to consider the tradeoffs required as we slide along the line. The isoprofit line drawn was $7C + 10A = 70$. For each Approxymate we give up, we lose $10 in contribution. But, in order for our equation to balance, we must gain $\frac{10}{7}$ cases of Computrons. Since they have a profit of $7 each, the $7(\frac{10}{7}) = \$10$ gain will just offset the $10 lost for the case of Approxymates given up. Thus all points on the line must have the same objective function value of $70.

Finding the Optimal Extreme Point Using the Isoprofit Line   Next we need to use the isoprofit line to find the optimal solution. We do this by sliding our ruler up to the right until it reaches the last feasible point. As we slide our ruler, we must be careful to keep it parallel with the original isoprofit line. The last feasible point occurs, as we found through enumeration, where $C = 8$ and $A = 6$ with an objective function value of 116. The isoprofit line passing through this point is shown in Figure 5-6. Note that all other points on that line correspond to solutions with objective function values of 116. However, none of these points are feasible.

INSTANT REPLAY   Suppose that each case of Computrons contributes $5 to profit and each case of Approxymates contributes $10. Using an isoprofit line, determine the optimal solution.

CHECK   Since the isoprofit line lies parallel to the assembly constraint line, all points between extreme points II and III along the assembly constraint are optimal.

A difficulty with this procedure is that once the optimal point is found we may not be able to read the correct values for the decision variables accurately from the graph. It may be difficult to tell which of several closely positioned points is the optimal point. Or the values may be fractional, which is an additional complication.

These problems can be overcome by solving for the exact values of the decision variables using the methods we considered for the enumeration procedure. Suppose that after sliding our ruler up, we are unsure which of, say, two points is optimal. We first observe which constraints generated those points and solve constraint equations simultaneously for each point to find the decision variable values. Then we can calculate the objective function value for each point to find the optimal solution.

Minimization Problems

Although minimization problems are solved in the same general way as maximization problems, it is instructive to work through a sample problem to illustrate the few basic differences. The problem used is representative of a general class of linear programming problems called *mixing problems*.

An Example

The Battle Creek Breakfast Company has developed a new process for the manufacture of a cereal combining both rice and corn. The company wants to know the *least-cost mixture* of the two grains which will meet the United States recommended daily allowances (RDA) for vitamins A and D. Each ounce of rice costs $.08 and provides 20 percent of the RDA for vitamin A and 40 percent of the RDA for vitamin D. Each ounce of corn costs $.12 and furnishes 50 percent of the RDA for vitamin A and 20 percent for vitamin D.

Formulating the Problem

The decision variables are the number of ounces of each type of grain used for the "mix," and the objective is to find the minimum cost mix. Thus, the company seeks to

$$\text{Minimize } .08R + .12C$$

where R and C are the ounces of rice and corn used.

The minimum nutritional values for the two vitamins provide the only two resource constraints. For vitamin A

$$\begin{pmatrix} \% \text{ of RDA for} \\ \text{vitamin A} \\ \text{provided by rice} \end{pmatrix} + \begin{pmatrix} \% \text{ of RDA for} \\ \text{vitamin A} \\ \text{provided by corn} \end{pmatrix} \geq \begin{pmatrix} \text{recommended} \\ \text{daily allowances} \\ \text{for vitamin A} \end{pmatrix}$$

$$.2R + .5C \geq 1$$

Note that this inequality allows the amount of vitamin A provided by the rice and corn to exceed the recommended daily allowances. This is necessary because it is possible that in order to meet the other constraint, we may have to use grains with more vitamin A than we need.

In a similar manner we can derive the second constraint for vitamin D,

$$.4R + .2C \geq 1$$

After adding nonnegativity constraints, we have the complete problem formulation, which is to

$$\begin{aligned} \text{Minimize:} \quad & .08R + .12C \\ \text{Subject to:} \quad & .2R + .5C \geq 1 \\ & .4R + .2C \geq 1 \\ & R \geq 0, C \geq 0 \end{aligned}$$

Determining the Feasible Solutions

Because there are only two variables, we can construct a graph of the set of feasible solutions. Recall that the nonnegativity constraints reduce the region to the upper right-hand quadrant (see Figure 5-1d).

To this quadrant we first add the constraint for vitamin A. At the limit we have $.2R + .5C = 1$. We now obtain the two points necessary to plot this line.

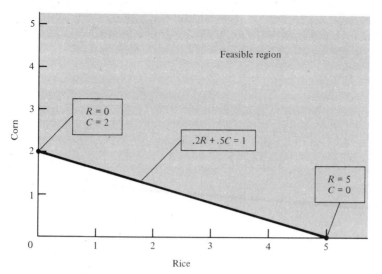

151

INTRODUCTION TO
LINEAR
PROGRAMMING:
PROBLEM
FORMULATION
AND GRAPHICAL
SOLUTION

FIGURE 5-7 Adding the vitamin A constraint.

We first set $R = 0$, which yields $C = 2$, and then set $C = 0$, getting $R = 5$. We then plot this line as shown in Figure 5-7.

Observe that the area in the region of the origin is infeasible, while the area above the constraint line is feasible. The reason for this is that the "greater than" constraint eliminates those low values of the decision variables which do not meet the nutritional requirements. We can substantiate this by checking the feasibility of any point not falling directly on the constraint line. For instance, take the origin, where $C = 0$ and $R = 0$. The constraint requires that

$$.2R + .5C \geq 1$$

Substituting for R and C, we find that the constraint calls for

$$.2(0) + .5(0) \geq 1$$
$$0 + 0 \ngeq 1$$

But since $0 \ngeq 1$, the constraint is not satisfied and the origin is infeasible. This point is the cheapest combination of grains, but hardly suitable since nothing is purchased. Figure 5-8 shows the graph with the second (vitamin D) constraint line added.

There is a significant difference between the feasible region for this minimization problem and the one for the maximization problem: The feasible region for this minimization problem is unbounded and unlimited because any combination of, say, large quantities of corn and rice will satisfy the constraints. Although this may be disquieting, it is actually of little consequence in solving this problem. After all, what we wish to do is minimize the cost of the mix, which is certainly going to call for small values for the decision variables.

Although the two problems so far treated in the text have contained constraints all of one type, either all "less than or equal to" (Nevada Instruments) or all "greater than or equal to" (Battle Creek), it is possible to have sets of mixed constraints. (See problem 5-1, sets 5 and 6.) These pose little difficulty. The addition of "greater than or equal to" constraints to maximization problems simply chops away additional infeasible solutions. The same is

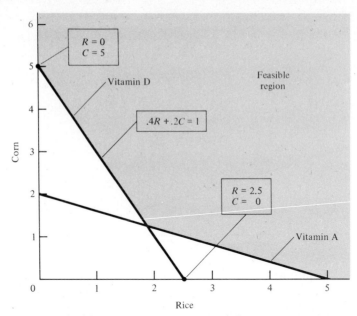

FIGURE 5-8 Adding the vitamin D constraint.

true for the inclusion of "less than or equal to" constraints in minimization problems.

Determining the Optimal Extreme Point

Figure 5-9 illustrates the three extreme points for this problem, each identified with a Roman numeral. Suppose we follow the equal cost line approach. We select a specific cost figure to obtain our initial line. In this case we choose $.24 because it is evenly divisible by the objective function coefficients or the costs for both grains ($.08 for rice and $.12 for corn). After plotting this line (Figure 5-9), we note that it lies below the feasible region. We therefore need to find the least-cost parallel line that has at least one feasible point. We do this by sliding a ruler parallel to the first equal cost line upward to the right until it just touches the feasible region. This occurs at extreme point II, which therefore corresponds to the optimal solution.

Calculating the Optimal Solution Values

Since point II corresponds to the intersection of the two constraints, we can find the optimal values of the decision variables by solving for the values of R and C that satisfy both constraint limit equations. Thus we wish values of R and C that satisfy both

$$.2R + .5C = 1$$

and

$$.4R + .2C = 1$$

Multiplying the first equation by 2 and subtracting the second one from it, we eliminate variable R and can then solve for C.

$$.4R + 1.0C = 2$$
$$\underline{-(.4R + .2C = 1)}$$
$$.8C = 1$$
$$C = \tfrac{5}{4} \text{ ounces}$$

153

INTRODUCTION TO
LINEAR
PROGRAMMING:
PROBLEM
FORMULATION
AND GRAPHICAL
SOLUTION

Substituting this value of C back into one of the original equations, we can then solve for the value of R.

$$.4R + .2(\tfrac{5}{4}) = 1$$
$$.4R \quad = 1 - \tfrac{1}{4}$$
$$R \quad = (\tfrac{3}{4})(\tfrac{5}{2}) = \tfrac{15}{8} \text{ ounce}$$

Then, to find the cost of this solution, we substitute the values of R and C into the objective function.

$$\text{Cost} = \$.08(\tfrac{15}{8}) + \$.12(\tfrac{5}{4})$$
$$= .15 + .15 = \$.30$$

If we had followed the enumeration approach, we would have found the values for R, C, and the cost for extreme point II just as we did above. The equivalent values for the other two points are quite easy to find and are shown in Figure 5-9. Since point II had the lowest cost of the three points, we would have chosen it as the optimal solution. Thus, regardless of the approach we choose, the graphical solution of a minimization problem is really no more difficult than for a maximization problem.

FIGURE 5-9 Identification and evaluation of extreme points for Battle Creek problem.

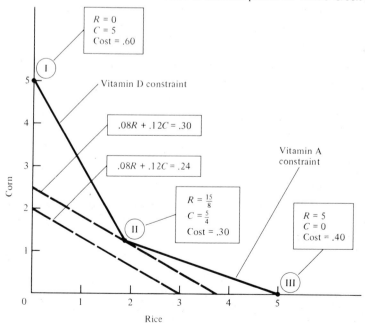

INSTANT REPLAY   Suppose we have the following minimization problem:

$$\text{Minimize:}\quad 5P + 10Q$$

$$\text{Subject to:}\quad P + Q \geq 10$$

$$2P + 3Q \geq 24$$

$$P \geq 0,\ Q \geq 0$$

What is the optimal solution to this problem?

CHECK   This problem has three extreme points as shown below:

Decision values		Objective
P	Q	function
0	10	100
6	4	70
12	0	60

The optimal solution is $P = 12$ and $Q = 0$, with the objective function equal to 60.

Note that the optimal solution to the Battle Creek problem requires $\frac{5}{4}$ ounces of corn and $\frac{15}{8}$ ounces of rice, for a total of $\frac{5}{4} + \frac{15}{8} = \frac{25}{8}$ ounces of grain. It is not likely that the cereal will be packaged in boxes containing exactly $\frac{25}{8}$ ounces; instead, standard package sizes, such as 40 ounces, will be used. It is not difficult, however, to convert our solution into a simple packaging formula. Note that the ratio of rice to corn is

$$\frac{\text{Ounces of rice}}{\text{Ounces of corn}} = \frac{\frac{15}{8}}{\frac{5}{4}} = \frac{15}{8}\frac{4}{5} = \frac{3}{2}$$

Thus the optimal solution can be restated to require that 3 ounces of rice be used with every 2 ounces of corn, whatever package sizes are actually used. The machinery used to prepare the cereal can be adjusted to provide the optimal mix of 3 to 2.

INSTANT REPLAY   How many ounces of corn and rice would be contained in a 40-ounce box?

CHECK   24 ounces of rice and 16 ounces of corn.

Further Examples of Linear Programming Problems

It is instructive at this point to consider briefly other types of linear programming problems and how they might be formulated. Our purpose here is threefold: (1) By examining other types of linear programming problems, we may get a sense of the nature of problem situations that are amenable to the linear programming approach. (2) We want to indicate the breadth and diversity of the areas in business and society where linear programming can and has been used. (3) We want to shed some light on the formulation process itself.

With respect to point (3), it has been said that formulating linear programming problems is an art rather than a science. Indeed, most people have much greater difficulty learning to formulate problems than to solve them. Any linear programming problem can be solved by computer. Thus the managerial requirements are necessarily more concerned with the difficulties in developing the model, gathering the right data, interpreting results, etc. At the end of this chapter we will see how easy it is to solve these problems with the computer. Here we will explore the formulation process. Although creativity may help in formulating more difficult problems, we can learn much by first studying how to formulate simpler examples.

Budgetary Allocation Problems

A common business problem involves allocating funds from a fixed budget to various alternative uses in such a way as to maximize some related measure, such as market share or profit. For example, a common marketing problem involves allocating a fixed advertising budget among alternative media choices, including newspaper, radio, television, magazines, and direct mail. The relative value of expenditures in each media class can be based on a variety of criteria such as the number of persons who see the ad, how often they see it, and what are the demographics (age, income level, marital status, etc.) of the people who see it. To illustrate, consider the following.

Wedge Brothers Company is about to test market a new brand of toothpaste, called Teeth Gloss. A total of $200,000 has been budgeted for the initial advertising campaign. The company is considering advertising in four different media: television, at a cost of $10,000 per ad; radio, at a cost of $1,000 per spot; magazines, at a cost of $7,000 per page; and newspapers, at a cost of $2,500 per page.

The aim of the advertising campaign is to introduce the public to the new toothpaste. Management has therefore decided that the effectiveness of the ads should be measured by the number of persons exposed to the ads. The company's marketing department has developed an *exposure index* for each type of ad, a higher index representing a more desirable exposure level. The exposure indices are: television 140, radio 35, magazines 70, and newspaper 40.

Several limitations restrict the actual advertising plan. Because of the frequency of publication, no more than 12 magazine ads can be used. Company policy dictates that the number of ads in print should never exceed 40 percent of the ads broadcast on radio and television. The radio and television ads chosen for the campaign depend on repeat exposures, which requires that at least 10 ads on each of these media be used.

Obviously the decision variables in this problem are the number of ads placed in each media. (An alternative way to formulate this problem is to let the decision variables represent dollars spent in each media; see the Instant Replay below.) The objective is to get the most out of the budget. Since effectiveness has been defined in terms of the exposure indices, we wish to maximize the sum of the index points. Thus, we wish to

$$\text{Maximize } 140T + 35R + 70M + 40N$$

where T, R, M, and N are the number of ads placed in television, radio, magazines, and newspapers, respectively.

The first major constraint is that no more than $200,000 is to be spent. We therefore have to ensure that

$$\left(\begin{array}{c}\text{Cost of}\\\text{television}\\\text{ads}\end{array}\right) + \left(\begin{array}{c}\text{cost of}\\\text{radio}\\\text{ads}\end{array}\right) + \left(\begin{array}{c}\text{cost of}\\\text{magazine}\\\text{ads}\end{array}\right) + \left(\begin{array}{c}\text{cost of}\\\text{newspaper}\\\text{ads}\end{array}\right) \le 200,000$$

or
$$10,000T + 1,000R + 7,000M + 2,500N \le 200,000$$

Next we need to limit the number of magazine ads to 12, as

$$M \le 12$$

The number of magazine and newspaper ads is to be limited to no more than 40 percent of those for radio and television. In its simplest form this is

$$M + N \le .4(R + T)$$

It is usually best to group all decision variables on the left of the equation; so we rearrange as follows:

$$M + N - .4R - .4T \le 0$$

Finally, we have the minimum limit of 10 radio and 10 television ads, which translates into two simple constraints:

$$R \ge 10 \qquad T \ge 10$$

Putting all this together and adding the nonnegativity constraints leads to:

Maximize: $140T + 35R + 70M + 40N$
Subject to:

$$10,000T + 1,000R + 7,000M + 2,500N \le 200,000$$

$$M \le 12$$

$$-.4T - .4R + M + N \le 0$$

$$R \ge 10 \qquad T \ge 10$$

$$T \ge 0, R \ge 0, M \ge 0, \text{ and } N \ge 0$$

Note that R and T were already constrained to be greater than 10. We need not have included the restriction that they both be nonnegative, since the first implies the latter.

INSTANT REPLAY Reformulate this advertising problem such that the decision variables represent *dollars spent* in each media rather than the *number of ads*.

CHECK The budget constraint now becomes

$$T + R + M + N \le 200,000$$

Blending and Mix Problems

157

INTRODUCTION TO
LINEAR
PROGRAMMING:
PROBLEM
FORMULATION
AND GRAPHICAL
SOLUTION

Other common linear programming problems are those in which ingredients are to be either *blended* or *mixed* to form some end product. The *blending problem* involves determining the most profitable blend of available input ingredients to produce a variable mix of outputs. Typical of this type of problem is that faced by petroleum companies. The inputs include the various types of crude oil available and existing refinery capacity. Within certain specified limits, the outputs from the refining process can be varied proportionally between gasoline, home heating fuel, and other fuel products. Profitability is affected by demand and selling price for the outputs as well as the cost of the crude oils used and the related refining cost.

The *mixing problem* consists of finding the *least-cost mix* of ingredients necessary to provide a sufficient quality to the mixture, such as nutrition level. The Battle Creek Breakfast Food cereal mix problem that we treated earlier in this chapter is an example.

Labor Scheduling Problems

Another application of linear programming that has received much attention recently is concerned with determining the minimum number of employees needed to meet required service levels.

One variation of this class of problems involves determining the minimum number of employees needed to work various shifts to meet a time-varying workload. Examples include staffing decisions for bank teller operations, telephone operators, police officers, firefighters, toll booth operators, etc.

Suppose, for example, that we wish to determine the minimum number of police officers needed to meet target levels that vary with crime activity throughout the day and night. We will assume that each officer works a consecutive 8-hour shift and that these shifts can begin at any one of six times: midnight, 4 A.M., 8 A.M., noon, 4 P.M., and 8 P.M. The decision variables represent the number of officers whose shift is to begin at one of these times. Suppose we let N_1 represent the number whose shift begins at midnight, N_2 the number that begin at 4 A.M., and so on. The objective is to minimize the total number of officers required, or

$$\text{Minimize } N_1 + N_2 + N_3 + N_4 + N_5 + N_6$$

The constraints for this problem ensure that a sufficient number of police officers are on duty during each time period to meet the target levels. Suppose the police commissioner has set target levels of 100 officers during the midnight to 4 A.M. period, 80 officers during the 4 to 8 A.M. period, 95 between 8 A.M. and noon, 100 from noon to 4 P.M., 120 from 4 to 8 P.M., and 150 from 8 P.M. to midnight. One constraint will be required for each of these time periods.

Consider the midnight to 4 A.M. period: 100 officers are required during this time period. The number actually on duty during this period include those that start at 8 P.M. (N_6) as well as those that start at midnight (N_1). Thus, we need the following constraint:

$$N_6 + N_1 \geq 100$$

Similar constraints would be added for each of the other target levels:

$$N_1 + N_2 \geq 80$$

$$N_2 + N_3 \geq 95$$

$$N_3 + N_4 \geq 100$$

$$N_4 + N_5 \geq 120$$

$$N_5 + N_6 \geq 150$$

Thus, after adding nonnegativity constraints, the police labor scheduling problem is formuated as

Minimize: $N_1 + N_2 + N_3 + N_4 + N_5 + N_6$

Subject to: $N_6 + N_1 \geq 100$

$$N_1 + N_2 \geq 80$$

$$N_2 + N_3 \geq 95$$

$$N_3 + N_4 \geq 100$$

$$N_4 + N_5 \geq 120$$

$$N_5 + N_6 \geq 150$$

$$N_1 \geq 0, N_2 \geq 0, N_3 \geq 0, N_4 \geq 0, N_5 \geq 0, N_6 \geq 0$$

Capital Budgeting Problems

The financial area of the firm also frequently uses linear programming applications. We shall consider here a simple form of a *capital budgeting problem*.

The Novato Supply Company sells its product through its own retail outlets. The company is considering expanding the number of these outlets. The number of potential sites for the new outlets is likely to require more funds than the company has available. Thus, it must choose which sites to adopt from the set of potential sites.

The decision variables in this case are of a special type. The decision is essentially a "yes" or "no" choice for each site rather than a "how much" choice. Thus we use what are called *zero-one variables*. These variables are allowed to take on one of only two values, either zero or one. For the present example we use a zero-one variable for each potential site: If this site is to be developed, the variable will have a value of one. If it is not to be developed, the variable will have a value of zero.

Suppose, for example, Novato has identified six potential sites for retail outlets. Let $x_1, x_2, \ldots, x_6$ be the zero-one variables corresponding to the selection decisions for the six potential sites. Based on estimates of demand for the product, various costs, and other factors, the expected profitability of each site has been developed. These are $100,000 for site 1, $85,000 for site 2, $70,000 for site 3, $95,000 for site 4, $110,000 for site 5, and $90,000 for site 6. The objective is to maximize the total expected profit for the set of selected sites. This means that the objective function is (amounts in thousands)

Maximize $100x_1 + 85x_2 + 70x_3 + 95x_4 + 110x_5 + 90x_6$

A variety of constraints can be specified for this problem. One is simply a limitation on the number of sites developed. Suppose Novato specifies that they are unwilling to open more than two retail outlets at this time. This would require that

$$x_1 + x_2 + x_3 + x_4 + x_5 + x_6 \leq 2$$

Another restriction relates to the amount of cash required to develop each site. The total spent cannot exceed budget amounts specified for each of the next 2 years. That is, development costs for the selected sites cannot exceed $100,000 in each of the next 2 years. Suppose that the required development costs for each proposed site during the next two years are:

Proposed site	Development cost	
	Year 1	Year 2
1	$50,000	$30,000
2	60,000	10,000
3	30,000	20,000
4	50,000	25,000
5	35,000	70,000
6	40,000	40,000

A separate constraint is required for each year. Thus (amounts in thousands):

$$50x_1 + 60x_2 + 30x_3 + 50x_4 + 35x_5 + 40x_6 \leq 100$$
$$30x_1 + 10x_2 + 20x_3 + 25x_4 + 70x_5 + 40x_6 \leq 100$$

The zero-one conditions can be handled in several ways. One of these is to specify that each decision variable x_i be zero or one:

$$x_i = \begin{cases} 0 \\ 1 \end{cases}$$

Another is to constrain the variables to values between zero and one, such as

$$0 \leq x_i \leq 1$$

but this may produce fractional values which must then be rounded up or down.

Regardless of the way that the zero-one conditions are specified, the solution procedure itself ultimately must force the decision variables to take on values of either zero or one in the final solution.

The complete formulation for Novato's site selection problem is

Maximize: $100x_1 + 85x_2 + 70x_3 + 95x_4 + 110x_5 + 90x_6$

Subject to:

$$x_1 + x_2 + x_3 + x_4 + x_5 + x_6 \leq 2$$
$$50x_1 + 60x_2 + 30x_3 + 50x_4 + 35x_5 + 40x_6 \leq 100$$
$$30x_1 + 10x_2 + 20x_3 + 25x_4 + 70x_5 + 40x_6 \leq 100$$

$$x_1, x_2, x_3, x_4, x_5, x_6 = 0 \text{ or } 1$$

We have examined the more difficult managerial problem of formulating linear programming problems. And we have seen how to solve two-variable problems graphically. We now consider how we can use the computer to solve these and larger problems. Numerous computer programs exist for solving linear programming problems, ranging from simplified procedures designed for classroom use to sophisticated and complex programs constructed to solve much larger and more complex practical problems.

The purpose in this section is to become familiar with the use of the simpler type of linear programming computer package. The system described in this text may not be identical to the one in use at your institution, but the vast majority of packages have enough standard components in common that you are likely to find that what you learn here is easily transferred to your own system. Your instructor should provide more detailed instructions on the linear programming computer packages available for your use.

There are three types of information that you will need to know in order to use a computer linear programming package: (1) how to access it, (2) how to provide input data, and (3) how to interpret the output. Each of these will be discussed below.

Gaining Access

To use a linear programming package you must learn how to get access to the program. Two basic types of packages are generally available. A *batch* program is one that requires the user to prepare the input in advance, usually on punched cards. The data, together with a set of control cards identifying the program to be used, are normally turned over to a computer facility. At some later point the user can retrieve the program output from the computer service facility.

The second type of package is generally referred to as a *time-shared* package. With this type of system, the user provides input and receives output while sitting at a computer terminal. In either case, your instructor will provide details on access requirements tailored to your computer system.

Providing Input

For batch programs the order and placement (format) of the input data will be specified by a program write-up (available from your instructor or the computer facility). With time-shared programs the computer, through the terminal, normally prompts or asks the user for the input data in some specified order. For instance, Figure 5-10 shows such a dialogue between the computer and user. To show clearly which statements were made by the computer and which were entered by the user, those provided by the user are *underlined*. (This underlining was added for clarification and would *not* be a part of the actual dialogue. An identifying Roman numeral is also added to the left of each question for reference purposes.)

The problem for which the data are being input in Figure 5-10 is the Nevada Instruments problem discussed earlier. For convenience, the formulation of this problem is repeated here:

$$\text{Maximize:} \quad TC = 7C + 10A$$

Subject to: $3C + 2A \leq 36$

$$2C + 4A \leq 40$$

$$1C \quad\quad \leq 10$$

161

INTRODUCTION TO
LINEAR
PROGRAMMING:
PROBLEM
FORMULATION
AND GRAPHICAL
SOLUTION

The nonnegativity constraints were omitted because they are not needed for input to the computer. (The method used to solve the problem assumes that all variables are to be nonnegative.)

The information asked for by the computer in the series of questions shown in Figure 5-10 is the minimum amount necessary in order for it to solve the problem.

Question I asks for the number of constraints and variables. The Nevada Instruments problem has three constraints (one each for fabrication, assembly, and IC chips) and two variables (number of cases of Computrons and of Approximates). Thus the user entered 3,2. (Note the use of the comma to separate numbers.)

The computer needs to know what type each of the three constraints is. Thus, in question II it asks for the number of less than (or equal to), greater than (or equal to), and equality constraints. All three constraints for the Nevada Instruments problem are of the less than or equal to variety: The user enters 3,0,0 in answer to the question. Note that even though there were no greater

FIGURE 5-10 Input steps for typical time-shared linear programming computer program. (Underlined statements were made by the user. Roman numerals identify each question.)

```
LPRUN


I    PLEASE ENTER THE NUMBER OF CONSTRAINTS AND VARIABLES, IN THAT ORDER?
     3,2

II   HOW MANY CONSTRAINTS ARE LESS THAN, GREATER THAN OR EQUALITY
     CONSTRAINTS, IN THAT ORDER?
     3,0,0

III  WHAT TYPE OF OPTIMIZATION IS DESIRED.  ENTER 0 FOR MAXIMIZATION,
     1 FOR MINIMIZATION?
     0

IV   ENTER THE RIGHT HAND SIDE COEFFICIENTS FOR EACH CONSTRAINT
     IN THE ORDER: LESS THAN, GREATER THAN, AND EQUALITY?
     36,40,10

V    ENTER THE OBJECTIVE FUNCTION COEFFICIENTS?
     7,10

VI   ENTER THE CONSTRAINT COEFFICIENTS FOR EACH CONSTRAINT
     IN THE SAME ORDER AS THE RIGHT HAND SIDE COEFFICIENTS
     WERE ENTERED ABOVE?
     3,2,2,4,1,0

VII  ENTER RUN CODE FOR TYPE OF OUTPUT DESIRED (0=OPTIMAL
     SOLUTION ONLY, 1=INCLUDE SENSITIVITY ANALYSIS,
     2=INCLUDE INITIAL AND FINAL TABLEAUX, 3=INCLUDE
     ALL TABLEAUX)?
     0
```

than or equality constraints, the user must nevertheless actually enter zero. A response of 3 is likely to cause the computer to repeat the question until three numbers are provided.

Question III asks whether the objective function is to be maximized or minimized. The computer in this case provides information concerning coded responses necessary to indicate whether maximization or minimization is desired. Since the Nevada Instruments problem requires maximization (of total contribution) the user enters 0.

Question IV asks for the right-hand-side constraint coefficients, which for the Nevada Instruments problem are the number of available fabrication hours (36), assembly hours (40), and cases of IC chips (10). In order to distinguish between constraint types, the computer requests that these values be entered in a strict order: first, all less than or equal to coefficients; second, all greater than or equal to coefficients; third, all equality coefficients.

Question V calls for the objective function coefficients. The user entered 7,10, representing the coefficients for Computrons and Approxymates, respectively.

The constraint coefficients (those to the left of the inequality) are entered in response to question VI. Caution must be exercised here to ensure that the coefficients are entered in the same order as the right-hand-side coefficients were in response to question IV. Recall that the response to question IV was in the order *fabrication, assembly,* and *IC chips*. Thus the response to question VI must be in that same order. Furthermore, since each constraint has (in this case) two coefficients to be entered, the order in which they are entered must be the same as was used for the objective function coefficients. In response to question V, the objective function coefficients were entered in the order Computron and Approxymate. This same order must therefore be followed here.

In summary, the response to question VI was to enter

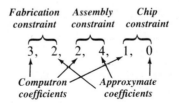

Also note that although the chip constraint contained no mention of Approxymates, a coefficient of zero was nevertheless required to be explicitly entered.

The final question asked users to specify how detailed they wished the output to be. Four coded responses are available of which the user selected code 0, indicating that only the optimal solution is desired. The other options provide additional types of output, which we will cover in later chapters.

Interpreting Output

Figure 5-11 shows the output the computer provided in response to the user-provided input. The first 10 lines of the output repeat the input information that was provided by the user. This allows the user to check that the formulation was correct. The variables representing the number of cases of Computron and Approxymate calculators to be produced are referred to in the computer output as variables 1 and 2. (They were called *C* and *A* in the formulation of the

```
LPRUN

NUMBER OF CONSTRAINTS    3    NUMBER OF VARIABLES    2

NUMBER OF LE CONSTRAINTS    3    GE CONSTRAINTS    0    EQ CONSTRAINTS    0

MAXIMIZATION OBJECTIVE

      VARIABLE         1      2

      COEFFICIENT     7.0    10.0

CONSTRAINTS

      VARIABLE         1      2       RELATION      RHS

         3           3.0    2.0         LE         36.0
         4           2.0    4.0         LE         40.0
         5           1.0    0.0         LE         10.0

FINAL SOLUTION     NUMBER OF ITERATIONS    2

MAX OBJECTIVE FUNCTION VALUE       116.0

BASIC DECISION VARIABLES

         1           8.0
         2           6.0

BASIC SLACK/SURPLUS VARIABLES

         5           2.0

STOP
```

| LE = less than or equal to |
| GE = greater than or equal to |
| EQ = equal to |
| RHS = right-hand side |
| Variable 1 = Computron |
| Variable 2 = Approxymate |

FIGURE 5-11 Output for computer solution of Nevada Instruments linear programming problem.

problem.) Some computer programs permit the use of simple alphabetic symbols, such as CTRON and AMATE (for Computron and Approxymate), in place of numeric variable designations. These would have to be provided during the input phase and are generally limited to a specific number of characters.

Note that all three constraints are listed, echoing the data provided during the input phase. Each constraint is assigned a number as shown to the left, 3 referring to the fabrication constraint, 4 referring to the assembly constraint, and 5 referring to the IC chip constraint. As with variable names, some computer programs allow the user to substitute alphabetic designations for the numeric names. Examples might be FABR, ASSEM, and CHIP for the three constraints in the Nevada Instruments problem.

The bottom portion of the output presents the optimal solution found. The results shown here correspond to those found earlier (see Figure 5-6). The maximum objective function value of 116 refers to the total contribution to profit earned. The values of variables 1 and 2 are the values of the decision variables, representing the number of cases of Computrons (variable 1) and of Approxymates (variable 2). The solution calls for 8 cases of Computrons and 6 cases of Approxymates, the same as we found graphically.

Chapter 6 will cover more about the meaning of the last section, labeled "BASIC SLACK/SURPLUS VARIABLES." But we can provide a simple explanation at this time. Recall that each of the constraint equations was assigned an identifying number (3, 4, and 5). The information shown in the last section refers, in this case, to the chip constraint, since that constraint was assigned the number 5. The value of 2.0 shown to the right represents the unused portion, or *slack,* with respect to that constraint. That is, the optimal solution did not use up all the available IC chips. Two cases of chips were left over. The fact that neither of the other two constraints are listed in this section implies that the capacities associated with these constraints were entirely used up; no slack remains. We will hear more about this in Chapter 6.

INSTANT REPLAY Answer the questions in Figure 5-10 for the Battle Creek Breakfast Food problem.

CHECK 2,2
0,2,0
1
1,1
.08,.12
.2,.5,.4,.2
0

Nature of Linear Programming Problems

This chapter examined a class of resource allocation problems referred to as linear programming problems. We must now look at certain implicit assumptions that must be met if a resource allocation problem is to be considered a linear programming problem.

Linearity Requirement

A major assumption is that the relationships among the decision variables, objectives, and constraints must all be described in *linear* terms. This means that the decision variables must have a *constant proportional, or linear, contribution to the objective function as well as a linear utilization rate for the constrained resources.* To see what that means, suppose that the first unit produced earns a $10 profit. The linearity requirement ensures that the same profit will be earned on the 100th or 1,000th or 1,000,000th unit. Similarly, if one unit requires 10 minutes of assembly time, then the same amount of time will be needed to assemble the hundredth, thousandth, or millionth unit. We first considered such linear relationships in our discussion of the break-even model in Chapter 1.

If these linearity requirements are not met sufficiently well, the problem is not a linear programming problem. In fact, such a problem is usually referred to as a *nonlinear programming problem.* Procedures do exist for solving nonlinear problems. But they are considerably more complex than those for linear problems and are beyond the scope of this text.

Feasibility of Fractional Values

165

INTRODUCTION TO
LINEAR
PROGRAMMING:
PROBLEM
FORMULATION
AND GRAPHICAL
SOLUTION

Another important assumption is that fractional values are permitted for the decision variables. Recall that the solution to the Battle Creek Breakfast Food problem gave fractional values for the decision variables. The number of ounces of rice and corn to be mixed were $\frac{15}{8}$ and $\frac{5}{4}$, respectively.

Many decision problems, however, require that the solution result in nonfractional, or *integer,* values for the decision variables. For example, an airline might want to determine the number of aircraft of various sizes to purchase. A solution calling for the purchase of 2.76 DC-10s would not be acceptable. The airline can purchase 2 or 3 DC-10s but not 2.76. Problems such as these are usually referred to as *integer programming problems,* emphasizing the integer requirements for the solution variables. We will examine how these problems can be solved in Chapter 11.

How Much Do We Need to Know about Linear Programming?

Success in solving linear programming problems has been achieved largely because of two major innovations. The first was the development of a systematic procedure, or solution method, for determining the optimal solution to linear programming problems. The ideas underlying linear programming existed for many years. But the solution of realistic problems was not possible until George B. Dantzig developed the *simplex method* in the late 1940s. We were able to solve the two-variable problems graphically in this chapter. But it is impossible to generalize that approach to more than three variables. The simplex method can handle any number of variables, which is why its development was so important.

The second development was the rapid growth of and improvement in high-speed electronic computers. The simplex method can be applied manually, as we shall see in Chapter 6. However, the level of computation required can be excessive, even for relatively few variables and constraints. For this reason, almost all practical linear programming problems are solved by computer. Without the development of digital computers, the practicality of using the simplex method to solve business problems would never have been possible.

If what we said above about the use of computers to solve linear programming problems is true, you may be wondering why we are devoting four chapters of the text to this topic. If the computer can do it, why do you need to know how it does it? There is actually several reasons why you should learn more about linear programming than just how to use the computer.

Ability to Formulate

First of all, the computer will provide the correct solution only if the problem is formulated properly. In the case of formulation errors, the computer will provide a solution that is not designed for the true problem. For this reason, a considerable portion of this chapter has been devoted to problem formulation.

A second major reason for learning more about linear programming results from general observations concerning what leads to successful implementation and use of management science models. If managers do not have an adequate understanding of the "how and why" of such models and techniques, they are more likely not to use them or to use them incorrectly. People are generally reluctant to put much faith in "black box" solutions. Documented cases exist in which managers were forced to use a model they neither understood nor believed in. Their "use" of the model consisted of modifying the formulation until the model provided a solution that fit with their own perception of what should be done.

Each of the chapters in this section has attempted to provide an explanation of not only how linear programming problems can be solved but why the solution methods work. This chapter began with the graphical method of solution. Chapter 6 examines the simplex method, which is the basis for most computerized linear programming solution procedures.

Ability to Test Solutions

A third reason for our extensive coverage is that problem solution is only one step in the management science process. As a by-product of obtaining a solution to a linear programming problem, a number of additional pieces of information can be obtained that deal with the *sensitivity* of the solution to changes in the input data.

This *sensitivity analysis* can be performed after a solution has been obtained. And it can provide answers to questions with significant managerial impact: How much should we be willing to pay to obtain additional units of each of the scarce resources? How far off do our estimates of the objective coefficients have to be before the optimal solution changes? Would the availability of another decision alternative change the optimal solution?

We will examine sensitivity analysis in Chapter 7. But in order to understand how to apply sensitivity analysis, we must first have a basic understanding of the simplex method, which is discussed in Chapter 6.

Ability to Handle Complications

A fourth reason for learning the essentials of linear programming is to develop the ability to take corrective action when the computer is unable to solve the problem as formulated. It is not too difficult in practice to formulate problems for which no feasible solution exists. Sometimes this results from an incorrect formulation. Other times it arises from specifying a set of constraints for which no feasible solution can be found.

Chapter 8 considers some of these problems and how they can be handled. The major portion of Chapter 8 deals with one way in which a problem with no apparent feasible solution can be solved.

Final Comments

This is the first of four chapters treating a general category of resource allocation problems called linear programming problems. We have seen that these problems have certain common elements (objective, decision variables, and resource constraints) that can be identified. The relationships between these elements can be expressed mathematically—a step we called problem formulation.

We can solve these problems, once they have been formulated, in several ways. We have examined the graphical approach in some detail. This requires first identifying the set of feasible solutions (those combinations of decision variable values that satisfy all the constraints). The optimal solution (the feasible solution with the best objective function value) was shown to always belong to the small, finite set of extreme point solutions. To find the optimal solution we needed to search only among these extreme point solutions (formed by the intersection of two constraints). We saw two ways that this search could be conducted: (1) enumerate and evaluate all the extreme points and (2) use the isoprofit/isocost approach to select the best solution visually.

The graphical approach provides a good conceptual introduction to linear programming problems. However, its usefulness in solving practical problems is quite limited. Our ability to graph the set of feasible solutions is generally limited to two variables. Furthermore, as the number of constraints increases, so does the number of extreme points. Thus, enumerating and evaluating all the extreme points becomes impractical for large problems.

Fortunately, a procedure exists that can be used to solve large linear programming problems. This procedure, called the simplex method, was the approach used by the computer program illustrated in this chapter. Chapter 6 will examine the simplex method in more detail. In Chapter 7 we will see how knowledge of the simplex method will allow us to use sensitivity analysis to provide the answers to a number of managerially important questions. In Chapter 8 we will see how resource allocation problems with multiple objectives can be treated.

Key Words

Problems

5-1. For each of the following sets of constraints, assuming nonnegativity for all variables, (a) plot each constraint, (b) identify the feasible region, and (c) enumerate the extreme points.

Set 1	Set 2	Set 3
$X \leq 10$	$X \leq 10$	$2X + Y \leq 30$
$Y \leq 20$	$X + Y \leq 20$	$X + Y \leq 20$

Set 4	Set 5	Set 6
$2X + 3Y \leq 30$	$3X + Y \leq 30$	$4X + 2Y \leq 40$
$X + Y \leq 20$	$X + Y \leq 20$	$2X + 2Y \leq 30$
	$X \geq 5$	$X + Y \geq 10$

5-2. Find the optimal solution to the problems defined by the following objective functions applied to the constraint sets in problem 5-1 as indicated below:

a. Maximize $6X + 4Y$ (sets 1 to 4).

b. Minimize $2X + 4Y$ (sets 5 and 6).

5-3. The Modular Furniture Company manufactures plastic shelf modules. These can be stacked and arranged in a variety of patterns, thus providing considerable flexibility to the homeowner. At the moment, management is troubled by what they consider low output on the production line. They produce two basic units, standard and deluxe.

The production process consists of two basic stages: injection molding and finishing. Shown below are the standard times for each unit in each stage, contribution to profit that each unit makes, and available hours per week of capacity in the two departments.

	Standard	Deluxe	Capacity
Molding department	3 hours	5 hours	40 hours
Finishing department	5 hours	5 hours	50 hours
Contribution margin	$2	$4	

a. Formulate this as a linear programming problem.

b. Identify the feasible solutions and extreme points.

c. Find the optimal solution.

5-4. Admiral Jack "Sea Dog" Hornblower is charged with the responsibility for forming a special task force to participate in Armed Forces Day celebrations at Norfolk, Virginia. His main problem is to determine the number and types of ships that will participate. Available for assignment are 2 aircraft carriers, 6 cruisers, and 24 destroyers. The operating costs associated with the celebration have been estimated at $100,000 per carrier, $35,000 per cruiser, and $12,000 per destroyer.

The government has directed Sea Dog to furnish at least 15 ships. For military reasons, at least 2 cruisers must be assigned for each carrier assigned and at least 3 destroyers must be assigned for each cruiser that is assigned.

Based on past Armed Forces Day celebrations, Sea Dog estimates that each carrier will draw 10,000 spectators, each cruiser 4,000 visitors, and each destroyer 1,000.

Sea Dog has turned the above information over to his staff with instructions to determine the best allocation of ships.

a. Ensign Benson, the junior staff officer, mindful of the large costs involved, suggests that an attempt should be made to minimize these costs while at least equaling

169

INTRODUCTION TO
LINEAR
PROGRAMMING:
PROBLEM
FORMULATION
AND GRAPHICAL
SOLUTION

the number of spectators that turned out last year—35,000. Formulate the problem as Ensign Benson sees it, taking into account all relevant constraints.

   b. Commander Oleander, Sea Dog's public relations officer, recommends that an attempt be made to maximize the crowd size while holding costs to no more than was spent last year—$475,000. Formulate the problem as Commander Oleander views it, taking account of all relevant constraints.

5-5. The Evans Office Equipment Company sells two different products, a stapler and a tape dispenser. The two items are produced in a common production facility which has an annual capacity of 15,000 labor hours. It takes $1\frac{1}{2}$ hours to produce a stapler and $\frac{1}{2}$ hours to produce a tape dispenser.

   The market has been surveyed, and company officials estimate that the maximum number of staplers that can be sold is 8,000 and that at most 12,000 tape dispensers can be sold. Subject to these limitations, the two products can be sold in any combination.

   The accounting department has provided the following information about profitability:

	Stapler	Tape dispenser
Selling price	$1.20	$.80
Variable cost	.60	.20

   a. Formulate this as a linear programming problem.
   b. Solve this problem graphically.
   c. What is the objective function value of the optimal solution?

5-6. The financial advisory board for the Mergatroid Company is reviewing new investment proposals for the coming year. Five projects have been identified as desirable. The *net present value* of the profits from each project, the cash requirements for each during the next 4 years, and the amount of cash that will be available for investment in each of these same 4 years are shown below.

	Cash needs (thousands of dollars) for year				Net present value of profits over planning horizon (thousands of dollars)
Project	1	2	3	4	
A	50	100	120	80	1,250
B	200	125	70	40	800
C	100	100	100	100	1,000
D	80	60	40	10	400
E	30	70	100	120	600
Cash available	200	300	250	200	

   Formulate this problem in the linear programming format so as to maximize the total net present value of profits from the projects over the planning horizon.

5-7. The Athens Dog Food Company produces and sells Progrow brand dog food. The dog food has two basic ingredients: meat by-products, which presently cost $.25 per pound, and cereal, which costs $.18 per pound.

   The purchasing agent is charged with the responsibility of purchasing the least-cost mix of ingredients. However, government standards require that all dog food contain at least 70 percent meat or meat by-products by weight. In addition, the nutritional contents, as stated on the can, require that each pound of dog food contains at least $\frac{1}{2}$

pound of protein. Assume that meat by-products contain 60 percent protein by weight and cereal 35 percent protein by weight.

The advertising campaign is based in part on the redness of Progrow dog food as an indication of the meatiness, or goodness, of the product. Thus the mix must meet a company-imposed redness standard. Each pound of meat by-products contributes 75 redness units (a company defined measure). Each pound of cereal contributes 50 redness units. The standard requires that each pound of dog food have no fewer than 60 redness units present.

a. Formulate the purchasing agent's decision as a linear programming problem.

b. Find the least-cost mix of meat by-products and cereal that satisfies the relevant constraints.

c. Can any of the constraints be discarded?

5-8. The Plains Peanut Company is attempting to decide what to do with this year's peanut crop. The latest estimate is that 1,000,000 pounds of peanuts will be harvested, of which approximately 40 percent are considered top quality. The company has traditionally disposed of its peanut crop in one of three ways: (*a*) seed peanuts sold to peanut farmers for use in planting next year's crop, (*b*) process peanuts sold for manufacturing peanut butter and other processed food items, and (*c*) whole peanuts that are packaged, after roasting, in cans, jars, and bags for resale.

The table below provides estimates per pound of the selling prices, variable costs, and contribution margins for the three methods of sale.

	Seed peanuts	Process peanuts	Whole peanuts
Selling price	$1.80	$3.10	$2.20
Variable costs	$1.10	$1.85	$1.60
Contribution	$ .70	$1.25	$ .60

The marketing manager for Plains Peanuts estimates that at those prices, the company can sell at most 200,000 pounds of process peanuts, 500,000 pounds of seed peanuts, and 800,000 pounds of whole peanuts.

Because of quality restrictions, whole peanuts must contain at least 75 percent top-quality peanuts, and seed peanuts must be at least 50 percent top-quality. Process peanuts can all be lower-quality peanuts, if necessary.

Set this up as a linear programming problem so as to maximize total contribution for the Plains Peanut Company.

5-9. The Champ Brothers Department Store Company is about to embark on an expansion of its discount department store chain. The brothers plan on building a series of stores each of which is to have 100,000 square feet of display space. At the moment they are contemplating how this space is to be allocated among the various departments. An analysis of existing stores has determined the following estimated profitability rates per square foot:

Department	Profit per square foot
Housewares	$2.50
Men's clothing	2.10
Women's clothing	3.80
Furniture	1.40
Appliances	1.90

Further analysis showed that each department requires different amounts of investment and also carries different risks, as shown below:

171

INTRODUCTION TO
LINEAR
PROGRAMMING:
PROBLEM
FORMULATION
AND GRAPHICAL
SOLUTION

Department	Investment per square foot	Risk as a % of investment
Housewares	$ 8	4
Men's clothing	10	12
Women's clothing	12	18
Furniture	18	9
Appliances	25	7

The brothers have established a limit of $1,750,000 on total investment per store. They also wish to keep the average risk to no greater than 10 percent of the total investment.

Furthermore, the brothers wish to limit the size of the women's clothing department to no more than 30 percent greater than the men's clothing department. Finally, they have established minimum sizes for each department, as shown below.

Department	Minimum size in square feet
Housewares	7,000
Men's clothing	12,000
Women's clothing	15,000
Furniture	10,000
Appliances	10,000

a. Formulate the space allocation decision as a linear programming problem.

b. Suggest how this problem might be formulated if the brothers were to relax the store size requirement (100,000 square feet) and wished to determine the most profitable store size instead.

5-10. The Collins Lawn Mower Company has been very successful in selling its low-noise mower. But it has had some problems in planning and controlling production. Owing to the seasonal nature of the demand for the product, the company has been experiencing severe differences between peak and slack production needs.

To illustrate, the expected quarterly demand for the coming year is

Quarter	Quarterly retail expected demand
1	14,000
2	28,000
3	24,000
4	10,000

At the moment the company expects to have 3,000 units in inventory at the beginning of the year and has established a target inventory of 5,000 units for inventory at the end of the year. Present production capacity is set at 18,000 units per quarter, using regular production only. Capacity can be expanded an additional 4,000 units per quarter through overtime.

The cost per unit produced on regular time is $50, and an additional $10 per unit is required for overtime. A unit produced in one period and not sold but carried in inventory until next period is estimated to cost $8 in storage costs. A unit back-ordered, that is, demanded in one period but not produced for sale until the following period, is estimated to cost $9 per period back-ordered.

Formulate the Collins Lawn Mower problem as a linear programming model, so as to minimize the production, storage, and back-order costs.

5-11. The ABCD Game Company manufactures computer-designed sports games. The firm currently manufactures football and basketball tabletop games. These games produce profits and require processing as shown in the table below.

	Processing requirements		Hourly capacity
	Basketball	Football	
Printing boards	2 minutes	3 minutes	60 minutes
Stamping parts	2 minutes	1 minute	50 minutes
Packaging	1 minute	1 minute	40 minutes
Profit	$3	$2.50	

    a. Formulate this as a linear programming problem.

    b. Find the most profitable production mix of basketball and football games.

    c. What is the hourly rate of profit for the production schedule determined in b?

    d. How much change can occur in the profit for basketball games without changing the optimal allocation found in b?

    e. How much change can occur in the profit per football game without changing the optimal allocation found in part b?

    f. How much change can occur in the packaging capacity constraint without changing either the mix or the quantities of the optimal solution in b? How much does the capacity have to change before one of the products is dropped from production?

    g. How much additional profit could be earned if the hourly stamping capacity could be increased?

5-12. Using the linear programming computer package available at your school, find the optimal solution to the Battle Creek Breakfast Food problem described in the text.

5-13. Using the linear programming computer package available at your school, find the optimal solution to the Nevada Instruments problem described in the text.

5-14. Using the linear programming computer package available at your school, find the optimal solution to the Modular Furniture Company problem (problem 5-3).

5-15. Using the linear programming computer package available at your school, find the optimal solution to the Armed Forces Day problem (problem 5-4): (a) as Ensign Benson sees it and (b) as Commander Oleander sees it.

5-16. Using the linear programming computer package available at your school, find the optimal solution to the Evans Office Equipment problem (problem 5-5).

6

Solving
Linear Programming
Problems
with the Simplex Method

In Chapter 5 we solved simple linear programming problems using graphical procedures. However, when the number of independent decision variables is greater than two, the graphical approach is inappropriate. A graph of the feasible region is limited to two dimensions, and we normally require one dimension for each variable.

Nevertheless, we can solve linear programming problems with more than two variables by using a systematic procedure called the *simplex method*. This method allows us to evaluate a series of extreme points in such a way that each successive extreme point is the same or better than the last one. We proceed by examining successive extreme points until no better solution can be found. Thus, we recognize that the last solution examined is the optimal solution.

We will examine the simplex method in detail in this chapter. We will begin by discussing the concepts that underlie simplex. Then we will see how simplex computations are performed algebraically. This will provide a more complete understanding of how simplex works. At that point we will observe how the algebraic calculations can be more efficiently organized and simplified by using what is called the simplex tableau. The use of the tableau will be demonstrated first for a maximization problem and then for a minimization problem. This will be followed by a brief discussion of several special issues that may arise when using simplex. The chapter concludes with a discussion of computer-related simplex issues.

Underlying Concepts

Consider again the set of feasible solutions for the Nevada Instruments problem, which are shown in Figure 6-1. Note that labels I, II, III, IV, and V   173

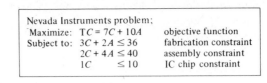

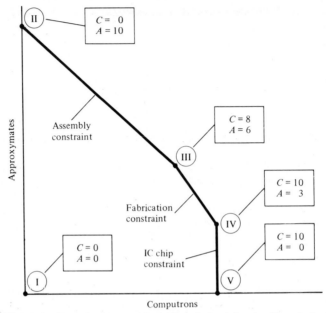

FIGURE 6-1 Formulation and feasible solutions for the Nevada Instruments problem.

identify the extreme points. We will now consider briefly how the simplex procedure would be used to solve this problem. We first require an initial solution, which can be any feasible solution. For convenience we will select the extreme point corresponding to the origin (I). Having selected an initial solution, we then check to see whether or not it is optimal. In the simplex method we determine optimality by examining whether or not changes to that solution can improve the objective function. If there is a change that improves the objective function, the solution is *not* optimal.

Our initial solution, the origin, corresponds to zero production quantities for Computrons and Approximates. Because we are attempting to maximize the total contribution to profit, that extreme point will not be optimal. Any changes in the initial values of the decision variables (production quantities for Computrons and Approximates) will increase the objective function value (total contribution to profits).

During our search for the optimal solution, we always proceed from the current extreme point to one of the neighboring, or *adjacent*, extreme points. An *adjacent extreme point* is one that can be reached by moving along one of the constraint lines. Thus each of the extreme points shown in Figure 6-1 has two adjacent extreme points. For example, points II and V are adjacent to point I.

Because the initial extreme point (I) has two adjacent points (II and V), two changes in the values of the decision variables are possible at this point.

175

SOLVING LINEAR
PROGRAMMING
PROBLEMS WITH
THE SIMPLEX
METHOD

Moving to extreme point II, we can produce as many Approxymates as possible, or moving to point V, we can produce as many Computrons as possible. Recall that the objective function will increase by $10 for each Approxymate produced and by $7 for each Computron. Therefore, extreme point I is not optimal. Furthermore, the relative size of the changes to the objective function also suggests the direction in which we should move: Because Approxymates promise a higher per-unit increase in profits, we next examine extreme point II.

Two extreme points are adjacent to point II. One of these (I), however, represents a return to the first point. We can therefore eliminate it from consideration because we know that it will decrease profits. So we turn our attention to the other point (III).

Notice that as we move from point II to point III we are in essence sliding along a constraint line. In this case, the constraint represents available assembly hours. A total of 40 assembly hours are available. Each case of Computrons requires 2 hours of assembly time, and each case of Approxymates needs 4 hours. If we assemble 1 less Approxymate, we save 4 hours of assembly time. This permits us to assemble 2 Computrons. Thus, for every Approxymate we give up, we gain 2 Computrons. In terms of profit, we are giving up $10 to gain $14. By adding 2 ($7) Computrons in place of 1 ($10) Approxymate, profit increases by $4. Since this exchange improves the objective function, we know that extreme point II is not optimal. Thus by sliding to point III, we exchange 4 Approxymates to gain 8 Computrons. We thereby increase the objective function by $16 $[-4(\$10) + 8(\$7) = \$16]$.

The two options available at extreme point III are either to return to point II or to move to point IV. We obviously need not consider point II. Moving to point IV involves further exchanges of Approxymates for Computrons. In this case the rate of exchange is different from what it was when we moved from point II to point III. We are now sliding along the fabrication constraint line.

A total of 36 hours of fabrication time is available. Each Computron requires 3 hours of fabrication time and each Approxymate requires 2 hours. Thus for each Approxymate we give up, we get 2 hours of fabrication time. In 2 hours we can fabricate two-thirds of a Computron. From a profit standpoint we would be giving up $10 to gain $4.67 ($\frac{2}{3} \times \$7$). Obviously this exchange is not profitable. We need not further consider a move to point IV.

Neither of the two potential changes (II and IV) from extreme point III is profitable; that is, neither increases the objective function. We have therefore determined that extreme point III is optimal. Note that we found the optimal solution by examining only three of the five possible extreme points. For larger problems, we will find that the simplex method actually considers a very small proportion of the potential extreme point solutions. In fact, the power of the simplex method does not come just from its capacity to solve large linear programming problems. It comes from the efficiency with which this method finds the optimal solution by systematically examining a relatively small number of potential solutions.

INSTANT REPLAY   Would point III be optimal if the contribution rates for the products were instead $12 for each Computron and $7 for each Approxymate?

CHECK No. An exchange of Approxymates for Computrons in moving from point III to point IV would gain $1 for each Approxymate given up. (Point IV would now be optimal.)

At this point you may question the benefit of the simplex method, when we could have solved the Nevada Instruments problem more easily using the graphical method described in Chapter 5. For a two-variable problem such as Nevada Instruments, there is no benefit. We used that problem only to illustrate the underlying concepts of the simplex method.

In Chapter 5 we saw how to use the computer to solve linear programming problems. The procedure used by the computer to find the optimal solution is nothing more than the simplex method. The purpose of studying the simplex method in this chapter is to remove some of the mystery surrounding the procedure. An understanding of simplex is valuable. Such knowledge will increase the success of your application of linear programming and help you to take advantage of the power of sensitivity analysis (to be covered in Chapter 7).

Steps of the Simplex Procedure

Before moving on, let us review the general solution steps that make up the simplex procedure. These are shown in the flowchart in Figure 6-2 and are discussed in detail below.

The simplex procedure involves four separate steps, two of which are carried out repetitively. These are:

1. The first step is to formulate the problem mathematically by specifying the decision variables, objective function, and constraints. Chapter 5 dealt with this.

2. The second step is to choose one of the extreme points as the initial feasible solution. Although any extreme point could be selected, it is usually convenient (for maximization problems) to choose the origin, where the decision variables all have zero values.

3. The third step is to determine whether or not the current extreme point is optimal. We do this by examining the change in the value of the objective function that will result from a move to one of the adjacent extreme points. If none of the adjacent points has a better objective function value, the current extreme point is optimal and our search can terminate. If, however, one or more of these adjacent points is better than the current point, we go to step 4.

4. The fourth step is to select the most promising adjacent point and to solve for the values of the decision variables at that point.

Note the loop in Figure 6-2 connecting steps 3 and 4. It calls for repeating steps 3 and 4 as often as necessary until the optimal solution is found.

Algebraic Basis of Simplex

177

SOLVING LINEAR
PROGRAMMING
PROBLEMS WITH
THE SIMPLEX
METHOD

An understanding of the mechanics of the various steps of the simplex method is needed now. This section will trace through the calculations required at each of the four steps (Figure 6-2). For convenience the Nevada Instruments problem will be used again. A later section will show how to use the simplex tableau, a more efficient way of organizing these calculations.

Step 1: Formulating the Problem: Adding Slack Variables

The Nevada Instruments problem was formulated first in Chapter 5 (see Tables 5-1 and 5-2). The problem as stated was to:

$$\text{Maximize:} \quad TC = 7C + 10A \qquad \text{objective function}$$

$$\text{Subject to:} \quad 3C + 2A \le 36 \qquad \text{fabrication constraint}$$

$$2C + 4A \le 40 \qquad \text{assembly constraint}$$

$$1C \qquad \le 10 \qquad \text{IC chip constraint}$$

Recall from Chapter 5 that in order to graph the set of feasible solutions, we had to convert each constraint inequality to an equality. The simplex method also requires conversion of the constraint inequalities to equalities. We

FIGURE 6-2 Flowchart of simplex procedure.

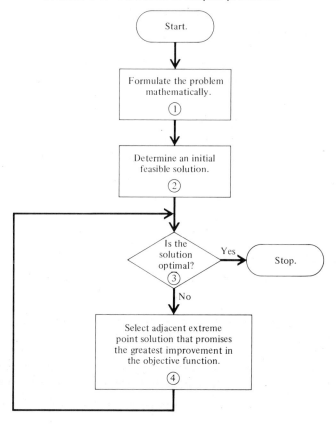

do this by adding a *slack variable* to each constraint. Each slack variable corresponds to *unused capacity for the constraint to which it is added.*

We will use the symbol S to represent slack variables. Thus S_1 will represent unused fabrication hours, S_2 excess assembly hours, and S_3 the number of unused IC chips. Slack variables are always added to the "less than" side of the constraint to bring the two sides of the constraint into balance. For example, we convert the fabrication constraint ($3C + 2A \leq 36$) to an equality by adding the slack variable to the left-hand side of the constraint so that both sides of the equation will always be equal:

$$3C + 2A + S_1 = 36$$

In general, we are converting an inequality of the form

(Capacity utilized by decision variables) $\leq$ (total available capacity)

to an equality of the form

$$\left(\begin{array}{c}\text{Capacity utilized by}\\\text{decision variables}\end{array}\right) + \left(\begin{array}{c}\text{unused}\\\text{capacity (slack)}\end{array}\right) = \left(\begin{array}{c}\text{total}\\\text{available capacity}\end{array}\right)$$

These slack variables must be nonnegative. Otherwise, the capacity utilized by the decision variables will exceed the total available capacity. Note that we now have two types of variables: *decision variables,* which represent the number of cases of each type of calculator to be produced, and *slack variables,* which represent the amount of unused capacity for each constraint.

We do not need to add the slack variables to the objective function because they do not directly affect the total contribution to profit. It is convenient, however, to include the current value of the objective function. That is, the objective function equation is written as

$$\left(\begin{array}{c}\text{Current value of}\\\text{objective function}\end{array}\right) + \left(\begin{array}{c}\text{potential changes in}\\\text{objective function}\end{array}\right)$$

Initially the objective function has a zero value. Thus, for the Nevada Instruments problem we would write

$$TC = 0 + 7C + 10A$$

This indicates that the current value of the objective function is 0 but that it can be increased by \$7 for each Computron produced and \$10 for each Approxymate.

Our revised formulation of the Nevada Instruments problem is now

$$\text{Maximize:} \quad TC = 0 + 7C + 10A$$

$$\text{Subject to:} \quad 3C + 2A + S_1 = 36$$

$$2C + 4A + S_2 = 40$$

$$1C \qquad + S_3 = 10$$

For convenience, we will pause here to obtain the values for the decision and slack variables at the five extreme points in Figure 6-3. (We can use the results from Chapter 5 for the values of the decision variables.)

At the origin (point I) we are not producing anything; therefore, $A = 0$, $C = 0$, and of course $TC = 0$. We can find values for the slack variables by substituting zeros for the two decision variables in each constraint and then

179

SOLVING LINEAR
PROGRAMMING
PROBLEMS WITH
THE SIMPLEX
METHOD

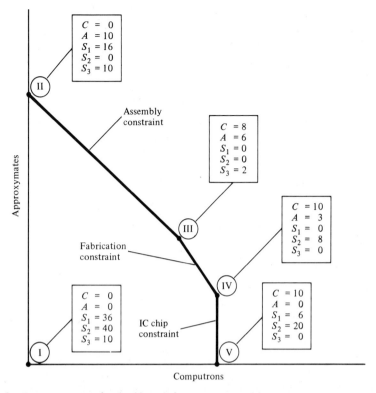

FIGURE 6-3 Extreme points for the Nevada Instruments problem with corresponding values for decision and slack variables.

solving for the slack variables. To do this, we first rearrange the constraint equation as

$$S_1 = 36 - 3C - 2A \qquad \text{fabrication constraint}$$

$$S_2 = 40 - 2C - 4A \qquad \text{assembly constraint}$$

$$S_3 = 10 - 1C \qquad\qquad \text{IC chip constraint}$$

Substituting values of 0 for A and C, we find that $S_1 = 36$, $S_2 = 40$, and $S_3 = 10$ at point I. Looking at Figure 6-3, we see that these values are summarized as

$$C = 0 \qquad S_1 = 36$$

$$A = 0 \qquad S_2 = 40$$

$$S_3 = 10$$

Referring back to Figure 6-3, we find that at point II, $C = 0$ and $A = 10$. Solving for the slack variables at this point, we find that

$$S_1 = 36 - 3(0) - 2(10) = 16 \qquad \text{fabrication constraint}$$

$$S_2 = 40 - 2(0) - 4(10) = \ \ 0 \qquad \text{assembly constraint}$$

$$S_3 = 10 - 1(0) \qquad\quad = 10 \qquad \text{IC chip constraint}$$

Thus at extreme point II:

$$C = 0 \qquad S_1 = 16$$
$$A = 10 \qquad S_2 = 0$$
$$S_3 = 10$$

Continuing in the same manner, we find

Extreme point III	Extreme point IV	Extreme point V
$C = 8$	$C = 10$	$C = 10$
$A = 6$	$A = 3$	$A = 0$
$S_1 = 0$	$S_1 = 0$	$S_1 = 6$
$S_2 = 0$	$S_2 = 8$	$S_2 = 20$
$S_3 = 2$	$S_3 = 0$	$S_3 = 0$

The values for the variables are shown next to each extreme point in Figure 6-3. As the steps required in applying the simplex are described, you may find it convenient to refer to this figure.

Step 2: Determining an Initial Feasible Solution

Having now formulated the problem, the second step in solving the problem is to select an initial feasible solution. We choose the origin (extreme point I in Figure 6-3) as the initial solution. In most cases we are assured that it represents a feasible, though not profitable, solution. In a later section we shall see how to select an initial solution when the origin does not represent a feasible solution, which is normally the situation with minimization problems.

Step 3: Checking Optimality of the Solution (Point I)

We determine the optimality of the current solution (extreme point I) by examining the objective function, which we defined earlier as

$$\text{TC} = \underbrace{0}_{\substack{Current \\ value}} + \underbrace{7C + 10A}_{\substack{Potential \\ changes}}$$

We see that the objective function has a value of zero and that both the decision variables have positive coefficients. Thus, any increase in the values of the decision variables will cause the objective function to increase. Because we are trying to maximize the value of the objective function, if the potential changes in its value are positive, the current solution is not optimal. Therefore, we conclude that extreme point I is not optimal because increases in either C or A will also increase the objective function. If all the potential changes would only reduce the objective function, the current solution would have been optimal. Since the current solution is not optimal, we now must see how to find a better solution.

Step 4: Selecting a Promising Adjacent Extreme Point

181

SOLVING LINEAR
PROGRAMMING
PROBLEMS WITH
THE SIMPLEX
METHOD

We need next to look at the process of moving from the current solution to one of the adjacent extreme points very closely. This is an essential aspect of the simplex procedure. At any extreme point each variable (decision or slack) is classified as *basic* or *nonbasic*. To move from one extreme point to the next, one of the nonbasic variables (called the *entering variable*) becomes a basic variable. Corresponding to this change, one of the basic variables (called the *departing variable*) becomes a nonbasic variable. To help in understanding this process, let us begin with basic and nonbasic variables.

Basic and Nonbasic Variables   Referring to Figure 6-3, we note that the current solution (point I) has three variables with nonzero values (the slack variables) and two with zero values (the decision variables). Variables with nonzero values are called *basic variables* and those with zero values are called *nonbasic variables*. The designation of which variables are basic and which are not will continually change as we move from one extreme point to another. But the *number* of basic, or nonzero, variables will remain constant. In fact, the fundamental theorem of linear programming states that:

> There will always be the same number of basic variables as there are constraints.

Observe that we began with three constraints. There are three nonzero, or basic, variables for the initial solution: the three slack variables.

Now, consider what changes take place when we move from the current solution to one of the adjacent extreme points. (It will be useful in this discussion to refer to Figure 6-3.) The values of many of the variables, both decision and slack, change. Some increase and some decrease. For example, compare the values of the variables for extreme points I and II:

Variable	Extreme point I	Extreme point II
C	0	0
A	0	10
S_1	36	16
S_2	40	0
S_3	10	10

Although the values of variables C and S_3 remain the same, each of the other three variables does change. Decision variable A increases from 0 to 10, while slack variables S_1 and S_2 each decrease. What causes these changes to occur? Extreme point I represents no production ($C = A = 0$). Extreme point II differs from I in that as many cases of Approxymates as the constraints allow are produced. We were limited by the assembly constraint to 10 cases of Approxymates—each case requires 4 hours of assembly time, and only 40 hours were available. Slack variable S_2, representing unused assembly capacity, decreased in value from 40 to 0 because producing 10 cases of Approxymates uses up every available hour of assembly capacity. Slack variable S_1, corresponding to unused fabrication capacity, declined from 36 to 16 hours. The 20-hour decrease is a direct result of the requirement that each of the 10 cases of Approxymates uses 2 hours of fabrication time.

Since extreme point II does not call for any Computron production, the values of C, representing the number of cases of Computrons produced, and S_3, the unused Computron IC chip capacity, remain the same as for extreme point I: 0 and 10, respectively.

Let us now take a different perspective and review the change with respect to which variables are basic and which are nonbasic between the two extreme points. The three slack variables (S_1, S_2, and S_3) were previously identified as the basic variables for extreme point I. S_1 and S_3 remain basic variables at extreme point II. However, decision variable A has replaced slack variable S_2 in the set of basic variables at point II. A now has a nonzero value while variable S_2 is zero.

It is not surprising that the creation of one new basic variable (A) is accompanied by the creation of one new nonbasic variable (S_2). As the fundamental theorem stated, there can be only one basic variable for each problem constraint. Thus, if a new basic variable is added, one of the old basic variables must become nonbasic by assuming a zero value. Compare the values of the variables in Figure 6-3 for any two adjacent extreme points. In every case the move from one point to another always results in one basic variable becoming nonbasic and one nonbasic variable becoming basic.

INSTANT REPLAY   In moving from extreme point II to extreme point III which basic and nonbasic variables change in status?

CHECK   Basic variable S_1 becomes nonbasic and nonbasic variable C becomes basic.

Entering and Departing Variables   We refer to the new basic variable as the *entering variable,* because it "enters" the set of basic variables. We call the new nonbasic variable the *departing variable* because it "leaves" the set of basic variables. Thus, in moving from extreme point I to extreme point II we found

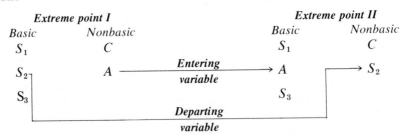

Next we will consider how to choose the entering and departing variables.

Selecting the Entering Variable   Returning to our example, for the first solution (extreme point I), we had two nonbasic variables A and C. The simplex procedure requires that the most promising variable be selected as the entering variable. That is, the variable with the highest per-unit objective function coefficient must be chosen. Since at extreme point I, A has a higher coefficient ($10), it is selected as the entering variable.

Selecting the Departing Variable   To select the departing variable, we must examine the constraints imposed on the value of the entering variable. Since variable A occurs only in the first two constraints, we need not consider the IC chip constraint. The two constraints to be examined are

$$S_1 = 36 - 3C - 2A \qquad \text{fabrication constraint}$$
$$S_2 = 40 - 2C - 4A \qquad \text{assembly constraint}$$

Recall that at extreme point I, both A and C are 0 and $S_1 = 36$. Now, as shown by the fabrication constraint, each unit of A produced requires slack variable S_1 to decrease by 2 units. If it is profitable to substitute 1 unit of A for 2 units of S_1, we should try to substitute as many units as possible. In this case we could increase variable A by as much as 18 units ($36 \div 2$) before slack variable S_1 reaches zero.

Examining the assembly constraint, we note that each unit of variable A produced requires slack variable S_2 to decrease by 4 units. Since we started with 40 units of S_2, variable A is limited by this constraint to a maximum value of $10\,(40 \div 4)$. Since a limit of 10 units is more constraining than a limit of 18, we find that the assembly constraint determines the size of variable A in the new solution. If, therefore, $A = 10$ in the next solution, slack variable S_2 will drop to zero. Thus variable S_2 is the departing variable and will become nonbasic.

We know that at extreme point I variables S_1, S_2, and S_3 were basic and C and A were nonbasic. To move to the next extreme point, we saw above that A, the entering variable, becomes basic and S_2, the departing variable, becomes nonbasic. Therefore, variables A, S_1, and S_3 are basic at extreme point II and C and S_2 are nonbasic.

To form the new solution we need to solve for the changed values of the basic variables. We first rewrite the assembly constraint so that the new basic variable (A) is on the left. Thus,

$$S_2 = 40 - 2C - 4A \qquad \text{assembly constraint, point I}$$
$$4A = 40 - 2C - S_2$$

And now we solve for A:

$$A = 10 - \tfrac{1}{2}C - \tfrac{1}{4}S_2 \qquad \text{assembly constraint, point II}$$

Because C and S_2 are now both nonbasic and have zero values, variable A has taken on a value of 10 (as was predicted above).

We now reflect the exchange of variable A for variable S_2 in the other constraints by substituting the value of A, as defined by the assembly constraint equation at point II, wherever it appears. Thus, we would update the fabrication constraint

$$S_1 = 36 - 3C - 2A \qquad \text{fabrication constraint, point I}$$

by substituting for A

$$S_1 = 36 - 3C - 2(10 - \tfrac{1}{2}C - \tfrac{1}{4}S_2)$$
$$= 36 - 20 - 3C + 1C + \tfrac{1}{2}S_2$$
$$= 16 - 2C + \tfrac{1}{2}S_2 \qquad \text{fabrication constraint, point I}$$

Because C and S_2 are nonbasic (zero values), the value of S_1 (fabrication slack) is now 16.

The value of variable S_1 has changed from 36 in the first solution to 16 here because of the 10-unit increase in variable A. The IC chip constraint is unchanged because variable A did not appear there. However, the objective function needs to be revised to reflect the change in variable A. We achieve this, as before, by substituting the value of A, as specified by the assembly constraint, into the objective function:

$$TC = 0 + 7C + 10A \qquad \text{objective function, point I}$$
$$= 0 + 7C + 10(10 - \tfrac{1}{2}C - \tfrac{1}{4}S_2)$$
$$= 0 + 100 + 7C - 5C - 2\tfrac{1}{2}S_2$$
$$= 100 + 2C - 2\tfrac{1}{2}S_2 \qquad \text{objective function, point II}$$

Because variables C and S_2 are nonbasic (zero values), the total contribution is 100. This is precisely what we should expect because we increased the value of variable A by 10 units and we were promised an increase in profit of $10 per unit for each A added.

Step 3: Checking Optimality of the New Solution (Point II)

We can now check the optimality of this new solution (extreme point II). As required by the simplex procedure, we examine the coefficients of the nonbasic variables in the objective function:

$$TC = 100 + 2C - 2\tfrac{1}{2}S_2 \qquad \text{objective function, point II}$$

Variable C has a positive coefficient of $2. This promises to increase total profits by $2 for each unit of variable C produced. Variable S_2 has a negative coefficient of $-2\tfrac{1}{2}$. This indicates that the contribution to profits will *decrease* by $2.50 for each unit that variable S_2 is increased. Clearly, since one nonbasic variable (C) has a positive contribution, the current solution is not optimal.

We should pause a moment and examine where the objective function coefficients come from. When we began, variable C had an objective function coefficient of $7; why has this now fallen to $2? To answer this question, first note that slack variable S_2 in the new solution has a zero value. This means that all available assembly hours have been used in producing Approxymates. Therefore, if we intend to produce any Computrons, we need to obtain additional assembly hours. The only way to do that is to reduce the number of Approxymates produced. Recall that each Computron requires 2 assembly hours and each Approxymate requires 4 hours. Thus, to produce one Computron we must reduce production for Approxymates by $\tfrac{1}{2}$ unit. This can also be read directly from the assembly constraint for point II:

$$A = 10 - \tfrac{1}{2}C - \tfrac{1}{4}S_2 \qquad \text{assembly constraint, point II}$$

The coefficient of $-\tfrac{1}{2}$ in front of variable C shows that an increase of 1 unit in that variable causes a $\tfrac{1}{2}$ unit decrease in variable A.

A gain of 1 Computron yields an increase in contribution of $7. This must be offset, however, by the loss of $\tfrac{1}{2}$ Approxymate. Since each Approxymate is worth $10, we must give up $5 to gain $7, or a net gain of $2. This is precisely where the $+2$ coefficient for variable C in the revised objective function came from.

INSTANT REPLAY   Why does variable S_2 have a value of $-2\frac{1}{2}$ in the revised objective function?

CHECK S_2 represents slack assembly capacity, which is now zero. If S_2 increases in value, A must decrease. Each unit of increase in S_2 requires a decrease of $\frac{1}{4}$ unit in A, as seen from the assembly constraint. The loss of $\frac{1}{4}$ unit of A costs us $\frac{1}{4}$ ($10) = $2.50.

Step 4: Selecting a New Adjacent Extreme Point

Since extreme point II is not optimal, we proceed to an adjacent extreme point by first selecting an entering variable. Examining the objective function at point II (TC $= 100 + 2C - 2\frac{1}{2}S_2$) shows that the choice here is clearly variable C. It is the only nonbasic variable with a positive objective function coefficient.

To find the departing variable, we need to determine which constraint imposes the tightest limit on the value of the entering variable (C). For the fabrication constraint

$$S_1 = 16 - 2C + \tfrac{1}{2}S_2 \qquad \text{fabrication constraint, point II}$$

we see that each unit increase in C will cause S_1 (which is now 16) to decrease by 2. This results in a limit of 8 units for variable C ($16 \div 2$).

For the assembly constraint

$$A = 10 - \tfrac{1}{2}C - \tfrac{1}{4}S_2 \qquad \text{assembly constraint, point II}$$

the value of A (now 10) must decrease by $\frac{1}{2}$ unit for each unit increase in C. This results in a limit of 20 units for variable C ($10 \div \frac{1}{2}$).

The IC chip constraint

$$S_3 = 10 - 1C \qquad \text{IC chip constraint, point II}$$

must also be considered because C is included in that constraint as well. Each unit increase in C will cause S_3 (now 10) to decrease by 1. Thus C is limited to 10 by this constraint ($10 \div 1$).

The tightest of these limits on the value of C is imposed by the fabrication constraint, which limits C to a value of 8. Observe that if $C = 8$, variable S_1 (defined by the fabrication constraint) will decrease to 0.

$$S_1 = 16 - 2C + \tfrac{1}{2}S_2 \qquad \text{fabrication constraint, point II}$$

$$= 16 - 2(8) + \tfrac{1}{2}S_2$$

$$= 0 + \tfrac{1}{2}S_2$$

Thus, variable S_1 is the departing variable and will become nonbasic in the next solution. Variable C is the entering variable and will take S_1's place in the set of basic variables. In general, *the basic variable* (in this case S_1) *associated with the limiting constraint* (in this case the fabrication constraint) *will be the departing variable.*

Note that a constraint is limiting only if the coefficient of the entering **185** variable is negative. A positive coefficient means that any increase in the entering variable will also cause the basic variable for that constraint to rise as well. For instance, note the current fabrication constraint:

$$S_1 = 16 - 2C + \tfrac{1}{2}S_2 \qquad \text{fabrication constraint, point II}$$

Variable S_2 has a positive coefficient. This indicates that if variable S_2 becomes nonzero, variable S_1 must also increase to keep the equation balanced. You may ask how increasing one variable can cause an increase to occur in another variable. Recall that this solution (point II) requires production of as many Approxymates as possible, completely using up all the available assembly hours. This drives the value of S_2, the slack variable for the assembly constraint, to zero. If variable S_2 is to increase from zero, variable A must make a corresponding decrease. Each Approxymate produced requires fabrication time. Thus, any decrease in Approxymate production will free up both fabrication time and assembly time. This will show up as an increase in the associated slack variables (S_1 and S_2).

Next we need to reflect the replacement of the departing variable (S_1) by the entering variable (C) in each of the equations. We begin by rewriting the limiting constraint (fabrication) and solving for C.

$$S_1 = 16 - 2C + \tfrac{1}{2}S_2 \qquad \text{fabrication constraint, point II}$$

$$2C = 16 - S_1 + \tfrac{1}{2}S_2$$

$$C = 8 - \tfrac{1}{2}S_1 + \tfrac{1}{4}S_2 \qquad \text{fabrication constraint, point III}$$

Then we substitute the value of C, as defined by the fabrication constraint, into each of the other two constraints. The assembly constraint now becomes

$$A = 10 - \tfrac{1}{2}C - \tfrac{1}{4}S_2 \qquad\qquad \text{assembly constraint, point II}$$

$$= 10 - \tfrac{1}{2}(8 - \tfrac{1}{2}S_1 + \tfrac{1}{4}S_2) - \tfrac{1}{4}S_2$$

$$= 10 - 4 + \tfrac{1}{4}S_1 - \tfrac{1}{8}S_2 - \tfrac{1}{4}S_2$$

$$= 6 + \tfrac{1}{4}S_1 - \tfrac{3}{8}S_2 \qquad\qquad \text{assembly constraint, point III}$$

Note that the increase in 8 units for variable C caused a drop of 4 units in variable A. This was promised by the coefficient of $-\tfrac{1}{2}$ for variable C in the assembly constraint before we made the substitution.

The IC chip constraint becomes

$$S_3 = 10 - 1C \qquad\qquad \text{IC chip constraint, point II}$$

$$= 10 - 1(8 - \tfrac{1}{2}S_1 + \tfrac{1}{4}S_2)$$

$$= 10 - 8 + \tfrac{1}{2}S_1 - \tfrac{1}{4}S_2$$

$$= 2 + \tfrac{1}{2}S_1 - \tfrac{1}{4}S_2 \qquad\qquad \text{IC chip constraint, point III}$$

Then we make a similar substitution in the objective function:

$$TC = 100 + 2C - 2\tfrac{1}{2}S_2 \qquad\qquad \text{objective function, point III}$$

$$= 100 + 2(8 - \tfrac{1}{2}S_1 + \tfrac{1}{4}S_2) - 2\tfrac{1}{2}S_2$$

$$= 100 + 16 - S_1 + \tfrac{1}{2}S_2 - 2\tfrac{1}{2}S_2$$

$$= 116 - S_1 - 2S_2 \qquad\qquad \text{objective function, point III}$$

Step 3: Checking the Optimality of the New Solution (Point III) 187

SOLVING LINEAR
PROGRAMMING
PROBLEMS WITH
THE SIMPLEX
METHOD

The addition of 8 units of Computrons caused the total contribution to increase by \$16. This is an increase of \$2 per unit added, as promised. It is important to note here that both nonbasic variables, S_1 and S_2, have negative objective function coefficients. Since neither nonbasic variable can increase the objective function value, we have reached the optimal solution. This solution calls for production of 8 units of Computrons and 6 units of Approxymates, with a total contribution of \$116. This is, of course, the same solution that we obtained graphically in Chapter 5 and earlier in this chapter.

Notice that the optimal solution contained a nonzero value (2) for slack variable S_3. This indicates that two cases of IC chips are left over. That is, they were not used up by the optimal solution. The slack variables for the other two constraints were nonbasic ($S_1 = S_2 = 0$). That indicates that all available fabrication and assembly time is used up by the optimal production plan. That also suggests that profits could be increased if additional fabrication and/or assembly time could be made available.

INSTANT REPLAY Explain why the objective function coefficient for slack variable S_2 was -2 in the optimal solution.

CHECK The fabrication constraint for the optimal solution shows that an increase of 1 unit in S_2 results in a gain of $\frac{1}{4}$ unit of C. The assembly constraint shows that an increase of 1 unit in S_2 results in a loss of $\frac{3}{8}$ unit of A. Thus, the net change is $\frac{1}{4}(7) - (\frac{3}{8})(10) = -2$.

Solving Maximization Problems with Simplex

We have now followed the simplex procedure through the steps necessary to determine an optimal solution to a linear programming problem. In this section we see how the calculations required at each step can be simplified and organized in a logical manner.

The Simplex Tableau

As you are surely aware by now, the calculations required by the simplex method can be messy. It is easy to lose direction if we are not careful. This section presents the *simplex tableau*. It is a means by which the simplex calculations can be simplified and organized. With an understanding of the basic logic behind the simplex procedure, considerable effort can be saved by using the simplex tableau. Furthermore, most computerized linear programming packages provide simplex tableaus as part of the output. (See the last section of this chapter for an example.) Experience gained here will thus help you to interpret the computer-generated output.

A word of assurance: The simplex tableau is nothing more than a tabular display of the same equations that we were manipulating in the preceding section. Appropriate column and row labels have been added, where possible, to help you to familiarize yourself with the tableau.

First, forming the initial tableau is explained. Then we will see how to

TABLE 6-1
Basic Format of Simplex Tableau

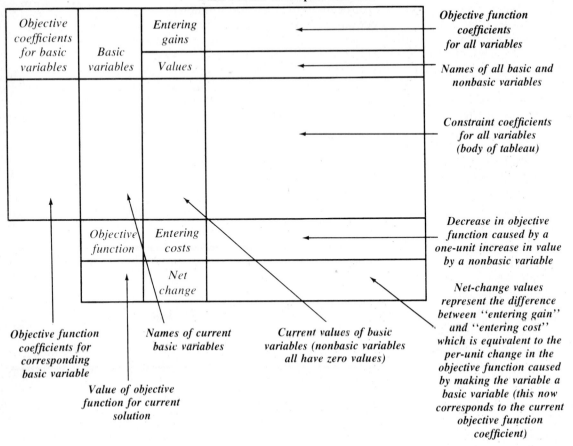

modify the initial tableau to generate succeeding tableaus. A separate tableau will be prepared for each extreme point solution examined. Finally, we will see how to interpret the values shown in the tableaus.

Table 6-1 illustrates the basic structure of the simplex tableau. Some of the labels will be easily understandable. Those that aren't will be explained shortly. The initial steps in using the simplex tableau are the same as those for the algebraic approach: formulating the problem, adding slack variables to the constraints, and choosing an initial feasible solution. We will again use the Nevada Instruments problem for convenience.

We previously formulated the Nevada Instruments problem, which, after the three slack variables (S_1, S_2, and S_3) were added, appeared as

$$\text{Maximize:} \quad TC = 0 + 7C + 10A \qquad \text{objective function}$$

$$\text{Subject to:} \quad 3C + 2A + S_1 = 36 \qquad \text{fabrication constraint}$$

$$2C + 4A + S_2 = 40 \qquad \text{assembly constraint}$$

$$1C \qquad + S_3 = 10 \qquad \text{IC chip constraint}$$

188

189

SOLVING LINEAR
PROGRAMMING
PROBLEMS WITH
THE SIMPLEX
METHOD

TABLE 6-2
Partially Completed Simplex Tableau

Objective coefficients for basic variables	Basic variables	Entering gains	7	10	0	0	0
		Values	C	A	S_1	S_2	S_3
0	S_1						
0	S_2						
0	S_3						
	Objective function	Entering costs					
		Net change					

We also chose the origin (extreme point I) as the initial feasible solution. At the origin the basic variables are $S_1 = 36$, $S_2 = 40$, and $S_3 = 10$. The nonbasic variables are $A = 0$ and $C = 0$.

Preparing the Initial Tableau

Tableau Headings The first step in preparing the initial simplex tableau is to enter the names of all the variables and their respective objective function coefficients in the top two rows of the right-hand side of the tableau. We can also complete the two columns at the far left of the tableau by entering for each constraint the appropriate initial corresponding basic variable (S_1 for the fabrication constraint, S_2 for the assembly constraint, and S_3 for the IC chip constraint) and its respective objective function coefficient (all zeros in this case). These items are entered in the tableau of Table 6-2.

Body of the Tableau The middle or *body of the tableau* is used to record the three constraint equations. The column labeled "Values" contains the initial value for each basic variable corresponding to the right-hand side of the appropriate constraint equation (36 for S_1, 40 for S_2, and 10 for S_3). In the row to the right of each constraint value, we record the constraint coefficient appropriate to each variable. These are entered in the order in which the columns are labeled. For example, for the fabrication constraint, the coefficient for C is 3, which is entered in the first column (labeled C). The coefficient for A is 2, which is entered in the second column. The coefficient for S_1 is 1, which is entered in the S_1 column. Zeros are entered in the columns labeled S_2 and S_3, since those variables do not appear in the fabrication constraint. Table 6-3 shows the insertion of the three constraint equations in the body of the tableau.

Also note that the portion of the body of the tableau for the basic variables has a special structure, called the *basic matrix*. This can be seen by isolating that portion of the table corresponding to the rows and columns for the basic variables. Thus, for our initial tableau we obtain the following basic matrix:

$$
\begin{array}{cccc}
 & S_1 & S_2 & S_3 \\
S_1 & 1 & 0 & 0 \\
S_2 & 0 & 1 & 0 \\
S_3 & 0 & 0 & 1
\end{array}
$$

Observe that a 1 appears at the intersection of the row and column corresponding to each basic variable, while zeros appear everywhere else. This same pattern will occur in every tableau, the relative positions of the ones and zeros shifting with changes in the set of basic variables.

The final portion of the tableau requires some calculations before we can complete it. However, those calculations are almost trivial for the initial tableau.

Objective Function   The objective function section of the tableau is used to record the current value of the objective function, which we know initially is zero. We could have reached this same conclusion by multiplying the objective coefficient for each basic variable by its current value and then adding the results:

$$
\begin{array}{l}
\text{Objective} \\
\text{function}
\end{array}
= \Sigma \left[\left(\begin{array}{c} \text{objective coefficient} \\ \text{for basic variable} \end{array} \right) \times \left(\begin{array}{c} \text{current value of} \\ \text{basic variable} \end{array} \right) \right]
$$

$$
= 0(36) + 0(40) + 0(10) = 0
$$

Entering Costs   The entering-costs row in the tableau represents the loss in the current objective function value that results from an increase by one unit in the value of each of the nonbasic variables. This loss is derived from the decreases in the values of the basic variables that would result. These losses are normally zero for the first tableau because the initial basic variables usually have objective function coefficients of zero. Thus, decreases in these basic variables cost nothing. We can obtain these same results by multiplying the objective coefficient for each basic variable by the corresponding constraint coefficient and then adding these results:

TABLE 6-3
Nearly Completed Simplex Tableau

Objective coefficients for basic variables	Basic variables	Entering gains	7	10	0	0	0
		Values	C	A	S_1	S_2	S_3
0	S_1	36	3	2	1	0	0
0	S_2	40	2	4	0	1	0
0	S_3	10	1	0	0	0	1
	Objective function	Entering costs					
		Net change					

$$\begin{pmatrix} \text{Entering cost for} \\ \text{each variable} \end{pmatrix} = \sum \left[\begin{pmatrix} \text{objective coefficient} \\ \text{for basic variable} \end{pmatrix} \times \begin{pmatrix} \text{constraint} \\ \text{coefficient for} \\ \text{that variable} \end{pmatrix} \right]$$

191

SOLVING LINEAR
PROGRAMMING
PROBLEMS WITH
THE SIMPLEX
METHOD

Entering costs for variable C are

$$0(3) + 0(2) + 0(1) = 0$$

and for variable A

$$0(2) + 0(4) + 0(0) = 0$$

and for S_1

$$0(1) + 0(0) + 0(0) = 0$$

and so on for the entering cost values for the remaining variables.

Net Change   The net-change row records the difference between the entering gain values and the entering costs. We simply subtract the entering costs from the entering gains shown at the top of the tableau.

$$\text{Net change} = (\text{entering gain}) - (\text{entering cost})$$

For variable C, for example, we obtain

$$\text{Net change} = 7 - 0 = 7$$

The other net-change values are calculated in the same way. Observe that the net-change values represent the per-unit change in the objective function that results from an increase in the corresponding variables. We will use the values in this row to determine the optimality of each solution. The completed tableau for the initial solution is shown in Table 6-4.

INSTANT REPLAY   Prepare an initial simplex tableau for the following problem:

$$\text{Maximize:} \quad \text{Profit} = 4A + 5B + 8C$$

$$\text{Subject to:} \quad A + B + C \le 100$$

$$3A + 2B + 4C \le 500$$

We will be referring to this problem in future Instant Replays as the *ABC* problem.

CHECK

Objective coefficients for basic variables	Basic variables	Entering gains	4	5	8	0	0
		Values	A	B	C	S_1	S_2
0	S_1	100	1	1	1	1	0
0	S_2	500	3	2	4	0	1
	Objective function	Entering costs	0	0	0	0	0
0		Net change	4	5	8	0	0

TABLE 6-4
Initial Simplex Tableau

Objective coefficients for basic variables	Basic variables	Entering gains	7	10	0	0	0
		Values	C	A	S_1	S_2	S_3
0	S_1	36	3	2	1	0	0
0	S_2	40	2	4	0	1	0
0	S_3	10	1	0	0	0	1
	Objective function	Entering costs	0	0	0	0	0
0		Net change	7	10	0	0	0

Checking Optimality (Step 3)

Once we have prepared the initial tableau, we need to check the initial feasible solution for optimality. We do this by noting the signs of the values in the *net-change row*. These values correspond to the *per-unit change in the objective function* caused by an increase in each variable. Positive values indicate potential increases in the objective function, and negative values indicate decreases. Therefore, as long as at least one of the net-change values is positive, the solution represented by the tableau is not optimal. An optimal tableau would have nothing but zero or negative values in the net-change row.

The current solution is not optimal because the tableau contains two positive values in the net-change row, 7 for variable C and 10 for variable A. Therefore, we must find a better solution and prepare a second tableau.

INSTANT REPLAY   Refer to the initial tableau for the *ABC* problem shown in the preceding Instant Replay. Is the initial solution optimal?

CHECK   No. Three variables (*A*, *B*, and *C*) have positive net-change values.

Improving the Solution (Step 4): Preparing the Second Tableau

We start by choosing the entering variable. The entering variable for the next solution is the variable with the largest positive net change value. This is because that variable offers the highest per-unit increase in the objective function (which we are trying to maximize).

The highest net-change coefficient for the initial tableau was 10, which is in the column corresponding to variable *A* (see Table 6-5). Thus, we select variable *A* as the entering variable. As before, we determine the departing variable by finding the constraint that most restricts the size of the entering variable. We do this conveniently in the margin to the right of the table, as shown in Table 6-5.

Recall that to find the limit on the size of the entering variable imposed by

193

SOLVING LINEAR
PROGRAMMING
PROBLEMS WITH
THE SIMPLEX
METHOD

each constraint, we divide the current solution value for the basic variable by the constraint coefficient for the entering variable. Thus, for the fabrication constraint, we divide the current solution value for variable S_1 (36) by the corresponding coefficient for variable A (2). This yields a limit of 18, as shown to the right of Table 6-5. We then calculate a similar ratio for the assembly constraint by dividing the value for S_2 (40) by the corresponding coefficient for variable A (4). This leads to a limit of 10. Since variable A is not included in the IC chip constraint (as indicated by the coefficient of 0 for variable A in that constraint), we need not consider it. The value of variable A is unconstrained by the IC chip constraint.

The tightest limit on variable A is imposed by the assembly constraint. We conclude, then, that S_2, the basic variable corresponding to that constraint, is the departing variable.

INSTANT REPLAY   Refer to the initial tableau for the ABC problem shown in a previous instant replay. Which nonbasic variable will be selected as the entering variable? Which basic variable will be the departing variable?

CHECK   Variable C will be the entering variable because its net-change value is the highest. The departing variable is S_1 as shown below:

	Basic variables	Values		C			
Departing variable	S_1	100	÷	1	=	100 ←	Most limiting
	S_2	500		4		125	

Having selected the entering (A) and departing (S_2) variables, we can now prepare the second tableau for the Nevada Instruments problem. This corresponds to evaluating extreme point II. Some elements in the new tableau will

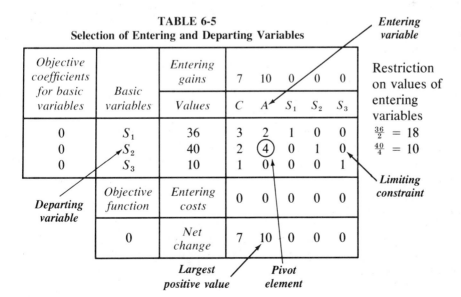

TABLE 6-5
Selection of Entering and Departing Variables

Objective coefficients for basic variables	Basic variables	Entering gains	7	10	0	0	0	Restriction on values of entering variables
		Values	C	A	S_1	S_2	S_3	
0	S_1	36	3	2	1	0	0	$\frac{36}{2} = 18$
0	S_2	40	2	(4)	0	1	0	$\frac{40}{4} = 10$
0	S_3	10	1	0	0	0	1	
	Objective function	Entering costs	0	0	0	0	0	
0		Net change	7	10	0	0	0	

Entering variable

Departing variable

Limiting constraint

Largest positive value

Pivot element

TABLE 6-6
Initial Entries in Second Simplex Tableau

Objective coefficients for basic variables	Basic variables	Entering gains	7	10	0	0	0
		Values	C	A	S_1	S_2	S_3
0	S_1						
10	A						
0	S_3						
	Objective function	Entering costs					
		Net change					

always be exactly the same as in the initial tableau and can therefore be copied directly: the column and row labels and the objective function coefficients shown in the top rows. We next substitute the entering variable for the departing variable. Then we can enter the current basic variables and their objective coefficients at the left of the tableau. The second tableau reflecting only these elements is shown in Table 6-6.

The next step in preparing the new tableau is to complete the constraint row for entering variable A. Recall that when we applied the simplex procedure algebraically, our first step in finding the next solution was to rewrite the limiting constraint so as to solve for the value of the entering variable. The initial limiting constraint for variable A was

$$S_2 = 40 - 2C - 4A \qquad \text{assembly constraint, point I}$$

Solving for variable A, we obtained

$$A = 10 - \tfrac{1}{2}C - \tfrac{1}{4}S_2 \qquad \text{assembly constraint, point II}$$

We can perform the identical operation quite easily on the simplex tableau by dividing the entire assembly constraint row in the initial tableau by the coefficient for variable A. This coefficient is commonly referred to as the *pivot element*, as shown in Table 6-5. Thus, the elements in the assembly constraint row in the initial tableau:

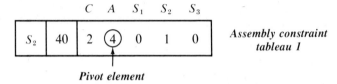

are each divided by the pivot element to form the assembly constraint row in the new tableau:

		C	A	S_1	S_2	S_3	
A	10	$\tfrac{1}{2}$	1	0	$\tfrac{1}{4}$	0	Assembly constraint tableau 2

Comparing the elements in the new row with the coefficients we derived algebraically shows that they are identical except for a change of sign. The change in sign results simply from the manner in which the equation is written. For instance, if the equation was rewritten with 10 on the left and everything else on the right, we would obtain

195

SOLVING LINEAR
PROGRAMMING
PROBLEMS WITH
THE SIMPLEX
METHOD

$$10 = \tfrac{1}{2}C + 1A + \tfrac{1}{4}S_2$$

which now corresponds exactly to the coefficients in the tableau.

The other constraint rows require slightly different operations to convert them to the correct form for the new tableau. Recall again our algebraic analysis. Once we solved the limiting constraint in terms of the entering variable, we substituted that constraint wherever the entering variable appeared in each of the remaining constraints.

For example, the fabrication constraint originally was

$$S_1 = 36 - 3C - 2A \qquad \text{fabrication constraint, point I}$$

We revised this constraint by substituting the value of variable A as defined by the new assembly constraint

$$A = 10 - \tfrac{1}{2}C - \tfrac{1}{4}S_2 \qquad \text{assembly constraint, point II}$$

in place of A in the fabrication constraint:

$$S_1 = 36 - 3C - 2(10 - \tfrac{1}{2}C - \tfrac{1}{4}S_2)$$

$$= 16 - 2C + \tfrac{1}{2}S_2 \qquad \text{fabrication constraint, point II}$$

We can easily accomplish this substitution using the simplex tableau. Note that the algebraic substitution first required multiplying the coefficient for entering variable A in the fabrication constraint by the new values for the limiting constraint. Then we subtracted the result from the corresponding coefficients of the fabrication constraint. In tableau form, we multiply the new coefficients of the limiting constraint

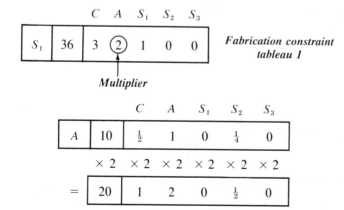

		C	A	S_1	S_2	S_3
A	10	$\tfrac{1}{2}$	1	0	$\tfrac{1}{4}$	0

Assembly constraint
tableau 2

by the *multiplier* coefficient of variable A in the initial fabrication constraint

		C	A	S_1	S_2	S_3
S_1	36	3	②	1	0	0

Fabrication constraint
tableau 1

Multiplier

thus

		C	A	S_1	S_2	S_3
A	10	$\tfrac{1}{2}$	1	0	$\tfrac{1}{4}$	0

	$\times 2$	$\times 2$	$\times 2$	$\times 2$	$\times 2$	$\times 2$
=	20	1	2	0	$\tfrac{1}{2}$	0

and subtract the result from the initial fabrication constraint to obtain the new fabrication constraint:

		C	A	S_1	S_2	S_3
S_1	36	3	2	1	0	0

$-$

	20	1	2	0	$\frac{1}{2}$	0

$=$

S_1	16	2	0	1	$-\frac{1}{2}$	0

In general, to find the values in the new tableau for constraints other than the limiting constraint:

$$
\begin{pmatrix} \text{Value of} \\ \text{constraint} \\ \text{coefficient} \\ \text{in} \\ \text{new tableau} \end{pmatrix} = \begin{pmatrix} \text{value of} \\ \text{constraint} \\ \text{coefficient} \\ \text{in} \\ \text{old tableau} \end{pmatrix} - \begin{pmatrix} \text{corresponding} \\ \text{coefficient in} \\ \text{limiting} \\ \text{constraint of} \\ \text{new tableau} \end{pmatrix} \times \begin{pmatrix} \text{coefficient of} \\ \text{entering variable} \\ \text{in old tableau for} \\ \text{this constraint} \\ (\textit{multiplier}) \end{pmatrix}
$$

as we did above:

$$16 = 36 - (10 \times 2) \qquad 1 = 1 - (0 \times 2)$$
$$2 = 3 - (\tfrac{1}{2} \times 2) \qquad -\tfrac{1}{2} = 0 - (\tfrac{1}{4} \times 2)$$
$$0 = 2 - (1 \times 2) \qquad 0 = 0 - (0 \times 2)$$

The values derived here are, as before, the same as those we calculated algebraically (adjusted for the change in sign).

We could normally follow the same approach for the IC chip constraint. However, no substitution is possible because variable A does not appear in that constraint. Thus, the IC chip constraint in the new tableau will be the same as in the initial tableau. We can show this mathematically by noting that the multiplier coefficient (of variable A in the IC chip constraint) is zero. The second tableau with completed constraint rows is shown in Table 6-7.

TABLE 6-7
Nearly Completed Second Tableau

Objective coefficients for basic variables	Basic variables	Entering gains	7	10	0	0	0
		Values	C	A	S_1	S_2	S_3
0	S_1	16	2	0	1	$-\frac{1}{2}$	0
10	A	10	$\frac{1}{2}$	1	0	$\frac{1}{4}$	0
0	S_3	10	1	0	0	0	1
	Objective function	Entering costs					
		Net change					

We complete the final two rows of the new tableau much as we did for the initial tableau. We find the objective function value by multiplying the objective coefficients of each basic variable by the current values for those variables and then summing the results:

Objective coefficients for basic variables		Values	
0		16	0
10	$\times$	10	$=$ 100
0		10	0
			100

Objective function → 100

We then calculate the values for the entering-costs row. To do this, we multiply the constraint coefficients in each column by the objective coefficients for the corresponding basic variable and then add the results. Thus, for column C

Objective coefficients for basic variables		C	
0		2	0
10	$\times$	$\frac{1}{2}$	$=$ 5
0		1	0
			5

We find the entering cost values for the other columns in a similar manner. For the last step in completing the new tableau, we subtract the entering costs from the entering gains to obtain the net-change values.

Entering gains	7	10	0	0	0

Less

Entering costs	5	10	0	$2\frac{1}{2}$	0

Equals

Net change	2	0	0	$-2\frac{1}{2}$	0

The completed tableau is shown in Table 6-8.

INSTANT REPLAY Refer again to the *ABC* problem we have been considering in the Instant Replays. Prepare the second tableau for this problem.

Objective coefficients for basic variables	Basic variables	Entering gains	4	5	8	0	0
		Values	A	B	C	S_1	S_2
8	C	100	1	1	1	1	0
0	S_2	100	-1	-2	0	-4	1
	Objective function	Entering costs	8	8	8	8	0
	800	Net change	-4	-3	0	-8	0

Checking Optimality of the Second Tableau (Step 3)

Having completed the second tableau, we then simply examine the net-change coefficients to determine optimality. Variable C has the only positive coefficient in Table 6-8. Thus, the objective function can be increased further by selecting variable C as the entering variable and generating a new tableau. The current solution is therefore not optimal.

INSTANT REPLAY   Is the second tableau for the ABC problem (see preceding Instant Replay) optimal?

CHECK   Yes. All the net-change values are zero or negative.

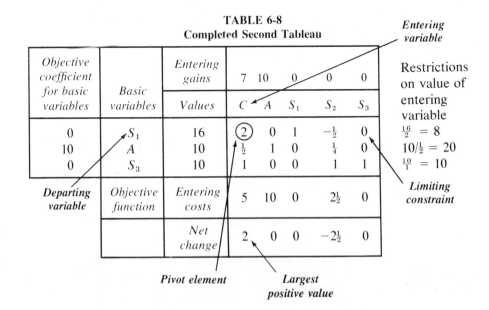

TABLE 6-8
Completed Second Tableau

Entering variable

Objective coefficient for basic variables	Basic variables	Entering gains	7	10	0	0	0	Restrictions on value of entering variable
		Values	C	A	S_1	S_2	S_3	
0	S_1	16	②	0	1	$-\frac{1}{2}$	0	$\frac{16}{2} = 8$
10	A	10	$\frac{1}{2}$	1	0	$\frac{1}{4}$	0	$10/\frac{1}{2} = 20$
0	S_3	10	1	0	0	1	1	$\frac{10}{1} = 10$
Departing variable	Objective function	Entering costs	5	10	0	$2\frac{1}{2}$	0	Limiting constraint
		Net change	2	0	0	$-2\frac{1}{2}$	0	

Pivot element   *Largest positive value*

We can quickly find the departing variable for the Nevada Instruments problem by calculating the restriction on the value of the entering variable, as shown in the right margin of Table 6-8. In each case we divide the current value for the basic variable by the corresponding constraint coefficient for the entering variable. Thus, we find that S_1 is the departing variable.

Basic variables	Values		C	
S_1	16		2	8 ← *Tightest limit*
A	10	÷	$\frac{1}{2}$ =	20
S_3	10		1	10

We begin the third tableau by filling in the objective function coefficients and row and column labels. We then turn to the constraint equations. The fabrication constraint was the limiting constraint

S_1	16	②	0	1	$-\frac{1}{2}$	0

Pivot element

We adjust it for the new tableau by dividing every element in that row by the pivot element and replacing the departing variable name with that of the entering variable.

C	8	1	0	$\frac{1}{2}$	$-\frac{1}{4}$	0

We next adjust the other constraints by multiplying the elements in the new limiting constraint by the coefficient for the entering variable in that constraint (the multiplier). We then subtract the new values from those of the constraint in the second tableau. Thus, for the assembly constraint we select the multiplier

A	10	①	1	0	$\frac{1}{4}$	0

Multiplier

and multiply each element of the new limiting constraint by that number

C	8	1	0	$\frac{1}{2}$	$-\frac{1}{4}$	0
	$\times\frac{1}{2}$	$\times\frac{1}{2}$	$\times\frac{1}{2}$	$\times\frac{1}{2}$	$\times\frac{1}{2}$	$\times\frac{1}{2}$
	4	$\frac{1}{2}$	0	$\frac{1}{4}$	$-\frac{1}{8}$	0

We then subtract the results from the assembly constraint in the second tableau to obtain the new assembly constraint.

| A | 10 | $\frac{1}{2}$ | 1 | 0 | $\frac{1}{4}$ | 0 |

| $-$ | 4 | $\frac{1}{2}$ | 0 | $\frac{1}{4}$ | $-\frac{1}{8}$ | 0 |

| $=$ A | 6 | 0 | 1 | $-\frac{1}{4}$ | $\frac{3}{8}$ | 0 |

We do the same thing for the IC chip constraint:

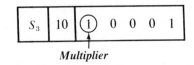

Multiplier

In this case the calculations are simplified. Multiplying by 1 does not change the values of the limiting constraint, and we can simply subtract the coefficients of the limiting constraint in the third tableau:

| S_3 | 10 | 1 | 0 | 0 | 0 | 1 |

| $-$ | 8 | 1 | 0 | $\frac{1}{2}$ | $-\frac{1}{4}$ | 0 |

| $=$ S_3 | 2 | 0 | 0 | $-\frac{1}{2}$ | $\frac{1}{4}$ | 1 |

We now find the objective function by summing the contribution of each basic variable:

Objective coefficients for basic variables		Values	
7		8	56
10	$\times$	6	$=$ 60
0		2	0

Objective function $=$ 116

We then calculate the entering costs by multiplying the basic variable objective coefficients by the corresponding constraint coefficients. For example, we would calculate the entering cost for variable S_1 by

Objective coefficients for basic variables		S_1	
7		$\frac{1}{2}$	$\frac{7}{2}$
10	$\times$	$-\frac{1}{4}$	$= -\frac{5}{2}$
0		$-\frac{1}{2}$	0
			1

Assuming that we have calculated the entering costs for the other variables, we must determine the net-change values. Recall that the net-change

201

SOLVING LINEAR
PROGRAMMING
PROBLEMS WITH
THE SIMPLEX
METHOD

TABLE 6-9
Third Tableau

Objective coefficients for basic variables	Basic variables	Entering gains	7	10	0	0	0
		Values	C	A	S_1	S_2	S_3
7	C	8	1	0	$\frac{1}{2}$	$-\frac{1}{4}$	0
10	A	6	0	1	$-\frac{1}{4}$	$\frac{3}{8}$	0
0	S_3	2	0	0	$-\frac{1}{2}$	$\frac{1}{4}$	1
Objective function	Entering costs		7	10	1	2	0
116	Net change		0	0	-1	-2	0

values are equal to the difference between the entering-gain values and the entering-cost values.

		C	A	S_1	S_2	S_3
	Entering gains	7	10	0	0	0
$-$	Entering costs	7	10	1	2	0
$=$	Net change	0	0	-1	-2	0

Checking Optimality of the Third Tableau (Step 3)

Notice that all the net-change values are zero or negative. The current solution is thus optimal. An attempt to increase the value of any of the nonbasic variables can only decrease the objective function. Therefore, we can stop our search for a solution. The solution represented by the third tableau is optimal and is shown in Table 6-9.

To see the relationship between the simplex tableaus and the extreme points, you may wish to refer back to Figure 6-3. You should be able to show that the values in the figure for extreme points I, II, and III are the same as those we found in tableaus 1, 2, and 3.

Summary of the Simplex Procedure

It would be a good idea at this point to review the steps and procedures required to use the simplex method to solve linear programming problems:

1. Formulate the problem and add slack variables to each constraint.

2. Determine the initial feasible solution. This is usually done by designating the slack variables as the basic variables and the decision variables as nonbasic. Then prepare the initial simplex tableau.

3. Check the optimality of the tableau by examining the net-change values. If all the net-change values are zero or negative, the solution is optimal (for maximization problems). If one or more of these values are positive, the solution can be improved by going to step 4.

4. Identify the next extreme point solution and prepare the tableau for that solution. This step is the most complicated, and it is useful to organize the tasks required as follows:

  a. Prepare a new tableau outline and fill in the identifying labels. Record the objective function coefficients of each variable in the top row.

  b. Select the entering variable by choosing that variable with the largest positive net-change value in the previous tableau.

  c. Calculate the restrictions on the size of the entering variable by dividing the current value of each basic variable by the corresponding constraint coefficient for the entering variable. Ignore negative or zero coefficients.

  d. Select the departing variable by choosing that basic variable whose constraint was most restrictive on the size of the entering variable.

  e. List the basic variables in the new tableau. Be sure to replace the departing variable with the entering variable.

  f. Identify the pivot element. This is the coefficient of the entering variable in the constraint associated with the departing variable.

  g. Determine new values for the limiting constraint (associated with the departing variable) by dividing each element by the pivot element. Record these values in the new tableau.

  h. Determine new coefficients for each of the other constraints. In each case, first identify the multiplier (the old coefficient for the entering variable in that constraint). Multiply each element in the limiting constraint by the multiplier. Then subtract those results from the old coefficients of the constraint being adjusted to find the new coefficients. Enter these in the new tableau.

  i. Calculate a new value for the objective function by multiplying the new value of each basic variable by its objective function coefficient and summing the results. Enter this in the new tableau.

  j. Determine the entering costs for each variable by multiplying that variable's constraint coefficients by the objective function coefficients for each corresponding basic variable and summing the results. Record these in the entering-cost row of the new tableau.

  k. Subtract the entering costs from the entering gains and enter the results in the net-change row of the new tableau.

Now that the new tableau has been completed, return to step 3 to check for optimality.

When concentrating on the mechanical details of the simplex tableau, it is easy to lose sight of the significance of the information it displays. In this section we shall briefly examine the meaning of the various tableau elements.

First it should be noted that the tableau is actually a kind of shorthand for the algebraic equations that we manipulated earlier in the chapter. The convenience of placing the variable names at the top of the columns and placing the coefficients below avoids the need to list the variable name next to each coefficient, or the plus or equal signs necessary for mathematical completeness.

Despite the reliance on shorthand, no information is lost. We can at any stage in the process translate the tableau elements back into equations. For instance, refer to the final, optimal tableau as shown in Table 6-9. By placing an equals sign between the element in the value column and the constraint coefficients, we can easily convert the three constraint rows into the equivalent constraint equations. Thus, we can convert the first constraint row from

	C	A	S_1	S_2	S_3
8	1	0	$\frac{1}{2}$	$-\frac{1}{4}$	0

to

$$8 = 1C + \tfrac{1}{2}S_1 - \tfrac{1}{4}S_2$$

which, if rearranged as

$$C = 8 - \tfrac{1}{2}S_1 + \tfrac{1}{4}S_2$$

is identical to the final fabrication capacity constraint equation that we developed algebraically.

This relationship, between tableau constraint row and algebraic constraint equation, helps us to understand the basic tableau elements. The constraint coefficients represent the number of units of each basic variable exchanged for one unit of each potential basic variable. Look at Figure 6-4. A positive coefficient in the tableau indicates the amount by which the basic variable will have to decrease for a unit increase in a nonbasic variable. Negative coefficients indicate that the basic variable will increase as the nonbasic

FIGURE 6-4   Explanation of constraint coefficients.

Basic variables		C	A	S_1	S_2	S_3
C		1	0	$\frac{1}{2}$	$-\frac{1}{4}$	0
A		0	1	$-\frac{1}{4}$	$\frac{3}{8}$	0
S_3		0	0	$\left(-\frac{1}{2}\right)$	$\left(\frac{1}{4}\right)$	1

Number of units of S_3 we *gain* by increasing the value of S_1 by one unit (*negative* coefficient)	Number of units of S_3 we *give up* to gain one unit of S_2 (*positive* coefficient)

variable is increased. A zero coefficient represents the absence of a relationship between the two variables.

Clearly, then, the constraint coefficient represents the change to a basic variable for a unit increase in one of the other variables. Thus, we can find the cost of such a change by weighting the basic variable changes by their respective objective function coefficients. This is precisely what we did when we obtained the entering-cost elements.

The final objective function equation can also be taken directly from the tableau by combining the objective function value with the net-change values. Thus, for the final tableau, we can convert the following

Objective function		C	A	S_1	S_2	S_3
116	Net change	0	0	-1	-2	0

to

$$TC = 116 - S_1 - 2S_2$$

which is identical to what we obtained algebraically.

INSTANT REPLAY   The table below represents an initial simplex tableau for a maximization problem. Convert the information shown into equation form, corresponding to the original problem formulation without slack variables. Assume that each of the constraints is the "less than or equal to" variety.

Objective coefficients for basic variables	Basic variables	Entering gains	5	4	3	0	0	0	0
		Values	A	B	C	S_1	S_2	S_3	S_4
0	S_1	40	1	1	1	1	0	0	0
0	S_2	125	2	4	3	0	1	0	0
0	S_3	400	14	11	12	0	0	1	0
0	S_4	10	1	0	0	0	0	0	1
	Objective function	Entering costs	0	0	0	0	0	0	0
0		Net change	5	4	3	0	0	0	0

CHECK   The original problem was

Maximize: $5A + 4B + 3C$

Subject to: $A + B + C \le 40$

$2A + 4B + 3C \le 125$

$$14A + 11B + 12C \leq 400$$

$$A \qquad\qquad\qquad \leq 10$$

$$A, B, C \geq 0$$

Solving Minimization Problems with Simplex

Until now we have limited the application of the simplex procedure exclusively to maximization problems. Now that you have developed some proficiency with, and understanding of, the simplex method, you are ready to apply it to minimization problems.

Although minimization problems can be easily solved with the simplex method, it is necessary to make a few modifications to the procedure as we shall see shortly.

For convenience we will use the Battle Creek Breakfast Food Company problem that we solved graphically in Chapter 5. Recall that we want to find the minimum cost combination of rice and corn that meets the United States recommended daily allowances for vitamins A and D. We previously formulated the problem as

$$\text{Minimize:} \quad TC = .08R + .12C$$

$$\text{Subject to:} \quad .2R + .5C \geq 1 \qquad \text{vitamin A}$$

$$.4R + .2C \geq 1 \qquad \text{vitamin D}$$

Formulating the Problem (Step 1)

The first step in translating the problem into the proper format for simplex is, of course, to add slack variables to each constraint. As before, we add them to the "less than" side of each constraint:

$$.2R + .5C = 1 + S_1$$

$$.4R + .2C = 1 + S_2$$

In minimization problems the slack variables are actually referred to as *surplus variables*. Rather than representing unused capacity, they represent the excess amount by which a particular requirement is met. The two constraints are of the general form:

$$\begin{pmatrix} \text{Vitamin} \\ \text{provided by} \\ \text{decision variables} \end{pmatrix} = \begin{pmatrix} \text{required} \\ \text{daily allowance} \\ \text{of vitamin} \end{pmatrix} + \begin{pmatrix} \text{excess} \\ \text{vitamin allowance} \\ \text{(surplus variables)} \end{pmatrix}$$

You may wonder why we would ever need to consider a solution that provides an excess over the minimum requirements if we are trying to minimize costs. The key to understanding is to recognize that there are two constraint requirements. In order to satisfy one constraint, say vitamin A, we may have to use more corn and rice than is necessary to satisfy the vitamin D constraint. This will produce an excess, or surplus, of vitamin D over that required.

205

Whether we call them (negative) slack variables or surplus variables, a serious problem does develop when we attempt to establish an initial solution. Having added slack variables to a maximization problem, we would solve for the values of the slack variables, assuming that all decision variables have initial values of zero (corresponding to the origin). If we attempt to do the same for a minimization problem, we quickly find that the surplus variables take on negative values, which violates the nonnegativity constraints.

$$S_1 = -1 + .2R + .5C \qquad\qquad S_2 = -1 + .4R + .2C$$
$$= -1 + .2(0) + .5(0) = -1 \qquad = -1 + .4(0) + .2(0) = -1$$

This, of course, results because we added the surplus variables to the right-hand side of the constraint equation, rather than the left-hand side as we did for maximization problems. To understand why this should be so, look at Figure 6-5, which depicts the constraints and feasible region for the Battle Creek problem.

Recall that for convenience we chose the origin, where all decision variables are zero, as our initial feasible solution for simplex. We do this because we are reasonably sure that the origin represents a feasible solution for a maximization problem. Examining Figure 6-5, we quickly see that the origin does not lie in the feasible region for the Battle Creek problem. This will normally be true for any minimization problem.

We obtained negative values for the surplus variables (after setting all decision variables to zero) because the origin is infeasible. The simplex method must always start with a feasible solution, moving from that solution to a better feasible solution until the optimal solution is found.

FIGURE 6-5 Feasible solutions and extreme points for the Battle Creek problem.

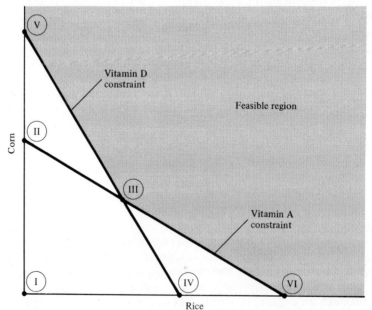

Suppose we chose to pretend that the origin was feasible and tried to force the simplex method to proceed from there. Would it work? No. We are attempting to minimize costs. By starting at the origin we begin with a solution that must have a lower cost (cost at the origin is zero) than that for the true optimal solution. In fact, the first tableau would indicate that the initial solution is optimal, although the constraints are not met.

207

SOLVING LINEAR
PROGRAMMING
PROBLEMS WITH
THE SIMPLEX
METHOD

Artificial Variables   To overcome that problem, we need to add an additional variable to each constraint that has a negative value with a surplus variable. These new variables are called *artificial variables* because they are used to convert the origin artificially from infeasible to feasible. They can best be thought of, for the Battle Creek problem, as artificial ingredients that would allow us to meet the minimum daily vitamin requirements without using any of the decision variables, corn and rice.

Thus artificial variable A_1 can be thought of as an artificial ingredient, one unit of which completely satisfies the minimum daily requirements for vitamin A. Artificial variable A_2 then represents a similar artificial ingredient that meets the minimum requirements for vitamin D. The two constraints thus become

$$.2R + .5C + A_1 = 1 + S_1$$

$$.4R + .2C + A_2 = 1 + S_2$$

The simplex procedure would then select the artificial variables as the initial basic variables. Therefore, the decision and surplus variables are non-basic and can be set to zero. This allows us to solve for the initial values of the artificial variables as

$$A_1 = 1 - .2R - .5C + S_1 \qquad A_2 = 1 - .4R - .2C + S_2$$

$$= 1 - .2(0) - .5(0) + 0 = 1 \qquad = 1 - .4(0) - .2(0) + 0 = 1$$

Thus, the addition of the artificial variables has allowed us to convert the origin from an infeasible point to a feasible one. However, we also need to modify the objective function. If we don't, when we check the initial tableau we will find it to be declared optimal. The reason for this is easy to explain. The artificial variables are not in the objective function and therefore are treated as if they have no cost. We would not want to substitute one of the decision variables, which have costs, for one of the artificial variables, which do not.

To correct this problem, we must add each artificial variable to the objective function. To ensure that the artificial variables are not basic in the optimal solution, we assign them very high costs. One convenient way of doing this is to assign each artificial variable a cost of M, where M is defined to be a very large number. Thus, the objective function for the Battle Creek problem would be

$$\text{Minimize TC} = .08R + .12C + MA_1 + MA_2$$

This approach is often called the Big-M method.

Computationally it is often easier to substitute an actual numeric cost rather than retain the designation M throughout the problem. For the Battle Creek problem we can assign the cost of $1 per unit to each artificial variable. This amount is larger than the cost coefficients for the real decision variables. Although $1 is not a very large number, it is sufficiently large in this case. Thus, the objective function now becomes

$$\text{Minimize TC} = .08R + .12C + A_1 + A_2$$

To avoid dealing with fractions such as .08 or .12, we can multiply each coefficient in the objective function by 100, thus effectively converting the amounts from dollars to cents. This leaves

$$\text{Minimize TC} = 8R + 12C + 100A_1 + 100A_2$$

In general, as long as we apply the same operation to all coefficients, we can transform the objective function, as we wish, by multiplying or dividing by a constant.

Finally, we can convert the decimal constraint coefficients to fractions. We do this to facilitate the calculations necessary to prepare subsequent tableaus. We thus avoid rounding errors from trying to express in decimal terms such repeating fractions as $\frac{1}{9}$. Thus the two constraints become

$$\tfrac{1}{5}R + \tfrac{1}{2}C - S_1 + A_1 = 1$$

$$\tfrac{2}{5}R + \tfrac{1}{5}C - S_2 + A_2 = 1$$

The modified problem is now to

Minimize: $TC = 8R + 12C + 100A_1 + 100A_2$ objective function

Subject to: $\tfrac{1}{5}R + \tfrac{1}{2}C - S_1 + A_1 = 1$ vitamin A constraint

$\tfrac{2}{5}R + \tfrac{1}{5}C - S_2 + A_2 = 1$ vitamin D constraint

Preparing the Initial Tableau   We can now set up the initial simplex tableau exactly as we did for the maximization problem. The completed initial tableau is shown in Table 6-10.

Checking Optimality of the First Tableau (Step 3)

The objective function for this initial tableau shows a total cost of 200 ($2). The net-change values represent the increases and decreases in that total cost that will result from each unit increase in the corresponding nonbasic variables. Since we are trying to minimize total cost, the solution will *not* be optimal as long as one or more of the net-change values are negative. The tableau corresponding to the optimal solution will contain all zero or positive net-change values. Note that this is exactly the reverse of the optimality condition for maximization problems.

The net-change row in our initial tableau (Table 6-10) indicates that total cost can be reduced by selecting either variable R or variable C as the entering variable. Therefore, the initial solution is not optimal, and a new extreme point must be examined.

Improving the Solution (Step 4)

As we saw before, the first step in selecting a new extreme point is to determine the entering and departing variables. The rule for choosing the entering variable for minimization problems is the reverse of what it is for maximization problems. Since we are trying to minimize costs, we select the variable with the largest *negative* net-change value as the entering variable. For our initial tableau, variable C has the highest negative coefficient, -58. We therefore pick C as the entering variable.

TABLE 6-10
Initial Tableau: Battle Creek Problem

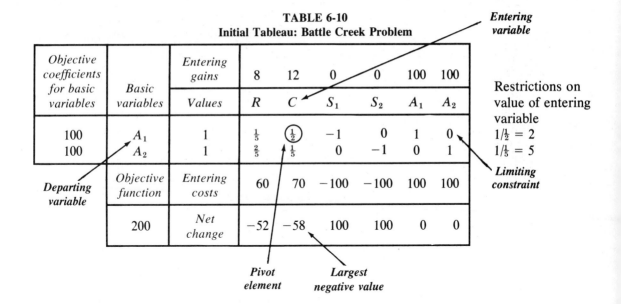

Objective coefficients for basic variables	Basic variables	Entering gains / Values	8 / R	12 / C	0 / S_1	0 / S_2	100 / A_1	100 / A_2
100	A_1	1	$\frac{1}{5}$	$\frac{1}{2}$	-1	0	1	0
100	A_2	1	$\frac{2}{5}$	$\frac{1}{5}$	0	-1	0	1
	Objective function	Entering costs: 60	70	-100	-100	100	100	
200		Net change: -52	-58	100	100	0	0	

Entering variable

Restrictions on value of entering variable

$1\frac{1}{2} = 2$
$1\frac{1}{5} = 5$

Limiting constraint

Departing variable

Pivot element

Largest negative value

The selection of the departing variable is made exactly as it is for maximization problems. Thus artificial variable A_1 is chosen as the departing variable on the basis of the restrictions imposed by the two constraints on the value of the entering variable. The relevant calculations are shown to the right of the tableau (Table 6-10).

Having selected the entering and departing variables, we can form the second tableau as we did for the maximization problem. The completed second tableau is shown in Table 6-11.

Several facts concerning the artificial variables need to be reviewed at this point. First, the purpose of the artificial variables is to convert what was originally an infeasible solution to one that is feasible. Second, we assigned each artificial variable a high cost so as to force it not to be a basic variable in the optimal solution. Finally, when an artificial variable is chosen as the departing variable and thereby becomes nonbasic, we should recognize that its departure from the set of basic variables was possible because the constraint that it was used to satisfy is now being satisfied by one or more of the decision variables.

We conclude from this that once an artificial variable becomes nonbasic, it will always remain nonbasic and can therefore be *eliminated from* the tableau. When we moved from the initial tableau to the second tableau of the Battle Creek problem, we replaced artificial variable A_1 with decision variable C. Note that C has a value of 2, which now allows the vitamin A constraint to be satisfied without the artificial variable:

$$.2R + .5C - S_1 + A_1 = 1$$
$$.2(0) + .5(2) - 0 + 0 = 1$$
$$1 = 1$$

Since variable C satisfies that first constraint, we can drop artificial variable A_1 from further consideration. Notice that the column for variable A_1 does not appear in the second tableau. The obvious advantage of eliminating artificial **209**

TABLE 6-11
Second Tableau: Battle Creek Problem

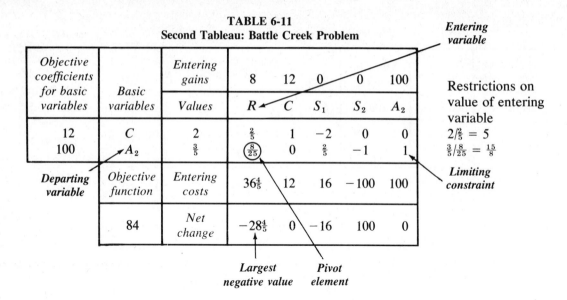

Objective coefficients for basic variables	Basic variables	Entering gains	8 R	12 C	0 S_1	0 S_2	100 A_2	
		Values						*Entering variable*
12	C	2	$\frac{2}{5}$	1	-2	0	0	*Restrictions on value of entering variable* $2/\frac{2}{5} = 5$
100	A_2	$\frac{3}{5}$	$\left(\frac{8}{25}\right)$	0	$\frac{2}{5}$	-1	1	$\frac{3}{5}/\frac{8}{25} = \frac{15}{8}$
Departing variable	*Objective function*	*Entering costs*	$36\frac{4}{5}$	12	16	-100	100	*Limiting constraint*
	84	*Net change*	$-28\frac{4}{5}$	0	-16	100	0	

Largest negative value   *Pivot element*

variables, as they become nonbasic, is the reduced computational effort to prepare new tableaus.

The initial tableau represents the origin (point I in Figure 6-5) which was made artificially feasible by the addition of the artificial variables (A_1 and A_2). But what does the second tableau represent? The second tableau corresponds to extreme point II in Figure 6-5. Note that it is also an infeasible point. By moving to point II we have satisfied the vitamin A constraint but not the vitamin D constraint. Thus we are able to drop artificial variable A_1 (which was added to the problem to meet the vitamin A constraint artificially), but we must continue using A_2 (added to meet the vitamin D constraint artificially).

Checking Optimality of the Second Tableau (Step 3)

We determine the optimality of the second tableau by examining the net-change values in Table 6-11. Since variables R and S_1 have negative net-change values, we know that this tableau is not optimal.

Improving the Solution (Step 4)

Look again at Figure 6-5. Note that from point II, two new adjacent extreme points are available: point V, which meets both the vitamin A and D constraints by using only corn, and point III, which meets the two vitamin constraints by using both corn and rice. In both cases, since the vitamin D constraint will be met, the artificial variable (A_2) for that constraint will no longer be needed. Thus A_2 will be the departing variable for either of the two new extreme points. Moving to extreme point V requires increasing the use of corn and represents an oversupply of vitamin A. Thus, the entering variable if this extreme point is chosen will be the vitamin A surplus variable S_1. Moving to extreme point III represents the use of rice, which was nonbasic at point II. Thus, variable R will be the entering variable if extreme point III is chosen.

The choice of variable S_1 or R as the entering variable is made on the basis of their net-change values. Variable R is chosen because it has the highest negative net-change value. Variable A_2 is designated the departing variable (as we saw above) since its constraint is the most limiting, as shown in the margin of the tableau. The third tableau is completed as shown in Table 6-12. Observe that the column for artificial variable A_2 has now been dropped because it is no longer a basic variable.

Checking Optimality of the Third Tableau (Step 3)

Examining the net-change row for the third tableau, we find that there are no negative values. Thus this solution is *optimal*. Although both the Nevada Instruments and the Battle Creek problems required exactly three tableaus, you should not conclude that this will always be the case. The number of tableaus required will depend on each specific problem. (The *ABC* problem treated in the instant replays required only two tableaus.)

Interpretation of the values shown in the tableau is exactly the same as for maximization problems.

INSTANT REPLAY Why is the final net-change value for surplus variable S_1 equal to 20?

CHECK An increase of 1 unit in S_1 will cause variable R to decrease by $\frac{5}{4}$ units and variable C to increase by $2\frac{1}{2}$ units. The net change to costs would be $+2\frac{1}{2}(12) - \frac{5}{4}(8) = 30 - 10 = 20$.

Other Uses of Artificial Variables

We saw above how artificial variables can be used with minimization problems to convert otherwise infeasible extreme points into artificially feasible points. We should also point out that artificial variables have two other related uses: They can be used in maximization problems and with any problem that includes constraints with strict equality (not less than or greater than but exactly equal to). These uses are briefly discussed below.

TABLE 6-12
Third and Optimal Tableau: Battle Creek Problem

Objective coefficients for basic variables	Basic variable	Entering gains	8	12	0	0
		Values	R	C	S_1	S_2
12	C	$\frac{5}{4}$	0	1	$-2\frac{1}{2}$	$\frac{5}{4}$
8	R	$\frac{15}{8}$	1	0	$\frac{5}{4}$	$-\frac{25}{8}$
	Objective function	Entering costs	8	12	-20	-10
	30	Net change	0	0	20	10

Although we have used artificial variables only with minimization problems, it is also possible that a maximization problem would require their use. For example, suppose that in the Nevada Instruments problem a contract had been signed to provide five cases of Computrons to a particular customer. This would require the addition of the following "greater than or equal to" constraint:

$$C \geq 5$$

Adding a surplus variable to this constraint would lead to the same problems that developed with the "greater than" constraints in the minimization problem. We would have to rely on the use of an artificial variable to transform the above constraint into a form usable by the simplex method. Note that the objective function coefficient for an artificial variable in a maximization problem must be a large negative value, such as $-M$.

Using Artificial Variables with Equality Constraints

Another use of artificial variables concerns constraints of the strict "equality" type. An equality constraint does not require either slack or surplus variables because both sides of the constraint are already in balance. To illustrate, suppose an additional requirement for the Battle Creek problem was that the total amount of cereal per package was to be exactly 10 ounces, no more or no less. This requires the constraint

$$R + C = 10$$

Since both sides balance, we don't need to add surplus or slack variables. However, if we start at the origin with decision variables R and C set to zero, the equation is unbalanced. To correct this, we would need to add an artificial variable, say A_3, to the same side of the constraint as the decision variables. The packaging constraint would thus become

$$R + C + A_3 = 10$$

We would then need to adjust the objective function to prevent this artificial variable from being in the optimal solution.

INSTANT REPLAY   Why couldn't a slack variable be used instead of an articificial variable with an equality constraint?

CHECK   There is no way of ensuring that the slack variable would not appear as a basic variable in the optimal tableau. If this were to happen, the equality constraint would not really be met.

Computer Solution: Tableau Output

Chapter 5 examined how the computer could be used to solve linear programming problems. Recall that the hypothetical computer package that was used offered a choice of output information. The example shown at that time requested that only the optimal solution be provided (in addition to the listing of input data which is always provided). This section will briefly show how the user can also obtain a printout of the simplex tableaus.

Frequently, linear programming computer packages offer the user a choice of (1) seeing just the first and last tableaus or (2) having all tableaus printed. Although it may be instructive to trace through the problem solution steps by examining all the tableaus, the availability of option (1) is convenient. It provides the most important tableaus while saving the time and effort necessary to print out the intermediate tableaus. For large problems, with many tableaus, this can be an important savings.

The computer-generated question concerning the output desired (see Figure 5-10) is repeated here for convenience:

ENTER RUN CODE FOR TYPE OF OUTPUT DESIRED (0 = OPTIMAL SOLUTION ONLY, 1 = INCLUDE SENSITIVITY ANALYSIS, 2 = INCLUDE INITIAL AND FINAL TABLEAUS, 3 = INCLUDE ALL TABLEAUS)?

The user provides the coded response indicating which output form is desired. Thus, if only the first and last tableaus are desired, the user would respond 2. If all tableaus are wanted, the user would respond 3. Figure 6-6 contains an illustration of the type of tableau output generated in response to the output code 2 request. Other information, such as input data and optimal solution, would also be included but has not been shown here to simplify the illustration. The problem solved is the Nevada Instruments problem.

Note that the form of the tableau printed by the computer, although quite similar to the simplex tableau used in the text, is different from what you are used to. The solution values of the basic variables are shown on the far right, under the column headed RHS (for right-hand side). The computer uses several symbolic abbreviations with which you may not be familiar. What we referred to as "entering gains" is called "C(J)" by the computer; what was referred to as "entering costs" is identified as Z(J) by the computer; the "net change" values are shown in the row labeled "C(J)-Z(J)." Not all computers use the same notation.

Variables 1 and 2 can be readily identified [look at the initial C(J) values row] as the number of cases of Computrons and Approxymates, respectively. Likewise, the three slack variables can be identified by the RHS (right-hand-side) values in the initial tableau. Thus variable 3 is the slack variable for the fabrication constraint, variable 4 is the slack for the assembly constraint, and variable 5 is the slack for the IC chip constraint.

You should compare the tableau printout of Figure 6-6 with the corresponding tableaus in the text (Table 6-4 for the initial tableau and Table 6-9 for the final tableau) to familiarize yourself with the location of tableau components. You may wish to run this same problem on the linear programming package available at your institution to obtain tableau printouts for purposes of comparison. Since there are many different ways in which the tableau can be printed, you may have some difficulty initially in interpreting the data.

Final Comments

The use of the simplex method was introduced in this chapter as a way of solving linear programming problems. The simplex method is a fairly complicated and mechanical procedure that is not easy to grasp at first glance. When

INITIAL SIMPLEX TABLEAU

	VARIABLE	1	2	3	4	5	RHS
	C(J)	7.0	10.0	0.0	0.0	0.0	
0.0	3	3.0	2.0	1.0	0.0	0.0	36.0
0.0	4	2.0	4.0	0.0	1.0	0.0	40.0
0.0	5	1.0	0.0	0.0	0.0	1.0	10.0
	Z(J)	0.0	0.0	0.0	0.0	0.0	0.0
	C(J)-X(J)						
	C(J)-Z(J)	7.0	10.0	0.0	0.0	0.0	

FINAL SIMPLEX TABLEAU

	VARIABLE	1	2	3	4	5	RHS
7.0	1	1.0	0.0	0.500	-0.250	0.0	8.0
10.0	2	0.0	1.0	-0.250	0.375	0.0	6.0
0.0	5	0.0	0.0	-0.500	0.250	1.0	2.0
	Z(J)	7.0	10.0	1.0	2.0	0.0	116.0
	C(J)-Z(J)	0.0	0.0	-1.0	-2.0	0.0	

C(J) = entering gain	Variable 1 = Computrons	Variable 4 = assembly slack
Z(J) = entering cost	Variable 2 = Approxymates	Variable 5 = IC chip slack
C(J) − Z(J) = net change	Variable 3 = fabrication slack	RHS = right-hand side

FIGURE 6-6 Tableau output for computer solution of Nevada Instruments linear programming problem.

first exposed to simplex, most people are confused by the mechanics and lose sight of the fundamental purpose in using it. It is useful, therefore, to review the role of simplex in solving linear programming problems. We need to consider again how simplex works in general and why it is important.

We saw that simplex solves linear programming problems by examining a series of adjacent feasible extreme points. Each extreme point considered had a better objective function value than the preceding one. The search for the optimal solution was stopped whenever no better solution could be found. The simplex tableau was used to organize and simplify the calculations required in evaluating the current extreme point and moving to the next one.

Most of you undoubtedly found the graphical solution approach of Chapter 5 much easier to carry out as well as understand. It must be emphasized again, however, that the graphical method can be used only for problems with two variables. This severely restricts its application because most practical problems involve large numbers of variables and constraints. Even if you could

graphically represent the set of feasible solutions for such large problems, the identification of the optimal solution would not be easy. Recall that every extreme point was the result of the intersection of a pair of constraints. A large number of constraints will thus lead to a large number of extreme points.

For these reasons we are fortunate that a systematic procedure such as simplex exists. It allows us to solve large problems quickly and efficiently. We recognize that speed and efficiency or the ability to handle large problems depends on the use of a computerized version of the simplex method.

The next chapter will demonstrate that there are many kinds of sensitivity analysis that can be performed using the solution to a linear programming problem. Much of this will be of extreme managerial importance. You must have a fundamental knowledge of how simplex works and what the elements of the simplex tableau reveal if you are to get the maximum benefit from sensitivity analysis.

Key Words

Problems

6-1. The XYZ television network is completing its selection of programs for the new fall schedule. Network executives have identified three types of prime-time programs. After discussions with potential sponsors, management estimates the revenue per program hour to be:

Program type	Revenue per hour
Situation comedies	$200,000
Detective/police	300,000
Westerns	250,000

Three hours of prime time viewing per evening are available each night for a total of 21 hours per week. The network is under considerable pressure from outside organizations to reduce the number of hours devoted to programs with violence. Detective/police shows are thought to be twice as violent as westerns, while situation comedies are assumed to be completely nonviolent. The network has agreed to limit the total hours of violent programming to no more than the equivalent of 12 hours of detective/police shows. This limit can be allocated on a violence-equivalent basis among the two categories of violence programming (detective/police and westerns), as the network decides. Thus, the whole 12 hours could all be used for detective/police shows. Or, for example, they could be distributed 10 hours to detective/police shows and 4 hours to westerns (equivalent to 2 hours of detective/police shows).

On the basis of these constraints, determine the allocation of programming hours among the three categories of programming that maximizes total revenue. Use the simplex method to solve this problem.

6-2. The Blanton Drug Company is planning to introduce a new time-release cold medication, Meditemp, for which they have very high sales expectations. The marketing department has been given a $1,000,000 budget for advertising Meditemp during its initial year. The company traditionally utilizes three media categories for its advertising campaigns, with average costs per advertisement shown below:

Media type	Cost per ad
Consumer journals	$30,000
Medical journals	20,000
Television	50,000

Based on analysis of past advertising campaigns, the company has determined an advertising effectiveness index for each media type which takes into account the relative advantages of each. These indices are:

Media type	Effectiveness index
Consumer journals	20
Medical journals	30
Television	25

Company policies dictate that no more than half the budget be placed in television advertising and because of journal frequencies no more than 12 ads may be placed in either type of journal.

Find the best allocation of advertising among the three media types that meets the above constraints and generates the highest total of advertising index points. Use the simplex method to solve this problem.

6-3. The Fischer Electric Company manufactures air conditioners, furnaces, and dehumidifiers for commercial applications. Net contribution for these products is estimated to be:

Product	Per-unit contribution
Air conditioner	210
Furnace	170
Dehumidifier	45

Each of these products requires processing time in the fabrication, assembly, and testing departments as shown below.

Product	Fabrication	Assembly	Testing
Air conditioner	3	3	1
Furnace	4	2	$\frac{3}{4}$
Dehumidifier	1	$\frac{1}{2}$	$\frac{1}{2}$

Time required in labor hours per unit

217

SOLVING LINEAR
PROGRAMMING
PROBLEMS WITH
THE SIMPLEX
METHOD

Total labor hours available for processing in three departments during the coming week are estimated to be

Department	Processing hours available
Fabrication	400
Assembly	350
Testing	200

Using the simplex method, determine the production schedule for the coming week that maximizes the total net contribution.

6-4. The Petgrow Feed Company produces and sells an extensive line of animal feed. Although a certain amount of flexibility exists in determining the exact mix of ingredients for the company's various products, they have been reluctant to change the mix once formulated so as to avoid confusion in the production operations. However, because of recent changes in the costs for ingredients, the company has decided to reformulate its product mix for Feed Bag, its popular line of horse feed. Three ingredients are used in this product, with the following costs:

Ingredient	Cost per pound
A	.10
B	.12
C	.15

Feed Bag is produced in 10-pound bags, made up by combining the three ingredients shown above. Certain restrictions are imposed on the relative mix of these ingredients. Each bag may contain no more than 5 pounds of ingredient A. Furthermore, the amount of A used must be no more than twice the amount of C used. Finally, the company promises that each bag of Feed Bag must contain at least 60 percent protein by weight. The ingredients are known to contain the following protein proportions:

Ingredient	Proportion of protein, %
A	50
B	80
C	60

Determine, using the simplex method, the least-cost mix of these ingredients per 10-pound bag that satisfies the restrictions given above.

6-5. The First Federal Financial Funds investment firm has just contracted to manage a $2,000,000 investment fund for an important new client. First Federal has identified three major investment categories and has arrived at estimates of the rates of return of investments (including dividends, interest, and capital gains) in each category as shown below:

Investment category	Rate of return, %
High-grade stocks	8
Speculative stocks	12
Bonds	6

The client, of course, desires the largest possible return on his investment, but he also has specified certain restrictions on the nature of the investment allocation. For one thing, he wishes to limit the amount invested in speculative stocks to no more than 40 percent of the total fund. For another, he desires a minimum cash return in the form of dividends and interest of $80,000 per year. The cash-flow provisions for the three types of investments are estimated to be

Investment type	Estimated cash return, %
High-grade stocks	4
Speculative stocks	1
Bonds	6

Given these constraints, determine the investment allocation that yields the highest expected rate of return, using the simplex method.

6-6. Refer to problem 5-8, in which you were asked to formulate a linear programming approach to determining the allocation of peanut harvest to one of three end uses that maximizes the total contribution. Solve this problem using the simplex method.

6-7. The Raybold Petroleum Company purchases the crude oil that it needs from three distinct sources. The costs, capacities, and characteristics of the three sources are somewhat different, as shown below.

Crude source	Cost per barrel	Annual capacity in thousands of barrels	Grade	Maximum proportion of gasoline, %
Soamer Oil	$43	12,000	70	45
Northslope Oil	$52	5,000	85	50
Mideast Oil	$60	20,000	90	55

Raybold estimates that it needs to purchase 20,000,000 barrels of crude during the coming year, and it wishes to determine the least-cost purchase schedule. Complicating the decision is the requirement that the average crude grade purchased must be at least 80 and that the total crudes must be capable of yielding at least 50 percent gasoline.

In addition the company is obligated, under contract, to purchase a minimum of 5,000,000 barrels of crude from Mideast Oil.

Formulate the purchasing decision problem in the linear programming format and prepare the initial simplex tableau.

6-8. The White and Cardwell Power Tool Company is just completing construction of a new production facility with which it plans to produce a series of power hand tools, whose estimated profitability and minimum production quantities are shown below

219

SOLVING LINEAR
PROGRAMMING
PROBLEMS WITH
THE SIMPLEX
METHOD

Product	Contribution per unit	Minimum weekly demand
Drill	2	5,000
Jigsaw	5	None
Circular saw	4	3,000
Router	3	None

Each item requires production time in the fabrication and assembly departments, as shown below, and it is estimated that 900 labor hours are available for production in both departments each week.

Product	Fabrication time (labor hours per 1,000)	Assembly time (labor hours per 1,000)
Drill	20	20
Jigsaw	25	20
Circular saw	30	12
Router	15	10

The company wishes to develop the most profitable production schedule given the various constraints described above. It has formulated this problem in the linear programming format, as shown below (D = thousands of drills, J = thousands of jigsaws, C = thousands of circular saws, R = thousands of routers, and TC = total contribution in thousands of dollars.

$$\text{Maximize:} \quad TC = 2D + 5J + 4C + 3R$$

$$\text{Subject to:} \quad 20D + 25J + 30C + 15R \leq 900$$

$$20D + 20J + 12C + 10R \leq 900$$

$$D \qquad\qquad\qquad \geq 5$$

$$C \qquad\quad \geq 3$$

$$D, J, C, R \geq 0$$

After adding slack, surplus, and artificial variables the following initial simplex tableau was prepared:

Objective coefficients for basic variables	Basic variables	Entering gains / values	2 D	5 J	4 C	3 R	0 S_1	0 S_2	0 S_3	0 S_4	-100 A_1	-100 A_2
0	S_1	900	20	25	30	15	1	0	0	0	0	0
0	S_2	900	20	20	12	10	0	1	0	0	0	0
-100	A_1	5	1	0	0	0	0	0	-1	0	1	0
-100	A_2	3	0	0	1	0	0	0	0	-1	0	1
Total contribution	Entering costs		-100	0	-100	0	0	0	100	100	-100	-100
-800	Net change		102	5	104	3	0	0	-100	-100	0	0

a. Why does this tableau have a negative total contribution?
b. Identify the entering and departing variables.
c. What will be the new total contribution figure for the second tableau?
After several iterations we obtain the following tableau:

Objective coefficients for basic variables	Basic variables	Entering gains	2	5	4	3	0	0	0	0
		Values	D	J	C	R	S_1	S_2	S_3	S_4
0	S_1	710	0	25	0	15	1	0	20	30
0	S_2	764	0	20	0	10	0	1	20	12
2	D	5	1	0	0	0	0	0	−1	0
4	C	3	0	0	1	0	0	0	0	−1
	Total contribution	Entering costs	2	0	4	0	0	0	−2	−4
	22	Net change	0	5	0	3	0	0	2	4

d. What are the values for the decision variables for this tableau?
e. Is the solution feasible?
f. Is the solution optimal?
g. How can a surplus variable, such as S_4, have a positive net-change value?
h. What are the values of the artificial variables at this point?
i. Identify the entering and departing variables.
The next iteration leads to this tableau:

Objective coefficients for basic variables	Basic variables	Entering gains	2	5	4	3	0	0	0	0
		Values	D	J	C	R	S_1	S_2	S_3	S_4
5	J	$28\frac{2}{5}$	0	1	0	$\frac{3}{5}$	$\frac{1}{25}$	0	$\frac{4}{5}$	$\frac{6}{5}$
0	S_2	196	0	0	0	−2	$-\frac{4}{5}$	1	4	−12
2	D	5	1	0	0	0	0	0	−1	0
4	C	3	0	0	1	0	0	0	0	−1
	Total contribution	Entering costs	2	5	4	3	$\frac{1}{5}$	0	2	2
	164	Net change	0	0	0	0	$-\frac{1}{5}$	0	−2	−2

j. What are the values of the decision variables represented by this tableau?
k. Is the solution optimal?
l. Why does variable R have a zero net-change value?
m. Which constraints are binding?
n. Suppose variable R is chosen as the entering variable for the next tableau. Select the departing variable and prepare the next tableau. What conclusions can you draw when comparing your new tableau with the one above?

6-9. Jack's All-Night Barbecue has been having difficulties establishing a work schedule for its employees. Under the present system Jack's has experienced periods of overstaffing, with idle employees, as well as understaffing, with impatient customers. Jack has worked hard, using past data, to determine the number of employees needed to meet demand during each 4-hour stretch as shown below:

Time period	Minimum employees needed
Midnight–4 A.M.	4
4–8	12
8–noon	8
Noon–4	14
4–8	18
8–midnight	10

Employees, by union rules, if used at all must be paid for a full 8 hours. Furthermore, no employee can work more than 8 hours, and the hours worked must be consecutive.

Assuming that employees may begin work at the beginning of each of the six time periods above, formulate this problem as a linear programming problem and solve it using the simplex method.

6-10. Using the linear programming computer package available at your school, find the optimal solution to the television programming mix problem of the XYZ network (see problem 6-1).

6-11. Using the programming computer package available at your school, find the optimal solution to the Petgrow Feed Company problem (see problem 6-4).

6-12. Using the linear programming computer package available at your school:

a. Find the optimal solution to the Fischer Electric Company problem (see problem 6-3).

b. Suppose the methods engineer has recommended the purchase of automated testing equipment which will reduce the time required to test each product by half. By how much will total net contribution increase during the coming week?

c. What if another person is available for the assembly department, raising the available hours by 50? What changes in the optimal solution to part *a* will result from the extra assembly capacity?

d. A price increase for the dehumidifier has been proposed which will increase the per-unit net contribution by $10. What effect would this price increase have on the optimal solution to part *a*?

e. The marketing department has proposed a special sales plan offering customers a discount for purchase of a combined air conditioner and furnace. This new unit would have a per-unit contribution of $350 and would require 6 hours of fabrication, 5 hours of assembly and 1½ hours of testing. Would the availability of this new unit affect the optimal solution to part *a*?

7

Postoptimality Analysis and Duality for Linear Programming

Chapters 5 and 6 dealt with formulating and solving linear programming problems. From a managerial standpoint, the actual solution of the problem is less important than the interpretation and analysis of the results. You may in fact be surprised at the scope and depth of information and insight that can be obtained through an analysis of the linear programming results. Thus this chapter is devoted to an intensive examination of the nature of the questions and answers that can be generated through *postoptimality*, or *sensitivity, analysis*.

Our focus in this chapter will be on developing an understanding of how the information in the final simplex tableau can be given managerial interpretations. In order to do this, we will see that every linear programming problem has a companion problem called the *dual*. Analysis of the solution to this dual problem provides additional insight concerning the solution to the original problem.

This chapter will begin by examining the application of sensitivity analysis to linear programming problems. We will see how the effects of changes in the objective function coefficients and constraint capacities can be examined without having to resolve the problem from scratch. We will consider how this can be done graphically as well as by using the information in the simplex tableau.

Next the concept of the dual problem will be introduced. We will see how this dual problem can be formulated and solved and how it relates to the original problem. Then we will consider the ways in which the dual can be used to answer additional sensitivity questions. These include determining the value of the constrained resources, the usefulness of adding new decision variables, and the effect of changes in the rate at which resources are used by the decision variables. The chapter will conclude by examining the sensitivity analysis functions usually available with linear programming computer packages.

Sensitivity Analysis

One of the main objectives of postoptimality analysis is to determine the sensitivity of the optimal solution to changes in the problem *parameters*. Linear programming parameters typically include the amount of resources available, the per-unit profit margins (or costs), the capacity utilization rates (or constraint coefficients), and other values that were used in formulating the problem. This analysis using these parameters is important because it tends to substantiate or refute the correctness of the optimal solution. This is essentially done by examining how far a specific parameter must change before the optimal decision has to be modified. Changes in the parameters can be caused by an actual shift in values over time, or they may simply reflect uncertainty in the true values. Many parameters are often only estimates of the correct values. The concept of sensitivity testing is appropriate to any management science model. Because of the special nature of linear programming problems, the procedures to follow in performing sensitivity tests are well defined and easy to follow. As we shall see later in the chapter, most linear programming computer packages provide sensitivity information automatically.

Changes in parameter values of linear programming problems do not necessarily lead to changes in the optimal decision. Frequently, in fact, small changes in a parameter value leave the optimal solution unchanged. Thus, sensitivity analysis for linear programming problems is concerned with *how large a change in a parameter value is necessary to cause a change in the optimal solution.*

If large changes in parameter values are necessary to cause a shift in the optimal decision, the manager can be much more confident that the solution is indeed correct. On the other hand, if the optimal decision is sensitive to small changes in the problem parameters, the decision maker may wish to spend more time and money either pinpointing the correct values of these parameters or controlling their values to lessen the chance that the decision chosen will not be optimal.

The kinds of sensitivity questions that can be examined include the effects of (1) changes in the objective function coefficients, (2) changes in the resource capacities or right-hand-side values of the constraints, (3) changes in the constraint coefficients or resource utilization rates, (4) consideration of additional constraints, and (5) the inclusion of other decision variables.

We will look at sensitivity analysis from several viewpoints. It will be easier to understand what sensitivity considerations entail if we first manipulate the problem parameters graphically. We will then consider how these manipulations can be accomplished using the final simplex tableau and with standard computer packages.

Analyzing Changes in Objective Function Coefficents

We will consider first changes in the objective function coefficients. We can view these changes as shifts, or changes, in the slope of the isoprofit line. We are concerned with identifying how large these shifts need to be in order to cause a change in the optimal solution.

Graphic Approach In order that the optimal extreme point may remain unchanged, the isoprofit line reflecting new values for the objective coefficients must pass through that point and not through any other feasible points. Suppose, instead, that after changing the original objective function coefficients, the revised isoprofit line that passes through the original optimal extreme point also passes through other points within the feasible region. It must then be cutting off a corner of that feasible region. The extreme point corresponding to that isolated corner will have a higher objective function value. To illustrate, consider Figure 7-1, which shows two isoprofit lines passing through extreme point I of the feasible region for the Nevada Instruments problem. Isoprofit line X touches no feasible points other than point I, and therefore point I is optimal for the set of objective function coefficients corresponding to isoprofit line X.

Isoprofit line Y, on the other hand, passes through the feasible region and touches many feasible solutions in addition to point I. It should be graphically evident that point II is more profitable than I because we can draw a profit line through point II parallel to isoprofit line Y that lies above and to the right (in the

FIGURE 7-1   Sensitivity of extreme point optimality to shifts in the slope of the profit line (Nevada Instruments problem).

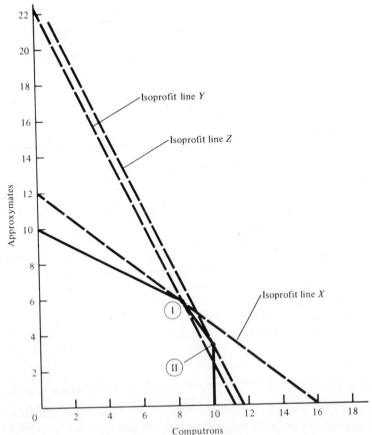

225

POSTOPTIMALITY
ANALYSIS AND
DUALITY FOR
LINEAR
PROGRAMMING

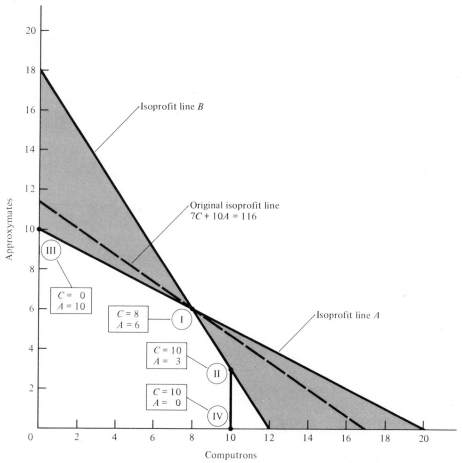

FIGURE 7-2 Optimal range for objective function isoprofit line passing through extreme point I.

direction of larger objective function values) of Y. This line is represented in Figure 7-1 as isoprofit line Z.

Now let us look at Figure 7-2. We can see there that as long as the profit line that passes through extreme point I (we know there can be only one such profit line for a given set of objective function coefficients) falls within the shaded area, point I remains optimal.

Suppose the isoprofit line passing through extreme point I rotates counterclockwise, thereby passing through the feasible region below extreme point III. Extreme point III then becomes optimal. If the isoprofit line rotates clockwise, it will eventually pass through the feasible region below extreme point II. Extreme point II will then be optimal. Thus, extreme point I will remain optimal only as long as it falls within the shaded area of Figure 7-2 defined by isoprofit lines A and B.

Rotation, either clockwise or counterclockwise, of the isoprofit line will occur if one of the objective function coefficients changes. It is useful to know how large a change is necessary to cause a change in the optimal extreme point. If the isoprofit line rotates counterclockwise, the point of change occurs when the line coincides with the constraint line that passes through extreme points I and III. This is referred to as isoprofit line A. Alternatively, if the isoprofit line rotates clockwise, the point of change occurs when it coincides with the constraint line passing through extreme points I and II. This is identified as isoprofit line B.

Recall that we originally estimated the objective function coefficients for the Nevada Instruments problem to be $7 per case of Computrons and $10 per case of Approxymates. Rotating the isoprofit line counterclockwise is equivalent to increasing the contribution for Approxymates or reducing the contribution for Computrons. A clockwise rotation is equivalent to decreasing the contribution for Approxymates or increasing the contribution for Computrons.

Suppose, for the moment, we are concerned with changes in the objective function coefficient for Computrons. If we let p represent the objective function coefficient for Computrons, we can write our objective function as

$$\text{Total contribution} = pC + 10A$$

As stated above, isoprofit line A represents the farthest that the isoprofit line can rotate counterclockwise and still leave extreme point I optimal. Note that isoprofit line A passes through extreme point III, with $C = 0$ and $A = 10$, and point I, with $C = 8$ and $A = 6$. Since the profits for all points on an isoprofit line are equal by definition, we can set the profits of extreme points I and III equal to each other and solve for p.

$$\text{Profit for extreme point III} = \text{profit for extreme point I}$$

$$p(0) + 10(10) = p(8) + 10(6)$$

$$100 = 8p + 60$$

$$p = 5$$

This indicates that the contribution for a case of Computrons can decline from our original estimate of $7 to as little as $5 without changing the optimal mix (extreme point I) of Computrons and Approxymates.

Next consider what happens if the isoprofit line rotates clockwise until it coincides with isoprofit line B in Figure 7-2. Again let us assume that the shift in the isoprofit line results from a change in the objective function coefficient for Computrons. Thus, a clockwise shift is equivalent to an increase in the contribution for Computrons.

In order to calculate the size of the increase for the Computron contribution, we first observe that isoprofit line B passes through extreme points I and II. If we again let p represent the Computron contribution, we can set the profits at extreme points I and II equal to each other and solve for p.

$$\text{Profit for extreme point I} = \text{profit for extreme point II}$$

Noting that $C = 8$ and $A = 6$ at extreme point I and $C = 10$ and $A = 3$ at extreme point II, we can then write

$$p(8) + 10(6) = p(10) + 10(3)$$

$$8p - 10p = 30 - 60$$

$$-2p = -30$$

$$p = 15$$

We find in this case that the objective function coefficient, or contribution, for Computrons would have to increase from $7 to more than $15 before the optimal solution would change from extreme point I to extreme point II.

In a similar manner we can determine the limits on changes in the contribution for Approxymates. Recall that a counterclockwise rotation of the isoprofit line can result from an increase in the contribution of Approxymates. Isoprofit line A represents the farthest counterclockwise rotation that leaves extreme point I optimal. Thus, the maximum increase in contribution for Approxymates can be found by equating the profit at extreme points I and III. Let q represent the contribution for Approxymates. Then,

$$\text{Profit for extreme point I} = \text{profit for extreme point III}$$
$$7(8) + q(6) = 7(0) + q(10)$$
$$56 + 6q = 10q$$
$$4q = 56$$
$$q = 14$$

Thus the contribution for Approxymates could increase from $10 to as high as $14 without changing the optimal solution.

INSTANT REPLAY The marketing department at Nevada Instruments has proposed a price drop for Approxymates. This would lower the contribution per case for Approxymates but would not affect the contribution for Computrons of $7. How large can the price decrease be without causing a change in the optimal production mix?

CHECK A decrease in Approxymate contribution will cause the isoprofit line to rotate clockwise. Using isoprofit line B, you should have found an objective function coefficient of $\frac{14}{3}$, or $4.67, for a case of Approxymates. Thus, the contribution margin would have to fall by $10 - 4.67 = $5.33 before the optimal production mix would change.

Table 7-1 summarizes the limits on changes to the objective function coefficients that will leave the original solution (extreme point I) optimal. For instance, we see that the contribution for Computrons, which was estimated to be $7, could be as low as $5 or as high as $15 without changing the optimal production mix. The percentage changes shown represent the corresponding percentage reduction or increase. Thus, a drop from $7 to $5 in the contribution for Computrons is a 28.6 percent decrease, while a rise from $7 to $15 is a 114.3 percent increase. Similar interpretation can be applied to the figures for Approxymates.

How can this information be used? One use concerns an analysis of proposed changes such as we saw with the preceding instant replay. As a second example, suppose a price increase is contemplated for Computrons that will raise the per-case contribution from $7 to $8. By referring to Table 7-1, we can see that this price increase will have no effect on the optimal mix between Computrons and Approxymates. The contribution for Computrons would have to be raised to more than $15 before we would need to change the optimal production mix.

TABLE 7-1
Limits on Objective Function Coefficients that Leave Optimum Solution Unchanged

	Percent decrease	*Lowest coefficient*	*Estimated coefficient*	*Highest coefficient*	*Percent increase*
Computrons	28.6	5	7	15	114.3
Approxymates	53.3	4.67	10	14	40

A second managerial use concerns errors in measuring the objective function coefficients. We used estimates of $7 and $10 for the contribution of each case of Computrons and Approxymates, respectively. Although these were the best estimates available, they may not be correct. The limits shown in Table 7-1 provide a means of determining how cautious management needs to be in using the optimal solution. If, for example, the lower limit for the Computron contribution had been $6.90 rather than $5, we would be much more concerned about the accuracy of the $7 estimate. In this case, a small error in our estimate could cause us to use the wrong production mix. If the correct contribution margin is, say, $6.80, the optimal mix is represented by extreme point III. Whenever either the upper or lower limits are close to the estimated coefficient, we need to ensure the accuracy of the estimate. This may justify the expenditure of additional time and money to refine the estimate.

Using the Simplex Tableau to Obtain Sensitivity Information   We will now consider similar analysis of the sensitivity of the optimal solution to changes in the objective function utilizing the information contained in the final simplex tableau. A slightly larger example problem will be used.

Consider the problem faced by the White and Cardwell Power Tool Company (see problem 6-8, modified slightly here). The company manufactures four power tools for the consumer market: drills, jigsaws, circular saws, and routers. The company formulated a linear programming problem to enable it to develop the most profitable production schedule for a new manufacturing facility. The decision variables were expressed in thousands of units of each of the four products: D = drills, J = jigsaws, C = circular saws, and R = routers.

Four constraints were recognized. The first acknowledged that the fabrication department was limited to 900 hours per week. Each 1,000 drills produced uses 20 hours of fabrication time; each 1,000 jigsaws needs 25 hours, circular saws 30 hours, and routers 15 hours. The second constraint limited assembly capacity to 900 hours per week. Each 1,000 drills requires 20 hours of assembly time, each 1,000 jigsaws 20 hours, circular saws 12 hours, and routers 10 hours. The third constraint was imposed to ensure that at least 5,000 drills are produced each week. The fourth constraint called for at least 3,000 circular saws to be produced.

Each 1,000 drills contributes $2,000 to profit, each 1,000 jigsaws $5,000, circular saws $4,000, and routers $2,000. Thus the objective function (in thousands of dollars) is TC = $2D + 5J + 4C + 2R$, and the complete formulation is

Maximize: TC = $2D + 5J + 4C + 2R$

Subject to: $20D + 25J + 30C + 15R \leq 900$

$$20D + 20J + 12C + 10R \leq 900$$
$$D \qquad\qquad\qquad \geq 5$$
$$C \qquad\quad \geq 3$$
$$D, J, C, R \geq 0$$

229

POSTOPTIMALITY
ANALYSIS AND
DUALITY FOR
LINEAR
PROGRAMMING

After slack, surplus, and artificial variables were added, the simplex method was applied. Three iterations were necessary to generate the final tableau, which is shown in Table 7-2.

The optimal solution calls for production of 28,400 jigsaws, 5,000 drills, and 3,000 circular saws, for a total contribution of $164,000. Note that the solution does not authorize production of the fourth product (routers).

In order to analyze the sensitivity of the optimal solution to changes in the objective function coefficients, it is necessary to discuss basic variables and nonbasic variables separately. We will first consider nonbasic variables.

Objective Coefficient Changes for Nonbasic Variables   Variable R, for routers, is the only nonbasic decision variable present in the final solution. We need not consider the other nonbasic variables, which were all slack or surplus variables. (The artificial variables were dropped out as the solution progressed.) By definition they do not have objective function coefficients.

How will a change in the objective function coefficient for a nonbasic decision variable affect the optimality of the final solution? Since that variable has a 0 value in the final solution, we can deduce that its contribution must not be high enough to allow a profitable exchange with one of the present basic variables. It should be obvious, then, that a *decrease in the objective function coefficient for any nonbasic decision* variable cannot possibly change the optimal solution. Such a decrease can only make the variable even less profitable than before.

On the other hand, it seems logical that if we were to increase that nonbasic objective function coefficient, at some point the increase would be large enough to convert that variable profitably from nonbasic to basic. The question to be answered is: How high is enough?

TABLE 7-2
Final Simplex Tableau for the White and Cardwell Power Tool Problem

Objective coefficients for basic variables	Basic variables	Entering gain	2	5	4	2	0	0	0	0
		Values	D	J	C	R	S_1	S_2	S_3	S_4
5	J	$28\frac{2}{5}$	0	1	0	$\frac{3}{5}$	$\frac{1}{25}$	0	$\frac{4}{5}$	$\frac{6}{5}$
0	S_2	196	0	0	0	-2	$-\frac{4}{5}$	1	4	-12
2	D	5	1	0	0	0	0	0	-1	0
4	C	3	0	0	1	0	0	0	0	-1
	Total contribution	Entering cost	2	5	4	3	$\frac{1}{5}$	0	2	2
	164	Net change	0	0	0	-1	$-\frac{1}{5}$	0	-2	-2

Recall that for a maximization problem the simplex method selects a nonbasic variable to become basic by considering those variables that have positive net-change values. As long as at least one nonbasic variable has a positive net-change value, the solution being examined is not optimal. Therefore, if the objective function coefficient for a nonbasic variable is to change by an amount sufficient to make the final tableau no longer optimal, it must increase by enough to cause the net-change value for that nonbasic variable to become positive. In other words, the maximum increase in the objective function coefficient for a nonbasic variable that will *not* change the optimality of the final tableau would be an increase just large enough to cause the net-change value for that variable to become zero.

For our example, the net-change value in the final tableau (Table 7-2) for variable R was -1. Consequently, the largest increase possible in the objective function coefficient for variable R is 1 (equivalent to $1,000). A larger increase will make it profitable to convert R to a basic variable, thus changing the optimal solution.

The reverse is true for minimization problems. That is, a decision variable is nonbasic if it is cheaper to use some combination of the basic variables. Thus, any increase in the objective function coefficient for a nonbasic decision variable will only make it more expensive. Any decrease in the coefficient greater than the final net-change value, however, will leave the solution nonoptimal.

In general, then, we can state the following sensitivity rule for objective coefficient changes for nonbasic variables in maximization (minimization) problems:

The objective function coefficient for a nonbasic variable can be decreased (increased) by any amount or increased (decreased) by an amount just sufficient to yield a zero net-change value without requiring a change in the optimal solution.

Objective Coefficient Changes for Basic Variables The analysis for basic variables is somewhat different because changes in either direction can cause a shift in the optimal solution. A decrease in the coefficient for a maximization problem can make it profitable to replace that basic variable with one of the nonbasic variables. An increase in the coefficient can make that basic variable so profitable that capacity now being used for one of the other basic variables should be shifted, instead, to the variable with the increased coefficient. Similar but opposite changes would result for minimization problems. These increases and decreases are equivalent to rotating the isoprofit line counterclockwise or clockwise, as we saw earlier.

For an understanding of how we can calculate the exact magnitudes of allowable changes in the coefficients for the basic variables, we need to recall that the optimal solution for a maximization problem is characterized by all zero or negative net-change values in the final tableau. These values were derived by subtracting the entering costs from the initial objective function coefficients for each variable. Note that the entering costs measure the value of the basic variables that must be given up to add one unit of each nonbasic variable. Thus, if we change the objective function coefficients for the basic variables, we are also changing the entering-cost values for the nonbasic variables. This in turn affects the net-change values for those nonbasic variables.

Now, as long as the net-change values for the nonbasic variables remain zero or negative, the solution represented by the final tableau remains optimal. Thus we can find the limits on changes in the objective function coefficients for basic variables by determining the maximum such changes, in both directions, that maintain negative or zero net-change values for *all* nonbasic variables. This normally requires that we do a separate calculation for each nonbasic variable.

Consider, first, variable J. Note that the constraint equation corresponding to variable J indicates the necessary changes in the size of variable J for a one-unit increase in the size of each of the nonbasic variables.

	R	S_1	S_3	S_4
J	$\frac{3}{5}$	$\frac{1}{25}$	$\frac{4}{5}$	$\frac{6}{5}$

If the objective function coefficient for variable J is changed by some amount, say α, the entering cost for each nonbasic variable will be increased by an amount equal to α times each respective constraint coefficient. To find the value for α that pushes the net-change value to zero for one of the nonbasic variables, we simply set the value of the change equal to the current net-change value for that variable and solve for α. The net-change values from Table 7-2 were

R	S_1	S_3	S_4
-1	$-\frac{1}{5}$	-2	-2

Thus, for nonbasic variable R the equation is

$$\tfrac{3}{5}\alpha = -1$$

Solving for α, we find

$$\alpha = -\tfrac{5}{3}$$

This says, in effect, that if the objective function coefficient for variable J decreased by $\frac{5}{3}$, the net-change value for nonbasic variable R will equal 0. Any greater decrease in the coefficient for J will give variable R a positive net-change value, causing the current tableau to become nonoptimal.

INSTANT REPLAY To convince yourself that the $\frac{5}{3}$ decrease in J's objective function coefficient does indeed cause the net change for R to go to 0, refer to the final tableau in Table 7-2 and recalculate R's net-change value using the revised objective coefficient for J.

CHECK Net change $= 2 - (\tfrac{3}{5})(5 - \tfrac{5}{3}) + (-2)(0) + (0)(2) + (0)(4)$

$$= 2 - (\tfrac{3}{5})(\tfrac{10}{3}) = 2 - 2 = 0$$

We must examine each of the other nonbasic variables in turn to find the appropriate value for α that drives their respective net-change values to zero. To simplify the calculations required, we can use the following equation:

$$\alpha_{ij} = \frac{NC_j}{CC_{ij}}$$

where α_{ij} = change in the objective function coefficient for basic variable i that causes the net-change value for nonbasic variable j to equal zero

NC_j = current net-change value for nonbasic variable j

CC_{ij} = constraint coefficient corresponding to rate of exchange of basic variable i and nonbasic variable j

Thus, we find

$$\alpha_{J,R} = \frac{-1}{\frac{3}{5}} = -\frac{5}{3}$$

$$\alpha_{J,S_1} = \frac{-\frac{1}{5}}{\frac{1}{25}} = -5$$

$$\alpha_{J,S_3} = \frac{-2}{\frac{4}{5}} = -\frac{5}{2}$$

$$\alpha_{J,S_4} = \frac{-2}{\frac{6}{5}} = -\frac{5}{3}$$

Each of the values computed for α_{ij} serves as a constraint on the changes to the objective function coefficient for basic variable i. Thus, to find the maximum change in the coefficient that will leave the solution optimal, we need to find which of these constraints are the tightest. This is done by finding the smallest positive and negative α_{ij} values (those that are closest to zero).

Note that for variable J all the α_{ij} values were negative. This implies that there is no limit on the amount of an *increase* in the objective coefficient for variable J. This means that no matter how much management can increase the contribution for jigsaws, the optimal production mix will not change. To convince yourself that this is correct, you may wish to pick some large value for J's objective coefficient and prove that the net-change values for the nonbasic variables do indeed remain zero or negative.

INSTANT REPLAY   What would the net-change values for the nonbasic variables be if J had an objective function coefficient of 100?

CHECK   The net-change values for the nonbasic variables are -58 for R, -4 for S_1, -78 for S_3, and -116 for S_4. Thus the solution remains optimal.

The maximum *decrease* allowed in J's objective coefficient is simply the *smallest* negative α_{ij} value. In this case $-\frac{5}{3}$ is the smallest negative α_{ij} (from the constraints for both R and S_4), which means that the objective coefficient for variable J can be decreased by as much as $\frac{5}{3}$ and the solution will remain optimal. Any larger decrease will cause the net-change values for nonbasic variables R and S_4 to become positive, indicating that the solution can be improved by selecting either R or S_4 as the entering variable for the next tableau.

We can carry out similar calculations for basic variable D using the constraint coefficients for the nonbasic variables in the constraint row corresponding to variable D:

	R	S_1	S_3	S_4
D	0	0	-1	0

and the corresponding net-change values

233

POSTOPTIMALITY
ANALYSIS AND
DUALITY FOR
LINEAR
PROGRAMMING

R	S_1	S_3	S_4
-1	$-\frac{1}{5}$	-2	-2

Note that the constraint coefficients for nonbasic variables R, S_1, and S_4 are zero. This signifies that the value of the objective coefficient for variable D has no effect whatsoever on the net-change value for these nonbasic variables. Thus, the only α_{ij} we need to calculate is that for variable S_3:

$$\alpha_{D,S_3} = \frac{-2}{-1} = 2$$

From this we conclude that for the solution to remain optimal, the objective function coefficient for variable D must not increase by more than \$2,000. The absence of any other limits implies that there is no limit on the size of a decrease to D's contribution coefficient. This is because no matter how small the contribution per 1,000 drills, the optimal value of D can be no less than its current value of 5 because of the minimum production constraint for variable D (drills).

INSTANT REPLAY Determine the appropriate limits on changes to the objective coefficient for basic variable C.

CHECK The coefficient for C cannot increase by more than 2 (from S_4) but is unlimited on the down side.

A summary of the appropriate limits on changes to the objective coefficients for all variables is shown in Table 7-3. Although the percentages vary somewhat, they are all relatively high. This should give the decision maker a fairly high degree of confidence in the optimal solution. The smallest percentage variation allowed is that for a decrease in the coefficient for jigsaws, 33.33 percent. If this margin of error is viewed uncomfortably, the decision maker may wish to invest further effort in pinpointing the precise nature of jigsaws' contribution or at least to monitor that contribution closely in the future.

The reader should be aware that although in the White and Cardwell problem the objective coefficient of each basic variable was unconstrained in one direction or the other, frequently the coefficients are constrained in both directions. For example, suppose that we were to calculate α_{ij} values for some basic variable and found them to be -4, $+5$, -3, and $+12$. What would be the limits on change for this basic variable? The two positive α_{ij} values would determine the limits on increases, and the two negative values would determine the limits on decreases. Thus, the coefficient for this variable would be constrained to an increase of no more than 5 and to a decrease of no more than 3.

In summary, then, to define limits on the changes to objective function coefficients for basic variables, we need to calculate the α_{ij} values and choose the smallest positive α_{ij} value (if any) as the maximum coefficient increase and the smallest negative α_{ij} (if any) as the maximum coefficient decrease.

Interpretation and use of the coefficient limits obtained using the simplex tableau are no different from that discussed with the graphical method. How-

TABLE 7-3
Summary of Limits on Changes in Objective Coefficients for Decision Variables in the White and Cardwell Problem That Leave the Optimum Solution Unchanged

	Maximum percent decrease	Lowest coefficient	Estimated coefficient	Highest coefficient	Maximum percent increase
Drills	N.L.*	N.L.	2	4	100
Jigsaws	33.3	$\frac{10}{3}$	5	N.L.	N.L.
Circular saws	N.L.	N.L.	4	6	50
Routers	N.L.	N.L.	2	3	50

*No limit.

ever, the advantages of being able to answer sensitivity questions directly from the final tableau should not be overlooked. For example, suppose White and Cardwell was considering a price increase for drills that would raise the contribution from $2,000 to $2,500 per thousand drills. To determine the effects of such a change, they could reformulate the problem with the higher coefficient for drills and resolve the problem using the simplex method. However, all this work is not really necessary. The effect on the optimal solution can be obtained by sensitivity analysis from the final tableau of the original problem. As shown in Table 7-3, a change in the contribution for drills from 2 to 2.5 would not affect the optimal production mix. Thus, we see that sensitivity analysis allows us to pose a number of "what if" questions that can be answered without resolving the problem from scratch. In this way sensitivity analysis is a powerful tool.

Analyzing Changes in the Resource Capacities

Changes in the objective function coefficients are but one of the many types of changes that can be examined with sensitivity analysis. In this section we consider the effects of changes in the resource capacities, or the right-hand-side values of the constraints. As before, we are interested in the sensitivity of the optimal solution to changes in the amount of resources available. Such changes may be unexpected or they may be the result of a specified managerial decision. For example, equipment failure may lead to a temporary unexpected decrease in productive capacity. Alternatively, management may wish to consider the effects of increasing capacity temporarily by using overtime.

In the sections below the Nevada Instruments problem will first be used to show how resource capacity changes can be examined graphically. Then the White and Cardwell example will illustrate how the simplex tableau can be used to examine the same issues.

Graphic Approach   Recall that each resource limitation is shown graphically by a constraint line. A change in the amount of resources available is equivalent to a shift in that constraint line. The direction of the shift is away from the origin for an increase in availability or toward the origin for a decrease. The effect of this shift in the constraint line on the optimal solution depends on which constraint is being shifted, the direction of the change, and the size of the change in the resource capacity. To demonstrate this, each of the three constraints for the Nevada Instruments problem will be examined in turn, beginning with the IC chip constraint.

IC Chip Constraint The IC chip constraint for the Nevada Instruments problem limited the number of cases of Computrons that could be produced to 10. Suppose that this limit could be changed. For instance, we may be able to purchase more of these chips from an alternate supplier. Alternatively, we may be concerned about the ability of the existing supplier to provide even enough chips to meet the 10-case limit. How far would we have to increase or decrease the chip capacity before the optimal production mix would change?

You should recall that the optimal solution is not constrained at all by the present chip capacity (10 cases) because the optimal production mix calls for only 8 cases of Computrons to be produced. If we increased the number of available IC chips, the solution would not change because the chips are already in excess supply. Increases are irrelevant, but what about decreases?

Since the optimal solution calls for 8 cases of Computrons, it is obvious that if the IC chip capacity is reduced to less than 8 cases, the optimal solution must change. Refer to Figure 7-3, which represents a decrease in chip capacity by a shift to the left of the IC chip constraint. No change in the optimal solution occurs until the chip capacity is reduced to 8 at extreme point I. At that point all three constraints intersect. As the chip capacity is further reduced, two things happen: the optimal solution moves with the constraint, and the fabrication constraint is no longer binding. As Figure 7-3 shows, when the chip constraint moves to limit Computrons to 6 cases, the optimal solution shifts from extreme point I to II. This shift leaves the fabrication constraint completely outside the feasible region. It is no longer binding because any solution that meets the assembly constraint and the tighter IC chip constraint requires less fabrication capacity than is available.

In summary, the IC chip capacity, which was originally listed at 10, can rise as much as possible or decrease as much as 20 percent (to 8) without

FIGURE 7-3 Effects of changes in IC chip capacity.

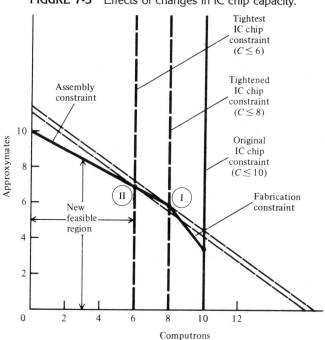

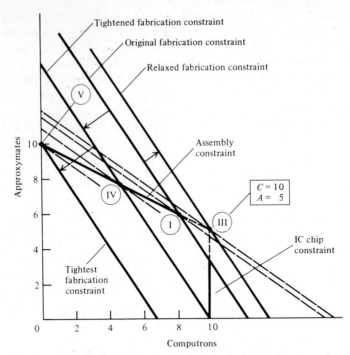

Approxymates

Tightened fabrication constraint

Original fabrication constraint

Relaxed fabrication constraint

Assembly
constraint

$C = 10$
$A = 5$

IC chip
constraint

Tightest
fabrication
constraint

Computrons

FIGURE 7-4   Effects of changes in fabrication capacity.

affecting the solution at all. Also of significance to management is that even if the chip capacity is less than 8, the same products are being produced; only the quantities change. Obviously this situation is preferred to one in which the product mix as well as the quantities change.

The Fabrication Constraint   Consider next the fabrication constraint. Since this constraint is one of the two that form the optimal extreme point, any change in the capacity for fabrication hours will cause a change in the optimal solution.

Examine first an increase in fabrication capacity. This is shown in Figure 7-4 as the relaxed fabrication constraint passing through extreme point III. Such an increase in capacity causes the optimal solution to shift from point I to point III, which, as before, causes a change in the decision variable quantities but no change in the product mix.

Further capacity increases will cause no further change in the optimal solution. The fabrication capacity will no longer be constraining because the set of feasible solutions satisfying both the assembly constraint and the IC chip constraint will require fewer fabrication hours than are available.

Next let us analyze changes in the other direction, representing decreases in fabrication capacity or a tightening of the constraint. As the fabrication constraint line shifts to the left, say to point IV, the optimal solution also shifts to point IV. This represents, as before, a shift in quantities but not in the mix. But as we push the constraint further, until the line passes through point V, a more substantial change occurs. At point V only one product, Approxymates, remains in the solution. Computrons have been forced out because of their heavier use of fabrication time, which is now very tightly constrained. Any

further reductions in fabrication capacity will lower the number of cases of
Approxymates produced.

237

POSTOPTIMALITY
ANALYSIS AND
DUALITY FOR
LINEAR
PROGRAMMING

Although we examined what would happen with shifts in the fabrication
constraint, we did not calculate the *magnitude* of the capacity changes necessary to bring about the more important shifts in the optimal solution. These
values are important in establishing limits within which the mix remains unchanged. In addition, as we shall see, we can determine whether or not capacity
change options, such as authorizing overtime, are economical. Such capacity
analysis is actually quite easy to carry out graphically.

Consider first a potential increase in fabrication capacity. We saw above
that the optimal solution is affected by increases in fabrication capacity only up
to the level represented by the line through extreme point III. At point III, $C =$
10 and $A = 5$, as shown in Figure 7-4. The fabrication constraint is based on
utilization rates of 3 hours for each case of Computrons and 2 hours for each
case of Approxymates. If the fabrication constraint passes through extreme
point III, the capacity must be defined by

$$\text{Capacity} = 3C + 2A$$

$$= 3(10) + 2(5) = 40$$

Thus, if fabrication capacity increases by 4 hours from 36 to 40, the
optimal solution quantities will change from 8 Computrons and 6 Approxymates with a total contribution of $7(8) + 10(6) = \$116$ to a mix of 10 Compu-
trons and 5 Approxymates with a profit of $7(10) + 10(5) = \$120$. Thus, an
increase of 4 hours in the fabrication capacity will yield an increase of $4 in
contribution.

This information can be valuable if, for instance, management was considering authorizing overtime in the fabrication department. We saw here that
such overtime could, at most, increase total contribution from $116 to $120 with
4 hours of overtime. If the cost of this overtime is greater than $4, management
would be ill advised to authorize it. Furthermore, as we saw previously, any
further increases in capacity will not cause any changes in the optimal solution.
Thus, even if the 4 hours of overtime cost less than the $4, any further overtime
has no benefit whatsoever.

INSTANT REPLAY   How far would the fabrication capacity have to decrease
before the Computron IC chip constraint is no longer a determinant of the
feasible region?

CHECK   30 hours of fabrication capacity (corresponding to the line passing
through point IV in Figure 7-4).

The Assembly Constraint   Finally, we turn to the assembly hours constraint. As
with fabrication, any change in assembly capacity will cause a change in the
optimal solution. If the assembly capacity increases, the optimal extreme point
will shift up from point I until it reaches point VI, as shown in Figure 7-5. At
point VI, $C = 0$, $A = 18$, and total contribution is $10(18) = 180$. This corresponds to an assembly capacity of $2(0) + 4(18) = 72$ hours.

Thus, 32 hours of overtime (or a second shift) will produce an increase in

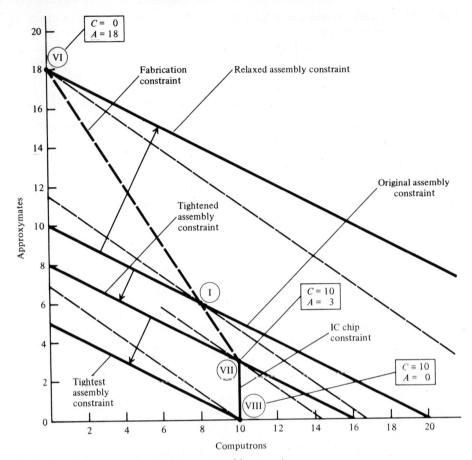

FIGURE 7-5 Effects of changes in assembly capacity.

contribution of $180 - 116 = \$64$. If the cost to increase this capacity was less than $64, it would raise the net contribution to do so. Note, however, that any further increases in assembly capacity would cause no further change in the mix or the quantities of the optimal solution.

If the capacity decreases, such that the constraint line now passes through point VII, the mix would not change, but the quantities produced would shift to 10 Computrons and 3 Approxymates. This reduces the contribution to $7(10) + 10(3) = 100$. This may be desirable if this capacity can be used for some other purpose that will generate more contribution than the $116 - 100 = \$16$ lost by the reduction in capacity available for the production of calculators.

Further decreases in assembly capacity will lead to no changes in the number of cases of Computrons but will lower the number of cases of Approxymates until point VIII is reached. Then only Computrons are produced. Continued reductions will lead to a decrease in the number of Computrons.

INSTANT REPLAY Suppose management desires to free up assembly capacity by restricting calculator production to Computrons. This extra capacity could be used in the production of other Nevada Instruments products. How many hours could be made available if extreme point VIII (corresponding to all-Computron production) is optimal?

239

POSTOPTIMALITY
ANALYSIS AND
DUALITY FOR
LINEAR
PROGRAMMING

CHECK Extreme point VIII requires 20 hours of assembly time to produce the 10 cases of Computrons called for. Thus $40 - 20 = 20$ hours are made available for other uses.

Using the Simplex Tableau to Analyze Changes in Constraint Capacities Next let us see how we analyze the effects of changes in resource capacity using the final simplex tableau. We refer again to the White and Cardwell example. For convenience the final tableau is shown in Table 7-4.

We analyze the effects of changes in constraint capacities by referring to the slack or surplus variables associated with each constraint. We will begin by considering slack variables. Surplus variables will be treated later.

Slack Variables Associated with each "less than or equal to" constraint is a slack variable. For the White and Cardwell problem we have two slack variables. S_1 corresponds to the existing fabrication constraint, and S_2 corresponds to the assembly constraint. We can examine the sensitivity of the optimal solution to changes in the capacities for these constraints by analysis of the status of each constraint's corresponding slack variable.

The status of these two slack variables in the final tableau differs in that S_1 is nonbasic and S_2 is basic. For convenience we will consider first the basic slack variable S_2.

Basic Slack Variables Slack variables represent the excess, or unused, capacity for their constraints. Slack variable S_2 is a basic variable in the final tableau and has a value of 196, as shown in Table 7-4. This value represents the amount of excess hours in the assembly department.

Since the optimal solution leaves the assembly department with excess capacity, any further additions to that capacity will not change the optimal

TABLE 7-4
Final Simplex Tableau for the White and Cardwell Power Tool Problem

Objective coefficients for basic variables	*Basic variables*	*Entering gain*	2	5	4	2	0	0	0	0
		Values	*D*	*J*	*C*	*R*	S_1	S_2	S_3	S_4
5	*J*	$28\frac{2}{5}$	0	1	0	$\frac{3}{5}$	$\frac{1}{25}$	0	$\frac{4}{5}$	$\frac{6}{5}$
0	S_2	196	0	0	0	-2	$-\frac{4}{5}$	1	4	-12
2	*D*	5	1	0	0	0	0	0	-1	0
4	*C*	3	0	0	1	0	0	0	0	-1
	Total contribution	*Entering cost*	2	5	4	3	$\frac{1}{5}$	0	2	2
	164	*Net change*	0	0	0	-1	$-\frac{1}{5}$	0	-2	-2

solution other than to increase the value of slack variable S_2 by the amount of the increased capacity.

Decreases, on the other hand, can affect the solution. Clearly we could have decreased the available assembly capacity by as much as 196 hours without changing the optimal solution. Further decreases would not be allowed, since slack variable S_2 would be forced to take on a negative value, which is, of course, infeasible. (Negative slack represents the utilization of more resource than is available.)

Thus, we conclude that the solution corresponding to the final tableau will remain optimal as long as the available capacity in the assembly department is not less than 704 hours (900 hours of original capacity less the maximum reduction permitted of 196 hours). In general, *if a slack variable is basic in the final solution, the capacity of the constraint to which that slack variable corresponds can be increased as much as desired or decreased by an amount equal to its final solution value without changing the optimality of the final solution.*

Nonbasic Slack Variables Next consider nonbasic slack variable S_1, which corresponds to fabrication capacity. Since this variable was nonbasic, it has a value of zero in the final solution. Thus, all the fabrication capacity was used up in the production of the basic decision variables, jigsaws, drills, and circular saws. Any increases or decreases in the fabrication capacity will change the values of these basic variables. We would like to determine the maximum size of capacity increases or decreases that will not affect the final solution mix. In other words, by how much does the fabrication capacity have to change before one of the nonbasic variables replaces one of the current basic variables?

Review, for a moment, the meaning of the constraint coefficients in the column corresponding to slack variable S_1 and their relationship to the solution values of the basic variables.

Basic variables	Values	S_1
J	$28\frac{2}{5}$	$\frac{1}{25}$
S_2	196	$-\frac{4}{5}$
D	5	0
C	3	0

In each case, the S_1 coefficient represents the amount of the basic variable given up to gain one unit of S_1; a positive coefficient indicates that a decrease in the basic variable is required, while a negative coefficient represents an increase.

Note that changes in the fabrication capacity can be viewed as increases or decreases in the value of slack variable S_1. For example, if the original fabrication capacity had been 800 hours instead of 900, basic variable J would have been $100 \times \frac{1}{25} = 4$ units smaller than it appeared in the final tableau, or $24\frac{2}{5}$ rather than $28\frac{2}{5}$. Likewise, if the original fabrication capacity had been 100 hours higher, or 1,000, the final value of basic variable S_2 would have been $(-100) \times (-\frac{4}{5}) = 80$ units smaller, or 116 rather than 196.

We are interested in the maximum changes in fabrication capacity that

241

POSTOPTIMALITY
ANALYSIS AND
DUALITY FOR
LINEAR
PROGRAMMING

will leave the *set* of basic variables unchanged (even though the *values* of those basic variables may change). As shown above, a decrease in fabrication capacity causes basic variable J to decrease at the rate of $\frac{1}{25}$ unit of J for each hour of decreased fabrication capacity. Such a decrease is permissible as long as the value of variable J does not become negative (i.e., it does not change the optimality of the final mix). Therefore, we can calculate the maximum allowable decrease in fabrication hours by solving for the size of the fabrication capacity decrease that reduces variable J to zero; any further decrease will make J's final value negative.

If we let b represent the maximum allowable change in the original fabrication capacity, we can solve for b according to

$$b = -\left(\frac{28\frac{2}{5}}{\frac{1}{25}}\right) = -(25)(\tfrac{142}{5}) = -710$$

Observe that it was necessary to insert a negative sign in the equation so that the final result shows the correct direction of allowable change. Thus, we conclude that fabrication capacity cannot be decreased any more than 710 hours if the final set of basic variables is to remain optimal.

Since there were four basic variables, a similar constraint on fabrication capacity change must be calculated for each. In general, the calculation required is

$$\begin{pmatrix} \text{Maximum allowable change} \\ \text{in the capacity for} \\ \text{nonbasic slack variable } S_i \\ \text{corresponding to basic variable } j \end{pmatrix} = - \frac{\begin{pmatrix} \text{final solution value} \\ \text{for basic variable } j \end{pmatrix}}{\begin{pmatrix} j\text{th constraint coefficient} \\ \text{for slack variable } S_i \end{pmatrix}}$$

Thus, for the second basic variable, slack variable S_2, we find

$$b = -\left(\frac{196}{-\frac{4}{5}}\right) = 245$$

Since S_1's constraint coefficients for the other two basic variables, D and C, are zero, we need not go further; variables D and C are unaffected by the fabrication capacity.

Therefore, we find that the fabrication capacity could have been as little as 190 ($900 - 710$) or as much as 1,145 ($900 + 245$) and the final tableau would have contained the same set of basic variables (although at different levels) as it did with the originally stated capacity of 900.

If we had found more than one positive or negative limit on change in fabrication capacity, we would select the smallest positive and negative limits (those closest to zero) as the actual constraints on capacity changes; these represent the tightest limits. Thus, if we had found values of, say, -710, $+245$, -140, and $+50$ for the respective values of b, we would conclude that fabrication capacity could not increase by more than 50 hours or decrease by more than 140 hours if the final set of basic variables was to remain optimal.

INSTANT REPLAY   Suppose that the fabrication capacity could be increased to 1,145 hours (instead of 900) through the use of overtime. What would be the final, optimal values for the basic variables? What is the maximum that the company would be willing to pay for this overtime?

CHECK The optimal values for the basic variables become $J = 38\frac{1}{5}$, $S_2 = 0$, $D = 5$, and $C = 3$. Total contribution would increase from \$164,000 to \$213,000, an increase of \$49,000. Thus, the maximum that the company would be willing to pay for the overtime is \$49,000, or \$200 per hour.

Surplus Variables Surplus variables are treated in a manner similar to slack variables, although the interpretation of what the changes represent is different. We add a surplus variable to each "greater than or equal to" constraint to represent the amount by which some minimum restriction is exceeded. The sensitivity testing performed on these "greater than or equal to" constraints thus consists of determining the effects of changes in these minimum levels.

Basic Surplus Variables If a surplus variable is present in the final tableau as a basic variable, the value for that variable is equivalent to the excess, or surplus, attained by that solution over and above the minimum stated requirement.

A reduction or relaxation in the original requirement can only cause the final value of the surplus variable to increase by an identical amount. Thus such decreases in the minimum level of the requirement will not affect the final solution, other than to increase the value of the surplus variable. For example, if the minimum production rate of 5 drills had been overachieved, with 7 drills produced, the corresponding surplus variable would have a value of 2. Relaxing the minimum production requirement from 5 to, say, 3 would increase the value of the surplus variable to 4, without changing any other part of the solution.

An increase in the minimum level of the requirement, on the other hand, causes a decrease in the value of the basic surplus variable. The size of this decrease is limited to the value for the surplus variable as shown in the final tableau.

For our example problem, both the two surplus variables (S_3 and S_4) were nonbasic in the final solution. They will be considered in the next section.

INSTANT REPLAY Suppose the basic variable S_2 was a surplus variable rather than a slack variable (see Table 7-4). What would be the maximum allowable increases or decreases to the original "minimum level" of 900 for that variable?

CHECK The minimum level could be as low as zero or as high as 1,096 (900 + 196).

Nonbasic Surplus Variables The treatment of nonbasic surplus variables is much the same as for nonbasic slack variables. Since a nonbasic surplus variable has a zero value in the optimal solution, we know that the minimum restriction was just met with no excess or surplus. Increases or decreases in the stated minimum level will cause changes to occur in the final solution. As with slack variables, we are concerned with determining how large the changes have to be in order to cause a change in the *set* of basic variables.

To determine the maximum allowable changes in the minimum level corresponding to each nonbasic surplus variable, we need to examine the effects that such changes have on the value of the basic variables. Consider, for example, surplus variable S_3, which corresponds to the constraint requiring a minimum level of production of 5 drills. The constraint coefficients for S_3 and the current values of the basic variables are extracted from the final tableau and repeated below.

243

POSTOPTIMALITY
ANALYSIS AND
DUALITY FOR
LINEAR
PROGRAMMING

Basic variables	Values	S_3
J	$28\frac{2}{5}$	$\frac{4}{5}$
S_2	196	4
D	5	-1
C	3	0

Clearly, a decrease in the original requirement for drills will cause a corresponding decrease in the optimal solution value of variable D. Since variable D has a current value of 5, the largest decrease that can occur is obviously 5. If we let c represent the maximum change that can occur in the original capacity of the constraint corresponding to variable S_3, while maintaining the same optimal set of basic variables, we can solve for c as follows:

$$c = \frac{5}{-1} = -5$$

In general, this is equivalent to

$$\left(\begin{array}{c} \text{Maximum allowable change} \\ \text{in the requirement for} \\ \text{nonbasic surplus variable } S_i \\ \text{corresponding to basic variable } j \end{array} \right) = \frac{\left(\begin{array}{c} \text{final solution value for} \\ \text{basic variable } j \end{array} \right)}{\left(\begin{array}{c} j\text{th constraint coefficient for} \\ \text{nonbasic surplus variable } S_i \end{array} \right)}$$

Note that in this case we did not need to insert a negative sign as we did for slack variables. This is because slack variables represent the amount by which constraints are *underachieved*; surplus variables represent the amount by which constraints are exceeded, or *overachieved*. Changes in the original constraint capacities or requirements will thus cause *opposite reactions* in surplus and slack variables. This is reflected by use of the negative sign for slack variables but not for surplus variables.

Using the formula shown for each of the basic variables, we find the following limits for surplus variable S_3:

$$c = \begin{cases} \dfrac{28\frac{2}{5}}{\frac{4}{5}} = \dfrac{71}{2} = 35\frac{1}{2} & \text{basic variable } J \\[3mm] \dfrac{196}{4} = 49 & \text{basic variable } S_2 \\[3mm] \dfrac{5}{-1} = -5 & \text{basic variable } D \end{cases}$$

No calculation was necessary for basic variable C because the constraint coefficient for S_3 in that row was zero, recognizing a lack of relationship between those variables.

The tightest constraints (those closest to zero) impose limits of $35\frac{1}{2}$ on increases and 5 on decreases for the original constraint requirements. As long as the constraint requires that no less than zero $(5 - 5)$ or no more than $40\frac{1}{2} =$

$(5 + 35\frac{1}{2})$ units of D be produced, the optimal set of basic variables will remain the same. Changes outside these limits will cause the optimal set of basic variables to change (equivalent to a change in extreme points).

INSTANT REPLAY   What would be the final values for the basic variables if a new order is received causing an increase in the minimum production quantity for drills to 20 (thousand)?

CHECK   The final values would be $J = 16\frac{2}{5}$, $S_2 = 136$, $D = 20$, and $C = 3$.

In a similar fashion we can calculate limits on changes to the original constraint requirements for S_4, based on the relevant tableau values:

Basic variable	Value	S_4
J	$28\frac{2}{5}$	$\frac{6}{5}$
S_2	196	-12
D	5	0
C	3	-1

Thus, the respective limits are

$$c = \begin{cases} \dfrac{28\frac{2}{5}}{\frac{6}{5}} = 23\frac{2}{3} \\[2ex] \dfrac{196}{-12} = -16\frac{1}{3} \\[2ex] \dfrac{3}{-1} = -3 \end{cases}$$

Selecting the tightest limits of 3 on decreases and $23\frac{2}{3}$ on increases, the constraint requirement for minimum production of circular saws can be as low

TABLE 7-5
Summary of Limits on Changes in the Constraint Requirements for the White and Cardwell Problem That Leave the Set of Basic Variables Unchanged

	Corresponding slack/surplus variable	Maximum percent decrease	Lowest requirement	Stated requirement	Highest requirement	Maximum percent increase
Fabrication capacity, hours	S_1	78.89	190	900	1,145	27.22
Assembly capacity, hours	S_2	21.78	704	900	N.L.*	N.L.
Minimum drill production, thousands	S_3	100.00	0	5	$40\frac{1}{2}$	710.00
Minimum circular saw production, thousands	S_4	100.00	0	3	$26\frac{2}{3}$	788.89

*No limit.

as zero $(3 - 3)$ or as high as $26\frac{2}{3} = (3 + 23\frac{2}{3})$ without changing the optimal set of basic variables.

245

POSTOPTIMALITY
ANALYSIS AND
DUALITY FOR
LINEAR
PROGRAMMING

A summary of the allowable changes in the constraint requirements for all four constraints is given in Table 7-5. In all cases the change in requirements must be relatively high before a change in the set of basic variables occurs. The two to watch most closely would be increases in fabrication capacity and decreases in assembly capacity.

Note that there is no point in performing sensitivity tests on artificial variables. They have no real-world counterparts and, as we have seen, drop out of the tableau when no longer needed.

Before continuing with our examination of solution sensitivity, we need to pause to consider the concept of *duality,* which is a powerful property of linear programming. We will see shortly how duality can be used to facilitate other sensitivity considerations.

Duality

Until now all the linear programming problems that have been formulated and solved can be classified as *primal* problems. In each case the linear programming formulation was derived directly from the manner in which the problem was described. If the problem dealt with the maximization of profits, we formulated the problem so as to maximize profits; if the problem involved costs, we formulated it as a cost minimization problem.

As we shall see shortly, for every primal linear programming problem there exists an alternate formulation, referred to as the *dual* problem. This dual problem has several important and distinct relationships with the primal problem. The most important relationship is that once we have solved either the primal or dual problem, we have also obtained the optimal solution to the other problem.

At this point you may question why we even need consider the dual problem if indeed we can find the solution to the dual from the final tableau for the primal. The importance of the dual problem is derived from the interpretation and analysis of the dual solution results. Also, in some cases it is easier to solve the dual formulation of a problem than it is to solve the primal form, although this is a less important property.

The dual formulation attacks the problem from a different perspective than does the primal. Suppose, for example, the primal problem involves determining the highest profit production mix for a set of products, given limited quantities of production resources. The dual problem would attempt to find the minimum values of these production resources that would leave the manufacturer indifferent between selling the resources at these prices or using them in producing the optimal product mix. These relationships and the interpretation of the dual problem will become clearer after we have considered an example problem.

Relationship of Primal and Dual Problems

It is informative first to compare the graphical representations of a primal problem and its corresponding dual. To do this we return again to the Nevada Instruments problem. In order to graph both primal and dual versions for this problem, we have modified the original problem by dropping the IC chip constraint. (This will not affect the solution, since as you will recall, the IC chip constraint was not binding on the optimal solution. More chips were available than required.)

The primal formulation for the modified problem is thus:

$$\text{Maximize:} \quad 7C + 10A$$

$$\text{Subject to:} \quad 3C + 2A \leq 36 \quad \text{fabrication}$$

$$2C + 4A \leq 40 \quad \text{assembly}$$

$$C \geq 0, A \geq 0$$

The primal problem formulation can be one requiring maximization, such as profits, market share, or volume, or one requiring minimization, such as cost or absenteeism. The dual formulation uses *new* variables based on the constraints of the primal, requires minimization of the dual objective if the primal problem was one of maximization, and calls for maximization of the dual objective whenever the primal involves minimization.

This reversal of objective from maximization to minimization, or vice versa, is necessary because of the different perspective taken with the dual. Suppose the primal is a product mix problem requiring profit maximization subject to scarce resource constraints. In essence, the dual attempts to minimize the value of the available resources but also ensures that the values of the resources consumed are at least equal to the per-unit contribution for each product.

To illustrate for the Nevada Instruments problem, the dual formulation will have two variables, one corresponding to the value of the fabrication hours and one corresponding to the value of assembly capacity. The objective function coefficients for the dual variables are the equivalent capacities (right-hand-side coefficients) of the primal resources. Let F represent the dual variable for the value of fabrication capacity and H represent the dual variable for the value of assembly capacity. The dual objective function can thus be written as

Primal   *Dual objective function*

$$\text{Max.} \quad 7C + 10A \qquad\qquad \text{Min.} \quad 36F + 40H$$

$$\text{S.T.} \quad 3C + 2A \leq \boxed{36}$$

$$2C + 4A \leq \boxed{40}$$

In other words, the dual objective function wishes to minimize the value of fabrication and assembly capacity and could have been written in more general terms as

$$\begin{pmatrix} \text{Value of} \\ \text{each} \\ \text{fabrication} \\ \text{hour} \end{pmatrix} \times \begin{pmatrix} \text{number of} \\ \text{available} \\ \text{fabrication} \\ \text{hours} \end{pmatrix} + \begin{pmatrix} \text{value of} \\ \text{each} \\ \text{assembly} \\ \text{hour} \end{pmatrix} \times \begin{pmatrix} \text{number of} \\ \text{available} \\ \text{assembly} \\ \text{hours} \end{pmatrix}$$

The dual problem will have one constraint corresponding to each decision variable in the primal. Thus the dual will have a constraint for Computrons and one for Approximates. The right-hand sides for these new constraints are equal to the primal objective function coefficient for the primal decision variable corresponding to the dual constraint. Since each constraint in the dual is equivalent to a decision variable in the primal, the constraint utilization coefficients (rates at which resources are consumed) in the dual are identical to the utilization coefficients for that variable in the primal constraints.

247

POSTOPTIMALITY
ANALYSIS AND
DUALITY FOR
LINEAR
PROGRAMMING

Again, F represents the value of fabrication capacity, and H represents the value of assembly capacity. Thus, the constraints for the dual to the Nevada Instruments problem could be formed as

$$
\begin{array}{ll}
\textbf{Primal} & \textbf{Dual constraints} \\
\text{Max.} \quad 7C + 10A & \\
\text{S.T.} \quad 3C + 2A \le 36 & 3F + 2H \ge 7 \\
\quad\quad\; 2C + 4A \le 40 & 2F + 4H \ge 10
\end{array}
$$

These constraints ensure that the value of the resources consumed in manufacturing each product are at least equal to the contribution that can be earned. The first dual constraint, corresponding to Computrons, could have been written in more general terms as

$$
\begin{pmatrix} \text{Hours of} \\ \text{fabrication} \\ \text{per} \\ \text{Computron} \end{pmatrix} \times \begin{pmatrix} \text{value of} \\ \text{each} \\ \text{fabrication} \\ \text{hour} \end{pmatrix} + \begin{pmatrix} \text{hours of} \\ \text{assembly} \\ \text{per} \\ \text{Computron} \end{pmatrix} \times \begin{pmatrix} \text{value of} \\ \text{each} \\ \text{assembly} \\ \text{hour} \end{pmatrix} \ge \begin{pmatrix} \text{contribution} \\ \text{earned} \\ \text{per} \\ \text{Computron} \end{pmatrix}
$$

After adding the nonnegativity constraints, we write the complete primal and dual formulations for the modified Nevada Instruments problem as

$$
\begin{array}{ll}
\textbf{Primal} & \textbf{Dual} \\
\text{Max.} \quad 7C + 10A & \text{Min.} \quad 36F + 40H \\
\text{S.T.} \quad 3C + 2A \le 36 & \text{S.T.} \quad 3F + 2H \ge 7 \\
\quad\quad\;\; 2C + 4A \le 40 & \quad\quad\;\; 2F + 4H \ge 10 \\
\quad\quad\;\; C \ge, A \ge 0 & \quad\quad\;\; F \ge 0, H \ge 0
\end{array}
$$

Figure 7-6 provides a pictorial comparison of the feasible regions and graphical solution to the primal and to the dual version of this problem. As the dotted lines indicate, there is an equivalency relationship between the extreme points of the two versions. Each extreme point in the primal corresponds to one point in the graphical version of the dual. Note, however, that only one of the extreme points for the primal feasible region has an equivalent point in the dual region that is also feasible. This equivalent pair of feasible points represents the optimal solution to both versions of the problem. In other words, the optimal extreme point to the primal problem is the *only* feasible point in the primal problem that corresponds to a feasible extreme point in the dual problem.

Note also that this feasibility equivalence works in both directions: The only feasible point in the dual problem that corresponds to a feasible extreme point in the primal problem is again the optimal solution. Furthermore, the values of the primal and dual objective functions are equal at their respective optimal points. The optimal solution of the primal corresponds to $C = 8$ and $A = 6$, yielding a primal objective function value of $7(8) + 10(6) = 116$. The

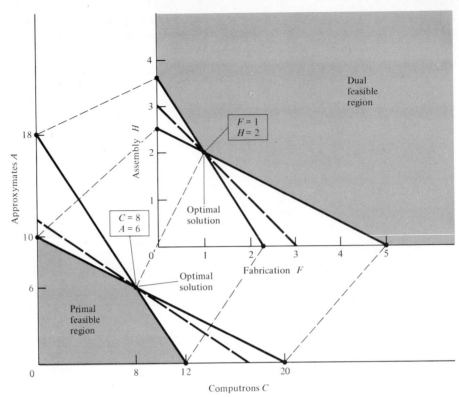

FIGURE 7-6 Comparison of primal and dual graphical solutions to Nevada Instruments problem (ignoring IC chip constraint).

optimal solution to the dual corresponds to $F - 1$ and $H - 2$, yielding a dual objective function value of $36(1) + 40(2) = 116$, which is identical to that for the primal solution.

Summary of Dual Problem Formulation

In general, the steps required to formulate the dual version of any linear programming problem can be summarized as follows:

1. For each constraint in the primal, establish a corresponding decision variable in the dual with an objective function coefficient equal to the right-hand side of the appropriate primal constraint.

2. If the primal problem is one of maximization with "less than or equal to" constraints, the dual problem will be one of minimization with "greater than or equal to" constraints.

3. For each variable in the primal problem, establish a corresponding constraint in the dual problem, with the right-hand-side constraint requirement equivalent to the corresponding objective function coefficient in the primal.

4. Since each constraint in the dual is equivalent to a decision variable in the primal, the constraint coefficients in the dual are equivalent to the coefficients for that variable in the primal constraints.

A complete summary of the primal/dual relationships is provided in Table 7-6.

Observe that although we have used a maximization example for the primal, thus generating a minimization problem for the dual, we could just as easily have begun with a minimization problem for the primal, which would produce a maximization problem for the dual. In this case we need only to reverse the column headings in Table 7-6 to show the corresponding relationships.

INSTANT REPLAY   Refer to the Battle Creek Breakfast Food problem first presented in Chapter 5. The original, or primal, formulation for that problem (where R = ounces of rice and C = ounces of corn) was given as

$$\text{Minimize:} \quad .08R + .12C$$

$$\text{Subject to:} \quad .2R + .5C \geq 1 \qquad \text{vitamin A constraint}$$

$$.4R + .2C \geq 1 \qquad \text{vitamin D constraint}$$

$$R \geq 0, \quad C \geq 0$$

Formulate the dual for this problem.

CHECK   Maximize: $K + L$

$$\text{Subject to:} \quad .2K + .4L \leq .08 \qquad \text{rice constraint}$$

$$.5K + .2L \leq .12 \qquad \text{corn constraint}$$

$$K \geq 0, L \geq 0$$

As is true for the dual of maximization problems, an economic interpretation of the dual variables can be provided for a primal minimization problem. Referring to the instant replay above, dual variable K corresponds to the vitamin A constraint and dual variable L corresponds to the vitamin D constraint. In each case, the dual variable represents the value of the corresponding vita-

TABLE 7-6
Summary of Duality Relationships

Primal element	Corresponding dual element
Maximization	"Greater than or equal to" constraints
"Less than or equal to" constraints	Minimization
Objective function coefficients	Right-hand-side constraint requirements
Right-hand-side constraint requirements	Objective function coefficients
Real variables	Constraints
Constraints	Real variables
Coefficients in the ith constraint	Constraint coefficients for the ith variable

min. In other words, if we could purchase one unit of vitamin A directly (rather than indirectly by purchasing rice or corn which contain vitamin A), we would be willing to pay K dollars to do so. The constraints ensure that the prices we would be willing to pay for these vitamins directly do not exceed the cost of obtaining the vitamins indirectly by purchasing corn or rice.

Relationship of Primal and Dual Solutions

We can solve the dual problem using the same linear programming solution methods we used for the primal: graphic, algebraic, and simplex. One advantage of the dual problem is that it may be easier to solve than the primal. If the primal problem is one of minimization with "greater than or equal to" constraints, artificial variables need to be added, as we saw in Chapter 6. The dual, on the other hand, would take the form of a maximization problem with "less than or equal to" constraints. Solution to this problem should be easier, since we do not need to add artificial variables.

Refer to Table 7-7, which contains the optimal tableau for the primal version of the Nevada Instruments problem (the full version including the IC chip constraint), and Table 7-8, which shows the optimal tableau for the dual version. (Dual variable I represents the now-added IC chip constraint.) Although it will not be obvious at this point, we can obtain the optimal solution to the dual problem from the optimal simplex tableau for the primal. Since the relationship between the primal and dual problems is reversible, the solution to the primal can also be found by examining the optimal simplex tableau for the dual. We will now compare the elements of the two tableaus to illustrate the close relationship between the primal and dual solutions.

Recall that for every decision variable in the primal there exists a corresponding constraint in the dual. Similarly, the dual contains one decision variable for every constraint in the primal. You may observe that the primal solution values are identical to the net-change values for the corresponding surplus variables in the dual, and that the solution values for the primal slack variables are equivalent to the net-change values for the corresponding dual decision variables:

TABLE 7-7
Optimal Tableau for Primal Version of Nevada Instruments Problem

Objective coefficients	Basic variables	Entering gains	7	10	0	0	0
		Values	C	A	S_1	S_2	S_3
7	C	8	1	0	$\frac{1}{2}$	$-\frac{1}{4}$	0
10	A	6	0	1	$-\frac{1}{4}$	$\frac{3}{8}$	0
0	S_3	2	0	0	$-\frac{1}{2}$	$\frac{1}{4}$	1
	Objective function	Entering costs	7	10	1	2	0
	116	Net change	0	0	-1	-2	0

251

POSTOPTIMALITY
ANALYSIS AND
DUALITY FOR
LINEAR
PROGRAMMING

Primal variables	Solution values
C	8
A	6
S_1	0
S_2	0
S_3	2

Dual variables	Net change
S_1	8
S_2	6
F	0
H	0
I	2

A similar relationship exists between the solution values for the dual variables and the net-change values for the corresponding primal variables, allowing for a change in sign:

Dual variables	Solution values
F	1
H	2
I	0
S_1	0
S_2	0

Primal variables	Net change
S_1	-1
S_2	-2
S_3	0
C	0
A	0

Thus, if we have solved the primal problem, we can find the optimal solution to the dual from the corresponding net-change values in the optimal primal tableau. Alternatively, if the optimal tableau for the dual problem is available, we can obtain the optimal values for the primal variables from the net-change row of the final dual tableau. If the tableau being examined, whether primal or dual, represents a maximization problem, the net-change values will be negative, requiring a simple change in sign to obtain the solution to the companion minimization problem.

A second point of agreement between the two tableaus is that the optimal objective function values (116) are identical, as was demonstrated graphically

TABLE 7-8
Optimal Tableau for Dual Version of Nevada Instruments Problem

Objective coefficients	Basic variables	Entering gains	36	40	10	0	0
		Values	F	H	I	S_1	S_2
36	F	1	1	0	$\frac{1}{2}$	$-\frac{1}{2}$	$\frac{1}{4}$
40	H	2	0	1	$-\frac{1}{4}$	$\frac{1}{4}$	$-\frac{3}{8}$
	Objective function	Entering costs	36	40	8	-8	-6
	116	Net change	0	0	2	8	6

earlier. For the primal this value represents the total contribution to profit achieved by producing the values shown for the decision variables, Computrons and Approxymates. An interpretation of this value for the dual is that it is equivalent to the optimal value of the scarce resources available for production of Computrons and Approxymates. Thus, for the optimal solution, the total value of the resources is exactly equal to the total contribution obtained. The value of the resources is equivalent to the contribution that can be earned by converting them into Computrons and Approxymates.

Another common point concerns the constraint coefficients. To illustrate, consider the constraint coefficients for variable S_1 in the primal problem. The analogue of S_1 in the dual is variable F. The constraint coefficients for variable F relating to the nonbasic variables in the dual tableau are identical, after a change of sign, to the constraint coefficients for variable S_1 relating to the basic variables in the primal tableau:

Nonbasic dual variables	Constraint coefficients relating to variable F		Basic primal variables	Constraint coefficients relating to variable S_1
I	$\frac{1}{2}$		S_3	$-\frac{1}{2}$
S_1	$-\frac{1}{2}$		C	$\frac{1}{2}$
S_2	$\frac{1}{4}$		A	$-\frac{1}{4}$

Similar identities exist with respect to the other companion variables.

It is also important to recognize the significance of the relationship between the solution values for the decision variables in the primal problem and the net-change values in the dual, as well as the corresponding relationship between primal net-change and dual-solution values. This relationship will be examined in the next section, to provide a new perspective on the simplex method.

Interpreting Nonoptimal Simplex Tableaus Recall that a nonoptimal tableau for a maximization problem is identified by one or more positive net-change values. For example, the initial tableau for the Nevada Instruments problem showed net-change values of $C = 7$ and $A = 10$ for the decision variables and net-change values of 0 for all three slack variables. Since the net-change values for primal slack variables are equivalent to solution values for the dual-decision variables, we can think of these values as trial-solution values for the dual problem. Substituting these trial values of zero into the constraint equations for the dual problem, we find that neither constraint is satisfied:

$$3(0) + 2(0) + 1(0) \geq 7 \qquad 2(0) + 4(0) + 0(0) \geq 10$$

$$0 \neq 7 \qquad\qquad 0 \neq 10$$

Thus the initial feasible solution to the primal problem is infeasible with respect to the dual. Furthermore, the degree of infeasibility, as represented by the difference between the left- and right-hand sides of the dual constraints, is exactly equal to the net-change values for the primal decision variables. This relationship will in fact be true at every step in the solution process.

As a further example, the second primal solution for the Nevada Instru-

253

POSTOPTIMALITY
ANALYSIS AND
DUALITY FOR
LINEAR
PROGRAMMING

ments problem corresponded to $C = 0$ and $A = 10$, and the net-change values for the slack variables were 0, $2\frac{1}{2}$, and 0 for S_1, S_2, and S_3, respectively. Substituting the net-change values for the slack variables as trial values for the dual decision variables yields the following dual constraint relationships:

$$3(0) + 2(2\tfrac{1}{2}) + 1(0) \geq 7 \qquad 2(0) + 4(2\tfrac{1}{2}) + 0(0) \geq 10$$

$$5 \neq 7 \qquad\qquad\qquad\qquad 10 = 10$$

Clearly, the first constraint, corresponding to variable C in the primal, is not satisfied. In fact, the difference between the two sides of the constraint, 2, is exactly equal to the net-change value for variable C in the primal tableau. The second dual constraint was satisfied, and the net-change value for variable A in the primal tableau was zero, the same as the difference between the two sides of that constraint.

If we take the net-change values for the primal slack variables in the optimal tableau and, after changing the signs, substitute them for the values of the dual variables in the dual constraints, we find

$$3(1) + 2(2) + 1(0) \geq 7 \qquad 2(1) + 4(2) + 0(0) \geq 10$$

$$7 = 7 \qquad\qquad\qquad\qquad 10 = 10$$

Both dual constraints are exactly balanced. The differences of zero correspond to the final net-change values for the primal decision variables.

From this we can develop a new understanding of the relationship between the primal and dual problems: The simplex algorithm is, essentially, a search among the extreme points that satisfy primal feasibility, in which the direction of the search is based on the degree of infeasibility for the dual problem. This search terminates as soon as a primal feasible extreme point is found that is also dual feasible.

Mixed Inequalities   In the preceding discussion of duality we assumed that the constraints for the primal problem were all of the same type, "less than or equal to" for a maximization problem or "greater than or equal to" for a minimization problem. If these conditions do not hold, a simple correction is necessary before the dual problem can be formulated.

If the primal problem is one of maximization and it contains a "greater than or equal to" constraint, we need to multiply both sides of that constraint by (-1). In so doing we reverse the direction of the inequality so that it becomes a "less than or equal to" constraint. A similar correction would be necessary if a minimization problem contained a "less than or equal to" constraint.

A simple example will demonstrate the soundness of the suggested adjustment. If, for example, we have an inequality requiring

$$2X \leq 10$$

substitution will show that $X = 4$ will satisfy that constraint but $X = 6$ will not.

As stated above, if we multiply both sides of the constraint by (-1), we must reverse the direction of the inequality. Thus, for our example, we obtain

$$-2X \geq -10$$

Substituting the values $X = 4$ and $X = 6$ will show that, as before, the constraint is satisfied for $X = 4$ but not for $X = 6$.

Earlier in this chapter the primal version of the White and Cardwell problem was formulated as

Maximize: $TC = 2D + 5J + 4C + 2R$

Subject to:
$$20D + 25J + 30C + 15R \leq 900$$
$$20D + 20J + 12C + 10R \leq 900$$
$$D \geq 5$$
$$C \geq 3$$
$$D \geq 0, J \geq 0, C \geq 0, R \geq 0$$

Since the third and fourth constraints are inequalities in the "wrong" direction for a maximization problem, we need to multiply each by (-1) before forming the dual. The revised primal is thus

Maximize: $TC = 2D + 5J + 4C + 2R$

Subject to:
$$20D + 25J + 30C + 15R \leq 900$$
$$20D + 20J + 12C + 10R \leq 900$$
$$-1D \leq -5$$
$$-1C \leq -3$$
$$D \geq 0, J \geq 0, C \geq 0, R \geq 0$$

The dual problem can now be correctly formulated as

Minimize: $900W + 900X - 5Y - 3Z$

Subject to:
$$20W + 20X - 1Y \geq 2$$
$$25W + 20X \geq 5$$
$$30W + 12X - 1Z \geq 4$$
$$15W + 10X \geq 2$$
$$W \geq 0, X \geq 0, Y \geq 0, Z \geq 0$$

Equality constraints require a slightly more complex adjustment. Before the dual problem is formed, the primal equality constraint must first be replaced with two inequalities. One of the replacing constraints is of the "greater than or equal to" form, and the other is of the "less than or equal to" form. Thus, if we had a constraint of the form

$$3A + 4B + 2C = 100$$

it would be replaced by

$$3A + 4B + 2C \geq 100$$
$$3A + 4B + 2C \leq 100$$

Since one of these two constraints will be in the "wrong" direction, it must be adjusted, as described earlier, by multiplying both sides by (-1). If, for example, the equality constraint given above applied to a maximization problem, the "greater than or equal to" form of the replacing constraints would need to be adjusted. In this case the final form of the replacing constraints would be

$$-3A - 4B - 2C \leq -100$$

$$3A + 4B + 2C \leq 100$$

On the other hand, if the primal problem required minimization, the adjustment would be applied to the "less than or equal to" constraint, leaving

$$3A + 4B + 2C \geq 100$$

$$-3A - 4B - 2C \geq -100$$

When all the constraints for a maximization problem are converted to "less than or equal to" form or for a minimization problem to "greater than or equal to" constraints, the dual problem can easily be formed by following the steps described earlier or by referring to Table 7-6.

INSTANT REPLAY Suppose we have the following primal problem:

Maximize: $3A + 4B + 2C$

Subject to: $A + B + C = 100$

$2A + 3B + 4C \leq 350$

$3A + 2B + C \geq 300$

$A \geq 0, B \geq 0, C \geq 0$

Formulate the dual for this problem.

CHECK Using W, X, Y, and Z as the dual variables we find

Minimize: $-100W + 100X + 350Y - 300Z$

Subject to: $-W + X + 2Y - 3Z \geq 3$

$-W + X + 3Y - 2Z \geq 4$

$-W + X + 4Y - Z \geq 2$

$W \geq 0, X \geq 0, Y \geq 0, Z \geq 0$

Using the Dual in Sensitivity Analysis

In the following sections we shall see how knowledge of the primal-dual relationship permits us to examine several postoptimality questions that have important managerial implications. These include: (1) What is the marginal value of additional resources? (2) What is the impact of considering additional decision variables? (3) What is the effect of changes in the resource utilization coefficients? The ability to answer these questions will allow us to test the impact of various optional formulations of the problem without having to resolve the problem from scratch. In this way we can easily deal with alternatives such as purchasing additional raw materials at higher than normal prices (due to supply shortages), producing a new product not included in the original problem formulation, or altering the method of producing one or more items so as to change the resource utilization rates.

Determining Marginal Resource Values   The optimal values for the dual variables provide important sensitivity information by themselves. If the dual variable corresponds to a "less than or equal to" constraint, its optimal solution values can be interpreted as the *marginal value of the scarce resource* to which the primal constraint refers. This marginal value is equivalent to the increase in the objective function that would result if one more unit of that resource was available. In the case of "greater than or equal to" constraints, the optimal value of the corresponding dual variable represents the *marginal cost associated with that minimum restriction*. Thus, marginal cost refers to the increase in the objective function (which we are trying to minimize) that would result from a unit increase in the minimum restriction.

To illustrate, recall that there were three constraints to the Nevada Instruments problem—fabrication time, assembly time, and number of IC chips. The optimal values of the three dual variables associated with these constraints were 1, 2, and 0, respectively. These amounts represent, respectively, the marginal value of an additional unit of fabrication time, assembly time, and IC chips. In other words, if 1 more hour of fabrication capacity was available, the objective function, or total contribution to profit, could be increased by $1.

Where did this $1 increase come from? Refer again to Table 7-7, the optimal primal tableau. The constraint coefficients for slack variable S_1 (corresponding to fabrication time) represent the amount of each basic variable to be given up in order to increase the slack variable by 1 unit. Since an increase in the slack variable is identical to a reduction of 1 hour in available fabrication time, it follows that a reduction of 1 unit in the slack variable should be equivalent to an increase of 1 hour in available fabrication time. Therefore, what were treated as *entering costs* for that slack variable when available fabrication capacity was reduced must be interpreted as *entering gains* for that slack variable when available fabrication time is increased. This is why the net-change value for S_1 of -1 can be interpreted as a marginal value of $1 per unit increase in fabrication time.

An identical analysis will show that the marginal value of an additional hour of assembly time is $2. Why did the third dual variable, corresponding to the IC chip constraint, turn out to have a zero value? The answer is found by noting that slack variable S_3 had a nonzero value of 2 in the optimal solution. That means that 2 cases of IC chips were unused in the optimal production schedule. If we have 2 cases of excess IC chips now, additional cases of these chips will add nothing to the total contribution of the optimal solution. Therefore, the marginal value of an additional case must be zero.

Observe that the values we are associating with these resources are different from the costs that we may incur to obtain them. For instance, we assigned a value of 0 to IC chips. Clearly these chips were not free, and it cost the company something to obtain them. The marginal resource values refer to the effect that changes in the quantity of the resources available will cause in the objective function value. Because the optimal solution leaves 2 cases of chips unused, 1 more or 1 less case of chips will not affect the optimal solution or the value of the objective function. Thus, the marginal value of 1 case of chips is 0 even though its real cost was nonzero.

Using Marginal Resource Values Marginal resource values are useful from a managerial standpoint because they can be used as a basis for deciding whether or not it is beneficial *to acquire additional units of the scarce resources*. For instance, it may be possible to authorize the fabrication and assembly departments to work overtime, thereby increasing the available capacity in those departments. But unless the marginal cost of overtime is less than $1 per hour in the fabrication department or $2 per hour in the assembly department, such overtime will not be profitable. Clearly, no matter how inexpensively we may be able to purchase additional IC chips, it would not pay to do so since their marginal value is 0.

You should, however, be aware that these marginal values are applicable only over a *limited range*. A preceding section examined how far we could change each of the resource capacities without changing the optimal set of basic variables. These limits in turn define the range over which the marginal resource values are applicable.

To illustrate, the marginal resource values for fabrication and assembly time for the the White and Cardwell problem are $0.20 and $0, respectively. See Table 7-4, where they are represented by the net-change values of slack variables S_1 and S_2 in the optimal tableau. The maximum changes in these constraint requirements are summarized in Table 7-5: Fabrication time can be increased by as much as 245 hours or decreased by as much as 710 hours. Assembly time can be increased as desired or decreased by as much as 196 hours. With this information we conclude that the marginal value for fabrication time is applicable to any changes in fabrication capacity that fall within the limits of up to a 245-hour increase or a 710-hour decrease. The marginal value for assembly time is similarly restricted to a maximum decrease of 196 hours with no limit on increases (because of its existing excess supply).

Note that the other two constraints (minimum production requirements for drills and circular saws) were of the "greater than or equal to" variety. The net-change values for slack variables S_3 (−2) and S_4 (−2) are therefore interpreted as the marginal cost associated with a change in the production restrictions. For example, if we increase the minimum production requirement for drills, the total contribution will decrease by $2 for each unit increase in the production requirement. Similarly, total contribution will fall $2 for each unit increase in the minimum production requirement for circular saws. Alternatively, decreases in either minimum requirement will produce a $2 increase in contribution for each unit of decrease.

As shown in Table 7-5, these marginal costs apply as long as the minimum production requirements for drills are not reduced by more than 5 or increased by more than $35\frac{1}{2}$ and as long as the requirement for circular saws is not decreased by more than 3 or increased by more than $23\frac{2}{3}$. (Recall that these requirements are in thousands of units.)

Adding New Decision Variables Another way in which the dual problem formulation is useful is in evaluating the impact of additional decision variables. For instance, White and Cardwell may be considering the introduction of a new product, such as an electric sander. Suppose that for purposes of the initial problem formulation, one or more of these potential decision variables had been excluded. Such exclusion might have been based on a low preliminary estimate of relative profitability. Alternatively, the excluded variable may represent a newly developed product, knowledge of which was not available at the time the original problem was formulated and solved.

Fortunately, an easy test is available to determine whether or not such excluded variables would cause the optimal solution to change if they are included. The test is simple to carry out and avoids the necessity of having to resolve the problem from scratch. Recall that there is a dual constraint associated with each primal decision variable. Thus, including a new decision variable in our problem formulation is equivalent to adding one additional constraint to the dual problem. If the previously obtained optimal values for the dual variables satisfy this additional dual constraint, the current solution remains optimal. It is therefore not worthwhile to consider the excluded decision variable. If, on the other hand, the additional dual constraint is not satisfied, the current solution can be improved by considering the new decision variable.

For example, suppose we consider a new line of calculators for the Nevada Instruments problem. This new calculator, the Supercalc, is estimated to have a contribution of $12 per case. Production requirements have been estimated at 3 hours of fabrication time and 5 hours of assembly time. The Supercalc uses a newly developed IC chip for which adequate supplies are available.

The dual constraint corresponding to the Supercalc would thus be

$$3F + 5H + 0I \geq 12$$

We found previously that the optimal values of the dual variables were $F = 1, H = 2$, and $I = 0$. Substituting these values into the new constraint yields

$$3(1) + 5(2) + 0(0) \geq 12$$

$$13 \geq 12$$

Since this new dual constraint is satisfied by the current values of the dual variables, the dual solution remains feasible and the original solution found is optimal. Thus, we would get the same optimal production decision (produce 8 cases of Computrons and 6 cases of Approxymates) whether or not we included the Supercalc in the formulation of the Nevada Instruments problem. In fact, we can see from the difference between the left and right sides of the constraint that the contribution from the Supercalc would have to be greater than $13 per case before it would be profitable to produce, given the existing resource constraints.

Since the values of the dual variables represent the marginal value of the scarce resources, we can interpret the above result as indicating that the value of resources used up in producing the Supercalc exceeds the value obtained (by $1 per unit), and therefore we should not add this item to the production line.

INSTANT REPLAY Suppose that Nevada Instruments is also considering a new, cheaper version of the Computron. This new Computron II is expected to require 2 hours per case in both the fabrication and assembly departments and will utilize the same IC chip as the regular Computron. What contribution per case would be required before we would consider altering the present production schedule?

CHECK The minimum contribution would be $6 per case as found from the dual constraint ($2F + 2H + 1I \geq$ contribution) and the optimal values of the dual variables ($F = 1$, $H = 2$, and $I = 0$).

Changes in Resource Utilization Rates We can also use dual constraints to examine changes in the resource utilization rates embodied in the resource constraints. In this way we can, for example, consider alternative production processes with different utilization rates for the resources. Thus, we might consider subcontracting some of the fabrication or assembly requirements for one of the calculators. This would reduce both the contribution received (due to subcontracting cost) and the fabrication or assembly requirements to manufacture the calculator. We restrict our attention to nonbasic decision variables. The analysis required for basic variables is beyond the scope of this text.

For primal nonbasic variables we can determine whether or not the change in the utilization rates or constraint coefficients maintains the feasibility of the corresponding dual constraint. To illustrate, we refer again to the Nevada Instruments problem. In the preceding section we considered the addition of a new calculator, the Supercalc, whose dual constraint required that

$$3F + 5H + 0I \geq 12$$

Substituting the optimal values of the dual variables showed that it was not profitable to produce the Supercalc. Thus, if we had included the Supercalc in the original problem, the final tableau would have shown the Supercalc to be a nonbasic variable.

Suppose that some of the fabrication and assembly requirements for the Supercalc can be subcontracted to other manufacturers. Assume that the subcontracting costs will reduce the contribution of the Supercalc from $12 to $9 but that concurrently the production requirements will be lowered to 2 hours of fabrication time and 4 hours of assembly time.

The profitability of this production alternative can be evaluated by examining the feasibility of the dual constraint. The new dual constraint becomes

$$2F + 4H + 0I \geq 9$$

Feasibility is ascertained by substitution of the current values of the dual variables:

$$2(1) + 4(2) + 0(0) \geq 9$$

$$10 \geq 9$$

Since the dual constraint remains feasible, we again conclude that it would not be profitable to produce the Supercalc even on a subcontracting basis.

INSTANT REPLAY By how much would assembly time have to decrease to make the subcontracting option profitable, assuming the fabrication time remains at 2 hours and that contribution is $9 per case of Supercalcs?

CHECK If assembly time is less than $3\frac{1}{2}$ hours per case, the subcontracting option will alter the optimal solution.

Using a Computer for Postoptimality Analysis

Most linear programming computer packages provide the option of obtaining sensitivity analysis information automatically. You may recall that the hypothetical computer program first presented in Chapter 5 had several run options, one of which (code 1) included sensitivity information as part of the program output.

Figure 7-7 illustrates the sensitivity-related output that would be provided for the White and Cardwell example problem introduced earlier. Note that four types of sensitivity information are provided: (1) shadow prices (marginal resource values) for each constraint, (2) net-change values for nonbasic decision variables, (3) upper and lower bounds on the right-hand-side coefficients for each of the constraints, and (4) upper and lower bounds on the objective function coefficients for the decision variables.

In interpreting the output shown in Figure 7-7, variables 1 to 4 correspond to the decision variables for the number of drills, jigsaws, circular saws, and routers, respectively, to be produced. Variables 5 and 6 correspond to the slack variables for the fabrication and assembly capacity constraints, respectively.

FIGURE 7-7 Sensitivity analysis output for linear programming computer solution of White and Cardwell example problem.

```
SENSITIVITY ANALYSIS

SHADOW PRICES FOR CONSTRAINTS

    5        0.200
    6        0.0
    7        2.000
    8        2.000
```

```
1 = number of drills
2 = number of jigsaws
3 = number of circular saws
4 = number of routers
5 = fabrication slack
6 = assembly slack
7 = minimum drill production surplus
8 = minimum circular saw production
    surplus
```

```
NET CHANGE VALUES FOR NONBASIC DECISION VARIABLES

    4       -1.000
```

```
SENSITIVITY ANALYSIS ON RIGHT HAND SIDE COEFFICIENTS
```

VARIABLE	LOWER BOUND	ACTUAL	UPPER BOUND
5	190.000	900.000	1145.000
6	704.000	900.000	NONE
7	0.0	5.000	40.500
8	0.0	3.000	26.666

```
SENSITIVITY ANALYSIS ON OBJECTIVE COEFFICIENTS
```

VARIABLE	LOWER BOUND	ACTUAL	UPPER BOUND
1	NONE	2.000	4.000
2	3.333	5.000	NONE
3	NONE	4.000	6.000
4	NONE	2.000	3.000

Variables 7 and 8 are the surplus variables for the minimum production constraints for drills and circular saws, respectively.

261

POSTOPTIMALITY
ANALYSIS AND
DUALITY FOR
LINEAR
PROGRAMMING

The marginal resource values (shadow prices) and final net-change values for the nonbasic decision variables shown in Figure 7-7 are exactly the same values shown in the final simplex tableau (see Table 7-4). The upper and lower bounds on the right-hand-side coefficients are identical to those calculated manually in the text and summarized in Table 7-5. The upper and lower bounds on the objective coefficients for the decision variables are the same as those found earlier and reported in Table 7-3.

Note, however, that several sensitivity analysis issues we treated earlier in the chapter—the addition of new decision variables and changes in the resource utilization rates—are not handled automatically by this hypothetical computer program. These issues can, however, be dealt with easily by using the dual formulation and the optimal values of the dual variables (as demonstrated earlier). The computer output lists the optimal values for the dual variables under the heading "Shadow Prices for Constraints."

Final Comments

The two preceding chapters on linear programming have treated the formulation and solution, by various means, of linear programming problems. This chapter is of considerable managerial significance because it shows how you, as a manager, can use the information embodied in the solution to examine a variety of questions dealing with the practical implementation of that solution. In particular, we have seen how the sensitivity of the optimal solution to changes in the problem parameters can be explored via postoptimality analysis.

Although, of necessity, a sizable portion of the chapter is devoted to the mechanics of performing sensitivity analysis, the kinds of managerial issues that can be considered are also illustrated. We have seen how potential price or cost changes related to the decision variables can be examined in regard to their effects on the optimal solution. We have also looked at the impact of resource constraints. This makes it possible to consider potential changes in the levels of these resources as well as to determine their value. These marginal resource values are particularly useful because they allow you to evaluate the economic implications of potential changes in resource availability. In addition, we have seen how other managerial decision alternatives can be incorporated. These include alternative manufacturing processes (by varying resource utilization rates) and previously unconsidered decision alternatives, such as new products.

One reason sensitivity analysis for linear programming problems is so powerful is that these "what if" questions can be answered easily and quickly by examining the original solution to the problem. This avoids the tedious alternative of reformulating the problem and resolving from scratch. As we have seen, many linear programming computer packages will provide most of the sensitivity information automatically.

We have also seen that there are two ways of formulating any linear programming problem. One of these was called the primal formulation and the other the dual. Consideration of the dual problem provides new insight into the operation of the simplex method and is also valuable in performing and understanding sensitivity analyses.

The next chapter will examine several complications that can arise in formulating and solving linear programming problems. A major portion of that chapter will be devoted to problems with multiple objectives. It will show how a modified version of the simplex method, called the goal programming procedure, can be used to solve a specific class of multiple-objective problems.

Key Words

Problems

7-1. Formulate the dual problem based on the following primal problem:

$$\text{Maximize:} \quad 3A + 2B + 7C$$

$$\begin{aligned}
\text{Subject to:} \quad A + B + C &\le 50 \\
2A + 5B + 2C &\le 200 \\
A \ge 0, B \ge 0, C &\ge 0
\end{aligned}$$

7-2. Formulate the dual problem based on the following primal problem:

$$\text{Minimize:} \quad 5X + 3Y + 4Z$$

$$\begin{aligned}
\text{Subject to:} \quad 3X - 2Y \quad &\ge 50 \\
X + Y + Z &\ge 30 \\
2X + \tfrac{1}{2}Y + Z &\ge 20 \\
X \ge 0, Y \ge 0, Z &\ge 0
\end{aligned}$$

7-3. Formulate the primal problem based on the following dual problem:

$$\text{Minimize:} \quad 4P + 3Q + 2R + 1S$$

$$\begin{aligned}
\text{Subject to:} \quad P + Q + R + S &\ge 7 \\
P + 2Q + R + 3S &\ge 25 \\
P \ge 0, Q \ge 0, R \ge 0, S &\ge 0
\end{aligned}$$

7-4. The commissioner of the Sanitation Department for the city of Metropolis is attempting to allocate sanitation crews among the available assignments. Each crew is capable of being assigned to one of three tasks: (1) street sweeping, (2) refuse collection, and (3) motorized litter patrols. The commissioner has 100 crews to be assigned to these tasks. The tons of refuse that can be collected per crew shift are shown in the table below.

263

POSTOPTIMALITY
ANALYSIS AND
DUALITY FOR
LINEAR
PROGRAMMING

Crew assigned to	Tons of refuse collected per shift
Street sweeping	7
Refuse collection	10
Motorized litter patrol	8

The number of crews assigned to refuse collection must be not less than 50 nor more than 80. The number of crews assigned to motorized litter patrol cannot exceed 25, and the number assigned to street sweeping cannot exceed 30.

    a. Formulate the commissioner's crew assignment problem so as to maximize the number of tons of refuse collected.

    b. Formulate the dual problem corresponding to your answer to part a.

7-5. Formulate the dual problem corresponding to the following primal problem:

$$\text{Minimize:} \quad .1A + .15B$$

$$\text{Subject to:} \quad 2A + 5B \geq 10$$

$$A + B = 8$$

$$.5A - 3B \leq 0$$

$$A \geq 0, B \geq 0$$

7-6. Provide an economic interpretation of the dual variables corresponding to each of the following constraints. In other words, what would the dual variables corresponding to these constraints represent?

    a. Capacity limitation on the number of hours available in the finishing department

    b. Capacity limitation on the amount of plywood available

    c. Restriction on the maximum amount of advertising dollars spent in television advertising

    d. Restriction on the minimum proportion by weight of protein

    e. Restriction on the minimum inventory level

    f. Restriction on the maximum number of retail outlets

    g. Restriction on the minimum amount of goods shipped to a specific market area

7-7. Consider the following linear programming problem:

$$\text{Minimize:} \quad 10A + 20B + 30C$$

$$\text{Subject to:} \quad A + B + C \geq 100$$

$$4A + 3B + 2C \geq 320$$

$$C \geq 40$$

$$A \geq 0, B \geq 0, C \geq 0$$

The dual for this problem was formulated and solved. The final tableau is given below:

Objective coefficients for basic variables	Basic variables	Entering gains	100	320	40	0	0	0
		Values	X	Y	Z	S_1	S_2	S_3
320	Y	$2\frac{1}{2}$	$\frac{1}{4}$	1	0	$\frac{1}{4}$	0	0
0	S_2	$12\frac{1}{2}$	$\frac{1}{4}$	0	0	$-\frac{3}{4}$	1	0
40	Z	25	$\frac{1}{2}$	0	1	$-\frac{1}{2}$	0	1
	Objective function	Entering costs	100	320	40	60	0	40
1,800		Net change	0	0	0	-60	0	-40

a. Formulate the dual mathematically.
b. What is the solution to the dual?
c. What is the solution to the primal?

7-8. Consider the following linear programming problem:

$$\text{Maximize: } 3A + 7B + 5C$$
$$\text{Subject to: } A + B + C \le 100$$
$$2A + 3B + C \le 200$$
$$A \ge 0, B \ge 0, C \ge 0$$

The final optimal tableau for this problem is

Objective coefficients for basic variables	Basic variables	Entering gains	3	7	5	0	0
		Values	A	B	C	S_1	S_2
5	C	50	$\frac{1}{2}$	0	1	$\frac{3}{2}$	$-\frac{1}{2}$
7	B	50	$\frac{1}{2}$	1	0	$-\frac{1}{2}$	$\frac{1}{2}$
	Objective function	Entering costs	6	7	5	4	1
600		Net change	-3	0	0	-4	-1

a. What is the optimal solution to this problem?
b. Formulate the dual problem.
c. What is the optimal solution to the dual?
d. For what range of objective function coefficients for variables A, B, and C will the solution remain optimal?
e. For what range of constraint capacities will the optimal set of basic variables remain unchanged?

f. What would the optimal objective function value be if the right-hand side of the first constraint were 120 instead of 100?

POSTOPTIMALITY
ANALYSIS AND
DUALITY FOR
LINEAR
PROGRAMMING

7-9. The Wando Toy Company manufactures and distributes a wide range of children's toys. Currently the company is experiencing some capacity problems in the production and distribution of their very successful Babsie Doll line.

Two basic dolls, Babsie and Lenny, are currently produced and sold in a variety of packaged combinations:

Product	Dolls required	Total contribution
Babsie only	1 Babsie	1.50
Lenny only	1 Lenny	1.25
Babsie and Lenny combination	1 Babsie and 1 Lenny	2.50
Babsie airline set	None	2.00

Production requirements for these combinations include time for construction of the dolls and for assembly and packaging as shown below:

	Construction time, minutes	Assembly and packaging time, minutes
Babsie	10	5
Lenny	10	5
Babsie and Lenny combination	20	8
Babsie airline set	15	12

The construction time available each day is currently 10 hours, and 8 hours are available for assembly and packaging. Market limitations dictate that no more than 20 of either the Babsie/Lenny combination or the Babsie Airline Set should be produced per day. As a final constraint, the supplier of artificial hair used in producing the Babsie doll can provide only enough hair to produce 50 Babsie dolls per day. The Lenny doll has no such limitation.

Letting B, L, C, and A represent the daily number of Babsie, Lenny, combination, and airline sets, respectively, the primal problem is

$$\text{Maximize:} \quad 1.5B + 1.25L + 2.50C + 2.00A$$

$$
\begin{aligned}
\text{Subject to:} \quad 10B + 10L + 20C + 15A &\leq 600 \\
5B + 5L + 8C + 12A &\leq 480 \\
C &\leq 20 \\
A &\leq 20 \\
B \quad + \quad C &\leq 50 \\
B \geq 0, L \geq 0, C \geq 0, A &\geq 0
\end{aligned}
$$

After surplus variables were added, the simplex method was used to develop the following optimal tableau:

Objective coefficients for basic variables	Basic variables	Entering gains	1.50	1.25	2.50	2.00	0	0	0	0	0
		Values	B	L	C	A	S_1	S_2	S_3	S_4	S_5
1.50	B	50	1	0	1	0	0	0	0	0	1
0	S_2	150	0	-3	-5	0	$-\frac{4}{5}$	1	0	0	3
2.00	A	$\frac{20}{3}$	0	$\frac{2}{3}$	$\frac{2}{3}$	1	$\frac{1}{15}$	0	0	0	$-\frac{2}{3}$
0	S_4	$\frac{40}{3}$	0	$-\frac{2}{3}$	$-\frac{2}{3}$	0	$-\frac{1}{15}$	0	0	1	$\frac{2}{3}$
0	S_3	20	0	0	1	0	0	0	1	0	0
Objective function	Entering costs		1.5	$\frac{4}{3}$	$\frac{17}{6}$	2	$\frac{2}{15}$	0	0	0	$\frac{1}{6}$
$88\frac{1}{3}$	Net change		0	$-\frac{1}{12}$	$-\frac{1}{3}$	0	$-\frac{2}{15}$	0	0	0	$-\frac{1}{6}$

a. Identify the value of all variables and the objective function for the optimal solution to the primal problem.

b. Formulate the dual for this problem.

c. Identify the value of all variables and the objective function for the optimal solution to the dual problem.

d. Provide an economic interpretation of the dual variables.

e. Suppose that the costs of overtime in the construction and assembly/packaging departments are $7 per hour. Would it be profitable to work either department on an overtime basis? What would be the maximum amount of overtime authorized, if any?

f. Suppose that a price change is under consideration for the Lenny doll. This would boost the contribution for the Lenny doll from $1.25 to $1.75. Would this change the optimum production plan? What is the largest change in contribution for the Lenny doll that would not change the optimum production plan?

g. Alternatively, suppose that a price decrease for the Babsie airline set is under consideration. This would decrease the contribution from $2 to $1.75. Would this change the optimum production plan? What is the largest decrease in contribution that would not change the optimum production plan?

h. Suppose that it is possible to purchase additional quantities of artificial hair for the Babsie doll from another supplier, at a cost of $0.20 more per doll than that paid the regular supplier. Should such a purchase be made? If so, for how many dolls?

i. Product developers have proposed adding a new Babsie doll package called the Babsie Beauty Parlor. This new item comes with a Babsie doll and requires 12 minutes of construction time and 14 minutes of assembly time. What contribution would be necessary before the company would consider production of this new unit?

7-10. Problem 5-11 considered the production plans for the ABCD game. The primal problem could be formulated as

$$\text{Maximize:} \quad 3B + 2.50F$$

$$\text{Subject to:} \quad 2B + 3F \leq 60 \quad \text{printing capacity}$$

$$2B + 1F \leq 50 \quad \text{stamping capacity}$$

$$1B + 1F \leq 40 \quad \text{packaging capacity}$$

The dual formulation for this problem is

267

POSTOPTIMALITY
ANALYSIS AND
DUALITY FOR
LINEAR
PROGRAMMING

$$\text{Minimize:} \quad 60W + 50X + 40Y$$

$$\text{Subject to:} \quad 2W + 2X + 1Y \geq 3$$

$$3W + 1X + 1Y \geq 2.50$$

$$W \geq 0, X \geq 0, Y \geq 0$$

After slack variables were added to the primal version of the problem, the following optimal tableau was generated:

Objective coefficients for basic variables	Basic variables	Entering gains	3	$2\frac{1}{2}$	0	0	0
		Values	B	F	S_1	S_2	S_3
$2\frac{1}{2}$	F	5	0	1	$-\frac{1}{2}$	0	0
3	B	$22\frac{1}{2}$	1	0	$\frac{3}{4}$	$\frac{1}{2}$	0
0	S_3	$12\frac{1}{2}$	0	0	$-\frac{1}{4}$	$-\frac{1}{2}$	1
Objective function	Entering costs		3	$2\frac{1}{2}$	1	$1\frac{1}{2}$	0
80	Net change		0	0	-1	$-1\frac{1}{2}$	0

Convert this optimal primal tableau into the corresponding optimal dual tableau.

7-11. Lois Foster has just received a sizable inheritance from her rich Uncle Herbert's estate. After taxes and fees were deducted, and allowing for a few necessities Lois wishes to purchase (trip to Paris, new Porsche, etc.), she has $100,000 available for investing. Lois has examined a number of investment alternatives and has narrowed the list to four alternatives, shown below together with relevant characteristics for each:

Investment	Risk, %	Dividend rate, %	Growth potential, %
Atlas Aluminum	3	7	5
Berkley Biscuits	5	5	8
California Uranium	20	0	30
Nevada Instruments	10	3	15

Lois wishes to invest the entire $100,000 in such a way that she minimizes the average risk. She has also specified that cash flow from dividends should be at least $5,000 per year. In planning for the future, she desires an average growth potential of at least 12 percent.

Having learned linear programming in school, Lois was able to formulate her investment problem as

$$\text{Minimize:} \quad 3A + 5B + 20C + 10N$$

$$\text{Subject to:} \quad A + B + C + N \geq 100$$

$$7A + 5B + \qquad 3N \geq 500$$

$$5A + 8B + 30C + 15N \geq 12(A + B + C + N)$$

$$A \geq 0, B \geq 0, C \geq 0, N \geq 0$$

where A, B, C, and N are thousands of dollars invested in the four investment alternatives.

After adding slack and artificial variables, Lois used the simplex method to generate the following optimal simplex tableau.

Objective coefficients for basic variables	Basic variables	Entering gains	3	5	20	10	0	0	0
		Values	A	B	C	N	S_1	S_2	S_3
5	B	3.448	0	1	0	1.034	.862	.241	−4.345
20	C	27.586	0	0	1	.276	−.103	−.069	.241
3	A	68.966	1	0	0	−.310	−.759	−.172	3.103
Objective function	Entering costs		3	5	20	9.760	−.027	−.691	−7.596
775.862	Net change		0	0	0	.240	.027	.691	7.596

a. What is the optimal investment decision?

b. Within what range of risk values for the four investment alternatives will the optimal solution remain unchanged?

c. How flexible can the dividend restriction be while maintaining the same set of optimal investment variables?

d. How flexible can the growth potential restriction be while maintaining the same set of optimal investment variables?

e. What is the value of reducing the dividend restriction?

f. What is the value of reducing the growth potential restriction?

g. Formulate the dual for this problem.

h. What conclusions should Lois draw from this information and analysis?

7-12. Using the linear programming computer package available at your school, solve the primal version of the Wanda Toy Company problem (7-9) and answer questions *a* to *i* based on the computer output.

7-13. Using the linear programming computer package available at your school, solve the *dual* version of the ABCD game problem (7-10) and perform the following.

a. Identify the optimal value of all dual variables.

b. Provide an economic interpretation of each dual variable.

c. Identify the optimal value of all primal variables.

7-14. Using the linear programming computer package available at your school, solve the *primal* version of the ABCD game problem (7-10) and answer the following questions:

a. Which of the two prices (for basketball and football games) would you say is the most critical (i.e., is the optimal solution most sensitive to)?

b. If capacity can be shifted from one department to another (among printing, stamping, and packaging), *from* which department would you remove capacity? To which department would you shift the capacity?

c. Suppose that a new game (baseball) is being considered by the company. If this product uses $1\frac{1}{2}$ hours in each of the three departments and returns a profit of $2, should the optimal mix of football and basketball games produced be changed to allow for production of this new game?

Capacity Planning for Outdoor Recreation Areas with Linear Programming*

The demand for outdoor recreation areas, such as national parks and forests, is growing. With this growth has come the realization that the administration of parks must maximize visitor's benefits from areas with limited visitor capacity. Visitor traffic has strained both manmade facilities as well as natural or ecological limits. The capacity of an outdoor recreation area (for brevity, henceforth referred to as a "park") is determined not only by the capacities of specific facilities at individual locations but also by how visitors move among the locations and utilize facilities (e.g., parking lots, campgrounds, trails, and restrooms). The objective of this study is to identify longer-range (5 to 10 years) park capacity and derive management policy which assumes park use within its capacity.

Management policy includes not only internal park policy but also the number of visitor admissions. Internal policy determines or influences the behavior of visitors within a park and presumably agrees with and supports the objectives of parks. Internal policy includes the laws and regulations establishing appropriate use of roads, trails, vehicles, and campgrounds. Sometimes via regulation and sometimes via pricing, it determines the types of people in campgrounds and lodging and the duration of their visit. Admittance policy is thus established from the modeling of internal policy in conjunction with visitor behavior. To the degree that internal policy cannot be managed so that the number of people desiring to use a park corresponds to park policy, the admittance policy regulates visitor volume via pricing, reservation systems, or a first-come, first-accepted operation.

The behavior of visitors within a park requires identification of both classes of visitors with similar behavior and the locations of visitors. Families may rush into a park, briefly observe the sights, and depart; nature-oriented groups may enter wilderness terrain for a week-long backpacking trip. Each of these types of people derives a different utility and places different demands upon the facilities of the park.

The problem was initially defined as one of formulating a policy for *admitting* people to a natural recreational area. A variety of objectives can be suggested, each with its own merits and disadvantages which depend upon local conditions and the legally established goals of the park. One objective may be simply to maximize the total number of people of all types entering the park. Alternatively, with the addition of differential weights the goal of maximizing the number of people may be biased in favor of some visitor types. These weights or coefficients might represent net income from fees collected. In some parks, where experiencing certain scenes is an integral value of the park, the objective may be to maximize the number of people visiting a particular location or traveling a particular link.

Three basic types of constraints are needed for this problem. The first type recognizes the various flow patterns into, within, and out of the park for each class of visitors. The second represents the capacity constraints of the various park facilities. The third models the maximum demand placed on the park by each visitor category.

The problem described above can be solved by currently available linear programming techniques. While the model outlined here directly determines visitor admittance policy for given internal park management policy, it also provides a means of interpreting or evaluating the effect of proposed internal policy changes on admittance policies and the goals of a park. Many parks are now reducing or eliminating the lodging facilities available within the park. How this policy affects the demand for food services, the number of bus tours, and the number of cars entering the park each day should be anticipated. In some parks, an examination of backpacker and hiking patterns may reveal that most people take

*Adapted from Alton J. Lenz, "Outdoor Recreation Areas: Capacity and the Formulation of Use Policy," *Management Science*, vol. 22, no. 2 (October 1975), pp. 139–147.

shallow or circular trails close to the road simply because they must return to their cars. If regular bus service were available to pick up and discharge passengers at any position on a road, trail capacity would change with shifts in use. In essence, the model can provide a means of evaluating experimental changes in internal policy to improve the efficiency of park use.

The use of values for the dual variables, which provide insights into the relative costs of various constraints, can also suggest improvements in internal policy. Constraints which seriously impair the enjoyment of the park by certain types of people can be identified, and issues about altering park facilities can be raised. Alternatively, one can establish which types of people are most demanding or expensive with respect to park ecology.

The adaptive manner in which the model can be implemented is relevant not only to the refined measurement of data but also for changing the park itself. For example, if other models of park wildlife management indicate that desired changes in, say, elk grazing land require the restriction of human use to certain levels for a period of time, then these restrictions can be studied via this linear programming model. Then, when subsequent observation indicates that the feeding grounds have achieved the desired state, the restrictions on human use can be altered to maintain the newly achieved conditions.

Discussion Questions

1. It was suggested that one objective for this model is to maximize a weighted sum of visitors, where the weights or objective function coefficients could represent income from fees collected. Use of this objective function implies what about the goals for park operation? What problems might develop with this type of objective function? Can you suggest other types of weighting schemes? How might these weights be developed?

2. Interpretation of the meaning of the dual variables depends on the type of objective function and the nature of the constraints. Discuss the meaning of the dual variables associated with capacity constraints for park facilities and demand constraints by visitor category assuming that the objective is (a) maximize total visitors, (b) maximize income-weighted total visitors, and (c) maximize people visiting a particular facility.

3. Much recent attention has been devoted to the costs of public regulation. How would you use the model described above to estimate the costs of restricting human use of the park facilities due to park wildlife management requirements?

4. Discuss how the park superintendent might use this model to prioritize facility expansion options. How might the model be used to justify Congressional appropriations for facility expansion?

5. Can you identify situations in the private sector where a similar model might be appropriate?

6. Suppose the decision variable for one of the park visitor categories turns out to be nonbasic in the final simplex tableau. What are the practical implications of this result? How might the model be changed to overcome any difficulties that this might present?

7. Suppose the park is considering the use of advertising to attract more visitors. How might the model be used to assist in formulating an effective advertising policy?

8

Multiple Objectives in Linear Programming and Other Special Problems

In this chapter several linear programming problem characteristics that present special difficulties will be examined. We will investigate how each of these characteristics manifests itself, both graphically and with the simplex tableau, and see how these difficulties may be overcome. We will spend the bulk of our time considering the use of *goal programming*, a specialized linear programming procedure that can be used to solve problems with *multiple objectives* and problems that have *no feasible solution* (two or more conflicting constraints). Two other topics to be treated are *degeneracy*, which can cause the simplex procedure to get stuck in a nonoptimal region, and an *unbounded feasible region*, which usually implies an incompletely specified problem.

Goal Programming

In the three preceding chapters on linear programming we have worked with problems that had a single objective and which always had at least one feasible solution. Many practical problems that might otherwise be formulated as linear programming problems have multiple objectives, which precludes the use of the standard simplex method on these problems.

As discussed in Chapter 4, there are many ways in which multiple objectives can be treated. One of these is to impose constraints for all but one of the objectives and then optimize the remaining objective. This means that any feasible solution (if one exists) satisfies, rather than optimizes, the constrained objectives. For example, we might treat a profit objective by including a constraint that requires some target profit level to be met. A major difficulty with **271** this approach is that the target levels for the objectives included as constraints may be so restrictive that no combination of decision variable values is feasible.

This section will consider a method for dealing with such multiple-objective problems. This method is called *goal programming* because it attempts to satisfy a set of multiple goals, or target levels, for the objectives. The method requires that these goals be placed in priority order. Starting with the highest-priority objective, the method attempts to satisfy or minimize the amount by which each goal is underachieved. In this way, even though no feasible solution exists that will satisfy all the goals simultaneously, a solution can be found that will minimize the amount of underachievement for any goal that cannot be attained without worsening the achievement of any higher-priority goal.

Before examining the use of goal programming in detail, we will first consider an example problem that demonstrates how situations can arise in which no feasible solution exists.

No Feasible Solution

The lack of a feasible solution to a linear programming problem can develop as the result of an error in formulating the problem (using "less than or equal to" when "greater than or equal to" was intended) or because the problem was too tightly constrained (the problem was formulated correctly but no solution can satisfy all the constraints). To illustrate the second of these infeasibility causes, we will look at the situation faced by the Maybar Watch Company.

Maybar Product Mix Problem   The operations manager of Maybar is attempting to schedule production for the coming week. The Maybar product line consists of two digital watches: the Pro model, which can be sold at a contribution margin of $10 each, and the Quad model, which has a contribution margin of $8 per watch. The operations manager's objective is to determine the most profitable (total contribution) product mix for the coming week.

The marketing department has acknowledged that orders have been received for 100 Pros and 200 Quads, which they would like to be able to ship by the end of the week. The operations manager is also aware that the current work force requires 3 labor hours to manufacture each Pro and 2 labor hours to produce a Quad, and that 600 labor hours are available during the week.

The operations manager recognizes that this situation can be formulated as a linear programming problem. Letting P represent the number of Pros produced and Q the number of Quads manufactured, he is able to write

$$\text{Maximize:} \quad 10P + 8Q$$

Subject to:	$P \geq 100$	Pros to meet orders received
	$Q \geq 200$	Quads to meet orders received
	$3P + 2Q \leq 600$	labor force constraint
	$P \geq 0, Q \geq 0$	

Unfortunately, there is no feasible solution to this problem, as can be seen in Figure 8-1. The large arrows in the figure indicate the direction of feasibility with respect to each of the constraints.

Although any two constraints taken together can identify a specific feasible region, the addition of the third constraint eliminates all remaining feasible

273
MULTIPLE
OBJECTIVES IN
LINEAR
PROGRAMMING
AND OTHER
SPECIAL
PROBLEMS

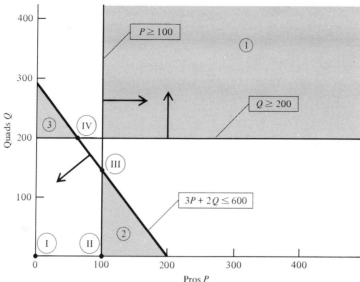

FIGURE 8-1   Graphical representation of the Maybar problem.

points. The shaded areas in the figure represent the three feasible sets formed by considering each possible pair of constraints. For example, the first two constraints, concerning the quantities of Pros and Quads necessary to satisfy existing orders, form the feasible region designated as ① in the figure. The addition of the labor hours constraint, however, leaves all the points in ① on the infeasible side of this constraint. Similar results occur with the other two-constraint feasible areas.

Clearly the problem is overconstrained, since it is not possible to produce enough Pros and Quads to meet existing orders and at the same time stay within the labor hour capacity constraint. In due time we will consider more fully the question of how the problem can be resolved. For the moment it seems clear that at least one of the existing constraints must be relaxed to the point where a feasible solution can be defined.

Infeasibility with Simplex   Suppose that we had attempted to solve the Maybar problem using the simplex routine. What characteristics of the simplex method would indicate that we have an infeasible solution? These characteristics can best be understood by means of our example.

After adding slack and artificial variables to the Maybar problem, the simplex algorithm would be applied, leading eventually to the tableau shown in Table 8-1. Since all the coefficients in the net-change row are zero or negative, the current solution appears optimal. But closer examination reveals that artificial variable A_1 is a basic variable. Recall that we add artificial variables so that an otherwise infeasible corner point can be temporarily treated as feasible until the simplex method reaches a truly feasible extreme point.

Refer again to Figure 8-1. The circled roman numerals refer to the sequence of extreme points examined by the simplex algorithm. Point ① requires two artificial variables, A_1 and A_2, in order that the two minimum sales constraints can be artificially satisfied. Variable P is then added to the basis in

TABLE 8-1
Fourth Simplex Tableau for Maybar Problem: No Feasible Solution

Objective coefficients	Basic variables	Entering gains	10	8	0	0	0	−100	−100
		Values	P	Q	S_1	S_2	S_3	A_1	A_2
8	Q	200	0	1	0	0	−1	0	1
10	P	$\frac{200}{3}$	1	0	$\frac{1}{3}$	0	$\frac{2}{3}$	0	$-\frac{2}{3}$
−100	A_1	$\frac{100}{3}$	0	0	$-\frac{1}{3}$	−1	$-\frac{2}{3}$	1	$\frac{2}{3}$
	Objective function	Entering costs	10	8	$\frac{110}{3}$	100	$\frac{196}{3}$	−100	$-\frac{196}{3}$
	$-\frac{3,200}{3}$	Net change	0	0	$-\frac{110}{3}$	−100	$-\frac{106}{3}$	0	$-\frac{104}{3}$

sufficient quantity to satisfy the minimum sales constraint for P, replacing the corresponding artificial variable A_1. This solution corresponds to point ⓘⓘ.

Variable Q is next added to the basis, leading to point ⓘⓘⓘ. Profitability can then be improved by moving to point ⓘⓥ. However, this change results in having artificial variable A_1 reenter the basis in place of artificial variable A_2. In order to satisfy the minimum sales constraint for Quads while not exceeding the labor hour capacity constraint, the number of Pros produced has to be reduced. The only way that the quantity of Pros can be reduced while maintaining the minimum sales requirement is by bringing artificial variable A_1 back into the solution as a basic variable.

No matter how large we make the penalty for the two artificial variables, there is no extreme point that can be found that is feasible with respect to all three constraints. Therefore, whenever an apparently optimal solution includes one or more artificial variables in the final basis, the problem, as formulated, has no optimal solution.

Such infeasibilities can, of course, arise because of errors in formulating the problem. In such cases, correcting the formulation should lead to a feasible and optimal solution. In other cases, however, the infeasiblity is due to correctly stated but conflicting constraints. In such cases, either the problem must be reformulated by relaxing one or more constraints or a method such as goal programming should be used to prioritize the constraints and objectives, as described in the next section.

Multiple Objectives: Establishing Priorities

Goal programming, which we will use to solve the apparently infeasible Maybar product mix problem, has in fact a much broader field of applicaton. It is an effective means of dealing with problems that have conflicting objectives where those objectives can be arranged in priority order. For instance, if a decision maker wishes to meet both a profit objective and a capacity utilization objective, goal programming would require that one objective or the other be given top priority. Thus the decision maker might choose to meet the profit objective before considering the capacity utilization objective. These goals, or objectives, do not have to be measured in the same units but can be expressed in entirely different units. For example, a firm might have (1) a profit objective, measured in dollars, (2) a productive capacity objective, measured in labor hours, and (3) a production target, measured in units of output.

If multiple objectives exist, the decision maker must be able to rank-order or prioritize these objectives for goal programming to be used. The manner in which goal programming operates is to ignore lower-priority objectives until all higher-priority goals have been achieved. Once each higher-level goal has been satisfied, goal programming attempts to satisfy each successive lower-level goal. In most multiple-objective situations, all goals cannot be simultaneously satisfied. The degree of satisfaction of each objective is measured by the deviation from the goal. Deviation can occur in two directions: a goal can be under-achieved or overachieved. For each goal we attempt to minimize *undesirable* deviations, which usually correspond to underachievement. For example, we might establish a target profit level of $2,000. The actual profit earned could be higher than $2,000 (overachievement) or lower than $2,000 (underachieve-ment). In this case we are not likely to worry about overachievement but we would desire to minimize underachievement.

INSTANT REPLAY   For the Maybar problem suppose the manager decides to produce 100 Pros and 200 Quads. What will the size of the deviation (if any) be from each of the following goals: (1) profit of at least $2,000, (2) no overtime, (3) produce at least 100 Pros, and (4) produce at least 200 Quads?

CHECK   The profit goal of $2,000 is overachieved by $600. The minimum production quantity goals of 100 Pros and 200 Quads are exactly met with no deviation. The no overtime goal is not achieved, since 700 labor hours will be required. Note that the profit deviation is desirable but that the overtime deviation is not.

Goal programming attempts to satisfy each goal or, failing that, to minimize the *undesirable deviations*, beginning with the highest-priority objective. As each higher-level goal is satisfied (or the deviation minimized), the lower-level goals are considered. The process terminates when improvement in some lower-level goal cannot be achieved without increasing the deviation for some higher-level goal.

To illustrate how goal programming works, we will apply it to the Maybar product mix problem, which has no feasible solution as originally formulated. Given that result, the operations manager now decides to reformulate the problem so that a goal programming approach can be used. The manager now requires that a profit of at least $2,000 be earned and the original three con-straints be met. Recall that no feasible solution exists to this problem (regard-less of the profit objective). To use goal programming, then, the manager has ranked these objectives in priority order: (1) meet the profit objective of at least $2,000, (2) produce at least 100 Pros, (3) produce at least 200 Quads, and (4) minimize overtime, given the labor hour capacity constraint of 600 hours without overtime. These objectives are shown in priority order in Table 8-2.

The goal programming solution ignores lower-priority goals until all higher-priority goals are achieved (their undesirable deviations minimized). Thus the minimum production requirement targets for Pros and Quads and the no overtime goal will all be ignored until a solution has been found that achieves

TABLE 8-2
Prioritized Goals for the Maybar Company Problem

Priority level of goal	Goal
1	Profits at least equal to $2,000
2	Produce at least 100 Pros
3	Produce at least 200 Quads
4	Avoid overtime (600 hours of capacity available)

the top-priority profit goal. Once some combination of Pros and Quads has been found that satisfies the profit goal, the second-priority goal (produce at least 100 Pros) can be considered. However, any new solution found that meets the second goal must also satisfy the first-priority profit goal. If no solution can be found that satisfies both goals, goal programming will pick the one that satisfies the first-priority objective and has the smallest undesirable deviation from the second objective. The search for a solution continues by successively considering the lower-priority objectives (minimum quantity of Quads and no overtime) while maintaining the minimum deviations previously derived for the higher-priority goals.

Having verbally formulated the Maybar problem in goal programming terms, we will next see how it can be solved graphically. Then we will see how we can use a modified simplex procedure to solve goal programming problems.

Graphical Approach

Goal programming problems (with two decision variables) can be solved graphically by successively adding constraints representing each goal or objective in precise priority order. The feasible points remaining after each goal constraint has been added represent those solutions that meet all goals considered to that point. Eventually, a goal constraint will be added that cannot be met by any of the solutions satisfying the higher-priority goal constraints. This unsatisfied goal constraint is then treated as if it were an objective function. The point that is feasible with respect to the higher-priority objectives that comes the closest (i.e., smallest undesirable deviation) to meeting that unsatisfied goal is designated as the optimal solution to the problem.

Looking at the Maybar problem, the first-priority constraint is that profit must be at least $2,000. This constraint is labeled ① in Figure 8-2. The arrow attached to the constraint line indicates that solutions lying on that line or above it will meet the profit objective. In other words, the undesirable deviation from the profit objective will be 0 for any point that lies on or above the line.

Next we consider the second-priority constraint, which requires a minimum production volume of 100 Pros. This constraint is labeled ② in Figure 8-2. Note that although some of the feasible points identified by the first-priority goal have been lost by the addition of this second goal constraint, many others remain that satisfy both constraints.

Adding constraint ③, which sets a minimum production volume of 200 Quads, leads to a similar result. The feasible set of solutions that satisfies the first three objectives is shown as the shaded area of Figure 8-2.

The fourth constraint, recognizing the normal production capacity of 600

277

MULTIPLE
OBJECTIVES IN
LINEAR
PROGRAMMING
AND OTHER
SPECIAL
PROBLEMS

labor hours, cannot be satisfied as were the first three constraints. This constraint is labeled ④, and the direction of the arrow indicates that none of the points that satisfy the first three constraints can also meet the fourth constraint. That is, the manager needs to find a solution that satisfies the first three constraints and *minimizes the deviation* from the fourth constraint. Thus some overtime is necessary. The objective is to determine a production schedule that minimizes the amount of overtime yet earns at least $2,000 in profit and produces at least 100 Pros and 200 Quads.

This is done in a manner similar to the way in which we used isoprofit (or isocost) lines to find the optimal solution graphically for an ordinary linear programming problem. Lines parallel to, but above, the fourth constraint represent a set of points, each of which correspond to the same level of deviation from that constraint. Thus we could refer to these lines as *isodeviation lines*. We seek the isodeviation line closest to that labor hour constraint that contains at least one point feasible with respect to the other three, higher-priority constraints. This occurs, as shown in Figure 8-2, at the point where $P = 100$, $Q = 200$, profit = $2,600, and overtime = 100 hours. Note that of the four objectives for the problem, three were met with no undersirable deviation, while the deviation from the fourth and lowest-priority goal (no overtime) was minimized. This is summarized in Table 8-3.

Reflection on the steps followed in solving this problem may provide a better understanding of goal programming. Note that the feasible solutions were determined by continuing to add constraints in priority order until some

FIGURE 8-2 Graphical solution of Maybar problem: goal programming method.

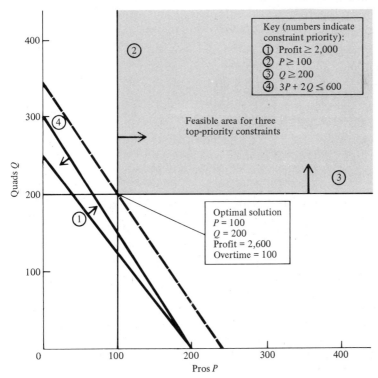

TABLE 8-3
Satisfaction of Goals for Maybar Company Problem

Priority level of goal	Goal	Was goal met?	How?
1	Profits at least equal to $2,000	Yes	Profits of $2,600 earned
2	Produce at least 100 Pros	Yes	$P = 100$
3	Produce at least 200 Quads	Yes	$Q = 200$
4	Avoid overtime (600 hours of capacity available)	No	$3P + 2Q =$ $3(100) + 2(200) = 700$ Overtime of 100 hours required

constraint could not be satisfied by one or more solutions feasible with respect to higher-order constraints. The deviation from this first unsatisfied constraint was then minimized. In essence, we could have formulated the problem as one of minimizing the amount of overtime subject to the profit and minimum production constraints. The solution obtained would have been identical to that found above. Of course, it would have been difficult to have known this in advance. And if there had been additional goals with deviations in the final solution, this simplification of the problem would not have been possible.

INSTANT REPLAY Suppose the priority ranking of the objectives for the Maybar problem were reordered such that they are (1) earn profit of $2,000 or more, (2) avoid overtime given the labor hour capacity of 600 hours, (3) produce at least 100 Pros, and (4) produce at least 200 Quads. Use the goal programming graphical approach to find the optimal solution.

CHECK The first three goals can be achieved but not the fourth. The optimal solution calls for 100 Pros, 150 Quads, a profit of $2,200, and no overtime. The target goal of 200 Quads was not met, resulting in an undesirable deviation of 50 Quads.

As the Instant Replay showed, different solutions are likely to result if the priority ranking of the objectives is changed or if the stated targets are altered. This issue will be considered later, along with other sensitivity issues.

Goal Programming with the Simplex Method

As with single-objective linear programming problems, the graphical method cannot be used for multiple-objective problems with more than two decision variables. Fortunately, we can modify the simplex procedure to handle more than one objective in the goal programming framework. In order to see how this can be done, we first need to be able to formulate goal programming problems mathematically. We begin by formulating a simple example problem with two objectives.

Formulating the Problem The production manager of the Photon Camera Company is in the process of setting production levels for the firm's two camera models, the Realist and the Trapper. The plant is operating at full capacity on a three-shift, 5-day basis, providing $24 \times 5 \times 60 = 7{,}200$ minutes of productive capacity for the coming week. Both cameras are produced on a common assembly line capable of turning out 1 Realist every 2 minutes or 1 Trapper every 1 minute.

279

MULTIPLE
OBJECTIVES IN
LINEAR
PROGRAMMING
AND OTHER
SPECIAL
PROBLEMS

The manager has identified two objectives to be met. The first and highest-priority objective is to achieve a total contribution of $70,000. Each Realist has a $15 contribution margin and each Trapper $10. The second and lower-priority objective is to limit the total number of cameras produced to 5,000 per week because of target inventory goals established for the plant.

Goal Programming Constraints   It is convenient to begin our discussion of formulating goal programming problems by developing the constraints. Goal programming problems have two types of constraints: technological and goal constraints. *Technological constraints* deal with resource capacities and other limitations that are not goal-oriented. They are similar to the types of constraints we have seen in preceding chapters. *Goal constraints* represent the target objectives that are established in priority order. These are similar to the four objectives considered in the Maybar problem.

The Photon production planning problem contains three constraints. One is technological and recognizes the production capacity of the assembly line. The other two are goal constraints, one related to the profit objective and the other to the target inventory level. It is important to distinguish between the two types of constraints because they require different treatment for formulation.

We formulate technological constraints, such as the capacity constraint, in the same manner as we did for a regular single-objective problem. Letting R represent the number of Realist cameras produced and T the number of Trapper models made, the capacity constraint requires

$$2R + T \leq 7{,}200$$

After adding slack variable S_1 to represent unused capacity, we write the constraint as

$$2R + T + S_1 = 7{,}200$$

The goal constraints are handled in a somewhat different manner. The stated level of a particular goal is a specific target that may not be exactly met. The goal might be exceeded or overachieved, on the one hand, or underachieved, on the other hand. To allow for this we need to add two variables to each goal constraint. These variables are called *deviational variables* because their values represent the amount by which the solution deviates from the goal. The positive deviational variable, denoted as D^+, represents overachievement of the target or goal. The negative deviational variable, or D^-, represents underachievement of the goal.

To illustrate, consider the Photon production manager's stated profit goal of earning at least $70,000. This could have been written as

$$15R + 10T \geq 70{,}000$$

Letting D_1^- represent the amount by which the goal is underachieved and D_1^+ represent the amount by which the profit goal is overachieved, the profit constraint is converted to the following equality:

$$15R + 10T + D_1^- - D_1^+ = 70,000$$

In essence, D_1^- is similar to a slack variable and D_1^+ is similar to a surplus variable. The use of both deviational variables recognizes that we may not be able to achieve a profit of \$70,000 exactly. In some cases profit may be less than \$70,000, in which case D_1^- will be equal to the difference between profits achieved and the \$70,000 target. In other cases profit may exceed \$70,000, in which case D_1^+ will be equal to the amount of the excess. (In any case both deviational variables must be nonnegative. That is, if one is positive the other must be 0.)

The second goal constraint (target inventory level for the two products) is formulated in the same manner by adding both an underachievement deviational variable D_2^- and an overachievement deviational variable D_2^+. In this way the goal of

$$R + T \leq 5,000$$

is converted to

$$R + T + D_2^- - D_2^+ = 5,000$$

INSTANT REPLAY What will the values of the deviational variables be for the solution to produce 400 Realist and 6,400 Trapper cameras?

CHECK Substituting $R = 400$ and $T = 6,400$ into the two goal constraints yields for the profit goal:

$$15(400) + 10(6,400) + D_1^- - D_1^+ = 70,000$$

$$6,000 + 64,000 + D_1^- - D_1^+ = 70,000$$

$$D_1^- - D_1^+ = 0$$

Hence

$$D_1^- = D_1^+ = 0$$

For the inventory goal:

$$400 + 6,400 + D_2^- - D_2^+ = 5,000$$

$$D_2^- - D_2^+ = -1,800$$

which requires $\quad D_2^- = 0 \quad$ and $\quad D_2^+ = 1,800$

Goal Programming Objective Function You may be concerned at this point, since the direction of the goals (less than or greater than) represented by the constraints appears to have been lost by the addition of the deviational variables. For example, the inventory target goal as originally formulated required that the total production of the two cameras be *no more than* 5,000 units. The revised constraint simply states

$$R + T + D_2^- - D_2^+ = 5,000$$

and does not indicate whether we desire $R + T$ to exceed 5,000, be less than 5,000, or equal 5,000. A similar loss of direction occurred with the profit constraint.

Fortunately this problem is corrected in the specification of the objective function. A goal programming objective function requires the minimization of *undesirable* deviations from the goal constraints. Thus, for example, since the production manager desires the profit to be at least equal to $70,000, we would consider underachievement of this goal, as measured by D_1^-, undesirable and would include this variable in the objective function to be minimized. We would not include the overachievement variable D_1^+, however.

281

MULTIPLE
OBJECTIVES IN
LINEAR
PROGRAMMING
AND OTHER
SPECIAL
PROBLEMS

The second goal was to limit production to no more than 5,000 cameras. Overachievement of that goal (producing more than 5,000 cameras) is undesirable. Thus, we would include D_2^+, the overachievement deviational variable, in the objective function, but not D_2^-.

In general, if the goal constraint is a "less than or equal to" constraint before the deviational variables are added, we would include the overachievement deviational variable (D^+) in the minimization objective function. If it is a "greater than or equal to" constraint, we would include the underachievement deviational variable (D^-). If it is an "equal to" constraint, we would include *both* deviational variables.

The *priorities* of the goals must also be specified in the objective function. For example, suppose there were two goals represented by the undesirable deviational variables D_i^+ and D_j^- and that goal i was at a higher priority level than goal j. Then we wish to

$$\text{Minimize } D_j^- \,\big|\, \text{minimum } D_i^+$$

which is read as: Minimize D_j^- given the minimum for D_i^+.

For our example problem, since the profit objective has a higher priority than the inventory target objective, we can write

$$\text{Minimize } D_2^+ \,\big|\, \text{minimum } D_1^-$$

which translates to: *Minimize the number of cameras produced in excess of 5,000 necessary to achieve a profit of at least $70,000.*

Thus our formulation of the Photon Camera problem is

$$\begin{aligned}
\text{Minimize:} \quad & D_2^+ \,\big|\, \text{minimum } D_1^- \\
\text{Subject to:} \quad & 2R + T + S_1 && = 7{,}200 \\
& 15R + 10T + D_1^- - D_1^+ && = 70{,}000 \\
& R + T + D_2^- - D_2^+ && = 5{,}000 \\
& R, T, S_1, D_1^-, D_1^+, D_2^-, D_2^+ \geq 0
\end{aligned}$$

INSTANT REPLAY Suppose for the Photon problem that the inventory goal was first priority and that the objective was to have *at least* 5,000 cameras produced. Assume that the $70,000 profit goal is now second priority. How would the objective function be written in this case?

CHECK The objective function would substitute D_2^- for D_2^+ and would now appear as

$$\text{Minimize } D_1^- \,\big|\, \text{minimum } D_2^-$$

Preparing the Tableau The initial simplex tableau for the Photon problem is shown in Table 8-4. Although much of the tableau is formed in the standard

TABLE 8-4
Initial Goal Programming Simplex Tableau for the Photon Camera Problem

Objective coefficients for basic variables		Basic variables	Value of basic variable	R	T	S_1	D_1^-	D_1^+	D_2^-	D_2^+	Restrictions on value of entering variable
L_1	L_2			*Departing variable*		*Pivot element*		*Entering variable*			
0	0	S_1	7,200	②	1	1	0	0	0	0	$\frac{7,200}{2} = 3,600$
1	0	D_1^-	70,000	15	10	0	1	-1	0	0	$\frac{70,000}{15} = 4,666\frac{2}{3}$
0	0	D_2^-	5,000	1	1	0	0	0	1	-1	$\frac{5,000}{1} = 5,000$
		Objective function	Entering gain	0	0	0	0	0	0	1	
0	L_2		Entering cost	0	0	0	0	0	0	0	
			Net change	0	0	0	0	0	0	1	
		Objective function	Entering gain	0	0	0	1	0	0	0	
70,000	L_1		Entering cost	15	10	0	1	-1	0	0	
			Net change	-15	-10	0	0	1	0	0	

manner, you will note some major differences. The initial basic variables are found in the usual manner by setting decision variables R and T equal to zero and then determining which of the deviational or slack variables will be basic in order to satisfy the constraints. For example, if R and T are zero, the capacity constraint is in balance only if slack variable S_1 is equal to 7,200:

$$2R + T + S_1 = 7,200$$
$$2(0) + 0 + S_1 = 7,200$$
$$S_1 = 7,200$$

Similarly, the profit goal constraint is balanced when underachievement deviational variable D_1^- is equal to 70,000 and overachievement variable D_1^+ is zero:

$$15R + 10T + D_1^- - D_1^+ = 70,000$$
$$15(0) + 10(0) + D_1^- - D_1^+ = 70,000$$
$$D_1^- = 70,000 + D_1^+$$
$$D_1^- = 70,000$$

The inventory target constraint is balanced when the underachievement variable is equal to 5,000 and the overachievement variable is zero.

Note that two objective coefficients are shown for each basic variable (on the far left). This is because there are two objectives (profit and inventory target). Designations L_1 and L_2 represent these two goals. L_1 is the first-priority profit goal, and L_2 is the second-priority inventory target objective.

283

MULTIPLE
OBJECTIVES IN
LINEAR
PROGRAMMING
AND OTHER
SPECIAL
PROBLEMS

Consider first the top-priority profit goal. The objective is to minimize the value of D_1^-, the underachievement deviational variable. Thus, the first-level objective function is to

$$\text{Minimize } 0R + 0T + 0S_1 + D_1^- + 0D_1^+ + 0D_2^- + 0D_2^+$$

Note that all variables except D_1^- have zero coefficients. Similarly the second-priority-level objective function can be written as

$$\text{Minimize } 0R + 0T + 0S_1 + 0D_1^- + 0D_1^+ + 0D_2^- + D_2^+$$

In this case the only variable with a nonzero objective coefficient is D_2^+, the undesirable overachievement deviational variable for the second-level objective. Since neither S_1 nor D_2^- appears in the two objective functions, objective coefficients of zero are shown for both of these basic variables at both priority levels L_1 and L_2. Basic variable D_1^-, however, has a coefficient of 1 in the first-level objective function and does not appear in the second objective. Thus the objective coefficients for D_1^- are listed in the tableau as 1 for L_1 and 0 for L_2.

The body of the tableau, showing the values of the basic variables and the constraint coefficients, is completed as for any standard linear programming problem as shown in Table 8-4.

Incorporating Multiple Objectives   The major modification to the simplex tableau is the result of there being two objectives. Observe that the lower portion of the tableau shows separate entering-gain, entering-cost, and net-change values for both the first- and second-level objectives. The entering-gain values normally appear at the top of the tableau (for single-objective problems). For convenience, they are grouped with the entering-cost and net-change values at the bottom of the goal programming tableau. These entering-gain values are simply the objective function coefficients for each variable at the appropriate priority level. Thus, for priority level L_1, the only nonzero entering gain applies to variable D_1^- (underachievement of the profit objective). At the second-level goal, L_2, the only nonzero entering gain applies to D_2^+ (overachievement of the inventory target).

The entering costs are calculated in the usual manner by multiplying the corresponding constraint coefficients by the objective coefficients (at each priority level) for each basic variable. For example, the entering cost for variable R at the first priority level is found by

Objective coefficients for basic variables L_1		R		
0	×	2	=	0
1	×	15	=	15
0	×	1	=	0
				15 entering cost

For the second priority level, the entering cost for variable R is given by

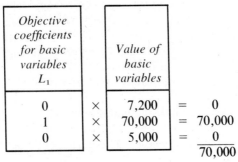

Objective coefficients for basic variables L_2		R		
0	$\times$	2	=	0
0	$\times$	15	=	0
0	$\times$	1	=	0
				$\overline{0}$ entering cost

The net-change values of each priority level are then found, as usual, by subtracting the entering cost from the entering gain. For example, for variable R, at priority level L_1 we find

$$\text{Net change} = (\text{entering gain}) - (\text{entering cost})$$

$$= 0 - 15 = -15$$

and at priority level L_2

$$\text{Net change} = 0 - 0 = 0$$

These net-change values represent the effect on each priority-level objective function of a one-unit increase in the values of the variables. Thus, a one-unit increase in variable R will reduce the value of the first-level objective by 15 but will have no effect on the second-level objective.

The current value of the objective function at each priority level can be found by multiplying the current value of each basic variable by the corresponding objective coefficient for that variable and summing the results. Thus, for priority level L_1 we find

Objective coefficients for basic variables L_1		Value of basic variables		
0	$\times$	7,200	=	0
1	$\times$	70,000	=	70,000
0	$\times$	5,000	=	0
				$\overline{70,000}$ objective function value L_1

and for priority level L_2

Objective coefficients for basic variables L_2		Value of basic variables		
0	$\times$	7,200	=	0
0	$\times$	70,000	=	0
0	$\times$	5,000	=	0
				$\overline{0}$ objective function value L_2

285

MULTIPLE
OBJECTIVES IN
LINEAR
PROGRAMMING
AND OTHER
SPECIAL
PROBLEMS

Thus, the solution corresponding to the first tableau shows an under-achievement of the profit objective by $70,000 and completely satisfies the target inventory goal. Both results were predictable since the solution calls for no cameras to be produced ($R = T = 0$). Thus no profit is earned, and the target of keeping the inventory below the 5,000-unit ceiling is easily met.

Test for Optimality   The test for optimality must be modified somewhat to take account of the priority structure of the goals. Since this is a minimization problem, an obvious condition for optimality is all positive or zero values in the net-change rows. The absence of negative values would indicate that the undesirable deviations of the goals cannot be reduced further.

Optimality is also indicated when the only variables with negative net-change values have positive (nonzero) net-change values *at higher priority levels*. This condition is optimal because of the priority structure of the goals. Although the negative value implies that some lower-priority deviational variable can be reduced, this gain will occur only at the cost of increasing the deviation from some higher-priority goal. The strict priority ordering of goals prevents us from doing this. In other words, we continue to bring variables into the solution if we can reduce one or more of the deviational variables without also increasing some higher-priority deviational variable. Because variables R and T in the initial tableau both have negative net-change values for the top-priority objective, L_1, the current tableau is not optimal.

Selecting the Entering and Departing Variables   The rule for selecting the next variable to enter the solution follows from the optimality condition. First identify the highest priority level that can be improved, which implies one or more negative net-change values at that level. Then select the variable with the largest negative net-change value as long as that variable has all zero net-change values for any higher-priority goals.

Consider Table 8-4 once more. Two variables, R and T, have negative net-change values for the highest priority level (L_1). Both variables promise to reduce the size of the undesirable deviation from the profit objective. Since variable R has the larger negative net-change value (-15 as opposed to -10), it is selected as the entering variable.

The variable chosen to depart the basis is selected in a manner identical to that for single-objective linear programming problems. Ratios are calculated by dividing the current value for each basic variable by the corresponding positive constraint coefficient for the entering variable. Whichever basic variable will first reach zero, as indicated by the smallest ratio, will thus be selected as the departing variable.

The ratios for our initial tableau are shown to the right in Table 8-4. The smallest ratio corresponds to basic variable S_1. Therefore, variable R will replace S_1 in the set of basic variables for the next tableau. The pivot element occurs at the intersection of the S_1 row and the R column and is identified in Table 8-4.

INSTANT REPLAY   Suppose that the priority order of the goals for the Photon problem is reversed and that the inventory goal is changed to require production of *at least* 5,000 cameras. What would be the departing and entering variables?

CHECK The objective coefficient for D_2^- would change from 0 to 1 for the top-priority inventory goal. This would yield net-change values of -1 for both R and T. Either could be chosen as the entering variable. If R is chosen, S_1 would be the departing variable. If T is chosen, D_2^- would be the departing variable.

Second Tableau Pivot operations to form the new tableau are carried out exactly as described for the simplex method. All elements in the pivot row are divided by the pivot element, and some multiple of this new row is added or subtracted to each of the other rows so as to obtain a zero in the pivot column. The net-change and objective function values are calculated as described above for the initial tableau. The second tableau for the Photon problem is shown in Table 8-5. You may wish to take a few moments to examine this tableau to check your understanding of where the numbers come from.

Observe that bringing variable R into the solution has dropped the first-priority objective function (deviation from the profit goal) from 70,000 to

TABLE 8-5
Second Goal Programming Simplex Tableau for the Photon Camera Problem

Objective coefficients for basic variables L_1	L_2	*Basic variables*	*Value of basic variables*	R	T	S_1	D_1^-	D_1^+	D_2^-	D_2^+	Restrictions on value of entering variable
0	0	R	3,600	1	$\frac{1}{2}$	$\frac{1}{2}$	0	0	0	0	$3{,}600/\frac{1}{2} = 7{,}200$
1	0	D_1^-	16,000	0	$\frac{5}{2}$	$-\frac{15}{2}$	1	-1	0	0	$16{,}000/\frac{5}{2} = 6{,}400$
0	0	D_2^- (Departing variable)	1,400	0	$\frac{1}{2}$ (Pivot element)	$-\frac{1}{2}$	0	0	1	-1	$1{,}400/\frac{1}{2} = 2{,}800$
Objective function 0		L_2	*Entering gain*	0	0	0	0	0	0	1	
			Entering cost	0	0	0	0	0	0	0	
			Net change	0	0	0	0	0	0	1	
Objective function 16,000		L_1	*Entering gain*	0	0	0	1	0	0	0	
			Entering cost	0	$\frac{5}{2}$	$-\frac{15}{2}$	1	-1	0	0	
			Net change	0	$-\frac{5}{2}$	$\frac{15}{2}$	0	1	0	0	

Pivot element — ***Entering variable*** (T) — ***Departing variable*** (D_2^-)

287

MULTIPLE
OBJECTIVES IN
LINEAR
PROGRAMMING
AND OTHER
SPECIAL
PROBLEMS

16,000, without changing the 0 value for the second-level objective function. As the second tableau shows, R has a value of 3,600, which is equivalent to producing 3,600 Realist cameras. At \$15 profit each, the 3,600 Realist cameras will yield a total profit of \$54,000, reducing the deviation from the profit objective by that amount and leaving an underachievement level of \$16,000. Since the 3,600 cameras produced is less than the maximum inventory target of 5,000, the second-level objective remains satisfied, as shown by the 0 value for the objective function (which measures only *undesirable deviations* from the target).

The second tableau is not optimal since one variable, T, shows a negative net-change value for the first-level goal. This promises a reduction in the first-level profit deviation of \$2.50 for each unit of T produced. Thus T is chosen as the entering variable.

The ratios shown to the right of Table 8-5 indicate that variable D_2^- will be the departing variable (replaced by variable T) because D_2^- has the smallest ratio. Recall that variable D_2^- represents underachievement of the maximum inventory target. Thus, the production of Trapper cameras will use up the remaining inventory capacity. The appropriate pivot element is identified in Table 8-5.

INSTANT REPLAY Suppose, as in the preceding instant replay, the priority order of the goals is reversed and the inventory goal is changed to require production of at least 5,000 cameras. What would be the entering and departing variables based on Table 8-5, modified as necessary?

CHECK Variable T would be the entering variable because it is the only variable with a negative net-change value for the inventory goal. D_2^- would be the departing variable.

Third Tableau The third tableau is prepared in the same manner as the second. The third tableau is shown in Table 8-6. Note that this tableau represents production of 2,200 Realist cameras and 2,800 Trapper Models. The deviation from the profit objective has been reduced from 16,000 to 9,000, and the second-level objective remains satisfied.

The solution represented by the third tableau is not optimal, however, since introduction of variable D_2^+ promises to reduce the profit deviation by \$5 per unit. Recall that variable D_2^+ represents the overachievement of the inventory goal. Although this is an *undesirable* deviational variable with respect to the second-level goal (note the $+1$ in the net-change row for this variable for priority level L_2), it is not undesirable from the perspective of the first-level goal. In fact, as the L_1 net-change value indicates, it is desirable because each unit increase in D_2^+ will decrease the deviation from the profit objective by \$5. Therefore, D_2^+ is selected as the entering variable.

There is a fundamental assumption of goal programming implicit in the identification of the third tableau as nonoptimal: *Any improvement in the higher-level objective* (in this case reduction of the deviation from the profit objective) *that is feasible to obtain is worthwhile no matter what effect this change might have on lower-priority objectives.*

For our example, the selection of variable D_2^+ as a basic variable will reduce the deviation of the profit objective but will, at the same time, increase

TABLE 8-6
Third Goal Programming Simplex Tableau for the Photon Camera Problem

Objective coefficients for basic variables L_1	L_2	Basic variables	Value of basic variables	R	T	S_1	D_1^-	D_1^+	D_2^-	D_2^+	Restrictions on value of entering variable
						Departing variable		Entering variable		Pivot element	
0	0	R	2,200	1	0	1	0	0	−1	1	$\frac{2,200}{1} = 2,200$
1	0	D_1^-	9,000	0	0	−5	1	−1	−5	(5)	$\frac{9,000}{5} = 1,800$
0	0	T	2,800	0	1	−1	0	0	2	−2	
Objective function	L_2	Entering gain		0	0	0	0	0	0	1	
0		Entering cost		0	0	0	0	0	0	0	
		Net change		0	0	0	0	0	0	1	
Objective function	L_1	Entering gain		0	0	0	1	0	0	0	
9,000		Entering cost		0	0	−5	1	−1	−5	5	
		Net change		0	0	5	0	1	5	−5	

the deviation from the inventory target objective. Goal programming does not explicitly permit cost/benefit tradeoffs to be made between goals at different priority levels. As long as any improvement can be made in a higher-level objective, goal programming will make it, even if the effect is highly adverse for some lower-level objective. In that sense, goal programming is a limited approach to handling multiple objectives. Unlike the utility approach discussed in Chapter 4, goal programming treats objectives at different priority levels separately and requires a strict ranking of the importance of these objectives.

The ratios to the right of Table 8-6 show that D_2^+, the entering variable, is to replace D_1^-, the departing variable. The fact that D_1^- is the departing variable indicates that the first-level profit goal will be completely satisfied by the next tableau. (Since D_1^- will become nonbasic, its solution value will be 0, indicating that the profit objective is no longer underachieved.)

Fourth Tableau The fourth tableau is completed in the usual manner and is shown in Table 8-7. As shown, the first-priority objective function value is now zero, indicating that the first-priority goal is now achieved. All the net-change values for this priority level are zero or positive.

The second-priority objective has not been met, however, as indicated by the objective function value of 1,800 for that goal (L_2). This means that the current solution produces 1,800 more units than the maximum inventory target

289

MULTIPLE
OBJECTIVES IN
LINEAR
PROGRAMMING
AND OTHER
SPECIAL
PROBLEMS

TABLE 8-7
Optimal Goal Programming Simplex Tableau for the Photon Camera Problem

Objective coefficients for basic variables L_1 L_2		Basic variables	Value of basic variables	R	T	S_1	D_1^-	D_1^+	D_2^-	D_2^+
0	0	R	400	1	0	2	$-\frac{1}{5}$	$\frac{1}{5}$	0	0
0	1	D_2^+	1,800	0	0	-1	$\frac{1}{5}$	$-\frac{1}{5}$	-1	1
0	0	T	6,400	0	1	-3	$\frac{2}{5}$	$-\frac{2}{5}$	0	0
Objective function			Entering gains	0	0	0	0	0	0	1
1,800	L_2		Entering costs	0	0	-1	$\frac{1}{5}$	$-\frac{1}{5}$	-1	1
			Net change	0	0	1	$-\frac{1}{5}$	$\frac{1}{5}$	1	0
Objective function			Entering gains	0	0	0	1	0	0	0
0	L_1		Entering costs	0	0	0	0	0	0	0
			Net change	0	0	0	1	0	0	0

called for. This resulted because the solution calls for production of 400 Realist cameras and 6,400 Trappers, a total of 6,800, which is 1,800 more than the target of 5,000.

At first glance it would appear that the deviation from this second-priority goal could be reduced by selecting variable D_1^- as an entering variable. The net-change value for variable D_1^- equals $-\frac{1}{5}$ at the second priority level. This promises to reduce the 1,800 deviation by $\frac{1}{5}$ for each unit increase in D_1^-. However, we are prohibited from doing this because of the $+1$ net-change value for variable D_1^- at the first priority level. Improvement in lower-level goals, such as the maximum inventory target, can be taken only when no higher-priority goal is adversely affected. Since an increase in D_1^- will increase the deviation from the first-level profit goal, D_1^- should not be increased no matter how much we can improve on the inventory target goal.

Optimizing or Satisficing

It is important to recognize the *satisficing* nature with which goals are achieved by goal programming. Each goal has a specific target level to be reached. Once that level has been achieved, attention turns to other objectives. For instance, the first-level goal for the Photon problem was a profit objective. A satisfactory level of $70,000 was specified. Even though profit was a first-level goal, we do *not* attempt to maximize profit. We only attempt to achieve the stated profit level.

For the Photon problem we were able to achieve the $70,000 profit goal but only by yielding on the second-level maximum inventory goal. To obtain the $70,000 profit, we had to exceed the inventory target by 1,800 units. The third tableau (Table 8-6) represented a solution in which profit of $61,000 was earned ($9,000 below the objective) and the maximum inventory target of 5,000 units was exactly met. To increase profits in order to meet the $70,000 target, the inventory goal was exceeded by 1,800 units. Thus, we gained $9,000 in profit at the expense of 1,800 additional units in inventory, a gain of $5 in profit for each excess unit.

Although goal programming does not make tradeoffs between priority levels, a decision maker who uses the goal programming solution is implicitly making such a tradeoff. In the Photon example, implementation of the solution represented by tableau 4 (rather than tableau 3) leads implicitly to the conclusion that the cost of exceeding the inventory target must have been less than the additional $5 profit generated by each excess unit.

Unfortunately, if we can accept the implicit conclusion that the cost of excess units is less than the $5 profit generated, why should we stop at tableau 4? Note that the net-change value for variable D_1^+ at the second priority level is $+\frac{1}{5}$. Recall that D_1^+ corresponds to profit in excess of the $70,000. Thus, a unit increase in D_1^+ corresponds to a $1 increase in profit. The $+\frac{1}{5}$ net-change value means that each $1 increase in profits causes a $\frac{1}{5}$ increase in the number of units in excess of the inventory target. In other words, each additional unit carried in inventory will generate a $5 increase in profits. If it was beneficial to trade off excess inventory to gain increased profits up to the $70,000 profit level, why is it not beneficial to continue making such a tradeoff beyond the $70,000 profit level?

The answer is that goal programming attempts only to *satisfy* goals or objectives. It is not an optimizing routine. Users of goal programming should be aware of this characteristic.

INSTANT REPLAY Consider again the third tableau for the Photon Camera problem as shown in Table 8-6. Suppose the priority order of the objectives is reversed such that the maximum inventory target is the first-level goal and the minimum profit objective is the second-level goal. Is the tableau in Table 8-6 optimal with respect to the revised priority order?

CHECK Yes. The (now) first-level priority has been achieved. Although the second (profit) objective has not been met, the only improvement that can be obtained requires selection of variable D_2^+ to enter the basis. This promises to reduce the profit deviation by $5 per unit. However, any increase in D_2^+ will cause an increase in the deviation from the inventory objective, and since this is now the top-priority objective, such a change is not allowed. Thus the tableau of Table 8-6 is optimal.

More Complex Goal Structures

At this point it is useful to consider a somewhat more complex example of a goal programming problem. For this purpose we return to the Maybar problem treated graphically earlier in the chapter.

291

MULTIPLE
OBJECTIVES IN
LINEAR
PROGRAMMING
AND OTHER
SPECIAL
PROBLEMS

You may recall that four objectives had been listed in priority order to be satisfied by the production schedule of Pros and Quads. These were:

1. Profit at least equal to $2,000.
2. Produce at least 100 Pros.
3. Produce at least 200 Quads.
4. Avoid overtime.

The addition of positive and negative deviational variables to each of the goals provides the following set of constraints:

$$10P + 8Q + D_1^- - D_1^+ = 2,000$$

$$P \qquad\quad + D_2^- - D_2^+ = \quad 100$$

$$Q + D_3^- - D_3^+ = \quad 200$$

$$3P + 2Q + D_4^- - D_4^+ = \quad 600$$

Considering each constraint and the direction of the goal, we conclude that variables D_1^- (underachievement of the profit objective), D_2^- (underachievement of the minimum production quantity for P), D_3^- (underachievement of the minimum production quantity for Q), and D_4^+ (overachievement of the production capacity requirement) are the undesirable deviational variables to be minimized. Note that D_4^+ is equivalent to overtime.

Thus the complete formulation of the Maybar problem is

Minimize: $D_4^+ |$ minimum $D_3^- |$ minimum $D_2^- |$ minimum D_1^-

Subject to: $10P + 8Q + D_1^- - D_1^+ = 2,000$

$$P \qquad\quad + D_2^- - D_2^+ = \quad 100$$

$$Q + D_3^- - D_3^+ = \quad 200$$

$$3P + 2Q + D_4^- - D_4^+ = \quad 600$$

$$P, Q, D_1^-, D_1^+, D_2^-, D_2^+, D_3^-, D_3^+, D_4^-, D_4^+ \geq 0$$

The initial simplex tableau for Maybar is shown in Table 8-8. Observe that the apparent complexity of the tableau results from the fact that there are four priority levels of objectives: L_1, L_2, L_3, and L_4. The first tableau shows that only the lowest-level objective (no overtime) has been satisfied. The existence of negative values in the net-change row for the highest-level objective ($L_1 =$ profit) shows that the first tableau is not optimal.

INSTANT REPLAY Which variable should be selected as the entering variable and which variable will it replace in the basis?

CHECK Variable P has the largest negative value in the L_1 net-change row and will be the entering variable. Variable D_2^- has the smallest ratio ($100/1 = 100$) and will be replaced by P.

Solution of the Maybar problem requires a total of six tableaus to be prepared. To avoid unnecessary complication, the intermediate tableaus are not shown. You may wish to try your hand at completing one or more of these

TABLE 8-8
Initial Goal Programming Simplex Tableau for Maybar Problem

L_1	L_2	L_3	L_4	Basic variables	Value of basic variables	P	Q	D_1^-	D_1^+	D_2^-	D_2^+	D_3^-	D_3^+	D_4^-	D_4^+
\multicolumn{4}{l}{*Objective coefficients for basic variables*}													
1	0	0	0	D_1^-	2,000	10	8	1	−1	0	0	0	0	0	0
0	1	0	0	D_2^-	100	1	0	0	0	1	−1	0	0	0	0
0	0	1	0	D_3^-	200	0	1	0	0	0	0	1	−1	0	0
0	0	0	0	D_4^-	600	3	2	0	0	0	0	0	0	1	−1
Objective function **0**			L_4		Gain	0	0	0	0	0	0	0	0	0	1
					Cost	0	0	0	0	0	0	0	0	0	0
					Net	0	0	0	0	0	0	0	0	0	1
Objective function **200**			L_3		Gain	0	0	0	0	0	0	1	0	0	0
					Cost	0	1	0	0	0	0	1	−1	0	0
					Net	0	−1	0	0	0	0	0	1	0	0
Objective function **100**			L_2		Gain	0	0	0	0	1	0	0	0	0	0
					Cost	1	0	0	0	1	−1	0	0	0	0
					Net	−1	0	0	0	0	1	0	0	0	0
Objective function **2,000**			L_1		Gain	0	0	1	0	0	0	0	0	0	0
					Cost	10	8	1	−1	0	0	0	0	0	0
					Net	−10	−8	0	1	0	0	0	0	0	0

tableaus. Summary information for intermediate tableaus 2 through 5 is given in Table 8-9.

In addition it is instructive to examine Figure 8-3, which traces the pattern of extreme points examined by the simplex method. The numbers refer to the corresponding tableau. The transition from tableau ① to tableau ② was based on production of enough Pros to meet the minimum production requirement of 100. Variable P was selected rather than Q at this stage because it offered a greater profit and the profit goal was top priority.

From tableau ② further reduction of the deviation from the profit goal could be achieved by producing Quads or increasing the production of Pros. Since P had the higher per-unit profit, its production volume was increased leading from tableau ② to ③.

At tableau ③ the profit objective has now been met. Note in Table 8-9 that the net-change row in the third tableau for this objective, L_1, contains all

293

MULTIPLE
OBJECTIVES IN
LINEAR
PROGRAMMING
AND OTHER
SPECIAL
PROBLEMS

zeros or ones, indicating satisfaction of the profit goal. Furthermore, second-level goal L_2 had also been satisfied, since that net-change row also contains only zeros and ones. The second-level objective of meeting the minimum production level for Pros had actually been achieved as early as the second tableau. With the first two goals satisfied, we turn our attention to the third goal, the minimum production quantity for Quads. As shown in Table 8-9, variable Q is the only variable with a negative net-change value in the L_3 row. Before selecting Q as the entering variable, we check the net-change values for that variable for all higher-level goals. Zeros were shown for both L_1 and L_2, indicating that the addition of Q will have no impact on the satisfaction of the higher-level goals. Therefore, variable Q was designated a basic variable, leading to tableau ④. Note that Quads were substituted for Pros at a rate consistent with the profit objective.

Examination of the net-change rows for the fourth tableau indicates that the two highest-level objectives remain satisfied while deviations from the third-level objective can be further reduced by bringing variable D_1^+ into the solution. Variable D_1^+ represents profits in excess of the stated target level of

TABLE 8-9
Summary Information Taken from Second, Third, Fourth, and Fifth Tableaus
for Maybar Goal Programming Problem

Basic variables	Value of basic variables	Net change for objective	P	Q	D_1^-	D_1^+	D_2^-	D_2^+	D_3^-	D_3^+	D_4^-	D_4^+	Objective function
					Tableau 2								
D_1^-	1,000	L_4	0	0	0	0	0	0	0	0	0	1	0
P	100	L_3	0	-1	0	0	0	0	0	1	0	0	200
D_3^-	200	L_2	0	0	0	0	1	0	0	0	0	0	0
D_4^-	300	L_1	0	-8	0	1	10	-10	0	0	0	0	1,000
					Tableau 3								
D_2^+	100	L_4	0	0	0	0	0	0	0	0	0	1	0
P	200	L_3	0	-1	0	0	0	0	0	1	0	0	200
D_3^-	200	L_2	0	0	0	0	1	0	0	0	0	0	0
D_4^-	0	L_1	0	0	1	0	0	0	0	0	0	0	0
					Tableau 4								
Q	125	L_4	0	0	0	0	0	0	0	0	0	1	0
P	100	L_3	0	0	$\frac{1}{8}$	$-\frac{1}{8}$	$-\frac{5}{4}$	$\frac{5}{4}$	0	1	0	0	75
D_3^-	75	L_2	0	0	0	0	1	0	0	0	0	0	0
D_4^-	50	L_1	0	0	1	0	0	0	0	0	0	0	0
					Tableau 5								
Q	150	L_4	0	0	0	0	0	0	0	0	0	1	0
P	100	L_3	0	0	0	0	$-\frac{3}{2}$	$\frac{3}{2}$	0	1	$\frac{1}{2}$	$-\frac{1}{2}$	50
D_3^-	50	L_2	0	0	0	0	1	0	0	0	0	0	0
D_1^+	200	L_1	0	0	1	0	0	0	0	0	0	0	0

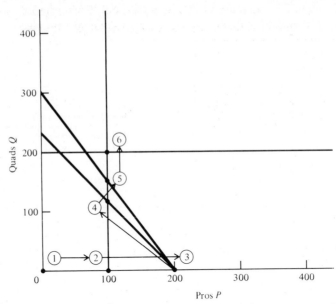

FIGURE 8-3 Pattern of extreme points traced by simplex solution to Maybar goal programming problem.

$2,000 which is accomplished here by producing more Quads until the available production capacity is reached. This change is reflected in tableau ⑤.

The net-change rows for tableau ⑤ continue to indicate satisfaction of the first two goals. Two variables, D_2^- and D_4^+, have negative net-change values for the third objective. The larger net-change value belongs to D_2^-. However, it was not selected as the entering variable because it had a $+1$ in the net-change row for objective L_2.

Observe that variable D_2^- corresponds to underachievement of the minimum production requirement for Pros. Since this requirement corresponds to the second objective, any increase in D_2^- will cause a corresponding increase in the deviation from the second goal. Because the second-priority goal always takes precedence over the third goal, we are prohibited from selecting D_2^- as the entering variable.

Fortunately D_4^+ has no effect on satisfaction of the two top-priority goals and therefore can be selected as the entering variable. The improvement in the third-level goal by adding D_4^+ is accomplished at the expense of the fourth-level goal. The fourth-priority objective refers to minimizing overtime, and D_4^+ represents the amount of overtime required. Note that this fourth objective is currently satisfied in tableau ⑤ as indicated by the presence of all zeros and ones in the L_4 net-change row. However, the $+1$ in the column for D_4^+ shows that selecting D_4^+ as the entering variable for tableau ⑥ will lead to a deviation from the fourth goal. Nevertheless, goal programming insists that all lower-priority goals be disregarded if the satisfaction of higher-level goals can be improved.

The final tableau is shown in its entirety in Table 8-10. Note that the first three priority goals have been completely satisfied, as indicated by the zero values for the objective function for levels L_1, L_2, and L_3. Two variables, D_2^- and D_3^-, have negative net-change values for the fourth goal. However, neither

TABLE 8-10
Final Tableau for Maybar Goal Programming Problem

Objective coefficients for basic variables L_1 L_2 L_3 L_4	Basic variables	Values of basic variables		P	Q	D_1^-	D_1^+	D_2^-	D_2^+	D_3^-	D_3^+	D_4^-	D_4^+
0 0 0 0	Q	200		0	1	0	0	0	0	1	−1	0	0
0 0 0 0	P	100		1	0	0	0	1	−1	0	0	0	0
0 0 0	D_4^+	100		0	0	0	0	3	−3	2	−2	−1	1
0 0 0 0	D_1^+	600		0	0	−1	1	10	−10	8	−8	0	0
Objective function 100	L_4	Gain		0	0	0	0	0	0	0	0	0	1
		Cost		0	0	0	0	3	−3	2	−2	−1	1
		Net		0	0	0	0	−3	3	−2	2	1	0
Objective function 0	L_3	Gain		0	0	0	0	0	0	1	0	0	0
		Cost		0	0	0	0	0	0	0	0	0	0
		Net		0	0	0	0	0	0	1	0	0	0
Objective function 0	L_2	Gain		0	0	0	0	1	0	0	0	0	0
		Cost		0	0	0	0	0	0	0	0	0	0
		Net		0	0	0	0	1	0	0	0	0	0
Objective function 0	L_1	Gain		0	0	1	0	0	0	0	0	0	0
		Cost		0	0	0	0	0	0	0	0	0	0
		Net		0	0	1	0	0	0	0	0	0	0

can become basic because each will adversely affect satisfaction of one of the higher-level goals; D_2^- will increase the deviation from the second-priority goal and D_3^- will adversely impact on the third-level goal.

An examination of the final set of basic variables shows that the optimal solution calls for 100 Pros and 200 Quads to be produced. This will require 100 hours of overtime, as shown by the value for D_4^+, but will yield profits $600 larger than targeted, as shown by the value for D_1^+.

INSTANT REPLAY Suppose the minimum production requirements for Pros and Quads are dropped as goals, leaving only the profit and production capacity constraints in the same priority order as before. What optimal solution would result?

CHECK   Two corner points, ($P = 200, Q = 0$, profit $= 2,000$) and ($P = 0, Q = 300$, profit $= 2,400$), satisfy both goals. Although the $2,400 profit point is clearly preferred, the simplex method would first reach the lower profit point and indicate that no further improvement in satisfying the goals could be achieved. This is due to the satisficing nature of goal programming. Goal programming, as applied here, seeks to minimize the deviations below $2,000 for profit. This is not the same as maximizing profit, as discussed earlier.

Using the Computer for Goal Programming

As should be evident by now, the calculations required to solve a goal programming problem manually can be complex and tedious. Of course, in practice, we would use the computer to handle these calculations. Although computer procedures exist for solving goal programming problems, you may find that one is not available at your institution. The relative newness of the approach and the difficulty in understanding the method, its assumptions, and problem formulation have slowed the distribution of efficient computer solution procedures.

Sensitivity Analysis

Because of the multiple objectives for a goal programming problem, sensitivity analysis becomes more complex but also more important. We will briefly consider the following three sensitivity questions for goal programming problems:

1. What effect do changes in the target levels of the goals have on the final solution?
2. What relative tradeoffs are implied among the goals?
3. What effect do changes in the priority ranking of the goals have on the final solution?

Changes in Goal Target Levels   Recall that goal programming is a satisficing approach that attempts to achieve prespecified target levels for each goal rather than to maximize or minimize the objectives. One question of primary concern, then, is the impact caused by changes in these prespecified targets. We will consider again the Photon Camera problem. For convenience the final optimal goal programming simplex tableau for this problem is repeated in Table 8-11.

The original target levels for the two goals were $70,000 for the profit objective (higher priority) and 5,000 units produced for the maximum inventory objective (lower priority). Recall that these goals were treated much like constraints except that both a slack variable (underachievement deviational variable D^-) and a surplus variable (overachievement deviational variable D^+) were added to the goal constraints. The target levels for these objectives are similar to the right-hand-side values for normal constraints.

Chapter 7 discussed how we could use the final status (basic or nonbasic) and solution value for slack and surplus variables to determine the largest increases and decreases that could be made to the original right-hand-side coefficients or constraint capacities that would leave the set of optimal basic variables unchanged. We can apply these same procedures to the deviational variables in a goal programming problem to determine the maximum increase and decrease in the original target levels for the goals.

297

MULTIPLE
OBJECTIVES IN
LINEAR
PROGRAMMING
AND OTHER
SPECIAL
PROBLEMS

TABLE 8-11
Optimal Goal Programming Simplex Tableau for the Photon Camera Problem

Objective coefficients for basic variables L_1	L_2	Basic variables	Value of basic variables	R	T	S_1	D_1^-	D_1^+	D_2^-	D_2^+
0	0	R	400	1	0	0	$-\frac{1}{5}$	$\frac{1}{5}$	0	0
0	1	D_2^+	1,800	0	0	-1	$\frac{1}{5}$	$-\frac{1}{5}$	-1	1
0	0	T	6,400	0	1	-3	$\frac{2}{5}$	$-\frac{2}{5}$	0	0

Objective function	Basic variables									
		Entering gain	0	0	0	0	0	0	1
1,800 (L_2)		Entering cost	0	0	-1	$\frac{1}{5}$	$-\frac{1}{5}$	-1	1
		Net change	0	0	1	$-\frac{1}{5}$	$\frac{1}{5}$	1	0
Objective function		Entering gain	0	0	0	1	0	0	0
0 (L_1)		Entering cost	0	0	0	0	0	0	0
		Net change	0	0	0	1	0	0	0

Nonbasic Deviational Variables   Consider the profit goal for the Photon Camera problem. The deviational variables, D_1^- and D_1^+, for this goal are both nonbasic in the final solution, as shown in Table 8-11. Chapter 7 developed formulas for determining the maximum allowable changes in constraint capacities for nonbasic slack and surplus variables. These formulas are repeated below, restated in terms of the goals and deviational variables:

$$\begin{pmatrix} \text{Maximum allowable change in} \\ \text{the goal level for nonbasic} \\ \text{underachievement variable } D_i^- \\ \text{corresponding to basic variable } j \end{pmatrix} = - \begin{pmatrix} \text{final solution value} \\ \text{for basic variable } j \\ \hline \text{jth constraint coefficient} \\ \text{for variable } D_i^- \end{pmatrix} \quad (8\text{-}1)$$

$$\begin{pmatrix} \text{Maximum allowable change in} \\ \text{the goal level for nonbasic} \\ \text{overachievement variable } D_i^+ \\ \text{corresponding to basic variable } j \end{pmatrix} = \begin{pmatrix} \text{final solution value} \\ \text{for basic variable } j \\ \hline \text{jth constraint coefficient} \\ \text{for variable } D_i^+ \end{pmatrix} \quad (8\text{-}2)$$

Note that each goal has both an underachievement variable D_i^- and an overachievement variable D_i^+. Since maximum changes in a goal level could be calculated for either of these deviational variables, which limits should be used? Actually it makes no difference, as we shall see, since both variables provide the same limits.

Consider first profit underachievement variable D_1^-. With three basic variables, three separate calculations are required. We use equation (8-1):

Basic variables	Value of basic variables	D_1^-	
R	400	$-\frac{1}{5}$	$-400/-\frac{1}{5} = 2{,}000$
D_2^+	1,800	$\frac{1}{5}$	$-1{,}800/\frac{1}{5} = -9{,}000$
T	6,400	$\frac{2}{5}$	$-6{,}400/\frac{2}{5} = -16{,}000$

The tightest limits on changes to the profit goal are an increase of $2,000 or a decrease of $9,000. Thus the original target profit level could have been as low as $61,000 (70,000 − 9,000) or as high as $72,000 (70,000 + 2,000) without changing the final optimal set of basic variables.

Note that the same results would have been obtained if we had used overachievement variable D_1^+. To demonstrate, we use equation (8-2) to find the limits for this variable:

Basic variables	Value of basic variables	D_1^+	
R	400	$\frac{1}{5}$	$400/\frac{1}{5} = 2{,}000$
D_2^+	1,800	$-\frac{1}{5}$	$1{,}800/-\frac{1}{5} = -9{,}000$
T	6,400	$-\frac{2}{5}$	$6{,}400/-\frac{2}{5} = -16{,}000$

Again we find that the limits on changes to the original profit target are an increase of $2,000 or a decrease of $9,000.

Consider next the maximum-inventory target, which set a goal of no more than 5,000 cameras produced. Observe from Table 8-11 that underachievement deviational variable D_2^- for this goal is nonbasic in the optimal solution while overachievement variable D_2^+ is basic.

We saw above how a nonbasic deviational variable could be used to obtain limits on changes to the original target level. Thus for D_2^- we use equation (8-1) to find

Basic variables	Value of basic variables	D_2^-	
R	400	0	No limit
D_2^+	1,800	−1	$-1{,}800/-1 = 1{,}800$
T	6,400	0	No limit

These results show that the original maximum-inventory target of 5,000 cameras could have been increased by as much as 1,800 or decreased as much as desired (unlimited decreases) without changing the final set of basic variables. Thus the target level for this goal could have been as low as zero or as high as 6,800 units without changing the mix of basic variables.

299

MULTIPLE
OBJECTIVES IN
LINEAR
PROGRAMMING
AND OTHER
SPECIAL
PROBLEMS

Basic Deviational Variables   Suppose we look at deviational variable D_2^+, which was basic in the final solution. Recall from Chapter 7 that the right-hand side of constraints with basic *slack* variables can be *increased* in any amount without changing the optimal set of basic variables. The same is true of *decreases* for constraints with basic *surplus* variables. Changes in the opposite direction are limited to the current value of that basic slack or surplus variable in the optimal solution. Thus, for a basic slack variable, the original right-hand side could be decreased by an amount equal to the final value of that basic slack variable. For a basic surplus variable, the right-hand side could be increased by an amount equal to the solution value of that basic surplus variable.

Since D_2^+ is, in effect, a basic surplus variable with a final solution value of 1,800, we conclude that the original maximum-inventory target could have been increased by as much as 1,800 units or decreased as much as desired without changing the optimal basis. Again we see that whether we look at limits based on the overachievement or the underachievement deviational variables, the calculated limits on changes to goal levels are the same.

Relative Tradeoffs among Goals   Although goal programming does not attempt to make tradeoffs among goals, it is possible to determine *implicitly* the relative values of the different goals by examining the final tableau. Looking at the final Photon tableau in Table 8-11, we see that the second-level deviation of 1,800 could be reduced by bringing variable D_1^- into the set of basic variables. We were prevented from doing this because of the $+1$ in the first-priority net-change row for this variable. Note also that D_1^- is, in fact, the underachievement deviational variable for the profit objective. If D_1^- is made basic, whatever value it takes on is equivalent to an underachievement of the profit objective.

Considering the net-change value for D_1^- for the second-priority objective, we see that each dollar that we miss the profit objective by will allow a $\frac{1}{5}$ decrease in the number of units produced in excess of the maximum-inventory target. Or, in other words, each unit by which we reduce the inventory deviation will cost $5 in profit. Thus, we have determined that the implied tradeoff between the two objectives is $5 in profit for each excess unit in inventory.

If management desired, profit could be increased at the expense of additional inventory units, the rate of exchange being $5 per unit. On the other hand, the excess inventory could be decreased if management was willing to give up $5 in profit for each unit of inventory reduction. The preferred direction of change depends on the relative values management places on the two targets.

INSTANT REPLAY   Examine the final simplex tableau for the Maybar production problem as shown in Table 8-10. What is the implied relative tradeoff between hours of overtime (L_4) and the minimum production quantities for Pros (L_2) and Quads (L_3)?

CHECK   Each Pro is worth 3 hours of overtime and each Quad is worth 2 hours of overtime.

Changes in Priority Rankings   Changes in the priority rankings for the various objectives can have a significant impact on the optimal solution. One form of sensitivity testing that we can perform with goal programming problems is to reorder the objectives to determine what impact the reordering will have on the optimal solution.

For instance, consider the Photon Camera problem's two objectives, profit (top priority) and maximum inventory (second priority). Suppose we were to rearrange these objectives such that the maximum-inventory objective was given top priority. Does this rearrangement of priorities require resolving the problem from scratch? Although restarting from scratch is a feasible alternative, it is not really necessary.

To see this, reexamine the Photon optimal tableau for the original priority order (Table 8-11). This tableau was declared optimal because further improvement in the inventory goal could be accomplished only at the expense of underachievement of the profit goal. However, if these goals are reversed in priority, the tableau is no longer optimal because the inventory objective now takes precedence over the profit goal.

Thus we can improve the solution by bringing variable D_1^- into the solution, which causes variable D_2^+ to depart. The resulting tableau is identical to the third tableau for the original priority order (Table 8-6). Observe that this new tableau is *optimal* with respect to the revised priority ranking. The net-change row for the top-priority goal (now L_2) contains all zero or positive values, indicating no further improvement in that objective. Although the profit objective has not been met and can be improved by bringing variable D_2^+ into the basis, the new goal priorities prevent us from doing this because D_2^+ has a +1 value in the net-change row for the higher inventory objective.

As shown by this small example, rearrangement of goal priorities can often be examined with relatively little extra effort. The benefit of such analysis is that management now has more solutions to choose from. For our example, the following two solutions have been found:

Priority rankings		Values of decision variables		Levels of goal achievement	
1	*2*	*R*	*T*	*Profit*	*Inventory*
Profit	Inventory	400	6,400	70,000	6,800
Inventory	Profit	2,200	2,800	61,000	5,000

Multiple Objectives at the Same Priority Level   As a final sensitivity point, we will consider an extension to goal programming that permits treatment of more than one objective at the same priority level. For example, suppose that for the Maybar problem we consider the two minimum production requirement objectives, for Pros and Quads, to be at the *same* priority level.

We can easily handle this with goal programming by assigning the two corresponding deviational variables the same priority weight and adding their values. Thus our objective function for the Maybar problem would be stated as

$$\text{Minimize } D_4^+ \mid \text{minimum } (D_2^- + D_3^-) \mid \text{minimum } D_1^-$$

Note that we now have only three priority levels to worry about. In essence, the objectives have been rearranged as follows:

1. Achieve a profit of $2,000.
2. Produce at least 100 Pros and 200 Quads.
3. Avoid overtime.

301

MULTIPLE
OBJECTIVES IN
LINEAR
PROGRAMMING
AND OTHER
SPECIAL
PROBLEMS

As shown above, we have given equal weight (1) to each of the deviational variables at priority level 2. It is not necessary to do this, and we can specify differential weights for these deviational variables. This may be necessary if the variables are measured in different units (i.e., dollars, units produced, labor hours) in order to achieve some sort of parity. On the other hand, we may wish to use differential weights to indicate that these variables do not have the same impact. For example, we may decide that missing deliveries for Pros is more serious than for Quads and therefore assign a greater weight to the deviational variable for Pros. Suppose a missed delivery for a Pro is considered three times as important as a missed delivery for a Quad. This could be reflected in the objective function as

$$\text{Minimize } D_4^+ \mid \text{minimum } (3D_2^- + D_3^-) \mid \text{minimum } D_1^-$$

Degeneracy

A condition that often occurs with certain kinds of linear programming problems is *degeneracy*. In graphical terms the situation arises when three or more constraints intersect at a common extreme point. Such a point is referred to as a *degenerate point*. Degeneracy is of some concern because it is possible for the simplex method to become stuck at a degenerate point and never reach the optimal solution. In practice, such sticking is rare and can be taken care of when it occurs.

There is a special class of linear programming problems, called *transportation problems,* for which degeneracy is a common event. A specialized solution procedure that is more efficient than the simplex method exists for solving transportation problems and will be described in the next chapter. One method for dealing with degenerate extreme points will be treated in that chapter.

Unbounded Feasible Region

Another linear programming problem can develop when the feasible region fails to constrain one or more of the decision variables. Recall from our discussion of minimization problems that the decision variables are normally unbounded or unconstrained for large values (upward and to the right). This was not a problem, however, because the minimization objective forced us to search extreme points in the area of the feasible region where the decision variables have small values (downward and to the left).

But suppose that an error is made in the formulation of a maximization problem. Then it is possible for the feasible region to be unbounded from above for one or more of the decision variables. This means that the objective function can be made as large as desired by choosing successively larger values for the unbounded variables.

Most linear programming computer packages are programmed to detect the condition of an unbounded feasible region. When such conditions are observed, the program will stop and print out a message to the user that says something like "UNBOUNDED SOLUTION."

Final Comments

This chapter has examined a number of special problems related to linear programming. The goal programming method was discussed as a means of dealing with two of these: problems with multiple objectives and problems with no feasible solution. In addition we considered situations with degenerate solutions and with unbounded solutions.

The objective was to make you familiar with each of these issues and to show you how they are commonly resolved. The major emphasis in the chapter was on goal programming. Although goal programming can be an effective means of dealing with multiple and conflicting objectives, you should by now be aware that the assumptions required in order for a problem to fit the goal programming format are rather restrictive. Of major concern is that the decision maker must be able to rank all the objectives in strict priority order. This prioritizing is important because improvements in lower-priority objectives cannot be accomplished with goal programming if some higher-priority objective will be affected.

We also saw that the optimal goal programming solution may be sensitive to the priority order of the goals and the target levels established for these goals. We saw how implicit tradeoffs could be measured based on the goals established.

As promising as goal programming may seem as a way of handling multiple-objective problems, the decision maker should be aware of these assumptions and sensitivity considerations. Otherwise, inappropriate decisions with unfortunate economic consequences may result.

Key Words

Basic deviational variable **299**
Degeneracy **301**
Degenerate point **301**
Departing variable **285**
Deviational variable **279**
Entering cost **283**
Entering gain **283**
Entering variable **285**
Goal constraint **279**
Goal programming **271**
Goal target levels **296**
Implicit goal tradeoff **299**
Infeasible problem **272**
Isodeviation line **277**

Multiple objectives **274**
Net change **273**
Nonbasic deviational variable **297**
Optimizing **289**
Overachievement deviational variable **279**
Prioritized goals **275**
Satisficing **289**
Sensitivity analysis **296**
Simplex tableau **273**
Technological constraint **279**
Unbounded feasible region **301**
Underachievement deviational variable **279**

Problems

8-1. The Balapro Sports Company has been experiencing capacity problems with its baseball bat manufacturing facility. The company uses a single two-stage process to manufacture baseball bats in two basic sizes, little league and standard. The contributions, processing requirements, and available labor hour capacities in each stage for the coming week are shown below:

303

MULTIPLE
OBJECTIVES IN
LINEAR
PROGRAMMING
AND OTHER
SPECIAL
PROBLEMS

	Little league	Standard model	Capacity available
Labor hours, stage 1	1	2	100
Labor hours, stage 2	2	3	160
Contribution	$2	$4	

In addition, the available storage for standard bats will not permit more than 40 standard bats to be produced in the coming week. After slack variables were added, this problem was solved using the standard linear programming approach (X_1 = number of little league bats and X_2 = number of standard bats). The final simplex tableau is shown below.

Objective coefficients	Basic variables	Entering gains	2	4	0	0	0
		Values	X_1	X_2	S_1	S_2	S_3
2	X_1	20	1	0	1	0	-2
0	S_2	0	0	0	-2	1	1
4	X_2	40	0	1	0	0	1
	Objective function	Entering cost	2	4	2	0	0
	200	Net change	0	0	-2	0	0

Identify the solution obtained and discuss any special characteristics that it has.

8-2. The Frame Furniture Company manufactures three types of chairs, all of which are assembled in one department. The company is attempting to determine the best assembly schedule for the coming week. Each Aristocrat chair and Bentwood chair takes 1 hour of assembly time; each Colonial chair takes 2 hours to assemble. Company policy is to maintain level employment throughout the year. Therefore, any assembly schedule should require at least 50 hours of assembly labor. Because of the uncertainty of sales volume for Aristocrat and Bentwood chairs, a limitation has been imposed on the schedule that no more than 60 chairs combined of these two types can be produced. The contribution margins on the chairs have been found to be $3 for an Aristocrat, $4 for a Bentwood, and $5 for a Colonial.

This problem was formulated as a linear programming problem (where X_1 = number of Aristocrat chairs, X_2 = number of Bentwood chairs, and X_3 = number of Colonial chairs). After artificial and slack variables were added, the following tableau was eventually obtained:

Objective coefficient	Basic variables	Entering gains / Values	3 X_1	4 X_2	5 X_3	0 S_1	0 S_2	-100 A_1
5	X_3	25	$\frac{1}{2}$	$\frac{1}{2}$	1	$-\frac{1}{2}$	0	$\frac{1}{2}$
0	S_2	60	1	1	0	0	1	0
Objective function	Entering cost	$2\frac{1}{2}$	$2\frac{1}{2}$	5	$-2\frac{1}{2}$	0	$-2\frac{1}{2}$
125	Net change	$\frac{1}{2}$	$1\frac{1}{2}$	0	$2\frac{1}{2}$	0	$-102\frac{1}{2}$

Identify the solution obtained and discuss any special characteristics that it has.

8-3. The Sanitation Department of the city of Metropolis has been asked by the mayor's budget commission to recommend the best way to allocate its equipment purchase budget of $1,000,000 for the coming fiscal year. The sanitation commissioner would like to purchase as many street sweepers and sanitation trucks as possible. Each street sweeper costs $50,000 and each sanitation truck $40,000. Given the increased load placed on the department, the commissioner feels that a minimum of 12 street sweepers and 15 sanitation trucks are needed.

One of the commissioner's aides formulated the budget allocation problem as a linear programming problem (where X_1 = number of street sweepers and X_2 = number of sanitation trucks) and obtained the following final simplex tableau:

Objective coefficient	Basic variables	Entering gains / Values	1 X_1	1 X_2	0 S_1	0 S_2	0 S_3	-100 A_1	-100 A_2
1	X_1	8	1	0	$\frac{1}{50}$	0	$\frac{4}{5}$	0	$-\frac{4}{5}$
-100	A_1	4	0	0	$-\frac{1}{50}$	-1	$-\frac{4}{5}$	1	$\frac{4}{5}$
1	X_2	15	0	1	0	0	-1	0	1
Objective function	Entering costs	1	1	$\frac{101}{50}$	100	$79\frac{4}{5}$	-100	$-79\frac{4}{5}$
-377	Net change	0	0	$-\frac{101}{50}$	-100	$-79\frac{4}{5}$	0	$-20\frac{1}{5}$

Identify the solution obtained and discuss any special characteristics that it has.

8-4. The plant manager for the Hendlick Company is concerned with the production line for microwave ovens. Two oven models, the Standard and Deluxe, are produced in the same facility, and each requires several integrated circuits, which are in short supply. These integrated circuits are purchased by Hendlick from another firm, and only 150 are available at the moment, with an additional shipment not due in for another week.

Each Standard oven requires three of the integrated circuits and produces a contribution margin of $60 per unit. Each Deluxe oven needs five of the integrated circuits and yields $100 in contribution. The plant manager has inventory limits that restrict this week's production to no more than 40 Standard and 20 Deluxe ovens. Since performance is judged on a total contribution basis, the plant manager would like to determine the most profitable production schedule consistent with the integrated circuit and inventory capacity constraints. The problem was formulated as a linear programming problem (where X_1 = number of Standard ovens and X_2 = number of Deluxe ovens), which yielded the following final simplex tableau:

Objective coefficient	Basic variable	Entering gains	60	100	0	0	0
		Values	X_1	X_2	S_1	S_2	S_3
60	X_1	$16\frac{2}{3}$	1	0	$\frac{1}{3}$	0	$-\frac{5}{3}$
0	S_2	$23\frac{1}{3}$	0	0	$-\frac{1}{3}$	1	$\frac{5}{3}$
100	X_2	20	0	1	0	0	1
Objective function	Entering costs		60	100	20	0	0
3,000	Net change		0	0	-20	0	0

Identify the solution obtained and discuss any special characteristics that it has.

8-5. The Grasspro Corporation is about to launch a new microcomputer-controlled lawnmower product. Management is preparing a national advertising plan to launch this product. A total of $300,000 has been budgeted for the campaign. Each magazine insert is expected to cost $20,000 and will reach an estimated 200,000 people. Each TV ad will cost $30,000 and reach an estimated 700,000 people. Management has agreed that the following goals are to be met in the order listed:

1. The total exposures should be at least 6,000,000 people.
2. The amount spent should not exceed the $300,000 budget. Set this problem up in the goal programming format and find the optimal solution *graphically*.

8-6. Refer again to the Grasspro advertising problem (8-5). Suppose that management has identified two additional objectives to be met. The priority ranking for all objectives is now:

1. Total exposures should be at last 6,000,000.
2. Amount spent should not exceed $300,000.
3. Number of magazine inserts should not exceed 12.
4. Number of television ads should be at least 6.

Set this problem up in the goal programming format and find the optimal solution *graphically*.

8-7. Solve the Grasspro advertising plan problem (8-5) using the goal programming version of the simplex procedure.

8-8. The financial officer for the Lifecycle Insurance Company is attempting to make target allocations of available company funds among several investment options. A total of $4,000,000 is available for investment subject to certain limitations specified below: In addition to holding cash, three options are available: government securities, commercial credit, and mortgages. Expected returns on these investments are 8, 10, and 11 percent, respectively. The financial officer has identified the following goals or constraints which must be satisfied in the order specified:

1. Total amount invested (including cash holdings) cannot exceed the $4,000,000.
2. Cash reserves must be maintained equal to no less than 10 percent of commercial credit and mortgage investments.
3. The total return for the $4,000,000 must be at least $360,000.
4. Mortgage investments cannot exceed 10 percent of the total.

Set this problem up in the goal programming format.

8-9. Solve the Lifecycle Insurance Company problem (8-8) using the simplex goal programming procedure.

8-10. The production manager for the Omega Appliance Company is attempting to develop a production schedule for the toaster line that meets, as well as possible, a set of conflicting objectives. The line is capable of producing two versions of the Omega toaster, a Standard and a Deluxe model. Production requirements and contribution are shown in the following table:

	Fabrication time	Assembly time	Contribution
Standard	2	3	$3
Deluxe	2	4	$5

The production manager has identified the following set of goals, which need to be satisfied in the order listed:

1. Total contribution earned should be at least $250.
2. A total of 120 fabrication hours and 200 assembly hours are available for production. The schedule should ensure that no idle time occurs in either department (equal priority for the two departments).
3. The amount of overtime required in the fabrication department should be minimized.
4. The amount of overtime required in the assembly department should be minimized.

Set this problem up in the goal programming format and find the optimal solution *graphically*.

8-11. Solve the Omega Appliance problem (8-10) using the goal programming simplex procedure.

8-12. How sensitive is your solution to the Omega Appliance problem (8-11) to changes in the priority ordering of the goals?

8-13. What changes in the original target levels for contribution, fabrication capacity, and assembly capacity will leave the optimal set of basic variables for the Omega Appliance problem (8-10 or 8-11) unchanged?

8-14. What tradeoffs are implicitly made among the goals for the Omega Appliance problem (8-10 or 8-11)?

Part Three

Network Flow Problems

In this section we will consider a special class of problems called network flow problems. They are so called because in each case the problem can be represented graphically as a network. A *network* consists of a set of activities or nodes connected by flow routes or arcs. A simple network with four nodes, lettered *A* to *D,* and four arcs, numbered 1 to 4, is shown below:

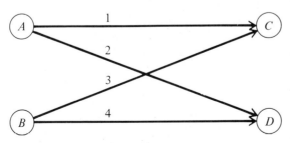

Note that the arcs show direction, indicating that flows can occur in only one direction. This is called a *directed network.*

The specific characterization of these nodes and arcs depends upon the type of network problem being examined. Chapter 9 will consider what are called transportation problems. A transportation problem involves determining the least-cost shipment pattern from one set of nodes, called supply points, to another set of nodes, called demand points. The supply points might represent factories and the demand points distribution warehouses. The arcs represent specific shipping routes from a supply point to a demand point. If the network illustrated above represented a transportation problem, nodes *A* and *B* would be supply points, nodes *C* and *D* would be the demand points, and arcs 1 to 4 would represent the four possible shipment routes. The objective is to determine the quantities to be shipped along these routes in a way that minimizes the total shipping cost, meets the demand requirements at each demand point, and does not exceed the capacities at each supply point.

Another network problem, to be considered in Chapter 10, is the assignment problem. An assignment problem consists of one set of objects that are to be assigned to another set of objects. An example would be the assignment of a set of jobs to a set of workers. Thus, nodes *A* and *B* above could represent the jobs to be assigned, nodes *C* and *D* the workers, and the arcs the possible assignments. For instance, arc 1 represents the assignment of job *A* to worker *C*. The cost of assigning jobs to workers depends on the job and worker. The objective is to minimize the total cost of completing the jobs.

A final category of problems to be treated in this section is what are called minimal spanning tree problems. A minimal spanning tree is defined as the minimum-cost set of arcs that connects a specified set of nodes. For instance, suppose we had the following set of nodes and arcs:

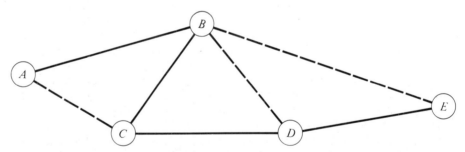

The solid arcs form a spanning tree in that they form a connection between all the nodes. The dotted arcs are not on the spanning tree shown but could be used to form other spanning trees for this set of nodes.

Spanning tree problems arise in a number of network design situations. For instance, the nodes above might represent neighborhoods to be served by a new subway system, and the arcs could be possible routes that the subway might follow. Each arc would have a cost associated with it corresponding to the cost of building a subway line along that route. The objective is to find the least-cost set of routes that serve to link the five neighborhoods. Other spanning tree problems include interstate highway design, electrical transmission system design, and so on.

9

The Transportation Method

One major area of success in the application of linear programming methods is the *transportation,* or *distribution, problem.* Like other linear programming situations, the transportation problem involves resource allocation issues. For the typical transportation problem, however, the allocation decision relates to the physical movement of goods from one set of locations, called *supply points,* to another set of locations, called *demand points.* The decision variables concern the quantity of goods to be moved or shipped from each supply point to each demand point. The supply points typically represent factories where the goods are produced. The demand points often correspond to distribution warehouses where the goods are needed to supply customers' demands. The problem objective is to ship the goods needed to each warehouse using the available stocks at the factories while minimizing the total shipping costs. Figure 9-1 depicts the essential elements of a transportation problem.

The transportation problem can be formulated as a standard linear programming problem. We will see how this is done later. However, the characteristics of a transportation problem are such that it is usually solved by a specialized procedure, appropriately called the *transportation method,* rather than by the simplex procedure. The transportation method is a simpler and more efficient way of solving transportation problems, as we shall see.

The descriptive title "transportation problem" is somewhat misleading because the types of problems for which the transportation method is suited are widely varied and by no means limited to the physical movement of goods or merchandise. The transportation method has been successfully applied to such diverse problems as production planning, machine scheduling, location analysis, work force scheduling, and media scheduling, to name but a few. We

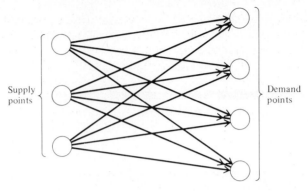

Supply
points

Demand
points

Question: How much to send from each supply point
to each demand point?

FIGURE 9-1   Pictorial view of transportation problem.

will consider some of these nontransportation examples later in this chapter. For now we will focus on the standard physical distribution problem.

Our discussion begins with the presentation of a simple example problem. Then we will see how this problem can be formulated as a standard linear programming problem. The major portion of the chapter will be concerned with an explanation and illustration of the transportation method itself. Then we will consider several special situations that can develop and how these are handled by the transportation method. Finally, we will examine types of problems that do not fit the standard model of physical movement of goods, as well as the transshipment problem.

Formulating the Problem

To illustrate the elements of a transportation problem and how it is formulated, let us consider the following situation. The Modor Oven Company produces microwave ovens at three different factories located in Atlanta, Boston, and Chicago. The ovens are moved from the factories to one of four distribution warehouses that Modor operates for later delivery to customers. The warehouses are located in Kansas City, Los Angeles, Memphis, and New Orleans.

Rising shipping costs, due to higher fuel costs, have led to increased concern on the part of Modor management for developing the least-cost shipping schedule of ovens from factories to warehouses. Consider, for instance, the distribution problem faced by the company for the coming week. Modor will have 175 ovens available for shipment based on next week's production plan: 75 at Atlanta, 60 at Boston, and 40 at Chicago. Based on inventory levels and anticipated needs at each of the warehouses, Modor management has allocated these 175 ovens to the four warehouses as follows: 30 to Kansas City, 65 to Los Angeles, 55 to Memphis, and 25 to New Orleans.

The transportation decision to be made consists of determining the number of ovens to be shipped from each factory to each warehouse. For instance, although we know that the Los Angeles warehouse is to receive 65 ovens, we have not yet determined how many are to be supplied from Atlanta, from Boston, or from Chicago. Clearly, the cost of shipping from Atlanta to

Los Angeles will not be the same as from Boston to Los Angeles. Shipment

costs such as these will necessarily influence our shipment decision.

Fortunately, shipping costs are often easy to obtain. The shipping costs per oven from each of the three factories to each of the four warehouses are shown in Table 9-1 for the Modor problem. Thus, we see that it costs $22 to ship an oven from Atlanta to Los Angeles. If we were concerned only with shipments to Los Angeles, we would clearly designate the Chicago factory to suppy 40 of the 65 ovens needed. The $21 cost per oven from Chicago to Los Angeles is obviously cheaper than the cost from Atlanta ($22) or Boston ($31). The remaining 25 ovens needed at Los Angeles could be shipped from Atlanta, the next cheapest route. Unfortunately, the problem is not quite so simple as finding the least expensive pattern of shipments for each warehouse independently. For example, note that Chicago is also the least costly location for shipments to the Kansas City warehouse. If all 40 ovens at Chicago are shipped to Los Angeles, the ovens needed at Kansas City will have to be shipped from Atlanta or Boston at a higher cost than if they were shipped from Chicago. Thus, the optimal, or least-cost, shipment pattern must take account of the interdependencies among the factories, the warehouses, and the shipping costs from one to another.

Relationship to Linear Programming

It was stated earlier that a transportation problem, such as Modor's, is a special type of linear programming problem. To illustrate this, let us see how the Modor problem can be formulated as a linear programming problem. Then we will see the special characteristics that set transportation problems apart from other linear programming problems. Because transportation problems are easier to solve with the transportation method than with the simplex method, it is worthwhile to be able to identify transportation problems by their special characteristics.

The decision variables for the Modor problem correspond to the quantity of ovens to be shipped from each factory to each warehouse. Each factory can potentially supply all four warehouses. Because there are three factories, there are $4 \times 3 = 12$ possible shipping routes or decision variables. In general, then, the number of decision variables is equivalent to the number of supply points (factories) multiplied by the number of demand points (warehouses).

To identify these decision variables for the Modor problem, we will use a two-letter designation, such as AK. The first letter will identify the factory (A

TABLE 9-1
Per-Unit Shipping Costs for Modor Oven Problem

Warehouse location

Factory location	Kansas City	Los Angeles	Memphis	New Orleans
Atlanta	11	22	6	5
Boston	16	31	14	15
Chicago	5	21	4	9

for Atlanta) and the second letter the warehouse (K for Kansas City). Thus BL will represent the number of ovens to be shipped from Boston to Los Angeles, CN the number shipped from Chicago to New Orleans, and so on.

The objective is to minimize the total cost of shipping the 175 ovens from the factories to the warehouses. Therefore, the objective function will represent the total shipment cost and requires that the number of ovens shipped along each route be multiplied by the cost of shipping an oven along that route. Using the shipping costs of Table 9-1, we can write the Modor objective function as:

Minimize: $11AK + 22AL + 6AM + 5AN + 16BK + 31BL + 14BM + 15BN$

$+ 5CK + 21CL + 4CM + 9CN$

Two basic sets of constraints are required for transportation problems such as Modor's. One set applies to the supply points and one applies to the demand points. The first set recognizes that we cannot ship more ovens from a factory than are available. This requires a separate constraint for each supply point of the form:

$$\left(\begin{array}{c}\text{Quantity shipped from}\\ \text{each supply point}\end{array}\right) \leq \left(\begin{array}{c}\text{quantity available at}\\ \text{that supply point}\end{array}\right)$$

Because the Modor problem has three factories, we will need three of these supply constraints. These would be written as:

$AK + AL + AM + AN \leq 75$ Atlanta

$BK + BL + BM + BN \leq 60$ Boston

$CK + CL + CM + CN \leq 40$ Chicago

The second set of constraints ensures that the total number of ovens shipped to each warehouse meets the requirements at that warehouse. This requires, in general, a separate constraint for each demand point of the form:

$$\left(\begin{array}{c}\text{Quantity shipped to}\\ \text{a demand point}\end{array}\right) \geq \left(\begin{array}{c}\text{quantity needed at}\\ \text{that demand point}\end{array}\right)$$

With four warehouses, we will need four of these demand point constraints:

$AK + BK + CK \geq 30$ Kansas City

$AL + BL + CL \geq 65$ Los Angeles

$AM + BM + CM \geq 55$ Memphis

$AN + BN + CN \geq 25$ New Orleans

Finally, we add the nonnegativity constraints (shipments ≥ 0), which leads to the complete problem statement:

Minimize: $11AK + 22AL + 6AM + 5AN + 16BK + 31BL + 14BM + 15BN$

$+ 5CK + 21CL + 4CM + 9CN$

Subject to: $AK + AL + AM + AN \leq 75$

$BK + BL + BM + BN \leq 60$

$CK + CL + CM + CN \leq 40$

$$AK + BK + CK \quad\quad \geq 30$$
$$AL + BL + CL \quad\quad \geq 65$$
$$AM + BM + CM \quad\quad \geq 55$$
$$AN + BN + CN \quad\quad \geq 25$$
$$AK, AL, AM, AN, BK, BL, BM, BN, CK, CL, CM, CN \geq 0$$

It is apparent that even a relatively simple transportation problem can lead to a rather large linear programming problem. With, say, 10 supply points and 50 demand points, the problem would contain 500 decision variables (10×50) and 60 constraints ($10 + 50$). Although a problem of this size is certainly not unmanageable with a computer, it is considerably easier to solve with the specialized transportation method, as will be demonstrated shortly.

Identifying the Special Structure of Transportation Problems

A transportation problem such as Modor's appears to have the same structure as any other linear programming problem. However, transportation problems do have certain characteristics which differentiate them from other problems. Observe that, unlike the linear programming problems we have dealt with, the constraint coefficients of the decision variables are all either 0s or 1s. For instance, the constraint corresponding to the supply capacity at the Atlanta factory is:

$$AK + AL + AM + AN \leq 75$$

The decision variables AK, AL, AM, and AN, which correspond to shipments from Atlanta to each of the four warehouses, all have constraint coefficients of 1 (implied). The other decision variables (BK, BL, BM, BN, CK, CL, CM, and CN) are not present in this constraint because they correspond to shipments from factories other than Atlanta. Thus, in effect, the coefficients of these other decision variables are all 0. Each of the other constraints have similar coefficient combinations of 0 or 1. This characteristic will be true for all transportation problems.

INSTANT REPLAY   For a transportation problem with 7 factories and 12 warehouses, how many decision variables, constraints, and nonzero constraint coefficients will the equivalent linear programming problem have?

CHECK $7 \times 12 = 84$ decision variables, $12 + 7 = 19$ constraints, and $(12 \times 7) + (7 \times 12) = 168$ nonzero constraint coefficients.

The Transportation Method

We now turn our attention to the transportation method, which is the specialized solution procedure developed for transportation problems. Conceptually the transportation method is similar to the simplex method. We begin with an initial feasible solution and test for optimality. If the solution is not optimal, we improve it by changing the shipping pattern (called *reallocating*).

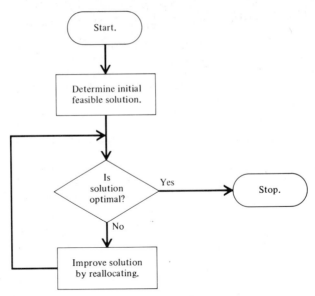

FIGURE 9-2   General solution approach for the transportation problem.

We continue checking and reallocating until an optimal solution is found. These steps are outlined in Figure 9-2 and should be strongly reminiscent of those followed by simplex.

One key difference between the transportation method and simplex concerns the determination of an initial feasible solution. When simplex is used to solve a minimization problem, we must add artificial variables in order to make the origin (where all decision variables are 0) artificially feasible. As simplex progresses from tableau to tableau, the artificial variables are dropped as they became nonbasic. Eventually a truly feasible solution is found, at which point all artificial variables have been dropped. The transportation method eliminates the need to use artificial variables because it is quite easy to find an initial solution that is feasible without them.

Finding an Initial Feasible Solution

There are a number of procedures available for generating an initial feasible solution for a transportation problem. We will consider one of these here: the *northwest-corner method,* which is fast and simple to use.

Feasible Solutions   Before considering how to find an initial feasible solution, we need to identify the characteristics of a feasible solution. Recall our earlier discussion of the Modor Oven problem and its corresponding linear programming formulation. That problem had seven constraints, one for each factory, to ensure that no more is shipped from a factory than is available, and one for each warehouse, to ensure that each warehouse's needs are fulfilled. Any combination of shipments that meets the warehouse needs without violating the factory capacities is a feasible solution to the problem.

Consider Table 9-2, which illustrates a feasible solution for the Modor Oven problem. The format followed in this table will be used throughout the chapter, so you should be sure that you understand the format. Each row

TABLE 9-2
Feasible Solution for the Modor Oven Problem

Factory location	Warehouse location — Kansas City	Los Angeles	Memphis	New Orleans	Factory capacity, ovens
Atlanta	11	22 / 50	6	5 / 25	75
Boston	16	31 / 15	14 / 45	15	60
Chicago	5 / 30	21	4 / 10	9	40
Warehouse requirements, ovens	30	65	55	25	

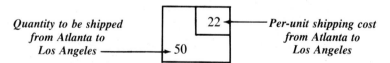

Quantity to be shipped — ← Per-unit shipping cost

Total shipping cost = 50($22) + 25($5) + 15($31) + 45($14) + 30($5) + 10($4)
= $2,510

corresponds to a specific factory and each column corresponds to a specific warehouse. Factory capacities are shown to the right of the table, and warehouse requirements are shown below. The larger box at the intersection of a specific row and column contains both shipping quantity and shipping cost along the route from the factory corresponding to that row and to the warehouse represented by that column. The shipment quantity is given (if any) in the lower left of that box while the per-unit shipping cost is shown in the smaller box at the upper right. Thus, for example, the box at the intersection of the Atlanta row and the Los Angeles column shows that 50 units are to be shipped from Atlanta to Los Angeles at a cost of $22 each:

Quantity to be shipped from Atlanta to Los Angeles — → 50   22 ← Per-unit shipping cost from Atlanta to Los Angeles

The feasibility of this solution can be verified by noting that the total quantity shipped from each factory is equal to the capacity at that factory and that the total quantity shipped to each warehouse equals the quantity required. For example, Table 9-2 shows 50 ovens being shipped from Atlanta to Los Angeles and 25 ovens from Atlanta to New Orleans. These are the only shipments shown from Atlanta and equal the 75 available.

The total shipping cost for this solution is computed by multiplying the quantities shipped by the appropriate per-unit shipping costs and summing the results. This is shown to be $2,510.

Observe that the total number of ovens available at the factories (175) exactly equals the total number of ovens needed at the warehouses (175). This is an important condition for feasibility. If the number of ovens available at the factories is less than the number needed at the warehouses, no feasible solution exists. No matter what shipping plan is chosen, one or more warehouses will not have its requirements met. In a later section we will see how the total supply (at the factories) and the total demand (at the warehouses) can be artificially balanced. For now we will assume that such a balance already exists.

Since we have identified the properties of a feasible solution, let us now see how such solutions can be generated.

Northwest-Corner Method   The simplest of the procedures used to generate an initial feasible solution is the northwest-corner method. It is so called because we begin with the northwest, or upper left, corner of our shipping table. For the Modor Oven problem the northwest corner corresponds to the shipping route from the Atlanta factory to the Kansas City warehouse, as shown in Table 9-3. The quantity to be shipped along that route is made as large as possible considering the amount available at that factory and the amount needed at that warehouse. Successive shipping quantities are determined for the other routes by moving to the next factory or warehouse, as needed, allocating the maximum amount along that route, and continuing in a general diagonal direction until all supply and demand constraints are met.

Table 9-3 shows the initial feasible solution that would be generated by the northwest-corner method for the Modor Oven problem. Let us consider how these shipping quantities were arrived at. We previously identified the Atlanta to Kansas City route as the northwest corner. Note that the amount that can be shipped along that route is limited by both the amount needed at Kansas City, 30 ovens, and the amount available at Atlanta, 75 ovens. Therefore, we can ship at most 30 ovens along that route.

This satisfies Kansas City's requirements but leaves 45 ovens at Atlanta available to be shipped elsewhere. Thus we move to the right, as the arrow in Table 9-3 indicates, and determine the maximum amount that can be shipped from Atlanta to Los Angeles. Since Los Angeles requires more ovens than Atlanta has available, the maximum amount shipped is limited to 45. This allocation is shown in Table 9-3.

All available units at Atlanta have now been allocated, but a 20-oven requirement still remains for Los Angeles. To satisfy this requirement we drop down one row to the Boston plant, and since Boston has 60 units available we can ship the 20 units needed to Los Angeles. This exhausts Los Angeles' needs, so we move to Memphis, which requires 55 units. Since Boston has only 40 units remaining, we can ship only 40 units from Boston to Memphis. We then drop down to Chicago, which has more than enough units to satisfy the remaining demand for 15 units at Memphis. The final allocation of 25 units from Chicago to New Orleans satisfies exactly the remaining requirement of 25 units needed at New Orleans and also uses the last 25 units available at Chicago. This method of obtaining an initial feasible solution always works.

We find the total cost of the initial solution by multiplying each of the

TABLE 9-3
Northwest-Corner Method: Initial Feasible Solution to Modor Problem

Factory location	Warehouse location				Ovens available
	Kansas City	Los Angeles	Memphis	New Orleans	
Atlanta	11 / 30——►45	22	6	5	75 − 30 = 45 − 45 = 0
Boston	16	31 / 20	14 / 40	15	60 − 20 = 40 − 40 = 0
Chicago	5	21	4 / 15——►25	9	40 − 15 = 25 − 25 = 0
Ovens required	30 −30 0	65 −45 20 −20 0	55 −40 15 −15 0	25 −25 0	

Total shipping cost = 30($11) + 45($22) + 20($31) + 40($14) + 15($4) + 25($9) = $2,785

quantities shipped by the appropriate shipping costs. Note that this cost of $2,785 is higher than the cost of $2,510 that we obtained for the solution shown in Table 9-2. Recall that the only purpose of using the northwest-corner method is to find an *initial* feasible solution. Later in this chapter we will see that we can improve on our methods to eventually obtain the optimal solution.

INSTANT REPLAY Although tradition calls for starting at the northwest corner, other corners could be used as well. Using the Modor Oven problem, apply the north*east*-corner method to obtain an initial feasible solution. In other words, start at the northeast corner (Atlanta to New Orleans) and proceed in a similar manner as with the northwest-corner method to find a feasible solution.

CHECK Initial feasible solution by the northeast-corner method has a cost of $2,560.

The northwest-corner method is a quick and easy way to find an initial feasible solution. Observe, however, that the shipping decisions (how much to ship along each route) ignore the shipping costs. Thus, the initial solution may be a high-cost solution. A comparison of the costs we obtained as the initial solutions by the northwest- and northeast-corner methods illustrates the variability possible. The northeast-corner method generated a solution ($2,560) that is 8 percent cheaper than that generated by the northwest-corner method ($2,785).

317

Finding an initial feasible solution is only the first step in solving a transportation problem. As shown in Figure 9-1, we need a means of determining whether or not a solution is optimal and, if not, a way of improving it. Actually these two steps are related. The test used to indicate the optimality of the current solution also points to an improved solution if the current solution is nonoptimal.

The optimality test for a transportation problem is in principle the same as that used by the simplex method. For this reason it is useful to review the simplex optimality test here. You should recall that simplex optimality was determined by evaluating each nonbasic variable. This was done by comparing what we gained from making that variable basic (entering gains) with what we had to give up (entering costs). The optimal solution was indicated when none of the nonbasic variables offered further improvement.

The same approach is followed for the transportation problem. For each unused route (nonbasic variable) we compare the cost of a shipment along that route (direct cost) with the net change in cost along the other routes (indirect costs) that would result from a reallocation along the route under investigation. The current solution is optimal if the direct cost of a shipment along each unused route exceeds the net reduction in indirect costs caused by a reallocation along the other routes.

When the current simplex solution was nonoptimal, we chose the nonbasic variable for which the per-unit improvement was greatest to become basic. We use the same approach with the transportation problem. If the current solution is nonoptimal, the cost of a direct shipment along at least one unused route must be less than the indirect costs along the other routes. If more than one unused route meets the condition for nonoptimality, we will choose the route that offers the largest per-unit savings to become basic.

Thus, the optimality test for transportation problems is, in principle, the same as that for the linear programming simplex method. However, in application, we exploit the special structure of the transportation problem to reduce the computations needed to complete the check.

To illustrate how this is done, let's look at a simple example problem. The shipment costs and a feasible allocation are shown below:

Factory	Warehouse X	Warehouse Y	Units available
A	4 / 40	7 / 10	50
B	5	12 / 50	50
Units needed	40	60	

Note that three routes, *AX*, *AY*, and *BY*, are basic in that they all have shipments assigned. The only nonbasic route is *BX*, which is unused at the moment. If this solution is optimal, the cost of shipping along route *BX* must be greater than the savings that result from reallocations on the other routes.

Route BX has a direct shipment cost of $5; that is easy to find. But what of the changes in the other routes? Suppose we ship 1 unit, say, along route BX. Shipments from B to Y must be reduced by 1 unit, or the capacity limit of factory B will be exceeded. If shipments along route BY are reduced by 1 unit, the shipments along route AY must be increased by an identical amount in order that warehouse Y has all its needs satisfied. Furthermore, the amount shipped along route AX must be reduced by 1 unit, both because the route AY shipments are increased by that amount and because BX shipments increased as well.

What is the net result of all these reallocations with respect to cost? The direct shipment along route BX will cost $5. The changes along the other routes include increases and decreases and can be summarized as:

1-unit decrease along route AX	−$ 4
1-unit increase along route AY	+$ 7
1-unit decrease along route BY	−$12
Net reduction in indirect costs	−$ 9

Thus, although the direct cost of reallocating 1 unit along route BX is $5, the indirect costs along the other routes will decrease by $9. Thus, the total change in shipping costs will be a $4 decrease. This indicates that the current solution is not optimal and that we can improve the solution by reallocating along route BX. If we can save $4 by shipping 1 unit along that route, the cost savings can be maximized by shipping as many units as possible along that route. How many can we ship?

Refer to Table 9-4, which shows the current shipment pattern for the solution we are evaluating. Note the pluses and minuses, corresponding to each route. These pluses and minuses indicate whether each of the current shipments must increase or decrease due to a reallocation along route BX. That is, shipments along routes BX and AY are to increase and those along AX and BY must decrease. It was these changes upon which we based the $4 cost-change figure.

Once again recall the linear programming simplex process. The limiting factor on the size of the entering variable is the allowable amount of decrease in the size of the current basic variables. The entering variable can be increased in size until one of the current basic variables declines to zero. Any further increase in the size of the entering variable causes at least one other variable to take on negative values, violating the nonnegativity constraints.

TABLE 9-4
Increase or Decrease in Basic Variables on Reallocation

	X	Y
	4	7
A	40 (−)	10 (+)
	5	12
B	(+)	50 (−)

The same principles apply in determining the maximum amount that can be reallocated when changing the transportation shipment pattern. This is easy to do in the transportation problem. Those routes that are to decrease will all decrease by the same amount. That is, any amount that we ship along route BX must be deducted from the amount currently shipped along routes AX and BY and added to the amount shipped on route AY. The same amount must be added and subtracted in order to keep the solution feasible. Thus, of those routes that are to decrease, the one with the smallest current shipment level determines the largest amount that can be reallocated.

In our example routes AX and BY have minuses, indicating that shipments along these routes are to decrease in the reallocation. Because the 40 units currently shipped along route AX is less than the 50 units along BY, the largest amount that can be reallocated is 40. Table 9-5 shows how the revised allocation would be formed.

If you compare the costs of these two solutions, you will find that they have dropped from $830 to $670. This decline of $160 is expected. We were able to reallocate 40 units at a predicted cost savings of $4 per unit.

INSTANT REPLAY   Using the new allocation shown in Table 9-5, calculate the net cost change for a reallocation to route AX.

CHECK   Because this is the reverse of the change we made above, the net cost change is +$4 per unit.

As the Instant Replay shows, the only nonbasic variable, shipments along route AX, has a positive net cost change. Thus, the solution shown in Table 9-5 is optimal.

This simple example illustrates the basic steps involved in checking a transportation solution for optimality and improving it if it is not optimal. We have to evaluate each of the unused, or nonbasic, routes. In each case we need to compare the direct shipment cost of the unused route with the cost of changes that will occur along the used, or basic, routes. If a reallocation along one or more of the unused routes will lower total costs, the current solution is

TABLE 9-5
Determination of Revised Allocation

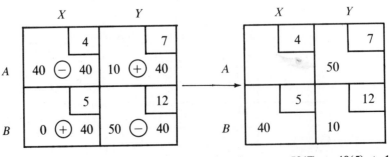

$$\text{Total cost} = 50(7) + 40(5) + 10(12)$$
$$= \$670$$

TABLE 9-6
Stepping Stone Reallocation Pattern for Boston to Kansas City Route

		Warehouse location			
Factory location	Kansas City	Los Angeles	Memphis	New Orleans	Ovens available
Atlanta	11 30 (−) ← (+)	22 45	6	5	75
Boston	16 (+) → (−)	31 20	14 40	15	60
Chicago	5	21	4 15	9 25	40
Ovens required	30	65	55	25	

not optimal. In that case, a reallocation is made to the unused route that promises the greatest per-unit decrease in shipping costs. The amount that can be reallocated is determined by the smallest quantity now shipped along the routes which are to decrease.

Stepping Stone Method   For problems larger than that treated above, tracing the pattern of changes required by a reallocation is sometimes difficult. One method for doing this is to trace through the increases and decreases necessary to keep the solution feasible, as we did above. This method is often called the *stepping stone method,* for reasons that will soon be apparent.

To illustrate the complexities in tracing this pattern, consider again the Modor Oven problem. Table 9-6 shows the northwest-corner solution for this problem found earlier. Suppose we wished to evaluate the optimality of this solution. This requires an examination of each of the nonbasic routes. Consider first the Boston to Kansas City route, which is nonbasic and has a direct cost of $16. A reallocation along this route will involve a series of increases and decreases, as traced in Table 9-6. Any shipment along the Boston to Kansas City route must be accompanied by a corresponding decrease along the Atlanta to Kansas City route (otherwise Kansas City will receive more than needed and some other warehouse will come up short). A decrease in the Atlanta to Kansas City shipment is met by an increase in that for Atlanta to Los Angeles. This in turn causes a decrease along the Boston to Los Angeles route.

To understand why this method is called the stepping stone method, examine the route-change path traced in Table 9-6. The allocation squares can be thought of as areas in a pond. Those squares that have allocations, representing shipments along a particular route, can be thought of as stepping stones. Imagine that a frog is sitting on a lily pad in the middle of the square being evaluated (Boston to Kansas City in this case). The frog wishes to exercise by hopping around the pond but realizes that takeoff and landing are confined to the stepping stones. The frog is constrained to move only in right-angle directions. As soon as the frog lands on a stone, it will leave that stone by jumping directly to the left or to the right, never straight ahead or diagonally.

Given these simple rules, there is *one and only one path* that the frog can trace. In the case of the Boston to Kansas City route, it is the one shown in Table 9-6. In fact, for any nonbasic route that needs to be evaluated, the path of the jumping frog (that is, the stepping stone path) can be used to determine the cost tradeoffs caused by a reallocation. After tracing the path, the routes need to be identified as representing positive or negative changes. We can easily do this by placing a plus in the cell being evaluated (a reallocation will involve an increase along this route) and starting around the path placing a minus in the first stepping stone square and then alternating pluses and minuses as the path is traced (to reflect the shipment changes needed to keep the solution feasible). It makes no difference in which direction the path is traced, because the two "stones" adjacent to the square being evaluated will both contain minuses. (If they don't, it is a signal that something is wrong.)

The following calculations summarize the cost changes that would occur if a reallocation was attempted along any of the empty routes:

Route	Direct cost, $	Cost of changes in other routes, $	Net change, $
Atlanta–Memphis	6	$-22 + 31 - 14 = -5$	$+1$
Atlanta–New Orleans	5	$-22 + 31 - 14 + 4 - 9 = -10$	-5
Boston–Kansas City	16	$-11 + 22 - 31 = -20$	-4
Boston–New Orleans	15	$-14 + 4 - 9 = -19$	-4
Chicago–Kansas City	5	$-11 + 22 - 31 + 14 - 4 = -10$	-5
Chicago–Los Angeles	21	$-31 + 14 - 4 = -21$	0

Since some of these cost changes are negative, the solution being tested is not optimal.

As you can see, the stepping stone method is rather tedious and time-consuming. It is but one of several approaches that can be used to find the net-change values for transportation problems. Shortly we will examine another, more efficient method. The stepping stone method was presented first because it is easier to understand and because the stepping stone path-tracing technique is used in either case to determine the shipment pattern changes whenever a reallocation is required to be made.

Using Dual Variables   We can exploit our knowledge of the dual to the transportation problem to provide an easy and efficient check on the optimality of any feasible solution to a transportation problem. This can be done without tracing the stepping stone paths. You will recall, from Chapter 7, that the optimality of a linear programming solution is in effect determined by whether or not the solution is *dual-feasible*, or satisfies the constraints of the dual. The constraints for the dual of a transportation problem have a special form which allows this check for dual feasibility (hence optimality) to be carried out very easily.

To illustrate, let us consider the primal and dual formulations of the Modor Oven problem as shown in Table 9-7. Note that there is one dual variable for each primal constraint. The primal constraints are of two types: those associated with supply capacities at each factory and those corresponding to

TABLE 9-7
Linear Programming Formulations (Primal and Dual) of Modor Oven Problem

Primal

Minimize: $11AK + 22AL + 6AM + 5AN + 16BK + 31BL + 14BM + 15BN + 5CK + 21CL + 4CM + 9CN$

Subject to: $AK + AL + AM + AN = 75$ Atlanta supply capacity

$BK + BL + BM + BN = 60$ Boston supply capacity

$CK + CL + CM + CN = 40$ Chicago supply capacity

$AK + BK + CK = 30$ Kansas City demand requirement

$AL + BL + CL = 65$ Los Angeles demand requirement

$AM + BM + CM = 55$ Memphis demand requirement

$AN + BN + CN = 25$ New Orleans demand requirement

Dual

Maximize: $75u_1 + 60u_2 + 40u_3 + 30v_1 + 65v_2 + 55v_3 + 25v_4$

Subject to: $u_1 + v_1 \leq 11$ Atlanta–Kansas City

$u_1 + v_2 \leq 22$ Atlanta–Los Angeles

$u_1 + v_3 \leq 6$ Atlanta–Memphis

$u_1 + v_4 \leq 5$ Atlanta–New Orleans

$u_2 + v_1 \leq 16$ Boston–Kansas City

$u_2 + v_2 \leq 31$ Boston–Los Angeles

$u_2 + v_3 \leq 14$ Boston–Memphis

$u_2 + v_4 \leq 15$ Boston–New Orleans

$u_3 + v_1 \leq 5$ Chicago–Kansas City

$u_3 + v_2 \leq 21$ Chicago–Los Angeles

$u_3 + v_3 \leq 4$ Chicago–Memphis

$u_3 + v_4 \leq 9$ Chicago–New Orleans

demand requirements for each warehouse. This same division is maintained in the dual by using u_i as the dual variable corresponding to the ith factory and v_j as the dual variable for the jth warehouse.

As shown in Table 9-7, each dual constraint corresponds to a specific shipping route. Observe that the left-hand side of each dual constraint is the sum of two dual variables, one representing a factory (u_i) and the other a warehouse (v_j). The right-hand side is the direct shipment cost from that factory to that warehouse, which we can refer to as c_{ij}. Thus, these constraints have the form:

$$u_i + v_j \leq c_{ij}$$

For any feasible solution to the primal problem, the differences between the left- and right-hand sides of these dual constraints are equal to the net-change values for the primal variables. Recall that the net-change values for basic variables will always be 0. In other words, the left- and right-hand sides of each dual constraint corresponding to a basic primal variable will be equal. Thus, if the solution has a shipment from factory i to warehouse j, the corresponding dual inequality $u_i + v_j \le c_{ij}$ can be written as an equality:

$$u_i + v_j = c_{ij}$$

This condition is important because it allows us to solve directly for the values of the dual variables.

To illustrate, let us suppose we are evaluating the northwest-corner method solution to the Modor Oven problem. This solution has shipments along six routes (thus, six basic variables). The dual constraints for these routes are shown below:

$$u_1 + v_1 = 11 \quad \text{Atlanta–Kansas City}$$
$$u_1 + v_2 = 22 \quad \text{Atlanta–Los Angeles}$$
$$u_2 + v_2 = 31 \quad \text{Boston–Los Angeles}$$
$$u_2 + v_3 = 14 \quad \text{Boston–Memphis}$$
$$u_3 + v_3 = 4 \quad \text{Chicago–Memphis}$$
$$u_3 + v_4 = 9 \quad \text{Chicago–New Orleans}$$

We have six equations and seven unknowns (u_1, u_2, u_3, v_1, v_2, v_3, and v_4). In order to solve for the values of the dual variables, we need to determine a value for one of these unknowns so that we can solve for the other six. Fortunately, we can pick any one of the seven dual variables and arbitrarily assign it a value of 0. It does not matter which dual variable we choose.

The reason that we can arbitrarily set one of the dual variables equal to 0 is that the linear programming formulation of a transportation problem (with balanced supply and demand[1]) has one more constraint than is actually needed. Using the Modor problem as an example, suppose we are told the shipment patterns to each of the warehouses from only the Boston and Chicago factories. Could we deduce from this the shipment plan for the Atlanta factory? A moment's reflection should convince you that we could.

INSTANT REPLAY: Suppose we know that Boston is to ship 30 ovens to Kansas City and 30 to Los Angeles and that Chicago is to ship 35 to Los Angeles and 5 to Memphis. Given that Kansas City is to receive 30 ovens, Los Angeles 65, Memphis 55, and New Orleans 25, determine the shipping plan for the Atlanta factory.

CHECK The Boston and Chicago shipments satisfy all the needs at Kansas City and Los Angeles, leaving Memphis with a shortage of 50 ovens and New Orleans with a need for 25. Thus, Atlanta will ship 50 to Memphis and 25 to New Orleans. Note that the required shipments from Atlanta equal its capacity of 75 ovens.

[1]Supply and demand can always be made equal by use of either a dummy supply or dummy demand point. This will be covered later in the chapter.

Thus we can always eliminate one of the primal constraints. The marginal value of this redundant constraint is zero, and the dual variable corresponding to that constraint must as well be equal to zero.

Suppose for the Modor Oven problem we designate the Atlanta supply capacity constraint as redundant. This means that the dual variable $u_1 = 0$. That allows us to solve the six dual constraints for the remaining six dual variables. If $u_1 = 0$, we can solve for v_1:

$$u_1 + v_1 = 11$$
$$0 + v_1 = 11$$
$$v_1 = 11$$

and for v_2:

$$u_1 + v_2 = 22$$
$$0 + v_2 = 22$$
$$v_2 = 22$$

Using the value for v_2, we can determine u_2:

$$u_2 + v_2 = 31$$
$$u_2 + 22 = 31$$
$$u_2 = 9$$

The value for u_2 can be used to find v_3:

$$u_2 + v_3 = 14$$
$$9 + v_3 = 14$$
$$v_3 = 5$$

This allows us to find u_3:

$$u_3 + v_3 = 4$$
$$u_3 + 5 = 4$$
$$u_3 = -1$$

and then to find v_4:

$$u_3 + v_4 = 9$$
$$-1 + v_4 = 9$$
$$v_4 = 10$$

Thus we have found the values of all seven dual variables for the *northwest-corner method* solution to the Modor Oven Problem. These are: $u_1 = 0$, $u_2 = 9$, $u_3 = -1$, $v_1 = 11$, $v_2 = 22$, $v_3 = 5$, and $v_4 = 10$.

Now that we have found the values for the dual variables, we can check the solution for optimality by testing the remaining constraints (those associated with the nonbasic routes) for dual feasibility. This is shown in the table at the top of page 326, where we see that some of the dual constraints for the nonbasic routes are not satisfied: the left-hand side of the constraint is not less than or equal to the right-hand side. Thus the northwest-corner method solution for the Modor Oven problem is not optimal. Observe that the values shown on the left-hand side are the same as the values found by the stepping stone method for the reduction in cost for basic variables brought about by a shipment along one of the unused (nonbasic) routes.

Nonbasic route	Dual constraint	Left-hand side	Constraint met?
Atlanta–Memphis	$u_1 + v_3 \leq 6$	$0 + 5 = 5$	Yes
Atlanta–New Orleans	$u_1 + v_4 \leq 5$	$0 + 10 = 10$	No
Boston–Kansas City	$u_2 + v_1 \leq 16$	$9 + 11 = 20$	No
Boston–New Orleans	$u_2 + v_4 \leq 15$	$9 + 10 = 19$	No
Chicago–Kansas City	$u_3 + v_1 \leq 5$	$-1 + 11 = 10$	No
Chicago–Los Angeles	$u_3 + v_2 \leq 21$	$-1 + 22 = 21$	Yes

The optimality check using the dual variables can be carried out in an easier manner than shown above, as will now be demonstrated. Consider Table 9-8 which shows the direct shipment costs (circled) in the body of the table corresponding to the northwest-corner method solution for the Modor Oven problem. The values of the dual variables for this solution are shown in the margins of the table. They are calculated by first setting one dual variable equal to 0 and then using the direct shipment costs to find the other dual variables. Thus, we set $u_1 = 0$ and since $u_1 + v_2 = 22$, we know $v_2 = 22$. Likewise, since $u_1 + v_1 = 11$, we find $v_1 = 11$. The other dual variable values are found in a similar manner.

The dual variables are then used to find the left-hand-side values for the dual constraints corresponding to each nonbasic route. These left-hand-side values are what we referred to as indirect costs because they correspond to the reduction in cost along the basic routes caused by a reallocation to a nonbasic route. These indirect costs are shown in Table 9-9. They are calculated by adding the factory and warehouse dual variable values corresponding to each nonbasic route. For example, the Atlanta to Memphis indirect cost is found by adding the Atlanta and Memphis dual variable values, $0 + 5 = 5$.

Optimality is then easily confirmed by subtracting these indirect costs from the direct shipment cost (Table 9-6) for each nonbasic route. This will yield net-change values for each nonbasic variable. If these are all zero or positive, the solution is optimal. If one or more net-change value is negative, the total cost can be reduced by reallocating along that route. The lack of optimality for the northwest-corner method solution to the Modor Oven prob-

TABLE 9-8
Using Direct Shipment Costs to Calculate Dual Variable Values

Factory location	Warehouse location				Supply point dual variables
	Kansas City	Los Angeles	Memphis	New Orleans	
Atlanta	⑪	㉒			$u_1 = 0$
Boston		㉛	⑭		$u_2 = 9$
Chicago			④	⑨	$u_3 = -1$
Demand point dual variables	$v_1 = 11$	$v_2 = 22$	$v_3 = 5$	$v_4 = 10$	

TABLE 9-9
327

THE
TRANSPORTATION
METHOD

TABLE 9-9
Using Dual Variable Values to Calculate Indirect Costs

Factory location	Kansas City	Los Angeles	Memphis	New Orleans	Supply point dual variables
		Warehouse location			
Atlanta	⑪	㉒	5	10	$u_1 = 0$
Boston	20	㉛	⑭	19	$u_2 = 9$
Chicago	10	21	④	⑨	$u_3 = -1$
Demand point dual variables	$v_1 = 11$	$v_2 = 22$	$v_3 = 5$	$v_4 = 10$	

lem is reconfirmed by the net-change values shown in Table 9-10. Four of the net-change values are negative.

Improving the Solution

What do we do when the solution being evaluated is shown to be nonoptimal? We do as we did with a nonoptimal linear programming solution: we improve it, by shipping along a route that is currently unused or nonbasic. This requires two steps: the first is the identification of the best route to become basic, and the second is the determination of the revised solution. Actually, we already know all that is required to perform either of these steps since the test for optimality will pinpoint the route to become basic and the stepping stone path will be used to perform the reallocation.

To illustrate, let us consider the northwest-corner method solution for the Modor Oven problem repeated here in Table 9-11. Table 9-12 shows the completed cost-change values or indirect costs for all nonbasic routes and the corresponding net-change values (direct shipment costs less the indirect costs).

TABLE 9-10
Net-Change Values for Northwest-Corner Method Solution to Modor Oven Problem

Factory location	Kansas City	Los Angeles	Memphis	New Orleans
		Warehouse location		
Atlanta	—	—	6 − 5 = 1	5 − 10 = −5
Boston	16 − 20 = −4	—	—	15 − 19 = −4
Chicago	5 − 10 = −5	21 − 21 = 0	—	—

TABLE 9-11
Northwest-Corner Method Solution to the Modor Oven Problem

Factory location	Kansas City	Los Angeles	Memphis	New Orleans	Ovens available
Atlanta	11 / 30	22 / 45	6	5	75
Boston	16	31 / 20	14 / 40	15	60
Chicago	5	21	4 / 15	9 / 25	40
Ovens required	30	65	55	25	

Selecting a Route for Reallocation Table 9-12 indicates that the solution is nonoptimal since there are four negative-value routes. These negative values not only indicate that the solution is nonoptimal but also identify the *per-unit* change in costs offered by the unused routes.

For instance, the -5 shown for the Atlanta to New Orleans route indicates that each unit shipped along that route will save $5. An interpretation of the amounts shown in Table 9-12 suggests a means for choosing one of the unused routes to be a basic route in the next solution tested. Because the amounts shown represent per-unit net change in costs, the largest negative value should be the preferred choice.

In our case we do not have a clear-cut choice since the Chicago to Kansas City and Atlanta to New Orleans routes both promise a $5-per-unit reduction in total costs. Actually, it makes very little difference as to which of these two routes we select. Either will move us closer to the optimal solution. One option is to select the route along which the larger number of units can be shipped.

Suppose we select the Atlanta to New Orleans route as the entering variable, or new basic route. The next question to be decided is how much can be shipped along that route, and ultimately, what will the new solution look like.

Actually, both of these questions can be answered simultaneously by use of the stepping stone method. Referring to Table 9-13, we see that if we are to ship along the Atlanta to New Orleans route we must reduce our shipments from Chicago to New Orleans. This reduction can be reallocated along the Chicago to Memphis route, which calls in turn for a reduction along the Boston to Memphis route. The Boston to Memphis reduction is offset by an increase along the Boston to Los Angeles route, which calls for a decrease from Atlanta to Los Angeles. This last decrease is also necessary to accommodate the increase from Atlanta to New Orleans that we started with.

Determining the Amount to Reallocate We have now determined the pattern of reallocation required to make the Atlanta to New Orleans route basic. We next need to determine the amount to be reallocated for shipment along this new basic route. That amount can be obtained only from shipments now being made on other routes. Those shipment quantities to be changed will increase or decrease by the amount shipped along the new route. Thus, the size of the entering variable (the amount to be shipped along the new route) will be limited by the previous shipment quantities along the routes to be decreased. The amount shipped along the new route can be no greater than the smallest quantity now shipped along the routes to be decreased.

For example, as the shipments increase along the Atlanta to New Orleans route, they must correspondingly decrease along the Atlanta to Los Angeles, Boston to Memphis, and Chicago to New Orleans routes. The size of the increase along the Atlanta to New Orleans route is thus limited by the amounts currently being shipped along the routes that are to be decreased. In this case the Chicago to New Orleans route is limiting, and only 25 units can be reallocated. If we try to reallocate more units than 25, a negative shipment will result along the Chicago to New Orleans route, which is, of course, not allowed. Thus the departing variable will always be the route with the smallest current allocation from among those routes that the stepping stone pattern indicates must decrease.

TABLE 9-12
Checking Optimality for the Northwest-Corner Solution to the Modor Problem

Factory location	Warehouse Location				u_i
	Kansas City	Los Angeles	Memphis	New Orleans	
Atlanta	⑪	㉒	5	10	0
Boston	20	㉛	⑭	19	9
Chicago	10	21	④	⑨	−1
v_j	11	22	5	10	

(a) Calculation of Indirect Costs

Factory location	Warehouse location			
	Kansas City	Los Angeles	Memphis	New Orleans
Atlanta	—	—	1	−5
Boston	−4	—	—	−4
Chicago	−5	0	—	—

(b) Calculation of Net-Change Values

TABLE 9-13

Improving the Solution by Reallocating Along the Atlanta to New Orleans Route

Warehouse location

Factory location	Kansas City	Los Angeles	Memphis	New Orleans
Atlanta	30	45 $\ominus$		$\oplus$
Boston		20 $\oplus$	$\ominus$ 40	
Chicago			$\oplus$ 15	$\ominus$ 25

(a) Identifying the Stepping Stone Reallocation Pattern

Warehouse location

Factory location	Kansas City	Los Angeles	Memphis	New Orleans
Atlanta	30	45 − 25 = 20		0 + 25 = 25
Boston		20 + 25 = 45	40 − 25 = 15	
Chicago			15 + 25 = 40	25 − 25 = 0

(b) Making the Reallocation

The reallocation would then be achieved by adding 25 units to those routes with a $\oplus$, subtracting 25 units from those routes with a $\ominus$, and not changing the remaining route allocations. The completed allocation is shown at the bottom of Table 9-13.

The next step in the solution of the problem is to evaluate the new solution for optimality. Table 9-14 shows the calculation of indirect costs and net changes for the solution of Table 9-13.

This time only two net changes are negative, and the Chicago to Kansas City route promises a $1-per-unit greater savings than the Boston to Kansas City route. Thus, the next solution will be formed by reallocating shipments along the Chicago to Kansas City route. The reallocation pattern and the new allocation are displayed in Table 9-15. Note that 30 units were reallocated.

INSTANT REPLAY In moving from the solution in Table 9-13 to Table 9-15, which variable is the departing variable?

CHECK The Atlanta to Kansas City route is the departing variable. Table 9-13 shows a shipment of 30 ovens along that route. Table 9-15 shows no shipments along that route.

TABLE 9-14
Checking Optimality for the Second Solution to the Modor Problem

Warehouse location

Factory location	Kansas City	Los Angeles	Memphis	New Orleans	u_i
Atlanta	⑪	㉒	5	⑤	0
Boston	20	㉛	⑭	14	9
Chicago	10	21	④	4	-1
v_j	11	22	5	5	

(a) Calculating the Indirect Costs

Warehouse location

Factory location	Kansas City	Los Angeles	Memphis	New Orleans
Atlanta	—	—	1	—
Boston	-4	—	—	1
Chicago	⊝5	0	—	5

(b) Calculating Net-Change Values

An examination of this new solution requires completion of the indirect cost and net-change values, as shown in Table 9-16. Because all net-change values are now positive or zero, the solution shown in Table 9-15 is optimal.

Complications with Transportation Problems

Now that we have seen how to solve transportation problems, we next need to consider several complications that can arise. These include: (1) multiple optimal solutions, (2) degenerate solutions, (3) maximization objectives, (4) unbalanced supply and demand, and (5) prohibited routes. An understanding of how to handle these complications in the transportation problem framework will allow you to apply this method to a wide variety of practical situations. Each of these complications will now be considered in turn.

Multiple Optimal Solutions

As with other linear programming problems, a transportation problem can have more than one optimal solution. This would be indicated by a value of 0 in the final net-change table. For instance, the final net-change table (Table 9-16) for

TABLE 9-15
Improving the Second Solution by Reallocating
Along the Chicago to Kansas City Route

Warehouse location

Factory location	Kansas City	Los Angeles	Memphis	New Orleans
Atlanta	30 (−)─(+)	20		25
Boston		(−)─45─(+)	15	
Chicago	(+)		(−) 40	

(a) Identifying the Stepping Stone Reallocation Pattern

Warehouse location

Factory location	Kansas City	Los Angeles	Memphis	New Orleans
Atlanta		50		25
Boston		15	45	
Chicago	30		10	

(b) Third Solution

the solution to the Modor Oven problem shows a 0 net change for the Chicago to Los Angeles route. This indicates that a reallocation including this route as a basic variable will have no effect on the total cost. This reallocation would lead to a solution with the same total cost as the optimal solution just found, thus identifying another optimal solution.

The identification of multiple optimal solutions and even those within a certain percentage of the optimal cost may be an important managerial consideration. There might, for instance, be many considerations which management is unable or unwilling to express explicitly as costs or constraints but which nevertheless are important in choosing among equal or nearly equal cost solutions. For example, management may be reluctant to rely on one of the routes because of past history of abnormal transportation delays. If two optimal solutions are available, one using this unreliable route and the other not, it is likely that the latter solution would be preferable even though the two solutions have identical costs.

INSTANT REPLAY Using the allocation shown at the top of page 333 as a starting point, apply the test/reallocation steps to obtain one of the two optimal solutions to the Modor Oven problem.

	Kansas City	Los Angeles	Memphis	New Orleans
Atlanta			50	25
Boston		55	5	
Chicago	30	10		

CHECK Only one reallocation is required (along the Atlanta to Los Angeles route) leading to the alternate optimal solution.

Degeneracy

Chapter 8 covered degeneracy, a condition that sometimes develops in linear programming problems. As you will recall, *degeneracy* results when more than two constraints intersect at a single extreme point. This results in one or more of the basic variables having a zero value. Degeneracy is a fairly common occurrence with transportation problems. Thus, it is useful to know how to

TABLE 9-16
Checking Optimality for the Third Solution to the Modor Problem

Factory location	Kansas City	Los Angeles	Memphis	New Orleans	u_i
			Warehouse location		
Atlanta	6	(22)	5	(5)	0
Boston	15	(31)	(14)	14	9
Chicago	(5)	21	(4)	4	−1
v_j	6	22	5	5	

(a) Calculating the Indirect Costs

Factory location	Kansas City	Los Angeles	Memphis	New Orleans
		Warehouse location		
Atlanta	5	—	1	—
Boston	1	—	—	1
Chicago	—	0	—	5

(b) Net-Change Values

TABLE 9-17
Degenerate Northwest-Corner Method Solution to the Modified Modor Oven Problem

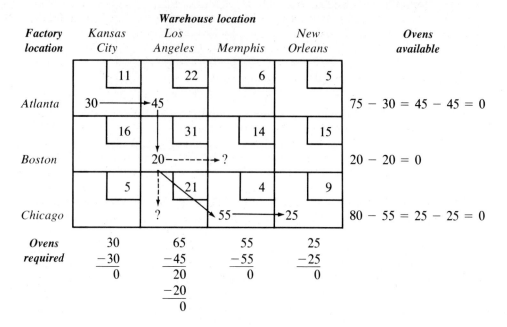

Factory location	Warehouse location				Ovens available
	Kansas City	Los Angeles	Memphis	New Orleans	
Atlanta	11 / 30———▸	22 / 45	6	5	75 − 30 = 45 − 45 = 0
Boston	16	31 / 20 ------▸	14 / ?	15	20 − 20 = 0
Chicago	5	21 / ?	4 / 55———	9 / ▸25	80 − 55 = 25 − 25 = 0
Ovens required	30 −30 ——— 0	65 −45 ——— 20 −20 ——— 0	55 −55 ——— 0	25 −25 ——— 0	

handle it when it occurs. We will begin with an example to show how degeneracy develops in a transportation problem.

To illustrate, let us suppose that in the Modor Oven problem the capacities of the Boston and Chicago factories are 20 and 80, respectively, while all else remains the same. Table 9-17 shows this modified situation and traces the northwest-corner allocation sequence (shown by the arrows). Observe that the path takes an unusual direction after the allocation to the Boston to Los Angeles route. Normally we would move either horizontally to the next warehouse, if Los Angeles had all its demand satisfied, or vertically to the next factory, if all of Boston's capacity had been used up. In this case, both events happen simultaneously. All of Boston's remaining capacity is just sufficient to meet the residual demand in Los Angeles. Thus, we need to move diagonally (a combination horizontal and vertical move) to a new factory *and* a new warehouse. The rest of the allocation sequence proceeds normally.

One immediate consequence of this situation is that one less shipping route is used in this initial allocation. A recheck of the past allocation tables for the Modor Oven problem will show that a feasible solution always used exactly six routes. The allocation in Table 9-17 requires that only five routes be used. Although this solution is feasible, it is degenerate. The reason there are five nonzero routes in the solution is that one other route, which is a basic variable and would normally have a nonzero value, has a zero value.

Table 9-7 showed the linear programming formulation of the Modor Oven problem. As described earlier, one of the seven constraints is redundant and can be eliminated. This leaves six nonredundant or independent constraints and signifies that there are six basic variables, one for each constraint.

334

Thus, since only five routes show nonzero shipments, the sixth basic variable has a zero value and the solution is degenerate. In general, with m rows or supply points and n columns or demand points, a solution must have exactly $m + n - 1$ nonzero routes in order to be nondegenerate. This number, $m + n - 1$, is simply the number of independent constraints or the number of basic variables. (As pointed out earlier, one of the $m + n$ constraints is redundant, which is why we subtract 1.) Recall that the fundamental theorem of linear programming requires one basic variable for each constraint.

In Chapter 8 we saw that degeneracy is largely a technical problem that usually is resolved without much effort. A degenerate solution to a transportation problem, however, causes special difficulties for the transportation method because we cannot evaluate its optimality without taking corrective action.

As an illustration, Table 9-18 shows an attempt to complete the indirect cost table for a degenerate solution. The table cannot be completed as shown. We are only able to obtain the dual variables for the Atlanta and Boston factories and for the Kansas City and Los Angeles warehouses. The only indirect cost we are able to determine is that for Boston to Kansas City.

Using an Artificial Allocation The solution to this dilemma is actually quite simple; we need an additional allocation to eliminate degeneracy. The problem arose when the Boston to Los Angeles allocation satisfied the factory and warehouse constraints simultaneously. Normally we would have had an allocation to either the Boston to Memphis route or the Chicago to Los Angeles route.

Therefore, we can force the solution to be nondegenerate by making an artificial allocation of some small quantity, usually represented by the symbol ϵ, along either of these routes. Suppose that the Boston to Memphis route is chosen and the shipment quantity ϵ is assigned to it, as shown in Table 9-19. An evaluation of this modified solution is shown in Table 9-20. This evaluation was successfully completed because the direct cost along the Boston to Memphis route allowed us to complete the indirect costs for the remaining routes.

Although we chose the Boston to Memphis route, we could just as well have assigned the ϵ to any of the routes for which we were unable to find the indirect cost in Table 9-18. This includes Atlanta to Memphis, Atlanta to New

TABLE 9-18
Incomplete Indirect Cost Table for Modor Degenerate Solution

Factory location	Warehouse location				
	Kansas City	Los Angeles	Memphis	New Orleans	u_i
Atlanta	⑪	㉒			0
Boston	20	㉛			9
Chicago			④	⑨	
v_j	11	22			

TABLE 9-19
Resolution of Degeneracy for Modified Modor Problem

Factory location	Warehouse location			
	Kansas City	Los Angeles	Memphis	New Orleans
Atlanta	11 — 30	22 — 45	6	5
Boston	16	31 — 20	14 — ε	15
Chicago	5	21	4 — 55	9 — 25

Orleans, Boston to Memphis, Boston to New Orleans, Chicago to Kansas City, and Chicago to Los Angeles, but *not* Boston to Kansas City.

INSTANT REPLAY Show that the indirect cost table can be completed if the ϵ is assigned to the Atlanta to Memphis route.

CHECK The indirect cost of the Boston to Memphis route is $15.

Degeneracy can also appear in the process of reallocating from a non-degenerate solution. For instance, consider Table 9-21, which illustrates a simple two-factory, three-warehouse problem. The upper table illustrates a reallocation path designed to make route AZ a basic route. Note that the amount to be reallocated is 10 units, limited, in this case, by both routes that are to decrease, AY and BZ, since both have the same quantity allocated.

The reallocation of the 10 units causes both of the decreasing routes to

TABLE 9-20
Completing the Indirect Cost Table for the Modified Degenerate Solution

Factory location	Warehouse location				u_i
	Kansas City	Los Angeles	Memphis	New Orleans	
Atlanta	⑪	㉒	5	10	0
Boston	20	㉛	⑭	19	9
Chicago	10	21	④	⑨	−1
v_j	11	22	5	10	

TABLE 9-21
Illustration of Degeneracy as a Result of a Reallocation

	X	Y	Z
A	30	10 ⊖—⊕	
B		20 ⊕—⊖	10

↓

	X	Y	Z
A	30		10
B		30	

drop to 0. This leaves three nonzero routes, while four ($m + n - 1 = 2 + 3 - 1 = 4$) routes must be nonzero in order for the solution to be nondegenerate. An attempt to complete the indirect cost table for this allocation will result in failure. We are unable to obtain the indirect costs for all of the unused routes.

As before, the problem can be corrected by adding ϵ to one of the unused routes. Any of the routes BX, AY, or BZ are appropriate here for allocation of the ϵ, since we are unable to find their indirect costs.

Interpreting Artificial Allocations Once the ϵ has been used to correct for degeneracy, it is treated much the same as any other shipment quantity. The only exceptions occur with respect to arithmetic operations involving ϵ. A summary of the important operations together with examples is presented below:

Operation		Result	Example
$0 + \epsilon$	=	ϵ	$0 + \epsilon = \epsilon$
$\epsilon + \epsilon$	=	ϵ	$\epsilon + \epsilon = \epsilon$
$\epsilon - \epsilon$	=	0	$\epsilon - \epsilon = 0$
$k + \epsilon$	=	k	$4 + \epsilon = 4$
$k - \epsilon$	=	k	$7 - \epsilon = 7$
$k \times \epsilon$	=	0	$5 \times \epsilon = 0$

The key to interpreting these calculations is to remember that ϵ is a minuscule quantity. It is just big enough to cause the route to which it is assigned to be treated as a basic variable, but not large enough to affect other nonzero amounts. Consequently, an ϵ route, although treated computationally as if a shipment was made on that route, in fact, represents an unused route.

In the process of reallocation, only one of three results is possible for the

TABLE 9-22
Possible Reallocation Results for ϵ

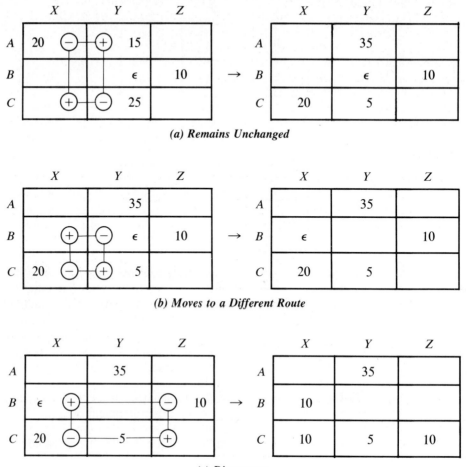

(a) Remains Unchanged

(b) Moves to a Different Route

(c) Disappears

ϵ: (*a*) it remains where it is, unchanged; (*b*) it moves to a different route; or (*c*) it disappears. These results are illustrated in Table 9-22.

The first allocation (Table 9-22*a*) is nondegenerate only because we assign an ϵ to route BY. The reallocation path required for a reassignment to route CX is also shown: 20 units are reallocated to the right. The ϵ remains where it was because it was not on the reallocation path.

The second illustration, Table 9-22*b*, shows a reallocation to route BX. In this instance routes BY and CX are to decrease, as shown by the reallocation path. Because the ϵ of route BY is less than the 20 of route CX, the amount to be reallocated is ϵ. As shown on the right, ϵ is added to the 0 of route BX, leaving ϵ; added to the 5 of route CY, leaving 5; subtracted from the 20 of route CX, leaving 20; and subtracted from the ϵ of route BY, leaving 0. (The arithmetic operation rules shown in the lower table on page 337 governed each of these transactions.) The net result of this second reallocation is to move the ϵ from route BY to route BX. Nothing else changes.

In the last case, Table 9-22c, ϵ disappears. A reallocation is desired along route CZ. The reallocation path is traced as shown. The amount to be reallocated is found to be 10 units, based on the amount shipped along route BZ. This amount is added to route CZ and subtracted from routes CX and BZ. It is added to the ϵ in route BX. Since $10 + \epsilon = 10$, the final allocation table shows a 10 on route BX. Note that the ϵ has disappeared and for good reason. It is no longer needed to correct for degeneracy. The last allocation has the required five non-zero routes (factories plus warehouses minus 1, or $m + n - 1 = 3 + 3 - 1 = 5$).

Although the last solution, Table 9-22c, does not contain an ϵ, it is important to note that an optimal solution can contain one or more ϵ's. When this happens, we simply ignore the ϵ's owing to their artificial nature. The optimal shipment plan would then include only those routes with actual numerical quantities.

INSTANT REPLAY Assume that the factory capacities and warehouse demands for the Modor Oven problem are modified as shown below, the shipping costs unchanged. Starting with the solution below, find the optimal solution.

Factory location	Kansas City	Los Angeles	Memphis	New Orleans	Ovens available
	Warehouse location				
Atlanta	11	22 ____ 20	6	5	20
Boston	16	31	14 ____ 10	15 ____ 10	20
Chicago	5 ____ 20	21	4	9	20
Ovens needed	20	20	10	10	

CHECK The total cost of the optimal solution is $820, and only one ϵ is present in the optimal solution (on either the Chicago to Los Angeles or the Chicago to Memphis route).

Maximization Problems

Although the transportation problems we have been dealing with have all had cost minimization objectives, there are transportation problems with maximization objectives. As an illustration, consider Agroproducts, Inc., which is a large grower of food products. It has three growing areas—in the Midwest, South, and West. The company sells its products on the domestic market, to Russia, and to Third World countries. Management wants to determine how best to allocate its current wheat crop among these three main markets. The amounts allocated cannot exceed the supplies available in its three growing

TABLE 9-23
Profit per Ton ($), Available Supplies, and Market Demands for Agroproducts Problem

Growing areas	Market area			Available supply, tons
	Domestic	Russia	Third World	
South	14	20	14	140
Midwest	15	19	14	120
West	16	18	12	40
Market demand, tons	100	100	100	

areas, nor can they exceed the quantities demanded by the three markets. The profit per ton that can be earned depends upon the cost of producing the wheat in each of the growing areas, transportation costs from the growing areas to the markets, and the market price that can be obtained (which varies with the market area). The available supply in each growing area, the demand for each market area, and the profit per ton for each combination of growing area and market area are shown in Table 9-23.

Maximization problems of the transportation type are actually quite easy to solve; several methods are available. We will consider two of these: one which converts the problem from a maximization to a minimization objective and then solves it in the normal manner, and another which modifies the procedures for checking optimality and for improvement of a solution for the standard transportation method.

Minimizing Opportunity Costs A transportation problem with a maximization objective can easily be converted to a minimization problem. This is done by subtracting each of the profits associated with the transportation routes from some large constant. A convenient constant to use is the largest profit. The largest profit for the Agroproducts problem is $20, which represents the profit per ton of selling the southern wheat to Russia. We can convert the problem from maximization to minimization by subtracting the profit for each of the other routes from $20. The resulting values represent opportunity costs because they correspond to the difference in profit earned by that route and the largest profit that could be earned by any of the routes. These opportunity costs are shown in Table 9-24.

After converting the profits to opportunity costs, we attempt to minimize these opportunity costs by solving the problem in the same manner as the other cost minimization problems we considered earlier. Thus, this approach requires only a simple adjustment to the data of the initial problem formulation.

INSTANT REPLAY Using the opportunity costs of Table 9-24, find the optimal solution to the Agroproducts problem.

CHECK The optimal solution calls for shipments of 100 tons along the route from the South to Russia, 40 tons from the South to the Third World, 60 tons from the Midwest to the domestic market, 60 tons from the Midwest to the Third World, and 40 tons from the West to the domestic market. Total profit for the optimal solution is $4,940. (Be careful when computing the final total profit to use the per-unit profits of Table 9-23 and not the opportunity costs of Table 9-24.)

Revising the Optimality Check An alternate approach is to revise the optimality check and reallocation process to reflect the fact that we are maximizing rather than minimizing. This approach requires no alterations to the shipment profits.

To illustrate, let us consider the net-change values for the northwest-corner method solution to the Agroproducts problem as shown in Table 9-25. The net-change amounts reflect the per-unit changes in total profit caused by a reallocation along the unused routes. An optimal minimization solution is indicated by the absence of any negative net-change values: any reallocations will only cause total cost to increase. For maximization problems we desire positive increases in the objective function, and therefore we will continue to reallocate to *positive* net-change routes as long as they exist. An optimal maximization solution is thus denoted by all negative or zero net-change values. If any of the net-change values is positive, we select the route with the highest positive net-change value and reallocate along that route.

In our example problem, the West to Domestic route has the highest positive net-change value, as shown in Table 9-25, calling for a reallocation along that route. This same process is used to evaluate and improve each subsequent solution: reallocate along the route with the highest positive net-change value until the net-change values are all negative or zero.

TABLE 9-24
Calculating Opportunity Costs for the Agroproducts Problem

Growing area	Domestic	Market area Russia	Third World
South	20 − 14 = 6	20 − 20 = 0	20 − 14 = 6
Midwest	20 − 15 = 5	20 − 19 = 1	20 − 14 = 6
West	20 − 16 = 4	20 − 18 = 2	20 − 12 = 8

TABLE 9-25
Net-Change Values for the Northwest-Corner
Method Solution to the Agroproducts Problem

Growing area	Market area		
	Domestic	Russia	Third World
South	—	—	−1
Midwest	2	—	—
West	5	1	—

INSTANT REPLAY   Using the modified optimality check and reallocation rule described above, find the optimal solution to the Agroproducts problem.

CHECK   Total profit for the optimal solution is $4,940, the same as computed in the previous Instant Replay.

Unbalanced Supply and Demand

One simple assumption that we have been making may seem rather naive: we have assumed that the amounts to be supplied equal the amounts demanded. In reality supply and demand are not likely to be exactly equal. Often, companies maintain greater capacity than average demand so that they are able to meet peak demand. Other companies maintain capacity at average demand levels, preferring to build inventories in low demand periods to meet peak demands. Policies such as these inevitably lead to supply and demand being unbalanced during some periods.

The solution procedure we have been considering requires that the total amount supplied and the total amount demanded be equal. Fortunately, we can always meet this assumption by adding either a *dummy supply point* or a *dummy demand point* to bring about a balance. The dummy supply (or demand) point is assigned a supply capacity (or demand requirement) equal to the excess of demand over supply (or supply over demand). If, for instance, the total demand exceeds the available supply by, say, 40 units, we would have to add a dummy supply point with a capacity of 40 units. On the other hand, if the total supply exceeds the total demand by, say, 100 units, we simply add a dummy demand point with a demand of 100 units.

Because no shipments will actually be made to or from these dummy activities, it does not matter what costs (or profits) are assigned to the dummy routes so long as all dummy routes are assigned the same cost (or profit). Unequal costs or profits will unfairly bias the real allocations. It is computationally convenient to use zero costs or profits for all dummy routes.

After the dummy facility has been added, the problem is solved exactly as described earlier. The dummy facility is treated no differently than a real facility. The interpretation of the optimal solution should include an adjustment for the dummy facility. If a dummy supply point is added, the amounts scheduled to be shipped from that supply point have to be treated as unfulfilled demand by

TABLE 9-26
Balancing Supply and Demand by Adding a Dummy Supply Point

	X	Y	Z	Capacity
A	7	5	3	50 ⎫
B	2	6	4	40 ⎬ 120
C	1	7	6	30 ⎭
Dummy supply point	0	0	0	80 (200 − 120)
Required	50	70	80	

200

the demand points that are to receive those shipments. In a similar manner, amounts scheduled to be received by a dummy demand point represent unused capacity at those supply points that are to make the shipments.

Tables 9-26 and 9-27 illustrate the proper manner of adding dummies. Table 9-26 illustrates a dummy supply point and Table 9-27 a dummy demand point.

In the first case, the total number of units available at the three supply

TABLE 9-27
Balancing Supply and Demand by Adding a Dummy Demand Point

	X	Y	Z	Dummy demand point	Capacity
A	7	5	3	0	50
B	2	6	4	0	70
C	1	7	6	0	60
Required	45	35	25	75 (180 − 105)	

105   180

points, A, B, and C, is 80 less than that needed by the three demand points, X, Y, and Z. Thus, we need to add a dummy supply point with a capacity of 80, equal to the supply deficit. Note that all of the routes from the dummy supply point show zero costs.

In the other case shown, the total number of units demanded by the three demand points, X, Y, and Z, is 75 units less than that available at the supply points, A, B, and C. Accordingly, a dummy demand point with total demand equal to the deficit of 75 units is added to bring the problem in balance.

Prohibited Routes

Another special situation that deserves attention is the existence of *prohibited routes*. This occurs whenever one or more routes are not available as shipment options. This can happen for a number of reasons, such as poor weather conditions, weight or size restrictions, environmental restrictions for hazardous materials, and transportation strikes.

Such restrictions, or prohibitions, can be handled in the transportation problem by assigning the prohibited routes a very high cost (or a large negative profit). This ensures that these routes will not be included in the optimal solution.

INSTANT REPLAY   Suppose, in the Agroproducts example, the dockworkers have refused to load grain from the Agroproducts southern growing area onto ships bound for Russia. This prevents Agroproducts from shipping southern wheat to Russia. What modified shipping plan should Agroproducts use? How much profit does the dockworkers' prohibition cost Agroproducts?

CHECK   The modified solution calls for shipments of 40 tons of southern wheat to the domestic market and 100 tons to the Third World; 20 tons of midwestern wheat to the domestic market and 100 tons to Russia; and 40 tons of western wheat to the domestic market. The total profit of this solution is $4,800. This is $140 less profit than could be earned without the dockworkers' refusal.

Applications to Nontransportation Situations

Although we have been using the terms "supply," "demand," "shipment," and "distribution," it should be emphasized that the procedures described in this chapter are in no way constrained to situations involving the physical transportation of goods. On the contrary, in many cases the allocation may require a movement in time rather than in space, such as where goods produced in one time period are sold to customers whose demand is received in another time period. Alternatively, the allocation may refer to the assignment of one class of items to another. An example is the assignment of a set of jobs or tasks to a set of employees. In the next few paragraphs a number of applications are described which are not pure "transportation" situations although all can be solved using the transportation method.

Production Planning

Production planning problems can be modeled as transportation problems by considering the plant capacities during specific time periods as the supply points and expected sales during those time periods as the demand requirements. The allocation costs consist of production and inventory carrying costs. Table 9-28 shows a simple form of such a problem including beginning and target ending inventories.

This illustration represents a production planning problem for a 3-month period (January, February, and March). Sales requirements for any specific month can be met in one of three ways: (1) produced that month, (2) produced in some previous month and carried in inventory until needed, or (3) carried forward from beginning inventory. The production capacity for any specific month can be disposed of in one of three ways: (1) used to meet demand for that month, (2) carried in inventory to meet some subsequent month's demand, or (3) carried in inventory to the end of March to meet the target for the ending inventory.

The allocation costs shown in Table 9-28 include both production costs of $10 per unit and inventory carrying costs of $2 per unit per month carried in inventory. Thus, the allocation cost is $10 for any month in which the demand is met by that month's production (no inventory carrying charges are incurred). An allocation cost of $12 is used whenever demand is met by the previous month's production ($2 inventory carrying charge added). This cost increases to $14 per unit if demand is met by production 2 months prior. Similar arguments will support the other cost figures shown.

The problem as formulated in Table 9-28 can be solved using the standard transportation method. Note the existence of three prohibited routes in the

TABLE 9-28
A Production Planning Problem Formulated as a Transportation Problem

Supply points	*Demand points*				
	Sales requirements for			*Target ending inventory*	*Capacity*
	January	*February*	*March*		
Beginning inventory	0	2	4	6	50
January production	10	12	14	16	100
February production	—	10	12	14	110
March production	—	—	10	12	120
Demand	120	100	150	10	

lower left corner of the table. These routes are prohibited here because they correspond to demand in one month being met by production in some subsequent month. This is equivalent to back ordering demand and, although not permitted here, could be considered in more complex situations. In addition to back ordering, other more realistic situations can be handled in the transportation format. These include alternate forms of production (overtime, second shift, subcontracting), multiple plants, multiple demand points, etc.

Assignment of Jobs to Machines

Another production-related application of the transportation method concerns the assignment of tasks or jobs to a set of machines, employees, or work centers. A special version of this problem, in which jobs cannot be split among machines and each machine can be used for only one job, is referred to as the assignment problem and will be treated in some depth in the next chapter. We now consider the more general, transportation-type case in which the requirements of any one job can be assigned to more than one machine and, if capacity exists, any machine can handle all or part of several jobs (setup costs are assumed to be minimal).

The key to treating this type of problem as a transportation problem is ensuring that the capacities of the machines and the requirements of the jobs are expressed in common units, such as *standard hours*. For example, suppose we have two machines each with 40 actual hours of capacity available, but machine A is twice as efficient as machine B. In other words, machine A can perform in 20 hours the amount of work that machine B can perform in 40 hours. One way of standardizing the available hours would be to adjust the hours available for machine B from 40 hours to 20 hours, recognizing that B can be assigned one-half the amount of work that A can be assigned. To be consistent, the costs (or profits) of assignments must also be based on the common units chosen (using machine A as the "standard machine"). Table 9-29 illustrates a simple version of this problem in which costs, capacities, and requirements are expressed in terms of standard machine-hours.

Location Analysis

The standard transportation problem assumes that the facility locations, such as for factories and warehouses, are known and fixed. The solution derived is optimal in the sense that it minimizes transportation costs for the given set of factory and warehouse locations. An important extension of the basic problem is to consider alternative factory or warehouse locations such as when the company is considering expansion or relocation. Although transportation or shipment costs are only one element that management will consider in making such a location decision, the transportation method can be used to provide relative transportation costs for potential or proposed sites.

Other Examples

The examples listed above are but a small representative set of nondistribution-type problems that can be modeled as transportation problems. Numerous other applications exist which also fit the transportation format, including work force planning, media scheduling for advertising, and traffic routing.

TABLE 9-29
Job-to-Machine Assignment Problem in Transportation Format*

Supply points	Job 1	Job 2	Job 3	Capacities in standard machine-hours
	Demand points			
Machine A	7	5	9	30
Machine B	11	13	10	50
Machine C	5	7	8	40
Machine D	16	14	12	40
Requirements in standard machine-hours	40	50	70	

*Costs are expressed per standard machine-hour.

Transshipment Problem

Up to this point we have treated various shipping points as either supply points or demand points. In practice, shipping points can act as *transshipment points*. Transshipment points can receive goods from one shipping point and then reship to another destination. This extension to the transportation problem can be conveniently handled by a few simple modifications to the standard transportation format. To illustrate, let us consider an example.

Suppose that the Modor Oven Company is considering using the Atlanta factory, the Chicago factory, and the Memphis warehouse as transshipment points, in addition to their normal supply and demand functions. The first adjustment necessary to allow transshipments is to ensure that each transshipment point is treated as both a supply and demand point. Thus, we need to add two columns to represent Atlanta and Chicago as demand points and one row to represent Memphis as a supply point. This modification is shown in Table 9-30.

Assume that the cost of shipping from Memphis to Atlanta is the same as from Atlanta to Memphis ($6 in this case) and from Memphis to Chicago is the same as in the reverse direction ($4). Note, however, that this condition is *not* necessary in order to use this approach. Further assume that the cost of shipping one unit from Memphis to the other locations is $4 to Kansas City, $10 to Los Angeles, and $3 to New Orleans. Also, let the cost from Atlanta to Chicago be $5 per unit, from Boston to Atlanta be $8, and from Boston to Chicago be $4.

The only remaining costs to be added are those for Atlanta to Atlanta, Chicago to Chicago, and Memphis to Memphis. Since no shipment will actually

TABLE 9-30
Formulation of the Modor Oven Transshipment Problem in the Transportation Format

Shipping points	Receiving points						Shipping capacity
	Kansas City	Los Angeles	Memphis	New Orleans	Atlanta	Chicago	
Atlanta	11	22	6	5	0	5	75 + 100 = 175
Boston	16	31	14	15	8	4	60
Chicago	5	21	4	9	5	0	40 + 135 = 175
Memphis	4	10	0	3	6	4	120
Receiving capacity	30	65	55 +120 175	25	100	135	

be made along these "routes," we can assume a zero shipping cost. Any allocation along these routes in the final solution *represents unused transshipment capacity*.

The final adjustment concerns the capacity and demand amounts for each of the transshipment points. Consider first Atlanta. The most that could be shipped into Atlanta would be the 100 units produced at Boston and Chicago. These 100 units plus the 75 units actually produced at Atlanta yield a combined shipment capacity from Atlanta of 175. Thus, in the revised problem, Atlanta is shown with shipping capacity of 175 and a receiving capacity of 100.

In a similar way Chicago has a receiving capacity of 135 units, the total produced at Atlanta and Boston. These 135 units plus the 40 Chicago produces leads to a shipping capacity of 175 units.

Memphis, on the other hand, will reship at most the 120 units demanded by Kansas City, Los Angeles, and New Orleans. Thus, the shipping capacity at Memphis is 120 units. The receiving capacity is 175, made up of the 55 units needed at Memphis plus the 120 units that might be received for reshipping elsewhere.

Table 9-30 shows the revised cost/capacity/demand table for the Modor Oven problem as adapted for transshipment. Once the problem has been modified as described above, it is solved in the same manner as any standard transportation problem.

INSTANT REPLAY If Boston and New Orleans had also been used as transshipment points, what would be the revised shipping and receiving capacities

for these points?

CHECK Boston would have a receiving capacity of 115, and New Orleans would have a shipping capacity of 150 units.

Final Comments

This is the first of two chapters dealing with what are called network problems. The transportation problem, which we considered here, is a network problem in that the supply points, demand points, and shipping routes can be viewed as a transportation network. The solution to the problem consists of identifying the optimal set of shipments to be made along these routes. In network terms we are attempting to find the least-cost flow through this network that meets demand requirements without exceeding supply capacities.

As it was pointed out, the transportation problem can also be thought of as a special type of linear programming problem. It is special because a solution procedure can be used that is more efficient than the standard simplex approach. In general, we are able to solve transportation problems by finding a good initial feasible solution, checking it for optimality, and then improving it by reallocating or changing the shipment pattern. This continues until no further improvements can be found.

An initial feasible solution can be found by a variety of methods. We considered one of these, the northwest-corner method. The northwest-corner method is quick and easy to use, but because it does not use any of the shipping cost data it does not always lead to good initial solutions.

The optimality check consists of examining the unused shipping routes to see whether or not the solution can be improved by using one of these routes. We are able to easily calculate the dual variables and use these to determine the net-change values of each nonbasic, or unused, route.

If any of these nonbasic routes has a negative net-change value, the total shipping cost can be decreased by using that route. This requires a reallocation affecting many of the currently used routes. The pattern of changes is identified by the stepping stone method.

In the latter portions of this chapter we saw how to extend the basic transportation model to include additional complications. These included the treatment of maximization objectives, the prohibition of specific routes, the balancing of supply and demand, allowing transshipments, and the identification of multiple optimal solutions. We also saw how degeneracy can arise in transportation problems and how the transportation solution method can be modified to handle it.

In the next chapter we will examine two other types of general network problems. These include such applications as finding the least-cost assignment of work to employees and the minimum-cost design of transportation systems.

Key Words

Allocation **309**
Artificial allocation **335**
Assignment problem **346**
Basic route **320**

Constraint coefficients **313**
Cost changes **319**
Degenerate solution **333**
Demand point **309**

Problems

9-1. The officer detailer for the Naval Intelligence Command is responsible for making job assignments for all officers attached to the command. The detailer is presently concerned with making assignments of 120 new officers who will be completing their training at the three basic intelligence schools:

Schools	Number of graduates
Richmond	30
Great Lakes	75
San Diego	15

These officers are to be assigned to one of four intelligence centers whose needs have been established as follows:

Centers	Positions available
Norfolk	22
Newport	31
Oakland	37
Seattle	30

As a first step, the detailer wishes to determine a set of assignments that minimizes the costs of transporting the officers, their families, and their household effects to their new duty stations. Adjustments to this least-cost assignment plan will be made later to meet the officers' preferences. Average costs of past transfers have been obtained and are shown below in hundreds of dollars.

	Norfolk	Newport	Oakland	Seattle
Richmond	15	22	38	40
Great Lakes	29	27	33	35
San Diego	39	41	16	19

a. Set up this problem in the transportation format.
b. Find an initial feasible solution using the northwest-corner method.

9-2. Formulate the Naval Intelligence Command problem (9–1) as a standard linear programming problem.

9-3. Use the stepping stone method to evaluate the optimality of the northwest-corner method solution to the Naval Intelligence Command problem (9–1).

9-4. Use the dual variables (u_i and v_j) to calculate the indirect costs and net-change values for the northwest-corner method solution to the Naval Intelligence Command problem (9–1). Is this solution optimal?

9-5. Find the optimal solution to the Naval Intelligence Command problem (9–1) starting with the northwest-corner method solution.

9-6. The Spitz Brewing Company has experienced unprecedented high demand for its low-calorie brew, Wings. The sales manager has obtained the following requests for deliveries for next month from each of the five regional distributors:

Distributor	Millions of gallons required
Birmingham	16
Miami	17
Memphis	14
Raleigh	12
Wilmington	23

The company currently has three breweries producing Wings. The production managers have provided the following estimates of next month's production volumes:

Brewery	Production volume in millions of gallons
Atlanta	15
New York	20
Washington	25

The costs of transporting the beer from each brewery to the distributor's warehouses are known to be (in thousands of dollars per million gallons):

	Birmingham	Miami	Memphis	Raleigh	Wilmington
Atlanta	8	10	15	13	19
New York	28	25	21	14	6
Washington	22	20	18	12	4

a. Formulate this problem as a transportation problem.

b. Find the least-cost or optimal allocation of the available beer to the distributors.

c. Which distributors, if any, will not receive all the beer desired?

9-7. Suppose that because of different pricing arrangements, the amount received from selling Wings beer (problem 9-6) differs from one distributor to another. Specifically, let the price received for each million gallons in thousands of dollars be:

Distributor	Price per million gallons in thousands of dollars
Birmingham	100
Miami	105
Memphis	115
Raleigh	110
Wilmington	120

a. Reformulate the Spitz Brewing Company problem as a transportation problem with the objective to maximize net revenue or revenue less transportation costs.

b. Solve this reformulated problem.

c. What differences, if any, exist between the solution you found here and the one you found for problem 9-6?

d. If the supply and demand quantities were equal (no dummy facilities required), would the differential prices shown above affect the solution to the problem?

9-8. The production manager for the Brown Air Conditioning Corporation is preparing a production schedule for the first calendar quarter of the coming year. Demands, or shipping requirements, have been estimated as follows:

Month	Units demanded
January	2,200
February	2,800
March	3,100

It is estimated that the on-hand inventory on January 1 will be 1,800 units, somewhat lower than would be normally desired due to increased demand for the unit. A target ending inventory for March 31 has been set at 2,500 units.

Plant capacity is being expanded by hiring additional personnel, although a tight labor market has limited the rate of growth. The production manager estimates the following unit capacities for the first 3 months, including additional capacity possible through overtime.

Month	Production capacity: regular hours of production	Additional capacity using overtime
January	2,400	600
February	2,600	650
March	2,800	700

Production costs are estimated to be the same in all months, $100 for units produced during regular hours and $110 for those produced on overtime. Inventory carrying costs are estimated to be $4 per month.

a. Formulate this problem as a transportation problem, assuming that back orders (producing in a later month to satisfy an earlier month's demand) are not permitted due to company policy.

b. Find the optimal, or least-cost, solution to the problem as formulated in part *a*.

c. Suppose that back orders are permitted and that the costs of back ordering (i.e., expediting, additional paperwork, customer impatience) have been estimated at $8 per unit per month back ordered. Reformulate the problem allowing for potential back orders.

d. Find the least-cost, or optimal, solution to the problem as formulated in part *c*.

9-9. The National Beef Growers Cooperative maintains three feedlots at Abilene, Topeka, and Des Moines. Cattle are fattened at these feedlots and then transported to one of three processing plants in Kansas City, St. Louis, and Memphis. Transportation costs per hundred head of cattle are estimated to be:

	Kansas City	St. Louis	Memphis
Abilene	42	45	38
Topeka	25	20	30
Des Moines	33	26	28

The number of cattle now available at the three feedlots, in hundreds, is:

Feedlots	Cattle available
Abilene	30
Topeka	40
Des Moines	30

Capacities at the three processing facilities are currently:

Processing plant	Capacity in hundreds
Kansas City	30
St. Louis	30
Memphis	40

Traditionally the allocation of feedlot cattle to processing plants has been based on matching capacity to demand with secondary attention to cost. On this basis the following shipment schedule has been proposed:

	Kansas City	St. Louis	Memphis
Abilene	30		
Topeka			40
Des Moines		30	

   a. Is this solution degenerate?

   b. Does it minimize transportation costs? If not, find the least-cost solution.

   c. How much more does the traditional solution cost them than the optimal solution? Can you think of a situation where the traditional capacity-matching solution might be preferred to the minimum-cost solution as derived by the transportation procedure?

9–10. The Prince Power Company supplies electric power to a large portion of southern New England. The company is vertically integrated in that it owns four coal mines as well as the power generating plants and distribution system. The costs of transporting the coal from the mines to the generating plants has been found to be (in dollars per ton):

	Generating plants			
Mines	1	2	3	4
A	4	7	9	8
B	5	4	6	7
C	10	3	6	8

Daily capacities for the mines and utilization rates for the generating plants, in thousands of tons per day, have been estimated at:

Mine	Capacity	Plant	Demand
A	40	1	30
B	30	2	25
C	50	3	35
		4	40

   a. Formulate this problem in the transportation format.

   b. Find the least-cost or optimal allocation of coal.

   c. Although the company owns the mines and the generating plants, it does not own the railroads which transport the coal from the mines to the plants. Suppose the railroad announced a change in rates along the A to 3 route. How far could this cost decrease without changing the optimal allocation found in part b? How much could the cost increase without changing the optimal solution?

   d. Suppose the transportation cost along the C to 2 route was to change. By how much, in either direction, could the cost change without causing a change in the optimal solution of part b?

   e. With the present supply and demand mix, one of the generating plants will not receive all the coal that it needs. If it is possible to expand the mine capacities, such as by hiring additional miners, which of the existing mines should be expanded and why?

9-11. The Five Star Fertilizer Company is attempting to allocate the output from its three plants to three regional warehouses. The supply capacities, demand requirements, and transportation costs per ton are shown below.

| | | Warehouses | | Output |
Plants	*Butte*	*Salt Lake City*	*Seattle*	*capacity, tons*
Denver	7	5	10	12
Reno	8	6	10	18
Portland	6	8	5	15
Tons required	15	20	10	

a. Find the optimal allocation of fertilizer from plant to warehouse.

b. Because of supply/demand mismatches, the company is considering using the existing plants and warehouses as transshipment points. Formulate this problem as a transshipment problem, given the following additional shipment cost information. (Assume that all costs are symmetric, being the same in one direction as they are in the other.)

Denver-Reno	4	Butte-Salt Lake City	6
Denver-Portland	7	Butte-Seattle	3
Reno-Portland	4	Salt Lake City-Seattle	5

c. Suppose that all points except Reno and Butte have been rejected as possible transshipment points. Formulate and solve this reduced transshipment problem.

9-12. The Gray Furniture Company manufactures end tables, chairs, and desks. These furniture items can be made from any of four different woods which at the moment are available in the following quantities.

Wood	*Supply, board feet*
Walnut	200
Oak	520
Pine	380
Maple	240

Each piece of furniture can be made from approximately the same quantity of wood, 20 board feet, and must be made wholly from one type of wood; no mixing of wood types in a single piece of furniture is permitted.

The company has received orders to manufacture the following quantities:

Furniture item	*Quantity to produce*
End tables	10
Chairs	20
Desks	30

The expected profit from each item produced is dependent on the type of wood used to manufacture it. These profits have been estimated to be:

	Walnut	Oak	Pine	Maple
		Wood used		
End table	11	8	10	7
Chair	20	18	16	15
Desk	40	20	30	—

Note that due to production difficulties, maple desks are not produced.

a. How many of each piece of furniture should be made from the various wood types?

b. What profit will be earned by the solution to part *a*?

10

Assignment and Minimal Spanning Tree Problems

In this chapter we consider two interesting network problems with a variety of practical applications. These are the assignment problem and the minimal spanning tree problem. Both of these problems can be represented graphically as a network, as demonstrated in the introduction to this section.

An *assignment problem* consists of a set of objects, such as jobs, that is to be assigned to another set of objects, such as machines. The assignment of a job to a machine is equivalent to specifying that the job is to be completed by that machine. The cost of each potential assignment is assumed to vary. For example, the cost of completing a particular job on one machine would differ from the cost of completing it on another machine if the operating costs for the two machines are different. Likewise, the cost of one job completed on a specific machine is not likely to be the same as the cost of completing another job on that machine because of different requirements for each job. The objective of the assignment problem is to determine the least costly set of assignments. Thus, for our example, we require an assignment of jobs to machines that will allow the jobs to be completed with the least total cost.

Many other problems of this type exist. Rather than machines, we might be concerned with an assignment of jobs to employees. The assignment "costs" might be expressed in terms of time (rather than cost) to complete the jobs. Another class of assignment problems concerns dispatching situations. In this case we might be assigning taxis to pick up customers or service trucks to respond to customer service calls. The objective might be to minimize the total travel time for the taxis or service truck to reach the customers.

We shall also consider the problem of finding a *minimal spanning tree*. A *spanning tree* is defined as a joined set of routes that provides a path from any **357** one activity in a network to every other activity. An example would be designing a subway system in which the activities are neighborhoods to be served by the system and the routes correspond to potential subway links. The objective is to determine the least-cost set of routes that connects each neighborhood with every other neighborhood. Similar problems which involve determining the minimal spanning tree include designing electrical transmission systems, communication networks, and interstate highway systems.

Assignment Problems

The assignment problem requires matching one set of objects with another set. Each match or assignment has a corresponding cost. The objective is to match each of the objects in one set with one of those in the other set in the least-cost manner. This can best be illustrated by means of the following example.

Formulating the Problem

One of the major duties of a Navy officer detailer is the determination of the next duty assignment for officers completing their current assignment. One such detailer has identified four officers of similar rank who will be completing their current tours of shore duty at approximately the same time. Each is next due to be assigned to sea duty according to the normal career pattern. The detailer has also identified four sea billets, or jobs, that require the rank and skills shared by this group of officers.

Because of budget restrictions, the detailer would like to assign the four officers to the available ships in a way that will minimize the travel costs of moving the officers from one duty station to another.

Travel costs for each relocation assignment are as shown in Table 10-1. As a preliminary attempt at solving this problem, the detailer might try sending each officer to the assignment that minimizes each officer's travel costs. In this case the best assignment for officer A would be to duty station Y since that assignment is clearly cheaper than for W, X, or Z. Note, however, that the least-cost assignment for officer B is also duty station Y, as is the case for officer D as well. Clearly a conflict exists that will have to be resolved.

An alternative approach might be to assign an officer to each duty station that minimizes the cost of transfer to that station. For instance, the least-cost assignment for duty station W is to send officer C. However, conflicts develop once more since officer C represents the lowest-cost assignment for duty stations X and Z as well.

Solving the Problem

Fortunately, a simple solution method exists for finding the best or lowest-cost allocation. This method, called the Hungarian method after the nationality of its originators,[1] will be described and demonstrated below.

Opportunity Costs of Assignments We begin by observing that no matter which duty station officer A is assigned to, we will have to incur a cost at least

---

[1] See H. W. Kuhn, "The Hungarian Method for the Assignment Problem," *Naval Research Logistics Quarterly*, vol. 2, 1955, pp. 83–97.

359

ASSIGNMENT
AND
MINIMAL
SPANNING
TREE
PROBLEMS

TABLE 10-1
Travel Costs for Relocation Assignments

Officer	*Next duty station*			
	W	X	Y	Z
A	$1,000	$1,200	$400	$ 900
B	600	500	300	800
C	200	300	400	500
D	600	700	300	1,000

equal to the minimum-cost assignment to station *Y*. For convenience, then, we can subtract this lowest cost ($400) from each of the assignment costs for officer *A*. These reduced costs are shown in the first row of Table 10-2.

Similarly, we can subtract the least cost for officer *B* from each of *B*'s assignment costs. Officer *B*'s lowest-cost assignment is to station *Y* for a cost of $300. Thus, as shown in Table 10-2, we can subtract $300 from every cost in the row corresponding to officer *B*'s assignments. An identical approach can be used for officers *C* and *D*, reducing their costs by $200 and $300, respectively. The costs subtracted from each row are shown to the right of Table 10-2.

Observe that the least-cost assignment for each officer now has a zero cost. All other costs are considered to be *opportunity costs*. That is, they represent the excess cost incurred by making an assignment to some duty station other than the least-cost duty station.

Further cost reduction is possible by considering the least-cost assignment for each duty station. Consider first station *W*. Here the least cost is achieved by assigning officer *C*. This cost is already zero so there is no need to reduce the costs in this column. On the other hand, observe that the least-cost

TABLE 10-2
Relocation Travel Costs ($) Reduced by Least-Cost Assignment for Each Officer

Officer	*Next duty station*				Cost removed
	W	X	Y	Z	
A	1,000 − 400 = 600	1,200 − 400 = 800	400 − 400 = 0	900 − 400 = 500	400
B	600 − 300 = 300	500 − 300 = 200	300 − 300 = 0	800 − 300 = 500	300
C	200 − 200 = 0	300 − 200 = 100	400 − 200 = 200	500 − 200 = 300	200
D	600 − 300 = 300	700 − 300 = 400	300 − 300 = 0	1,000 − 300 = 700	300

TABLE 10-3
Initial Opportunity Costs: Relocation Travel Costs ($) after Reduction by
Least-Cost Assignment for Each Officer and Each Duty Station

Officer	W	X	Y	Z	Cost removed
		Next duty station			
A	600	800 − 100 = 700	0	500 − 300 = 200	400
B	300	200 − 100 = 100	0	500 − 300 = 200	300
C	0	100 − 100 = 0	200	300 − 300 = 0	200
D	300	400 − 100 = 300	0	700 − 300 = 400	300
Cost removed	0	100	0	300	

assignment for station X is also officer C, at a cost of $100. Since we know that one officer must be assigned to station X, we are guaranteed to incur at least this lowest cost of $100 for that assignment. Therefore, all costs in the column corresponding to station X can be reduced by $100. This change is reflected in Table 10-3.

In a similar manner we see that the least cost for station Y is already zero but that for station Z is $300. Therefore, no changes are required for the column representing station Y, and all costs in the column for station Z must be reduced by the $300. Table 10-3 shows the initial opportunity costs. We should note that we could just as well have begun with column subtraction and then used row reduction in determining the initial opportunity costs. Similarly, our initial cost table could have associated officers with columns and duty stations with rows.

Note that at least one zero appears in each row and column, which is a natural result of the row and column cost reduction actions. Furthermore, the sum of the amounts that were subtracted from the rows and columns serves as a lower bound on the cost of an optimal assignment of officers to duty stations. In this case, the lower bound is:

$$\$400 + \$300 + \$200 + \$300 + \$0 + \$100 + \$0 + \$300 = \$1,600$$

Thus, if we can make an assignment of officers to duty stations such that each assignment corresponds to one of the zero-opportunity-cost elements of Table 10-3, that assignment will be optimal and will have a total cost of $1,600.

INSTANT REPLAY   Determine the initial opportunity costs for the following assignment problem:

361

ASSIGNMENT
AND
MINIMAL
SPANNING
TREE
PROBLEMS

	K	L	M
F	140	80	150
G	145	70	130
H	160	90	120

CHECK The initial opportunity costs can be found by subtracting 80 from row F, 70 from row G, 90 from row H, 60 from column K, and 30 from column M. This yields the following table:

	K	L	M
F	0	0	40
G	15	0	30
H	10	0	0

Checking Feasibility We now have to determine whether or not a feasible assignment can be made that will achieve this lower-bound cost of $1,600. For convenience, those assignments that have zero costs are shown in Table 10-4a. Whether or not an optimal solution can be identified at this stage depends on whether a feasible allocation can be made of officers to duty stations that involves only these zero-opportunity-cost assignments. A feasible allocation requires that each officer be assigned to a separate duty station. In other words, each officer must be assigned a single duty station, and each duty station must be assigned a single officer.

It is useful here to distinguish between so-called forced and unforced assignments. A *forced assignment* occurs if there is only one zero-cost cell in any row or column. For example, consider the row in Table 10-4a corresponding to officer A. There is only one zero in that row, corresponding to duty station Y. Thus, if a feasible solution is to be found at this point, officer A must be assigned to duty station Y. This is a forced assignment. If another zero had appeared in that row, say for station Z, an assignment would not be forced.

To determine whether a feasible set of assignments can be found, we need to make a trial set of assignments. This is done by making all forced assignments, if any, first. When this is done, if any unforced assignments remain, we can arbitrarily choose one of the zero cells and continue.

As we observed above, there is only one zero in the row corresponding to officer A (station Y). If this is to be an optimal solution, officer A must be assigned to station Y, since this is a forced assignment. This assignment is denoted by the asterisk (*) next to the zero in that cell of Table 10-4b. Because station Y has now been tentatively assigned to officer A, it is not available for assignment to any other officer. We can therefore cross out all other zeros in the column corresponding to station Y. This is shown in Table 10-4b.

Next consider officer B. No zeros remain in the row representing officer B, and we can immediately see that an optimal solution cannot be found. Note

TABLE 10-4
Determination of Feasibility for Initial Solution

	W	X	Y	Z
A			0	
B			0	
C	0	0		0
D			0	

(a) Potential Assignments with
Zero Opportunity Costs

	W	X	Y	Z
A			0*	
B			Ø	
C	0	0		0
D			Ø	

(b) Remaining Assignments with
Zero Opportunity Costs
after Assigning Officer A
to Station Y

	W	X	Y	Z
A			0*	
B			Ø	
C	0*	Ø		Ø
D			Ø	

(c) Feasible Assignments for
Initial Solution
(A to Y and C to W)

that it would have done us no good to start first by assigning officer *B* to station *Y* since such an assignment would have required us to cross out the only zero in the row for officer *A*.

Although we know that an optimal assignment cannot be made, it is important to complete any remaining feasible assignments, in order to find where future adjustments need to be made, as we will see shortly. An assignment for officer *C* is not forced at this point since *C* has three zero-cost assignments as indicated by the three zeros in that row. Officer *D* has no remaining zeros so we cannot make an assignment for that officer either.

Next consider the duty stations. Only one zero exists in the column corresponding to duty station W, so we are forced to make an assignment of the corresponding officer, officer C, to that duty station. Having assigned officer C to station W, we cannot assign officer C to any other stations, and we therefore must cross out the other two zeros in C's row. This exhausts the set of potential assignments since no zeros remain that are not starred or crossed out, as shown in Table 10-4c.

363

ASSIGNMENT
AND
MINIMAL
SPANNING
TREE
PROBLEMS

Clearly we are not able to make an optimal assignment because the only assignments we are able to complete are officer A to station Y and officer C to station W. It is useful to summarize the steps that we followed in checking for feasibility. These are:

1. Make all forced assignments first (those where only a single zero appears in any row or column). Cross out any other zeros in the row and column corresponding to each forced assignment made.
2. When only unforced assignments remain, make an arbitrary assignment to one of the zero-cost cells. Cross out any other zeros in the row and column corresponding to that assignment.
3. When all feasible assignments have been made, stop. If the set of assignments includes each row and each column, a feasible and therefore optimal solution has been found.

It is important to note that this procedure will always find an optimal feasible assignment if one exists.

INSTANT REPLAY   Using the procedure described above, check the feasibility of an assignment to zero-opportunity-cost cells for the following table:

	K	L	M
F	0		0
G		0	
H		0	

CHECK   The solution shown is not feasible. A forced assignment of G to L eliminates the only zero-cost cell for H.

Reducing Infeasibility   If it is not possible to achieve a feasible allocation using the minimum-cost allocation options, it should be clear that the optimal solution can be found only by making one or more assignments that incur some opportunity costs. Consider for a moment where such a nonzero-opportunity-cost allocation is likely to be required. Referring to Table 10-4c, we note that officers B and D were not assigned. Clearly one option would be to assign each to the next lowest cost duty station. Alternatively, however, note that both of these officers were prevented from being assigned to their lowest-cost stations because of the assignment of officer A to that station. (The assignment of A to station Y required the crossing out of the only zero-cost allocation for B and D.) Therefore, it may cost less to assign officer A to some other station, freeing up station Y for assignment to officers B or D.

We could not find a feasible assignment based on the zero-opportunity-cost allocation possibilities. So our goal is now to open up other assignment possibilities until a feasible set of assignments can be found. Each additional option will be chosen so as to minimize the incremental opportunity cost increase.

Increasing the Number of Assignment Options   In general, we seek then to identify low-opportunity-cost cells that either permit the assignment of one or more currently unassigned officers or allow reassignment of a presently assigned officer so that that officer's current assignment can be given to one of the unassigned officers. This search can easily be accomplished in a systematic manner as described below.

The desirability of finding additional assignment options for those cases in which assignments could not be previously made is indicated by placing a check next to those rows. Thus, in Table 10-5, which shows the original opportunity costs, checks are placed next to rows corresponding to officers *B* and *D* because it was not feasible to assign either officer to a duty station. The possibility of reassigning officer *A*, whose present assignment prevents the unassigned officers *B* and *D* from being allocated to their lowest-cost duty stations, is indicated by checking the column corresponding to station *Y*, the one they are competing for. This in turn requires that the row for officer *A* be checked. As a final step, lines are drawn through the *unchecked rows* and *checked columns* because we do not need additional assignment options there. These checks and lines are also shown in Table 10-5. Observe that every zero cell has at least one line going through it. This condition will be true if the checking/lining process is accomplished successfully and thus serves as a simple check on that process.[1]

The candidates for additional assignments are those assignment options whose cells are not covered by one or more lines. Each such option permits assignment of a previously unassigned officer either directly or indirectly by reassigning a currently assigned officer. Because we wish to increase costs as little as possible, we *select the smallest uncovered opportunity cost,* which in this case is the circled 100 corresponding to an assignment of officer *B* to station *X* in Table 10-5.

[1]The checking process can be bypassed and the minimum number of lines to cover all zeros can be drawn directly. Finding the minimum number of lines may be difficult to do for larger problems, which is why we describe the more thorough checking method.

TABLE 10-5
Determination of Additional Assignment Options
Based on Infeasibility of Initial Assignment

	W	X	Y ✓	Z	
✓ A	600	700	0*	200	*Smallest uncovered opportunity cost*
✓ B	300	(100)	0	200	
C	0*	0	200	0	
✓ D	300	300	0	400	

Revising the Opportunity Costs **365**

ASSIGNMENT
AND
MINIMAL
SPANNING
TREE
PROBLEMS

Revising the Opportunity Costs   Recall that we obtained zero-opportunity-cost values in our initial opportunity cost table by subtracting amounts from each row and column. To achieve a zero opportunity cost for the additional assignment option of officer B to station X, we need to subtract the current $100 opportunity cost for that assignment from each opportunity cost in row B or column X. Suppose we subtract this $100 cost from all the costs in the row corresponding to officer B. This leaves the revised opportunity costs as shown in Table 10-6a. Observe that this table has a -100 entry corresponding to the allocation of B to Y. Since we desire all potential assignments to have zero costs, we must correct for this negative cost. We can do this by adding 100 to the column in which it appears. (A negative opportunity cost is equivalent to a negative slack variable, which of course is not permitted.) The revised costs are shown in Table 10-6b.

Although no negative numbers remain, Table 10-6b is not quite ready for determining feasibility. This is because the rows corresponding to officers A and D now have no zero-cost assignments. The costs in these rows can be reduced by subtracting the lowest cost from every cost in those rows. The lowest cost in both cases is $100. Subtracting $100 from rows A and D leaves the revised opportunity costs of Table 10-6c.

The cost-removed figures shown in the margins of the opportunity cost tables (Table 10-6) reflect the changes made at each step in the aggregate amounts subtracted from the original cost figures. Table 10-6a shows a subtraction of $100 from each cost element for officer B. We had originally subtracted $300 from this row (see Table 10-2), which leaves a total reduction of $300 + $100 = $400, as shown. Table 10-6b records a $100 *addition* to the column for station Y. Note that a $100 addition to the opportunity costs is equivalent to a $-$100 subtraction from the costs to be removed. Because nothing had been previously added to or subtracted from this column, the net result is a $-$100 subtraction, as shown in the bottom margin of Table 10-6b. The subtractions of $100 from rows A and D shown in Table 10-6c are reflected in the cost-removed figures, increasing that for row A from $400 to $500 and that for row D from $300 to $400.

Summary of Steps to Revise the Opportunity Cost Table

Now that we have examined the steps involved in revising the opportunity cost table to reflect additional assignment options, we can next summarize these steps in a computationally efficient manner.

Whenever a feasible solution cannot be found for a given opportunity cost table, additional assignment options for a revised opportunity cost table are found as follows:

1. Check each row without an assignment.

2. Check each column that has a zero in a checked row.

3. Check each row that has an assignment in a checked column.

4. Repeat steps 2 and 3 as necessary until no new checks can be made.

TABLE 10-6
Revision of Initial Opportunity Cost Table

	W	X	Y	Z	Cost removed
A	600	700	0	200	400
B	300 − 100 = 200	100 − 100 = 0	0 − 100 = −100	200 − 100 = 100	300 + 100 = 400
C	0	0	200	0	200
D	300	300	0	400	300
Cost removed	0	100	0	300	

(a) Subtraction of $100 from Row B

	W	X	Y	Z	Cost removed
A	600	700	0 + 100 = 100	200	400
B	200	0	− 100 + 100 = 0	100	400
C	0	0	200 + 100 = 300	0	200
D	300	300	0 + 100 = 100	400	300
Cost removed	0	100	0 − 100 = −100	300	

(b) Addition of $100 to Column Y

	W	X	Y	Z	Cost removed
A	600 − 100 = 500	700 − 100 = 600	100 − 100 = 0	200 − 100 = 100	400 + 100 = 500
B	200	0	0	100	400
C	0	0	300	0	200
D	300 − 100 = 200	300 − 100 = 200	100 − 100 = 0	400 − 100 = 300	300 + 100 = 400
Cost removed	0	100	−100	300	

(c) Subtraction of $100 from Rows A and D

367

ASSIGNMENT
AND
MINIMAL
SPANNING
TREE
PROBLEMS

TABLE 10-7
Shortcut Method of Obtaining Revised Opportunity Cost Table

	W	X	Y ✓	Z
✓ A	600 − 100 = 500	700 − 100 = 600	0	200 − 100 = 100
✓ B	300 − 100 = 200	100 − 100 = 0	0	200 − 100 = 100
C	− − 0 − −	− − 0 − −	200 + 100 = 300	− − 0 − −
✓ D	300 − 100 = 200	300 − 100 = 200	0	400 − 100 = 300

5. Draw a line through each unchecked row and each checked column.

6. Circle the smallest uncovered cost.

7. Subtract the circled cost from every cost element not lined through, add it to any cost element covered by two lines, and leave the remaining cost elements (those covered by a single line) unchanged.

The first six steps are exactly as we performed in our example. The seventh step is a shortcut way of accomplishing the cost adjustments shown in Table 10-6. Table 10-7 demonstrates that the shortcut seventh step achieves the same revised opportunity cost table we obtained earlier. The dotted lines are included in Table 10-7 to show which elements are not lined through, which are covered by a single line, and which are covered by two lines. Note that the cost for assigning officer C to station Y is the only cost element covered by two lines. Therefore, this is the only cost element to which the circled cost is added. The other costs in the row corresponding to officer C and the column corresponding to station Y are all covered by a single line and according to step 7 remain unchanged. The remaining costs in the table are not covered by either line, and therefore the circled cost of \$100 is subtracted from each. Compare the costs obtained in Table 10-7 with those in Table 10-6c to assure yourself that they are the same.

INSTANT REPLAY   Suppose that you have obtained the following opportunity cost table:

	K	L	M
F	0	10	0
G	12	0	15
H	9	0	8

Check this solution for feasibility. If not feasible, prepare a revised opportunity cost table.

CHECK Assignments of G to L and F to K are possible. Since neither H nor M are assigned, the solution is not feasible. The checking/lining process leads to the following:

	K	L ✓	M
F	~~0*~~	~~10~~	~~0̸~~
✓ G	12	0*	15
✓ H	9	0̸	8

The smallest uncovered cost is 8. Using this cost to adjust the current table, the following revised cost table is developed:

	K	L	M
F	0	18	0
G	4	0	7
H	1	0	0

Checking Feasibility of Revised Opportunity Cost Table Having found a revised opportunity cost table, we next test to see whether or not a feasible, and hence optimal, assignment can be made using the zero-opportunity-cost cells. This check is illustrated in Table 10-8. A comparison of Table 10-8 with Table 10-4c shows that the revised table contains one additional zero not found in the original table.

TABLE 10-8
Optimality Check for Second Opportunity Cost Table

	W	X	Y	Z
A			0* ①	
B		0* ②	0̸ ①	
C	0* ③	0̸ ②		0̸ ③
D			0̸ ①	

① Officer A to station Y
② Officer B to station X
③ Officer C to station W

Let us review the steps followed in Table 10-8 to check for feasibility. For **369**

ASSIGNMENT
AND
MINIMAL
SPANNING
TREE
PROBLEMS convenience, we have numbered the cells in the table to show the order of the assignments. As before, we see that we are forced to assign officer A to station Y because that remains the only feasible assignment for A. This assignment ① results in the other zeros in the Y column being crossed out. At that point officer B has one zero remaining, which corresponds to station X. Therefore, we are forced to assign B to X and cross out the other zero in column X. This is shown as assignment ②.

Officer C has two zeros remaining (stations W and Z), and we are not forced to make an assignment here. Officer D, on the other hand, has no feasible assignment because his only zero-cost station was crossed out when the assignment of officer A was made to station Y.

Turning next to station W we note that only one feasible assignment exists, that of officer C. The assignment of officer C to station W precludes the assignment of officer C to any other station and causes us to cross out the final zero, corresponding to row C and column Z. This is shown as assignment ③.

Preparing the Third Opportunity Cost Table Since only three assignments were possible using the zero-cost cells of the second opportunity cost table, we know that one additional assignment must be made to find the optimal solution. You might be tempted at this point to conclude that officer D should be assigned to station Z because these are the only unassigned officer and duty station remaining. This would be incorrect because it may cost less to assign either A, B, or C to station Z and D to the station freed up by reassignment of A, B, or C.

Refer now to Table 10-9, which summarizes the first six steps of the procedure used to determine a revised opportunity cost table. The starred (*) elements represent the only feasible assignments found in Table 10-8. Since officer D was not assigned, we first check row D. Step 2 requires that any column be checked that has a zero in a checked row. The only zero in row D occurs in column Y, so column Y is checked. Step 3 asks that any row be checked that has an assignment in a checked column. Row A has an assignment in column Y, leading to a check for row A. If row A had zeros in any unchecked column, we would be required to check those columns as in step 4. In this case, however, the only zero in row A occurs in column Y, which is already checked. Further application of steps 2 and 3 will not cause any additional rows or columns to be checked, so we move on to step 5.

TABLE 10-9
Determination of New Assignment Options
Using Second Opportunity Cost Table

	W	X	Y ✓	Z	
✓ A	500	600	0*	(100)	← Smallest uncovered cost
B	~~200~~	~~0*~~	~~0~~	~~100~~	
C	~~0*~~	~~0~~	~~300~~	~~0~~	
✓ D	200	200	0	300	

Since rows B and C were unchecked and since column Y was checked, step 5 calls for lines to be drawn through rows B and C and column Y. The smallest uncovered cost, 100 for row A and column Z, is circled, as called for by step 6.

Step 7 requires that 100 (the circled cost) be added to those costs covered by two lines, which in this case are the B to Y and C to Y elements. The circled cost must also be subtracted from the uncovered costs, or A to W, A to X, A to Z, D to W, D to X, and D to Z. The remaining costs are to be left unchanged. These changes are summarized in Table 10-10.

In the margins of Table 10-10 we show the necessary adjustments to the cost-removed figures. A brief analysis of Table 10-10 will show that, in essence, we subtracted \$100 from rows A and D and added \$100 to column Y. In general, the revisions to the opportunity cost table are equivalent to subtracting the circled cost (smallest uncovered cost) from each *checked row* and adding it to each *checked column*. Thus, the cost-removed figures for rows A and D must be increased by \$100 (yielding \$600 and \$500, respectively) and that for column Y must be decreased by \$100 (leaving −\$200).

Checking Feasibility of the Third Opportunity Cost Table The next step is to determine whether or not the revised opportunity cost table will permit a feasible set of assignments using zero-cost cells. This test is shown in Table 10-11. Again for convenience we numbered the order of the assignments. Since officer A has two potential assignments, Y and Z, we are not yet forced to make an assignment. Officer B, however, has only one feasible assignment, to station X. This assignment requires us to cross out the other zero in column X because it is no longer feasible to assign officer C to that station.

Officer C has two feasible assignments remaining, so we pass on to officer D. The only feasible assignment for D is to station Y, which eliminates the zero in that column for officer A. Officer A now has one zero remaining, so we are forced to assign him to station Z. This eliminates the option of assigning officer

TABLE 10-10
Determination of Third Opportunity Cost Table

	W	X	Y	Z	Cost removed
A	500 − 100 = 400	600 − 100 = 500	0	100 − 100 = 0	500 + 100 = 600
B	200	0	0 + 100 = 100	100	400
C	0	0	300 + 100 = 400	0	200
D	200 − 100 = 100	200 − 100 = 100	0	300 − 100 = 200	400 + 100 = 500
Cost removed	0	100	−100 −100 −200	300	

371

ASSIGNMENT
AND
MINIMAL
SPANNING
TREE
PROBLEMS

TABLE 10-11
Optimality Check for Third Opportunity Cost Table

	W	X	Y	Z
A			Ø ②	0* ③
B		0* ①		
C	0* ④	Ø ①		Ø ③
D			0* ②	

① Officer B to station X   ③ Officer A to station Z
② Officer D to station Y   ④ Officer C to station W

C to that station, leaving officer C with a single feasible assignment, to station W.

As shown, a feasible assignment of officers to stations using only zero-opportunity-cost allocations is possible at this point and represents the optimal solution to the detailer's assignment problem. Total cost for this solution can be found by referring to the original costs of Table 10-1 and the assignments determined in Table 10-11:

A to Z	$900
B to X	500
C to W	200
D to Y	300
	$1,900

This same total cost can be found by summing the total cost removed from each of the rows and columns. This is shown below:

Removed from	Cost removed
Row A	$ 600
Row B	400
Row C	200
Row D	500
Column W	0
Column X	100
Column Y	−200
Column Z	300
	$1,900

The total cost removed is equivalent to the cost of the optimal assignment because these costs were the amounts subtracted from the original costs in order to yield the zero opportunity costs on which the assignments were based. For example, the assignment of officer A to station Z will cost $900 as shown in the original cost table. This $900 cost was reduced to a zero opportunity cost by subtracting $600 from row A and $300 from column Z ($600 + $300 = $900).

Enumeration   It may have occurred to you that the solution to this problem could have been found simply by enumerating all possible assignment combinations, comparing the cost of each feasible combination, and selecting the least-cost combination as the optimal solution. For our example problem there are 24 possible combinations, certainly a small enough number to enumerate. In general, however, the number of feasible combinations is equivalent to n! (n factorial), where n is the number of rows or columns. This number grows very large quite quickly, precluding the practical use of enumeration for solving assignment problems. For example, with 10 officers to be assigned, there would be 10! = 3,628,800 combinations to be evaluated.[1]

Relationship to Linear Programming

The assignment problem is a special case of the transportation problem in which all the supply capacities and demand requirements are 1. Because the transportation problem is a special type of linear programming problem, it follows that the assignment problem is also a linear programming problem.

Any assignment problem could be solved as either a linear programming problem, using the simplex algorithm, or as a transportation problem, using the procedure described in Chapter 9. However, the network-based Hungarian assignment algorithm described in this chapter is a computationally more efficient method of solving such problems. The Instant Replay that follows demonstrates one reason why the transportation method is not very effective for this type of problem.

INSTANT REPLAY   Suppose you are to use the transportation method to solve the officer relocation problem of Table 10-1. Determine an initial feasible transportation solution. How many artificial allocations, ϵ, do you need to add to remove degeneracy?

CHECK   Three artificial allocations must be added to bring the number of allocations to 7 (rows + columns $- 1 = m + n - 1 = 4 + 4 - 1 = 7$). One such allocation is shown below:

	W	X	Y	Z
A	1	ϵ		
B		1	ϵ	
C			1	ϵ
D				1

---

[1] $n! = n(n - 1)(n - 2) \cdots (2)(1)$. Thus, $10! = 10(9)(8)(7) \cdots (3)(2)(1) = 3,628,800$.

373

ASSIGNMENT
AND
MINIMAL
SPANNING
TREE
PROBLEMS

TABLE 10-12
Officer Assignment Problem Modified to
Prohibit Assignment of Officer C to Station X

	W	X	Y	Z
A	$1,000	$ 1,200	$400	$ 900
B	600	500	300	800
C	200	10,000	400	500
D	600	700	300	1,000

Large cost used for prohibited assignment (pointing to 10,000 cell)

Complications

Compared with the degeneracy problem when using the transportation method, there are relatively few complications that need to be considered with the assignment method. In this section we will discuss four situations that cause slight modifications to the solution procedure outlined earlier: (1) prohibited assignments, (2) multiple optimal solutions, (3) maximization objective functions, and (4) unequal assignment options.

Prohibited Assignments Occasionally an assignment problem will be formulated in which one or more assignment options are prohibited. For example, in the officer detailing problem discussed earlier, suppose that officer C is currently stationed overseas, that duty station X represents a ship whose home port is also overseas, and that Navy policy prohibits back-to-back overseas tours. In this case the assignment of officer C to station X is a *prohibited assignment*. Although the optimal solution we found previously did not include such an assignment, how could we ensure that such an assignment could not result? This issue is quite easily resolved by artificially placing a very large cost on that assignment. This is what we did in Chapter 9 when a transportation problem contained one or more prohibited routes.

Thus, for the example described, we could associate some large cost, say $10,000, to the assignment of officer C to station X. The initial, modified cost table would therefore appear as shown in Table 10-12. As another alternative we could have simply crossed out this cell completely to indicate that an assignment there is not permitted. The solution of this modified problem would otherwise proceed as before.

Multiple Optimal Solutions Another situation worth noting is that which occurs when more than one optimal assignment exists. This is easy to recognize when making the optimality check to see if a feasible assignment can be made using only zero-opportunity-cost cells. Multiple optimal solutions exist if a feasible (and thus optimal) solution has been found and at least one unforced, tie-breaking assignment had to be made.

To illustrate, let us suppose our final opportunity cost table for the officer detailing problem had zeros as shown in Table 10-13. Consider first the solution labeled solution 1. This was found in the usual manner by looking always for forced assignments. Since officers A, B, and C all had two or more zero cells,

TABLE 10-13
Illustration of Multiple Optimal Solutions to Assignment Problems

	W	X	Y	Z
A			Ø	0*
B	Ø	0*		
C	0*	Ø		Ø
D			0*	

(a) Solution 1

	W	X	Y	Z
A			Ø	0*
B	0*	Ø		
C	Ø	0*		Ø
D			0*	

(b) Solution 2

the first forced assignment was of officer D to station Y. This eliminated the option of A being assigned to Y, forcing an allocation of A to Z. At that point officers B and C each have two zeros remaining, and stations W and X have two zeros remaining. Since these are the only unassigned officers and stations, there are no further forced assignments. To complete the assignment process we need to break this "tie" by *arbitrarily* selecting one of these unforced assignments. In solution 1 we selected the assignment of officer B to station X. This forced us then to cross out the zeros corresponding to assignments of B to W and C to X, leaving one zero for both officer C and station X, which is, of course, a forced assignment.

Solution 2 begins exactly as solution 1 by first assigning D to Y and then A to Z. In this case, however, we made an unforced assignment of B to W. After crossing out the zeros corresponding to assignments of B to X and C to W, we were forced to complete the solution by assigning C to X.

These are the only two solutions that can result no matter which unforced

FIGURE 10-1 Use of tree diagram to enumerate multiple optimal solutions to assignment problem.

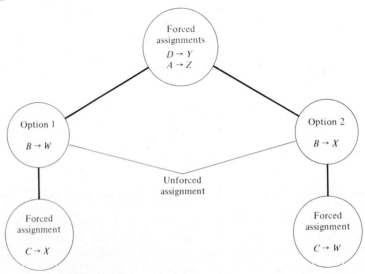

assignment we first select. Both solutions are optimal and will therefore have the same total cost. For large problems with multiple forced assignments, it is useful to construct a tree diagram such as shown in Figure 10-1 to ensure that all optimal solutions have been found.

INSTANT REPLAY   Determine *all* optimal solutions using the following final opportunity cost table (zero costs only are shown):

	W	X	Y	Z
A		0	0	0
B	0	0	0	
C	0	0	0	
D		0		

CHECK   Two solutions are optimal (*D* to *X*, *A* to *Z*, *B* to *W*, *C* to *Y*; and *D* to *X*, *A* to *Z*, *B* to *Y*, *C* to *W*) as shown by the following tree diagram:

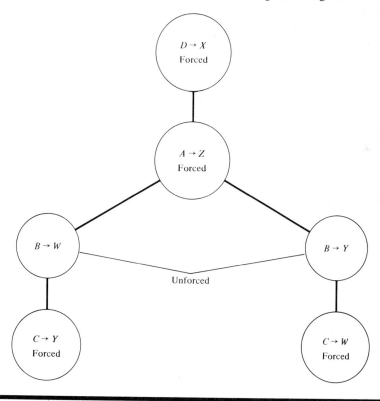

Maximization Objective Function   A third situation frequently encountered with assignment problems is that where the objective function is to be maximized rather than minimized. Suppose that our detailing problem, for example, has as an objective the maximization of some artificial fitness measure **375**

TABLE 10-14
**Conversion of Assignment Maximization Problem
to Equivalent Opportunity Cost Minimization Problem**

	W	X	Y	Z
A	10	12	4	9
B	6	5	3	8
C	2	3	4	5
D	6	7	3	10

	W	X	Y	Z
A	12 − 10 = 2	12 − 12 = 0	12 − 4 = 8	12 − 9 = 3
B	8 − 6 = 2	8 − 5 = 3	8 − 3 = 5	8 − 8 = 0
C	5 − 2 = 3	5 − 3 = 2	5 − 4 = 1	5 − 5 = 0
D	10 − 6 = 4	10 − 7 = 3	10 − 3 = 7	10 − 10 = 0

*Maximization of
fitness measure* ⟶ *Equivalent to* ⟶ *Minimization of
opportunity cost*

which determines the fit in terms of each officer's skills and background with
the requirements for the job. Suppose that the fitness of each officer for each
assignment is given by the number shown in Table 10-14. Assume that a higher
number represents a preferred assignment. Thus, we desire to find the set of
assignments that *maximizes* the sum of the fitness measures corresponding to
these assignments.

Recall that the solution method previously described for assignment
problems converts the initial cost data into a set of opportunity costs, by
subtracting the smallest cost from every entry in each row and column. Any
assignment problem with a maximization objective can also be easily converted
to an opportunity cost minimization problem. This is done by *subtracting every
coefficient in each row from the largest coefficient in that row*,[1] thus converting
these coefficients into their corresponding opportunity costs. From that point
on the problem is solved just as if it is a minimization problem.

For purposes of our illustration refer to the objective function coefficients
or fitness measures for each job as shown in Table 10-14. Note that the largest
or best fitness measure in the first row (officer A) is 12. So long as that assignment (A to X) can be achieved in the final solution, we will incur no lost
opportunity with respect to that officer (row). If, however, an assignment is
made of officer A to station W, the resulting fitness measure is only 10, 2 less
than that for the best assignment. Thus we would have incurred an opportunity
loss of 2 with this assignment. In a similar manner you should be able to see that
the opportunity cost of any assignment is equal to the difference between the
best fitness measure in that row and the fitness measure achievable for that
assignment.

Therefore, the opportunity cost row for officer A can be found by subtracting each fitness measure from 12, the best measure achievable by A. This

[1] An alternative approach requires subtracting each coefficient from some constant chosen to
be as large or larger than every original coefficient. The advantage of the method above is that at
least one zero is created for each row. Note that columns could be used in place of rows.

leads to the row as shown to the right in Table 10-14. In a similar manner we subtract each fitness measure from 8 for officer B, 5 for officer C, and 10 for officer D to calculate the remaining opportunity costs.

377

ASSIGNMENT
AND
MINIMAL
SPANNING
TREE
PROBLEMS

At this point the opportunity cost table has not been completely reduced since every column does not have at least one zero. The next step would be to subtract the smallest opportunity cost in each column from every element in that column. From there the solution procedure is applied exactly as for a cost minimization problem. But you must be careful to read the value of the solution in terms of the original fitness table for the final result of total fitness measure.

INSTANT REPLAY   Determine the optimal assignment of officers to stations so that fitness measure total is maximized. What is the total fitness measure?

CHECK   The fully reduced initial opportunity cost table is:

	W	X	Y	Z
A	0	0*	7	3
B	0*	3	4	0
C	1	2	0*	0
D	2	3	6	0*

The optimal assignments can be obtained directly from this table as shown from the starred (*) zero-cost elements above. The combined fitness total can then be calculated from:

A to X	12
B to W	6
C to Y	4
D to Z	10
	32

Unequal Assignment Options   A final situation of interest is that in which the number of assignments is unequal. This could result if more officers are available for assignment than there are duty stations, or vice versa. In other words, the number of rows does not equal the number of columns.

Recall that when we had an unbalanced transportation problem—total supply was not equal to total demand—we forced a balance by establishing either a dummy supply point or a dummy demand point with a supply or demand quantity equal to the amount of the imbalance. A similar method is used to balance assignment problems; as many dummy rows or columns as necessary are added to bring the number of each into balance.

For instance, suppose we had six officers to assign to four duty stations. The problem as stated is not in balance and must be modified by adding two dummy duty stations. For convenience, the cost of any assignment involving a dummy is assumed to be zero. An example of how two dummy duty stations

TABLE 10-15
Use of Dummy Columns to Balance an Assignment Problem

| | Next duty station | | | | | |
Officer	W	X	Y	Z	D_1	D_2
A	1,000	1,200	400	900	0	0
B	600	500	300	800	0	0
C	200	300	400	500	0	0
D	600	700	300	1,000	0	0
E	600	500	400	800	0	0
F	900	700	500	700	0	0

Six officers

Four real duty stations   *Two dummy duty stations*

are added to a modified version of the officer assignment problem to achieve a balanced problem is shown in Table 10-15. Of course, if we had started with more duty stations than officers, we would add dummy rows until the number of rows equaled the number of columns.

INSTANT REPLAY Determine the optimal assignment of officers to stations so that costs are minimized for the problem shown in Table 10-15. How do we interpret the assignment of an officer to a dummy station?

CHECK Several optimal solutions are possible. One is A to D_2, B to D_1, C to W, D to Y, E to X, and F to Z, for a total cost of $1,700. The assignment of officers to dummy stations is equivalent to no assignment made for these officers. Presumably, their next assignment will come from some other subset of duty stations. The existence of more than one optimal (equal-cost) solution gives the officer detailer the opportunity to introduce other noncost items into the decision. For example, the preferences of the officers themselves could be used by the detailer to make the final choice.

Minimal Spanning Tree Problems

Another type of network problem to be discussed in this chapter is that normally called the *minimal spanning tree problem*. As described earlier, a spanning tree is a joined set of routes that provides a path from any one activity in a network to every other activity. Each of these routes has a fixed cost associated with it. The total cost for any spanning tree is equal to the sum of the fixed costs for the routes that it contains. The *minimal spanning tree* is the spanning tree with the minimum total cost.

Consider, for example, the network shown in Figure 10-2. The activities to be connected by the spanning tree are represented by the circled letters.

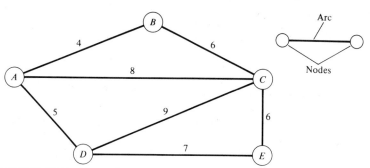

379

ASSIGNMENT
AND
MINIMAL
SPANNING
TREE
PROBLEMS

FIGURE 10-2 Network representation of a minimal spanning tree problem.

These are frequently referred to as *nodes*. The potential routes connecting the activities are represented by the lines connecting the circles. These lines are often referred to as *arcs*. The fixed costs associated with each route, or arc, are also shown.

As defined above, a spanning tree consists of a set of routes, or arcs, that form a joined path from each activity, or node, to every other activity. Numerous spanning trees can be formed using the network in Figure 10-2. For example, both of the following are spanning trees:

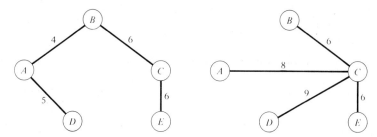

Note that 4 routes, or arcs, were required to connect the 5 activities. In general, if there are n activities, a spanning tree will contain $n - 1$ routes, or arcs.

The minimal spanning tree is that which has the lowest-total-cost set of arcs. The cost of the spanning tree on the left above is $5 + 4 + 6 + 6 = 21$. The cost of the tree on the right is $6 + 8 + 9 + 6 = 29$. Clearly, the spanning tree on the left is preferred to that on the right. In fact, the tree on the left is the minimal spanning tree for the network of Figure 10-2. No other spanning tree can be found with a total cost less than 21.

Before learning how to identify the minimal spanning tree, let us see how such problems arise in practice. Suppose the nodes, or activities, represent communities in a metropolitan area and that the arcs represent distances between these communities. Given this framework, there are several minimal spanning tree problems that can be hypothesized. For instance, suppose we wish to build a subway system to serve every community shown. Given the high cost of construction, we are likely to be interested in the shortest possible subway system that can be constructed that will serve each community. This is equivalent to finding the minimal spanning tree.

Alternatively, we may wish to build an electric power system connecting these communities. If the arc costs represent the cost of linking communities electrically, the lowest-cost power system is again defined by the minimal spanning tree. In place of electric power or subway systems, we could substitute sewer, water, cable television, or many other systems, where in each case the total cost of the system is minimized if connections are constructed to cover the arcs of the minimal spanning tree.

Suppose that the nodes represent major cities distributed regionally or nationally. Then we may be interested in the lowest-cost transportation system, highway system, or communication system that will interconnect each of these cities. The solution is again to find the minimal spanning tree.

Clearly, then, many real-world problems can be formulated as minimal spanning tree problems. Given that high costs are usually associated with the problems described, an optimal solution has a high potential payoff. Let us now examine by means of an example how such problems are solved.

Formulating the Problem

The city of Metropolis is faced with a budget crisis which has forced the city to cut back on many traditional city services. After a heavy snow the Metropolis sanitation department is responsible for snow removal. First priority has always been the removal of snow from specially designated snow emergency streets. These streets were selected for designation in such a way as to provide at least one cleared route between nearby major city sections. The current emergency routes are indicated, together with the length of each route (in blocks) in Figure 10-3. The current routes require a total of 350 blocks to be plowed.

Due to cutbacks in the size of the sanitation department, the current set of snow emergency routes is viewed as too extensive to complete snow removal on these routes in a satisfactory time limit. Therefore, city management would like to determine a reduced set of snow emergency routes that will permit emergency travel between any two communities and that can be cleared in the least possible time. This is clearly equivalent to finding the minimal spanning tree for the network of Figure 10-3.

Finding the Minimal Spanning Tree

Fortunately, a simple procedure exists for determining the minimal spanning tree. We begin by selecting the shortest of all the arcs, breaking any ties arbitrarily. We then find the shortest arc connecting any node not on the original arc with one of the nodes that was on the original arc. These two arcs must by definition join at some common node and will be on the minimal spanning

FIGURE 10-3 Metropolis snow emergency routes.

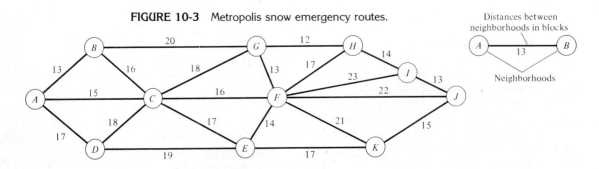

381

ASSIGNMENT
AND
MINIMAL
SPANNING
TREE
PROBLEMS

TABLE 10-16
Distances Between Nodes for Metropolis Snow Removal Problem

	A	B	C	D	E	F	G	H	I	J	K
A	—	13	15	17							
B	13	—	16				20				
C	15	16	—	18	17	16	18				
D	17		18	—	19						
E			17	19	—	14					17
F			16		14	—	13	17	23	22	21
√ G		20	18			13	—	(12)			
√ H						17	12	—	14		
I						23		14	—	13	
J						22			13	—	15
K					17	21				15	—

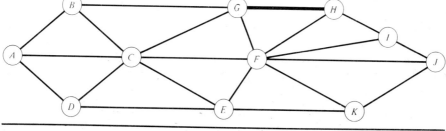

tree. We continue this process, always adding to the tree the shortest arc that connects the tree with some node not already on the tree. Eventually, no more nodes will remain unconnected, and the arcs so far selected constitute the minimal spanning tree.

Although this process could be carried out using the network diagram of Figure 10-3, a tabular approach, which will now be demonstrated, is less prone to error. Suppose we write the distances between nodes in tabular form as shown in Table 10-16.

Selecting the Initial Arc We begin by selecting the shortest route, which is that between communities G and H, a distance of 12 blocks. We circle that route distance. Then we check the rows labeled G and H and draw lines through the columns for G and H since they are now included on the spanning tree. These steps are reflected in Table 10-16. At the bottom of the table we show the snow removal network with the thick line between G and H indicating that the route between these two communities will be on the minimal spanning tree.

Selecting Additional Arcs At any stage, we build our spanning tree by connecting one node not currently on the tree with some node that is. If the tree is to be a minimal spanning tree, the new node to be added must be the one which lies closest to one of the nodes already on the tree.

For our example problem, the selection of the route connecting nodes G and H is equivalent to defining a tree with two nodes, G and H. The checks next to both of those rows are used to designate that those nodes are already on the

TABLE 10-17
Distance Table for Snow Removal Problem after Nodes F, G, and H Are Assigned to the Spanning Tree

	A	B	C	D	E	F	G	H	I	J	K
A	—	13	15	17							
B	13	—	16				20				
C	15	16	—	18	17	16	18				
D	17		18	—	19						
E			17	19	—	14					17
✓ F			16		14		13	17	23	22	21
✓ G		20	18			(13)	—	(12)			
✓ H						17	12	—	14		
I						23		14	—	13	
J						22			13	—	15
K					17	21				15	—

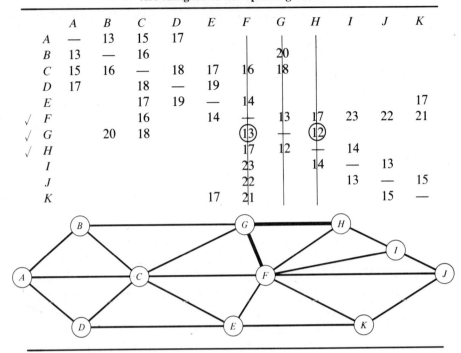

tree. The next node to be added is that which lies closest to either G or H. To determine this we scan the rows for G and H to find the closest node.

F is the closest node to G, lying just 13 blocks away, and I is the closest node to H, 14 blocks away. Since F is closer to the tree than I, F is the next node added to the tree by connecting the arc from F to G.

To indicate this change, the route distance from F to G is circled, row F is checked, and column F is lined through, as shown in Table 10-17. At this point you may wonder why the columns corresponding to nodes on the tree are crossed out. This is simply to avoid connecting any two nodes that are already on the tree. For example, we have now added nodes F, G, and H to the tree with connections between F and G and G and H. If the distance between F and H is less than the distance connecting F, G, or H with any other node, we might make the mistake of adding the arc from F to H to our tree. Since F and H are already connected through node G, adding the arc from F to H unnecessarily increases the length of the tree. To prevent this from happening, we put a line through the column of each node as it is added to the tree.

Referring to Table 10-17, we search each of the checked rows, F, G, and H, to determine the cheapest route to any unconnected node. At this point a tie occurs since node E is 14 blocks from F, the same distance that node I is from H. It does not make any difference how ties are broken; any arbitrary choice will lead to a minimal spanning tree. Of course, the existence of ties may indicate more than one optimal solution, and it might be desirable to explore each of these, for other managerial reasons.

TABLE 10-18

TABLE 10-18
Distance Table for Metropolis Snow Removal Problem
with Minimal Spanning Tree Arcs Circled

Order of selection		A	B	C	D	E	F	G	H	I	J	K
8	A	—	(13)	15	(17)							
9	B	13	—	16				20				
7	C	(15)	16	—	18	17	16	18				
10	D	17		18	—	19						
3	E			17	19	—	14					17
2	F			(16)		(14)	—	13	17	23	22	21
1	G		20	18			(13)	—	(12)			
1	H						17	12	—	(14)		
4	I						23		14	—	(13)	
5	J						22			13	—	(15)
6	K					17	21			15	—	

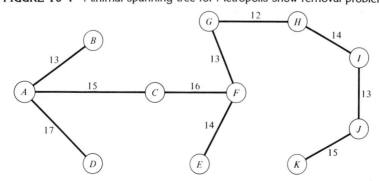

Suppose we arbitrarily select node E to add to the tree. A continued application of this selection procedure will then lead to the final table shown as Table 10-18. The minimal spanning tree arcs are those identified by the circles. For convenience, the order in which each new node was added to the tree is indicated in the left margin. You should trace the solution through with pencil and paper to ensure that you understand the procedure.

The actual spanning tree is shown in Figure 10-4. Note that the length of the spanning tree is equivalent to the number of blocks to be plowed to clear these newly designated snow emergency routes; this system totals 142 blocks compared to 350 blocks with the previous snow emergency plan.

FIGURE 10-4 Minimal spanning tree for Metropolis snow removal problem.

INSTANT REPLAY Suppose the city is divided into two districts (district I serving communities *A* through *E;* district II, *F* through *K*), and separate snow emergency routes are to be developed connecting communities within each district. Determine the minimal spanning tree for each district. Assuming that arc *EF* will be plowed to connect the two districts, compare the total number of blocks plowed under the two-district plan with that for the city as a whole.

CHECK The minimal spanning tree for district I contains arcs *A* to *B*, *A* to *C*, *A* to *D*, and *C* to *E* for a total length of 62 blocks. That for district II contains arcs *F* to *G*, *G* to *H*, *H* to *I*, *I* to *J*, and *J* to *K* for a total length of 67 blocks. The total number of blocks is thus $62 + 67 + 14 = 143$, 1 more than for the city treated as a whole.

The procedure described here of building the minimal spanning tree by always adding the node closest (lowest fixed cost) to the current tree will always produce an optimal solution. As you can see, the procedure is quite simple and fast. It is important because of the wide variety of problems to which it can be applied and the large costs associated with the decision alternatives.

Final Comments

In this chapter and the previous one we have examined three different categories of network problems. In Chapter 9 we considered the transportation problem. In this chapter we have looked at the assignment problem and the minimal spanning tree problem. Both problem types can be represented graphically as networks, and each has certain similarities and differences.

The transportation and assignment problems involve the assignment of resources, or flow of objects, from one set of nodes to another. They are similar in that the arcs have costs associated with them. The objective is to choose the least-cost set of arcs which corresponds to specific routes over which goods are transported or which corresponds to specific assignments. Capacities are assigned to each node for transportation and assignment problems. These represent supply and demand capacities for the transportation problem. For the assignment problem each node has a single-unit capacity representing the object to be assigned.

Minimal spanning tree problems are least like the other two. In this case we are concerned with ensuring that each node can be connected with minimum cost to the others. The connecting arcs have fixed costs. We wish to find the least-cost set of arcs that allows the node-to-node connections.

Two other types of network problems will be covered in later chapters. In Chapter 12 we will see how dynamic programming can be used to solve what is called the shortest-route problem. The shortest-route problem is concerned

with finding the shortest (if time or distance is the objective measure) or least-cost path from one node in a network to another. Each arc in the network has a "cost" associated with it that corresponds to the time, distance, or dollar cost required to move from one node to the next. The shortest route between any two nodes is thus the path between these nodes with the least-total-cost set of arcs.

In Chapter 16 we will consider project planning and control systems. As part of that analysis, we will develop a procedure for determining the longest path through a network. The length of the longest path is equivalent to the shortest total time in which the project can be completed.

385

ASSIGNMENT
AND
MINIMAL
SPANNING
TREE
PROBLEMS

Key Words

Arcs **379**

Assignment problem **357**

Cost reduction **359**

Dummy column **377**

Dummy row **377**

Dynamic programming **384**

Enumeration **372**

Forced assignment **361**

Hungarian method **358**

Minimal spanning tree **378**

Minimal spanning tree problem **378**

Multiple optimal solutions **373**

Nodes **379**

Opportunity cost **359**

Prohibited assignment **373**

Project planning and control **385**

Removed cost **360**

Shortest-route problem **384**

Spanning tree **357**

Unequal assignment options **377**

Unforced assignment **361**

Problems

10-1. The law firm of Crachett, Tim, and Dickens employs five law students on a part-time basis to perform pretrial research. Owing to different backgrounds the students are not equally adept at accomplishing the different research tasks. At the moment five research tasks are available for assignment to the five students. Estimated times, in hours, for each student on each task are shown below.

Student	Research task V	W	X	Y	Z
A	4	10	12	6	8
B	5	7	9	8	6
C	9	13	10	7	12
D	6	8	8	5	10
E	3	9	12	6	9

    a. Assuming that the firm wishes to minimize the labor costs to complete these research tasks (all five students are paid the same hourly rate), determine the best assignment.

    b. How many hours will it take to complete these five tasks?

10-2. Refer to the law student assignment situation of problem 10-1.

a. Assuming that the firm wishes to improve the skills of the five students by assigning them to the tasks for which they are least prepared, determine the best assignment.

b. How many hours will it take to complete these tasks?

10-3. The police dispatcher for the Wembley police department has received four requests for police assistance. At the moment six patrol cars are available for assignment and the estimated response times (minutes) are shown in the table below.

	Patrol unit					
Incident	1	2	3	4	5	6
I	6	5	3	4	5	8
II	8	6	2	3	7	6
III	4	4	7	6	5	5
IV	3	7	9	8	4	7

a. Which patrol units should respond?

b. What will be the average response time?

10-4. A government purchasing agent is now analyzing a set of bids received for five projects from six bidders. Guidelines established for selecting the successful bidders require the purchasing agent to (1) minimize the total cost to complete the five projects, (2) not award more than one contract to each bidder, and (3) disregard the lowest bid whenever it is more than 25 percent below the next lowest bid (the assumption being that the quality of the work will not be up to standards). The bids on the projects are shown in the table below (in thousands of dollars).

	Bidders					
Contracts	1	2	3	4	5	6
A	7	9	3	17	8	10
B	8	13	7	17	12	10
C	8	10	6	7	7	10
D	12	14	13	8	15	16
E	7	5	11	8	16	8

a. Identify the successful bidders for the five contracts.

b. How much will these five contracts cost the government?

10-5. The director of a holiday basketball tournament is attempting to determine the first-round pairings for the tournament. Based on knowledge of each team's drawing power, national ranking, etc., the director estimates that the following attendance figures (in thousands) would result for each of the first-round games between a group of local schools and a group of visiting schools.

387

ASSIGNMENT
AND
MINIMAL
SPANNING
TREE
PROBLEMS

	Iona	St. John's	Princeton	Columbia
Duke	12	17	14	13
North Carolina	17	18	16	15
Michigan	14	16	13	11
Notre Dame	13	19	15	14

    a. What pairings should the director select so as to maximize attendance for the first-round games?

    b. What will the average attendance be for these games?

10-6. The American Broadcasting System (ABS) network is planning its television coverage for the summer Olympics. They wish to establish a communications system that will connect each of the major sports competition areas with the others but in a way that will minimize the total amount of cable necessary to make such connections. The sports areas (nodes) and the distances (in miles) to adjacent areas are shown in the diagram below:

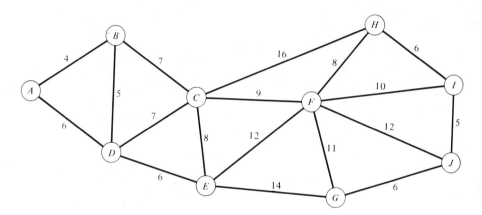

    a. Select the arcs on which ABS should establish its cable network connecting the sports competition areas.

    b. How many miles of cable will be required?

10-7. The Interstate Highway Commission is planning to build new sections of interstate highway to serve the cities (nodes) shown in the figure at the top of page 388. The potential routes (arcs) and their distances in miles are also shown.

    a. If the objective of the commission is to complete the smallest interstate system that will permit travel from each of these cities to any other, which routes should be included?

    b. How many miles of interstate highway will need to be constructed to serve the cities?

    c. Suppose that an alternate route from E to F has been suggested that would cut the distance from 125 to 100 miles. Would this proposed modification cause your answer to parts a and b to change?

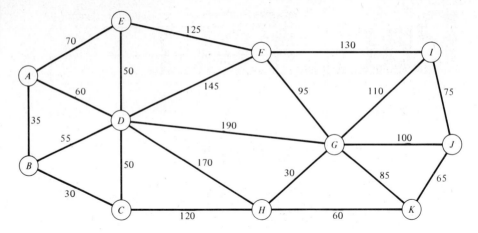

10-8. The voters in the Metropolis regional area recently approved a referendum in favor of a regional subway system. The system is to serve each of 10 communities within the region. The subway planning commission is now attempting to decide where the subway should be constructed. Costs of making various connections between these communities are shown below (in hundred thousands of dollars).

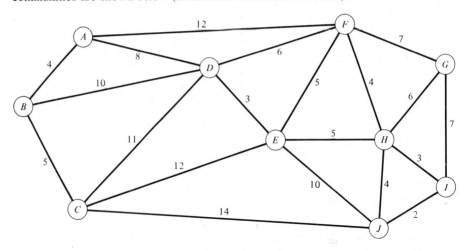

    a. Which routes will yield the lowest total construction cost for the system and will allow a citizen in any community to take a subway to any of the other nine communities?

    b. How much will this system cost?

Part Four

Other Programming Techniques

Our treatment of management science decision-making procedures continues in this section with a discussion of three general-purpose programming techniques: integer programming, dynamic programming, and heuristic programming.

Integer programming problems, to be covered in Chapter 11, are an important class of linear programming problems. Integer problems are characterized by the inclusion of a special category of constraints called integer constraints. These constraints are added to ensure that the solution contains integer nonfractional values for the decision variables. Two types of integer problems are considered: positive integer problems and zero-one problems. Positive integer problems contain decision variables that are restricted to having positive integer values (0, 1, 2, . . .). These problems occur in practice when the items corresponding to the decision variables cannot be divided but must be in integral units. Zero-one problems contain decision variables that must be either 0 or 1. Such problems arise when yes-no-type decisions are required.

Integer programming problems occur frequently in practice. For that reason they are important. Unfortunately, the solution of such problems is not always easy. We will consider several solution approaches that can be used.

Chapter 12 deals with what are called dynamic programming problems. These problems consist of a set of sequential, interrelated decisions. This series of decisions, because they are interrelated, cannot be made independently but must be treated collectively. An example might be a production planning problem over several time periods. A production level decision in one period will affect the production level decision in another period.

Dynamic programming is unlike other programming approaches. This is because dynamic programming is really a conceptual approach to solving a problem rather than a specific procedure. Although the conceptual approach is the same from problem to problem, the specific steps to be carried out will differ, depending on the nature of the problem to be solved.

In Chapter 13 we consider heuristic programming. Heuristic programming differs from other programming procedures in that the solutions obtained cannot be guaranteed to be optimal. That is, a heuristic solution procedure attempts to find good solutions to a problem but has no provision for guaranteeing optimality.

Heuristic procedures are important for dealing with large-scale, practical problems of many types. They are often simple and fast and therefore capable of handling such large problems. Many optimizing procedures, such as integer programming procedures, have difficulty in solving large problems. It is precisely these problems for which heuristics are most useful.

11

Integer Programming

In this chapter we treat an important class of linear programming problems in which some or all of the decision variables are required to have *integer,* or whole number, *values.* This class of problems is commonly referred to as *integer programming.* If *all* the decision variables are to be integer-valued, the problem is further categorized as a *pure integer problem.* When some of the variables may be fractional and others are restricted to integers we have a *mixed integer problem.*

In our previous treatment of linear programming problems we have not been concerned whether the decision variables resulted in integer values, such as 2, 10, and 24, or fractional, noninteger values, such as $\frac{33}{2}$, .157, and $\frac{5}{12}$. In some cases this lack of concern resulted from the fact that the fractional portion of the value had little effect on the decision. For example, suppose the decision variable represents the number of units of a product to be produced. If the optimal value for this decision variable turns out to be $990\frac{1}{5}$, it makes little difference if we ignore the fractional portion of this value and use 990 as our answer. In other cases we did not need to worry about fractional values because the nature of the problem formulation was such that the solution always resulted in integer values. This was the case for the transportation and assignment problems, for instance. For these problems the constraint coefficients were always 0 or 1, the right-hand-side values were always integer, and the optimal values for the decision variables will always be integer, as a result.

There are, however, many managerial problems for which fractional decision variable values are very important. These problems typically have high costs or benefits associated with the decision variables, such that the fractional portion of the solution cannot be ignored. This would be the case if the decision variables represented such items as the number of hospitals to build for a community, whether to fund a capital budgeting project, the number of warehouses needed for a distribution system, and the number of airplanes to be purchased by an airline. Each of these decision variables has a high associated cost. In most cases the standard linear programming problem structure cannot guarantee that integer values will result. Thus, it is useful to be able to add integer restrictions to such problems and to find the optimal integer solution.

At first glance it might appear that integer programming problems are easier to solve than standard linear programming problems. For instance, with a pure integer problem, the number of feasible solutions is restricted to those integer-valued combinations that satisfy the noninteger constraints. This is a considerably smaller number of solutions to examine than without the integer restrictions. To illustrate, suppose we were attempting to determine the number of hospitals to build for a set of communities, where each community is limited to a maximum of five hospitals. A standard linear programming constraint of the form

$$\text{Hospitals for community } i \leq 5$$

would permit any fractional or integer solution between 0 and 5 (an infinite number of combinations). Thus, solutions such as 1.38 hospitals would be permitted, although not practical. Limiting the number of hospitals to the integers 0, 1, 2, 3, 4, and 5 reduces the number of feasible solutions to six for each community.

Despite this reduction in the number of feasible solutions, integer programming problems are considerably more difficult to solve than normal linear programming problems. Although a number of solution procedures exist for finding the optimal solution to an integer linear programming problem, the size of the problem they can solve is somewhat limited. The simplex method is easier and less costly to use than one of the integer programming procedures that will be presented in this chapter. Therefore, as a general rule, simplex should be used unless the benefits to be obtained from forcing integer solutions outweigh the additional costs of using an integer programming procedure.

Formulating Integer Programming Problems

Before we see how to solve integer programming problems, it is worthwhile to examine the nature of such problems and how they are formulated. Formulation is particularly important for several reasons. As with linear programming problems, computer procedures exist for solving integer programming problems. Thus, from a managerial perspective, you are more likely to be involved in formulating such problems than in solving them. Furthermore, there is frequently more than one way in which an integer programming problem can be formulated. The ease with which a problem can be solved may depend to a large extent on how the problem is formulated. This is why it is generally recognized that the formulation of integer programming problems is even more of an art than the formulation of standard linear programming problems.

One of the keys to determining a good formulation is to reduce as much as possible the number of integer variables. The ability of any of the available computerized procedures to solve integer programming problems is significantly improved whenever the number of integer variables is kept small.

This is because the solution time is normally related to the number of integer variables in an exponential fashion. For instance, an integer programming problem with 10 decision variables, each potentially taking 1 of 20 integer values, has 20^{10} or 10,240 billion potential solutions. Each additional variable considered for this example multiplies the number of potentially optimal solutions by a factor of 20.

It is useful to distinguish between two types of integer variables: positive integer variables and zero-one variables. *Positive integer variables* are decision variables that are limited to positive integer values, such as 0, 1, 2, 3, and so on. *Zero-one variables* are more restricted in that these decision variables must be either 0 or 1. This distinction is useful because specialized procedures have been developed that are more efficient at solving problems with zero-one variables than those for problems involving positive integer variables. Later in this chapter we will solve both types of problems. Next let us see how such problems arise in practice.

Positive Integer Problems

Positive integer programming problems are like standard linear programming problems except that at least some of the decision variables are limited to positive integer values. For example, many decision problems require determining the optimal number of specific types of resources to be assigned, purchased, produced, constructed, and so on. These resources might be the number of scientists to assign to specific research projects, the number of different types of aircraft to purchase, or the number of different types of power generators to produce.

Product Mix Problem   As an example of a positive integer problem, suppose we reconsider the *product mix problem,* which we first treated in Chapter 5. Suppose in this case we are scheduling production of airplanes for an aircraft manufacturer. Two types of airplanes can be produced: DC 727's and DC 747's. Each DC 727 provides contribution to profits of $400,000 and each DC 747 provides $600,000.

During the next year the company will have available a total of 2,520,000 labor hours in the assembly department and 201,600 labor hours in the testing department. Each DC 727 requires 27,000 labor hours in the assembly department and 2,000 labor hours in the testing department. Each DC 747 requires 38,000 labor hours in the assembly department and 3,200 labor hours in the testing department.

If we let X represent the number of DC 727's produced and Y the number of DC 747's, we can formulate this problem as a standard linear programming problem:

> Maximize: $\$400,000X + \$600,000Y$
>
> Subject to:
>
> $27,000X + 38,000Y \le 2,520,000$ assembly constraint
>
> $2,000X + 3,200Y \le 201,600$ testing constraint

Nothing in this formulation will prevent the answer from containing fractional, or noninteger, values. (In fact, the answer requires $X = 40.9615$ and $Y =$

37.2115.) Clearly, we cannot manufacture fractional portions of an airplane. To prevent this we can add the additional constraints that the two decision variables, X and Y, can take on only positive integer values. These *integer constraints* can be written in several ways, such as

$$X \text{ and } Y \text{ integer} \quad \text{or} \quad X \text{ and } Y = 0, 1, 2, 3, \ldots$$

Note that the difference between this product mix problem and those treated in earlier chapters is the high value associated with the two decision variables. (X and Y have objective function coefficients of $600,000 and $400,000, respectively.) Ignoring the fractional portions of the solution represents a significant dollar value. Therefore, the benefits from considering only all-integer solutions may be high.

Cargo Loading Problem   As another example, consider the *cargo loading problem*, where several sizes of cargo are available for loading in a ship, airplane, truck, or train. The solution to this problem requires the determination of the number of cargo units of each size to load so as to maximize total contribution subject to capacity restrictions for the carrier.

For an illustration, suppose we are loading a cargo ship, and three different sizes of cargo container are available for loading. The cargo capacity of the ship is constrained both by a maximum volume, 100,000 cubic feet, and a maximum weight, 500,000 pounds. Let us designate the three sizes of cargo container as A, B, and C. Each A container has a volume of 100 cubic feet, a weight of 800 pounds, and a contribution of $1,000. Each B container has a volume of 500 cubic feet, a weight of 2,000 pounds, and a contribution of $4,000. Each C container has a volume of 1,000 cubic feet, a weight of 5,000 pounds, and a contribution of $9,000. Suppose that there are 300 A containers, 200 B containers, and 100 C containers available for loading.

We can define the following integer programming formulation for this problem:

Maximize: $1,000A + $4,000B + $9,000C$

Subject to:

$$100A + 500B + 1,000C \leq 100,000 \quad \text{volume constraint}$$

$$800A + 2,000B + 5,000C \leq 500,000 \quad \text{weight constraint}$$

$$\left. \begin{array}{l} A = 0, 1, 2, \ldots, 300 \\ B = 0, 1, 2, \ldots, 200 \\ C = 0, 1, 2, \ldots, 100 \end{array} \right\} \quad \text{integer constraints}$$

The first two constraints ensure that the cubic volume and weight capacities, respectively, are not exceeded. The last three constraints ensure that the quantity to be loaded of each size does not exceed the number of available containers (300 As, 200 Bs, and 100 Cs) and that only integer quantities are considered. The integer condition is necessary for this problem because cargo containers cannot be subdivided and the profit coefficients are quite large.

INSTANT REPLAY   Suppose the problem above is modified to include a fourth size of cargo, D, of which 75 containers are available. Each D container contributes $10,000, has a volume of 1,200 cubic feet, and weighs 6,000 pounds.

Furthermore, suppose that loading time is also limited because the ship is due
to sail in 48 hours. Loading time for the various cargo containers is 15 minutes
for each A, 20 minutes per B, 30 minutes per C, and 40 minutes for each D.
What modifications would be necessary to our formulation?

CHECK The new formulation would be:

Maximize: $\$1,000A + \$4,000B + \$9,000C + \$10,000D$

Subject to:

$$100A + 500B + 1,000C + 1,200D \leq 100,000$$
$$800A + 2,000B + 5,000C + 6,000D \leq 500,000$$
$$15A + 20B + 30C + 40D \leq 2,880$$
$$A = 0, 1, 2, \ldots, 300$$
$$B = 0, 1, 2, \ldots, 200$$
$$C = 0, 1, 2, \ldots, 100$$
$$D = 0, 1, 2, \ldots, 75$$

Zero-One Problems

Another major category of integer programming problems includes those with
zero-one variables. Zero-one variables are particularly useful for modeling
situations in which yes-no decisions must be made. These include, for example,
selecting a set of research and development projects for funding from among a
large set of proposals, or deciding which potential locations are to be used for
fire stations needed to serve a new community.

Each of the potential alternatives (R&D proposals and fire station locations) requires a yes-no decision. They can be formulated as zero-one decision
variables. A value of 0 corresponds to a "no" decision (R&D proposal not
funded) and a value of 1 corresponds to a "yes" decision (R&D proposal
funded). Fractional values are not permitted for these variables to avoid impractical solutions. (How do you build one-third of a fire house?)

In the sections below we will see how zero-one problems can arise in
practice and how they can be formulated.

Capital Budgeting Problem We will first consider a *capital budgeting problem*.
Suppose a firm has a set of investment opportunities, or projects, each of which
requires a specific pattern of funds invested and is expected to yield a given
return on that investment. If the funds available for investment in these projects
are limited, the decision problem can be stated as selecting some subset of
projects so as to maximize the expected return without exceeding the investment budget restrictions.

To illustrate, consider the American Burger Company, a fast food chain
that specializes in a hamburger pattie cooked so that the charcoal markings give
the appearance of an American Flag on each pattie. The company is busily
expanding the number of outlets around the country, but is somewhat constrained by the amount of cash available to support this expansion.

At the moment they are considering four potential sites for their next new outlets: Athens, Dacula, Winder, and Jefferson. On the basis of demand estimates, costs, and other factors, they estimate the expected return for each site to be $180,000 for Athens, $90,000 for Dacula, $120,000 for Winder, and $140,000 for Jefferson. In addition, they have estimated what their cash needs will be for each site during the next four accounting periods. The Athens site will require $10,000 in period 1, $12,000 in period 2, $8,000 in period 3, and $7,000 in period 4. Dacula will need $9,000 in each of the four periods. Winder will require $7,500 in period 1, $7,000 in each of periods 2 and 3, and $5,000 in period 4. The Jefferson site will require $5,000 in period 1, $7,500 in period 2, and $9,000 in each of periods 3 and 4. Available cash is constrained to no more than $25,000 for each of the first two periods and $30,000 for each of the last two.

The objective is to choose a set of sites that maximizes the expected return but does not require more cash invested than is available. To formulate this problem, we use a zero-one variable for each potential site. If the site is to be developed, the variable will have a value of 1. If it is not to be developed, the variable will have a value of 0. Letting A, D, W, and J represent the zero-one variables for the Athens, Dacula, Winder, and Jefferson sites, the objective function is then:

$$\text{Maximize } \$180,000A + \$90,000D + \$120,000W + \$140,000J$$

Thus, if we decide to open American Burger shops at Athens and Winder but not at Dacula and Jefferson, the variables would be valued as $A = 1$, $D = 0$, $W = 1$, and $J = 0$. The total expected return would be $180,000(1) + $90,000(0) + $120,000(1) + $140,000(0) = $300,000.

Because each period has a limitation on the amount of cash available and cash needs vary from period to period, we need a constraint equation for each period:

$$\$10,000A + \$9,000D + \$7,500W + \$5,000J \leq \$25,000 \quad \text{period 1}$$

$$\$12,000A + \$9,000D + \$7,000W + \$7,500J \leq \$25,000 \quad \text{period 2}$$

$$\$8,000A + \$9,000D + \$7,000W + \$9,000J \leq \$30,000 \quad \text{period 3}$$

$$\$7,000A + \$9,000D + \$5,000W + \$9,000J \leq \$30,000 \quad \text{period 4}$$

The zero-one conditions can be handled by adding the constraints A, D, W, and $J = 0$ or 1.

INSTANT REPLAY What modifications to the above formulation would be necessary if the American Burger Company wished to limit the number of openings to no more than two?

CHECK An additional constraint would need to be added, requiring that

$$A + D + W + J \leq 2$$

Capacitated Warehouse Location Problem Another common use of zero-one variables occurs when decision variables affect both fixed and variable costs. In previous linear programming situations we safely ignored fixed costs because they were not affected in any way by the values of the decision variables.

However, many problems with yes-no decisions require consideration of fixed cost. This is because the fixed costs will be incurred only if the decision is "yes."

As an example, consider the *capacitated warehouse location problem* (which will be treated in a different manner in Chapter 13). The problem involves selecting a subset of warehouses from among a set of potential warehouse sites to supply customers. The costs to be minimized include the variable shipping cost, which depends on the number of units to be shipped from each warehouse to each customer, and a fixed operating cost for each warehouse selected.

To illustrate, suppose we consider the simple example of the Claxton Video Company. Claxton manufactures videorecorders which it sells to four major retail chains, referred to here as W, X, Y, and Z. Annual requirements are 400 recorders for customer W, 500 for customer X, 600 for Y, and 300 for Z. The company is about to establish a distribution warehouse system that will allow it to supply its customers more quickly than at present. Three potential locations, referred to as A, B, and C, have been identified. A warehouse at location A will cost $20,000 per year to operate, has an annual capacity of 1,000 recorders, and can supply customers at a shipping cost per recorder of $10 for W, $12 for X, $15 for Y, and $8 for Z. A warehouse at location B will cost $32,000 to operate, has a capacity of 1,200 units, and has shipping costs of $9, $16, $13, and $10 for W, X, Y, and Z, respectively. Warehouse location C has fixed costs of $18,000, a capacity of 1,800, and variable shipping costs of $13, $10, $12, and $13, respectively. The decision is to choose which of these three warehouses should be operated and which customers will be supplied from the selected warehouses.

The objective is to minimize the total of the fixed operating costs and the variable shipping costs. Thus, the objective function consists of two parts corresponding to the variable shipping costs and the fixed operating costs:

Minimize: (Variable shipping costs) + (fixed operating costs)

The variable shipping costs are equal to the number of units shipped along each potential route multiplied by the per-unit shipping cost. Suppose we use a two-letter designation to represent the quantity shipped. Thus AX would correspond to the number of recorders shipped from warehouse A to customer X. This yields

$$\text{Variable shipping costs} = \begin{cases} 10AW + 12AX + 15AY + 8AZ \\ + \quad 9BW + 16BX + 13BY + 10BZ \\ + \quad 13CW + 10CX + 12CY + 13CZ \end{cases}$$

Incorporating the fixed operating costs is a little more difficult. This can be done by using a zero-one variable for each warehouse. Suppose we let A, B, and C be the zero-one variables for the three warehouses. A value of 0 corresponds to a decision not to operate that warehouse; a value of 1 represents the opposite. Thus, the fixed costs can be written as

$$\text{Fixed operating costs} = 20,000A + 32,000B + 18,000C$$

The complete objective function is thus:

Minimize: $10AW + 12AX + 15AY + 8AZ$

$+ 9BW + 16BX + 13BY + 10BZ$

$+ 13CW + 10CX + 12CY + 13CZ$

$+ 20{,}000A + 32{,}000B + 18{,}000C$

Three sets of constraints are necessary. The first ensures that each customer's demand is satisfied by one or more of the warehouses:

$$AW + BW + CW \geq 400 \qquad \text{customer } W$$
$$AX + BX + CX \geq 500 \qquad \text{customer } X$$
$$AY + BY + CY \geq 600 \qquad \text{customer } Y$$
$$AZ + BZ + CZ \geq 300 \qquad \text{customer } Z$$

The second set of constraints accomplishes two purposes. One is to restrict the amount shipped from any warehouse to no more than its capacity (thus the use of "capacitated" in the name of the problem). The other is to ensure that customer demands can only be satisfied from warehouses that are to be operated (their zero-one variables equal 1). This is accomplished by multiplying the capacity of each warehouse by its corresponding zero-one variable and using the result as the effective warehouse capacity. These constraints will have the general form

$$\binom{\text{Amounts shipped}}{\text{from a warehouse}} \leq \binom{\text{true}}{\text{warehouse capacity}} \times \binom{\text{zero-one variable}}{\text{for warehouse}}$$

For our problem this results in the following three constraints:

$$AW + AX + AY + AZ \leq 1{,}000A \qquad \text{warehouse } A \text{ capacity constraint}$$
$$BW + BX + BY + BZ \leq 1{,}200B \qquad \text{warehouse } B \text{ capacity constraint}$$
$$CW + CX + CY + CZ \leq 1{,}800C \qquad \text{warehouse } C \text{ capacity constraint}$$

Note that because zero-one variable A is limited to 0 or 1, the right-hand side of warehouse A's constraint is either 0, if $A = 0$, or 1,000, if $A = 1$. Thus, we can ship either 0 recorders or a maximum of 1,000 recorders, depending on whether warehouse A is not to be operated ($A = 0$) or operated ($A = 1$).

The final set of constraints represent the zero-one restrictions on each warehouse: A, B, $C = 0$ or 1.

Covering Problem Providing public emergency services, such as fire, police, or ambulance service, often requires the solution of a special form of a facility location problem called a *covering problem*. A covering problem is similar to the warehouse location problem in that a set of locations is to be selected from a larger set of potential locations. The covering problem differs from the warehouse problem in that only fixed costs are minimized. A feasible solution is defined as one that *covers* or meets some specified service objective for all customers.

Suppose, for example, that we are locating fire stations to serve a particular community by choosing from among a set of potential locations. The stations are to be located so that at least one station is within 5 minutes travel time of every neighborhood within the region being served. Thus, a station covers a neighborhood if it is within 5 minutes' travel time of that neighborhood. A feasible solution is any set of stations, at least one of which covers every neighborhood.

To illustrate, suppose we have four potential fire station sites, P, Q, R, and S, that are to serve six neighborhoods, F, G, H, I, J, and K. Suppose that the fixed costs of operating a station are assumed to be \$150,000 at site P, \$130,000 at site Q, \$185,000 at site R, and \$170,000 at site S. Site P is within 5 minutes, or covers, neighborhoods, F, I, and J. Site Q covers neighborhoods F, G, and H. Site R covers G, H, I, J, and K. Site S covers I, J, and K.

The objective is to minimize the total fixed costs for the selected station sites. If we let P, Q, R, and S be zero-one variables corresponding to whether each location is selected (i.e., $P = 1$) or not (i.e., $P = 0$), we can define the following objective function:

$$\text{Minimize } \$150,000P + \$130,000Q + \$185,000R + \$170,000S$$

Two sets of constraints are needed. The first ensures that each neighborhood is covered by at least one station. Observe, for instance, that neighborhood F is covered by stations located at sites P or Q. Thus, to ensure that neighborhood F is covered, we require

$$P + Q \geq 1 \quad \text{neighborhood } F$$

In a similar manner we add

$$Q + R \geq 1 \qquad \text{neighborhood } G$$
$$Q + R \geq 1 \qquad \text{neighborhood } H$$
$$P + R + S \geq 1 \qquad \text{neighborhood } I$$
$$P + R + S \geq 1 \qquad \text{neighborhood } J$$
$$R + S \geq 1 \qquad \text{neighborhood } K$$

The second set of constraints restricts each decision variable to values of 0 or 1:

$$P, Q, R, \text{ and } S = 0 \text{ or } 1$$

Sequencing Problem Another large category of problems involving zero-one variables consists of decisions requiring a *sequencing*, or scheduling, of objects. A common example is the job sequencing problem, which consists of determining the order in which a set of jobs are to be processed by a specific work center. Let us illustrate with a simple example.

Suppose we have two jobs to be processed at a single work center. Job 1 will take 5 hours to process and job 2 will take 2 hours. Clearly, this simple problem has only two solutions: either we process job 1 first and then job 2 or we process them in reverse order.

A number of objectives can be proposed for determining which order, or sequence, is best. Suppose we wish to minimize the average finish time. Letting F_1 be the time job 1 finishes processing and F_2 be the time that job 2 finishes, we can define the average finish time as

$$\text{Average finish time} = \frac{F_1 + F_2}{2}$$

Because the denominator 2 is a constant (unaffected by the job sequence), we can ignore it and attempt to minimize the sum of the finish times. In other words, we seek to

$$\text{Minimize } F_1 + F_2$$

The constraints for this problem will be used to define the actual finish times. These finish times obviously depend on the sequence in which the jobs are processed. Consider job 1. If it is processed first, its finish time will not be earlier than 5 hours:

$$F_1 \geq 5 \quad \text{if job 1 first}$$

If, however, job 2 is processed first, the finish time for job 1 will be equal to the sum of the processing times for the two jobs. Thus,

$$F_1 \geq 5 + F_2 \quad \text{if job 2 first}$$

Situations such as this, where the right-hand side of the constraint depends upon some other condition, can be conveniently handled by use of a zero-one variable. Suppose we define S as a zero-one variable where $S = 1$ if job 1 is processed first and $S = 0$ if job 2 is processed first. This allows us to write the finish time constraint for job 1 as

$$F_1 \geq 5 + F_2(1 - S)$$

Observe that if job 1 is processed first, S will equal 1 and the term inside the parentheses will be $1 - 1 = 0$. This will leave the constraint as $F_1 \geq 5$. On the other hand, if $S = 0$, the constraint will be $F_1 \geq 5 + F_2$.

A similar constraint is needed for the finish time of job 2, F_2. This requires

$$F_2 \geq 2 + F_1(S)$$

Note that, in this case, the zero-one sequence variable is not subtracted from 1 but is multiplied directly by the finish time for job 1. This is because job 1's finish time is only relevant to job 2 if job 1 is processed first ($S = 1$). The complete formulation is thus

$$\text{Minimize:} \quad F_1 + F_2$$
$$\text{Subject to:} \quad F_1 \geq 5 + F_2(1 - S)$$
$$F_2 \geq 2 + F_1(S)$$
$$S = 0 \text{ or } 1$$

This problem, purposely simplified for explanatory purposes, is quite easy to solve. The zero-one variable S is the only decision variable and must be either 0 or 1. If $S = 0$, implying that job 2 is to be processed first, the objective function can be minimized by setting $F_2 = 2$ and $F_1 = 7$. If $S = 1$, implying that job 1 is first, the objective function can be minimized by setting $F_1 = 5$ and $F_2 = 7$. The sum of the finish times is less with job 2 first ($2 + 7 = 9$) than with job 1 first ($5 + 7 = 12$). Therefore, the solution that minimizes the average completion time is to process job 2 then job 1. Average completion time will be $9/2 = 4\frac{1}{2}$ hours.

Sequencing problems are not always so simple to solve. As we increase the number of jobs and the number of work centers through which those jobs are to be processed, the problem complexity increases substantially.

INSTANT REPLAY   Suppose we are to find the sequence of three jobs that minimizes the average completion time. Job 1 takes 3 hours, job 2 takes 5 hours, and job 3 takes 4 hours. Formulate this problem as a zero-one integer programming problem.

CHECK   The formulation requires three zero-one sequence variables. We let $R = 1$ if job 1 precedes job 2, and $R = 0$ otherwise. We let $S = 1$ if job 2 precedes job 3 and $S = 0$ otherwise. We let $T = 1$ if job 1 precedes job 3 and $T = 0$ otherwise. This leads to:

$$\text{Minimize:} \quad F_1 + F_2 + F_3$$
$$\text{Subject to:} \quad F_1 \geq 3 + F_2(1 - R)$$
$$F_1 \geq 3 + F_3(1 - T)$$
$$F_2 \geq 5 + F_1(R)$$
$$F_2 \geq 5 + F_3(1 - S)$$
$$F_3 \geq 4 + F_1(T)$$
$$F_3 \geq 4 + F_2(S)$$
$$R, S, T = 0 \text{ or } 1$$

Now that we have seen how to formulate integer programming problems, let us turn our attention to solving them. We will first examine solution procedures for positive integer problems. Then we will discuss methods for solving zero-one problems.

Solving Positive Integer Problems

A number of procedures exist for solving linear programming problems with positive integer variables. An intuitive approach is to ignore the integer restrictions, solve the problem as if it were a standard linear programming problem, and round off or ignore any fractional values. This approach is not always very effective, as we shall see. Other procedures, such as the *cutting-plane method*[1] and *branch and bound*,[2] add additional constraints to the problem, as needed to eliminate fractional solutions. In this way, fractional (noninteger) solutions are made infeasible. Eventually, the set of feasible solutions is narrowed until an integer solution can be found by the simplex method.

In this section we will examine two of these approaches: the rounding method and the branch-and-bound method. To provide a comparison we will use a common example problem of the cargo loading type discussed earlier.

---

[1]R. E. Gomory, "An Algorithm for Integer Solutions to Linear Programs," pp. 269–302 in *Recent Advances in Mathematical Programming*, Robert L. Graves and Philip Wolfe (eds.), McGraw-Hill, New York, 1963.

[2]A. Land and A. Doig, "An Automatic Method for Solving Discrete Programming Problems," *Econometrica*, vol. 28 (1960), pp. 497–520.

Consider the cargo loading problem faced by the Southern Express Company. The company has built a thriving business by promising overnight delivery for air freight. The rapid growth in business has led to occasional problems where the volume of freight to be shipped has exceeded capacity on certain runs. This has led to late deliveries which has cost the company lost revenue (the shipping cost is refunded to the customer if overnight service is not provided) and potential damage to their reputation for reliability. Although capacity can be increased in the long run, it is the short-run scheduling problem that concerns them now.

Typical of the problem is the situation faced at Atlanta recently. Only one aircraft was available for shipments to Washington, and the cargo accepted for shipment far exceeded the capacity of the single aircraft. Two types of cargo, referred to here as A and B, were available. Enough units of either type were available to fill the aircraft independently of the other. Two capacity restrictions were in effect, one related to cubic volume of cargo and the other related to weight. Each unit of cargo type A contributed $560 in revenue, had a size of 10 cubic yards, and weighed 600 pounds. Each unit of cargo type B contributed revenue of $540, used up 12 cubic yards, and weighed 500 pounds. The aircraft had room for 30 cubic yards and 1,500 pounds.

The integer programming formulation for this problem, if A and B represent the number of units of cargo types A and B carried, is

$$\text{Maximize:} \quad 560A + 540B$$
$$\text{Subject to:} \quad 10A + 12B \le 30$$
$$6A + 5B \le 15$$
$$A \text{ and } B = 0, 1, 2, \ldots$$

Forgetting for the moment the integer restrictions on A and B, we can easily find the optimal *noninteger* solution to the problem graphically, as shown in Figure 11-1. This calls for $1\frac{4}{11}$ units of both A and B to be loaded and will provide $1,500 in revenue. Obviously this solution is not practical because the cargo units cannot be divided into fractional parts for loading. Next let us consider how we can resolve this situation.

Rounding

One obvious way of converting a noninteger solution to an integer solution would be to simply round the noninteger values for the decision variables to their closest integer values, while maintaining feasibility. Note that the optimal noninteger solution can be visualized as falling within a box (shown by dashed lines in Figure 11-1) defined by the closest integer values for the decision variables. Since the optimal values for A and B were both $1\frac{4}{11}$, we could round either up or down, finding four possible rounded combinations ($A = 1$ and $B = 1$; $A = 2$ and $B = 1$; $A = 1$ and $B = 2$; $A = 2$ and $B = 2$). Each of these combinations corresponds to a corner of the dashed-line box in Figure 11-1.

However, only one of these four rounded combinations is feasible or satisfies both of the cargo capacity constraints. This point corresponds to loading one unit of each cargo type and yields total revenue of $1,100. This best rounded solution is *not* the optimal integer solution, however. Consider the

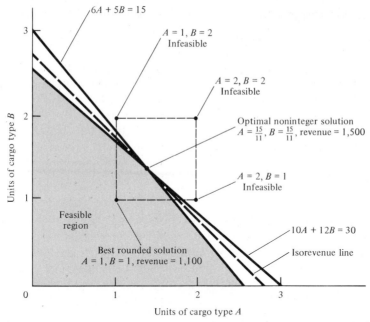

FIGURE 11-1 Optimal noninteger solution to Southern Express problem rounded to yield integer solutions.

feasible integer solution $A = 2$ and $B = 0$. This solution has a revenue of $1,120$, which is 20 higher than the best rounded solution. Thus, we see that rounding noninteger values will not always lead to the optimal integer solution.

For larger problems than dealt with here, the process of rounding becomes much more complex. With two variables we had four possible rounded combinations. In general, with n integer variables to be rounded there are 2^n possible combinations, which leads to a large number of alternatives. For example, with 20 integer variables to be rounded there are $2^{20} = 1,048,576$ rounding alternatives. Checking each of these for feasibility and then identifying the feasible rounded solution with the best objective function value can therefore be quite time-consuming, even with a computer. As shown above, this set of rounding alternatives does not necessarily include the optimum integer solution.

Because of these difficulties, a great deal of research has gone into developing methods that can be used to find the optimal integer solution in a more systematic manner. Although some success has been achieved, all of the procedures developed suffer from excessive computation time requirements for large problems.

INSTANT REPLAY Suppose we have the following integer programming problem:

$$\text{Minimize:} \quad 100W + 70X$$
$$\text{Subject to:} \quad 5W + 4X \geq 20$$
$$6W + 3X \geq 18$$
$$W \text{ and } X = 0, 1, 2, 3, \ldots$$

What is the optimal noninteger solution? What is the best rounded solution? Can you spot any other integer solutions with a better objective function value than that for the best rounded solution?

CHECK The optimal noninteger solution is $W = \frac{4}{3}$ and $X = \frac{10}{3}$. The objective function value for that solution is 1,100/3. Three of the rounded solutions are feasible. These are $W = 2, X = 3$, and objective function $= 410$; $W = 1, X = 4$, and objective function $= 380$; and $W = 2, X = 4$, and objective function $= 480$. The best of these is $W = 1$ and $X = 4$. In this case no better integer solution can be found.

Branch-and-Bound Method

Another approach used for solving integer programming problems, and one that has had wide application, is the *branch-and-bound method*. The branch-and-bound approach successively adds constraints that chop away noninteger solutions until the optimal integer solution is obtained. However, as we shall show, we must use a controlled search to ensure that the optimal solution is not missed.

Creating Complementary Subproblems with Upper- and Lower-Bound Constraints We begin the branch-and-bound method by solving the original problem without considering the integer restrictions. If the solution yields noninteger values for one or more of the integer variables, the original problem is replaced by two *complementary subproblems*. Each complementary subproblem is identical to the original problem except for the addition of one constraint forming either an *upper bound* or a *lower bound* on the value of one currently fractional but integer restricted variable. The subproblems are complementary in that one contains an upper bound on the integer variable and the other a lower bound. These bounds are chosen such that the optimal fractional value for the bounded variable is infeasible for both complementary problems.

For example, note that the optimal noninteger solution to the Southern Express Company problem (Table 11-1) required both decision variables, A and B, to take on values of $\frac{15}{11}$, or $1\frac{4}{11}$. We need to select one of these two variables as

TABLE 11-1
Optimal Noninteger Simplex Tableau for Southern Express Problem

Objective coefficients for basic varibles	Basic variables	Entering gain	560	540	0	0
		Values	A	B	S_1	S_2
540	B	$\frac{15}{11}$	0	1	$\frac{3}{11}$	$-\frac{5}{11}$
560	A	$\frac{15}{11}$	1	0	$-\frac{5}{22}$	$\frac{6}{11}$
	Objective function	Entering costs	560	540	20	60
1,500		Net change	0	0	-20	-60

the basis for forming the complementary subproblems. Although no general rule exists for selecting from among two or more fractional variables, we can select variable A because it has the higher objective function coefficient (560 vs. 540 for variable B).

Two complementary subproblems can be created from the original problem by adding an upper-bound constraint for variable A to form one subproblem and a lower-bound constraint to form the other subproblem. The bounds are formed by separating the current value for the selected variable A into an integer portion b and a fractional portion f. In our case, variable A has a value of $\frac{15}{11}$, or $1\frac{4}{11}$. Thus $b = 1$ and $f = \frac{4}{11}$. One subproblem is formed by adding an upper-bound constraint of the form

$$\text{Selected variable} \leq b$$

and the other is formed by adding a lower-bound constraint of the form

$$\text{Selected variable} \geq b + 1$$

Thus, for variable A we would add the constraint $A \leq 1$ to one subproblem (subproblem $P1$) and the constraint $A \geq 1 + 1 = 2$ to the other subproblem ($P2$). The upper-bound constraint added to subproblem $P1$ limits variable A to values that do not exceed 1. The lower-bound constraint added to $P2$ limits A to values no smaller than 2.

Interpreting the Results of Adding Upper- and Lower-Bound Constraints It should be clear that one or the other of these two complementary subproblems contains every feasible *integer* solution that the original problem contained. The only feasible solutions not included are those for which variable A takes on fractional values between 1 and 2, the lower and upper bounds just added for variable A. This can be seen pictorially by examining Figure 11-2. It shows the partitioning of the feasible region that results from replacing the original problem with the two complementary subproblems. The original feasible region is partitioned into three separate and distinct portions. The portion on the left (subproblem $P1$) corresponds to the feasible region that remains after adding the constraint $A \leq 1$. The portion on the far right (subproblem $P2$) contains the feasible solutions that remain after adding the restriction that $A \geq 2$. The portion in the middle represents those solutions not represented by either of the two subproblems.

Inspection of these regions should convince you of two things. First, none of the solutions eliminated represented one in which *both* decision variables (A and B) were integer-valued. In other words, any all-integer solution contained in the original problem is represented in one or the other of the two complementary subproblems. Second, the original, optimal, noninteger solution ($A = B = 1\frac{4}{11}$) is not feasible with respect to either of the subproblems created. Therefore, although the optimal solution to either of the subproblems will be worse than that for the original problem, the optimal integer solution that we seek will be found in the feasible region of one of these subproblems.

The operation of replacing the original problem with two complementary subproblems is referred to as *partitioning*, or *branching*. The use of the term "branching" is derived from the treelike relationship between the original problem and its complementary replacement problems, as shown in Figure 11-3. Note that the three problems are identical except for the lower- and upper-bound constraints in subproblems $P1$ and $P2$, respectively.

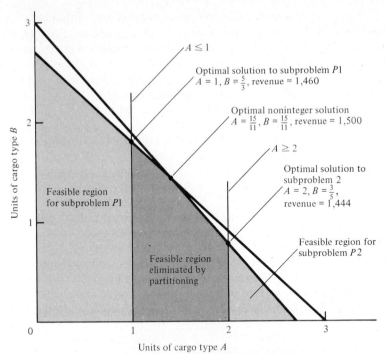

FIGURE 11-2 Partitioning of feasible region by adding additional constraints on variable A to create two complementary Southern Express subproblems.

Interpreting Optimal Subproblem Solutions Next we need to solve the two newly created subproblems. Their optimal solutions are shown in Figure 11-3 and can easily be identified graphically (see Figure 11-2). Observe that the optimal revenue for the original problem is higher than that obtained for either of the subproblems. It is not difficult to see why this occurred. Each subproblem has one more constraint than the original problem. In both cases the constraint was selected so that the optimal solution to the original problem is no longer feasible for either subproblem. Clearly the optimal solution to either subproblem cannot be as good as that for the original problem.

It should also be apparent that the revenue obtained from the optimal integer solution to this problem cannot be as good as the revenue obtained from the solution to the original problem: the optimal noninteger solution contains noninteger values for both of the decision variables. In other words, the optimal revenue for the original problem is an *upper bound on the value of the revenue for the optimal integer solution.* This upper bound is an important tool in knowing when we have found the optimal integer solution, as will soon be demonstrated.

So far we have succeeded in replacing the original problem with separate and distinct but complementary subproblems. If a unique optimal integer solution exists to the problem,[1] only one of these two subproblems will contain that solution because their respective feasible regions are mutually exclusive.

---

[1] If multiple optimal solutions exist, it is possible that both subproblems contain one or more of these optimal solutions. Nonetheless, this will not affect the procedure described.

Consider for a moment the solution to subproblem $P1$. Observe that decision variable A has an integer solution value ($A = 1$), but that variable B does not ($B = \frac{5}{3}$). Just as we were able to replace the original problem with two subproblems, we can also branch on subproblem $P1$, creating two new complementary subproblems ($P3$ and $P4$) to replace it. The optimal value in subproblem $P1$ for variable B was $\frac{5}{3}$, which suggests that subproblem $P3$ can include a constraint requiring B to be less than or equal to 1 ($B \leq 1$), and subproblem $P4$ can restrict B to values greater than or equal to 2 ($B \geq 2$).

Replacing subproblem $P1$ with its complementary subproblems $P3$ and $P4$ subdivides the feasible region associated with subproblem $P1$ into three parts: one corresponding to subproblem $P3$, another corresponding to subproblem $P4$, and a third segment (which includes the optimal solution to subproblem $P1$) representing fractional values for variable B in the range from 1 to 2.

The optimal solution to subproblem $P1$ has been excluded from either subproblem $P3$ or $P4$ by the addition of the upper- and lower-bound constraints on variable B. Thus, we know that neither of these new subproblems can have a solution as good as that for subproblem $P1$. The optimal revenue for subproblem $P1$, therefore, serves as an *upper bound* on the revenue for subproblems $P3$ and $P4$. Furthermore, any further subdividing of these new subproblems, through additional branching operations, in an effort to yield integer solutions, can never lead to an integer solution better than (or as good as) the optimal (noninteger) solution found for subproblem $P1$.

FIGURE 11-3 Branching relationship of complementary subproblems to original problem.

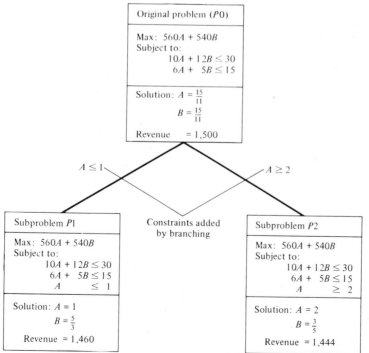

Using the Upper Bound to Identify Optimal Solutions This upper bound conclusion is fundamental to the effectiveness of branch-and-bound methods. The upper bound can be used to eliminate unnecessary branching. To demonstrate this, suppose that the optimal solution to subproblem $P3$ contained integer values for variables A and B and that the revenue was $1,450. Note that because that solution was an *integer solution,* no further branching from subproblem $P3$ would be necessary. Any additional subproblems would only contain poorer solutions. Does this mean that the solution found is optimal? The answer can only be *maybe,* until subproblems $P2$ and $P4$ have been considered.

Note that subproblem $P2$ had an optimal solution of $1,444. Since this is smaller than that found for the integer solution to subproblem $P3$ ($1,450), we know that the feasible region associated with subproblem $P2$ cannot possibly contain a solution better than that found with subproblem $P3$. Therefore, no further branching is necessary from subproblem $P2$.

This leaves subproblem $P4$. If its optimal solution was also smaller than that for subproblem $P3$, we could eliminate subproblem $P4$ as well. Since no other subproblems would then remain to be considered, the integer solution found for subproblem $P3$ would be optimal and our search could be terminated. On the other hand, if subproblem $P4$ had a higher optimal revenue, say $1,455, than that for subproblem $P3$, we have no guarantee that one of the integer solutions contained in the feasible region for subproblem $P4$ is not better than the one found at subproblem $P3$. Thus, we would have to branch from subproblem $P4$ and, possibly, its successors until either a better integer solution is found or the optimal revenue from any remaining subproblems is no better than the value of the solution for subproblem $P3$.

Selecting a Subproblem for Branching Since at any one stage in the solution process more than one subproblem can be available for branching, it is useful to have a rule for selecting which problem to branch on next. Two approaches are commonly used. One is to select the problem with the best bound (e.g., highest revenue in the Southern Express problem). Another method is to select the last subproblem created. Both approaches have their advantages. The *best bound rule* usually will find the optimal solution in less time (fewer problems solved), but the *newest problem rule* will generate fewer active subproblems, requiring less computer storage. Both approaches are otherwise identical.

Eliminating Subproblems Branching on a subproblem is terminated when any one of three conditions exists: (1) the subproblem is infeasible, (2) the subproblem has an integer solution, or (3) the subproblem has a noninteger solution that is not as good as a known integer solution. Infeasibility can result when lower- and upper-bound constraints are added as the result of several branching steps that force the decision variables to take on values that exceed one or more of the real problem constraints. For example, if one branching operation added the constraint $A \geq 2$ and a later step added the constraint $B \geq 2$, both the volume constraint ($10A + 12B \leq 30$) and the weight constraint ($6A + 5B \leq 15$) would be violated. Thus, the solution to this subproblem would be infeasible. No further branches are necessary from this subproblem because any new subproblems created will also be infeasible.

If the subproblem results in an integer solution, branching can also be terminated. Further branching can only lead to a poorer solution (by adding more constraints). If the value of a noninteger solution to a subproblem is not as

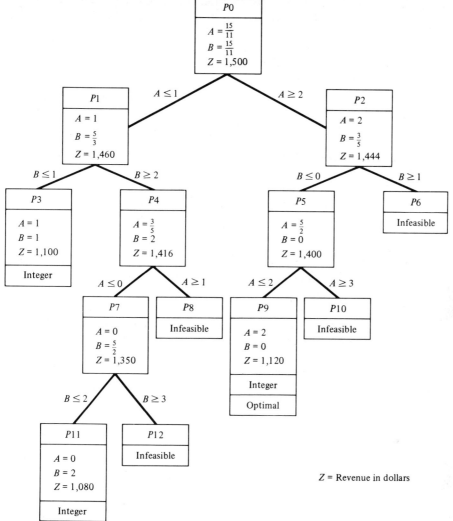

FIGURE 11-4 Branching tree for branch-and-bound solution to Southern Express problem.

good as some known integer solution, additional branching is also not necessary. This is because any integer solution that might be found will not be as good as one already known, and therefore cannot be optimal.

Using Branch and Bound to Solve the Problem   Figure 11-4 shows the complete branching tree for the Southern Express problem based on the use of the best bound subproblem selection rule. The subproblem numbers refer to the order in which the subproblems were created. If we had used the newest problem selection rule, the same subproblems would have been generated, but in a slightly different order.

Refer to Figure 11-4 as we briefly review the steps followed in solving the problem. As described earlier, subproblems $P1$ and $P2$ were created to replace the original problem. Both $P1$ and $P2$ yielded feasible but noninteger solutions. At that point both subproblems are candidates for further branching.

Subproblem $P1$ was selected first, according to the best bound selection rule, and replaced by subproblems $P3$ and $P4$. Subproblem $P3$ yielded an integer solution, with $A = 1, B = 1$, and revenue of $1,100. This solution was then recorded as the best all-integer solution found up to this point. Subproblem $P4$ had a higher revenue ($1,416) but contained one noninteger variable ($A = \frac{2}{3}$).

The active subproblems (those that are potential candidates for further branching) at this point were $P4$ and $P2$. Since $P2$ had a higher revenue, it was next selected for branching, leading to subproblems $P5$ and $P6$. Subproblem $P6$ did not permit a feasible solution and was not added to the list of active subproblems. The solution to $P5$ had revenue of $1,400 and contained one noninteger value.

Subproblems $P4$ and $P5$ remained at this point as candidates for branching. Since $P4$ had a higher revenue value it was next branched on, and $P7$ and $P8$ were created. $P8$ was infeasible, but $P7$ could be added to the list of active subproblems because it contained a fractional solution value.

Since $P5$ had a higher revenue value than $P7$ it was next selected for branching, leading to subproblems $P9$ and $P10$. The solution to $P10$ was not feasible. $P9$, on the other hand, yielded an all-integer solution with a revenue value of $1,120 which is $20 better than our previous best all-integer solution, $P3$. Thus $P9$ is now recorded as the best solution found to date.

The only remaining active subproblem is $P7$. Since its revenue value of $1,350 is higher than that for the best all-integer solution ($P9$), we cannot eliminate $P7$ but must branch on that subproblem next. This yields $P11$ and $P12$. Subproblem $P12$ was infeasible and could be eliminated. $P11$ yielded an all-integer solution ($A = 0, B = 2$) but its revenue value of $1,080 was less than that for the previously best all-integer solution, so $P11$ could also be eliminated.

At this point no more active subproblems remain. Note in Figure 11-4 that each subproblem not branched on corresponds to either an infeasible solution or an all-integer solution. Thus, all potentially optimal solutions have been examined. The optimal all-integer solution has been found to be that corresponding to subproblem $P9$, where $A = 2, B = 0$, and revenue = $1,120.

Summary of Branch-and-Bound Procedure

You may find it helpful to use a formal list of the steps required to apply the branch-and-bound method to integer programming problems. The following list of steps should serve that purpose as well as review what we have covered:

1. Solve the noninteger version of the original problem using normal linear programming procedures. If the solution results in integer values for all integer-constrained variables, stop. Otherwise go to step 2.

2. Select an integer-constrained variable which has a noninteger value. A suggestion: choose the variable with the largest (smallest) objective function coefficient for maximization (minimization) problems.

3. Form two subproblems to replace the current problem by adding a lower-bound constraint to one and an upper-bound constraint to the other for the variable selected in step 2. If b is the integer portion of the current value of that selected variable, the variable will be constrained to be less than or equal to b in one subproblem and greater than or equal to $b + 1$ in the other subproblem.

Determine the optimal solution to both of the newly created subproblems using normal linear programming methods. If the solution to either contains integer values for all integer variables, compare the value of this solution to that for the best known integer solution (if any exists), recording whichever is best.

5. Update the list of active subproblems. Delete any subproblems for which no feasible solution exists. Delete the problem just branched on. Delete any subproblems with noninteger solutions if their optimal solution is no better than the best known integer solution found in step 4 (if any exists).

6. Select one of the subproblems on the active list using one of the problem selection rules discussed earlier (subproblem with the best bound or the most newly created subproblem). If no subproblems remain on the list, the best integer solution found to date is the optimal solution. If no integer solution has been found and no subproblems remain, no feasible integer solution exists for the problem. If a subproblem has been selected for branching, return to step 2.

Solving Zero-One Problems

Many practical decision problems include decision variables representing yes-no choices, referred to earlier as zero-one variables. We found zero-one variables present in the formulation of several types of integer programming problems, including capital budgeting, warehouse location, job sequencing, and covering problems.

Although zero-one variables are only a special category of integer variables, they frequently permit a specialized procedure to be used to find the optimal solution. A specialized procedure is an approach that can be used to solve one type of zero-one problem but not another. The assignment problem, dealt with in Chapter 10, is an example of such a zero-one problem with a specialized solution procedure. In this section we will examine three more-general approaches for solving zero-one problems: brute force enumeration, simplex linear programming, and branch and bound. For illustration purposes, we will use a common example problem, as described below.

Formulating the Problem

The operations manager at the Swift Lawnmower Company must decide how to allocate his capital improvements budget for the coming year. He had initially proposed five projects to top management, which would have required a total expenditure of $160,000. Project A requires an investment of $30,000 and has expected benefits of $90,000. Project B requires a $40,000 investment with expected benefits of $100,000. Project C will cost $35,000 and is expected to return $70,000 in benefits. Project D will cost $25,000 and return $40,000.

Project E requires an investment of $30,000 and is expected to return $45,000. Because of financial constraints, top management has authorized a capital expenditure budget of only $100,000 for the operations department, but the operations manager can decide how that money is to be spent.

As a first step in deciding which of the five projects to fund, the operations manager has formulated the problem as an integer programming problem. His objective is to maximize the total benefits received from the projects funded. If zero-one variables A, B, C, D, and E represent funding decisions for the five projects, the objective function can be written as

Maximize: $90,000A + $100,000B + $70,000C + $40,000D + $45,000E$

The budget constraint requires that the total amount spent on the projects funded not exceed $100,000, or

$30,000A + $40,000B + $35,000C + $25,000D + $30,000E \leq $100,000

Finally, a set of zero-one constraints are needed: A, B, C, D, E = 0 or 1.

Brute Force Enumeration

One method of solving a zero-one problem is to enumerate all feasible solutions, determine the total benefits achieved by each, and select the best combination. In other words, we need to identify and evaluate all possible funding alternatives. We could decide to fund none of the projects, project A only, projects C and E only, and so on. *Brute force enumeration* will find the optimal solution because every single alternative is considered. For a problem with n zero-one variables, there are 2^n potentially optimal solutions. For the Swift Lawnmower problem there are five zero-one variables and thus $2^5 = 32$ potentially optimal funding options.

Each of the 32 options is shown in Table 11-2, together with the total

TABLE 11-2
Enumeration of all Funding Options for Swift Lawnmower Problem

Funding option	Total benefits	Funding option	Total benefits
None	0	ABC	Infeasible
A	90,000	ABD	230,000
B	100,000	ABE	235,000*
C	70,000	ACD	200,000
D	40,000	ACE	205,000
E	45,000	ADE	175,000
AB	190,000	BCD	210,000
AC	160,000	BCE	Infeasible
AD	130,000	BDE	185,000
AE	135,000	CDE	155,000
BC	170,000	ABCD	Infeasible
BD	140,000	ABCE	Infeasible
BE	145,000	ABDE	Infeasible
CD	110,000	ACDE	Infeasible
CE	115,000	BCDE	Infeasible
DE	85,000	ABCDE	Infeasible

*Optimal.

TABLE 11-3
Calculation of Benefit/Cost Ratios for Swift Lawnmower Projects

Project	Benefits, thousands of dollars	Costs, thousands of dollars	Benefit/cost ratio
A	90	30	3.0
B	100	40	2.5
C	70	35	2.0
D	40	25	1.6
E	45	30	1.5

benefits achieved for those options that are feasible. Observe that some options, such as *BCE*, are infeasible. This is because the total funding required to support these options exceeds the $100,000 available. For example, option *BCE* would require $40,000 + $35,000 + $30,000 = $105,000 funds to be invested and is therefore infeasible.

As can be seen from Table 11-2, the best combination is to fund projects *A*, *B*, and *E*, for a total return of $235,000. The brute force method was not difficult to apply here. However, as the number of zero-one variables increases, the computational effort required becomes impractical. For instance, with 20 zero-one variables, 1,048,576 potential optimal solutions to the problem would have to be enumerated and evaluated.

Linear Programming Approach

If the zero-one constraints are ignored, the Swift Lawnmower problem becomes a simple linear programming problem. Because of the special structure of the Swift Lawnmower problem, a solution can be easily obtained without recourse to the simplex method. Note that the right-hand column of Table 11-3 contains a ratio of benefits to cost for each project. A benefit/cost ratio for project A was found by dividing the total benefits by the total cost or

$$\text{Benefit/cost ratio for } A = \frac{90}{30} = 3$$

When the zero-one constraints are ignored, each dollar invested in project *A* will return $3 in benefits. A dollar invested in any of the other projects will return less than $3, as shown in the benefit/cost ratio column of Table 11-3. Therefore, as long as dollars are available we will prefer to put them in project *A*. The most we can invest in project *A* is $30,000, which leaves $100,000 − $30,000 = $70,000 to be invested in the remaining four projects.

Using similar analysis, we would invest $40,000 in project *B*. Its benefit/cost ratio is higher than the other three remaining projects. This would leave $70,000 − 40,000 = $30,000 to invest in *C*, *D*, or *E*. Since project *C* has a higher benefit/cost ratio than *D* or *E*, we would invest the remaining $30,000 in this project. Note that the $30,000 represents $30/35 = \frac{6}{7}$ of the total that could have been invested in *C* if we were not constrained by the $100,000 capital investment budget.

The total benefits received from this investment plan would be $250,000 as shown below (benefits received equal amount invested times benefit/cost ratio):

Project funded	Amount invested	Benefit/cost ratio	Benefits received
A	30,000	3.0	90,000
B	40,000	2.5	100,000
C	30,000	2.0	60,000

From a zero-one standpoint this solution (funding projects A, B, and C) is not feasible (see Table 11-2) since only $\frac{6}{7}$ of project C was funded (equivalent to the zero-one variable for project C taking on a value of $\frac{6}{7}$ rather than 0 or 1). To fund all three projects (A, B, and C) in full would require an investment of \$105,000 which is more than the available budget of \$100,000. Thus, the linear programming solution was not feasible.

Although linear programming (with zero-one constraints relaxed) was not of much help here, it can be used in conjunction with branch and bound to solve the zero-one variable for project C taking on a value of $\frac{6}{7}$ rather than 0 or 1). To fund all three projects (A, B, and C) in full would require an investment of the linear programming solution. *First,* observe that, as with positive integer programming problems, the linear programming solution represents an upper bound for a maximization problem (or a *lower bound* on a minimization problem) on the value of the best zero-one solution.

Second, the special nature of this linear programming problem (a single constraint if we ignore the zero-one constraints) permitted an easy, nonsimplex solution. We simply invested as much as possible in each project, selecting the projects in *benefit/cost-ratio order,* starting with the highest ratio, proceeding to the next highest, and so on.

Branch-and-Bound Method

To use the branch-and-bound method to solve this zero-one problem, we proceed essentially as we did with positive integer programming problems. First, the problem is solved without the zero-one constraints (as we did above). Then, this problem is replaced by two subproblems, which divide or partition the set of feasible solutions in half. One of the subproblems will constrain a zero-one variable to be 1 and the other subproblem will constrain that variable to be 0. In other words, one of the subproblems will specify that a project is to be funded and the other subproblem will designate that the specified project is not to be funded.

Figure 11-5 illustrates the nature of this partitioning (branching) operation. It assumes that project A was selected for constraining to 1 in subproblem $P1$ and 0 in subproblem $P2$. Observe that the solution to subproblem $P2$ resulted in zero-one values for all variables: $A = E = 0$ and $B = C = D = 1$. No further branching or partitioning from this subproblem is required. The optimal linear programming solution for this subproblem is also a feasible solution to the zero-one problem. The objective function value for this solution, \$210,000, also serves as a threshold, or lower bound, for any further solutions considered.

Since subproblem $P1$ has a higher objective function value than that for the best known all zero-one solution (subproblem $P2$) but is not itself an all zero-one solution, we next replace subproblem $P1$ with two additional subproblems. These subproblems will be formed by constraining the value of one

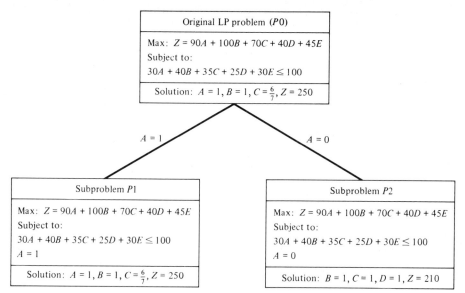

FIGURE 11-5 Initial partitioning operation for Swift Lawnmower problem.

of the as yet unconstrained variables B, C, D, or E. Although any of these variables could be selected, we will follow the convention of selecting them in alphabetical order, thus selecting variable B next.

Figure 11-6 shows the complete branch-and-bound tree for this problem. As shown, subproblem $P3$ constrains variable B to a value of 1 and $P4$ constrains B to a value of 0. The solution to $P3$ is identical to that for $P1$. The solution to $P4$ calls for a fractional value of $\frac{1}{3}$ for variable E and has a lower objective function value than that for $P3$. Two subproblems, $P3$ and $P4$, are thus available for further partitioning. Which should be chosen first? Since $P3$ has a higher objective function value than $P4$, it is chosen first (best bound selection rule).

Subproblem $P5$ and $P6$ constrain variable C to 1 and 0, respectively. $P5$ is infeasible since funding of projects A, B, and C in full requires more than the $100,000 budget, as we saw earlier. $P6$ results in a fractional solution ($E = \frac{1}{6}$) with an objective function value of $237,500. Again two subproblems, $P4$ and $P6$, are available for further branching. Since subproblem $P6$ has the higher objective function value, it is next chosen.

Variable D is constrained to 1 to form $P7$ and to 0 to form $P8$. The solution for $P7$ is identical to that for $P6$. Subproblem $P8$, however, results in no fractional values and thus is a feasible solution to the zero-one problem. Observe that $P8$'s objective function value is higher than that for the only other feasible solution found, $P2$. Furthermore, consider again subproblem $P4$. This subproblem has not yet been branched from, nor will it ever be. The reason is that the zero-one feasible solution to subproblem $P8$ has a *higher objective function value* than that for $P4$. Since further branching from $P4$ can only lower the objective function value (from the current $215,000) it will not be possible to find a zero-one solution, by branching on $P4$, that is as good as or better than that represented by $P8$. Therefore, we mark subproblem $P4$, as shown in Figure 11-6, as *pruned,* meaning that no further branches from $P4$ need to be taken.

This leaves subproblem $P7$ as the only remaining unpruned, infeasible

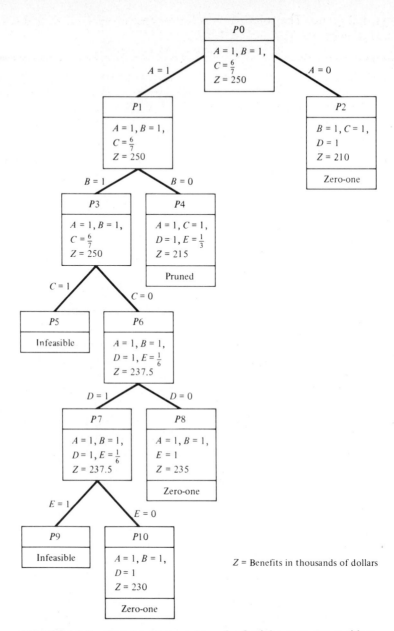

FIGURE 11-6 Branch-and-bound tree for Swift Lawnmower problem.

solution. Therefore we branch on $P7$, forming subproblems $P9$ and $P10$ by alternately constraining variable E to 1 and 0. The solution to $P9$ is infeasible because the investment budget constraint is violated by funding projects A, B, D, and E. The solution to $P10$ is an all zero-one solution. However, the objective function value is less than that for the best previous integer solution, $P8$.

At this point no more subproblems remain for branching. Each has either been branched from ($P1$, $P3$, $P6$, and $P7$), been pruned ($P4$), been found to be infeasible ($P5$ and $P9$), or resulted in a feasible zero-one solution ($P2$, $P8$, and $P10$). Thus, the branch-and-bound tree has been completed and the optimal solution, *P8*, found. The solution calls for funding projects *A, B,* and *E* and is expected to generate $235,000 in benefits.

INSTANT REPLAY In the branch-and-bound solution to the Swift Lawn-mower problem we always selected the variables to constrain for the subproblems in alphabetical order. Suppose instead the variable with the largest fractional value is always selected for the upper- and lower-bound constraints. What branch-and-bound tree would result?

CHECK The following branch-and-bound tree would result for this modified selection rule:

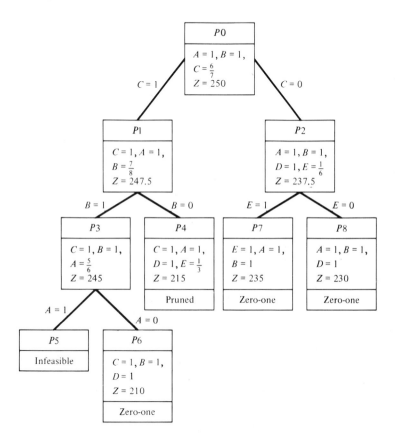

The optimal solution, as before, calls for funding projects *A, B,* and *E,* with total benefits of $235,000.

A comparison of the branch-and-bound tree for the instant replay with that obtained earlier indicates that the number of subproblems that need to be examined is sensitive to the branching rules used. Earlier we selected variables for constraining in alphabetical order. In the instant replay we selected the variable with the largest fractional value. Other variable-selection rules are possible, such as selecting the variable with the largest objective function coefficient, the smallest objective function coefficient, the smallest benefit/cost   **417** ratio, and so on. In general, the success of a particular selection rule is dependent on the nature of the problem. That is, one rule may work well on one problem and not so well on another. Because large problems (many zero-one variables) lead to large branch-and-bound trees, we may have to experiment with different selection rules.

In practice, the amount of time required to solve large problems may be prohibitive. One advantage of branch and bound is that the procedure can be stopped at any point and the best all zero-one solution found will usually be a good solution. Often this solution will even be optimal, although we cannot guarantee it because the tree has not been completed.

Final Comments

Integer programming problems are an important category of management science problems. This is because they occur so frequently in practice. Unfortunately they are difficult to solve efficiently. In this chapter we have seen how such problems arise in practice, how they can be formulated, and how they might be solved.

We divided our attention between two classes of integer problems: those with zero-one variables and those in which the decision variables are limited to positive integer values. Such a division was convenient both from a formulation and from a solution viewpoint.

An important solution approach for both types of problem is branch and bound. It attempts to eliminate noninteger solutions by adding additional constraints to the problem. Unlike previous solution methods presented (e.g., simplex, transportation method, and so on) the speed with which the branch-and-bound method can find the optimal solution is sensitive to certain decision rules employed. The choice of subproblem for branching and the selection of a variable for upper- and lower-bound constraints have an impact on the efficiency of this method. Unfortunately, the best decision rules are often dependent on the problem itself. Our intention here was to describe the types of approaches that have been used for integer problems, as well as some of the difficulties that can be encountered. The widespread applicability of integer problems ensures that continued research will be devoted to finding better solution methods.

Key Words

Problems

11-1. The manager of research and development for the Harrington Textile Company is currently reviewing a set of research and development project proposals prepared by his staff. As his contribution to the company's budgeting and planning process, by the end of the week he must recommend to his boss those projects which the company should fund.

For each of the five proposals he is reviewing, his staff has provided an estimate of the potential benefits to the company of pursuing the project as well as an estimate of the cost of the project in terms of dollar expenditures and worker requirements over the 3-year planning horizon. These are shown below.

Project	Dollar cost in year, thousands of dollars			Worker requirements in year			Net benefits to firm
	1	*2*	*3*	*1*	*2*	*3*	
1	200	300	300	1	2	2	5.0
2	200	200	0	2	2	0	2.8
3	300	300	0	2	2	0	4.0
4	0	300	300	0	1	2	6.0
5	100	500	400	1	3	3	5.4

The R&D manager's boss has directed that the set of recommended projects should maximize the expected net benefits to the firm but must not require dollar expenditures exceeding $700,000 the first year, $800,000 the second year, nor $900,000 the third year. In addition, the manager knows that he has only four people available to assign to the projects in the first year, although he expects to be able to hire an additional two people beginning with the second year and a third additional person beginning in year 3.

Formulate the R&D manager's problem as an integer programming problem.

11-2. George Steingold, the owner of the New York Bombers baseball team, is concerned about the lack of hitting on his ball club. He hopes to improve the team by signing several free agents with demonstrated hitting ability. At present he is negotiating with four players of whom he hopes to sign no more than two. The players, their career batting averages, and the estimated financial costs of signing each are shown below.

Player	Career batting average	First-year bonus, thousands of dollars	Average annual salary, thousands of dollars	Deferred compensation payments, millions of dollars
Rod Career	.341	700	500	1.5
Charlie Hustle	.305	300	700	.8
Dave Porker	.335	200	600	1.7
Reggie Action	.295	600	400	.9

George has carefully estimated his available financial resources, given current salary levels, etc., and feels he can spend no more than $1,000,000 on first-year bonuses, no more than $1,100,000 in annual salaries, and no more $3,000,000 in deferred compensation benefits.

Formulate George's hiring problem as an integer programming problem such that he obtains the best hitting players that he can afford.

11-3. The Landspread Corporation is investigating the possibility of operating its own regional warehouse system to supply retailers directly, rather than rely on wholesalers. A preliminary study has been conducted of potential sites and cost data obtained with regard to fixed and variable operating and delivery costs, which are summarized below.

Warehouse	Per-unit variable costs to supply customer							Annual fixed warehouse cost
	1	*2*	*3*	*4*	*5*	*6*	*7*	
A	1.43	1.25	1.17	1.38	1.65	1.95	1.48	3,000
B	1.27	1.17	1.15	1.50	1.63	1.70	1.40	1,500
C	1.62	1.75	1.50	1.22	1.75	1.68	1.92	2,200
D	1.50	1.63	1.28	1.30	1.98	1.48	1.62	2,900
E	1.15	1.72	1.40	1.29	1.80	1.38	1.75	1,750
Annual customer demand, thousands	10	12	25	18	7	32	14	

Each warehouse has sufficient capacity to supply any customers assigned.

Formulate this decision problem as an integer programming problem so that the company can determine the least-cost means of operating its own warehousing distribution system.

11-4. Consider the Harrington Textile Company problem (11-1). Suppose that the problem were simplified by ignoring the manpower requirements completely and adding the cost requirements for the 3 years together. Thus the problem is to maximize the net benefits to the firm given a total dollar expenditure limit, as summarized below.

Project	Dollar cost over the 3 years, thousands of dollars	Net benefits to the firm
1	800	5.0
2	400	2.8
3	600	4.0
4	600	6.0
5	1,000	5.4

Assuming that $2,200,000 is available for funding these projects, use the zero-one branch-and-bound procedure described in the text to find the optimal solution.

11-5. The Raynor Company is developing a system of regional service centers to provide service for its computerized energy management systems. The company has at present 12 such systems either operating or being installed. They estimate that each service center will cost the company about $100,000 annually to operate. Because of sales contract guarantees, these service centers need to be located within 500 miles of each customer served. Five potential service center sites have been tentatively selected and those customers within a 500-mile radius have been identified as shown below ("yes" indicates that a center is within a 500-mile radius).

Customer	Service center site				
	A	B	C	D	E
1	Yes	No	Yes	No	Yes
2	No	Yes	No	Yes	No
3	No	No	Yes	Yes	No
4	Yes	Yes	No	Yes	No
5	Yes	No	No	No	Yes
6	No	Yes	Yes	No	No
7	Yes	Yes	No	No	No
8	No	No	Yes	Yes	Yes
9	No	No	Yes	Yes	Yes
10	Yes	No	No	Yes	Yes

Formulate as an integer linear programming problem the selection of the least-cost set of service centers so that each customer is served by a least one warehouse within a 500-mile radius.

11-6. The service manager for the Rickshaw Airline Company is concerned with the backlog of aircraft engines needing repair that has accumulated in the past week. The repair facility uses a single maintenance crew to disassemble, overhaul, and reassemble each engine. At the moment five engines are available for overhaul and the maintenance crew is ready for its next assignment. Estimated overhaul times are given for each engine below:

Engine	Estimated overhaul time, hours
1	22
2	16
3	35
4	12
5	28

The service manager's performance is judged in part on the average time an engine spends in the shop awaiting or receiving an overhaul. He would like to determine the best order in which to process the engines so as to minimize the average time spent in the shop.

Formulate this problem as an integer linear programming problem.

11-7. The Bandolier Sportswear Company reduces the cost of seasonal downturns in demand for their products by contracting to process work for other garment manufacturers. During the coming week Bandolier expects to have 110 hours of excess capacity in the cutting department and 140 hours of extra capacity in the sewing department. Two companies, Alpha and Brava, have approached Bandolier concerning contracting for Bandolier's extra capacity. Alpha has five jobs it can contract for, each offering Bandolier $1,000. Each such job requires 20 hours of cutting time and 30 hours of sewing time. Brava Company has offered to pay $1,200 for each of six jobs. Each Brava job requires 25 hours of cutting time and 24 hours of sewing time.

Formulate Bandolier's capacity subcontracting problem in the integer linear programming format.

11-8. Solve the Bandolier subcontracting problem (see problem 11-7) graphically.

11-9. Use the branch-and-bound method to solve the Bandolier subcontracting problem (see problem 11-7).

11-10. The Universal Broadcasting Network (UBN) is in the process of preparing its fall schedule of programs for the new season. Although many of the schedule openings are already filled with successful holdover shows from previous seasons, there are eight spots open for new shows. At the moment the programming director for UBN is reviewing a total of 20 new shows that could potentially fill the open time slots in the schedule. These shows could be roughly classified in three distinct categories: eight of the shows are situation comedies, seven are of the detective/police variety, and five are musical variety.

The program director knows that the potential earnings from each category differ because of production cost differentials as well as some differences in commercial rates that can be charged. Typical revenue and budget figures per program are shown below.

Program category	Commercial revenue, thousands of dollars	Production costs, thousands of dollars
Situation comedy	1,000	400
Detective/police	900	550
Musical variety	1,300	900

For budgetary reasons the eight shows selected should not require more than $5,000,000 per week for production costs. In addition, in order to maintain programming balance, it is necessary to limit the number of new situation comedies to no more than the combined number of new shows in the other two categories.

Formulate the new show selection problem in an integer programming format.

11-11. Use the branch-and-bound method to solve the Universal Broadcasting Network problem (see problem 11-10).

12

Dynamic Programming

In this chapter we consider an important class of problems which require a set of interdependent decisions. The method used to solve such problems is referred to as *dynamic programming*.[1] In many cases these decisions are *time-sequential* in that separate, but related, decisions are to be made for a sequential set of time periods. The number of time periods for which decisions are to be made is usually referred to as the *planning horizon*. For example, the production planning decision problem involves determining the least-cost production pattern to satisfy expected demand levels over some specified time horizon. The solution to this problem requires a separate production level decision for each time period included in the planning horizon. These decisions are interdependent in that the best production level decision in one period is dependent on production level decisions for prior periods as well as those for following periods.

In other cases, although the decisions are not really time-sequential, it is convenient, from a solution viewpoint, to treat them as if they *were* made sequentially. For instance, resource allocation problems, such as those we considered as linear programming or integer programming problems, require a simultaneous allocation decision. However, as we shall see, it is often useful to decompose, or separate, these problems into sets of subproblems, which are then solved sequentially, rather than simultaneously.

To illustrate, in a capital budgeting problem the aim is to allocate the scarce resource, capital, to competing projects. We saw previously how these

[1] Richard Bellman is considered the originator of dynamic programming. His work at the RAND Corporation in the 1950s led to a number of significant developments in the field, which resulted in his book *Dynamic Programming*, Princeton University Press, Princeton, N.J., 1957.

problems could be solved by linear or integer programming methods. Another way of solving this problem is to use dynamic programming. This is done by treating the allocation decision for a particular project as a set of subproblems. Each subproblem assumes that a specific portion of the available capital remains to be allocated at that stage. The best decision for each of these subproblems compares the return from capital invested in that project with alternate allocations to other competing projects.

Dynamic Programming Concepts

Dynamic programming is really not a specific procedure that, once learned, can be applied to any sequential, interdependent decision problem by mechanically following a set of steps. Instead, it is more of a conceptual approach, or solution strategy. Although we identify a basic set of steps required to apply dynamic programming, the details of how these steps are accomplished depend on the nature of the problem being solved and may require a certain amount of intuition to develop.

Some of the problems that dynamic programming can be used to solve can also be formulated and solved by alternate methods. We mentioned above that a capital budgeting problem can be formulated as a dynamic programming problem as well as a linear or integer programming problem. You may recall from the previous chapter that integer programming procedures, such as branch and bound, become ineffective when the number of integer variables becomes large. Dynamic programming offers an alternative solution approach that, at least in some cases, may be more effective than integer programming.

Furthermore, dynamic programming offers capabilities for handling certain problem characteristics that other methods cannot deal with. Two of these characteristics are *nonlinear objective function coefficients* and *probabilistic, or stochastic, outcomes.* Linear and integer programming problems assume that the objective function coefficients are linear. That is, if we use a decision variable to represent the number of salespersons to be assigned to a sales territory and one salesperson will generate sales of $1,000 per month, we assume that two salespersons will generate $2,000 in sales, three salespersons will generate $3,000, and so on. In dynamic programming we are not constrained to such constant, or linear, returns. We can easily use dynamic programming to solve problems where the returns are nonlinear. This is an important characteristic because it allows us to consider cases with decreasing or increasing marginal returns. In reality, we would expect that each additional salesperson would not be able to generate the same amount of sales as the last. Such nonlinear situations are readily handled in dynamic programming.

Probabilistic, or stochastic, outcomes are another frequent situation that cannot be easily dealt with in linear or integer programming. In linear programming problems we assume, for example, that the cost of a particular item is known with certainty. In practice, such certain knowledge may not be possible. Instead, the best we might be able to do is express probabilities for different levels of cost. Again dynamic programming can be used to handle such situations.

The bulk of this chapter will consist of three distinctly different decision problems which will be formulated and solved by dynamic programming. These problems are representative of the types of situations in which dynamic programming can be used. Our first problem is an example of what is sometimes called the *shortest-route problem*. This is another type of network problem. The problem involves finding the shortest or least-cost route from one location in a network to another.

Our second example problem illustrates the use of dynamic programming to solve problems with nonlinear objective function coefficients. We will refer to this as a *nonlinear allocation problem*. The last example we will consider includes events that are probabilistic or stochastic. We will use a purchasing problem to illustrate this class of *stochastic time-sequential problems*.

Shortest-Route Problem

In Chapters 9 and 10 we examined a number of what we called network problems. One that was *not* considered there is the problem of finding the shortest, or least-cost, route from one point in the network to another. We chose not to present this problem earlier because it can be effectively solved using dynamic programming.

Although it is easiest to visualize a shortest-route problem in geographical terms—finding the shortest route from one geographical location to another—we should emphasize that many shortest-route problems do not fit this geographical model. Many time-sequential (rather than geographic-sequential) problems can be viewed as shortest-route problems. In this case the locations would refer to specific decision outcomes, while the alternative paths or routes would refer to decision alternatives. The concept of the shortest-route problem and the use of dynamic programming to solve it can best be introduced by means of a simple example.

Formulating the Problem

Consider the problem faced by the planning committee for a traveling exhibit of art treasures from a major European museum. The committee has made arrangements for the display of these items at five, yet to be selected, American museums. The committee has identified museums in 11 cities as potential exhibition sites. Each of these museums has met all of the committee's qualifications, including a minimum guarantee rental fee.

Two criteria have been agreed upon by the committee members in selecting the five museums for display of the exhibit. One is that the cities are to be chosen so that no more than one comes from any specific geographical region, so as to give the exhibit national exposure. The five geographical regions and the cities in each are: San Francisco and Los Angeles in the Far West region; Salt Lake City, Denver, and Phoenix in the Rocky Mountain region; Chicago, Cincinnati, and St. Louis in the Midwest region; Pittsburgh and Atlanta in the Mideast region; and New York in the East Coast region.

The second criterion is that the cost of transporting the exhibit between sites must be minimized. These costs are considered important because of the fragility and irreplaceable value of the exhibit pieces. These transport costs have been estimated and are shown in Figure 12-1 for each potential transport route. It is assumed that the exhibit will begin in one of the Far West cities, move eastward from one region to the next, and finish in the East Coast region at New York. Thus, for example, if the exhibit is shown first in San Francisco,

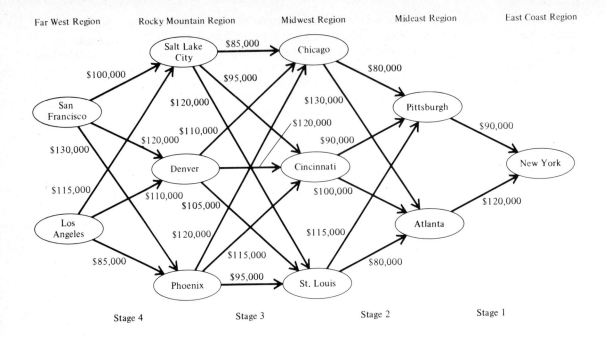

three routes are possible for transporting it to its Rocky Mountain exhibition site. It can be moved from San Francisco to: Salt Lake City at a cost of $100,000, Denver at a cost of $120,000, or Phoenix at a cost of $130,000. Shipment costs for the other routes can be interpreted similarly. Those costs incurred in transporting the exhibit to and from the United States are to be borne by the exhibit owners and are not a factor for the committee to consider.

Solving the Problem

Rather than view this problem as one of selecting cities, we can look on it as one of choosing routes. A solution to the problem is completely specified by a set of four routes, one route for each adjacent pair of regions. For example, if we select the San Francisco to Phoenix, Phoenix to St. Louis, St. Louis to Atlanta, and Atlanta to New York routes, we have, in effect, chosen San Francisco, Phoenix, St. Louis, Atlanta, and New York as the five exhibition sites. Thus, the problem can be seen as attempting to select the least-cost set of routes that will allow the exhibit to be moved from the Far West region to each subsequent eastward region. In this sense it is a shortest-route problem.

Defining the Interdependent Decision Stages The shortest, or in this case least-cost, route from the Far West to the East Coast region consists of four sequential, interrelated decisions, which we call *decision stages*. That is, we need to choose sequentially a route from the Far West to the Rocky Mountain region, from the Rocky Mountain to the Midwest region, from the Midwest to the Mideast region, and from the Mideast to the East Coast region. Each of these route choices is a separate decision stage. However, they are interdependent decisions because any routes chosen must be consistent with the other

426

routes. For example, we cannot select the Los Angeles to Phoenix route to move the exhibit into the Rocky Mountain region and the Salt Lake City to Chicago route to move it out of the Rocky Mountain region. The route into any region and out of any region must involve a common city in that region.

Furthermore, the lowest-cost route from a city in one region to some city in the next region is not necessarily the best route to choose. For example, suppose the exhibit is in Denver. The lowest-cost route from Denver to the Midwest region can be seen in Figure 12-1 to be from Denver to St. Louis. This will cost $105,000, as opposed to $110,000 from Denver to Chicago or $120,000 from Denver to Cincinnati. The Denver to St. Louis route is not the best choice because it ignores the cost of moving the exhibit from St. Louis to the Mideast and then to the East Coast regions. In this case, the best routes from St. Louis are to Atlanta and then to New York. The total cost of moving the exhibit from Denver to New York via St. Louis is $305,000 as shown below:

$105,000	Denver to St. Louis
80,000	St. Louis to Atlanta
120,000	Atlanta to New York
$305,000	

Even though the Denver-to-Chicago route has a higher cost ($110,000) than the Denver-to-St. Louis route ($105,000), it is a better choice because of lower transport costs between subsequent regions. The total cost from Denver to New York via Chicago is $280,000, as shown below:

$110,000	Denver to Chicago
80,000	Chicago to Pittsburgh
90,000	Pittsburgh to New York
$280,000	

This is $25,000 less than the set of routes including Denver to St. Louis.

Determining the Ordering of the Stages   This example of the interdependence of route selection decisions points out a basic difficulty in making these decisions. In order to make a route selection decision from Denver to one of the Midwest cities, we need to know not only the cost from Denver to each Midwest city, but the lowest cost from each Midwest city to the East Coast as well. Our dilemma is that we do not know what these latter costs are until we make route selection decisions from the Midwest to the Mideast and from the Mideast to the East Coast.

To resolve this dilemma we can reverse the order in which we consider the decision stages and make the route selection decisions. That is, we can begin in the East Coast region and first consider available routes from the Mideast to the East. Then we can consider route selection choices from the Midwest to the Mideast, incorporating cost information for the best Mideast to East Coast routes. Working backward in this manner, we will eventually choose a route from the Far West to the Rocky Mountain region that will be based on the cost of the best routes from each Rocky Mountain city to the East Coast as well as the Far West to Rocky Mountain costs. This *backward orien-*

tation of starting with the last sequential decision and working toward the first sequential decision is typical of many dynamic programming problems. We will have further occasion to use this approach in this chapter.

Identifying the Subproblem for Each Stage We are able to use this backward approach to solving the problem by anticipating all possible outcomes of earlier decisions. To illustrate, the last sequential decision for our traveling exhibit problem consists of selecting a route from the Mideast to the East Coast region. If we start with this decision, we do not know what routes will be chosen to move the exhibit from the Far West to the Mideast region. Therefore, we must allow for all possible choices. This is easier than it might seem. Observe that no matter what decisions will be made concerning routes taken to move the exhibit from the Far West to the Mideast region, only two possible outcomes will result: either the exhibit is sent to Pittsburgh or it is sent to Atlanta. These are the only two Mideast cities and the exhibit must be moved to one of them.

Therefore, in order to anticipate the possible outcomes of the route decisions from the Far West to the Mideast, we need consider only two cases. Either the exhibit is in Pittsburgh or it is in Atlanta. Because either of these cases may result, we must treat both of them. We do this by, in effect, solving two subproblems. One subproblem assumes that the exhibit is in Pittsburgh and the other subproblem assumes it is in Atlanta. We then solve each subproblem separately by selecting the lowest-cost route from Pittsburgh to the East Coast region, on the one hand, and from Atlanta to the East Coast, on the other hand.

Each of the decision stages will be treated similarly. That is, a separate subproblem will be developed for each possible city in one geographic region and the shortest route will be found from that city to the East Coast region. This shortest route represents the solution to that subproblem.

INSTANT REPLAY Suppose the sales manager for a nationally marketed product wishes to visit one sales office in each of three sales regions while traveling from the New York office to a marketing convention in San Francisco. The sales offices, regions, possible routes, and travel costs along each route are shown in the network diagram below.

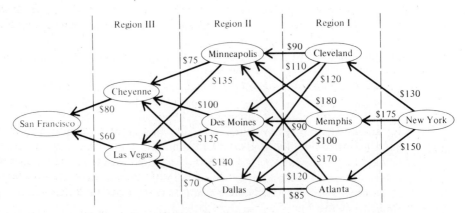

Assume that the sales manager will visit one city in each of the three regions and wishes to complete the trip with the least total cost to the company. If this problem is viewed as a shortest-route problem, how many decision stages are there and what decisions do they represent? In what order should these stages be considered? How many subproblems does the stage 1 decision have and what do they represent?

CHECK The problem has four decision stages corresponding to a route choice into and out of each region. The stages are from New York to region I, from region I to region II, from region II to region III, and from region III to San Francisco. The stages should be examined in reverse order, beginning with the region III to San Francisco decision. The stage 1 decision will have two subproblems, corresponding to the possibility that the sales manager visits Cheyenne or Las Vegas.

Solving the Stage 1 Subproblems Now let us use dynamic programming to solve the traveling exhibit problem. We begin with the stage 1 decision concerning the Mideast to East Coast routes. Actually there is no real decision to make for either of the stage 1 subproblems. This is because New York is the only city in the East Coast region. If the exhibit is in Pittsburgh it must be shipped to New York at a cost of $90,000. If it is in Atlanta, it will be shipped to New York at a cost of $120,000. Although of trivial importance here, this information will be useful in making the remaining route selection choices in stages 2, 3, and 4.

Note that at this point we can make no judgment that Pittsburgh is preferred to Atlanta as the Mideast exhibition site, even though the cost from Pittsburgh to New York is $30,000 less than that from Atlanta to New York. No preference can yet be stated because we have not considered the costs of shipping along routes leading into Pittsburgh or Atlanta.

Solving the Stage 2 Subproblems Having solved the two subproblems for routes leading out of the Mideast region, we next need to consider the choice of routes leading into the Mideast (from the Midwest region). Observe that no matter which routes are to be selected leading into the Midwest region, the exhibit will be moved to one of the three Midwest cities—Chicago, Cincinnati, or St. Louis. In effect, stage 2 consists of three subproblems, one for each of the three Midwest cities. Each is solved without regard to how we got to that particular city, by determining the lowest-cost, or optimal, route out of that city. Two routes exist to the Mideast region for each of the three subproblems. The choice of one of these two routes is not decided solely on the basis of the cost from the Midwest to the Mideast (e.g., Chicago to Pittsburgh), but also on the basis of the cost from the Mideast to the East Coast region.

For an illustration, suppose we are solving the Chicago subproblem. This is equivalent to assuming that the exhibit is in Chicago. The solution to any subproblem must be optimal with respect to any previous route decisions. That is, we must choose a route leaving Chicago that lies along the least-cost route from Chicago to New York. Two options exist: we can go from Chicago to New York via Pittsburgh or via Atlanta. The total cost for either option is made up of two parts:

$$\begin{matrix} \text{Total cost from} \\ \text{Chicago to New York} \end{matrix} = \left(\begin{matrix} \text{cost from Chicago} \\ \text{to Mideast} \end{matrix} \right) + \left(\begin{matrix} \text{cost from Mideast} \\ \text{to New York} \end{matrix} \right)$$

Observe that, in the previous stage of the problem, we found the optimal-cost routes from both of the Mideast region cities to New York. These were \$90,000 from Pittsburgh and \$120,000 from Atlanta. To these optimal costs must be added the cost to get from Chicago to Pittsburgh and from Chicago to Atlanta, respectively. Thus,

$$\text{Chicago to New York via Pittsburgh} = \left(\text{Chicago to Pittsburgh}\right) + \left(\text{Pittsburgh to New York}\right)$$

$$= \$80{,}000 + \$90{,}000 = \$170{,}000$$

$$\text{Chicago to New York via Atlanta} = \left(\text{Chicago to Atlanta}\right) + \left(\text{Atlanta to New York}\right)$$

$$= \$130{,}000 + \$120{,}000 = \$250{,}000$$

Clearly, if the exhibit is in Chicago, the cheapest route from Chicago to New York is via Pittsburgh, at a cost of \$170,000, which is \$80,000 less than via Atlanta.

We solve the other subproblems at this stage in a similar manner. For Cincinnati,

$$\text{Cincinnati to New York via Pittsburgh} = \$90{,}000 + \$90{,}000 = \$180{,}000$$

$$\text{Cincinnati to New York via Atlanta} = \$100{,}000 + \$120{,}000 = \$220{,}000$$

For St. Louis,

$$\text{St. Louis to New York via Pittsburgh} = \$115{,}000 + \$90{,}000 = \$205{,}000$$

$$\text{St. Louis to New York via Atlanta} = \$80{,}000 + \$120{,}000 = \$200{,}000$$

Thus, if the exhibit is sent to Cincinnati, we know that the optimal route across the remainder of the country must go through Pittsburgh at a cost of \$180,000. Likewise, if the exhibit is in St. Louis, the cheapest way to reach New York is via Atlanta at a cost of \$200,000.

Solving the Stage 3 Subproblems   Having solved all the subproblems for stage 2, we now move to stage 3 and consider shipment routes from the Rocky Mountain region to the Midwest. Since there are three Rocky Mountain cities, we have three subproblems to solve for this stage of the problem, each based on the assumption that the exhibit resides in one of the three Rocky Mountain cities.

Consider first Salt Lake City. Note that three routes exist from Salt Lake City to the Midwest: via Chicago, Cincinnati, and St. Louis. In the previous stage of the problem we determined the lowest-cost route to New York from each of these Midwest cities. For the current stage of the problem, we now need to select the cheapest route from each Rocky Mountain city to New York. The cost is again made up of two components:

$$\text{Total cost from Rocky Mountain region to New York} = \left(\text{cost from Rocky Mountain region to Midwest region}\right) + \left(\text{optimal cost from Midwest region to New York}\right)$$

For Salt Lake City, three options exist which have the following costs:

$$\text{Salt Lake City to New York via Chicago} = \$85{,}000 + \$170{,}000 = \$255{,}000$$

$$\text{Salt Lake City to New York via Cincinnati} = \$95{,}000 + \$180{,}000 = \$275{,}000$$

$$\text{Salt Lake City to New York via St. Louis} = \$120{,}000 + \$200{,}000 = \$320{,}000$$

Obviously, if the exhibit is in Salt Lake City, the cheapest remaining route to New York is via Chicago (as determined above) and subsequently via Pittsburgh (as determined in the previous stage).

Similar analysis is used to solve the other subproblems. For Denver we find

$$\text{Denver to New York via Chicago} = \$110{,}000 + \$170{,}000 = \$280{,}000$$

$$\text{Denver to New York via Cincinnati} = \$120{,}000 + \$180{,}000 = \$300{,}000$$

$$\text{Denver to New York via St. Louis} = \$105{,}000 + \$200{,}000 = \$305{,}000$$

Thus, if the exhibit is in Denver, it should be routed next to Chicago, then to Pittsburgh, and finally to New York, for a total cost of $280,000.

The analysis for Phoenix yields|

$$\text{Phoenix to New York via Chicago} = \$120{,}000 + \$170{,}000 = \$290{,}000$$

$$\text{Phoenix to New York via Cincinnati} = \$115{,}000 + \$180{,}000 = \$295{,}000$$

$$\text{Phoenix to New York via St. Louis} = \$95{,}000 + \$200{,}000 = \$295{,}000$$

From Phoenix the cheapest route goes through Chicago, then Pittsburgh, and finally New York.

Solving the Stage 4 Subproblems Having solved all subproblems for stage 3, we next consider the stage 4 decision, which is to choose a route from the Far West region to the Rocky Mountain region. Since there are two Far West cities, we have two subproblems to solve at this stage. One assumes that the exhibit starts in San Francisco and the other that the exhibit begins in Los Angeles.

As in previous stages, the optimal subproblem solution will be based on two costs: that from the Far West region to one of the Rocky Mountain cities and the optimal cost from the designated Rocky Mountain city to New York. The optimal Rocky Mountain costs were determined in the previous stage of the problem as $255,000 from Salt Lake City, $280,000 from Denver, and $290,000 from Phoenix.

Therefore, the San Francisco subproblem has three options:

$$\text{San Francisco to New York via Salt Lake City} = \$100{,}000 + \$255{,}000 = \$355{,}000$$

$$\text{San Francisco to New York via Denver} = \$120{,}000 + \$280{,}000 = \$400{,}000$$

$$\frac{\text{San Francisco to New York}}{\text{via Phoenix}} = \$130,000 + \$290,000 = \$420,000$$

This shows that if the exhibit begins in San Francisco, the cheapest route through the remaining regions to New York has a cost of $355,000, and will go to Salt Lake City, Chicago, and Pittsburgh along the way.

If the exhibit begins in Los Angeles, the cost of the three possible routes out of Los Angeles are given by

$$\frac{\text{Los Angeles to New York}}{\text{via Salt Lake City}} = \$115,000 + \$255,000 = \$370,000$$

$$\frac{\text{Los Angeles to New York}}{\text{via Denver}} = \$110,000 + \$280,000 = \$390,000$$

$$\frac{\text{Los Angeles to New York}}{\text{via Phoenix}} = \$85,000 + \$290,000 = \$375,000$$

We see that the cheapest route from Los Angeles to New York is via Salt Lake City, Chicago, and Pittsburgh, for a total cost of $370,000.

INSTANT REPLAY   Refer to the sales manager's travel problem first discussed in the previous instant replay. Determine the optimal decisions for each of the subproblems in the four decision stages.

CHECK   The stage 1 decisions are straightforward: if he is in Cheyenne he travels to San Francisco for a cost of $80; if he is in Las Vegas he travels to San Francisco for a cost of $60. There are three subproblems for stage 2: Minneapolis, Des Moines, and Dallas. If he is in Minneapolis, he should travel to San Francisco via Cheyenne for a total cost of $75 + $80 = $155. If he is in Des Moines, he should travel via Cheyenne for a cost of $100 + $80 = $180. If he is in Dallas, he should travel via Las Vegas for a cost of $130. There are also three subproblems for stage 3: Cleveland, Memphis, and Atlanta. If he is in Cleveland, he should travel via Minneapolis for a cost of $90 + $155 = $245. If he is in Memphis, he should travel via Dallas for a cost of $100 + $130 = $230. If he is in Atlanta, he should travel via Dallas for a cost of $85 + $130 = $215. Stage 4 has only a single subproblem because his trip will begin in New York. If he goes via Cleveland his total cost will be $130 + $245 = $375. If he goes via Memphis, his cost will be $175 + $230 = $405. If he goes via Atlanta, his cost will be $150 + $215 = $365. Thus, the solution to the stage 1 subproblem is to go via Atlanta.

Determining the Optimal Solution   Now that all subproblems have been solved for each of the stages, we can determine the optimal solution to the entire problem. Observe that the solution of the two subproblems in the last stage consisted of the optimal, or lowest-cost, routes from the *two possible starting points* of the exhibit tour—San Francisco and Los Angeles—to the ending point of the tour—New York.[1] The lowest total cost of a complete tour from

[1]The problem dealt with here had only a single city in the last region. If there is more than one city in the last region (e.g., New York, Washington, D.C., and Boston), the same general procedure would be followed. The only change is that the first decision stage (from Mideast to East) would no longer be trivial but would involve finding the cheapest route from each Mideast city to one of the set of East Coast cities. From there the solution is similar.

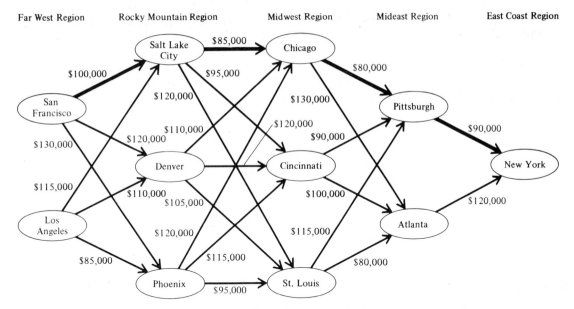

FIGURE 12-2 Optimal set of exhibition sites for art treasures exhibition.

San Francisco to New York was $355,000 and from Los Angeles was $370,000. Clearly the cheapest tour route is the one that begins in San Francisco and, as determined in other stages of the problem, goes through Salt Lake City, Chicago, and Pittsburgh before reaching New York. The optimal route is indicated by the thicker lines in Figure 12-2.

This problem could have been solved by enumerating all possible sets of routes and then selecting the lowest-cost set. In this case there were 36 possible sets of routes, equal to the product of the number of cities in each region (2 × 3 × 3 × 2 × 1 = 36). We actually solved 10 subproblems, equal to the sum of the cities in all regions except the last (2 + 3 + 3 + 2 = 10). The number of subproblems in any stage is equivalent to the number of cities in the prior region. Thus, for stage 1 there were two cities in the Mideast region and hence two subproblems, for stage 2 there were three cities in the Midwest and therefore three subproblems, etc.

As a problem grows in size (with, say, the inclusion of additional cities in each region), the difficulty in enumerating all possible routes makes brute force enumeration very time-consuming if not impractical. The number of subproblems to be solved with dynamic programming also increases, but at a slower rate. For instance, suppose that in our example each region, including the East Coast, had five competing cities. There would be $(5)^5 = 3,125$ routes to enumerate. But there would be only 5 + 5 + 5 + 5 = 20 subproblems to solve with dynamic programming because there will be five subproblems for each of the four decision stages. Thus, the efficiency of dynamic programming will improve in comparison with enumeration as the problem becomes larger.

INSTANT REPLAY Using the results of the previous instant replay, identify the least-cost route for our sales manager. How many subproblems did we solve? How many routes would need to be evaluated if we had used complete enumeration?

CHECK The optimal route is from New York to Atlanta to Dallas to Las Vegas to San Francisco for a total cost of $365. We solved two stage 1 subproblems, three subproblems each for stages 2 and 3, and one subproblem for stage 4, which is a total of $2 + 3 + 3 + 1 = 9$. Total enumeration would have required $1 \times 3 \times 3 \times 2 \times 1 = 18$ routes to be examined.

Characteristics of Dynamic Programming

At this point it is useful to draw some generalizations concerning dynamic programming problems from our shortest-route example. First of all, note that the problem consisted of a number of distinct *decision stages,* in this case represented by the geographical regions. Each decision stage consisted of a set of subproblems. There was one such subproblem for each possible museum site in a region. In dynamic programming terminology we would refer to these museum sites as *states* or *state variables.* (We use the term "state" to refer to status or current situation, not to refer to a geographical state, such as Ohio.) Note that we found the optimal decision for any subproblem by considering the best way of moving from a state in one stage to a state in the next stage or, in our terms, from a museum site in one region to a museum site in the adjacent region.

We based the decision about which state-change option was best on the combination of two costs: the cost of the immediate state change plus the previously determined *optimal* cost of remaining state changes.

In effect the decision at each stage *collapses the decision problem by one stage.* For instance, in the final stage of the problem, the Los Angeles subproblem could have been viewed as shown in Figure 12-3. Since at each stage we solve subproblems optimally, the best solution for each of the Rocky

FIGURE 12-3 Illustration of Los Angeles subproblem showing collapsed problem.

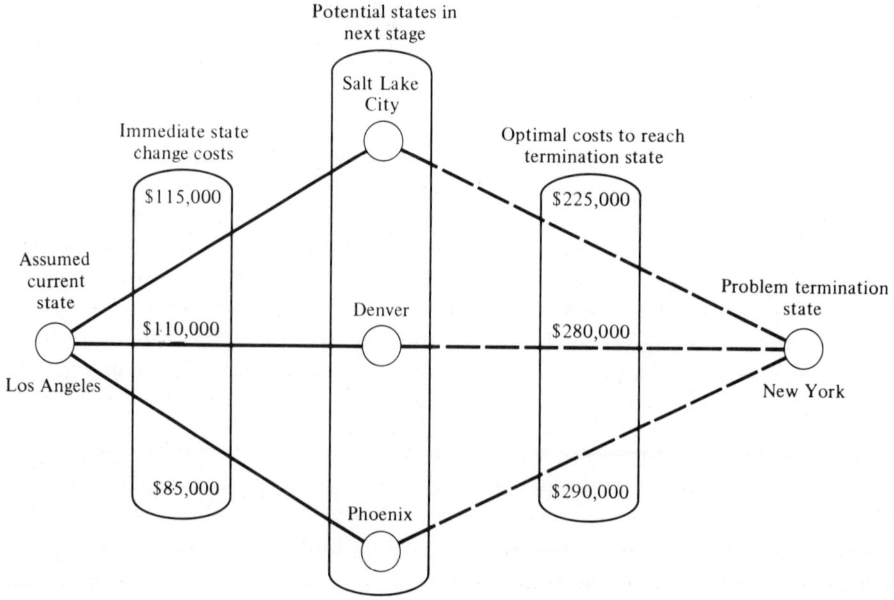

Thus, to find the optimal route from Los Angeles we need only add the cost
from Los Angeles to these Rocky Mountain cities to the now known optimal
cost from these same cities to New York.

This collapsing of the problem so that we need consider only the current stage and the optimal solutions to the previous stage is a common element of dynamic programming problems. A fundamental principle of dynamic programming that must hold if this problem-collapsing property is to yield an optimal solution is called the *principle of optimality*. This principle states, in essence, that an optimal decision at any stage (i.e., for some subproblem) must be based on an optimal set of decisions with regard to the state resulting from that first decision. This is why we started at the back of the problem and always made an optimal decision for each subproblem that incorporated the results of optimal decisions from previous stages.

Nonlinear Allocation Problem

In this section we shall examine another type of dynamic programming problem, one which does not have a natural set of sequential decisions but which can, nonetheless, be formulated and solved as if it did. We will consider a resource allocation problem. However, this problem differs from resource allocation problems treated in earlier chapters in that benefits received are not linearly related to the resources allocated. This nonlinear allocation problem can best be illustrated by the following example.

Formulating the Problem

The Neptune Sea Food Company has recently been expanding its chain of fast food retail outlets. The company is currently examining its plans for expansion in the coming year. Financial and manpower resources are available in sufficient quantity to open, at most, five new outlets.

Neptune is organized on a regional basis with four distinct geographical regions, for simplicity here identified as *A, B, C,* and *D*. Because of different past expansion rates and potential for future growth in the four regions, the estimated incremental profits from opening new outlets will differ from region to region. These incremental profits are shown in Table 12-1.

At first glance this problem may seem to be quite similar to some of the integer programming situations treated in Chapter 11. It is similar in many ways, but there is one very important difference: the incremental profit earned from each additional outlet opened in any specific region is not constant. For an illustration, consider region *A*. Opening one outlet in that region will earn Neptune an additional $15,000. Opening two outlets will earn a total of $27,000. Thus, the second outlet contributes only $12,000. Similarly, we see that a third outlet will add ($37,000 − $27,000) or $10,000, a fourth outlet $8,000, and a fifth outlet $6,000. Total profit increases with each additional outlet, but the size of the increase is decreasing. This is often called *decreasing marginal returns* and results in a nonlinear objective function. Fortunately, this can be easily handled with dynamic programming. Let us see how this can be done.

Designating Decision Stages   Clearly, the allocation of outlets to the geographic regions is a simultaneous decision. However, we can solve the problem using

TABLE 12-1
Additional Profits Generated by Opening Increasing Numbers of New Neptune Fast Food Outlets by Geographical Region*

Number of new outlets opened	Geographical region			
	A	B	C	D
1	$15,000	$12,000	$14,000	$16,000
2	$27,000	$23,000	$27,000	$28,000
3	$37,000	$32,000	$39,000	$36,000
4	$45,000	$40,000	$50,000	$42,000
5	$51,000	$47,000	$60,000	$45,000

*Five at most can be opened.

dynamic programming if we treat the allocation decision for *each region as a separate stage*. Thus, we might proceed by allocating first to region A, then to region B, next to region C, and finally to region D. The actual order chosen makes little difference here because there is no natural decision sequence as there was in the previous problem. Clearly the allocation decision at any stage is dependent on (1) how many outlets are available to be assigned and (2) what is the most profitable allocation of these outlets between the region considered at that stage and those regions yet to be treated.

Identifying Subproblems for Each Stage Suppose we decide to allocate outlets among the regions in the order A, B, C, and D. In order to be able to make these decisions, it is necessary to work backward as we did the shortest-route problem. In other words, we begin at the end with region D. Since it is possible that as few as zero or as many as five outlets can be allocated to regions A, B, and C, we must consider each possibility when selecting the optimal decision for region D. There are, in effect, six separate subproblems for region D, corresponding to the six possible outcomes of the allocation decisions for regions A, B, and C. If five outlets are assigned to regions A, B, and C, there will be zero outlets available for D. If four outlets are allocated to A, B, and C, one will be available for D. Thus, no matter what allocation decisions we make for regions A, B, and C, there will be zero, one, two, three, four, or five outlets available for allocation in region D. Each of these cases will represent a separate subproblem for region D. The solution to each subproblem for this first stage is quite easy: however many outlets we assume are not assigned to regions A, B, or C should be assigned to region D.

The decisions at subsequent stages (regions A, B, and C) are somewhat more difficult. Consider the decisions at the next stage for region C. There are again six subproblems to solve, one for each possible number of available outlets (zero to five). The solution to any given subproblem requires determining the most profitable allocation of the remaining outlets between areas C and D.

For example, consider the subproblem corresponding to two outlets available for assignment to C. There are three decision options to this subproblem: (1) allocate both outlets to area C, (2) allocate one outlet to C and one to D, and (3) allocate both outlets to D. Whichever alternative yields the highest total profit will be selected as the optimal solution to this subproblem.

Each subsequent stage (areas *A* and *B*) will contain subproblems corresponding to the potential number of outlets that could be available for assignment. There will be six subproblems for region *B*, but only one subproblem for region *A*. Region *A* will have only one subproblem because all five outlets are available at that decision stage. (No decisions or possible allocations precede this stage.)

The optimal decision to these subproblems will be determined by the profit that can be earned in that region vs. the profit to be earned by "saving" outlets for allocation in one of the subsequent regions. For example, consider the subproblem where two outlets are available for allocation to region *B*. These can be allocated (1) both to region *B*, (2) one to region *B* and the other saved for allocation between regions *C* and *D*, or (3) both saved for allocation between regions *C* and *D*. The profit from saving outlets for allocation to regions *C* and *D* will have already been found by solution of the subproblems at the previous stage.

INSTANT REPLAY   The audit manager for a state income tax bureau is attempting to decide where to assign three new auditors that the bureau is about to hire. Three categories of returns, labeled I, II, and III, seem to offer the most promise. The following table indicates the amount of additional taxes that can be collected for different assignment patterns.

Number of auditors assigned	Additional taxes collected from audit category		
	I	*II*	*III*
1	$100,000	$ 90,000	$ 87,000
2	$180,000	$175,000	$172,000
3	$250,000	$245,000	$252,000

If this problem is formulated as a dynamic programming problem, how many stages will the problem have? How many subproblems will there be for each stage and what will they represent?

CHECK   There will be three stages, one for each audit category. The first two stages will have four subproblems, corresponding to whether there are zero, one, two, or three auditors available for assignment. The third stage will have a single subproblem representing the initial availability of all three auditors.

Solving the Problem

Solving the Stage 1 Subproblems   With this background let us now solve the Neptune problem. The six subproblems for the first stage are easy to solve with the profit figures shown in Table 12-1. Note that total profits for region *D* always increase with an increase in the number of outlets opened. Thus, however many of the five outlets that can be opened remain unassigned at this stage should be allocated to region *D*. Thus if five outlets are available, all five should be opened in region *D* at a profit of $45,000. If only four are unassigned, all four should be allocated to region *D* for a profit of $42,000. Similar choices exist for the other subproblems.

Solving the Stage 2 Subproblems The subproblem decisions are slightly more complex when we move back to stage 2, corresponding to the allocation for region C. Consider the subproblem that assumes five outlets remain to be assigned. There are six ways in which the five outlets can be allocated: (1) five to C and zero to D; (2) four to C and one to D; (3) three to C and two to D; (4) two to C and three to D; (5) one to C and four to D; and (6) zero to C and five to D. The total profit for each option can be found by adding the corresponding profits for the pair of allocations as obtained from Table 12-1. Thus,

Profit (5 to C, 0 to D) = \$60,000 + 0   = \$60,000

Profit (4 to C, 1 to D) = \$50,000 + \$16,000 = \$66,000

Profit (3 to C, 2 to D) = \$39,000 + \$28,000 = \$67,000

Profit (2 to C, 3 to D) = \$27,000 + \$36,000 = \$63,000

Profit (1 to C, 4 to D) = \$14,000 + \$42,000 = \$56,000

Profit (0 to C, 5 to D) = 0   + \$45,000 = \$45,000

The best allocation, and therefore the solution to this subproblem, is to assign three outlets to region C and two outlets to region D.

Table 12-2 contains the calculations necessary to solve the other subproblems for this stage. The optimal decision for each subproblem is indicated by the asterisk next to the total profit. Based on those results, we now know that if five outlets are available for assignment to regions C and D, three should be assigned to C and two to D. Similarly if four outlets are available, either three should go to C and one to D or two should go to each (both allocations have the same total profit). The solution to the other subproblems provide the optimal allocation of zero, one, two, or three outlets between the two areas C and D. These optimal solutions will be used in solving the subproblems at the next stage.

Solving the Stage 3 Subproblems The stage 3 subproblems are concerned with the distribution of unassigned outlets between area B, on the one hand, and areas C and D, on the other. For instance, if only one outlet remains unassigned at this stage (meaning four are assigned to region A), we have two decision options: (1) assign the remaining outlet to region B, or (2) save it for assignment in region C or D. The incremental profit of \$12,000 obtained by assigning one outlet to region B can be read directly from Table 12-1. The incremental profit of assigning one outlet to region C or D is equivalent to the profit obtained from the optimal solution to the previous stage's subproblem in which only one outlet was available for assignment to C or D. This is seen to be \$16,000 in Table 12-2 and corresponds to an assignment of the outlet to area D.

Table 12-3 shows the calculations necessary to solve each of the six subproblems for stage 3. The incremental profit for each option consists of the profit from an allocation of a specific number of outlets to B together with the profit from the optimal allocation of the remaining outlets to areas C and D (those identified by an asterisk in Table 12-2). Note that there are two optimal solutions to subproblem V since the profit of \$55,000 earned by allocating one outlet to B and three to C or D is the same as that earned by allocating all four outlets to C or D.

TABLE 12-2

Subproblem Solutions for Stage 2 of the Neptune Seafood Problem (Regions C and D)

Subproblem number	Number of outlets			Profit, dollars		
	Available	Assigned to C	Assigned to D	For C	For D	Total
I	0	0	0	0	0	0*
II	1	1	0	14,000	0	14,000
		0	1	0	16,000	16,000*
III	2	2	0	27,000	0	27,000
		1	1	14,000	16,000	30,000*
		0	2	0	28,000	28,000
IV	3	3	0	39,000	0	39,000
		2	1	27,000	16,000	43,000*
		1	2	14,000	28,000	42,000
		0	3	0	36,000	36,000
V	4	4	0	50,000	0	50,000
		3	1	39,000	16,000	55,000*
		2	2	27,000	28,000	55,000*
		1	3	14,000	36,000	50,000
		0	4	0	42,000	42,000
VI	5	5	0	60,000	0	60,000
		4	1	50,000	16,000	66,000
		3	2	39,000	28,000	67,000*
		2	3	27,000	36,000	63,000
		1	4	14,000	42,000	56,000
		0	5	0	45,000	45,000

*Optimal subproblem solution for stage 2.

Solving the Stage 4 Subproblem Having completed the subproblems for stage 3, we can now proceed to stage 4, which corresponds to the decision allocation between area A and the other three regions. Recall that the number of subproblems at any stage is determined by the possible numbers of unallocated outlets. Since no allocation options precede stage 4, we know that all five outlets *must* be available for assignment. Thus, there is only one subproblem to solve, which is the allocation of these five outlets between region A, on the one hand, and regions B, C, or D, on the other.

The incremental profits for the six options of this subproblem are found in a manner similar to that in the previous stage. The incremental profit for a specific allocation to region A is obtained directly from Table 12-1. The incremental profit from the assignment of the remaining units to regions B, C, and D is the optimal solution to the corresponding subproblem in stage 3 as shown in Table 12-3. Thus, the six options and their profits are

$$\text{Profit (5 to } A, \text{ 0 to } B/C/D) = \$51,000 + 0 \qquad = \$51,000$$

$$\text{Profit (4 to } A, \text{ 1 to } B/C/D) = \$45,000 + \$16,000 = \$61,000$$

Profit (3 to A, 2 to $B/C/D$) = \$37,000 + \$30,000 = \$67,000

Profit (2 to A, 3 to $B/C/D$) = \$27,000 + \$43,000 = \$70,000

Profit (1 to A, 4 to $B/C/D$) = \$15,000 + \$55,000 = \$70,000

Profit (0 to A, 5 to $B/C/D$) = 0   + \$67,000 = \$67,000

INSTANT REPLAY Refer to the tax auditor assignment decision discussed in the previous instant replay. Using the approach described above for the Neptune problem, determine the solution to the subproblems of each stage for the tax auditor problem. Start with tax audit category III as the stage 1 subproblem and work backwards to categories II and I.

CHECK The four subproblems for stage 1 refer to the availability of zero, one, two, or three auditors for assignment to audit category III. The solutions are straightforward: assign the remaining number of auditors to category III. With three auditors available, additional tax revenue of \$252,000 will be earned. With two auditors, \$172,000 will be earned. With one auditor, \$87,000 can be earned. With zero auditors, nothing can be earned.

TABLE 12-3

Subproblem Solutions for Stage 3 of the Neptune Seafood Problem (Regions B and C/D)

Subproblem number	Number of outlets			Profit, dollars		
	Available	Assigned to B	Assigned to C/D	For B	For C/D	Total
I	0	0	0	0	0	0*
II	1	1	0	12,000	0	12,000
		0	1	0	16,000	16,000*
III	2	2	0	23,000	0	23,000
		1	1	12,000	16,000	28,000
		0	2	0	30,000	30,000*
IV	3	3	0	32,000	0	32,000
		2	1	23,000	16,000	39,000
		1	2	12,000	30,000	42,000
		0	3	0	43,000	43,000*
V	4	4	0	40,000	0	40,000
		3	1	32,000	16,000	48,000
		2	2	23,000	30,000	53,000
		1	3	12,000	43,000	55,000*
		0	4	0	55,000	55,000*
VI	5	5	0	47,000	0	47,000
		4	1	40,000	16,000	56,000
		3	2	32,000	30,000	62,000
		2	3	23,000	43,000	66,000
		1	4	12,000	55,000	67,000*
		0	5	0	67,000	67,000*

*Optimal subproblem solution for stage 3.

Stage 2 subproblems correspond to zero, one, two, or three auditors available for assignment to audit categories II and III. With three auditors available, an assignment of two to category II and one to category III or an assignment of one to category II and two to category III will yield the highest revenue of $262,000. With two auditors available, the highest revenue of $177,000 can be earned by assigning one to both categories. With one auditor available, that auditor should be assigned to category II for $90,000 additional tax revenue. With zero auditors available, nothing can be earned.

Stage 3 has only one subproblem, corresponding to all three auditors available. The best solution to that subproblem is to assign one auditor to category I and the remaining two to categories II and III. This will yield $277,000 in additional tax revenue.

Identifying the Optimal Solution   Note that two optimal solutions exist for the stage 1 subproblem of the Neptune problem with profit of $70,000. One requires two outlets to be assigned to region A and the remaining three to regions B, C, and D. A second solution assigns one outlet to A with the other four given to regions B, C, and D.[1]

The solution to the total allocation problem can now be found by working back through the various stages. As noted, there were two optimal solutions at stage 4; suppose we select the one with two outlets assigned to region A. This left three to be assigned to regions B, C, and D at stage 3 of the problem. Referring to Table 12-3 we see that with three unassigned outlets, the optimal allocation is none to region B, leaving three to be allocated to C and D.

Moving further back to the analysis for stage 2, we find that the best allocation of three outlets between C and D was to assign two to C and one to D.

We have now identified an optimal solution to the allocation problem. That is, assign two outlets to region A, none to B, 2 to C, and 1 to region D. This allocation promises to add $70,000 in incremental profits, as shown in the stage 4 analysis. You may wish to check the original incremental profit figures in Table 12-1 to assure yourself that the chosen assignment will indeed produce the $70,000.

INSTANT REPLAY   Stage 4 analysis showed that at least one other optimal solution exists for the Neptune problem. Trace back through the stage to identify any additional optimal solutions.

CHECK   Three other optimal solutions can be found: (1) one outlet each to A and B, two to C, and one to D; (2) one outlet to A, none to B, three to C, and one to D; (3) one outlet to A, none to B, and two each to C and D.

Multiple Optimal Solutions

The existence of multiple optimal solutions can be beneficial in treating objectives other than profit. For example, the organizational costs of expansion are

---

[1]Since there are two equal-cost ways of allocating four outlets to regions B, C, and D (see subproblem V in Table 12-3) and one of these has two equal-cost alternatives as well (see subproblem V of Table 12-2), there are a total of four optimal solutions.

likely to be less if expansion is concentrated in one or two regions. Thus, management may desire to select the optimal profit solution which expands in the fewest number of regions. The optimal solution found above of one to A, one to B, two to C, and one to D would not be as desirable, under this criterion, as the other three solutions.

Suppose that management is instead concerned with the "fairness" of their expansion plan. They may prefer a plan which allocates at least one new outlet to each of the geographical regions. In this instance, the plan of one to A, one to B, two to C, and one to D would be preferred to the other three optimal profit allocations.

Originally we assumed that Neptune wishes to allocate all five available outlets to one or more of the regions. (This is why in stage 4 we solved only one subproblem, that with five outlets available.) However, Neptune may wish to know the incremental profits and optimal allocations that would result if it decided to open fewer than five outlets. This information can be easily found by solving additional subproblems in the fourth stage.

Table 12-4 shows the calculations necessary to solve all six possible subproblems for stage 4. The difference in incremental profit between the optimal

TABLE 12-4
Subproblem Solutions for Stage 4 of the Neptune Seafood Problem (Regions A and $B/C/D$)

Subproblem number	Number of outlets			Profit, dollars		
	Available	Assigned to A	Assigned to B/C/D	For A	For B/C/D	Total
I	0	0	0	0	0	0*
II	1	1	0	15,000	0	15,000
		0	1	0	16,000	16,000*
III	2	2	0	27,000	0	27,000
		1	1	15,000	16,000	31,000*
		0	2	0	30,000	30,000
IV	3	3	0	37,000	0	37,000
		2	1	27,000	16,000	43,000
		1	2	15,000	30,000	45,000*
		0	3	0	43,000	43,000
V	4	4	0	45,000	0	45,000
		3	1	37,000	16,000	53,000
		2	2	27,000	30,000	57,000
		1	3	15,000	43,000	58,000*
		0	4	0	55,000	55,000
VI	5	5	0	51,000	0	51,000
		4	1	45,000	16,000	61,000
		3	2	37,000	30,000	67,000
		2	3	27,000	43,000	70,000*
		1	4	15,000	55,000	70,000*
		0	5	0	67,000	67,000

*Optimal subproblem solution for stage 4.

subproblem solutions represents the opportunity cost of not opening each additional outlet. For instance, if Neptune decides to limit the number of new outlets to four, incremental profits will drop from the $70,000 achieved with five outlets to $58,000 for four, a decline or opportunity cost of $12,000. Management may decide that the start-up costs that would have been allocated to the fifth new outlet could be better spent increasing the sales at the other four.

INSTANT REPLAY   Refer again to the tax auditor assignment situation. Using the optimal subproblem solutions, identify all optimal solutions, assuming that three auditors are available for assignment. Suppose the tax bureau's budget is under review and there is some possibility that only two auditors will be hired rather than three. What justification can the audit manager use to support hiring the third auditor?

CHECK   Only one optimal solution exists. This calls for assigning one auditor to each of the three audit categories and will generate $277,000 in additional tax revenue. The audit manager can add an additional stage 3 subproblem which assumes two auditors are available for assignment. Solution of this subproblem yields a total of $190,000 in additional revenue. (One auditor is to be assigned to audit category I and the other to audit category II.) This represents a drop of $277,000 − $190,000 = $87,000 in additional tax revenue if one fewer auditor is hired. If the salary plus fringe benefits of one tax auditor is less than $87,000, the audit manager should be able to build a strong case for hiring the third auditor.

Stochastic Time-Sequential Problem

As a final example of dynamic programming, we shall consider a problem with probabilistic, or stochastic, outcomes. As an illustration of this class of problems we will examine a purchasing problem where the price paid for an item is subject to fluctuation over time. Problems of this type occur frequently for raw commodity items, such as grains, metals, and so on. Purchasing problems are not the only type of stochastic problem that can be solved by dynamic programming. We might be concerned, for instance, with the best time to sell off resources, where the price that can be obtained varies probabilistically. Let us now consider our example problem.

Formulating the Problem

The purchasing agent for the Rollzone Manufacturing Company is faced with a *purchase timing decision*. The company has signed a contract to supply 1,000 microwave ovens to a restaurant chain. Production for this order is scheduled to begin in 5 months. Most of the items needed are in stock or can be manufactured by Rollzone. However, sometime during the next 5 months they need to purchase 1,000 electronic control units for the ovens.

The purchasing agent knows that the cost of these control units has undergone substantial swings in recent months and she would like to be able to take advantage of any potential price drops while minimizing the risk of having to purchase the control unit at a high price. After combining data concerning past price behavior with information as to future expectations provided by

TABLE 12-5
**Probability Estimates of Purchase Cost for Microwave Oven Control Units
over Next 5 Months**

Cost per unit	January	February	March	April	May
$25	.10	.05	.05	.10	.05
26	.20	.15	.10	.20	.15
27	.30	.35	.50	.40	.50
28	.25	.25	.20	.20	.20
29	.15	.20	.15	.10	.10
Expected cost	$27.15	27.40	27.30	27.00	27.15

consultation with suppliers, she has estimated the probabilities of five possible prices ($25 to $29) for this unit over the 5-month period January–May. These are shown in Table 12-5. The table shows, for example, that the purchasing agent estimates that, in January, there is a .10 probability the units can be purchased for $25, a .20 probability of a $26 price, a .30 probability of a $27 price, a .25 probability of a $28 price, and a .15 probability of a $29 price. The probabilities of these prices differ from month to month as shown.

The expected prices, calculated by weighting each potential price by its probability, for each month are shown at the bottom of Table 12-5. Note that these expected prices do not vary much from month to month. However, the range of possible prices suggests that opportunities for a low price exist as well as risk of a high price. It should be obvious that if the price ever drops as low as $25 the agent should buy the units then. But what about other price levels? Suppose she waits for a $25 price and the price never drops that low. She will have to purchase during the last month and may have to pay a $29 price per unit.

The purchasing agent would like to develop a set of policies or purchasing rules that will enable Rollzone to buy at the lowest expected price. We can solve this problem quite easily using dynamic programming principles, although the details of analysis will be quite different from anything we have looked at so far.

Solving the Problem

This problem consists of a set of sequential purchase/no purchase decisions, one for each month. Each month therefore constitutes a stage, with separate subproblems corresponding to each potential price that may be in effect during that month. The solution of each subproblem consists of deciding whether to purchase at the existing price or to postpone the purchase decision to the next month.

Solving the Stage 1 Subproblems   We begin at the end with the month of May as stage 1. As should be evident, there is no decision to be made at that point; whatever price exists, the control units must be purchased at that price. This assumes that this stage is not reached if the units were purchased in some earlier month, which is correct since no decision exists for May if the units were bought prior to May.

Given that the units have not been purchased prior to May, what price can

the agent expect to pay in May? This is simply the expected price, which is shown to be $27.15 in Table 12-5 and was calculated by weighting each potential price by its probability:

$$.05(\$25) + .15(\$26) + .50(\$27) + .20(\$28) + .10(\$29) = \$27.15$$

Thus, if the agent waits until May to purchase the units, the expected price she will pay is $27.15.

Solving the Stage 2 Subproblems   Having determined the expected outcome for stage 1, we now move to stage 2, the decision for April. As mentioned earlier, if the price in April is $25, the units should be purchased at that price. Just as obvious is the conclusion that, if the price is $29, no purchase should be made and the agent should wait until May and hope for a lower price (she cannot do worse). What about prices between $25 and $29? The answer in each case is based on a comparison with the expected cost from stage 1.

Suppose that the price in April is $26. If she purchases now, she is guaranteed a cost of $26. If she waits until May, she does not know exactly what the price will be but she can use the expected cost for May of $27.15. If the purchasing agent uses an *expected value criterion* to make decisions (which we will assume she does), her best decision would be to purchase the control units at $26, rather than wait until May when the expected cost is $27.15.

As a general rule for stage 2, if the actual price in April is less than the expected price for May, the decision should be to purchase in April. But, if the price in April is greater than $27.15, the decision should be to wait until May. In summary, if the price in April is $25, $26, or $27, the agent should purchase the units then. If the price is $28 or $29, she should wait until May.

Given the optimal solutions to the April subproblems, an expected purchase price can now be determined for April and May. Observe that the probabilities of a $25, $26, or $27 price are given in Table 12-5 as .10, .20, and .40, respectively for April. The probability of waiting until May to purchase is thus $1 - (.10 + .20 + .40) = .30$. Therefore, taking April and May together, we see that there is a .10 probability she will purchase at $25, a .20 chance of purchasing at $26, a .40 chance of obtaining a $27 price, and a .30 chance of waiting until May, when the expected purchase price is $27.15. this leads to the following expected price for April and May:

$$.10(\$25) + .20(\$26) + .40(\$27) + .30(\$27.15) = \$26.65$$

This purchase price is the expected cost if the units are not purchased in January, February, or March, but are bought in either April or May. It is based on a set of optimal purchase decisions for April and May (buy in April if price is $27 or lower, otherwise take the available price in May).

Solving the Stage 3 Subproblems   Next let us consider March. Since the expected purchase price of waiting for April or May is $26.65, the agent should purchase the units in March only if the actual selling price is less than $26.65. There is a .05 probability in March of a $25 price, a .10 probability of a $26 price, which must mean there is a $1 - (.05 + .10) = .85$ probability that she will wait until April or May. This leads to an expected purchase cost of waiting until March, April, or May of

$$.05(\$25) + .10(\$26) + .85(\$26.65) = \$26.50$$

Solving the Stage 4 Subproblems Since the expected cost of waiting until March or later is $26.50, the agent should not purchase in February unless the actual price that month is less than $26.50. The probability that this will happen is .20 because there is a .05 probability of a $25 price and a .15 probability of a $26 price. The expected purchase price if the agent waits until February or later is therefore

$$.05(\$25) + .15(\$26) + .80(\$26.50) = \$26.35$$

Solving the Stage 5 Subproblems Finally we turn to the decision for January. Since the expected cost of waiting until February or later to purchase is $26.35, the agent should buy in January only if the price is $25, with probability .10, or $26, with probability of .20. This leads to an expected cost of

$$.10(\$25) + .20(\$26) + .70(\$26.35) = \$26.15$$

Identifying the Optimal Solution Having completed the last stage of the problem, we have now found an optimal set of purchase policies. They can be briefly summarized as:

1. If the price is $26 or less during January, February, or March, purchase at that price.
2. If the price is $27 or less during April, purchase at that price.
3. In May, purchase at whatever price is available.

The expected cost of this set of policies was shown above to be $26.15. These decisions and outcomes are shown in modified decision tree form in Figure 12-4.

FIGURE 12-4 Optimal purchase policies for Rollzone Manufacturing Company.

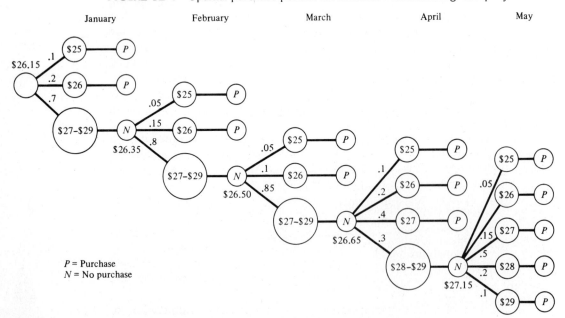

P = Purchase
N = No purchase

INSTANT REPLAY   Suppose the purchasing agent needs to buy another kind of element sometime during the next 3 months. Assume that the following probabilities exist for purchase costs of this item *during each month*:

Price	Probability
$10	.05
$11	.15
$12	.35
$13	.25
$14	.20

Determine a set of optimal purchase policies and the expected purchase cost for this element.

CHECK   Purchase in month 1 if cost is $11 or less, purchase in month 2 if cost is $12 or less, otherwise purchase at available price in month 3. Expected cost for this set of decisions is $11.69 as compared to an expected cost of $12.40 for waiting until the third month and taking what price exists at that time.

Final Comments

In this chapter we have examined the use of dynamic programming as a decision-making procedure. Dynamic programming is a conceptual approach to problem solving rather than a mechanical procedure. To provide some feeling for the breadth of application we have chosen to present three different types of problems and to discuss how they can be formulated and solved. These included a shortest-route problem, a nonlinear allocation problem, and a stochastic time-sequential problem.

By now you should have noticed that the approach we used in solving these problems had certain common elements. The decision problem was subdivided into a series of separate decisions referred to as decision stages. Each decision stage had a set of subproblems to be solved. The subproblems reflected all possible situations that might arise at each decision stage. In this sense dynamic programming is anticipatory. That is, decisions are made in anticipation of all possible situations.

The solution to a subproblem at any stage always reflects optimal decisions for subproblems in previous stages. Thus, the subproblem solutions for the last stage reflect optimal decisions for all stages of the problem. This requires a backward orientation, which involves starting at the end and working back to the beginning. We should note that this orientation appears backwards only when there is a natural sequential order to the decision stages.

Once the subproblems for all stages have been solved, the optimal solution for the entire problem can be found. This is done by choosing the best subproblem solution in the last stage. The remaining optimal decisions can then be traced by following the pattern of decisions that were assumed in the best subproblem of that last stage.

If the number of possible solutions (those obtained by enumeration) is **447** compared with the number of subproblems that have to be solved, dynamic programming is an efficient method. That is, the number of subproblems that need to be solved are considerably less than the total number of feasible solutions. Nonetheless, we should point out that dynamic programming, like integer programming, can require excessive computational effort for large problems. Therefore, it may not be practical for problems with a large number of decision stages and many subproblems for each stage.

In Chapter 13 we will examine what are called heuristic programming procedures. These methods are most useful for those large problems that integer and dynamic programming procedures have the most difficulty with. Heuristic methods, however, do not always generate optimal solutions. They are, in fact, designed to generate good solutions. This they can usually do quickly and easily. Thus we trade off solution optimality to gain speed and ease of application.

Key Words

Backward orientation **427**	Principle of optimality **435**
Capital budgeting problem **423**	Probabilistic outcome **424**
Decision stage **426**	Purchase timing decision **443**
Decreasing marginal return **424**	Shortest-route problem **425**
Dynamic programming **423**	State-change option **434**
Enumeration **433**	State variables **434**
Expected value criterion **445**	States **434**
Network problem **425**	Stochastic outcome **424**
Nonlinear allocation problem **435**	Stochastic time-sequential
Nonlinear objective function **424**	problem **443**
Opportunity cost **443**	Subproblem **424**
Planning horizon **423**	Time-sequential decision **423**

Problems

12-1. Admiral Alfred Jones has responsibility for naval bases distributed throughout four naval districts. He has to fly from his headquarters to an important meeting in Washington next week and wishes to visit one base in each district en route. The bases, districts, and transportation costs between bases are shown below.

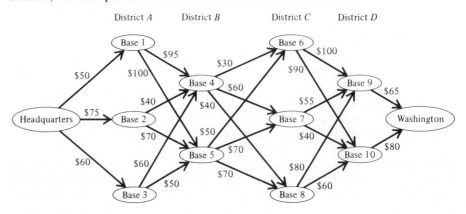

Determine which set of bases the admiral should visit so as to minimize the total cost of transportation.

12-2. Ruth Fillmore must replace her secretary who is leaving for a better-paying job. Ruth contacted an employment agency and arranged successive interviews with four candidates for the job. Each candidate will be given a typing test as part of the interview. Ruth wants to hire the candidate who can type fastest. From past experience, she estimates that the candidates are likely to have the following probabilities of typing speeds.

Typing speed, words per minute	Probability
40	.10
45	.15
50	.20
55	.25
60	.15
65	.10
70	.05

a. Suppose that Ruth interviews each candidate, administers the test, and chooses the candidate with the best speed. What is the probability that she will hire a candidate who can type as fast as 65 words per minute?

b. Suppose that Ruth must make a decision as to whether a candidate should be hired as soon as the interview for that candidate has been completed and before the remaining candidates have been seen. What hiring rules should Ruth use? What is the expected typing speed for the candidate hired?

12-3. The capital budgeting committee for the Tadley Corporation is reviewing research and development proposals for the coming year. The expected returns (in thousands of dollars) from these proposals are shown below for each of four departments.

Number of proposals funded	Department			
	A	B	C	D
1	5	7	4	6
2	12	10	12	11
3	17	16	16	18
4	25	22	21	22
5	28	25	25	29

The committee has determined that due to budget and personnel constraints, six projects at most can be funded. Clearly, no single department can have more than five projects funded. Determine the project funding allocation among departments that will yield the highest total expected return.

12-4. The Wister Company uses a 4-month planning horizon for manufacturing staffing decisions, which are based on aggregate sales estimates. The company estimates that it needs the following manufacturing work force to meet demands for the next 4 months:

Month	Work force needed
January	400
February	300
March	500
April	400

Hiring costs for any given month depend on the number hired, as shown below:

Number hired	Hiring cost
100	$10,000
200	$30,000

Because of the nature of the production process, employees must be hired in groups of 100. This is because 100 people are needed to staff an automated production line for one-shift operation. The personnel office has imposed a limit of no more than 200 employees hired in any given month. Thus, for any given month, three hiring options are available: (1) hire none, (2) hire 100, or (3) hire 200.

At present, the company has 300 manufacturing employees and at the end of the 4 months it has a specified target of 300 employed. Layoff costs are estimated to be:

Number laid off in 1 month	Layoff costs
100	$5,000
200	$12,000

As with hiring options, only three layoff options exist for any given month: (1) lay off none, (2) lay off 100, or (3) lay off 200. As an alternative to laying off excess employees, the company can keep them on the payroll as standby employees at an estimated cost of $9,000 per month per 100 employees.

Determine the optimal hiring/layoff plan for the Wister Manufacturing Company.

12-5. The Hayes Shipping Company is scheduling the loading of one of its oceangoing ships. The total capacity available for cargo is known to be 1,000 cubic feet. The following types of cargo are available for loading:

Cargo type	Number of units available	Revenue per unit	Size of unit, cubic feet
1	3	$2,600	125
2	3	$5,600	250
3	2	$9,000	375
4	2	$10,000	500

Determine the cargo loading plan that will yield the most revenue.

12-6. John Barker has invested $10,000 in 100 shares of stock currently selling at a price of $100 per share. John needs to sell the stock within the next 6 months, since he will be getting married at that time and wishes to use the money as a down payment on a house. A thorough reader of investment planning information, John has estimated that the following probabilities describe his expectations for the price he could get if he sells during any one of the 6 months:

Per-share selling price	Month					
	1	*2*	*3*	*4*	*5*	*6*
$80	.10	.15	.10	.10	.10	.15
$90	.20	.20	.15	.10	.15	.15
$100	.25	.25	.25	.20	.20	.20
$110	.25	.20	.25	.30	.25	.20
$120	.15	.10	.15	.20	.15	.20
$130	.05	.10	.10	.10	.15	.10

Determine an optimal selling plan for John that will maximize his expected return.

12-7. The Pigman Toy Company is about to bring out a new electronic game. The company is considering various options for this toy. The table below shows the profits the company expects over a 4-year period for various prices charged for the game, taking into account competitors' reactions, price elasticities of demand, and various other market factors.

Price charged	Expected profit, thousands of dollars, during year			
	1	*2*	*3*	*4*
$30	25	30	20	35
$31	18	22	28	32
$32	20	24	32	30
$33	32	28	24	28
$34	38	27	20	30
$35	34	25	18	32

   a. Assuming that the price can be changed freely from year to year, what prices would you recommend and what would be the total profit earned? (This can be solved by inspection and does not require the use of dynamic programming.)
   b. Assuming that the price can be changed up or down by only $1 from one year to the next, what pricing plan would you recommend and what would be the total profit earned?
   c. Assuming that company policy prohibits any price *increases,* what pricing plan would you recommend and what would be the total profit earned?

12-8. Jim Barrow is a contestant on the new Bell-Ringer Quiz Show. Jim is given $1,000 for answering a series of easy questions. He now has the option of playing the "Big Gamble." The Big Gamble has three rounds with the questions becoming progressively harder on each successive round.
   Two types of questions are available, easy and hard, with the following estimated probabilities of Jim's answering them correctly:

Question round	Probability of correct answer	
	Easy	*Hard*
1	.8	.4
2	.6	.25
3	.5	.2

If Jim answers any easy question correctly he doubles his money. If he answers a hard question correctly he quadruples his money. If he answers either question incorrectly, he loses all past winnings but is given a consolation prize of $1,000. If he wishes, Jim can pass any round without cost or he can stop at any point and take home his winnings. Determine an optimal question-answering strategy so that Jim can maximize his expected earnings.

12-9. The management training program of the Last National Bank is about to graduate eight trainees. Various bank departments were asked to identify how they might employ one or more of these trainees to improve operations. A summary of cost savings or profit improvements estimated by each of four departments is shown below in thousands of dollars.

Number of trainees assigned	Benefits obtained in department			
	W	X	Y	Z
1	7	10	5	8
2	13	8	10	13
3	18	19	15	22
4	22	25	21	19
5	29	28	25	24
6	33	31	26	30

Determine an assignment of trainees to departments that will maximize the total benefits to the firm.

Application: Scientific Worker Allocations to New Drug Screening Programs*

Pressures on research and development productivity and costs, and emphasis on earlier commercial exploitation of technology, coupled with an increasing number of attractive avenues for research, have made resource allocation an increasingly critical issue for R&D management.

In the late 1960s the authors were faced with a problem of allocating scientific and technical personnel at Smith Kline and French Laboratories to a number of primary screening programs which were clearly defined in terms of their product objective. We were able to solve this allocation problem through the application of dynamic programming as illustrated below.

The problem to be solved is that of assigning the available workers to the various research programs in such a manner as to optimize the total expected return from all the programs. In order to derive an expression for the total expected return, one requires:

1. A series of functions (one for each research program) which give probability of success in obtaining a marketable compound as a function of workers assigned to the research program.

*Adapted from E. B. Pyle III, B. Douglas, G. W. Ebright, W. J. Westlake, and A. D. Bender, "Scientific Manpower Allocation to New Drug Screening Programs," *Management Science*, vol. 19, no. 12 (August 1972), pp. 1433–1443.

2. A measure of the utility, or worth to the company, of a compound if it becomes a marketable product.

Once the above functions have been constructed, the assignment of workers to the research programs is a straightforward exercise in dynamic programming.

For each research program we had to screen a total of S compounds in order to find A of them that were active and worthy of secondary testing. Of the A actives, D of them would survive and would be taken into full-scale development. Out of the D compounds entering development, one of them would emerge as a marketable product. The probability P that at least one marketable product will be found for a specific program is defined as

$$p = 1 - \left(1 - \frac{1}{D}\right)^a \left(1 - \frac{1}{A}\right)^b \left(1 - \frac{1}{S}\right)^{cNt}$$

where a is the number of compounds in full-scale development, b is the number of active compounds undergoing secondary testing, c is the number of compounds that a single scientist can test per year in the primary screen, N is the number of scientists screening compounds (the decision variable), and t is the number of years over which the screen is to be considered active (usually equal to the planning horizon).

The second item required is the measure of utility of a compound if it becomes a marketable product. Originally, this measure was taken to be simply the expected peak sales.

Early in the development and implementation of the model, however, it became apparent that this measure had some severe drawbacks. Projects that would take a long time to produce were not differentiated from those that would produce early. It is also known that certain types of products are more costly to produce and market than other types. In addition, management became concerned about expected payoff from current and anticipated projects within specific time periods related to those for which long-range planning goals had been established.

Due to these deficiencies, we decided to use cumulative expected pretax profit over a specified time period as a function of workers assigned as the utility function. A computer program was developed for the model which determines optimal allocations for different levels of workers.

The model accepts the input data and produces a four-page output report. Page 1 is merely a recapitulation of all the input parameters for each project. Page 2 shows the cumulative expected pretax profit for the selected time periods as a function of worker levels for each project. This is the actual scoring table used by the dynamic programming algorithm and it is useful in determining the total payoff which would be obtained by assigning workers in some nonoptimal manner. It permits management to make tradeoffs between the economic factors and other qualitative factors influencing worker allocation and seeing the "price" which must be paid in making a nonoptimal allocation. Pages 3 and 4 show, respectively, the unrestricted and restricted allocations for each manpower level specified. The unrestricted allocations permit zero workers to be assigned to one or more projects in order to achieve the optimal return. The restricted allocations assume that every project will be operated with at least the minimum number of scientists required for screening. This necessarily results in a suboptimum solution for some worker levels. However, in many instances, qualitative factors dictate the necessity for maintaining some minimal effort on certain research programs and it is useful to see the economic effects for tradeoff purposes.

Since the initial problem was formulated in 1967, the model has been used as one input to the planning of research. Some of the benefits of a model as described here are that it assists in:

1. The definition (and thus understanding) of the problem and in making visible factors that bear on its solution.
2. The generation of many alternate solutions by modifying the inputs
3. The establishment of unknowns and uncertainty associated with the input which leads on some occasions to improving the procedures employed to gather relevant data.
4. The ability to test the impact of operational decisions on the outcome of the plan.

There are, of course, potential problems associated with the utilization of such techniques, and thus it is important to recognize what these are if they are to be minimized. One important area of concern is the impact that the use of these techniques by management may have on the generation of options and on the flow and transfer of technology. Or simply stated, the pursuit by management of quantitative methodologies can tend to limit people's thinking to only those options and alternatives which can fit the information requirement of the model. There is a potential, therefore, that the more certain and less risky projects will be suggested at the expense of the more risky and potentially more desirable projects. In this context, it should be emphasized that this model has been applied only to biological programs with fairly clear product objectives and also that it has served as one input to the process of resource allocation, with the final decision on allocation resting with management. On many occasions the "best solution" offered by the model has been rejected and other considerations included in reaching judgments concerning the best allocation of workers.

Discussion Questions

1. Explain in words the function for the probability that at least one marketable product will be found for a specific research program. What assumptions are implicit in this function?
2. Is this problem similar to any of the dynamic programming problems considered in the text? If so, what type of problem is this?
3. In terms of dynamic programming structure, how do you think the decision stages were defined? How were the subproblems for each stage defined?
4. What advantages does the use of cumulative expected pretax profit as the utility measure have over expected peak sales?
5. What type of sensitivity analysis was used? Can you identify any other areas where sensitivity analysis might be considered?
6. What might be done by management to minimize the problem described at the end of the article concerning the limitations that models impose on the generation of decision options?

13

Use of Heuristics in Problem Solving

Despite the great success achieved through the development and application of such management science optimization procedures as linear, integer, and dynamic programming, there remains a large number of practical problems for which these procedures are impractical. The size of these problems leads to computational requirements for such procedures that exceed the capability of current computers. For instance, although branch-and-bound procedures can be quite efficient at solving small to moderate combinatorial problems, the richness of potential solutions for large problems dooms even the most efficient methods to eventual failure.

Consider a sequencing or ordering problem which requires determining the best order of, say, 50 items, such as jobs to be processed by some machine facility. There are 50! possible orderings of these 50 items, which is equivalent to 3.04×10^{64}, an extremely large number. If a branch-and-bound procedure were used to solve this problem and it needed to explicitly examine as few as 2 percent of all the possible solutions, this would still leave $.02 \times 50! = (\frac{1}{50}) \times 50(49!) = 49!$ or 6.08×10^{62} solutions to consider. Even with a powerful computer that could examine as many as 1,000,000 solutions per second, it would take 1.9×10^{49} years to solve one problem. (This is roughly 19,000 billion billion billion billion billion years.)

Excessive computation time is not the only difficulty encountered in solving large problems. Required computer storage also tends to grow exponentially with an increase in problem size, rapidly exhausting available computer storage capacity.

These solution difficulties have led to the development of what are called *heuristic procedures.* They are used to generate *good* solutions to large problems but do not guarantee that these solutions will be optimal. In fact, except in a few instances, not only can we not guarantee optimality, we cannot even say how close the heuristic solution is to the optimal solution. Nevertheless, heuristic procedures have received increasing attention as models for problem solving. They are usually fast and easy to apply. Normally, they are based on sound, logical concepts and may offer the only means of handling difficult, realistic problems.

In this chapter we shall explore a few general approaches to developing good heuristic procedures. We shall see how heuristics can be used with optimizing techniques as well as on their own. We will also examine a few of the many areas to which heuristics have been applied. You may find this chapter of great practical interest because you can apply the concepts discussed to a multitude of problems by using a little ingenuity.

Heuristics as Problem Solvers

Although we will not be greatly concerned with precise definitions, it may be useful to think of a heuristic procedure as any *method of solving a problem that does not guarantee that the solution is optimal.* The word "heuristic" is derived from the Greek word *heuriskein*, which means "to discover." In general, heuristic procedures are an attempt to discover a good solution to a problem by applying a set of logically developed rules.

Heuristics as Search Procedures

It is useful to think of heuristic methods as *search procedures.* As discussed earlier, a characteristic common to problems for which heuristics are most useful is an extremely large number of potential solutions. Heuristic methods identify good solutions by searching a limited subset of the many solutions. The power and effectiveness of such a limited search is derived from the choice of logical rules that limit the search to regions, or areas, in which good solutions should exist. Frequently, these rules combine problem data with hypothesized characteristics of what good solutions should look like.

Classification of Heuristics

Although a number of different heuristic approaches exist, we will examine four broad categories: (1) *approximation heuristics*, (2) *truncation heuristics*, (3) *solution-generating heuristics*, and (4) *solution-improvement heuristics*. Approximation and truncation heuristics result from nonoptimal modifications to existing optimum procedures. Solution-generating heuristics use certain rules of thumb to develop problem solutions from scratch. Solution-improvement heuristics take some known solution and, through successive modifications, attempt to find better solutions.

As an example, consider a large integer programming problem with an objective function to be maximized and a single resource constraint. An illustration of an approximation heuristic would be to solve this problem as a straight linear programming problem, without the integer constraints. Then, round each noninteger result up or down, as necessary to stay within the resource constraint.

Alternatively, suppose that we use branch and bound to solve the problem. We could specify that if an optimal solution had not been found within a certain time limit (or after a certain number of steps have been performed), the best solution so far found is to be used as the solution to the problem. This is an example of a truncation heuristic in that solution has been stopped, or truncated, before completion.

A solution-generating heuristic for this integer problem might be based on a ratio of benefits to costs for each integer variable. Suppose each variable had an objective function coefficient c_i and a resource utilization rate a_i. We could define a benefit/cost ratio of c_i/a_i. A heuristic based on these ratios would be to add these variables to the solution in the order of the ratios c_i/a_i until all resources have been fully utilized.

A solution improvement heuristic begins with some known, feasible solution. The modifications made to this solution to obtain improvements might consist of all possible exchanges between some variable not now in the solution and one that is. If any such exchange of variables produces a better objective function value, we have found an improved solution. A similar series of exchanges can now be tried with this solution. Such exchanging can be continued until no further improvement is found.

Use of Heuristics with Optimizer

Usually, heuristics are considered as an alternative to optimization methods such as integer or dynamic programming procedures. But we should also point out that optimizing procedures themselves may incorporate or take advantage of heuristic methods. The simplex procedure for linear programming, for instance, uses a heuristic rule for determining which variable should next become basic. Recall that the simplex procedure always selected the variable with the highest positive (for maximization) or negative (for minimization) net-change value. Although this is a logical way in which to select the next variable to enter, it can easily be shown that this does not always lead to the best choice. Consider, for example, the following simple linear programming problem:

$$\text{Maximize:} \quad Z = 7A + 5B$$

$$\text{Subject to:} \quad 3A + B \leq 15$$

The graphical representation of this problem is shown in Figure 13-1. Observe that since variable A has the larger objective function coefficient (7), it would be chosen as the first variable to enter the solution (replacing the slack variable representing the single constraint). Clearly, however, variable B should be preferred to variable A because B is more conservative in its use of the scarce resource represented by the single constraint. Although A has the higher per-unit contribution, B can add more to total profit. The constraint will permit 3 units of B for every unit of A. Thus, a better rule to use in this case is to select the variable which will provide the largest total improvement in the objective function. However, this more sophisticated rule would entail more computation for each tableau and will not always be better than the one we use now.

Thus, the simplex rule of selecting the variable with the largest net change coefficient is in effect a heuristic rule. It does not guarantee that the variable so selected is in fact the best choice. Of course, this lack of guarantee that any individual choice is optimal is not a serious problem. Eventually the simplex

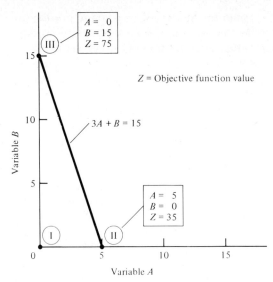

FIGURE 13-1   Graphical representation of simple linear programming problem.

method will reach the optimal solution. Indeed, in the simple example we used, represented by Figure 13-1, the very next iteration would have caused variable B to replace variable A. Thus, the optimal solution would have been found, although at the cost of one more iteration than necessary.

The procedures that we used to solve transportation problems, as described in Chapter 9, also illustrate how heuristic methods can be used with optimizing procedures. Recall that the choice of the next shipping route along which to reallocate was based on the per-unit net-change values. The unused route with the largest negative net-change value was always chosen for reallocation. Although this choice may be logical on a per-unit basis, the maximum reduction in total costs might be achieved by selecting a route with a smaller per-unit net-change value but which has a greater capacity for shipping units. Thus, it would have been better to ship, say, 30 units along a route which saves $3 per unit than to ship 10 units along a route that saves $5 per unit. For the same reasons discussed above for linear programming, the transportation method will eventually solve the problem optimally. The use of a heuristic route selection rule will, at worst, cost a few more iterations than would have been necessary if we could have chosen the routes optimally.

It should be pointed out that heuristic selection rules are used for both linear programming and transportation problems because no one knows of any selection rule, let alone an efficient selection rule, that will always make the optimal selection. To illustrate, suppose we had the following linear programming problem:

$$\text{Maximize:}\quad Z = 3C + 2D$$

$$\text{Subject to:}\quad C + D \le 10$$

$$C \le 5$$

$$D \le 8$$

$$C, D \ge 0$$

The feasible region for this problem is shown in Figure 13-2.

Now suppose that we use the more sophisticated variable selection rule in which the entering variable is that for which the (profit per unit) × (maximum number of units) is the greatest. Use of this rule would cause the simplex routine to move from node I to node V (rather than to node II), to node IV, and finally to the optimal node III.

Alternatively, if we had used the standard variable selection rule in which the entering variable is that with the highest profit per unit, we would have progressed from node I to node II, and finally to node III. Thus, the seemingly less sophisticated rule required one less tableau to be examined than did the more sophisticated rule.

Comparing the two selection rules for the problems shown in Figures 13-1 and 13-2 indicates that neither rule will always select the most efficient (i.e., smallest) set of tableaus. Thus both are heuristic rules.

Solving the transportation problem also illustrates another use of heuristics with optimizers. In order to apply the transportation procedure we required some feasible initial solution. We described one way that this initial solution could be generated, the northwest corner method. This method is heuristic because it does not guarantee that the solution found is optimal.

Approximation Methods

Approximation methods can be thought of as those that restructure the problem to be solved in such a way that it can be heuristically solved. This may involve relaxing or eliminating one or more constraints so that a problem that is intractable in its original form can be solved with some known procedure in its revised

FIGURE 13-2   Graphical representation of linear programming problem.

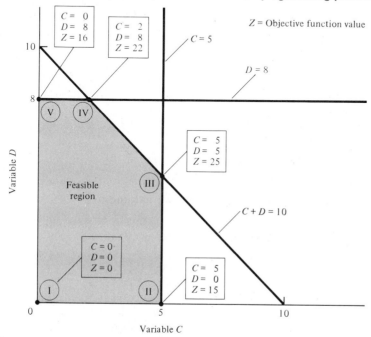

form. The solution to the revised problem may then have to be modified to make it a feasible solution to the original problem.

An example of this approach would be the *rounded linear programming* approach to solving integer or zero-one programming problems. The problem solved by the simplex linear programming algorithm is identical to the original problem except that the constraints requiring integer or zero-one values for the solution variables are temporarily ignored. The linear programming solution is then modified by rounding the variables to the nearest integer (or to 0 or 1 for a zero-one problem) value. Some care must be exercised when rounding to ensure that the resulting solution remains feasible. We saw an example of this in Chapter 11.

Truncation Methods

Truncation methods, as we discussed earlier, are normally optimization methods with prespecified stopping conditions that cause the procedure to finish its search prematurely without having identified, or at least proven, that the best solution found is optimal.

Truncation may result from a number of immediate effects, almost all of which are caused by a problem too large to solve optimally, given available computation resources. A common truncation condition is to specify a maximum amount of computer time to be used in the search. When that time has been exhausted, the procedure is halted and the best solution found in the time alloted is the heuristic solution to the problem. If the solution procedure is an iterative one, a limit can be placed on the number of iterations to be executed before truncation.

Another problem that may develop is a lack of sufficient computer storage to retain the results of calculations. This is a common problem with branch-and-bound methods, since each branching operation creates additional nodes for which some computer storage must be allocated. For large problems these nodes may be created at a faster rate than others are eliminated, and available computer storage becomes filled. One result of this is a need for a truncation of further search.

There are, however, ways in which the need for truncation caused by storage limitations can be reduced. As discussed in Chapter 11, where branch-and-bound methods were used to solve integer programming problems, the rule used to choose the next node to branch from can have a significant impact on storage requirements. One of the most efficient rules in terms of nodes examined is always to branch from the node with the best bound. However, it is also the most wasteful in terms of storage requirements. Always branching from the last node created is normally more efficient from a storage viewpoint. But it is less efficient in terms of computation time.

A combination of these two rules may be an effective compromise. Under this approach the best node rule could be used until storage requirements reached some specified maximum level. At that point, the newest node rule would be used until storage requirements dropped below some minimum level, when the procedure would revert to the best node rule.

Another approach to dealing with storage capacity problems is to discard a number of nodes when the storage limit is reached, freeing up capacity for further search. Of course, this tactic introduces some likelihood that the eventual solution found is not optimal; one of the discarded nodes could have led to the optimal solution. Another problem with this approach is developing a mechanism for deciding which nodes to discard.

Another truncation method is designed to yield a solution that is within some guaranteed distance from the optimum. With this approach the decision maker specifies some limit of acceptability for a heuristic solution, such as "within 5 percent of the optimum." This limit is then used as a criterion for stopping the search. In effect, this represents a satisfying approach. It recognizes that the benefits to be achieved from further search are likely to be less than the cost.

Recall that the value of the optimal solution is not normally known. However, when a branch-and-bound method is used, we do calculate a bound for each node, which represents an upper limit on the value of the solutions that can be obtained by further branching from that node. The best of these bounds thus represents an upper limit on the value of any solutions that might be found by further search. As soon as some feasible solution is found that is within the prespecified acceptability range from the current best bound, search would be truncated. Note that the acceptable error range is actually an upper bound on the true error. Although the best solution found may be 5 percent from the best bound at the time of truncation, there is no guarantee that this best bound can be achieved by some feasible solution. In fact, the best solution found may be optimal.

In the case of certain iterative procedures, successive iterations provide solutions whose value approaches that of the optimal solution asymptotically. In other words, each successive iteration provides a solution which is improved at a decreasing marginal rate.

Solution-Generating Heuristics

The largest category of heuristics is that in which a heuristic solution is built from scratch. Some of these are *deterministic methods* consisting of a set of rules that when applied lead to the development of a single heuristic solution. Other heuristics use rules that are *probabilistic* in nature and are capable of generating a number of solutions to the problem. By means of examples we will demonstrate both types below.

Deterministic Generating Heuristic

A common type of deterministic procedure is sometimes called the *greedy heuristic*. Greedy heuristics are so called because they take what appears to be the best immediate option. The variable selection rule in the linear programming simplex procedure is a greedy heuristic, always selecting the variable with the largest per-unit contribution to the objective function. The procedure we used to find the minimal spanning tree in Chapter 10 is also a greedy procedure. We always chose the shortest route to add to the spanning tree. For this problem, however, the greedy approach was optimal, rather than heuristic. Let us illustrate the use of a deterministic heuristic by means of an example.

The Raytone Television Company manufactures a complete line of television sets which it distributes on a regional basis. At present the company supplies these sets to wholesalers from its factory in Atlanta. Due to a proposed

**TABLE 13-1
Annual Fixed Operating Costs for
Potential Warehouse Sites**

Warehouse location	Annual fixed costs
Atlanta	$300,000
Charleston	$250,000
Knoxville	$220,000
Memphis	$200,000
Richmond	$240,000

expansion of its product line, existing warehouse space at the factory is to be taken over by manufacturing operations. This fact, plus complaints from some of the wholesalers concerning lengthy shipping delays from Atlanta, have caused Raytone to consider establishing a decentralized warehousing system with a number of smaller warehouses distributed throughout a geographical region.

As a first step they have identified a set of key cities as potential warehouse sites. Five cities—Atlanta, Charleston, Knoxville, Memphis, and Richmond—have been chosen. Table 13-1 shows the annual fixed operating costs estimated for each site.

Any warehousing system selected must satisfy the demands of eight major wholesalers. These are located in Atlanta, Birmingham, Charleston, Knoxville, Louisville, Memphis, Nashville, and Richmond. The cost of shipping from the factory to each potential warehouse site, and then from that warehouse to the wholesaler, has been estimated on the basis of annual demand from each wholesaler. These cost figures are shown in Table 13-2. These are not per-unit costs, but represent the cost of shipping the number of units required annually from the factory to the warehouse to the wholesaler. Thus, if the Charleston warehouse supplies the Atlanta wholesaler, it will cost the company $378,000 annually. For later convenience, the lowest cost for supplying each of the wholesalers is circled.

As can be seen from the analysis above, the problem of selecting a set of warehouses involves two costs: the fixed costs associated with each warehouse (Table 13-1) and the transportation costs of supplying each wholesaler from one of the warehouses (Table 13-2). The fixed warehouse cost can be minimized by opening a single warehouse. The transportation cost would be minimized by opening all five warehouses. Minimization of the total of these two costs will require tradeoffs. For example, although Memphis has the lowest fixed cost, it would *not* be the least-expensive single warehouse to operate because of higher transportation costs. Knoxville has the lowest annual cost for a single warehouse: $220,000 (fixed) + $1,102,000 (transportation) = $1,322,000 (total).

With only five potential warehouse sites, we could enumerate all possible combinations and evaluate each one. The number of potential solutions for n warehouses is $2^n - 1$. Thus, with 5 possible warehouses there would be $2^5 - 1 = 31$ possible solutions. Unfortunately, for larger, more practical problems, the number of possible solutions can be prohibitively large. For instance, with 25 potential sites, there would be 33,554,431 possible combinations, far too many to permit the enumeration and evaluation of each combination.

TABLE 13-2
Cost of Supplying Wholesaler Annual Demand from Potential Warehouse Sites

Wholesaler location	Warehouse sites				
	Atlanta	Charleston	Knoxville	Memphis	Richmond
Atlanta	$54,000	$378,000	$216,000	$432,000	$486,000
Birmingham	$64,000	$80,000	$48,000	$64,000	$176,000
Charleston	$182,000	$26,000	$130,000	$234,000	$104,000
Knoxville	$48,000	$60,000	$12,000	$72,000	$72,000
Louisville	$288,000	$144,000	$252,000	$216,000	$288,000
Memphis	$192,000	$216,000	$180,000	$24,000	$288,000
Nashville	$126,000	$147,000	$84,000	$63,000	$189,000
Richmond	$240,000	$120,000	$180,000	$360,000	$30,000

Note: Circled values represent the cheapest route for each wholesaler.

This suggests that a heuristic procedure may be quite useful. We shall examine two such heuristics developed by A. A. Kuehn and M. J. Hamburger which could be called greedy heuristics.[1] One is called the *add heuristic*. Here solutions are developed by iteratively adding warehouses to a set of warehouses to be opened until the total cost (fixed and variable) cannot be reduced further. The procedure begins by selecting the single warehouse that can satisfy all customer demand with the lowest total cost. Suppose, for example, that Knoxville turned out to be the cheapest single warehouse.

Next we try all possible combinations of the best single warehouse (Knoxville) with each of the remaining warehouses. Suppose the combination of Knoxville and Atlanta is the lowest-total-cost combination. If the total cost for the Knoxville/Atlanta pair is lower than that for Knoxville alone, we continue with the add procedure by trying all possible combinations of the best warehouse pair (Knoxville/Atlanta) with each of the remaining warehouses. As long as total costs are reduced by adding another warehouse, the procedure continues. As soon as the addition of one more warehouse fails to lower total cost, the procedure stops with the lowest total cost combination selected as the solution.

The second heuristic is called the *drop heuristic* and proceeds in a manner opposite to that of the add heuristic. We begin by evaluating all warehouse combinations in which a single warehouse is dropped or not used. If the cost of the best all-but-one combination is lower than the cost of opening all the warehouses, we continue by trying all possible combinations that delete a second warehouse from our best all-but-one combination. As with the add heuristic, the drop heuristic continues to drop successive warehouses until total costs cannot be lowered further.

Add Hueristic Let us illustrate how the add heuristic can be applied to our example problem. We begin by evaluating the total cost of using each of the five potential warehouse sites by itself. For instance, if Atlanta is the only open warehouse, we incur fixed costs of $300,000 (Table 13-1) and transportation

[1]A. A. Kuehn and M. J. Hamburger, "A Heuristic Program for Locating Warehouses," *Management Science*, vol. 9, no. 4 (1963), pp. 643–666.

TABLE 13-3
Evaluation of all Single-Warehouse Options

Warehouse	Fixed cost	Transportation cost	Total cost
Atlanta	$300,000	$1,194,000	$1,494,000
Charleston	$250,000	$1,171,000	$1,421,000
Knoxville	$220,000	$1,102,000	$1,322,000*
Memphis	$200,000	$1,465,000	$1,665,000
Richmond	$240,000	$1,633,000	$1,873,000

*Lowest-cost option.

costs equal to the sum of the entries in the first column of Table 13-2; these transportation costs come to $1,194,000. Thus, the total cost of supplying all wholesalers from an Atlanta warehouse would be $300,000 + $1,194,000 = $1,494,000. We can perform a similar analysis for each of the other warehouse sites, leading to the results shown in Table 13-3.

If the company decides to open only one warehouse, the lowest-cost site would be Knoxville with annual costs of $1,322,000, as shown in Table 13-3. The next step for the add heuristic is to see whether costs can be lowered by opening a second warehouse in addition to that at Knoxville. Four sites are available as second warehouses, Atlanta, Charleston, Memphis, and Richmond. We examine each of these options in turn.

Consider, for instance, the Knoxville and Memphis combination. Fixed costs for these two sites are $220,000 and $200,000, respectively, for a total fixed cost of $420,000. The appropriate transportation cost would be found by assigning each wholesaler to either Knoxville or Memphis depending on which warehouse can supply that wholesaler at the cheapest transport cost. For example, to supply the Atlanta wholesaler will cost $216,000 from Knoxville and $432,000 from Memphis. Thus, the Atlanta wholesaler would be assigned to Knoxville. Considering each of the wholesalers, we find that Knoxville should supply wholesalers at Atlanta, Birmingham, Charleston, Knoxville, and Richmond, while the remaining wholesalers will be handled by Memphis.

Adding the transportation costs based on these assignments, we find that the annual transportation costs necessary to supply all wholesalers from either Knoxville or Memphis is $889,000. Adding this to the fixed cost of $420,000, we find total annual costs to be $1,309,000, which is $13,000 cheaper per year than using Knoxville by itself. Thus, adding Memphis must have reduced transportation costs by $213,000 in order to offset the $200,000 fixed costs at Memphis and still lower total costs by $13,000.

Calculations for each of the other options are summarized in Table 13-4. The lowest total cost was achieved from the Charleston/Knoxville pair. Since this cost was cheaper than that for the best single warehouse, the add heuristic next considers all possible three-warehouse configurations that include Charleston and Knoxville. Three such combinations exist, with the added warehouse being Atlanta, Memphis, or Richmond.

INSTANT REPLAY Suppose we have the following set of potential warehouses, customers, annual fixed costs, and annual shipping charges.

	Potential warehouse site			
Customer	A	B	C	D
U	$14,000	$10,000	$12,000	$15,000
V	$22,000	$21,000	$19,000	$20,000
W	$3,000	$8,000	$7,000	$5,000
X	$13,000	$17,000	$10,000	$12,000
Y	$4,000	$5,000	$6,000	$7,000
Z	$10,000	$9,000	$8,000	$7,000
Warehouse fixed cost	$25,000	$32,000	$28,000	$30,000

Determine first the lowest-cost single warehouse. Then, using this warehouse, find the lowest-cost pair of warehouses.

CHECK The lowest-cost single warehouse is warehouse C, with transportation costs of $62,000 and fixed costs of $28,000, for a total cost of $90,000. The lowest-cost pair that includes C consists of A and C. This combination has shipping costs of $56,000 and fixed costs of $53,000 for a total of $109,000.

We find the costs for three-warehouse combinations in a manner similar to that for the warehouse pairs. Fixed costs for the three warehouses are added. Transportation costs are determined by assigning each wholesaler to the warehouse that can supply the wholesaler's demand with the lowest annual cost. For example, given the warehouse combination of Atlanta, Charleston, and Knoxville, we find that the Atlanta warehouse will supply only the Atlanta wholesaler, the Charleston warehouse will supply Charleston, Louisville, and Richmond, and the Knoxville warehouse will supply the rest. Transportation costs for this assignment total $668,000.

The cost calculations for each three-warehouse option are shown in Table 13-5. The best of these adds Memphis to the Charleston/Knoxville combination; however, the cost of this best three-warehouse combination is $1,323,000, which is $23,000 greater than that for the best two-warehouse combination. It should be obvious that continuing the add heuristic will be fruitless: if the addition of a fourth warehouse is beneficial, it should have been beneficial when that warehouse was considered as the third warehouse. Therefore the best solution found by the add heuristic is to operate warehouses at Charleston and Knoxville with total annual operating costs of $1,300,000.

TABLE 13-4
Evaluation of All Two-Warehouse Configurations that Include Knoxville

Warehouses	Fixed cost	Transportation cost	Total cost
Atlanta, Knoxville	$520,000	$940,000	$1,460,000
Charleston, Knoxville	$470,000	$830,000	$1,300,000*
Memphis, Knoxville	$420,000	$889,000	$1,309,000
Richmond, Knoxville	$460,000	$926,000	$1,386,000

*Lowest-cost option.

TABLE 13-5
Evaluation of All Three-Warehouse Configurations that Include Charleston and Knoxville

Warehouses	Fixed cost	Transportation cost	Total cost
Charleston, Knoxville, Atlanta	$770,000	$668,000	$1,438,000
Charleston, Knoxville, Memphis	$670,000	$653,000	$1,323,000*
Charleston, Knoxville, Richmond	$710,000	$740,000	$1,450,000

*Lowest-cost option.

INSTANT REPLAY   What would the total cost be for the three-warehouse combination of Knoxville, Memphis, and Richmond? Which customers would be served by each warehouse?

CHECK   Fixed costs of $660,000 and transportation costs of $713,000 yield a total cost of $1,373,000. Knoxville would serve wholesalers at Atlanta, Birmingham, and Knoxville. Memphis would serve Louisville, Memphis, and Nashville. Richmond would serve Charleston and Richmond.

Drop Heuristic   Next let us consider the drop heuristic. To do this we first calculate the cost of operating all five warehouses. Fixed costs total $1,210,000 and transportation costs are $401,000, based on each wholesaler being supplied by the lowest-cost warehouse (sum of the circled amounts in Table 13-2). This produces a total cost of $1,611,000.

The drop heuristic begins by examining the possible four-warehouse configurations that result from dropping each of the five potential sites. For instance, dropping Atlanta will lower fixed costs to $910,000 and will raise transportation costs by $162,000 to $563,000, a net decrease of $138,000. Observe that the transportation costs are calculated as before, each wholesaler supplied by the cheapest undropped warehouse. Results are shown in Table 13-6.

The best four-warehouse configuration results when Knoxville was dropped. The next step with the drop heuristic is to evaluate each of the possible three-warehouse configurations that remain after dropping one additional warehouse. A summary of these evaluations is reported in Table 13-7.

Since the best three-warehouse combination includes Atlanta, Charles-

TABLE 13-6
Evaluation of All Four-Warehouse Configurations

Warehouses	Fixed cost	Transportation cost	Total cost
Charleston, Knoxville, Memphis, Richmond	$910,000	$563,000	$1,473,000
Atlanta, Knoxville, Memphis, Richmond	$960,000	$551,000	$1,511,000
Atlanta, Charleston, Memphis, Richmond	$990,000	$453,000	$1,443,000*
Atlanta, Charleston, Knoxville, Richmond	$1,010,000	$578,000	$1,588,000
Atlanta, Charleston, Knoxville, Memphis	$970,000	$491,000	$1,461,000

*Lowest-cost option.

TABLE 13-7
Evaluation of All Three-Warehouse Configurations that Exclude Knoxville

Warehouses	Fixed cost	Transportation cost	Total cost
Charleston, Memphis, Richmond	$690,000	$789,000	$1,479,000
Atlanta, Memphis, Richmond	$740,000	$603,000	$1,343,000
Atlanta, Charleston, Richmond	$790,000	$684,000	$1,474,000
Atlanta, Charleston, Memphis	$750,000	$543,000	$1,293,000*

*Lowest-cost option.

ton, and Memphis and the total cost of this combination is $1,293,000, or $150,000 less than for the best four-warehouse configuration, the drop heuristic continues by examining each two-warehouse combination that can be formed by dropping one of the three warehouses. Table 13-8 contains the results of this search.

The Atlanta/Charleston pair had the lowest total cost among the group of two-warehouse combinations. Note, however, that this cost was actually higher than that for the best three-warehouse group by $31,000. Therefore, the drop heuristic would be terminated with the Atlanta, Charleston, and Memphis configuration designated as the best solution found.

Comparison of Add and Drop Solutions   A comparison of the best solutions found by the add and the drop heuristics shows that the combination found by the drop heuristic—Atlanta, Charleston, and Memphis—had the lowest total cost, $1,293,000 as opposed to $1,300,000 for the best add combination—Charleston and Knoxville.

It should be noted that the add and drop approaches used for this problem have one advantage not found with many heuristics. Both procedures generate several heuristic solutions as candidate solutions to the problem. This allows management to introduce other objectives in making their final selection, and if they select a solution other than that with the lowest cost, they have objective information concerning how much cost they are willing to absorb to achieve that objective.

In the Raytone case, the difference in cost between the add and the drop solutions was only $7,000. It may therefore be desirable for them to consider other intangible factors. For instance, does the firm have enough resources to open three warehouses now (as called for by the lowest-cost solution), or would it be better to expand more slowly by opening only two warehouses?

TABLE 13-8
Evaluation of All Two-Warehouse Configurations that Exclude Knoxville and Richmond

Warehouses	Fixed cost	Transportation cost	Total cost
Charleston, Memphis	$450,000	$879,000	$1,329,000
Atlanta, Memphis	$500,000	$891,000	$1,391,000
Atlanta, Charleston	$550,000	$774,000	$1,324,000*

*Lowest-cost option.

INSTANT REPLAY Suppose Raytone Television Company wishes to implement the decentralized distribution system in stages. Although the company eventually wishes to move to the best three-warehouse configuration, it wants to begin with some two-warehouse combination on a trial basis for 1 year. How should Raytone proceed, and what will this staged implementation plan cost it?

CHECK The best three-warehouse combination was Atlanta, Charleston, and Memphis. Table 13-8 shows total costs for any two of these three, the lowest being Atlanta and Charleston. Thus, the company should open the Atlanta and Charleston warehouses for the first year, adding the Memphis warehouse later. The cost of this staged policy is the difference between the three-warehouse combination and the chosen two-warehouse configuration, or $1,324,000 − $1,293,000 = $31,000.

Probabilistic Generating Heuristics

The add and drop heuristics used to solve the warehouse location problem are deterministic in that, if repeatedly applied to the same problem, they will always generate the same set of solutions. In this section we consider another class of heuristics which allows the generation of as many solutions as desired. This variety is achieved by making the heuristic rules probabilistic rather than deterministic. This approach will be illustrated by means of an example.

Consider the Carp Toy Company, which is designing a production line for a new action toy that the company hopes to introduce during the coming Christmas season. Assembling this toy requires nine separate tasks which must be accomplished in a somewhat limited order as shown by the *precedence diagram* in Figure 13-3. The letters *A* through *I* represent the individual tasks and the arrows indicate precedence. Thus, before task *E* can be accomplished, both tasks *C* and *D* must have been completed. The numbers next to each task represent the time in minutes necessary to complete that task.

On the basis of expected demand for the toy, management has set a target production rate of one unit every 16 minutes. This rate will produce 30 units

FIGURE 13-3 Precedence requirements and task times (in minutes) for Carp Toy Company problem.

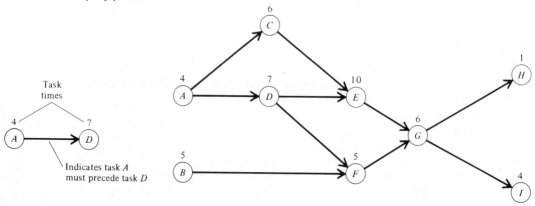

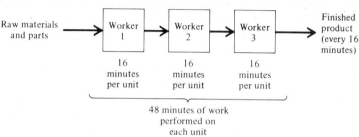

FIGURE 13-4   Division of work to achieve a 16-minute cycle time.

each 8-hour shift. The total time to complete one unit is 48 minutes, which is equal to the sum of the individual task times. The assembly process must, therefore, utilize at least three workers, each with 16 minutes of assigned work per unit. This division of work into 16-minute groupings will permit a unit to be assembled every 16 minutes, which is the desired production rate. This is illustrated in Figure 13-4.

The problem faced by management is to assign the tasks to these workers so that each has 16 minutes of work and none of the precedence relationships are violated. For example, one worker might be assigned tasks A, B, and D. This assigns $4 + 5 + 7 = 16$ minutes of work to that person, meeting the time requirement. In addition, none of the precedence requirements are violated: tasks A and B have no predecessors and task D can be done after task A. Note, however, that assigning task G to the second worker and task E to the third worker is not allowed. This would violate the precedence requirement that task E must be done before task G. An assignment of tasks A, C, and D to one worker would also not be permitted because the total work assigned requires $4 + 6 + 7 = 17$ minutes, which exceeds the 16-minute limit for each worker.

This example problem is simple enough that you can probably determine a feasible assignment by inspection. In practice, however, assembly operations may involve hundreds of tasks with many precedence relationships. For these problems solution by inspection is impractical.

We will examine a heuristic method of solving this problem which can generate as many solutions as desired. It is useful to view the solution of the problem as a series of interrelated decisions, each decision requiring the selection of one task from among those available for assignment to a particular worker. Tasks available for assignment at any decision point are constrained by whether their predecessor tasks have already been assigned and whether or not the worker has enough time to accomplish them. For instance, if we begin with the first worker, only two tasks, A and B, are available for assignment. All other tasks cannot be done until A, B, or both, have been finished. Until task B is completed, tasks F, G, H, and I cannot be started. Until task A is completed, tasks C, D, E, F, G, H, and I are prevented from being started. Since each worker has 16 minutes of available time, either A or B could be assigned at this point since neither takes more than 16 minutes.

As a further illustration, suppose previous decisions had first assigned tasks A and C to the first worker. Tasks B and D are now available for assignment since their precedence relationships have been satisfied. Note, however, that this first worker has only 6 minutes of time available for further work, since tasks A and C use up 10 of the worker's 16 minutes. Task B could be assigned to this worker since it requires only 5 minutes, but task D could not, since it takes

7 minutes to complete. Thus, only task B satisfies both precedence and time limitations, and is the only candidate task for this assignment decision.

The heuristic to be described here, which was developed by Albert L. Arcus, consists of three simple steps:[1]

1. Identify tasks available for assignment that satisfy precedence and time constraints.
2. Use a probabilistic rule to select one of the available tasks and assign it to the earliest worker with time available.
3. Return to step 1 if more tasks remain to be assigned.

Arcus proposed a number of different probabilistic rules that could be used in making a selection from the available tasks. These rules determine a probability of selection for each task that is based on some heuristic measure. The simplest is the pure random rule which gives each task an equal probability of being selected. Thus, with two available tasks, each would have a probability of .5 of being chosen. If there were five tasks, each would be given a .2 probability of selection.

The other rules proposed by Arcus attempt to bias the selection toward those tasks that seem better suited for a particular assignment. One such rule yields probabilities proportional to the task times. A task with a longer task time would be given a greater probability of selection than one with a shorter task time. For instance, suppose that tasks A and B are the only tasks available for selection. B would be given a higher probability than A because, as Figure 13-3 shows, it has a larger time. Specifically, each task would be assigned a probability equal to the ratio of its time relative to the total time for all available tasks. At this point either A or B must be chosen; no other tasks are available for assignment. Since the total time for tasks A and B is $4 + 5 = 9$, task A would be given a selection probability of $\frac{4}{9}$ and task B a probability of $\frac{5}{9}$. The rationale for this probability assignment is based on the hypothesis that if the longer tasks are assigned first, it will be easier to fit the smaller tasks in later.

Let us now illustrate how the heuristic can be applied to the example problem. To demonstrate, we will use the probability rule that assigns probabilities proportional to task times. The initial step, that of identifying the tasks available for assignment, was described earlier. Tasks A and B are the only tasks with all precedence relationships satisfied. Since the two tasks take 4 and 5 minutes, respectively, we determine that task A should have a $\frac{4}{9}$ chance of selection and task B a $\frac{5}{9}$ chance.

The exact method of selecting between these two tasks in a way representative of the assigned probabilities will be dealt with more fully in Chapter 20, where we deal with simulation. It is sufficient for our purposes here to note that if the selection of task A or B were repeated many times, on average we would expect task A to be chosen $\frac{4}{9}$ of the time and task B $\frac{5}{9}$.

Suppose, for purposes of illustration, that task A was selected. This task would be assigned to the first worker which reduces his available time to $16 - 4 = 12$ minutes. The assignment of task A completes the precedence requirements for tasks C and D, so that the tasks available for the second assignment are B, C, and D. All three tasks take less than 12 minutes, so any one could be assigned to the first worker.

[1]A. L. Arcus, "COMSOAL: A Computer Method of Sequencing Operations for Assembly Lines," in *Readings in Production and Operations Management*, E. Buffa (ed.), Wiley, New York, 1966, pp. 336–360.

The total time for the three tasks is $5 + 6 + 7 = 18$ minutes and they would be assigned probabilities of selection of $\frac{5}{18}$ for B, $\frac{6}{18}$ for C, and $\frac{7}{18}$ for D. Suppose that task D is chosen for assignment to the first worker. This reduces that worker's available time to $12 - 7 = 5$ minutes. The assignment of task D does not make any additional tasks available for selection. The two tasks blocked by D (E and F) remain blocked by as yet unassigned tasks C (blocks E) and B (blocks F). Thus, our candidate tasks are B and C. Note, however, that task C requires 6 minutes, which exceeds the remaining available time for the first worker, so task B, which does fit the worker's capacity, is the only remaining task available for assignment at this point.

Task B would therefore be automatically assigned to the first worker. This accomplishes two things. First, worker 1 now has tasks assigned that use up the full 16 minutes. Thus, the next assignment will be made to the second worker. Furthermore, now that task B has been assigned, the precedence requirements for task F have been completed, and the group of tasks available for assignment now includes tasks C and F, both of which will fit within the second worker's capacity.

Task C would be given a selection probability of $\frac{6}{11}$ and task F $\frac{5}{11}$. Suppose that task F is selected. The assignment of task F reduces the second worker's capacity to $16 - 5 = 11$ minutes but does not increase the set of tasks available for assignment. Since task C is the only candidate task at this point and requires less time than the second worker has available, it is assigned to that worker.

The second worker now has $11 - 6 = 5$ minutes of remaining capacity. The assignment of task C completes the precedence requirements for task E. However task E requires 10 minutes to complete, which exceeds the remaining time for the second worker and therefore cannot be assigned to that worker. Since no other candidates exist for assignment, we have no choice but to assign task E to the third worker.

This means that the second worker will only have 11 minutes of work to complete for each unit produced. In addition, since tasks E, G, H, and I are yet to be assigned and they total 21 minutes of work, we know that at least two additional workers will be needed to complete all assignments. Thus, the solution so far generated will require at least four workers and cannot possibly achieve a perfectly balanced assignment with three workers.

If we are insistent upon having a perfect balance, we would abandon this solution attempt and return to the start, hoping that the next or some future set of selections will achieve the desired goal. For our purposes, however, let us assume that we are unconvinced that a perfect balance can be found and therefore let us continue with the current solution.

As stated above, task E must be assigned to the third worker. This reduces that worker's available time to $16 - 10 = 6$ minutes and completes the precedence requirements for task G. Since this is the only task now available, it would also be assigned to the third worker completing his set of tasks for a total of 16 minutes of work. Tasks H and I are now available. Regardless of the order in which they are selected, they would be assigned to the fourth worker. The steps that we followed in making assignments are summarized in Table 13-9.

The solution obtained is not very good. Four workers are required, and the line is not well balanced. Two workers have 16 minutes of work assigned per unit (no idle time), one worker has 11 minutes of work (5 minutes of idle time), and the fourth has only 5 minutes of work (11 minutes of idle time). Of course, the advantage of a probabilistic heuristic is not that every solution will

TABLE 13-9
Summary of Assignment Decisions for Carp Toy Company Problem

Step	Available* tasks	Feasible† tasks	Task time	Probability‡ of selection	Task selected	Assigned to worker
1	A	A	4	$\frac{4}{9}$	A	1
	B	B	5	$\frac{5}{9}$		
2	B	B	5	$\frac{5}{18}$		
	C	C	6	$\frac{6}{18}$		
	D	D	7	$\frac{7}{18}$	D	1
3	B	B	5	1	B	1
	C					
4	C	C	6	$\frac{6}{11}$		
	F	F	5	$\frac{5}{11}$	F	2
5	C	C	6	1	C	2
6	E					
7	E	E	10	1	E	3
8	G	G	6	1	G	3
9	H	H	1	$\frac{1}{5}$		
	I	I	4	$\frac{4}{5}$	I	4
10	H	H	1	1	H	4

*Tasks whose precedence requirements have been met.
†Tasks whose precedence requirements have been met and fit the worker's capacity.
‡Selection probability proportional to task time.

be a good one, but that repeated application of the procedure will eventually lead to a reasonably good solution, if one exists. In addition, the cost of obtaining probabilistic solutions is relatively low.

Table 13-10 shows several task/worker assignment patterns that may have resulted from subsequent applications of this probabilistic heuristic. Note that the first solution is identical to the one that we developed. Also observe that a perfect assignment, requiring only three workers, is possible as shown by solutions 2, 4, and 6.

INSTANT REPLAY   What solution would result if the task with the highest probability (based on task time ratios) was always selected at each decision point?

CHECK   A three-worker assignment would have been found with tasks assigned (in order) as: B, A, and D to worker 1; C and E to worker 2; and F, G, I, and H to worker 3.

The variety of solutions achievable with this heuristic is enhanced by the availability of a number of probability assignment rules. Arcus proposed many rules that included, for example, those that assign probabilities proportional to: (1) the number of immediate followers of a task (those for which this task is an immediate predecessor), (2) the number of all followers of a task (those for which this task is a predecessor, immediate or otherwise), and (3) the sum of the time of a task and the times of its followers.

The rationale for (1) is that by assigning tasks with many immediate followers, we quickly expand the number of tasks available for assignment, increasing assignment flexibility. The rationale for (2) is that tasks with a large number of followers are in a sense key tasks since they block the assignment of many others. Rule (3) is similar to (2) except that the task times of blocked tasks are used rather than a simple count of the number of tasks. A task which blocks long-duration tasks is given preference to one which blocks short-duration tasks. (These are easier to fit in later than would be longer tasks.)

Thus, great flexibility exists for trying many repetitions to obtain better solutions to the problem. Variability can be introduced by using different probability biasing rules or by repeating the procedure over and over with the same biasing rule.

Solution-Improvement Heuristics

Solution-improvement heuristics are a very powerful class of general-purpose heuristics. They operate by transforming some known initial solution into successively better and better solutions, stopping when no further improvement can be found. Although they generally operate deterministically, they do offer the advantage of variety that probabilistic methods have. This variety is obtained by repeatedly restarting the process with some new initial solution.

Improvement heuristics are sometimes called *local optimizers*. The final solution obtained, after successive transformations of the initial solution, is optimal, in a limited sense, in that it cannot be improved by further transformations of the type used. These are *local optimals,* however, because there is no guarantee that some other transformation method would not lead to a better solution.

It is useful to view solution-improvement methods as consisting of three components: (1) a method of obtaining a starting, or base, solution; (2) a transformation procedure; and (3) a criterion for selecting the best transformed solution as the base for the next series of transformations.

Finding a Base Solution

The initial base solution is often obtained by applying one or more solution-generating heuristics. For example, the northwest-corner method solution

TABLE 13-10
Potential Worker/Task Assignments for Carp Toy Company Problem

Solution no.	Tasks assigned to worker			
	1	*2*	*3*	*4*
1	*ADB*	*FC*	*EG*	*IH*
2	*ABD*	*CE*	*FGHI*	
3	*BAC*	*DF*	*EG*	*HI*
4	*BAD*	*CE*	*FGIH*	
5	*BAD*	*CF*	*EG*	*HI*
6	*ADB*	*CE*	*FGHI*	

found for a transportation problem could serve as the base solution for a solution-improvement heuristic. The same could be said of the solutions found by the add and drop procedures or the Arcus probabilistic heuristics.

If a large number of base solutions are desired, it is frequently possible to generate them randomly. For instance, in the warehouse location problem, slips of paper with numbers corresponding to specific warehouse sites could be drawn from a hat to generate as many base solutions as desired.

Transformation Procedure

The method of transformation used depends on the type of problem being solved. Normally these transformations involve minor changes from one solution to the next and can be thought of as fine-tuning devices.

Solutions for some problems can be changed by rearranging elements. For instance, a solution to the sequencing problem consisted of a sequence of jobs. One method of rearranging might be to switch the order, or sequence position, of two adjacent jobs. Suppose that the base sequence was 2, 1, 3, 5, 4. Swapping adjacent jobs 2 and 1 would lead to a transformed sequence of 1, 2, 3, 5, 4. Applying this rule to other potential swaps would lead to 2, 3, 1, 5, 4 (jobs 1 and 3 swapped), 2, 1, 5, 3, 4 and 2, 1, 3, 4, 5. Note that this swapping always involved jobs that were adjacent in the original base sequence.

Solutions to many other problems can be transformed by dropping one item and adding another. The warehouse location problem is an excellent example of this class of problems. To illustrate, suppose the base solution consisted of warehouses at Atlanta, Charleston, and Richmond and that we were interested only in three-warehouse configurations. Dropping any one of the three warehouses in the current base solution and substituting one of the remaining two unused warehouses would lead to six new solutions. There would be $3 \times 2 = 6$ possible transformations for this example.

Choosing a New Base

Normally, then, a specific transformation rule is applied to a given base solution as often as possible, generating a set of transformed solutions. The third component of a solution improvement heuristic is a criterion, or rule, for selecting the next base solution. An obvious criterion is to select the best new solution after all new solutions have been evaluated; this rule is frequently used.

It should be noted, however, that with large problems some transformation methods can generate a fairly large number of new solutions. Suppose we were solving a warehouse location problem with 50 potential sites and we desired to find the best 10-warehouse configuration. The replace-one-warehouse transformation method would require evaluation of 400 new solutions. (Each of the 10 that could be dropped can be replaced by 1 of 40.) If we started from a relatively poor base solution, a number of new bases may have to be chosen before the local optimal solution has been found. Repeated application of this heuristic could lead to excessive computation costs.

As an alternative, instead of examining all new solutions before selecting the next base, it may be desirable to choose a new base whenever the transformation leads to a solution better than the last solution. Other alternative selection criteria include (1) probabilistic selection, where probabilities are based on

Department *A* Office 1	Department *B* Office 2

Department *E* Office 5	Department *C* Office 3	Department *D* Office 4

FIGURE 13-5   Present departmental assignment to offices for the White Knight Insurance Company.

the size of the improvement, (2) selecting all solutions that show improvement and using each in turn as a new base, or (3) selecting the solution that shows the smallest improvement.

In the next section we provide a demonstration of how an improvement heuristic can be applied.

Problem Formuation

The office manager for the White Knight Insurance Company was concerned with the flow of paperwork between departments in the central office. The office layout had developed historically without much regard for work flow and business had grown so much recently that the inefficiencies of the current layout had become quite apparent.

The office has five departments, here referred to as *A, B, C, D,* and *E,* each taking up roughly the same amount of office space. The five departments are currently located as shown in Figure 13-5. For reasons that will soon be apparent, we have labeled each of the office areas with a number as shown.

The office manager feels that the cost of transporting paperwork from one department to another can be lowered by reassigning or moving departments so that those departments with heavy interdepartmental flows are close to each other.

As a first step in the analysis of this problem he has identified the average weekly volume of paperwork flow between departments and the transport cost per unit from one office area to another. These are conveniently grouped in Table 13-11. Each row and column in the table represents a particular department and a specific office area. Thus, *A* 1 identifies that department *A* is assigned to office area 1. The pair of numbers corresponding to a flow from one department to another show the volume to the left and above the diagonal and the per-unit cost below and to the right of the diagonal in each box. Thus, for example, we see that from department *A* to department *D* a total weekly volume of 125 exists and the per-unit costs are \$10. Therefore the weekly costs of moving this flow from department *A* to *D* in the present locations is $125 \times \$10 =$ \$1,250.

Although we have shown all flows between a pair of departments as a single flow, as for example the 125 between *A* and *D,* the actual flows can go both ways. In this example, it may be that 95 units flow from *A* to *D* and 30 from *D* to *A.* It is convenient, however, to treat both flows in the aggregate, assuming the cost is the same in either direction.

The total cost of the present assignment can thus be found by summing the products of weekly flow times per unit cost:

TABLE 13-11
Paperwork Volume between Departments and per-Unit Transport Costs for Current Assignment

	A1	B2	C3	D4	E5
A1		100 / $5	20 / $5	125 / $10	40 / $10
B2			75 / $10	60 / $5	140 / $15
C3				35 / $5	75 / $5
D4					100 / $10

Key

Volume	
	Per-unit cost

$$\text{Total weekly cost} = 100(\$5) + 20(\$5) + 125(\$10) + 40(\$10) + 75(\$10)$$
$$+ 60(\$5) + 140(\$15) + 35(\$5) + 75(\$5) + 100(\$10)$$
$$= \$6{,}950$$

That this cost might be reduced is evidenced by the fact that the largest flow, 140, also has the highest per-unit transport cost, $15. Therefore, it would appear that a reassignment could possibly lead to lower weekly costs.

With n departments/locations there are $n!$ possible assignments of departments to office areas. In our case this means there are $5! = 120$ possible solutions to the problem. Although it may be feasible to examine each one to find the lowest-cost arrangement for this small problem, it is clear that such an approach would be impractical for a larger problem. With just 10 departments there would be well over 3 million possible layouts.

CRAFT Heuristic

Therefore, we shall apply a heuristic procedure to this problem which is based on a more flexible procedure called CRAFT. This stands for Computerized Relative Allocation of Facilities Technique and was developed by Gordon C. Armour and Elwood S. Buffa.[1] The procedure works by considering the effects of switching two departments so that they exchange locations. Although the CRAFT procedure can also examine switches among three departments as well, we will restrict our attention to those cases in which only two departments are swapped.

For a given starting assignment with n departments, if r of those departments are to be swapped, there is a total of

$$\frac{n!(r - 1)!}{r!(n - r)!}$$

[1]G. C. Armour and E. S. Buffa, "A Heuristic Algorithm and Simulation Approach to the Relative Location of Facilities," *Management Science*, vol. 9, no. 5 (1963), pp. 294–309.

possible swaps that can be attempted. For our problem with 5 departments,

with exchanges limited to pairs of departments, there are

$$\frac{5!(2-1)!}{2!(5-2)!} = \frac{120}{2(6)} = 10$$

exchanges that need to be evaluated to determine whether a given assignment is a local optimum.

Considerable computational effort can be saved by noting that the interchange of any two departments will affect only the cost of flows between those two departments and the departments that remain fixed. The cost of flows between those departments that remain fixed will not change, and if it is assumed that the cost of flows in one direction are the same as in the other direction, the cost of the flow between the two departments that exchange position must also remain the same.

With this background let us now apply the department interchange heuristic to the present layout to determine whether a better assignment can be found. Consider the exchange of departments A and B. As stated above, the only relevant costs to consider are those from A and B to the other departments. For the present layout we have

$A1$ to $C3$	$20(\$5) =$	$\$100$
$A1$ to $D4$	$125(\$10) =$	$\$1,250$
$A1$ to $E5$	$40(\$10) =$	$\$400$
$B2$ to $C3$	$75(\$10) =$	$\$750$
$B2$ to $D4$	$60(\$5) =$	$\$300$
$B2$ to $E5$	$140(\$15) =$	$\underline{\$2,100}$
	Total cost	$\$4,900$

If A and B swap positions, observe that the *flows* from A and B to C, D, and E will be the same but the *per-unit-costs* will change. In fact, the per-unit costs will be exchanged between A and B. Thus the cost of flows from A to C will be equal to the product of the current flow volume from A to C, or 20, and the per-unit cost from B's current location to C's location, or $\$10$, for a total of $\$200$. Therefore, the total relevant cost, after swapping A with B, is calculated as

$A2$ to $C3$	$20(\$10) =$	$\$200$
$A2$ to $D4$	$125(\$5) =$	$\$625$
$A2$ to $E5$	$40(\$15) =$	$\$600$
$B1$ to $C3$	$75(\$5) =$	$\$375$
$B1$ to $D4$	$60(\$10) =$	$\$600$
$B1$ to $E5$	$140(\$10) =$	$\underline{\$1,400}$
	Total cost	$\$3,800$

The exchange of A with B is clearly advantageous. The relevant costs will be lowered by $\$4,900 - \$3,800 = \$1,100$.

INSTANT REPLAY What change in costs will result from an exchange of departments *A* and *C*?

CHECK Relevant costs are $3,450 for the existing arrangement and $3,300 for the revised layout, for $150 in savings.

The cost savings for each of the 10 possible exchanges of departments are summarized in Table 13-12. Observe that 8 of the 10 exchanges promise to lower costs. The exchange of *A* with *D* will not change costs, while the exchange of *B* with *E* will actually increase costs by $100.

Since the biggest savings result from an exchange of departments *A* and *B*, we will make that change to the initial layout to generate our next base solution. Table 13-13 shows this new assignment with revised flows and per-unit costs. As a check, we can calculate the total weekly cost of flows as we did for the first layout:

$$\text{Revised weekly cost} = 100(\$5) + 20(\$10) + 125(\$5) + 40(\$15) + 75(\$5)$$
$$+ 60(\$10) + 140(\$10) + 35(\$5) + 75(\$5) + 100(\$10)$$
$$= \$5,850$$

The resulting weekly cost of $5,850 is $1,100 less than for the initial solution ($6,950), which is precisely the amount of the cost savings that we determined in our test calculations above.

Using our new base solution we again evaluate the 10 possible interdepartmental exchanges. Note, however, that the cost savings for the exchange of *A* with *B* are already known. If we swap *A* and *B* in our second base layout, we will be moving them back to their original positions, leaving the layout that we started with. Since we saved $1,100 by our original swap, a reexchange of *A* and *B* must cost us $1,100. This is borne out by the cost shown in Table 13-14, which summarizes the cost savings for all possible two-way swaps from the second base layout.

Table 13-14 shows that only two swaps promise to reduce costs. An exchange of *B* with *C* will lower costs by $50 while a swap of *C* with *E* will save $750. Clearly we should next exchange departments *C* and *E* so that *C* will now

TABLE 13-12
Cost Savings for Pairwise Interchanges of
Departments with Initial Layout

Exchange of department	*With department*			
	B	*C*	*D*	*E*
A	$1,100	$150	0	$400
B		$650	$525	−$100
C			$725	$750
D				$800

TABLE 13-13
Paperwork Volume between Departments and per-Unit Transport Costs for Second Base Layout

	A2	B1	C3	D4	E5
A2		100 / $5	20 / $10	125 / $5	40 / $15
B1			75 / $5	60 / $10	140 / $10
C3				35 / $5	75 / $5
D4					100 / $10

occupy office area 5 and *E* will be located in area 3. This transfer of departments leads to the revised flow volume and costs shown in Table 13-15.

INSTANT REPLAY   Verify that a savings of $750 has been achieved by this new layout.

CHECK   Multiplying the revised flows by the per-unit costs, we find a weekly cost for the third layout of $5,100. This is $750 less than the $5,850 cost of the second layout.

Next we examine the effects of exchanges of departments for the third layout. The cost savings for each possible exchange are summarized in Table 13-16. Note that, as anticipated, costs would increase by $750 if departments *C* and *E* are reexchanged.

Since none of the two-way exchanges shown in Table 13-16 promises any savings in cost, the heuristic procedure can be stopped at this point. Note that two solutions have the same total cost. These two layouts are shown in Figure

TABLE 13-14
Cost Savings for Pairwise Interchanges of Departments with Second Base Layout

Exchange of department	*With department*			
	B	*C*	*D*	*E*
A	−$1,100	−$350	−$575	−$200
B		$50	0	−$600
C			−$475	$750
D				−$850

TABLE 13-15
Paperwork Volume between Departments and per-Unit Transport Costs
for Third Base Layout

	A2	B1	C5	D4	E3
A2		100 / $5	20 / $15	125 / $5	40 / $10
B1			75 / $10	60 / $10	140 / $5
C5				35 / $10	75 / $5
D4					100 / $5

13-6. The top layout is the same as the third solution found earlier (see Table 13-15). The bottom layout is identical except that departments B and D have exchanged positions. This exchange results in no change in costs, as promised by the 0 cost savings figure in Table 13-16.

Observe that the final layouts will reduce costs from $6,950 to $5,100, a total weekly savings of $1,850, or approximately 27 percent. This amounts to nearly $100,000 on an annual basis.

Final Comments

Heuristics are an important tool for dealing with complex management science problems. In many cases they may be the only practical approach. They can be applied to almost any type of problem and are particularly useful for very large or complicated situations. The purpose of this chapter was to show you a few representative types of heuristics and to provide a structure in which these approaches can be classified.

TABLE 13-16
Cost Savings for Pairwise Interchanges for Departments
with Third Base Layout

Exchange of department	With department			
	B	C	D	E
A	−$1,100	−$750	−$575	−$550
B		−$800	0	−$500
C			−$1,050	−$750
D				−$1,025

Department B	Department A
Office 1	Office 2

Department C	Department E	Department D
Office 5	Office 3	Office 4

or

Department D	Department A
Office 1	Office 2

Department C	Department E	Department B
Office 5	Office 3	Office 4

FIGURE 13-6   Best layouts found for White Knight Insurance Company problem by pairwise departmental interchange procedure.

We saw that heuristics have several uses. They can be used as decision rules for optimizing procedures, such as the rule for selecting the entering variable in the simplex method. They can provide good initial feasible solutions for optimizing procedures, such as the northwest-corner method for the transportation procedure. In this way they help speed up the optimizing procedures. Heuristics are also used by themselves to provide good solutions. In this case, however, we are not guaranteed that the solution is optimal, or even close to optimal. Nevertheless, they are usually quite fast, easy to apply, and may be the only way of obtaining a solution.

We have classified heuristics into four categories: approximation methods, which modify the problem so that it can be solved approximately; truncation methods, which use stopping rules to control how long the search for good solutions will continue; solution-generating heuristics, which use problem data to provide solutions, either deterministically or probabilistically; and solution-improvement procedures, which modify some initial solution in order to provide better solutions.

Heuristics can be fun to develop and use. There are many opportunities for creative people to develop good heuristic methods for important problems. All that is required is an understanding of the nature of the problem being solved and a little ingenuity.

Key Words

Add heuristic **463**
Approximation heuristic **459**
Arcus' probabilistic heuristic **470**
Base solution **473**
Branch and bound **455**
CRAFT heuristic **476**
Deterministic generating
  heuristic **461**
Drop heuristic **463**

Entering variable **457**
Greedy heuristic **461**
Heuriskein **456**
Heuristic procedure **456**
Integer programming **460**
Interchange **477**
Linear programming **457**
Local optimizers **473**
Minimal spanning tree **461**

Problems

13-1. The maintenance garage for the Metropolis Sanitation Department has five refuse collection trucks that are in need of overhaul. Three crews are used in the overhaul operation: one to disassemble the components needing repair, one to repair or replace defective parts, and a third crew to reassemble any necessary components. The estimated time in hours to complete each of the tasks is shown below for the five trucks.

	Processing time requirements, hours		
Truck	Disassembly	Repair	Reassembly
A	3	7	5
B	6	2	4
C	1	3	2
D	4	8	5
E	3	5	4

a. How many different ways can the trucks be sequenced?

b. Using the principle that jobs with short times on the first machine should be sequenced early and jobs with short times on the last machine should be sequenced later, develop a heuristic procedure that will generate a single solution. What sequence do you get when you apply your heuristic to the five jobs shown above?

13-2. El Diablo, a chain of Mexican fast food outlets, is in the process of expanding to new geographical areas. The company has decided to open two new outlets in an area that will serve six local communities. Management is undecided as to which two of the six communities to locate the outlets in. The objective to be used in making the final decision is to minimize the sum of a population- and distance-weighted cost measure. This measure takes into account both the distance between communities and the size of the population. Minimization of this measure is an attempt to locate the outlets centrally, both with regard to travel distances and with regard to population. It is assumed that each outlet will serve those communities for which this weighted cost is minimized. The table below shows the weighted measures between communities.

If outlet located in community	Weighted cost to serve community					
	1	2	3	4	5	6
1	0	40	75	50	80	60
2	30	0	65	25	20	50
3	60	30	0	100	40	70
4	70	70	50	0	80	55
5	40	20	50	40	0	60
6	100	50	30	80	75	0

a. Use the add and drop procedures to determine the best location for the two outlets.

b. What is the weighted cost for your best locations?

13-3. Refer to the El Diablo situation in problem 13-2. Suppose that an executive of El Diablo prefers that the two outlets be located in communities 1 and 5. Using the solution-improvement procedure described below, determine whether a better *pair of locations* can be found, in terms of the weighted-cost measure. For a transformation method try replacing one of the two base locations with each of the unused locations. Thus, starting with 1 and 5 as your initial base, you could swap 1 out and replace it with 2, 3, 4, and 6 and then swap 5 out and replace it with 2, 3, 4, or 6. As soon as a better pair of outlets is found, call that a new base sequence. Continue until no further improvement can be found. No more than four iterations are necessary.

a. What is the best solution found by the improvement heuristic?

b. What is the weighted cost of this solution?

13-4. The Farraday Manufacturing Company is about to establish a decentralized distribution system for its product line, by opening regional warehouses. To a large extent, Farraday's products are sold to 10 wholesalers whose annual demand in tons is shown below.

Wholesaler	Demand	Wholesaler	Demand
1	40	6	17
2	15	7	8
3	24	8	55
4	65	9	48
5	32	10	34

Farraday has identified five potential warehouse sites and estimates that the fixed operating costs as well as per-ton transportation costs to serve these wholesalers through the warehouses are as shown below. Each warehouse has capacity sufficient to supply one or all of the warehouses.

Wholesaler	Warehouse				
	A	B	C	D	E
1	$6	$8	$5	$9	$2
2	$10	$6	$3	$3	$6
3	$12	$11	$11	$3	$15
4	$9	$8	$7	$5	$6
5	$7	$11	$17	$4	$9
6	$6	$8	$13	$14	$17
7	$6	$11	$12	$18	$16
8	$14	$14	$19	$13	$12
9	$7	$12	$7	$15	$5
10	$11	$17	$10	$11	$12
Fixed costs	$750	$900	$600	$1,200	$800

a. Use the add and drop heuristics to find the best number and location of warehouses for Farraday.

b. What is the total annual cost for the best set of locations?

13-5. Develop a greedy heuristic that considers fixed warehouse cost and potential transportation cost savings that could be used to generate a solution to the warehouse location problem. Apply that heuristic to the Farraday location problem (13-4).

13-6. The Tantamount Photo Equipment Company is in the process of revising its assembly operation to reflect changes in its most popular camera model. The new assembly process consists of the following tasks, precedence requirements, and task times (in seconds):

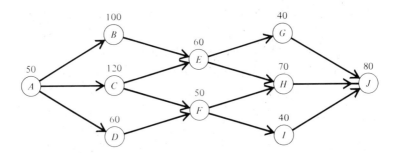

It is desired to establish a line that can produce at a rate of 30 units per hour with as few workers as possible.

    a. Use the Arcus probabilistic procedure to generate one assignment of tasks to workers. Use the same probability assignment rule as in the example in the text and select the task with the higher probability at each decision point.

    b. How many workers does your line require?

    c. |How well balanced is the line?

13-7. Refer to the Tantamount Photo Equipment line-balancing problem (13-6). This time, assign probabilities on the basis of the number of immediate followers that each task has.

    a. Use the Arcus probabilistic heuristic with the probability assignment rule described above. Select the task with the highest probability at each decision, breaking ties arbitrarily.

    b. Compare the solution you find with that for problem 13-6.

13-8. The Lansdowne Lamp Company is in the process of designing a new production facility. At the moment, the managers of the company are concerned with determining the best arrangement for layout of the four production departments. If they follow the layout in their existing plant, the following assignment of departments to areas would result:

Department W Area 1	Department X Area 2	Department Y Area 3
		Department Z Area 4

They estimate the following volume of materials will need to be transported between departments on a weekly basis:

	Department		
Department	**X**	**Y**	**Z**
W	120	40	130
X		70	100
Y			60

The per-unit costs of flows based on distance between areas are shown in the following table (costs are the same either direction):

	Area		
Area	**2**	**3**	**4**
1	10	20	30
2		10	20
3			10

a. Using the CRAFT two-way-swap procedure, determine an assignment of departments to areas with as small a total cost as possible. Use the existing layout as the initial base.

b. What would be the total cost savings per week of your best plan when compared with the layout used in the existing factory?

13–9. The Clean Sweep Laundry Company operates a pickup and delivery laundry for institutional customers such as restaurants and hotels. The senior dispatcher is concerned about what she feels are inefficient delivery routes for the trucks that pick up and deliver from the firm's customers. She has been studying one such route, and after referring to a city street map she has determined the following travel distances (in blocks) between each customer and the laundry plant. These are shown below. (Distances are the same in either direction.)

	Customer					
	1	**2**	**3**	**4**	**5**	**6**
Plant	10	11	6	7	11	7
Customer 1		5	4	7	7	11
Customer 2			5	3	4	12
Customer 3				3	5	7
Customer 4					4	4
Customer 5						8

a. Develop a heuristic procedure that will generate a route from the plant to each of the customers and then back to the plant again.

b. What route would your heuristic provide?

c. Suppose the present route has the truck visiting each customer in numerical order (1, 2, etc.). Suggest a solution-improvement procedure that could be used to reduce the total distance traveled.

13-10. The Blind Tiger Airline Company is in a predicament. A recent advertising campaign promised that if a customer's cargo was not flown to its destination within 24 hours, the cargo would be flown free (customer's money refunded) on the next available flight. The increase in business received as a result of this ad campaign has seemed to justify the cost. At the moment, however, the company is short of aircraft and has only one aircraft available for the New York-to-Boston run. The aircraft has 1,500 cubic feet of cargo capacity, but the available cargo that needs to be shipped on this flight (to avoid customer refunds) far exceeds this capacity as shown by the following size and revenue breakdown:

Cargo category	Size of unit, cubic feet	Number of units available	Revenue per unit
1	75	5	$100
2	100	6	$150
3	150	4	$235
4	250	3	$350
5	300	2	$400

a. Develop a solution-generating heuristic that could be used to minimize the amount of customer refunds.

b. What loading plan for the New York-to-Boston route would you recommend?

c. Consider whether a solution-improvement heuristic might be useful here.

Application: A Heuristic Approach to Solid-Waste Collection Routing*

In 1970 Huntsville, Alabama, city officials desired to improve the solid-waste collection routes which were then in existence. At that time, the solid-waste collection routes numbered 48 and many were fragmented and dispersed through the city in a somewhat haphazard manner.

The objectives of the city were to provide an improved (but not necessarily "optimal") collection routing system which would:

• Reduce the total number of routes from 48 to 42.
• Establish more-equitable routes in terms of workload.
• Maintain the collections on a two-day (either Monday/Thursday or Tuesday/Friday) basis.
• Provide an incentive to the workers by structuring the individual collection routes on a heavy-volume-day basis. (Thus, on light-collection-volume days the workers could possibly go home early.)

The limited amount of time and funds available precluded anything but a straightforward development of a simple improved routing system. It was decided that a heuristic procedure would best ensure a successful effort. A route structuring program was developed that utilized a combination of heuristics.

*Adapted from J. P. Ignizio, R. M. Wyskida, and M. R. Wilhelm, "Huntsville's Solid Waste Collection System," *Interfaces*, vol. 2, no. 4 (August 1972) pp. 69–71.

The set of heuristic rules and guidelines developed included the following:

1. Routes must not be fragmented. Each route must be continuous and cannot be broken into scattered subroutes.
2. Each route must be compact or clustered rather than widely dispersed or strung out.
3. Major thoroughfares, artificial boundaries (railroads, drainage canals, etc.), and natural boundaries (mountains, rivers, etc.) provide the constraints for item 2.
4. Contiguous streets have preference over streets which tend to leave the general location of the continuous path.
5. Ideally, each route is to require 8 hours of collection time, including driving time to and from the route and the unloading of the truck. In practice, however, routes were selected on the basis of an upper limit of 8 hours and lower limit of $7\frac{1}{2}$ hours (based on heavy collection volume).

These heuristic rules were then applied in the following manner. On a city map, a single continuous route for traveling through every street in Huntsville was drawn. This route was based on two major guidelines. The first was to satisfy the heuristic rules above and the second was to provide a reasonable, common-sense route through the entire city. The route was based on knowledge and experience gained by driving through the city and in riding trucks during actual workings hours.

The single continuous route was then divided into individual collection routes whose lengths were based on an estimated collection time of between $7\frac{1}{2}$ and 8 hours. The individual routes were each investigated and driven to ensure their plausibility. Minor modifications were made and the final routing system was presented to the city.

The solution provided a collection of 42 equitable-workload routes (varying in collection time from 455.33 to 475.71 minutes).[1] A listing of all city streets, by blocks, with estimated work time and volumes was punched onto computer cards. These cards were then sequenced according to the single continuous path previously identified. Consequently, any further collection route changes (caused by additional houses, etc.) can be easily incorporated via computer-card correction and addition. New routes can then be generated by a computer, which accumulates times and volumes and determines the start and end of each route.

Implemented in the summer of 1971, the new system worked as anticipated, to the satisfaction of the city. The total cost to develop the system was $13,401. The savings achieved by the new routing system were $43,200 per year.

Discussion Questions

1. What general category of management science problems does the situation described belong to?
2. What factors permitted a heuristic method to be used?
3. Identify those areas where heuristics were used.
4. How was sensitivity analysis applied to this situation?
5. What role should management play in evaluating the routing plan? How will the workers view this plan?
6. What other applications might this routing heuristic be used for?

[1] 7.59 and 7.93 hours, respectively.

Part Five

Inventory Models

This section explores the various ways that management science models can be used in managing and controlling inventories. It differs from the earlier sections in that it focuses on a specific problem area, inventories, rather than on a specific solution method such as linear programming. You will find, in fact, that a number of different models and solution methods can be used with inventory problems, including both optimizing and heuristic approaches.

Two chapters, 14 and 15, are devoted to inventory models. The reason for such extensive coverage is the wide variation in types of inventories and the specific characteristics of each. Almost all organizations maintain inventories of one type or another, ranging from paper clips to aircraft engines. Even within a single firm we find a variety of inventories. A typical manufacturing firm, for example, is likely to have inventories of raw materials, purchased parts, work-in-process, finished goods, office supplies, maintenance supplies, office furniture, and so on. Because the cost of maintaining these inventories and the benefits from doing so may differ with each type of inventory, management needs a diverse set of models to be able to manage and control them.

Chapter 14 examines more fully the types of inventories and the objectives or performance measures of interest. A series of inventory models for items with constant, or uniform, demand is also presented. Chapter 15 begins with a discussion of models dealing with items that have variable demand. This variability can be either predictable or unpredictable. Both of these cases are examined. The chapter concludes with a discussion of implementation choices for using computerized inventory models.

14

Constant Demand
Inventory Models

One area in which management science has had a significant impact in the business world is *inventory management*. The reason for this is clear to see from an examination of the financial statements of any manufacturing company. One of the largest controllable assets on any manufacturing company's balance sheet is classified under the heading "Inventory." Inventories for all United States manufacturing firms represent roughly 7 percent of total assets and 13 percent of sales.[1]

In addition, one of the major functions of inventory is to store manufacturing capacity. Many firms experience seasonal demand for their products. Rather than build a plant with capacity to meet peak demand, a company may decide to set plant capacity at a level sufficient to meet average demand. Then by producing at a rate in excess of needs during low demand periods and storing the excess output as inventory, the demand in peak periods can be met from current production and from inventories built during the low periods. The importance of this function of inventory can be seen by reference to a typical company's balance sheet, where the firm's capacity, as measured by the dollar value of plant and equipment, represents another very sizable asset. Thus, using inventory to reduce capacity needs will be reflected in fewer assets devoted to plant and equipment.

This and the next chapter will deal with the management, or control, of inventories and will focus on two major questions: *How much inventory do we*

---

[1]U.S. Bureau of the Census, *Statistical Abstract of the United States: 1979,* 100th edition, Washington, D.C., 1979, p. 561.

need? When do we need it? It is sometimes stated that the function of inventory management is to provide the right amount of materials at the right time. We will explore how management science is being used to provide the answers to these questions.

Functions of Inventories

For an understanding of the magnitude of the inventory management problem we must first consider the reasons for carrying inventory. One primary function that inventories serve is to provide materials, parts, or products when they are needed to meet expected demand or requirements. For example, if it takes 6 weeks to manufacture a product and customers expect immediate delivery on an order, sufficient finished goods inventory must be available to meet *expected customer demand*. In addition, most companies carry what is called *safety stock*, which consists of inventory in excess of expected demand. This safety stock provides protection against upside fluctuations in demand, such as a sudden, unexpected increase in orders.

Inventories permit the organization to *decouple* the various stages of the manufacturing and distribution process. For instance, even though a firm's demand may follow a marked seasonal pattern, production can be achieved at a smooth, uniform rate by allowing inventories to absorb or buffer the seasonal demand impact. Thus inventories would increase during low demand periods and then decrease during peak periods. Figure 14-1 indicates such a pattern. Observe that the use of inventories permits a reduction in the capacity require-

FIGURE 14-1 Using inventories to smooth production in the face of seasonal or cyclical demand.

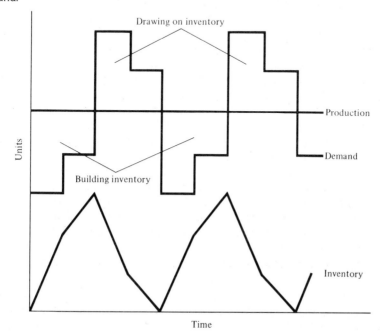

ments to meet peak demands by shifting production requirements from peak periods to periods in which capacity would otherwise be underutilized.

Decoupling can occur throughout the production system, where inventories accomplish two basic purposes. One is to reduce the dependency of successive stages in the system on each other so that fluctuations or malfunctions in one stage do not impact on later stages. The second purpose is to permit relatively independent scheduling of successive stages. Thus, by using fabricated parts inventory, the scheduling of parts fabrication operations can be done independently of the assembly operations. This independence makes it easier to manage the fabrication operation in an efficient and economical manner. Coordination is now accomplished by control of the intermediate inventory levels.

Another function provided by inventories is to facilitate cost savings and increase capacity utilization in manufacturing. For example, if a particular part requires a machining operation, this typically involves a fixed cost of adjusting, or setting up, the piece of equipment on which the machining operation is to be accomplished, regardless of the number of parts to be machined. By machining parts in large lots, or batches, the company can reduce the fixed setup cost that must be absorbed by each part, as well as increase capacity utilization, since the number of setups required per year will be less than would be the case if smaller batches were used. Fewer setups also improve capacity utilization, since setup times are nonproductive. Larger lots do, however, increase the average inventory carrying costs. A similar cost saving can be achieved for purchased rather than fabricated materials, when quantity purchase discounts are available.

Companies also frequently use inventories as a hedge against the uncertainty of price changes or availability of materials. If inflationary pressures suggest that the price for a particular item is likely to rise, a firm may increase its inventory of that item in the expectation that purchase price savings will more than offset any additional inventory costs. If, as many companies experienced in the mid-1970s, certain key materials are expected to be in short supply, inventories of these items may be increased to ensure their availability, thereby avoiding production shutdowns, back orders, lost sales, and so on.

Types of Inventories

It is useful, when determining the appropriate type of inventory model to use, to consider the nature of the inventory itself, since many different kinds of inventories will exist for any particular company.

Of major importance to most companies are those inventories directly related to the products being produced. These would include raw materials and purchased parts which serve as direct inputs to the system, intermediate or work-in-process inventories, and the finished products or system outputs.

Of increasing concern to many manufacturing companies, particularly those that are high-technology firms, are inventories of materials, parts, and supplies required to maintain the production system itself. Formal management of such maintenance inventories is extremely important for highly automated production systems.

It is also useful to distinguish between those items purchased from outside suppliers and those fabricated or produced internally. Items purchased externally normally arrive and are placed in inventory in batches or lots. Items produced internally, while often manufactured in batches, can also be produced serially so that portions of the lot are periodically added to inventory as they are produced rather than as a single batch. As we shall see, this distinction is important in determining the correct inventory model to be used.

Measures of Performance

Our major focus in this (and the next) chapter will be on the development of models that can be used to manage inventory systems successfully. An important aspect of those models will be the inclusion of costs and benefits that are related to inventory policy. Therefore, it is useful to know what these are and how they can be obtained.

Traditional inventory models attempt to minimize *relevant costs,* which can be classified in four major categories: (1) costs related to the number of orders, (2) costs related to the size of the inventory, (3) costs related to service provided, and (4) costs related to the size of the order. We will consider each of these costs in the sections that follow.

Costs Related to Number of Orders

Each time an order is placed with an outside supplier to replenish the inventory for a particular item, certain costs are incurred, regardless of the size of the order placed. These include telephone and postage costs, labor costs in preparing the order, computation and other record-keeping costs, and receiving costs. If the item is produced internally rather than purchased, similar costs are incurred each time the item is produced, including preparation of the production order, setting up the equipment, receiving the produced parts in inventory, and record keeping.

Costs Related to Size of Inventory

The costs related to the size of the inventory maintained include both out-of-pocket costs associated with handling and storing the inventory as well as the opportunity cost of capital invested in the inventory. Handling and storage costs include insurance, taxes, rental of warehouse space, heating and other energy costs, and losses due to spoilage, theft, or obsolescence.

If funds are borrowed to finance the inventories, the capital costs become out-of-pocket costs as well. Alternatively, if the funds needed to finance the inventory investment are generated internally, an appropriate interest rate needs to be identified that reflects the rate of return on alternative investments elsewhere in the firm. In other words, suppose the firm uses its scarce capital to finance inventory rather than finance some new piece of equipment. If this equipment would have produced a net return of, say, 20 percent through productivity increases, this lost opportunity should be reflected in the costs of financing the inventory.

Costs Related to Services Provided

In the preceding section, which described the functions that inventories provide, a number of benefits or services were enumerated, including meeting customer demands and decoupling the manufacturing stages. Since the orientation of most inventory models is cost minimization, these services or benefits are recognized by considering the costs incurred when they are reduced or not provided. If sufficient inventory of finished goods is not on hand to meet demand, higher costs may result from product substitution, lost sales, or back ordering and expediting the subsequent shipment if the customers are willing to wait. If the stockout occurs at the raw material or work-in-process stages, idle labor costs, higher material costs through substitution, or costs associated with expediting the missing parts may have to be expended.

Costs Related to Size of Order

As mentioned earlier, although the per-unit costs of materials purchased or manufactured may not change with the size of an order or batch, on some occasions the per-unit cost is affected. The availability of quantity discounts for purchased items or economies of scale for manufactured items is often a relevant consideration.

Problems with Costs

You should recognize that many of the costs discussed above are *interrelated*. As the size of an order increases, the number of orders needed to meet requirements decreases, while the average size of the inventory increases. Balancing these interrelated changes and their associated costs forms the essence of inventory modeling.

Although we may conveniently be able to identify the types of costs that need to be included in inventory modeling, it is often quite difficult to measure what these costs should be. To illustrate, it would be incorrect to compute the average cost per order by dividing the total cost of maintaining a procurement department by the number of orders processed. This would be inappropriate because the total cost includes certain types of costs that are fixed, at least in the short run, and are therefore not affected by the number of orders placed. What need to be identified are those costs that vary directly with the number of orders.

Those costs associated with providing customer service are almost always the most difficult to determine accurately. Consider, for instance, the cost of a lost sale due to a stockout. Although we may be able to measure the lost profit on this one sale, what are the long-run effects on the firm's reputation, or goodwill? This problem is compounded when the firm markets complementary products. For instance, stockouts for lipstick may affect sales for nail polish. Similarly, stockouts on cameras can affect demand for film.

As we shall see in a subsequent section, the problem of stockout-related costs is frequently overcome by specifying a surrogate measure expressed in terms of some *maximum level of stockout risk,* or conversely some *minimum level of service.* For example, the firm's management might establish a policy requiring sufficient inventory to limit stockouts to no more than 1 percent per year. This is equivalent to saying that they wish this item to be in inventory and available for immediate shipment to the customer for at least 99 percent of all customer orders. Thus a target of 1 percent stockout risk is often referred to as a 99 percent service level.

It should be pointed out that cost accounting systems are often an inadequate means of providing the costs necessary to use inventory models. In the first place, some costs such as stockout costs are simply not available. In other cases, the costs that can be obtained are *average* costs rather than *marginal* costs. The following example will illustrate the difference between average and marginal cost. Suppose we wish to obtain the cost related to the number of orders. We might find that the annual cost of operating the purchasing department is $40,000 and that the department handles 1,000 orders per year. You might be tempted to conclude that the cost of placing an order is equal to the average cost per order, or $40,000/1,000 = $40 per order. This would be incorrect, because at least some portion, probably the major portion, of that $40,000 annual cost is unaffected by the number of orders placed. For instance, the purchasing manager's salary is not likely to change if the number of orders increases to 1,100 per year.

What is needed is to determine the marginal ordering cost, which consists of those costs that vary in direct proportion to changes in the number of orders. These marginal costs include the cost of the purchase requisition form, the cost of sending this requisition to the vendor, and any other costs that vary with the number of requisitions. Not to be overlooked are opportunity costs associated with alternative uses of both time and equipment. Thus the ordering cost for a small retail shop must take into account the fact that time spent by the manager in preparing requisitions could be spent in serving customers, preparing financial statements, or redecorating the shop window.

Nature of Demand

A key factor in determining which inventory model should be used is the nature of demand or usage for the item being stocked in inventory. One distinction that can be made is whether the pattern of demand or usage is constant or variable. An item whose demand rate is predictably uniform is said to have *constant demand.* As an example, a company manufacturing a product, such as a bicycle, at a steady rate, say, 1,000 per week, would find that the usage rate for the parts and components needed to assemble the end item (bicycle) would have uniform or constant demand. Each bicycle requires, among other things, two wheels and one seat. At a production rate of 1,000 bicycles per week, the usage rates for wheels and seats would be 2,000 and 1,000 per week, respectively.

In other cases, the demand for inventory items may follow a less uniform, or *variable demand,* pattern. We have chosen to distinguish between two types of variablility, that due to lumpiness, or lack of uniformity, in the usage rate and that due to demand uncertainties.

Lumpy, or uneven, *demand* frequently results from the nature of the manufacturing process, particularly where products are assembled on an intermittent basis. To illustrate, consider a small firm that manufactures power tools. Suppose their product line consists of a power drill and a power saw. Even though the demand for both drills and saws may follow an approximately uniform pattern, the company may actually assemble these two products on an intermittent basis. This would occur if a common assembly line were used for both products. Thus they might use the line to assemble drills for 2 weeks, followed by saws for 3 weeks, alternating in a similar rotating pattern thereafter.

The importance of this intermittent assembly pattern from an inventory modeling standpoint is that the demand for some components used in these products will not follow a uniform pattern but will mimic the intermittent assembly pattern. Suppose, for example, the line can assemble 1,000 drills or saws per week. During those weeks that saws are being assembled, the usage rates for parts and components needed to assemble saws will be 1,000 per week (assuming one part per saw). During those weeks that drills are being assembled, however, the demand or usage rates for saw components will be zero. The demand for drill components will also follow a lumpy pattern, being zero when saws are being assembled and 1,000 when drills are being assembled.

The second type of variability results from *demand unpredictability*. Consider again our bicycle manufacturer. Although the demand for parts and components used in manufacturing bicycles was uniform at 1,000 per week, based on the stated assembly rate, the demand for bicycles is not likely to follow such a uniform pattern. Even though average demand for bicycles may be 1,000 per week, the actual demand for any given week could be above or below that figure, depending on the pattern of customer orders.

Similarly, although the demand pattern for parts and components used in the manufacture of power drills and saws was lumpy, it was predictable based on the assembly schedule. Nevertheless, the demand for the end items, drills and saws, will be subject to variation for reasons identical to that for demand variability for bicycles.

The remaining sections of this chapter will discuss inventory models appropriate to items with uniform or constant demand. Chapter 15 will consider models more appropriate for items with lumpy or uncertain demand.

Constant Demand Models

As we consider the various inventory models treated here, it is helpful to observe that in each case we will first carefully define the situation being considered, then identify the relevant costs to be included in the model formulation, and finally derive the characteristics of an optimum inventory policy. This common approach will be followed both throughout the remainder of this chapter and in Chapter 15.

Economic Order Quantity Model

First we shall consider what is called the *economic order quantity,* or EOQ, *model.* Although basically a simple model, it has been used for many years and applied to many diverse kinds of situations. Our discussion will begin with an example.

The Ackroyd Bicycle Company produces and sells a quality line of 10-speed racing bicycles. The Ackroyd manufacturing plant has been producing bicycles at a steady rate of 40 per week, or 2,000 per year. Demand has remained fairly steady at that rate, and is likely to do so, at least for the immediate future. Ackroyd is basically an assembly company. That is, they purchase almost all parts used in their bicycles from external suppliers, manufacturing only a few small parts themselves. Recent increases in interest rates have caused management to look more closely at its inventory and reordering policies.

The company uses at present a very simple inventory control system.

They place orders with their suppliers 10 times per year, ordering a sufficient quantity of parts to produce one-tenth of the 2,000 bicycles made annually. This present policy has come under question because of its uniform treatment of all items. That is, the question has been raised: Why should a $10 item be ordered at the same rate as a $.05 item? Therefore, management would like to know if a better ordering policy can be developed that reflects differential costs for each part.

Developing the Model   In order to analyze this situation and develop an appropriate model, we need first to identify the costs relevant to the problem. Previously we identified four major cost components. For the Ackroyd situation, however, the relevant costs will be restricted to those related to the number of orders and to the size of the inventory. We shall assume, for the moment, that purchase discounts are not available and that stockout-related costs are not relevant.

Since all costs must be expressed over a common time period, we shall specify, without loss of generality, that we are attempting to minimize *annual* relevant costs, which are defined to include

$$\begin{pmatrix} \text{Total annual} \\ \text{relevant costs} \end{pmatrix} = \begin{pmatrix} \text{costs related to} \\ \text{number of orders} \end{pmatrix} + \begin{pmatrix} \text{costs related to} \\ \text{size of inventory} \end{pmatrix}$$

In order to "flesh out" our relevant cost equation so that an optimum inventory policy can be determined, we need first to introduce the following notation. For any given item we can define

D = annual demand in units

Q = number of units per order (order quantity)

n = number of orders per year

Note that these three items are related in that $n = D/Q$. In other words, if we need D units per year and they are ordered in lots of Q, we need to place n orders to satisfy demand.

Furthermore, we can define

C_O = cost per order

C_H = cost associated with carrying $1 of inventory per year

p = per-unit cost of the item

Next observe that the annual cost related to the number of orders can be expressed as

$$\begin{pmatrix} \text{Annual cost relevant to} \\ \text{number of orders} \end{pmatrix} = \begin{pmatrix} \text{number of orders} \\ \text{per year} \end{pmatrix} \times \begin{pmatrix} \text{cost} \\ \text{per order} \end{pmatrix}$$

$$= nC_O$$

Or, since $n = D/Q$, we can also state annual ordering cost as

$$\begin{pmatrix} \text{Annual cost related to} \\ \text{number of orders} \end{pmatrix} = \frac{D}{Q}C_O$$

Furthermore, the costs related to the size of the inventory are equivalent to

$$\begin{array}{c} \text{Annual cost} \\ \text{related to} \\ \text{size of inventory} \end{array} = \left(\begin{array}{c}\text{average} \\ \text{inventory} \\ \text{in units}\end{array}\right) \times \left(\begin{array}{c}\text{per-} \\ \text{unit} \\ \text{cost}\end{array}\right) \times \left(\begin{array}{c}\text{cost associated} \\ \text{with carrying \$1} \\ \text{of inventory per year}\end{array}\right)$$

To express the costs related to inventory size in notational terms, we need to determine the average inventory in units. Refer to Figure 14-2, which illustrates the inventory pattern for the constant demand situation we are considering. We assume that each new order of Q items arrives just at the time that the on-hand inventory falls to zero and that demand occurs at a uniform rate. (These assumptions will be relaxed in Chapter 15 when we consider variable demand models.) Observe that the on-hand inventory balance follows a saw-tooth pattern, dropping at a constant rate from a high of Q units, the order size, to a low of zero, as the order is completely used up. It follows from these observations that the average on-hand balance is one-half the maximum level, or simply $Q/2$.

The other elements needed to determine the cost of carrying inventory have already been defined: the per-unit cost is p and the cost of carrying \$1 of inventory per year is C_H. Thus the annual costs related to the size of the inventory can be expressed in notational form as

$$\begin{array}{c}\text{Annual cost related to} \\ \text{size of inventory}\end{array} = \frac{Q}{2}pC_H$$

If Ackroyd purchases an item in lots of 200 units each, the average inventory in units will be 200/2, or 100. If each of these costs \$3, the average inventory investment will be \$300. Finally, if it costs the company 20 percent for each dollar of inventory carried per year, the annual carrying costs for this item will be $.2 \times \$300$, or \$60. This cost could have been obtained more directly from the formula as $(200/2)(\$3)(.2) = \$60$.

Combining our two cost expressions, we have

$$\text{Total annual relevant costs} = \frac{D}{Q}C_O + \frac{Q}{2}pC_H$$

Testing the Model for Reasonableness Before finding the minimum cost solution, it is useful to examine the structure of the model. Note that all the variables except Q are assumed to be known constants; the annual demand in units,

FIGURE 14-2 On-hand inventory pattern.

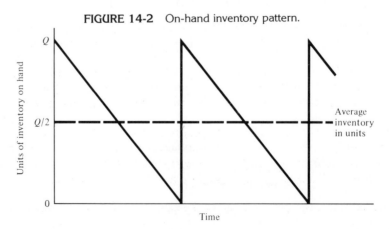

cost per order, per-unit item cost, and the cost per \$1 of inventory are assumed to be constant and known for the item at hand. Furthermore, observe that for a many-item inventory system it is likely that C_O and C_H are the same for most if not all items in the system. In practical applications, when the cost of ordering and the cost of carrying inventory are not the same for all items in the inventory, it is necessary to decompose the total inventory into subclasses or groups of items for which these costs are the same. For example, some items require special handling and storage, thus necessitating a higher carrying cost C_H than for the more standard items. Controlled drugs and narcotics would require such differential cost treatment in a hospital inventory system, because of the extra costs associated with their storage. Exploitation of cost commonalities, where they exist, reduces the amount of data required for an inventory management system.

It is always a good idea to examine any management science model to determine whether the model's behavior reasonably approximates the situation being modeled. One way this can be accomplished here is to observe the effects of changes in the size of the order quantity Q on total costs.

Note that as Q gets larger the costs associated with the number of orders, $(D/Q)C_O$, decreases, since Q is in the denominator. This is as we would expect, since larger order quantities reduce the number of orders required.

On the other hand, since Q is in the numerator of the second cost expression, $(Q/2)pC_H$, we see that the costs associated with the size of the inventory increase as Q gets larger. This is, of course, expected, since larger order sizes increase the average on-hand inventory. Thus the model passes our simple reasonableness test.

INSTANT REPLAY   Does the model respond in the proper way to an increase in annual demand?

CHECK   Annual demand D appears only in the first cost expression. A larger D causes the annual ordering cost to increase, because higher demand with a fixed order size necessitates a greater number of orders, as expected.

Determining the Minimum Cost Order Quantity   It is also useful to plot the relationship between cost and order quantity. This is done in Figure 14-3. As we observed earlier, when the order quantity increases, the costs associated with ordering decrease, while the costs associated with holding inventory increase. The total costs first decrease until reaching a minimum and then begin to rise again. This plot shows that there is a minimum cost point, and you should observe that this occurs at the point where ordering costs and holding costs are equal. This minimum cost order quantity has been designated as Q^*, the *optimal order quantity*.

The fact that the optimal order quantity occurred at the point where the cost components were equal was no coincidence but will always be true for cost functions of the form $A/Q + BQ$. This observation indicates that we can solve for the optimal order quantity by equating the two cost components:

$$\frac{D}{Q^*}C_O = \frac{Q^*}{2}pC_H$$

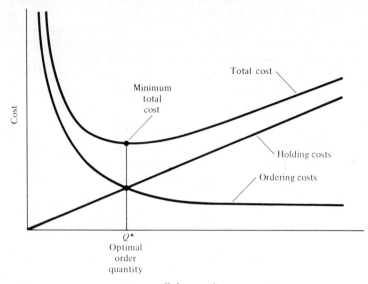

FIGURE 14-3 Relationship between order quantity and relevant inventory costs.

To solve for Q^*, we first multiply both sides of the expression by Q^*

$$DC_O = (Q^*)^2 \frac{pC_H}{2}$$

then multiply both sides by $2/pC_H$ and rearrange as

$$(Q^*)^2 = \frac{2DC_O}{pC_H}$$

To find the optimal value we take the square root of both sides:

$$Q^* = \sqrt{\frac{2DC_O}{pC_H}}$$

Again it is useful to examine the resulting optimal value equation for reasonableness. For instance, if the cost of ordering increases, the order quantity will also rise, although at a slower rate because of the dampening effects of the square root. This seems reasonable, since with increased ordering costs, all else held constant, we should be making larger but less frequent orders. Similar checks of the other variables lead to the same general conclusion, supporting the model.

Next the use of the model will be illustrated by seeing how it will affect the current ordering policies for the Ackroyd Bicycle Company. Suppose we consider two parts typical of those purchased by Ackroyd. One of these is a low-cost item, with a per-unit cost of $.50. The other is typical of higher-cost items with a purchase price of $12.50. Both parts have an annual demand of 2,000 units. A study of inventory related costs estimated ordering cost to be $9 per order and annual holding costs to be 20 percent of average investment in inventory.

Using our notation, we can define for the low-cost part:

$$D = 2,000 \qquad C_O = \$9$$

$$p = \$.50 \qquad C_H = .20$$

To find the optimal inventory quantity we substitute these values into the EOQ formula:

$$Q^* = \sqrt{\frac{2(2,000)(9)}{.50(.20)}} = \sqrt{360,000} = 600 \text{ units}$$

Thus we can minimize the sum of annual ordering and holding costs for the $.50 item by always ordering it in lots of 600 units. We can also determine the optimal number of orders n^* from the previously defined relationship:

$$n = \frac{D}{Q} \qquad \text{or} \qquad n^* = \frac{D}{Q^*}$$

$$n^* = \frac{2,000}{600} = 3\tfrac{1}{3} \text{ orders per year}$$

Note that the $3\tfrac{1}{3}$ orders per year does not mean we place 3 full orders and 1 partial order of $Q/3$ each year. Instead, it means we place 10 orders spread evenly over a 3-year period, which on *average* is $3\tfrac{1}{3}$ orders per year.

The total costs for this optimal policy can be found by substituting the appropriate values in our equation for total relevant costs (TRC).

$$\text{TRC}^* = \left(\frac{D}{Q^*}\right)C_O = \left(\frac{Q^*}{2}\right)pC_H$$

$$= \left(\frac{2,000}{600}\right)\$9 + \left(\frac{600}{2}\right)(\$.50)(.20)$$

$$= \$30 + \$30 = \$60 \text{ per year}$$

Observe that the total ordering costs and total holding costs were both $30, which is expected because we earlier learned that these two costs will always be equal for the optimal order quantity.

INSTANT REPLAY What would be the optimal inventory quantity, number of orders per year, and total annual relevant costs for the $12.50 part purchased by Ackroyd? Assume that ordering costs remain $9, annual holding costs are 20 percent of average investment inventory, and annual demand is 2,000 units.

CHECK In this case, $D = 2,000$, $p = \$12.50$, $C_O = \$9$, and $C_H = .20$. Thus,

$$Q^* = \sqrt{\frac{2(2,000)(\$9)}{\$12.50(.20)}} = 120 \text{ units per order}$$

$$n^* = \frac{D}{Q^*} = \frac{2,000}{120} = 16\tfrac{2}{3} \text{ orders per year}$$

$$\text{TRC} = \left(\frac{D}{Q^*}\right)C_O + \left(\frac{Q^*}{2}\right)pC_H$$

$$= \frac{2,000}{120}(\$9) + \frac{120}{2}(\$12.50)(.20)$$

$$= \$150 + \$150 = \$300$$

As the Instant Replay shows, even though annual demand, ordering cost, and holding costs were the same, the two parts ($.50 and $12.50 parts) should not be ordered with the same frequency and order size as current policy calls for. Instead, the low-cost item should be ordered less frequently than the high-cost item. This necessitates a larger order quantity for the low-cost item, as well.

It is also useful to compare the relevant costs for these two parts based on the optimal order quantities with those for the current ordering policy. Recall that current policy requires all parts to be ordered 10 times per year in quantities equal to one-tenth of annual demand. Thus current policy requires 10 orders per year for both the $.50 and $12.50 parts in quantities of $2,000/10 = 200$ units. This leads to the total relevant cost for the $0.50 item of

$$\text{TRC} = \frac{2,000}{200}(\$9) + \frac{200}{2}(\$.50)(.20)$$

$$= \$90 + \$10 = \$100$$

and for the $12.50 item:

$$\text{TRC} = \frac{2,000}{200}(\$9) + \frac{200}{2}(\$12.50)(.20)$$

$$= \$90 + \$250 = \$340$$

These costs of $100 and $340 should be contrasted with the costs of using the optimal ordering policies, which were $60 and $300. Thus, for these two items, use of the optimal ordering policies would have saved $100 − $60 = $40 and $340 − $300 = $40 per year, or an average savings for the summed total costs of more than 18 percent.

Sensitivity Analysis   At this point you may not be convinced that these total costs cannot be improved upon. Suppose, as a simple test, we vary the order quantity for the $.50 part by, say, 5 percent in either direction around Q^* and observe the effects on total cost. If, for instance, $Q = 630$ rather than 600, we find

$$\text{TRC} = \left(\frac{2,000}{630}\right)\$9 + \left(\frac{630}{2}\right)(\$.50)(.20)$$

$$= \$28.57 + \$31.50 = \$60.07$$

In this case the ordering costs decreased slightly, but not by as much as holding costs increased, so that total costs were $.07 higher.

Alternatively, suppose we use a lower Q of 570. Then

$$\text{TRC} = \left(\frac{2,000}{570}\right)\$9 + \left(\frac{570}{2}\right)(\$.50)(.20)$$

$$= \$31.58 + \$28.50 = \$60.08$$

Here we see that the decrease in holding costs was more than offset by the increase in ordering costs, although total cost increased only $.08.

The small changes in total cost resulting from minor deviations from the optimal order quantity result from the fairly flat nature of the total cost curve in the neighborhood of the optimal order quantity. This is best seen by examining Figure 14-3.

Given the difficulties in obtaining the cost and demand information necessary to derive the optimal order quantity, this flatness of the total cost curve is reassuring. Thus, if the estimated ordering cost differs from the true ordering cost by some small amount, we are assured that the order quantity based on the estimated cost will not be too far from the true optimal order quantity and that the cost penalty incurred will be relatively small.

In fact, this lack of sensitivity of TRC to errors is much more robust than implied above. This can be demonstrated by referring to the formula for Q^*:

$$Q^* = \sqrt{\frac{2DC_O}{pC_H}}$$

Suppose instead of the true ordering cost C_O, we use a cost that differs from C_O by some factor k. In other words, we use kC_O as our ordering cost, where k would equal 2 if the ordering cost estimate was twice as large as the true cost. Thus we would use

$$Q = \sqrt{\frac{2DkC_O}{pC_H}}$$

Note that this can easily be rewritten as

$$Q = \sqrt{k}\,\sqrt{\frac{2DC_O}{pC_H}}$$

and since the second square root form is simply Q^*, we find

$$Q = \sqrt{k}\,Q^*$$

In words, the order quantity used will deviate from the optimal quantity by a factor of $\sqrt{k}$. The square root tells us that errors in estimating C_O will be dampened because of the square root. For example, if $k = 2$, meaning that true ordering costs are one-half of those estimated, the order quantity used would be 1.414 times the optimal order quantity.

If we substitute $\sqrt{k}\,Q^*$ for Q^* in the total relevant cost equation, we find

$$TRC = \frac{1}{\sqrt{k}}\left(\begin{array}{c}\text{optimal} \\ \text{ordering costs}\end{array}\right) + \sqrt{k}\left(\begin{array}{c}\text{optimal} \\ \text{holding costs}\end{array}\right)$$

and since optimal ordering costs and optimal holding costs are equal, we can substitute $TRC^*/2$ for these costs and derive

$$TRC = \frac{TRC^*}{2}\left(\sqrt{k} + \frac{1}{\sqrt{k}}\right)$$

If $k = 1$, representing true ordering costs, we find $TRC = TRC^*$, as expected, and if $k = 2$,

$$TRC = \frac{TRC^*}{2}\left(1.414 + \frac{1}{1.414}\right) = 1.06\ TRC^*$$

which says that actual costs incurred using the erroneous estimate for ordering costs will be 6 percent higher than optimal. Thus we see that a 100 percent error in estimating ordering costs will lead to only a 6 percent error in total costs. Similar robustness results from errors in the other information needed for the EOQ formula.

Note that some errors tend to cancel each other out, while others reinforce each other. For instance, if both C_O and C_H are twice what they should be, the estimation errors are canceled and the correct order quantity would be found, since C_O is in the numerator of the EOQ equation while C_H is in the denominator. On the other hand, if both D and C_O are double what they should be, the factor k will be four times higher than the correct figure, and annual inventory costs will be 25 percent higher than they should be.

INSTANT REPLAY What percent error in total costs will result from an estimated holding cost that is one-half that of the true holding cost?

CHECK $Q = \sqrt{1/k}\; Q^*$ and total costs are 6 percent higher than they would have been if the true holding cost had been used.

Quantity Discounts

It is often possible to reduce the per-unit cost of an item by purchasing it in large lots, thereby taking advantage of quantity discounts offered by the supplier. The preceding inventory model that we considered limited our attention to ordering and holding costs and assumed that the cost per unit was a fixed constant. If we are to take advantage of quantity discounts, we must now incorporate costs related to the size of the order. Thus, when quantity discounts are offered, our inventory cost model becomes

$$\begin{pmatrix} \text{Total annual} \\ \text{relevant} \\ \text{costs} \end{pmatrix} = \begin{pmatrix} \text{annual} \\ \text{ordering} \\ \text{costs} \end{pmatrix} + \begin{pmatrix} \text{annual} \\ \text{holding} \\ \text{costs} \end{pmatrix} + \begin{pmatrix} \text{costs related} \\ \text{to size} \\ \text{of order} \end{pmatrix}$$

The new, third element of our cost expression is easy to incorporate, since our annual costs of buying the item can be found by multiplying the appropriate per-unit cost by the number of items used on an annual basis:

$$\begin{pmatrix} \text{Costs related to} \\ \text{size of order} \end{pmatrix} = \begin{pmatrix} \text{per-unit} \\ \text{item cost} \end{pmatrix} \times \begin{pmatrix} \text{annual} \\ \text{demand} \end{pmatrix}$$

$$= pD$$

Total relevant costs thus become

$$\text{TRC} = \frac{D}{Q} C_O + \frac{Q}{2} pC_H + pD$$

Unfortunately, the methods we used previously to derive an equation for the optimal order quantity will no longer work in this case. This is because the per-unit cost element p is now dependent on the size of the order quantity and this dependency is discontinuous; the correct per-unit cost is p up to the discount quantity and smaller thereafter. To illustrate, consider the relationship between costs and order quantity as shown in Figure 14-4. The situation illustrated is one in which the per-unit costs are p_1 if the order quantity is less than Q_1, p_2 if the order quantity is at least Q_1 but less than Q_2, and p_3 if the order quantity is Q_2 or larger, where $p_3 < p_2 < p_1$.

In this case the total relevant cost curve is no longer a smooth continuous curve but experiences discontinuities at points Q_1 and Q_2 because of the sudden drop in the per-unit item cost at those points.

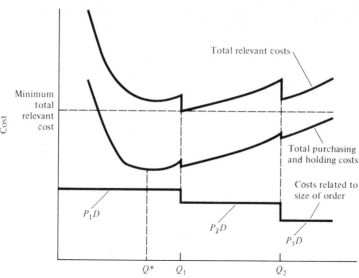

FIGURE 14-4 Effect of quantity discounts on relationship of order quantity to total relevant costs.

For the example shown in Figure 14-4, the minimum TRC occurs at one of the breakpoints or discontinuities, in this case Q_1. In other cases, the minimum TRC may occur at one of the breakpoints. A simple procedure exists for determining the minimum cost order quantity.

To illustrate how this done, consider the discount situation faced by the Gardner Appliance Company. They manufacture a food processor which is produced at a constant rate of 1,280 per week, or 64,000 units per year. One of the key components of the food processor is a 1-horsepower electric motor which is purchased from an outside supplier. The price paid by Gardner depends upon the quantity ordered, as shown in Table 14-1. Thus the motors will cost Gardner $10 each in order quantities of up to 999, $9.80 each (a 2 percent discount) in quantities between 1,000 and 4,999, or $9.50 (a 5 percent discount) in quantities of 5,000 or more.

Assuming, then, that annual demand is 64,000 motors ($D = 64,000$), ordering costs are $10 per order ($C_O = \$10$), and holding costs are 20 percent ($C_H = .20$), the management of Gardner Company would like to know the minimum cost order size.

The procedure used to solve this problem consists of three steps. First the optimal order quantity Q^* is calculated for all three prices. Thus,

$$Q_1^* = \sqrt{\frac{2DC_O}{p_1 C_H}} = \sqrt{\frac{2(64,000)(10)}{(10)(.20)}} = 800$$

$$Q_2^* = \sqrt{\frac{2DC_O}{p_2 C_H}} = \sqrt{\frac{2(64,000)(10)}{(9.80)(.20)}} = 808$$

$$Q_3^* = \sqrt{\frac{2DC_O}{p_3 C_H}} = \sqrt{\frac{2(64,000)(10)}{(9.50)(.20)}} = 821$$

Then, for any Q^* that is less than the minimum order quantity necessary to qualify for that price, we need to adjust the Q^* value to equal the minimum

TABLE 14-1
Discount Information for Gardner Appliance Problem

Price category	Required order quantity	Discount rate, %	Discounted unit cost
1	0–999		$10.00
2	1,000–4,999	2	9.80
3	5,000 or more	5	9.50

order quantity. In this case, only Q_1^* is larger than the minimum qualifying order quantity (0 units) and Q_2^* and Q_3^* must be adjusted upward to their respective breakpoints. To achieve a per-unit cost of $9.80, the order quantity must be at least 1,000; therefore, Q_2^* is adjusted to 1,000. Likewise, to be eligible for the $9.50 price, we must order at least 5,000 units and Q_3^* is therefore adjusted to that level.

Finally, the total relevant cost is calculated using each of the three adjusted order quantities:

$$\text{TRC}_1 = \frac{D}{Q_1^*} C_O + \frac{Q_1^*}{2} p_1 C_H + p_1 D$$

$$= \left(\frac{64,000}{800}\right)(\$10) + \left(\frac{800}{2}\right)(\$10.00)(.20) + (\$10.00)(64,000)$$

$$= \$800 + \$800 + \$640,000 = \$641,600$$

$$\text{TRC}_2 = \left(\frac{64,000}{1,000}\right)(\$10) + \left(\frac{1,000}{2}\right)(\$9.80)(.20) + (\$9.80)(64,000)$$

$$= \$640 + \$980 + \$627,200 = \$628,820$$

$$\text{TRC}_3 = \frac{64,000}{5,000}(\$10) + \left(\frac{5,000}{2}\right)(\$9.50)(.20) + (\$9.50)(64,000)$$

$$= \$128 + \$4,750 + \$608,000 = \$612,878$$

TRC_3 is lower than the costs at the other two order quantities. Thus the optimal ordering decision is to order in lots of 5,000.

Observe what happens to each of the three cost elements as the order quantity increases. Ordering cost decreases, as fewer orders are required; holding cost increases, since the average inventory is higher; and the cost of providing an annual supply of the item decreases, since the per-unit cost declines.

Thus, as long as the savings in ordering and supply costs decrease more than the inventory holding costs increase, it is advantageous to move up to the next highest price break. Although in our example the optimal order quantity occurred at the highest price break, the reader should be cautioned that this will not always be the case; each situation needs to be examined on its own merits.

Summary of the Discount Problem

For convenience we can summarize the three steps we followed in solving the discount problem. They were:

1. Using the standard EOQ equation, calculate the appropriate optimal order quantity Q^* for each price.

2. In each case, if Q^* is less than the minimum order quantity necessary to qualify for the per-unit cost used, adjust the Q^* values up to the minimum qualifying order quantity.

3. Calculate TRC, using the three cost elements described earlier, for each Q^* as adjusted, and select the Q^* with the lowest TRC as the optimal order quantity.

INSTANT REPLAY An item with annual demand of 2,500 units costs $1 per unit unless ordered in lots of 2,000 or more, at which point the price drops to $.98 per unit. Assuming that the cost per order is $10 and holding costs are 20 percent, what order quantity should be used?

CHECK The item should be ordered in lots of 500 because TRC is $58.50 less than when ordered in lots of 2,000. Observe that, in this case, it is not advantageous to take the discount.

Economic Lot Size Models

The models treated so far have implied that we were purchasing the items from an outside supplier. In this section we consider inventory models in which we are deciding on the appropriate lot size for items manufactured, fabricated, or assembled internally.

Here we need to make a distinction between two types of models, depending upon the manner in which the manufactured items enter inventory. In the first case, which we will refer to as the *batch model,* it is assumed that all items in a lot finish processing and are added to inventory simultaneously as one batch.

The second model is used to treat those cases where all items in a lot are not added to inventory simultaneously but are added at a constant rate over the life of the production run. This second situation will be referred to simply as the *nonbatch model.*

Batch Model Other than a change in terminology, the batch model turns out to have exactly the same characteristics as the EOQ model treated previously. Instead of an ordering cost, the batch production model includes an analogous *setup cost.* Setup costs, as described earlier, include the nonproductive time associated with setting up machinery and equipment. In many instances this cost is nontrivial and is generally higher than the analogous ordering cost.

The total relevant costs for the batch model are thus

$$\text{Total annual relevant costs} = \left(\begin{array}{c}\text{annual} \\ \text{setup costs}\end{array}\right) + \left(\begin{array}{c}\text{annual inventory} \\ \text{holding costs}\end{array}\right)$$

Let us define C_S to represent the cost per setup. We can now present the batch model in notational form as

$$\text{TRC} = \frac{D}{Q} C_S + \frac{Q}{2} p C_H$$

Solving this model would be identical to that for the standard EOQ model, leading to

$$Q^* = \sqrt{\frac{2DC_S}{pC_H}}$$

The only difference is the inclusion of a cost per setup C_S in place of the cost per order C_O.

To illustrate, suppose that the Gardner Appliance Company manufactures the plastic case used in its food processor and these cases are produced in batches. Annual demand for the case is 64,000 units, the cost of materials and labor is $4, carrying costs are 20 percent, and setup costs are $100 per setup. The optimal lot size would be found from

$$Q^* = \sqrt{\frac{2DC_S}{pC_H}} = \sqrt{\frac{2(64,000)(\$100)}{\$4(.20)}}$$

$$= 4,000 \text{ cases}$$

Thus the cases should be produced in lots of 4,000, which will require $64,000/4,000 = 16$ setups per year.

INSTANT REPLAY   Determine the optimal production lot size and total annual relevant costs for an item with annual usage of 4,900 units, a manufacturing cost of $2.00, cost per setup of $100, and a holding cost rate of 25 percent per year.

CHECK $Q^* = 1,400$ units and TRC* = $700.

Nonbatch Model   The nonbatch model presents a slightly different problem because items are being added to inventory throughout the production run rather than only at the end, as was the case for the batch model. Figure 14-5 presents the appropriate inventory pattern for the nonbatch case. Note that production begins when the inventory reaches zero. During the production run the inventory increases until it reaches its maximum at the end of the production run.

It is important to note that the maximum inventory level is not equal to the size of the production run Q, as it was in the batch case. This is because some of the units added to inventory during the production run are withdrawn from stock to satisfy demand during that period. If we let d represent the daily demand rate and r the daily production rate, the on-hand inventory grows at a daily rate $(r - d)$ during the production run. Furthermore, we can define the length of the production run in days as Q/r, which states that Q units are to be produced at a rate of r per day. Thus

$$\begin{pmatrix} \text{Maximum} \\ \text{inventory} \end{pmatrix} = \begin{pmatrix} \text{length of} \\ \text{production run} \\ \text{in days} \end{pmatrix} \times \begin{pmatrix} \text{daily rate of} \\ \text{inventory increase} \\ \text{during production} \end{pmatrix}$$

$$= \frac{Q}{r}(r - d)$$

The average inventory on hand, as shown in Figure 14-5, is half the maximum inventory level:

$$\text{Average on-hand inventory} = \frac{Q}{2}\left(\frac{r-d}{r}\right)$$

With this background we can now develop our total relevant cost model for the nonbatch case. We again are concerned only with setup and holding costs:

$$\left(\begin{array}{c}\text{Total annual}\\\text{relevant costs}\end{array}\right) = \left(\begin{array}{c}\text{annual}\\\text{setup costs}\end{array}\right) + \left(\begin{array}{c}\text{annual}\\\text{holding costs}\end{array}\right)$$

$$= \left(\begin{array}{c}\text{number of}\\\text{setups}\\\text{per year}\end{array}\right) \times \left(\begin{array}{c}\text{cost per}\\\text{setup}\end{array}\right)$$

$$+ \left(\begin{array}{c}\text{average}\\\text{inventory}\\\text{in units}\end{array}\right) \times \left(\begin{array}{c}\text{cost}\\\text{per}\\\text{unit}\end{array}\right) \times \left(\begin{array}{c}\text{annual holding cost}\\\text{per \$1 of}\\\text{inventory}\end{array}\right)$$

$$= \frac{D}{Q}\,C_S + \frac{Q}{2}\left(\frac{r-d}{r}\right)pC_H$$

Note that the only difference between this formulation and the one for the batch case is the inclusion of the $(r-d)/r$ factor in the holding cost.

Solving the model is achieved as for the EOQ or batch models. The two cost elements can be set equal to each other and the resulting equation solved in terms of optimal lot size Q^*. Thus

$$\frac{D}{Q}\,C_S = \frac{Q}{2}\left(\frac{r-d}{r}\right)pC_H$$

$$Q^* = \sqrt{\frac{2DC_S}{pC_H}\left(\frac{r}{r-d}\right)}$$

The only difference between Q^* for the nonbatch case and that for the batch case is the $r/(r-d)$ factor. Note that since production rate r must be larger than

FIGURE 14-5 Inventory pattern for nonbatch lot size model.

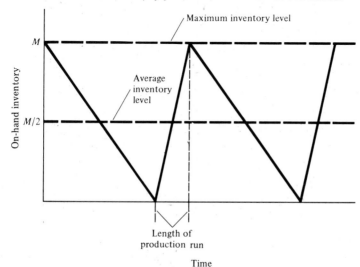

demand rate d (otherwise the situation is infeasible),[1] the factor $r/(r - d)$ will always be greater than 1. This means that the optimal lot size in the nonbatch case will *always be larger* than that for the batch case, all else equal.

INSTANT REPLAY   Can you provide a logical explanation for why the lot size in the nonbatch case should be larger than that for the equivalent batch situation?

CHECK   The maximum nonbatch inventory will always be less because some units are used to satisfy demand immediately. Thus, a larger nonbatch lot size can be produced for equivalent inventory holding costs.

As an example, consider the switch component used to control the operation of the Gardner food processor. This item is assembled by Gardner and is added to inventory in a nonbatch manner. Switches can be assembled at a rate of 1,280 per day and are used at a rate of 256 per day. Annual demand is 64,000 switches, setup cost to assemble the switches is $250, and holding costs are 20 percent. Each switch costs the company $8 to manufacture. Thus we see that

$$D = 64,000 \qquad p = \$8$$

$$C_S = \$250 \qquad r = 1,280$$

$$C_H = .20 \qquad d = 256$$

$$Q^* = \sqrt{\frac{2DC_S}{pC_H}\left(\frac{r}{r-d}\right)} = \sqrt{\frac{2(64,000)(\$250)}{\$8(.20)}\left(\frac{1,280}{1,280-256}\right)}$$

$$= 5,000 \text{ switches}$$

Thus the switches should be assembled in lots of 5,000.

INSTANT REPLAY   Suppose that the plastic case (discussed previously as a batch problem) used in the Gardner food processor was produced in a *nonbatch* manner. If the weekly demand is 1,280 and the weekly production rate is 3,200 cases, what is the optimal production lot size for the case?

CHECK   In this case, we use the nonbatch formula with $D = 64,000$, $C_S = \$100$, $p = \$4$, $C_H = .20$, $r = 3,200$, and $d = 1,280$. This yields $Q^* = 5,164$ cases. Note that the lot size has increased from the 4,000 cases found assuming batch production to 5,164 cases assuming nonbatch production.

A comparison of the batch and nonbatch results for the Gardner plastic case shows that in addition to higher lot sizes, lower inventory-related costs are also possible with nonbatch production. For instance, the total inventory-related costs for the food processor case are, in the *batch* case,

$$TRC = \frac{64,000}{4,000}(\$100) + \frac{4,000}{2}(\$4)(.20) = \$3,200$$

and in the *nonbatch* case,

[1] If the demand rate exceeded the supply rate, $r - d$ would be negative, yielding a negative quantity under the square root sign, which is unacceptable.

$$\text{TRC} = \frac{64,000}{5,164}(\$100) + \frac{5,164}{2}(\$4)(.20)\left(\frac{3,200 - 1,280}{3,200}\right) = \$2,478.71$$

Thus inventory-related costs are about 22.5 percent lower with nonbatch production. From this it may appear to be quite attractive to choose nonbatch over batch production methods. However, we should point out that the nature of the manufacturing process may dictate that a batch method be employed. For example, many chemical processes require that the entire lot be produced as a single batch.

Also note that as production rate r increases relative to demand rate d, the differences between the batch and nonbatch situations become less distinct. That is, as r becomes much larger than d, the term $r/(r - d)$ in the nonbatch formula approaches a value of 1. If that factor is equal to 1, the formulas for Q^* in both the batch and the nonbatch case are identical.

Final Comments

This is the first of two chapters dealing with the application of management science models to inventory problems. This chapter began by discussing the importance of the role that inventories can play in a firm's operations. We saw that inventories provide the raw materials, parts, and finished products to meet manufacturing and consumer requirements. We also saw how inventories serve to decouple the various stages of the manufacturing and distribution system. Decoupling reduces the dependency of various stages in this system on each other and increases the ability to schedule these stages independently. The use of inventories to achieve cost savings and increase capacity utilization was also discussed.

We briefly considered the various types of inventories that can exist. These include raw materials, purchased parts, work-in-process, maintenance materials, and finished products. The distinction between items purchased from external suppliers and those fabricated or assembled internally was pointed out. Different inventory models are used for these two kinds of items.

The models considered in this chapter and those that we will see in the next chapter use various costs as measures of inventory system performance. These costs were grouped in four categories: costs related to the number of orders, costs related to the size of the inventory, costs related to service provided, and costs related to the size of the order. It is important to reiterate that identifying the costs that need to be considered is much easier than determining actual values for these costs. The potential confusion between average and marginal costs was emphasized, as were the difficulties in measuring service-related costs such as back order or stockout costs.

The remaining portion of this chapter was used to present and discuss several constant demand inventory models. These models all assume that demand occurs at a steady and predictable rate. The economic order quantity model presented a means for balancing the costs of ordering with those related to holding inventory for items ordered from external suppliers. This model was then extended to include the availability of quantity discounts.

The modifications necessary to the economic order quantity model for application to inventory items manufactured internally were then discussed. This necessitated considering two such modified models. The batch model assumed that items were produced and added to inventory in batches. This model was similar to the EOQ model. The nonbatch model is appropriate whenever items are added to inventory as they are manufactured rather than in a single batch. This model leads to larger lot sizes and lower total costs than for the batch case, at least when setup costs are the same for both cases.

The next chapter will examine models with variable demand as well as the various methods used to implement both constant and variable demand models.

Key Words

Average cost **495**	Inventory model **496**
Back orders **494**	Lumpy demand **495**
Batch model **507**	Marginal cost **495**
Carrying cost **497**	Maximum inventory level **498**
Constant demand **495**	Maximum level of stockout risk **494**
Decoupling **491**	Minimum level of service **494**
Demand unpredictability **496**	Nonbatch model **508**
Economic lot size model **507**	Ordering cost **493**
Economic order quantity **496**	Per-unit cost **504**
Economic order quantity model **496**	Quantity discounts **504**
EOQ **496**	Relevant costs **493**
Expected customer demand **491**	Safety stock **491**
External supplier **492**	Sensitivity analysis **502**
Hedge **492**	Setup cost **492**
Holding cost **499**	Stockouts **494**
Inventory **490**	Variable demand **495**
Inventory management **490**	

Problems

14-1. The Katz Camera Store maintains an inventory of flashcubes to satisfy customer demand. Current policy calls for the inventory to be replenished once every 4 months, at which time 50 cases each costing $12 are received. Assuming demand occurs at a regular rate (150 cases per year):
    a. What is the maximum inventory (in cases)?
    b. What is the average inventory (in cases) during the 4-month order cycle?
    c. What is the average annual inventory (in cases)?
    d. What is the average dollar investment required to maintain this inventory?

14-2. Suppose that the cost of placing an order to replenish the flashcube inventory for Katz Camera Store (problem 14-1) is estimated to be $9 and the cost of carrying inventory is 25 percent of average investment per year:
    a. What should the optimal order quantity be (in cases)?
    b. What would the annual ordering costs be for this optimal policy?
    c. What would the annual holding costs be for the optimal policy?
    d. How many orders would be placed each year?
    e. How much would be saved each year if flashcubes are ordered in the optimal quantity as compared with the current policy?

14-3. Suppose that the supplier of flashcubes to Katz Camera Store (problems 14-1 and 14-2) offers quantity purchase discounts according to the following schedule:

Quantity (in cases)	Price per case
1–59	$12
60–99	11
100 or more	10

a. Should the Katz Camera store take advantage of the discounts offered?

b. How much would be lost or saved by each of the discount options when compared with the optimal nondiscount option?

14-4. The owner of the Katz Camera stores is quite interested in the inventory cost analysis as demonstrated for flashcubes (problems 14-1 through 14-3). She would like to implement an inventory control system for the many items stocked by the store, but she had several questions concerning the details of how this would be accomplished.

There was some question concerning the appropriate holding cost rate, for instance. Inventory was being financed through borrowing at a current interest rate of 10 percent. The cost of storage, insurance, obsolescence, and pilferage was estimated to be 12 percent of average inventory value. The cost of storing some items such as film was considerably higher, however, because of limited shelf life and special storage requirements.

The cost to place an order also varied somewhat, since some items, notably film, flash equipment, and cameras, required special shipping procedures; other items, such as camera cases, were considerably easier to replenish.

Another problem concerned the high variability in item value. At one extreme, the store stocked very expensive cameras with costs in the hundreds of dollars, while at the other, they stocked many inexpensive photographic supplies that cost under $5.

Discuss how these considerations could be dealt with in a formal inventory system.

14-5. The Inverness Manufacturing Company recently converted its entire ordering procedure to an EOQ system. Six months after the system had been implemented a follow-up study was made to determine the effectiveness of the system. In the process of this study, it was observed that one of the items stocked had high annual shipping costs under the new EOQ policy. The optimal order quantity, calculated using the standard EOQ formula, called for shipments to be made by rail in less than carload lots at a cost of $200 per shipment. If the same item was shipped in carload lots, the cost per shipment would be $300, but the item would have to be shipped in lots of 1,000. Shipping costs would be reduced, since fewer shipments would be necessary if the item was shipped in carload lots. Annual demand for the unit is expected to continue at 5,000 units, the per-unit cost is $200, carrying costs are estimated at 20 percent per year, and ordering costs (exclusive of freight charges) are estimated to be $40 per order.

a. Should Inverness order this item in lots of 1,000?

b. How much would they save or lose each year by ordering in lots of 1,000 units as opposed to the current EOQ policy?

14-6. Another item stocked by the Inverness Manufacturing Company (problem 14-5) has a constant annual demand of 20,000 units. The cost of the item is $10 per unit, ordering costs are $50 per order, and carrying cost is 20 percent per year.

a. What is the optimal purchase order quantity?

b. What is the optimal time between orders?

c. The supplier for this item offers quantity discounts according to the following schedule:

Order quantity	Cost per item
Less than 3,000	$10.00
3,000–9,999	9.00
10,000 and over	8.50

Should either of these discounts be taken? Substantiate your answer with annual cost comparisons.

d. Suppose that as an alternative strategy, the same item can be made in house with existing equipment that can produce 120 units per day. If demand is known to be 80 per day (20,000 per year), cost of producing the item is $6 per unit, and setup costs are figured to be $1,000 per production run, what is the optimal production lot size? (*Note*: Carrying costs remain 20 percent.)

e. Under the alternative listed in *d*, what will be the maximum inventory?

f. Which alternative policy *c* or *d* would you choose and why?

14-7. The Bastille Auto Parts Company manufactures various replacement parts for automobiles. One of the items they produce is a fuel pump which has an annual demand of 20,000 units, and the cost of production, including all labor, material, and overhead is $10.

The cost per production setup is estimated at $50 and the annual holding cost rate is assumed to be 25 percent. The plant operates 250 days per year and can produce pumps at the rate of 400 per day.

a. How many manufacturing runs should be scheduled per year if the pump is produced on a nonbatch basis?

b. What is the optimal lot size?

c. What is the maximum inventory level in units?

d. What would the optimal lot size be if the pump were produced in batches (assuming the same setup cost applies)?

14-8. The Broadway Electronics Company manufactures a video tape recorder that has an annual demand of 10,000 units and a cost of production of $500. Setup costs per production run are estimated to be $1,000, and the annual holding cost rate is 20 percent. The recorder can be assembled at a rate of 200 per day, and the plant operates 250 days per year.

a. If production follows a nonbatch pattern, what is the optimal production lot size?

b. If production follows a batch pattern, what is the optimal production lot size (assuming the same setup cost applies)?

14-9. The Broadway Electronics Company (problem 14-8) is also considering importation of a home video camera unit, made by Rising Sun Electronics of Japan, which would be distributed under the Broadway name. Annual demand is expected to be 1,000 units, and the cameras would cost Broadway $600 each. Purchase costs are expected to be $200 per order and carrying costs 20 percent.

a. What would be the optimal order quantity?

b. What would be the total annual relevant costs?

15

Variable Demand Models

The preceding chapter considered models that assumed constant, uniform demand rates. These models also assumed that the time to replenish inventories was instantaneous or of a fixed, known duration. This chapter examines models that relax the assumptions of the preceding chapter, treating situations where the demand is variable and considering issues related to the management of inventories, including computer implementation.

The first section deals with the case of lumpy, or nonuniform, demand. As pointed out in Chapter 14, lumpy demand is frequently the rule rather than the exception, resulting from intermittent manufacturing schedules. For these models we continue to assume that the demand variability is known and predictable, relating only to the nonuniformity of demand.

The second section considers models in which the demand variability results from the unpredictability of demand, as would be the case for the end items or finished goods. The demand for these items is subject to the vagaries of customer behavior.

The chapter concludes with a discussion of various ways in which inventory models can be implemented.

Lumpy Demand Models

We turn our attention to inventory models for items which have lumpy or nonuniform demand. As described earlier, demand for raw materials, parts, components, etc., is often nonuniform because of intermittent manufacturing or assembly requirements for the end items or subassemblies in which they are **515** used. If power drills, for example, are assembled the first week of each month, demand for the parts and components used exclusively in these drills will exist only during the initial week of each month.

The demand for parts and materials used in end items produced on a continuous basis is also frequently lumpy. This results because, even though the end item may be assembled continuously, it may be more economical to produce the subassemblies needed on an intermittent or batch basis. For instance, a bicycle manufacturer may operate a continuous assembly line but find it economically advantageous to produce pedal assemblies on an intermittent basis. The demand for pedals and other parts needed for a pedal assembly would therefore follow a lumpy or nonuniform demand pattern.

The models presented in this section are designed to match inventory decisions to these lumpy demand patterns and therefore are expected to perform better than would be the case if the uniform demand EOQ models were used instead. Nevertheless, we find that the same principles used to develop optimum decisions in the uniform case (balancing ordering and holding costs) are the basis for decision making in the lumpy demand case.

Wagner-Whitin Algorithm

An early approach to dealing with the lumpy demand situation was a dynamic programming procedure developed by Wagner and Whitin.[1] The assumptions necessary to describe this situation include: (1) demand is known with certainty but may vary from period to period, (2) replenishment orders are made periodically such that stock arrives at the beginning of the period, (3) shortages are not allowed, and (4) ordering and holding costs are known and constant. The model permits the optimal ordering decisions to be determined, as to both timing and quantity, over any specified planning horizon.

Heuristic Decision Rules

Although the Wagner-Whitin approach is fairly efficient from a computational standpoint, in practice one or more heuristic lot sizing rules frequently are used instead. This is partly due to management difficulties in understanding the logic of the Wagner-Whitin approach and partly due to the number of inventory items and length of the planning horizon for which the lot sizing decision must be made. It is not uncommon to find inventories that number in the tens of thousands of items for which a 50- to 100-period planning horizon would be necessary in practice. Even with heuristic decision rules, a high-speed computer's computation time is likely to be in hours. For these reasons, the Wagner-Whitin procedure will not be discussed. This section will describe several of the more commonly used heuristic ordering rules instead.

This type of problem is best illustrated by means of an example. The Kutz Company manufactures and sells a laser cutting machine for cutting fabric. The demand for the next 10 weeks for the control panel used in this machine is shown in Table 15-1. This item is ordered from a supplier, and ordering costs are assumed to be $100 per order. Inventory carrying costs are $1 per unit per period. The beginning inventory of control panels is assumed to be 0.

---

[1]H. Wagner and T. M. Whitin, "Dynamic Version of the Economic Lot Size Model," *Management Science*, vol. 5, no. 1 (1958), pp. 89–96.

TABLE 15-1
Ten-Week Demand Pattern for Kutz Company Control Panel

	Period									
	1	*2*	*3*	*4*	*5*	*6*	*7*	*8*	*9*	*10*
Demand	10	30	20	5	65	30	40	10	50	40

Lot-for-Lot The simplest procedure, called *lot-for-lot,* requires that an order be received in any period for which a nonzero demand exists. As you will recall (see Table 15-1), the control panel had a nonzero demand in each of the 10 periods. Thus, if the lot-for-lot heuristic were used, we would place a separate order for each of the 10 periods. Note that the lot-for-lot method always maximizes ordering costs, since an order is placed for every nonzero demand period, and minimizes inventory holding costs, since ending inventory is always expected to be zero. This method is most effective when setup or ordering costs are very low or demand is quite sporadic, with many zero-demand periods. For the Kutz Company control panel problem 10 orders would need to be placed as shown below:

	Period received									
	1	*2*	*3*	*4*	*5*	*6*	*7*	*8*	*9*	*10*
Quantity	10	30	20	5	65	30	40	10	50	40

This heuristic ordering pattern would thus incur ordering costs of $1,000 (10 orders at $100 each) and 0 holding costs (no ending inventory for any of the periods), for a total cost of $1,000.

EOQ The standard EOQ model can be applied in a lumpy demand situation, even though the EOQ assumption of uniform demand is not met. The effectiveness of this approach often depends upon by how much this uniformity assumption is violated.

In order to use the EOQ approach, we need to modify the standard formula slightly. Previously we have always expressed both demand and holding costs on an annual basis. None of the other elements in the EOQ formula involve time measurement. In our problem the holding costs are expressed per unit per period, or $pC_H = \$1$ per unit per period. Since holding costs are expressed per period, we must ensure that demand is also expressed per period so that the time units in our expression are compatible. This presents a small problem since the demand varies from period to period. To overcome that problem, we need to use average demand, which is easily calculated as

$$\frac{\text{Average demand}}{\text{per period}} = \frac{10 + 30 + 20 + 5 + 65 + 30 + 40 + 10 + 50 + 40}{10}$$

$$= \frac{300}{10} = 30 \text{ units per period}$$

The appropriate parameters for the EOQ formula are thus

$$D = 30 \qquad C_O = \$100 \qquad pC_H = \$1$$

which leads to

$$Q^* = \sqrt{\frac{2(30)(\$100)}{\$1}} = \sqrt{6,000} = 77.45 \approx 77 \text{ units}$$

Since we do not permit stockouts or back orders, an order (for 77 units) would need to be received in any period for which the demand exceeds the inventory balance left over from the previous period. For our example, the first order for 77 units received in period 1 would satisfy demand for the first 4 periods, requiring the second order to be received in period 5. The remaining orders, as shown below, would be determined in a similar manner:

	|| *Period received*									
	1	*2*	*3*	*4*	*5*	*6*	*7*	*8*	*9*	*10*
Quantity	77				77	77			77	

Note that the use of a fixed order quantity, as required by this rule, causes obvious order-demand mismatches. For instance, the first order of 77 units is intended to cover the first 4 periods (since the second order will be received in period 5), whose demand totals 65 units. Thus 12 units were carried for 4 periods that need not have been ordered in the first place. Costs could have been reduced by lowering the initial order from 77 to 65 units (covering the first four periods) or raising the order size to 130 (covering the first five periods).

Periodic Order Quantity   The *periodic order quantity* (POQ) procedure attempts to overcome the order-demand mismatch problem of the EOQ method, while basing the order timing decision on EOQ principles.

The POQ method requires the translation of the EOQ *quantity* into *time periods* rather than units. For our example, the EOQ quantity of 77 units is equivalent to slightly more than $2\frac{1}{2}$ periods of average demand ($77/30 = 2.6$ periods). This quantity would be rounded up to three periods and the POQ procedure would require that whenever demand in a period exceeds the ending inventory from the previous period, an order should be received that matches the total demand for the next three periods.

Thus the first order is placed for 60 units, which exactly covers the requirements for the first three periods, the second order covers demand for periods 4, 5, and 6, and so on, as shown below.

	|| *Period received*									
	1	*2*	*3*	*4*	*5*	*6*	*7*	*8*	*9*	*10*
Quantity	60			100			100			40

This leads to ordering costs of $400 (4 orders) and holding costs of $305 (average inventory of 30.5 units), for a total cost of $705.

Fixed Order Quantity Based on External Constraints   Frequently the size of the order may be restricted by considerations other than the holding or ordering costs. These include minimum order requirements (to obtain quantity discount, for instance), standard batch sizes (to fit material transport or process requirements), quantities based on unit of issue requirements (i.e., issued in 55-gallon drums), etc.

If, for the example problem, a fixed order quantity of 50 had been used, the pattern of orders would appear as below:

Period received

	1	2	3	4	5	6	7	8	9	10
Quantity	50		50		50	50		50	50	

Part Period Balancing A method frequently used in practice for dependent demand items is called the *part period balancing,* or least total cost, method. This approach attempts to balance ordering and holding costs in a manner similar to EOQ. Recall that the Optimal EOQ decision results in ordering and holding costs that are equal. The part period balancing procedure considers various order size options and chooses the one that most nearly balances the two cost elements. An exact balance cannot be achieved, as we could for EOQ, because demands occur in discrete period-by-period lumps rather than a consistent uniform pattern.

The first decision, for our example problem, concerns the size of the order to be received in period 1. If an order is received sufficient to cover demand for period 1 only, ordering costs will be $100 and there will be no holding costs. The holding costs can be increased by ordering enough units to cover more than one period's demand. The question of how many periods to include is answered by choosing the set of periods whose total holding costs are closest to the ordering cost, in this case $100.

Thus, if an order covers demand for periods 1 and 2, the 30 units needed in period 2 will be carried for one period at a cost of $1 per unit or total holding costs of $30. If the order covers periods 1, 2, and 3, an additional holding cost of $40 would be incurred to carry for two periods the 20 units needed in period 3. Thus total holding costs would be $70 for this option.

Expanding the order to include the demand for period 4 adds $15 in holding costs (5 units carried 3 periods), yielding a total of $85. Including the demand for period 5 costs an extra $260 (65 units carried for 4 periods) and brings the total holding costs to $345.

We need not consider any other options, since our total holding costs already exceed $100 and any further options can only increase this cost. Clearly the $85 holding cost associated with ordering to cover demand for periods 1 through 4 comes closest to the ordering cost of $100.[1] Therefore, the part period balancing procedure would conclude that the first order placed, which is to arrive in period 1, should be equal to the sum of the demands for the first four periods (10 + 30 + 20 + 5 = 65).

The second order must therefore arrive in period 5. If it covers only period 5's demand, holding costs would be zero. Including demand for period 6 would cost $30 (30 units carried 1 period) in holding charges. The addition of

---

[1] It is possible that the holding cost for one option could be as much above the ordering cost as the cost for another option is below. For instance, if the cost of including period 5 in the order had been $30, a $115 holding cost would result. Since the $115 is as much above the $100 ordering cost as the $85 is below, a tie results. Since no clear-cut procedure exists for breaking this tie, we can arbitrarily select one or we can try both and see which leads to a better solution.

TABLE 15-2
Determination of Part Period Balancing Order Quantities for
Kutz Company Control Panel Problem

Order number	Order to cover periods	Ordering cost, $	Holding cost, $
1	1	100	0
1	1, 2	100	$30(1) = 30$
1	1, 2, 3	100	$30 + 20(2) = 70$
1	1, 2, 3, 4	100	$70 + 5(3) = 85^*$
1	1, 2, 3, 4, 5	100	$85 + 65(4) = 345$
2	5	100	0
2	5, 6	100	$30(1) = 30$
2	5, 6, 7	100	$30 + 40(2) = 110^*$
3	8	100	0
3	8, 9	100	$50(1) = 50$
3	8, 9, 10	100	$50 + 40(2) = 130^*$

Total cost = $100 + $85 + $100 + $110 + $100 + $130 = $625

*Best option (closest to the $100 ordering cost).

period 7 adds $80 (40 units carried 2 periods) to the holding costs for a total of $110. Since the total now exceeds $100, no further options need be considered. The $110 figure is closest to $100; so our selected order for period 5 should cover demand for periods 5, 6, and 7 for a total of 135 units (65 + 30 + 40).

Our next order must arrive in period 8. If we include demand for period 9, we will incur $50 (50 units carried 1 period) in holding costs. The addition of demand for period 10 would raise holding costs by $80 (40 units carried 2 periods) to a total of $130. This last case is closest to $100, and our final order should therefore include demand for periods 8, 9, and 10 (10 + 50 + 40 = 100).

The calculations for each step are summarized in Table 15-2. As shown, the total cost for this solution is $625.

INSTANT REPLAY   Determine the part period balancing decisions that would result for the example problem if holding costs were $2.50 per unit per period rather than $1.

CHECK   Orders should be received as follows: 40 units in period 1, 25 units in period 3, 95 units in period 5, 50 units in period 7, and 90 units in period 9. Note that as might be expected, higher holding costs resulted in an increase in the number of orders and a decline in the average inventory. Total costs based on the $2.50 holding cost rate would be $787.50.

Least Unit Cost   The final heuristic considered is called the *least unit cost method*. This procedure determines the order quantities in a way that minimizes the per-unit ordering and holding costs of each order. In each case the ordering and holding cost total is divided by the number of units ordered to arrive at an average per-unit cost. Normally, as the order size is increased, this cost will

TABLE 15-3
Determination of Least Unit Cost Order Quantities
for Kutz Company Control Panel Problem

Order number	Order to cover periods	Ordering + holding costs	Units ordered	Average cost per unit
1	1	100	10	10.00
1	1, 2	130	40	3.25
1	1, 2, 3	170	60	2.83*
1	1, 2, 3, 4	185	65	2.85
2	4	100	5	20.00
2	4, 5	165	70	2.36
2	4, 5, 6	225	100	2.25*
2	4, 5, 6, 7	345	140	2.46
3	7	100	40	2.50
3	7, 8	110	50	2.20
3	7, 8, 9	210	100	2.10*
3	7, 8, 9, 10	330	140	2.36
4	10	100	40	2.50*

*Best option (lowest average cost per unit).

first fall and then begin to rise. As soon as an increase in average cost is detected, the decision with the lowest average cost can be selected.

To illustrate, refer to Table 15-3, which summarizes the necessary calculations for our example problem. The first decision considered four options ranging from ordering only for period 1 up to ordering for the first four periods. Average unit costs were calculated by dividing the total holding and ordering cost for each option by the number of units ordered. This average cost began at $10, fell first to $3.25, then to $2.83, and finally rose slightly to $2.85. At that point the third option (order to cover periods 1, 2, and 3) was selected and the second decision began with period 4. The lowest average cost for the second order was based on covering demand for periods 4, 5, and 6. The third decision selected periods 7, 8, and 9 as best, necessitating a fourth order to be received in period 10.

INSTANT REPLAY Determine the least unit cost ordering decisions that would result for the Kutz control panel if ordering costs were $60 rather than $100.

CHECK Orders should be placed to be received in period 1 for 60 units, in period 4 for 70 units, in period 6 for 70 units, in period 8 for 60 units, and in period 10 for 40 units.

Comparison of Methods

Table 15-4 provides a summary of the ordering decisions and inventory costs for each of the heuristics discussed above, as applied to the Kutz control panel

TABLE 15-4
Summary of Heuristic and Optimal Solutions and Costs for the Kutz Company Control Panel Problem

Heuristic rule	Orders to be received in period										Ordering cost	Holding cost	Total cost
	1	2	3	4	5	6	7	8	9	10			
Lot-for-lot	10	30	20	5	65	30	40	10	50	40	$1,000		$1,000
EOQ	77				77	77			77		400	$336	736
Periodic order quantity	60			100			100			40	400	305	705
Fixed order quantity (Q = 50)	50		50		50	50		50	50		600	265	865
Part period balancing	65				135			100			300	325	625
Least unit cost	60			100			100			40	400	305	705
Optimal solution	65				145				90		300	265	565

problem. Although it is dangerous to reach hard and fast conclusions on the basis of a single example problem, several observations can be made. The optimal solution to the problem, as found using the Wagner-Whitin algorithm, has a cost of $565. This is, in fact, lower than the cost of any of the heuristic solutions. Referring to Table 15-4, we see that the best heuristic solution was found by the part period balancing method, which had a cost 10.6 percent higher than the optimal cost. The importance of the decision is highlighted by the fact that the worst solution, based on the lot-for-lot rule, was 77 percent higher than the optimal solution. Although the absolute cost differential may be relatively small, when you consider that the total inventory may consist of 10,000 or more items, the total cost impact can be quite significant.

On the other hand, this same inventory size factor tends to restrict the procedures used in practice to those that are computationally quick, which supports the use of heuristics rather than optimizing procedures, such as Wagner-Whitin. The choice between heuristics is more difficult to make. Although part period balancing performed best on our example problem, it is easy to find demand patterns for which each of the other heuristics will perform best. In practice, most firms do not stick to the use of a single heuristic but attempt to match the right heuristic to each item or class of items. For example, the lot-for-lot rule might be used for items with sporadic and infrequent demand. A fixed order quantity rule might be used for items with relatively uniform demand or where external constraints dictate. Part period balancing might be used for items with lumpy but frequent demands.

A comparison of the uniform demand models discussed in Chapter 14 with the lumpy demand models presented above should highlight one major difference. Since lumpy demand models require demand information to be provided on a period-by-period basis, the information requirement when implementing any of these models is substantially greater than that necessary to use the uniform demand EOQ models.

Fortunately, many computer manufacturers offer software packages, usually called material requirements planning (MRP) systems, which among other benefits, provide just such a period-by-period breakdown of demand and ordering decisions. Most of these packages contain the various heuristic ordering procedures discussed in this chapter.

Uncertain Demand Models

The lumpy demand models dealt with the question of known but variable demand. The following sections treat demand variations due to uncertainty. In the preceding chapter, the constant demand models that were considered assumed that demand followed a predictable, uniform pattern. In practice, demand, whether lumpy or uniform, is often quite variable, and we can no longer ignore the possibility of stockouts and their related costs. Carrying additional inventory or safety stock is one way in which the risk of stockout can be reduced. As will soon be clear, the question of how much safety stock should be carried is essentially the same as answering the question: When should we order?

Determining When to Order

Until now our attention has been focused almost exclusively on determining the quantity to order. The following sections will concentrate on determining when the order should be placed. Assume for the moment that demand is completely predictable and uniform. Suppose, for example, that demand for an item is constant at 100 units per day. If we are to determine when a replenishment order should be placed, we need to know how long it takes from the time the order is placed until the stock is actually received. This time interval is commonly referred to as *replenishment lead time*.

Suppose for our example that lead time is always 8 days. The optimal time to order is clearly 8 days prior to when we use up the existing inventory. Ordering any earlier incurs additional holding costs and ordering any later will generate stockouts.

It is more practical to convert the replenishment lead time into an equivalent on-hand inventory level. This is done by calculating the usage during lead time:

$$\begin{array}{c}\text{Usage during}\\\text{lead time}\end{array} = \left(\begin{array}{c}\text{usage}\\\text{per day}\end{array}\right) \times \left(\begin{array}{c}\text{number of days}\\\text{of lead time}\end{array}\right)$$

For our example

$$\text{Usage during lead time} = (100)(8) = 800$$

Thus, when the on-hand inventory level drops to 800 units, we need to place a replenishment order. Since demand is 100 units per day and lead time is 8 days, the 800 units on hand at the time the replenishment order is placed will be exactly used up at the time the stock is replenished. This relationship is shown pictorially in Figure 15-1. The on-hand inventory level used to trigger a replenishment order is normally called the *reorder point*.

Of course, in practice it is not very likely that we would know with certainty either the lead time or the usage per day. In such cases we could use

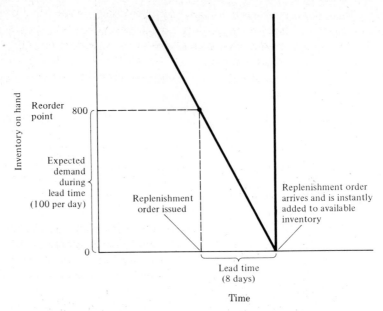

FIGURE 15-1 Calculation of reorder point with certain demand.

expected lead time and expected daily usage, but any deviations would lead to stockouts or excess inventory levels. This is illustrated in Figure 15-2 where two stockouts occur, the first due to greater than expected demand and the second due to longer than expected lead time.

To reduce the likelihood and severity of stockouts, we obviously can order earlier. This is equivalent to adjusting the reorder point to a higher level by adding safety or reserve stock. Thus our reorder point is calculated from

$$\text{Reorder point} = \left(\begin{array}{c}\text{expected demand} \\ \text{during lead time}\end{array}\right) + \left(\begin{array}{c}\text{safety} \\ \text{stock}\end{array}\right)$$

The safety stock provides a cushion against both longer than expected lead times and higher than expected demand. This is graphically depicted in Figure 15-3.

The key decision is, thus, to determine the best size of the safety stock. The tradeoff is between the holding costs incurred by carrying too much safety stock and the stockout costs associated with too little safety stock. In general, we choose a safety stock that permits us to satisfy "reasonable maximum demand" during the replenishment period.

Many factors will have an impact on deciding what constitutes reasonable maximum demand. Some are objective, measurable factors such as the ability to forecast demand accurately, the ability to forecast or control the length of the lead time, the frequency of reordering, the pattern and stability of demand, and the length of the lead time. Others are more subjective, such as the willingness to run the risk of stockout or the desired level of service to be achieved.

Frequently, the level of safety stock to be carried is defined as $k\sigma$, where σ represents an objective measure of demand variability for the replenishment lead time (standard deviation of demand) and k, the number of standard deviations, is set subjectively to limit the stockout risk or achieve a desired level of service.

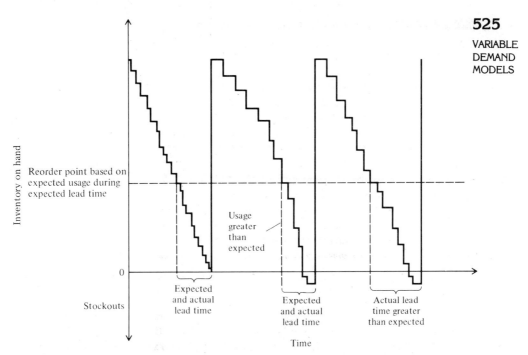

FIGURE 15-2 Effects of demand and lead time variability on inventory stockout patterns.

The tradeoff between the cost of carrying safety stock and the benefits gained through better service can be viewed as attempting to establish balance between these two elements; this balance is shown graphically in Figure 15-4.

To illustrate the nature of this tradeoff decision, consider a simple example problem. Suppose that the duplicating department of Ivy University pur-

FIGURE 15-3 Use of safety stock to deal with uncertainty.

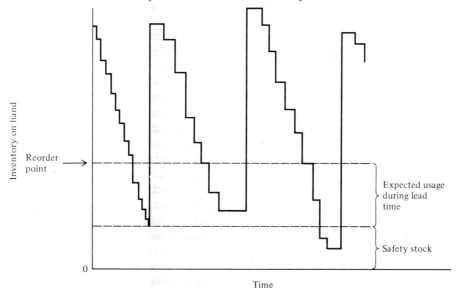

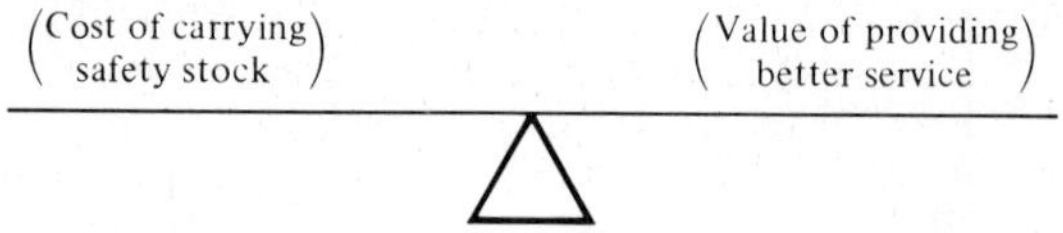

$$\left(\begin{matrix}\text{Cost of carrying} \\ \text{safety stock}\end{matrix}\right) \qquad \left(\begin{matrix}\text{Value of providing} \\ \text{better service}\end{matrix}\right)$$

FIGURE 15-4   Fundamental safety stock tradeoff between cost and service.

chases two sizes of paper from the same supplier: regular size ($8\frac{1}{2} \times 11$) and legal size ($8\frac{1}{2} \times 14$). This supplier has consistently filled all orders within 1 week. Thus we can assume a 1-week lead time for these two items. The demand past histories for both sizes of paper are shown for the last 10 weeks in Table 15-5. Note that the average demand for the two sizes is identical, although the demand patterns are different.

Suppose that the manager of the duplicating department has decided to carry enough safety stock to limit the risk of stockout to 10 percent. This is more commonly referred to as a 90 percent service level.

Although the average demand for the two items, as shown in Table 15-5, is identical, the variability of demand does differ, as shown in Table 15-6, where the demand data have been reorganized to show the probability of specific demands based on the past history.

Since lead time is 1 week, the reorder point for both items must be set so as to cover maximum reasonable demand, which in this case is defined (by management policy) to be 90 percent of possible demands. For regular size paper the reorder point should be set at 2,200 units, since 90 percent of the demands in past periods have been less than or equal to that level. Since the average demand is 1,800 units, a reorder point of 2,200 units implies a 400-unit safety stock (2,200 − 1,800 = 400).

Legal size paper, on the other hand, has a much more variable demand pattern, and a 90 percent service level requires a reorder point of 2,800. This, in turn, means that 1,000 reams of safety stock (2,800 − 1,800) must be carried to meet the stated service level objective. Thus, although the two items have the same average demand, the higher variability for legal size paper requires a higher level of safety stock to provide the same level of service.

TABLE 15-5
Past History of Demand (in Reams) for Ivy University
Paper Replenishment Example

Week	Regular size	Legal size
1	1,600	1,800
2	1,800	2,800
3	1,200	1,600
4	2,000	2,600
5	2,200	2,000
6	2,600	400
7	1,600	2,200
8	1,200	3,000
9	1,800	1,000
10	2,000	600
Total demand	18,000	18,000
Average demand	1,800	1,800

TABLE 15-6
Demand Probabilities for Ivy University
Paper Replenishment Problem

Demand, reams	Regular size paper		Legal size paper	
	Probability	Cumulative probability	Probability	Cumulative probability
400			.1	.1
600			.1	.2
1,000			.1	.3
1,200	.2	.2		
1,600	.2	.4	.1	.4
1,800	.2	.6	.1	.5
2,000	.2	.8	.1	.6
2,200	.1	.9	.1	.7
2,600	.1	1.0	.1	.8
2,800			.1	.9
3,000			.1	1.0

Interdependency of Order Size and Reorder Point

It is important to note that although we have treated the determination of the reorder point independently of the order quantity, these two decisions are, in fact, interdependent. The size of the order quantity chosen will affect the frequency of reordering. Since stockout risk occurs only during the replenishment phase, the relative reordering frequency will have a direct impact on the expected stockout risk.

In other words, specification of a 90 percent service level objective, as we have been using it, will generate different stockout rates, depending upon the reorder frequency.

To illustrate, consider first a 90 percent service level objective for an item that is replenished twice a year. The expected number of stockouts per year can be calculated from

$$\text{Expected stockouts per year} = \left(\begin{array}{c}\text{probability of a} \\ \text{stockout during a} \\ \text{replenishment period}\end{array}\right) \times \left(\begin{array}{c}\text{number of} \\ \text{replenishment} \\ \text{periods per year}\end{array}\right)$$

Thus, for our example we have

Expected annual stockouts = (.10)(2) = .2 stockout per year

This says, in effect, that we can expect 1 stockout to occur every 5 years.

Contrast this with the situation where the same 90 percent service level is used with an item ordered 10 times per year rather than twice.

Expected annual stockouts = (.10)(10) = 1 stockout per year

Thus the same service level policy leads to one stockout per year when the item is ordered 10 times per year and only one stockout every 5 years when ordered twice a year.

If the cost of experiencing a stockout can be specified, it is possible to determine an optimal reorder point that balances the cost of carrying safety stock with the cost of stocking out, recognizing the effect of replenishment frequency.

The optimal reorder point can be found by starting with some minimum value, say, expected demand during lead time, and then increasing the reorder point as long as the cost of adding one additional unit of safety stock is less than the marginal cost of not stocking that unit. At the optimal reorder level these two costs would be equal.

The marginal cost of adding one unit of safety stock is simply the cost of carrying that one unit in inventory, or pC_H (where p = cost per unit and C_H is the annual holding cost rate). The marginal cost of *not* carrying that one unit of safety stock is equal to the expected stockout cost or the probability that the additional unit will be demanded during a replenishment period times the number of replenishment periods, and multiplied in turn by the cost per unit short.

$$\begin{pmatrix} \text{Annual marginal} \\ \text{cost of not} \\ \text{carrying one} \\ \text{additional unit} \end{pmatrix} = \begin{pmatrix} \text{probability unit} \\ \text{will be demanded} \\ \text{during replenishment} \\ \text{period} \end{pmatrix} \times \begin{pmatrix} \text{number of} \\ \text{replenishment} \\ \text{periods} \\ \text{per year} \end{pmatrix} \times \begin{pmatrix} \text{cost} \\ \text{per} \\ \text{unit} \\ \text{short} \end{pmatrix}$$

Note that the probability that a unit will be demanded during a replenishment period is equivalent to 1 minus the service level provided when that unit is added to safety stock. Thus, if we let SL represent service level, the probability that a unit will be demanded during a replenishment period is $1 - \text{SL}$. If we also let C_U represent the per-unit stockout cost, we can then define

$$\begin{pmatrix} \text{Annual marginal cost of not carrying} \\ \text{one additional unit} \end{pmatrix} = (1 - \text{SL})\frac{D}{Q}C_U$$

This cost should be equal to the cost of adding that additional unit (pC_H) at the optimal service level. Thus we can set these two costs equal to each other.

$$\begin{pmatrix} \text{Annual marginal cost of carrying} \\ \text{one additional unit} \end{pmatrix} = \begin{pmatrix} \text{annual marginal cost of not carrying} \\ \text{one additional unit} \end{pmatrix}$$

$$pC_H = (1 - \text{SL})\frac{D}{Q}C_U$$

In this case the only unknown value is the appropriate service level (SL) to be used. Therefore, we need to solve for SL in terms of the other variables. This leads to

$$\text{SL} = 1 - \frac{Q}{D}\frac{pC_H}{C_U}$$

This equation can be used to find the optimal reorder point as follows: First, use the standard EOQ formula to find a value for Q. Then, substituting Q and other values into the equation above, solve for the appropriate service level, as shown below. Finally, using past demand history during lead time choose a reorder point that will yield the desired service level.

As an example, suppose the Ivy University duplication department also stocks boxes of blank transparencies. This item has an annual demand of 1,000 boxes, a cost of $10 per box, and lead time of 1 week. Further assume an ordering cost of $20 and carrying cost of 10 percent.

The first step is to calculate the appropriate order size. In this case we have

$$Q^* = \sqrt{\frac{2DC_0}{pC_H}} = \sqrt{\frac{2(1,000)(20)}{(10)(.1)}} = 200$$

Using this value, we next solve for the appropriate service level. Assume here that the per-unit stockout cost is $4.

$$SL = 1 - \frac{Q}{D}\frac{pC_H}{C_U} = 1 - \left(\frac{200}{1,000}\right)\left(\frac{10(.1)}{4}\right) = 1 - \frac{1}{20} = .95$$

The reorder point would then be chosen so that the duplicating department expects a stockout of transparencies only 5 percent of the time. Thus, if the demand past history was that appearing in Table 15-7, the reorder point would be set at 22 boxes, because demand has been less than or equal to that level 95 percent of the time.

INSTANT REPLAY Suppose that the cost per box short for transparencies was $10 rather than $4. What would the appropriate reorder point be then?

CHECK The reorder point would be 23 boxes, based on a calculated service level of 98 percent.

With the reorder point at 22 boxes and average demand during lead time of 19.46 (see Table 15-7), the duplicating department is carrying $22 - 19.46 = 2.54$ boxes of safety stock. The annual cost of carrying that safety stock is

$$\begin{array}{c}\text{Annual cost of} \\ \text{carrying safety stock}\end{array} = \left(\begin{array}{c}\text{per-unit} \\ \text{carrying costs}\end{array}\right) \times \left(\begin{array}{c}\text{units of} \\ \text{safety stock}\end{array}\right)$$

$$= (\$10)(.1)(2.54) = \$2.54$$

Annual stockout costs can be obtained using the demand history in Table

TABLE 15-7
Demand Past History Used to Determine
Reorder Point for Boxes of Blank Transparencies

Weekly demand, boxes	Probability	Cumulative probability
15	.03	.03
16	.04	.07
17	.06	.13
18	.12	.25
19	.23	.48
20	.28	.76
21	.13	.89
22	.06	.95
23	.03	.98
24	.02	1.00

Average demand = .03(15) + .04(16) + .06(17) + .12(18) + .23(19)

+ .28(20) + .13(21) + .06(22) + .03(23) + .02(24) = 19.46

15-7. With the reorder point at 22 boxes, 3 percent of the time demand will be 23 boxes and there will be a stockout of 1 box. Likewise, 2 percent of the time demand will be 24 boxes and there will be a shortage of 2 boxes. The other 95 percent of the time no stockouts will occur.

The expected boxes short can be found by multiplying the expected boxes short per replenishment period by the number of replenishments:

$$\begin{array}{c}\text{Annual expected} \\ \text{units short}\end{array} = [(.03)(1) + (.02)(2)]\left(\frac{1,000}{200}\right) = .35$$

This needs to be multiplied by the cost per box short to obtain the annual stockout cost:

$$\begin{array}{c}\text{Annual} \\ \text{stockout cost}\end{array} = \left(\begin{array}{c}\text{cost per} \\ \text{unit short}\end{array}\right) \times \left(\begin{array}{c}\text{annual expected} \\ \text{units short}\end{array}\right)$$

$$= \$4(.35) = \$1.40$$

Thus, using a reorder point of 22 boxes will lead to an expected annual stockout cost of $1.40.

Determining the Reorder Point for Normally Distributed Demand

In the previous cases, our knowledge of past demand history was given in empirical, tabular form. If past demand follows an approximately normal distribution, we can use normal tables to determine the safety stock and reorder point.

Figure 15-5 illustrates a typical normal demand curve. The vertical line drawn in the right tail of the curve represents a specified reorder point. The shaded area of the curve corresponds to the probability that demand during a replenishment period will not exceed the reorder point or, in other words, is equivalent to the service level. The unshaded area, in the right tail of the curve, corresponds to the probability that demand will exceed the reorder point or is equivalent to the risk of a stockout.

Our problem is, given a target service level, to determine the appropriate reorder point that provides that specified level of service. This is easily done using Table 15-8, which shows, among other things, the number of standard deviations of demand during the replenishment period that must be carried as safety stock in order to meet various service level objectives. Thus we can determine the required safety stock from

FIGURE 15-5 Normal demand curve relationship to service level and reorder point.

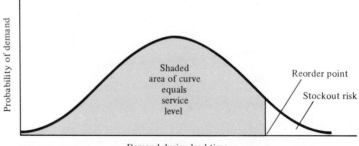

$$\begin{matrix} \text{Required} \\ \text{safety} \\ \text{stock} \end{matrix} = \begin{pmatrix} \text{number of standard deviations} \\ \text{required to achieve} \\ \text{desired service level} \end{pmatrix} \times \begin{pmatrix} \text{observed standard} \\ \text{deviation of demand} \\ \text{during replenishment} \end{pmatrix}$$

The first factor is obtained from Table 15-8, while the second factor comes from past demand history.

To illustrate, suppose our duplicating department also stocks staples with an average demand during lead time of 100 boxes and a standard deviation of 20 boxes. If we desire a 90 percent service level, Table 15-8 indicates that 1.28 standard deviations of safety stock are needed. Thus,

$$\text{Safety stock} = 1.28(20) = 25.6 \text{ or } 26 \text{ boxes}$$

The reorder point is equal to the sum of average demand during lead time and the required safety stock:

$$\text{Reorder point} = 100 + 26 = 126 \text{ boxes}$$

Frequently in practice the mean absolute deviation is used in lieu of the standard deviation. The mean absolute deviation, or MAD, is simply the average absolute deviation (without regard to sign) of a variable from its average. Thus if we had n periods of past history for demand d_i, and d is the average demand per period, the MAD would be calculated using

$$\text{MAD} = \frac{\sum_{i=1}^{n} |d_i - \overline{d}|}{n}$$

where the vertical bars indicate absolute value. The standard deviation and the MAD are approximately related as

$$\text{Standard deviation} \simeq (1.25) \text{ MAD}$$

Actually we don't need to remember this relationship because Table 15-8 pro-

TABLE 15-8
Safety Stock Factors for Normally Distributed Demand

Desired service level	Number of standard deviations required	Number of MADs (mean absolute deviations) required
50	.00	.00
55	.13	.16
60	.25	.31
65	.39	.49
70	.52	.65
75	.67	.84
80	.84	1.05
85	1.04	1.30
90	1.28	1.60
95	1.65	2.06
96	1.75	2.19
97	1.88	2.35
98	2.05	2.56
99	2.33	2.91

vides the number of MADs necessary to achieve a desired service level directly.

To illustrate, suppose that for our staples example we knew the MAD to be 16. From Table 15-8 we find that 1.60 MADs are needed to provide 90 percent service.

The safety stock would, in this case, be calculated as

$$
\begin{array}{c}
\text{Required} \\
\text{safety} \\
\text{stock}
\end{array}
=
\left(
\begin{array}{c}
\text{number of MADs} \\
\text{necessary to achieve} \\
\text{desired service level}
\end{array}
\right)
\times
\left(
\begin{array}{c}
\text{observed MAD} \\
\text{during} \\
\text{replenishment}
\end{array}
\right)
$$

$$= 1.60\,(16) = 25.6 \text{ or } 26 \text{ boxes}$$

Note that the safety stock calculated based on the MAD is exactly the same as we obtained using the standard deviation. This is because the standard deviation was exactly 1.25 as great as the MAD specified. In practice we would not expect to find the same safety stock value using both measures of variation, since the relationship between the standard deviation and MAD is only approximate. Note that MAD and standard deviation are both measures of demand variability. While both are used in industry, only one will be used with a given inventory. The choice is management's.

INSTANT REPLAY   Suppose, for an item with an average demand during lead time of 200 and a MAD of 50, that we desire no more than one stockout per year. What are the required service level and reorder point if the item is replenished 20 times per year?

CHECK   Service level is 95 percent and reorder point is 303.

Adjustments for Differences between Forecast Interval and Lead Time

Often in practice we find that the period of time over which we measure demand differs from the lead time. For instance, the average demand and MAD may be calculated on a weekly basis, while lead time may be some multiple of weeks. Heretofore we have assumed that lead time was always equal to the demand forecast interval; in fact, we always assumed lead time was 1 week.

The formulas used to calculate safety stock in the preceding section require that average demand and either the standard deviation or MAD be expressed for the duration of the lead time. If the forecast interval is not identical to the lead time, the values for average demand and either MAD or standard deviation must be adjusted so that they are stated in terms of the lead time.

This adjustment is straightforward insofar as average demand is concerned. If lead time is four weeks and the average demand is known to be 100 per week, we simply multiply the average demand per week by the number of weeks in the lead time. More generally, we calculate

$$
\begin{array}{c}
\text{Average demand} \\
\text{during lead time}
\end{array}
=
\left(
\begin{array}{c}
\text{average demand during} \\
\text{forecast interval}
\end{array}
\right)
\times
\left(
\frac{\text{length of lead time}}{\text{length of forecast interval}}
\right)
$$

For the example stated we find

$$\text{Average demand during lead time} = (100)\left(\frac{4}{1}\right) = 400$$

Unfortunately, it is not as simple to adjust either the MAD or the standard deviation. The reason for this has to do with the statistical relationship which says that although

$$\text{Variance for 4 weeks} = 4 \text{ (variance for 1 week)}$$

assuming all four weeks are the same, the same relationship does not hold for either the standard deviation or MAD.

To illustrate, assume that the variance for 1 week is 400. Therefore, the variance for 4 weeks is 1,600 (i.e., 4×400). Since the standard deviation is equal to the square root of the variance, the standard deviation for 4 weeks is 40 (i.e., $\sqrt{1,600}$).

Clearly the standard deviation for 1 week is 20 (i.e., $\sqrt{400}$) and it would have been incorrect to multiply this value by 4 to arrive at the standard deviation for 4 weeks, since this would lead to a value of 80 (i.e., 4×20) rather than the correct value of 40.

The correct adjustment can be found by first defining K as the ratio of lead time to the forecast interval, or

$$K = \frac{\text{length of lead time}}{\text{length of forecast interval}}$$

and noting that

$$\text{Variance for } K \text{ periods} = K \text{ (variance for 1 period)}$$

Then because

$$\text{Variance} = (\text{standard deviation})^2$$

we find

$$\left(\begin{matrix}\text{Standard deviation} \\ \text{for } K \text{ periods}\end{matrix}\right)^2 = K \left(\begin{matrix}\text{standard deviation} \\ \text{for one period}\end{matrix}\right)^2$$

Taking the square root of both sides

$$\begin{matrix}\text{Standard deviation} \\ \text{for } K \text{ periods}\end{matrix} = \sqrt{K} \left(\begin{matrix}\text{standard deviation} \\ \text{for one period}\end{matrix}\right)$$

Using the approximate relationship between the standard deviation and MAD, we can derive a similar adjustment formula for MAD, which is

$$\begin{matrix}\text{MAD for} \\ \text{lead time}\end{matrix} = \sqrt{\frac{\text{length of lead time}}{\text{length of forecast interval}}} \left(\begin{matrix}\text{MAD for} \\ \text{forecast interval}\end{matrix}\right)$$

$$= \sqrt{K} \text{ (MAD for forecast interval)}$$

Comprehensive Example Problem

To illustrate the use of the adjustment factor, as well as provide a review of other inventory concepts, we shall work through a comprehensive example problem. Demand, cost, and policy data are shown below.

$$\text{Average weekly demand} = 100 \text{ units}$$

$$\text{MAD per week} = 25$$

$$\text{Ordering cost} = \$40$$

Cost per unit = \$2

Holding costs = 20 percent

Desired service level = 1 stockout per year

Lead time = 4 weeks

Assuming a 50-week operating year, we find annual demand to be 5,000 (i.e., 50 × 100) units. We first need to determine the optimal order quantity

$$Q^* = \sqrt{\frac{2DC_0}{pC_H}} = \sqrt{\frac{2(5,000)(40)}{2(.20)}} = 1,000 \text{ units}$$

In order to calculate the reorder point, we need to determine the target service level. Since annual demand is 5,000 units and we will be ordering in lots of 1,000, we should reorder 5 times per year. A stated policy of 1 stockout per year implies, then, a probability of stockout of .2 per replenishment or, in other words, an 80 percent service level.

Note that both average demand and MAD are given per week while the lead time is 4 weeks. The average demand and MAD for the lead time would be calculated using the adjustment equation as

$$\begin{array}{l} \text{Average demand} \\ \text{for lead time} \end{array} = \left(\begin{array}{c} \text{average demand during} \\ \text{forecast interval} \end{array}\right) \times \left(\frac{\text{length of lead time}}{\text{length of forecast interval}}\right)$$

$$= 100\left(\frac{4}{1}\right) = 400$$

$$\begin{array}{l} \text{MAD for} \\ \text{lead time} \end{array} = \sqrt{\frac{\text{length of lead time}}{\text{length of forecast interval}}} \left(\begin{array}{c} \text{MAD for} \\ \text{forecast interval} \end{array}\right)$$

$$= \sqrt{\frac{4}{1}}\,(25) = 50$$

To achieve an 80 percent service level, Table 15-8 indicates that we need 1.05 MADs of safety stock. Thus

Safety stock = 1.05(50) = 52.5 or 53 units

Finally, the reorder point can be determined:

Reorder point = (average demand for lead time) + (safety stock)

$$= 400 + 53 = 453$$

INSTANT REPLAY   How many additional units of safety stock would be required to increase the service level to 95 percent, and what would be the annual cost of carrying those additional units?

CHECK   50 additional units are needed at an incremental annual cost of \$20.

Computer Implementation

Any study of inventory management models would not be complete without consideration of the manner in which these models are implemented in practice. Although all the concepts and models that have been discussed can be implemented in a manual system, the discussion will focus on computer-based systems for several reasons. First, the large number of inventory items carried by many firms and the need for an inventory system that responds quickly to changes in demand necessitate, in many instances, a computerized system to gain the speed, capacity, and economic advantages that computers provide over manual systems. Second, the rapid spread of minicomputers has allowed even relatively small firms to benefit from the advantages of computerization that were previously limited to larger systems. Finally, the technological advances made in data capturing devices, such as cash registers that automatically record sales item by item, have made it possible for many retail stores to obtain computerized inventory control, where previously it was uneconomical to do so.

The following sections will briefly treat three different types of computerized inventory control systems: (1) *perpetual inventory systems,* (2) *periodic inventory systems,* and (3) *material requirements planning systems.* Each differs to some extent as to the timing of replenishment decisions and the determination of order quantities.

Perpetual Inventory Systems

Many companies use perpetual inventory systems to control their inventories. A perpetual inventory system uses the computer to maintain a current on-hand balance for each item in the inventory. This requires that the inventory balance kept on the computer be increased whenver a replenishment order is received and decreased whenever items are withdrawn from that inventory. The need for a replenishment order is recognized automatically whenever the current on-hand balance reaches the *reorder point*. In some systems the computer prepares a purchase or manufacturing order as soon as the need is recognized. In other cases, the computer prepares a list of those items needing replenishment for action by the purchasing or production control departments.

The quantity to be ordered Q is usually determined by using the appropriate EOQ or ELS model as discussed in Chapter 14. The reorder point is calculated as discussed earlier in this chapter.

A variation of the perpetual inventory system frequently found in manual systems is that referred to as the *two-bin system*. Under this approach the actual physical stock for an item is segregated into two bins, usually adjacent to each other. One bin contains an amount equal to the reorder point quantity, the second bin containing the remaining stock. Stock is drawn as needed from this second bin until that bin is empty. The stockkeeper knows that the reorder point has been reached when that second bin is empty, and therefore notifies the purchasing or production control departments that this item needs replenishment. The first bin is then used to meet demand pending replenishment.

Periodic Inventory Systems

Periodic systems differ from perpetual systems in that the time between replenishments, called the *review period,* is normally fixed while the order quantity itself varies from order to order. Some items are reviewed weekly, others less frequently, once a month, quarterly, annually, etc., and possibly some on a daily basis (in which case the system more closely resembles a perpetual system). At the time of the review, the actual stock on hand is determined and an order is placed for the difference between an *order up to level M* and the actual on-hand balance. The derivation of the level M will be explained shortly.

So far in the discussion, inventory models have been stated in terms more properly suitable for perpetual inventory systems. Fortunately, it is quite easy to adapt these models for use with periodic systems. To do this we can define an optimal *review period* t^*, or time between orders, for the basic EOQ model as

$$t^* = \frac{Q^*}{D} = \sqrt{\frac{2DC_0/C_Hp}{D^2}} = \sqrt{\frac{2C_0}{DC_Hp}}$$

where t^* is in years. For example, suppose annual demand is 400,000, ordering costs are $20 per order, the holding cost rate is 20 percent, and the per-unit cost is $.05. Then the optimal review period would be

$$t^* = \sqrt{\frac{2(20)}{(400,000)(.2)(.05)}} = .1 \text{ years}$$

Thus this item would be optimally reviewed and an order placed every .1 years or 1.2 months or 5.2 weeks or 36.5 days.

INSTANT REPLAY   What should be the optimal time between orders for an item with annual demand of 2,500 units, ordering costs of $15, a purchase cost of $2, and a holding cost rate of 15 percent?

CHECK $t^* = .2$ year, or 5 orders per year.

In practice the review would be fixed at some *convenient interval*. For instance, the review period for the item above might be fixed at once a month, for processing convenience, which only approximates the optimal review period of 1.2 month. For those items purchased from the same supplier, it is often economical to assign each item a common review period so that joint replenishment orders can be placed. Joint replenishment frequently reduces the cost of ordering and provides savings through supplier discounts or reduced shipping costs.

The order up to level M is determined by calculating the maximum reasonable demand during the time equal to a *review period plus the replenishment lead time*. This is equivalent to the expected demand plus safety stock for the review and replenishment periods. Note that since the safety stock is based not only on the demand during the replenishment lead time (as previously assumed) but also on the demand during the review period, the size of the safety stock required for a periodic system will be larger than that required for the same item under a perpetual system.

The reason the safety stock must cover this larger period of demand is that the number of units ordered now plus those already in inventory must be sufficient to cover all demand between now and the time the *next* order will be received. This subsequent order will not be placed until one more review period elapses and will not arrive for an additional period equal to the replenishment lead time. Thus the safety stock must cover the sum of those two time periods. This is shown pictorially in Figure 15-6. Note that the stockout that occurs before the order for q_2 units is received could have been averted by increasing

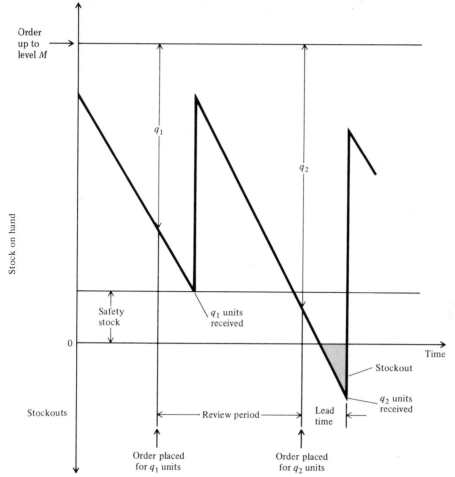

FIGURE 15-6   On-hand inventory balance for a periodic inventory system.

quantity q_1. It resulted from the fact that demand, over the period beginning with the order being placed for q_1 and ending with the order being received for q_2, exceeded the quantity available (q_1 plus that on hand at the time order q_1 was placed).

Although the periodic system requires that additional safety stock be carried, the clerical costs are often less than those for a perpetual system. This is because the reorder status for an item needs to be reviewed only periodically rather than perpetually. In addition the economic benefits of joint replenishment are easier to obtain with a periodic system.

Material Requirements Planning Systems

The most rapid growth in recent years for applied inventory systems has been experienced for our third category, material requirements planning systems (MRP). These systems are particularly useful in a manufacturing environment where the demand requirements for materials, parts, components, etc., can be calculated from the planned manufacturing or assembly schedule for end items.

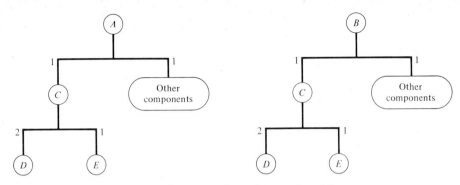

FIGURE 15-7 Simplified bill of materials for end items *A* and *B*.

As an example, consider a situation in which two end items, *A* and *B*, are produced. Suppose that both these items use a common component *C* and that each *C* consists of three parts, 2 *D*s and 1 *E*. These usages and relationships among the parts, components, and end items can be conveniently organized in a tree diagram, commonly referred to as a *bill of materials*. A simplified bill of materials for each of the two end items is shown in Figure 15-7.

The demand or requirements for component *C* and parts *D* and *E* can be derived or calculated from the assembly schedule for end items *A* and *B*. Table 15-9 provides a hypothetical assembly schedule for these two end items. The requirements for component *C* can be easily calculated from the master assembly schedules for items *A* and *B*, because 1 *C* is required for each *A* and each *B* that is to be assembled.

In Table 15-10 we see that the gross requirements or demand for item *C* are calculated by adding together the planned assembly quantities for *A* and *B*. An MRP system maintains a *component requirements plan* for all items similar to that shown for item *C* in Table 15-10. This plan shows the *anticipated* on-hand balance for item *C* projected into the future. Observe that the initial (current) on-hand balance is sufficient to meet the demand or gross requirements for the first two periods. In period 3, however, the projected on-hand balance of 75 is less than the projected demand for period 3, creating a net requirement for (150 − 75) 75 units in period 3. Likewise, the current on-hand balance will not be able to meet projected demands in periods 4, 5, and 6, creating additional net requirements in those periods.

A replenishment order will therefore need to be placed so as to arrive no later than period 3 in order to satisfy the net requirement in that and possibly subsequent periods. Earlier in this chapter we considered lot sizing procedures for lumpy demand situations, including lot-for-lot, periodic order quantity, part period balancing, etc. Most MRP systems have these lot sizing rules available as optional methods for determining order quantities. For our example let us assume that we use a fixed order quantity of 300 for component *C*. Thus an order for 300 units will have to be placed in time to meet the net requirement in period 3.

When should the order be placed? The answer depends on the replenishment lead time. Suppose it takes two periods to fulfill a replenishment order for component *C*. This means that the order must be placed in period 1 if the replenishment is to be received by period 3. You will observe that a *planned order* of 300 units is shown in period 1 in Table 15-10. Note that the 300 units to be received in period 3 will satisfy the net requirements not only for period 3

TABLE 15-9
Master Assembly Schedule for Items A and B

	Period 1	2	3	4	5	6
Item A	100	50	0	50	100	50
Item B	0	75	150	75	0	75

but for periods 4 and 5 as well. The total net requirement for these three periods is 75 + 125 + 100 = 300. Since this uses up all 300 units to be received in period 3, a second order will have to be placed to meet the net requirement of 125 in period 6. This second order will have to be placed in period 4, because of the 2-period lead time. Such a planned order, for the fixed order quantity of 300, is shown in Table 15-10.

Recall that each C is made up of 2 Ds and 1 E (see Figure 15-7). Since we have planned orders for 300 Cs in periods 1 and 4, we know we will need 600 Ds (2 × 300) and 300 Es in each of those periods; we can't make the required number of Cs otherwise. Thus C's planned orders become gross requirements or demands for Ds and Es, as shown in the component requirements plans for components D and E in Table 15-11.

The net requirements for D and E are calculated in the same manner as for C. Since item D has a net requirement of 500 in period 4 and a 1-period lead time, a planned order for the fixed order quantity of 700 is shown in period 3. Item E has a net requirement of 300, a 2-period lead time, and a fixed order quantity of 300. Thus a planned order for 300 is shown in period 2.

A similar logic is used to determine the planned replenishments for all items in inventory. Normally, each period is equivalent to 1 week and the total number of periods included in the planning horizon is 1 year or more. Although we used fixed order quantities for our example problem, in practice we find many of the lumpy demand lot sizing rules being used, particularly lot-for-lot and part period balancing.

TABLE 15-10
Determining Requirements and Planned Orders for Component C
Based on Master Assembly Schedule for Items A and B

A	1	2	3	4	5	6
	100	50	0	50	100	50

B	1	2	3	4	5	6
	0	75	150	75	0	75

Item C		1	2	3	4	5	6
Gross requirements		100	125	150	125	100	125
Stock on hand	300	200	75				
Net requirements				75	125	100	125
Planned orders		300			300		

TABLE 15-11
Computing Component Requirements Plans for Items *D* and *E*
Based on Planned Orders for Item *C*

Item C		Period 1	2	3	4	5	6
Planned orders		300			300		

×2   ×2

Item D		1	2	3	4	5	6	
Gross requirements		600			600			
Stock on hand	700	100	100	100				Lead time = 1 period
Net requirements					500			Order quantity = 700
Planned orders				700				

Item C		1	2	3	4	5	6
Planned orders		300			300		

×1   ×1

Item E		1	2	3	4	5	6	
Gross requirements		300			300			
Stock on hand	300							Lead time = 2 periods
Net requirements					300			Order quantity = 300
Planned orders			300					

When this inventory system is compared with the perpetual or periodic systems, several similarities and differences stand out. Like the periodic system, most MRP systems revise plans and issue orders on a periodic, usually once a week, basis. Like the perpetual system, orders are not placed unless the stock on hand is projected to be insufficient to meet demand (creating a net requirement).

Unlike either perpetual or periodic systems, the interrelationships among the items are exploited by MRP. In our example we saw that the demands and ordering requirements for items *C*, *D*, and *E* were all based on the assembly schedule for end items *A* and *B*.

Furthermore, the degree of detail maintained in an MRP system is considerably greater than for perpetual or periodic systems. Demand, stock on hand, net requirements, and planned orders are maintained for each item on a period-by-period basis (frequently 52 periods or more). This focus on detail necessitates the use of a computer-based system. The computer storage requirements are normally quite high, and it is not unusual for the run time necessary to update the system to be measured in hours.

Final Comments

This chapter has considered a number of practical extensions to the basic inventory concepts treated in Chapter 14. These extensions included variable demand situations and procedures for computer implementation of inventory models.

We considered two types of demand variability. The first, lumpy demand, often results from intermittent manufacturing requirements. Although the demand is predictable, it is not uniform. Although an optimizing procedure, the Wagner-Whitin algorithm, can be used to solve lumpy demand problems, the extensive computational requirements of most practical inventory situations limit the usefulness of this procedure. In practice, many companies turn to one or more heuristic methods designed for lumpy demand problems. We presented a number of these, including the lot-for-lot, EOQ, periodic order quantity, fixed order quantity, part period balancing, and least unit cost procedures.

The second category of variable demand situations was where the variability is due to demand unpredictability. We saw how demand variability could be compensated for by carrying additional stock called safety stock. We considered several methods for computing safety stock. These normally involved managerial specification of the amount of stockout risk considered acceptable.

In the last segment of this chapter we examined three common ways in which the various management science inventory models can be implemented using a computer. We looked at three such approaches: perpetual inventory systems, periodic inventory systems, and material requirements planning systems. Each of these, as discussed, offers certain advantages and disadvantages that need to be considered by management in making a choice of which system should be used.

Key Words

Problems

15-1. The Broadway Electronics Company uses a standardized tape drive unit in several items that it manufactures. The demand for the unit is lumpy because of intermittent assembly schedules for the various items that use this drive unit. The company wishes to determine which of several lot sizing rules should be used for this item. Demand for the coming 12-week period is shown below, based on the planned, end item assembly schedules:

	Week											
	1	*2*	*3*	*4*	*5*	*6*	*7*	*8*	*9*	*10*	*11*	*12*
Demand	200	30	10	0	325	100	50	0	50	10	400	10

If setup costs are $50 per production run and holding costs are $.50 per unit per week, determine the ordering schedule and total relevant costs for the 12-week period using the following lot size policies (assume zero initial inventory): (*a*) lot-for-lot, (*b*) EOQ, (*c*) periodic order quantity, (*d*) fixed order quantity of 400, (*e*) part period balancing, (*f*) least unit cost.

15-2. The Harrington Toy Company uses a certain plastic material in the manufacture of many of the toys that it produces and sells. The demand for this plastic can be calculated in advance from the planned assembly schedule. Demand for this plastic for the next 12 weeks in gallons is shown below:

	Week											
	1	*2*	*3*	*4*	*5*	*6*	*7*	*8*	*9*	*10*	*11*	*12*
Demand	200	200	200	250	250	300	300	250	200	200	200	200

Ordering costs for this plastic are $20 per order and carrying costs are $.10 per gallon per week. Determine the ordering schedule and total relevant costs for the 12-week period using each of the following lot size procedures (assume zero initial inventory): (*a*) lot-for-lot, (*b*) EOQ, (*c*) periodic order quantity, (*d*) fixed order quantity of 600 units, (*e*) part period balancing, (*f*) least unit cost.

15-3. Comparison of the relative total cost performance of the various lumpy demand lot sizing procedures in the two situations described in problems 15-1 and 15-2 should show marked differences. Provide an explanation that accounts for these differences in relative cost performance.

15-4. Dack and Blecker, a major power tool manufacturer, purchases 240,000 line cords per year from a single supplier at a cost of $.30 each. The average lead time between order placement and receipt of stock is 10 working days. The company operates 300 days per year. A study of the inventory system has shown that the cost of placing an order is $112.50 while annual carrying costs are 20 percent. The lead time usage rate has been determined from records of past usage and is shown below.

Usage during lead time	Probability
7,400	.04
7,600	.08
7,800	.12
8,000	.50
8,200	.11
8,400	.08
8,600	.07

a. Determine the optimal replenishment order quantity.
b. What level of safety stock will provide 85 percent service level?
c. Determine the reorder point for the 85 percent service level.
d. What service level should be used if per-unit out of stock costs are $1?
e. What reorder point should be used to obtain the service level of part d?

15-5. The producer of Maxigrow Hair Restorer uses, on the average, 400 gallons per week of a chemical compound which is ordered in quantities of 5,000 gallons at a price of $4 per gallon. Replenishment lead time is 2 weeks and the MAD is 250 gallons per week. Demand during lead time is assumed to be normally distributed. The company has established a 95 percent service level objective for this item. If holding costs are $.01 per gallon per week, find the (a) appropriate level of safety stock, (b) reorder point in gallons, (c) annual total cost of maintaining the safety stock.

15-6. Demand for a particular item is know to follow a normal distribution wtih average demand of 20 per day and MAD of 5 per day. Lead time is 9 days.
a. What reorder point will yield a service level of 50 percent?
b. What service level corresponds to a zero safety stock level?
c. What should the desired service level be if the item is ordered in lots of 6,000, annual demand is 60,000 units, out of stock cost is estimated to be $1 per unit, the item costs $5, and annual carrying costs are 10 percent.
d. Determine the required safety stock and reorder point necessary to achieve the service level in part c.
e. What will be the annual costs of carrying the safety stock found in part d?

15-7. The Gardner Publishing Company has in the past specified a target service level of 85 percent for inventory of books that they publish. Recent complaints from salespeople concerning lost sales due to stockouts have interested management in considering increasing the service level objective to some higher level.

To obtain a rough estimate of the costs associated with a change in the service level one particular book was chosen for study. This item has a lead time of 10 days, an average demand of 40 books per day, and a standard deviation per day of 10 books. Past demand patterns indicate that demand approximates a normal distribution.

Present stocking policy for this book calls for replenishment printing and binding 10 times per year. Annual carrying costs are 20 percent, and the average cost per book is $10.
a. What reorder points would be necessary to achieve alternate service levels of 85, 90, and 95 percent per replenishment?
b. What would be the annual carrying costs required to maintain safety stock levels for each alternative in part a?
c. If this item represents approximately 1 percent of all books carried in inventory, what would you estimate the incremental carrying costs to be for the 90 and 95 percent service level objectives compared with current policy for the total inventory?

Part Six

Predictive Models

This major section of the text considers what can be called *predictive models*. These are management science models that can be used to predict the consequences of specific actions, or alternatives. They differ from the models we have examined previously because, in general, the models do not provide solutions, optimal or heuristic. Instead, they predict the outcome for specific decision alternatives. These predictive models are grouped into five chapters, as briefly described below.

Chapter 16 examines project planning and control models. These are designed to help the manager plan for and control large projects, such as constructing a building or launching a new product. These models can be used to predict such things as the expected length of the project, the project activities that should be monitored more closely, and the probability of completing the project by a specific target date.

Models for designing and operating service systems are the focus of Chapter 17. A service system involves customers arriving at a facility for service. The facility consists of one or more servers and has limited service capacity. This leads to waiting lines developing, which is why the models examined in Chapter 17 are called waiting line models. These models can be used to predict a number of performance measures for a specific system. These include the average number of customers waiting, the average time spent waiting, and the utilization of the servers. Based on these predicted performance measures, management can select from among alternative design configurations for these systems.

Chapters 18 and 19 are concerned with forecasting models. These models are used to provide a forecast of future events or conditions. For example, the model may be used to forecast future sales, costs, interest rates, etc. The forecasts obtained are then often used as information for other decision models, including linear programming models, inventory models, and so on. Chapter 18 treats what are called *extrapolation models*. These models examine historical data for the variable to be forecast, identify historical patterns, and then project, or extrapolate, these patterns into the future. For example, an extrapolation model would provide forecasts of future demand on the basis of past demand. *Explanatory models* are covered in Chapter 19. These models attempt to identify relationships between the variable to be forecast and a set of explanatory variables, which are thought to influence the forecasted variable. For example, we may feel that sales are a function of product price, advertising expenditures, and gross national product. Thus sales is the variable to be forecast and the other three factors are the explanatory variables.

Simulation modeling is the subject of Chapter 20. Simulation is an important management science modeling approach and is particularly useful for treating complex decision problems. A simulation model is capable of incorporating as much complexity as desired and can be used to predict the effects of a variety of decision alternatives.

16

Project Planning and Control Models

Most organizations are at some point faced with the problem of planning for, organizing, and controlling large-scale, nonrepetitive projects. The managers who are faced with the responsibilities related to such projects are well aware of the difficulties that can arise when the inevitable delays and problems occur. They are also mindful of the enormous economic rewards and penalties riding on the successful or unsuccessful completion of these projects.

Successful management of these large projects depends on many related factors. An important cornerstone of this success is the ability to obtain correct and up-to-date status reports on every activity and other information concerning the project. This information base enables the manager to answer important questions such as:

1. When will the project be completed?
2. Which activities are most critical regarding the project's completion on time?
3. If the project is to be on time, what are the earliest dates that the various activities can be started and finished?
4. What are the latest points in time that the activities can be started and completed if the project is to be finished on time?
5. How long can individual tasks be delayed without causing the project itself to be delayed?

547

6. How should existing resources best be assigned if additional resources are available, and where should they be used?

These are representative of the kinds of questions that can be answered through the use of project planning and control techniques, such as those referred to as the *critical path method* (CPM) and the *program evaluation review technique* (PERT).

CPM was developed in the late 1950s by Du Pont, Remington Rand Univac, and Mauchly Associates. CPM was proposed as a means of applying computers to the management of complex engineering projects. PERT was developed by a team set up by the U.S. Navy Special Projects Office, which included representatives from Lockheed Aircraft Corporation and the consulting firm of Booz, Allen and Hamilton. PERT was developed as a planning and control system for the Polaris Fleet Ballistic Missile Program.

Although these approaches differed significantly at the time they were developed, years of application and refinement have caused many of the differences in the basic approach to disappear. Today the distinctions between CPM and PERT are of little importance, and both approaches can be covered under the same general heading of project methods, as in this chapter.

Despite the similarity of the basic approaches, you will find dozens of different computer packages available for project planning and control. While each generally follows the same fundamental approach, they offer different features and handle such issues as resource allocation in different ways. We will deal with these issues later in this chapter.

The procedures that we will examine in this chapter are applicable to a wide range of economic activities: (1) building construction, (2) highway construction, (3) planning and launching a new product, (4) start-up of a new production process, (5) planning and coordination of research and development projects, (6) installing a new information system, (7) scheduling and planning for building or overhauling ships and aircraft, (8) relocation of a major facility, and (9) filming of a motion picture, to name but a few.

Nature of a Project

A project is itself a combination of many varied and complex tasks or activities. These tasks are interdependent in that most cannot begin until some other task has been completed. Such relationships are called *precedence relationships*. These can be depicted in a network precedence diagram.

To illustrate, consider the situation faced by the Columbian Construction Company. They have contracted to build a warehouse for the Hargus Company. This construction project consists of a number of activities, or tasks, including excavation, erecting the frame, installation of plumbing, heating, and wiring, external and internal finishing, roofing, landscaping, painting, and cleanup. These activities, together with their estimated times and precedence relationships, are shown in Table 16-1. Observe, for example, that activity *B*, erecting the frame, cannot be done until activity *A*, excavation and pouring of the foundation, is completed. This is indicated by listing activity *A* as an immediate predecessor of activity *B*.

TABLE 16-1
Activities, Estimated Times, and Precedence Relationships
for Columbian Construction Company Problem

Activity designation	Description	Estimated time, working days	Immediate predecessors
A	Excavate and pour foundation	4	
B	Erect frame	12	A
C	Install plumbing	3	A
D	Install heating	6	B
E	Install wiring	4	B
F	Plaster	3	B,C
G	Brickwork	3	D
H	Roofing and gutters	2	E,F
I	Landscaping	5	G
J	Paint	3	H
K	Final cleanup	1	I,J

Graphic Representation

These activities, their estimated times, and the precedence relationships can also be shown graphically, as in Figure 16-1. The lettered circles, or nodes, refer to the activities in Table 16-1. The arrows, or directed arcs, connecting the nodes identify the precedence relationships. Thus we note that activity H cannot be carried out until both activities E and F have been completed. This is represented by the pair of arcs leading from activities E and F to activity H. The numbers next to each node refer to the estimated times in days that each activity is expected to take.

Observe that no precedence relationships exist, explicitly or implicitly, between activities B and C. This implies that these activities, erecting the frame and installing the plumbing, can be done one before the other or simultaneously. Although a direct line of precedence is not shown from task A to task D, there is an implied precedence. That is, activity B (erect frame) must be completed before D (install heating) can begin and activity A (excavate and pour foundation) must be finished before B can be started.

FIGURE 16-1 Project network for construction of warehouse by Columbian Construction Company.

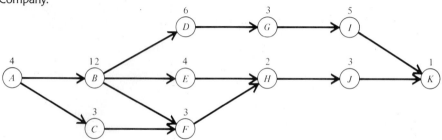

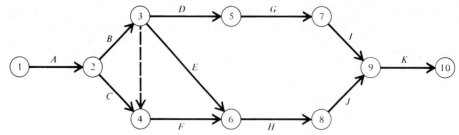

FIGURE 16-2 Activities on arcs (AOA) representation of project network for construction of warehouse by Columbian Construction Company.

AON and AOA Approaches

There are two graphical ways of showing the activities and their relationships. Figure 16-1 shows each node, or circle, corresponding to an activity and the arrows representing precedence. This type of diagram is called AON for *activities on nodes*. An alternate approach, *activities on arcs*, or AOA, is shown for the Columbian Construction project in Figure 16-2. In this case the arrows represent the activities as well as showing precedence. The nodes are used to represent *events*; an event is a point in time corresponding to the beginning or completion of one or more activities. Event 1 represents the beginning of activity A, event 2 the end of activity A and the beginning of activities B and C, and so on.

Dummy Activities

The AOA approach is probably more widely used than the AON, because many of the computer packages developed to do project analysis were based on the AOA format. However, AOA suffers from one major defect in that dummy activities sometimes need to be added to the diagram to show the correct precedence relationships clearly.

Figure 16-2 contains one dummy activity as represented by the dotted line between events 3 and 4. To see why this dummy activity was necessary, consider the abbreviated network in Figure 16-3a, which shows only activities B, C, E, and F for the Columbian project in the AON format. Figure 16-3b shows an incorrect AOA version without a dummy activity, and Figure 16-3c shows the proper AOA version with a dummy added.

The defect of Figure 16-3b concerns event 3. This event represents the completion of activity C and the beginning of activity F. Since activity B also

FIGURE 16-3 Three representations of activities B, C, E, and F for the Columbian warehouse project. (a) AON format. (b) Incorrect AOA format. (c) Correct AOA format.

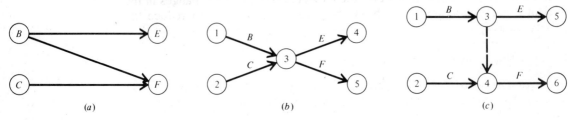

precedes activity *F*, its concluding event should be the same as the beginning event for activity *F*, which is event 3. But activity *B* must precede activity *E*, as well, and if *B* is to end at event 3, *E* must begin at event 3. However, this implies, incorrectly, that activity *E* follows activity *C*. This difficulty is eliminated (in Figure 16-3c) by separating the event signifying the end of activity *B* from the event representing the beginning of activity *F*. This requires, though, the addition of a dummy activity, shown as a dotted arrow, between events 3 and 4, the purpose of which is only to show that activity *B* precedes activity *F*. An estimated time of zero is normally assigned to dummy activities. It is now clear in the revised diagram that the completion of *C* does not influence the start of *E*.

INSTANT REPLAY   Convert the AON activity diagram shown below to the AOA format, adding dummy activities where necessary:

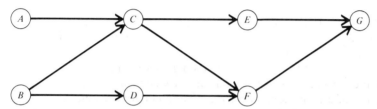

CHECK   Two dummy activities are necessary (from the end of *B* to the start of *C* and from the end of *C* to the start of *F*).

Critical Path and Critical Activities

At the beginning of this chapter a list of questions was provided that have managerial importance for project planning and control. Recall that the first two questions concerned determining how long the project would take and which activities were considered crucial to the project's successful completion. We will shortly see that the length of the project is equivalent to the length of the *longest* path through the precedence network. This longest path is referred to as the *critical path*. The activities that make up this path are called the *critical activities* because any delay in their completion beyond their expected duration will cause the entire project to take longer than necessary.

Associated with each activity of a project is an *activity time* which represents the expected duration of that activity for a specific assignment of resources. For the moment we will assume that these expected activity times are known and fixed. In later sections we will examine the effects of variability in these times as well as the impact on the expected times due to changes in the level of resources assigned (such as assigning more workers to reduce the activity time).

Identifying the Critical Path

Refer again to Figure 16-1 (or Figure 16-2). Simple inspection will show that the Columbian construction project network has four paths starting from activity *A* on the left and leading to activity K on the right. Each of these four paths, identified by Roman numerals, contains six activities:

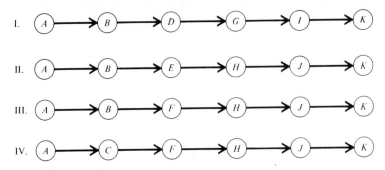

I. $A \longrightarrow B \longrightarrow D \longrightarrow G \longrightarrow I \longrightarrow K$

II. $A \longrightarrow B \longrightarrow E \longrightarrow H \longrightarrow J \longrightarrow K$

III. $A \longrightarrow B \longrightarrow F \longrightarrow H \longrightarrow J \longrightarrow K$

IV. $A \longrightarrow C \longrightarrow F \longrightarrow H \longrightarrow J \longrightarrow K$

Each path contains a set of activities that are to be performed in a specific, nonoverlapping order. The length of each path is equal to the sum of the times for all activities on that path. Assuming that the times for these activites are known and fixed, the activities on each path cannot be performed in less time than indicated by the length of that path. Because the project cannot be completed in less time than the length of any path, the *length of the longest path represents the shortest time in which the project is expected to be completed.* This longest path, then, is called the critical path and the activities of which it is composed are the critical activities.

To find the critical path, we must determine the length of each path. This is done by adding the estimated times for the activities on each path:

$$\text{I.} \quad 4 + 12 + 6 + 3 + 5 + 1 = 31$$

$$\text{II.} \quad 4 + 12 + 4 + 2 + 3 + 1 = 26$$

$$\text{III.} \quad 4 + 12 + 3 + 2 + 3 + 1 = 25$$

$$\text{IV.} \quad 4 + 3 + 3 + 2 + 3 + 1 = 16$$

Since path I is the longest, it is the critical path. Activities A, B, D, G, I, and K are the critical activities, since they all lie on the critical path.

INSTANT REPLAY For the moderately sized network shown below, identify the nine paths through this network.

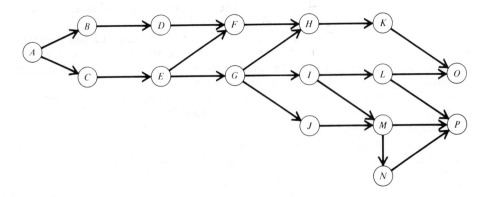

CHECK The paths can be identified by a tree diagram as shown below, each **553**
branch in the tree corresponding to a unique precedence path.

PROJECT
PLANNING AND
CONTROL
MODELS

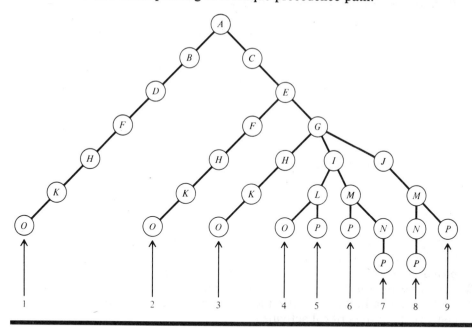

Although our discussion tends to focus on the critical activities, the noncritical activities cannot be disregarded. Some lie on paths that are almost as long as the critical path. If the activity times are not fixed, as we assumed above, a change in the time it takes actually to complete one or more of the activities can cause one of these near-critical paths to become critical. This issue will be considered later in the chapter.

Also note that noncritical activities will have available some potential delay, usually referred to as slack, or float. That is, because an activity is noncritical, its completion can be delayed a certain amount of time without affecting the completion of the project. The availability of this slack is useful because it provides scheduling flexibility and may permit shifting workers from a noncritical to a critical task when problems arise.

As easy as it was to enumerate all the paths in the example network to find the critical path, there are drawbacks to this approach. One is that as the networks become more complex, as they often do in practice, with many activities and many precedence relationships, the number of paths increases very rapidly. It becomes exceedingly difficult to identify all the paths through a large network successfully. Even if successful, the time consumed becomes excessive. A second drawback is that the enumeration procedure focuses on paths, which makes it more difficult to obtain information related to activities and events, particularly with a large number of paths.

Clearly what is needed is a systematic way of finding the critical path that focuses on either activities or events. As described earlier, the AON diagramming method tends to focus on activities. The AOA method concentrates on events. The AON approach will be described here (thereby avoiding the necessity of including dummy activities). We should note that a similar approach can be used with the event-oriented AOA formulation.

Finding Early Start and Finish Times   The method we will describe identifies the earliest and latest times that each activity can be started and completed. Completing a project in the time indicated by the length of the critical path requires that all the activities on that path start and finish as soon as they can. We refer to these start and finish times as *early start* and *early finish times*.

As was pointed out before, those activities not on the critical path can be delayed an amount of time equivalent to the slack time before they must begin and still allow the project to be completed on time. The starting time which gives the maximum amount of delay and yet permits the project to be completed on time will be called the *late start time*. Each late start time has a corresponding *late finish time*.

The early and late finish times can both be found by adding the expected activity time to their respective start times. Thus,

$$\left(\begin{array}{c}\text{Early}\\\text{start time}\end{array}\right) + \left(\begin{array}{c}\text{expected}\\\text{activity time}\end{array}\right) = \begin{array}{c}\text{early}\\\text{finish time}\end{array}$$

and

$$\left(\begin{array}{c}\text{Late}\\\text{start time}\end{array}\right) + \left(\begin{array}{c}\text{expected}\\\text{activity time}\end{array}\right) = \begin{array}{c}\text{late}\\\text{finish time}\end{array}$$

The difference between the two start times or between the two finish times is equivalent to the *slack time*.

$$\begin{array}{c}\text{Total}\\\text{slack}\end{array} = \left(\begin{array}{c}\text{late}\\\text{start}\\\text{time}\end{array}\right) - \left(\begin{array}{c}\text{early}\\\text{start}\\\text{time}\end{array}\right) = \left(\begin{array}{c}\text{late}\\\text{finish}\\\text{time}\end{array}\right) - \left(\begin{array}{c}\text{early}\\\text{finish}\\\text{time}\end{array}\right)$$

We also saw that the project completion time was equivalent to the length of the longest path, which is the same as the early finish time for the last activity, or

$$\left(\begin{array}{c}\text{Project}\\\text{completion}\\\text{time}\end{array}\right) = \left(\begin{array}{c}\text{length of}\\\text{critical}\\\text{path}\end{array}\right) = \left(\begin{array}{c}\text{largest early}\\\text{finish time of}\\\text{all activities}\end{array}\right)$$

How are these early and late start and finish times calculated? Essentially, they are computed in two steps. The first step starts at the beginning of the network, calculating the early start and finish times for each activity as we progress to the end of the network. The second step begins at the end, working backward to complete the late start and finish times for all the activities.

To begin, since we are determining early start and finish times, we need to start every activity that has no predecessors at time zero.[1] In other words, all activities that can start right away (those without predecessor activities) are available for starting at the end of day 0. Although it may seem more logical to say that they can begin on day 1, for computational reasons it is more convenient to show start and finish times as the end of the day. In the Columbian Construction Company problem, activity A was the only activity without predecessors; so its early start time is 0. We find the early finish time by adding the expected time to the early start time. Activity A has an expected duration of 4 days; so its early finish time is $0 + 4 = 4$. This means that activity A, excavation and pouring of the foundation, will be completed at the end of day 4.

Now that activity A's early start and finish times have been found, we can next calculate the start and finish times for activities B and C, since their only predecessor was activity A. The earliest either activity can start is equivalent to

---

[1]An alternate approach would be to use a specific calendar start date.

the earliest that A can be completed. Therefore, B and C have early start times of 4; their early finish times of 16 and 7, respectively, are found by adding the expected activity time of each.

Now that B and C have been completed, we can determine the start and finish times for D, E, and F. Activities D and E have only one predecessor, activity B, and therefore take the early finish time of that predecessor as their early start time. D and E thus take B's finish time of 16 as their early start time; early finish times of 22 and 20 are found for D and E, respectively, by adding their expected activity times.

Activity F is somewhat more complex in that it has two predecessor activities. The key to determining the early start time for F is to recall that both predecessors, B and C, must be completed before F can begin. Although activity C finishes at time 7, activity B cannot be completed any earlier than 16. Thus F must wait until time 16 before it can begin. This gives F an early start time of 16 and, after adding the expected time, an early finish time of 19.

In general, then, when an activity has more than one predecessor, it must wait until all predecessors are finished before it can begin. Therefore, the early start time for an activity is defined as

$$\binom{\text{Early start time}}{\text{for activity } i} = \binom{\text{maximum early finish time}}{\text{of } i\text{'s predecessors}}$$

Activity G is easy to complete, since it follows activity D. G takes D's early finish time of 22 as its early start time. This leads to an early finish time for G of 25.

Activity H is similar to F in that it has two predecessors, E and F. Activity E has an early finish time of 20 and activity F a finish time of 19. Since 20 is greater than 19, activity H has an early start time of 20; adding the expected time of 2, H has an early finish time of 22.

The start and finish times for activities I and J are also easy to find, since each has only one predecessor. Activity I follows G; so I has an early start time of 25 (G's early finish time) and an early finish time of 30 (25 + 5). Activity J has an early start time of 22 (H's early finish time) and an early finish time of 25.

Finally, we reach activity K, the last activity in the network. K has two

FIGURE 16-4 Project network for Columbian Construction Company problem showing early start and finish times.

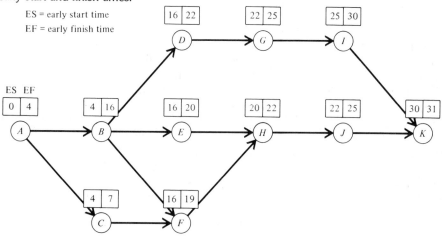

predecessors with finish times of 30 (activity I) and 25 (J). Therefore, K must have an early start time of 30 and since K takes 1 day it has an early finish time of 31. Figure 16-4 shows the early start and early finish times for each activity in the boxes near each corresponding node.

The earliest completion time for the project was defined earlier to be the largest early finish time. In this case it is obvious that since all activities precede activity K, the early finish time for K must be the largest. K's finish time of 31 is equivalent to the length of the critical path found earlier by enumerating and evaluating all the paths in the network.

After completion of this step, we not only know the length of the critical path but we also are able to determine the earliest times that each activity may start or finish. In addition it is possible, through close examination of the network, to determine which activities are the critical activities. As we will see, it is easier to identify the critical activities by first determining the latest start and finish times for each project activity.

INSTANT REPLAY   Study Figure 16-4 to see if you can determine which of the activities are critical.

HINT   By working backward from activity K, trace a continuous path along which each predecessor activity has the same early finish time as the early start time for one of its followers. This path will be the critical path, and the activities making up this path will be the critical activities.

CHECK   In this case we trace the critical activities: K to I to G to D to B to A.

Late Start and Late Finish Times   Determining the late start and finish times is quite similar to finding the early start and finish times. However, in this case we begin at the end and work backward through the network, determining first the late finish time and then the late start time for each activity.

In order to begin, we need to know the desired or target project completion date. We shall assume that the Columbian Construction Company desires to build the warehouse in as short a time as possible. Therefore, we will use 31 days (equivalent to the length of the critical path) as the target completion date. If some other target date was desired, it could be easily incorporated. For instance, if there is a contract due date of, say, 35 days for completing the warehouse, we could begin with 35 as the target project completion date.

Just as zero served as the early start time for all activities without predecessors, we will use 31 as the late finish time *for all activities without successors*. For our example problem, activity K is the only activity without successors; so we begin by setting K's late finish time at 31. Since K takes 1 day to complete, its late start time must be $31 - 1 = 30$.

Activities I and J are the only predecessors of K, and their late start and finish times can next be found. Both I and J must be completed in time for K to begin by its late start time. Since K must start no later than day 30, I and J must finish no later than that same day. Thus I and J take 30 as their late finish time; after subtracting the expected times for each, we find late start times of 25 for activity I and 27 for activity J.

We can next compute the late times for activities G and H, the predecessors of I and J. G precedes I, and therefore G's late finish time is equivalent to

I's late start time. Thus *G* must be finished no later than day 25 and must start no later than day 22. Likewise, *H* precedes *J* and takes *J*'s late start time of 27 as its late finish time. Since *H* takes 2 days to complete, it must begin no later than day 25.

Activity *D* precedes *G* and is found to have a late finish time of 22 (*G*'s late start time) and late start of 16 (*D* takes 6 days to complete). Activities *E* and *F* were predecessors of *H*, and both therefore have the same finish time of 25 (*H*'s late start time). After subtracting the expected activity times, we find the late start time for *E* to be 21 and for *F* to be 22.

Activity *C* precedes *F* and therefore has a late finish time of 22 (*F*'s late start time) and a late start time of 19 (*C* takes 3 days to complete).

Activity *B* is more difficult to compute than the others, since *B* has three follower activities, *D, E,* and *F*. Activity *B* must be finished early enough so that none of those three is delayed beyond their late start times. The late start times for *D, E,* and *F* are 16, 21, and 22, respectively. The earliest of these is 16, and *B* must be finished by then or activity *D* will be delayed. Therefore, *B* has a late finish time of 16, and since *B* takes 12 days, *B* must start no later than day 4.

In general, when an activity has more than one follower, it must take the earliest of the late start times of its followers as its late finish time:

$$\begin{pmatrix} \text{Late finish time} \\ \text{for activity } i \end{pmatrix} = \begin{pmatrix} \text{minimum late start time} \\ \text{of } i\text{'s followers} \end{pmatrix}$$

In a similar manner, we note that activity *A* has two followers, *B* and *C*. The late start times for *B* and *C* are 4 and 19, respectively. Since *B* has the earlier start time of the two, *B*'s late start time of 4 becomes *A*'s late finish time. Activity *A* is expected to take 4 days; so its late start time is day zero. Figure 16-5 provides a summary of the late start and finish times found for each activity. These are shown in the triangles next to each corresponding node.

Identifying Critical Activities and Total Slack

An examination of the completed diagram in Figure 16-5 will enable us to determine the critical activities. Note that for some activities, such as activity *A*, the early start and late start and the early finish and late finish times are identical. This means that the activity has no slack and is therefore critical. Any delay in that activity will cause the entire project to be delayed. Therefore, those activities that have 0 total slack, or equivalent 0 differences between the start times or finish times, must be critical activities and lie on the critical path. These were, in this case, *A, B, D, G, I,* and *K*. The critical path is shown by the heavier line in Figure 16-5.

Total slack for activities not on the critical path is found by subtracting either early start from late start times or early finish from late finish times. Thus activity *C* has slack of 15 days, activity *E* 5 days, etc.

Note that if we had used a target completion time of something other than 31 days, the 0 slack condition would not be a sufficient means of identifying the critical activities. Instead, the critical activities would all have slack equal to the difference between the earliest project completion time, as found in the first step, and the target completion time used to begin the second step. Thus, if the contract called for the project to be completed in 35 days and 35 was used as the late finish time for all activities at the end of the project (those without successors), every critical activity would have exactly 4 days of slack (35 − 31). Note

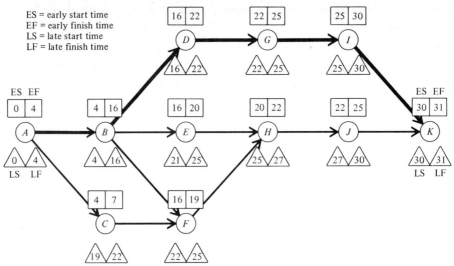

ES = early start time
EF = early finish time
LS = late start time
LF = late finish time

FIGURE 16-5 Project network for Columbian Construction Company problem showing early and late start and finish times.

also that it is possible to have negative slack, as would happen if the target completion time were set at less than the minimum completion time. If in the Columbian problem the target completion time was set at 28 days, every critical activity would have -3 days of slack. In such cases it is common to refer to these activities as *supercritical*.

Although the network diagram may be convenient for visualizing the activity relationships when determining the various start and finish times, the diagram becomes rather cluttered with the addition of the various boxes, triangles, etc. In addition, it is not a convenient form for computer implementation. For these reasons it is often more convenient and efficient to use a table to calculate and display the start and finish times and slack values for the various activities. Table 16-2 is an example of this approach for the Columbian

TABLE 16-2
Early and Late Start and Finish Times and Total Slack for Activities
of the Columbian Construction Company Problem

Activity	Expected time	Immediate predecessors	Early start	Early finish	Immediate successors	Late start	Late finish	Total slack
A	4		0	4	B, C	0	4	0
B	12	A	4	16	D, E, F	4	16	0
C	3	A	4	7	F	19	22	15
D	6	B	16	22	G	16	22	0
E	4	B	16	20	H	21	25	5
F	3	B, C	16	19	H	22	25	6
G	3	D	22	25	I	22	25	0
H	2	E, F	20	22	J	25	27	5
I	5	G	25	30	K	25	30	0
J	3	H	22	25	K	27	30	5
K	1	I, J	30	31		30	31	0

Construction Company problem. The start and finish times are found in the same manner as before.

INSTANT REPLAY The Wellvid Drug Company is about to launch a new prescription drug. To do this, it has planned an extensive promotional campaign involving detailed advertising brochures and free samples to be distributed by salespeople to doctors. The campaign involves six activities as shown below.

Activity	Estimated time, weeks	Immediate predecessors
A. Familiarize salespeople with product	3	
B. Develop advertising brochures	2	
C. Produce free samples	6	
D. Familiarize salespeople with brochures	1	A, B
E. Print advertising brochures	3	B
F. Distribute product and brochures	4	C, D, E

Determine the early start and finish times, late start and finish times, and total slack for each activity. Calculate the length of the critical path and identify the critical activities. Assume that management desires this campaign to be completed in 12 weeks.

CHECK The desired information is shown below.

Activity	Early start	Early finish	Late start	Late finish	Total slack
A	0	3	4	7	4
B	0	2	3	5	3
C	0	6	2	8	2
D	3	4	7	8	4
E	2	5	5	8	3
F	6	10	8	12	2

Activities C and F are critical, and the length of the critical path is 10 weeks.

Interpreting Slack Until now we have been using the term "slack" to describe the maximum amount an activity can be delayed without delaying the completion of the entire project. This kind of slack is often called *total slack*, or *total float*, to distinguish it from several other types of slack.

Free slack represents the amount of time that an activity can be delayed without delaying the early start of any other activity. *Interruptive slack* is the difference between free slack and total slack and represents potential delay time beyond the free slack time, which if used will cause at least one activity to start after its early start time but will not cause the project to be delayed beyond its early finish time. In other words,

$$\text{Total slack} = (\text{free slack}) + (\text{interruptive slack})$$

559

To illustrate, consider activity C of the Columbian Construction problem. Activity C had early start and finish times of 4 and 7 and late start and finish times of 19 and 22. We previously calculated total slack to be 15, the difference between the start times ($19 - 4$) or between the finish times ($22 - 7$) for activity C. Free slack is found by calculating the difference between activity C's early finish time and the early start time for activity F; thus the free slack is found to be 9 days ($16 - 7$). Activity C can be delayed 9 days without changing the early start time for any other activity, or it can be delayed as much as 16 days without changing the earliest project completion date (although if C is delayed more than 9 days, the early start time for some other activity will be postponed).

In general, the free slack can be found in either of two ways:

$$\begin{pmatrix} \text{Free slack for} \\ \text{activity } i \end{pmatrix} = \begin{pmatrix} \text{total slack for} \\ \text{activity } i \end{pmatrix} - \begin{pmatrix} \text{minimum total slack of} \\ \text{immediate successors of } i \end{pmatrix}$$

or

$$\begin{pmatrix} \text{Free slack for} \\ \text{activity } i \end{pmatrix} = \begin{pmatrix} \text{minimum early start time} \\ \text{for successors of } i \end{pmatrix} - \begin{pmatrix} \text{early finish time} \\ \text{for activity } i \end{pmatrix}$$

For activity C this was

$$\text{Free slack for activity } C = 15 - 6 = 9$$
$$= 16 - 7 = 9$$

Activity E, on the other hand, has total slack of 5 days, but since activity H, which follows E, has 5 days of total slack, E has no free slack at all. Interruptive slack would be 5 for activity E.

INSTANT REPLAY Calculate the free and interruptive slack for the other noncritical activities of the Columbian Construction Company problem, as was done above for activity E.

CHECK Free slack for activities F, H, and J is 1, 0, and 5, respectively. Interruptive slack is thus 5, 5, and 0, respectively.

Managerial Use of Slack Information about each activity's slack can be useful in making operational decisions for a project. It is important, however, to understand the differences between total, free, and interruptive slack if this information is to be used properly.

If resources are in tight supply, management may wish to smooth peak resource requirements by delaying the start of some noncritical activities. Total slack for an activity gives a measure of how much delay is possible for that activity without causing the project completion date to change. However, recall that total slack consists of two components, free slack and interruptive slack. As defined earlier, if an activity is delayed by an amount equal to its free slack, not only does the project completion date not change but the start and finish times (and hence slack) for all other activities remain the same. On the other hand, if an activity is delayed by an amount in excess of its free slack, thereby using some of the interruptive slack, the start and finish times of at least one follower activity will be affected. This will in turn reduce the slack available for these follower activities. If the delay uses up all of an activity's total slack (free and interruptive), the total slack for the follower activities will also disappear.

Thus, although free slack applies to each activity independent of other activities, interruptive slack is shared by several activities.

To illustrate, in our example problem activity C was seen to have 15 days of total slack and activity F 6 days. If activity C is delayed 15 days, the slack for activity F disappears. On the other hand, if activity C is delayed by the amount of the free slack, 9 days, the 6 days of slack for activity F remain. In that case both activities C and F will have 6 days of total slack remaining, and free slack for both activities will be zero.

Thus, from an operational viewpoint, if decisions concerning activity delay are to be decentralized by allowing the supervisors in the field to make these decisions, free slack should be used as the basis for such decisions rather than total slack. Otherwise each supervisor may decide to utilize the amount of interruptive slack that is not really available separately but is shared by two or more activities. Decisions concerning the use of interruptive slack can then be made centrally.

INSTANT REPLAY Refer again to the Wellvid Drug Company promotional campaign presented in an earlier Instant Replay. At a management meeting the sales manager requested a 4-week delay in beginning the 3-week training session to familiarize the salespeople with the new product (activity A). The advertising director reported that the printer has requested an additional week in which to print the advertising brochures (activity E). Will these changes still allow the campaign to be completed in 12 weeks?

CHECK A delay of 4 weeks in activity A will use up all the available slack for that activity (as well as that for activity D). The extra week needed for printing the brochures will reduce the slack for activity E by 1 week. Since activities A and E are independent of each other, both changes can be made without delaying the campaign beyond the 12-week deadline. (Note, however, that the critical path is now 12 weeks rather than 10 weeks and that activities A, D, and F, each with 0 slack, are now critical.)

Activity Variation

The preceding discussion has assumed that the activity time, or duration, was deterministic and known with certainty, although it was generally referred to as an expected time. In practice, of course, the degree of uncertainty about the actual activity time duration can vary considerably. Some activities that have been performed many times in the past can be estimated fairly closely. This would be true of many construction-related activities, for example. Alternatively there may be a high degree of uncertainty concerning other kinds of activities. Activities of many research-related projects, where this may be the first time such an activity has been performed, are indicative of the kind of task that has high uncertainty.

Traditionally the PERT approach, which grew out of research and development operations, was concerned with activity variability while CPM, which had its origins in construction-related projects, was not. As stated earlier, these distinctions have become somewhat blurred through time.

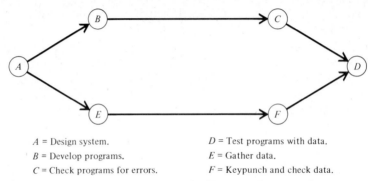

A = Design system.   D = Test programs with data.
B = Develop programs.   E = Gather data.
C = Check programs for errors.   F = Keypunch and check data.

FIGURE 16-6   Project network diagram for Harkness Research Company project.

Nevertheless, concern with activity variability is very much related to the nature of the project being modeled.

To illustrate how activity variability can be handled with project planning, consider the following example. The Harkness Research Company specializes in designing and installing computerized management science models. They have just signed a contract to design and install a market forecasting package for a regional distillery. This project is to be completed in 40 days and consists of six activities: (*A*) designing the system, (*B*) developing the programs, (*C*) checking the programs for errors, (*D*) testing the programs with the data, (*E*) gathering the data, and (*F*) keypunching and checking the data. These activities and their precedence relationships are shown in Figure 16-6.

With a 40-day deadline, Harkness management is concerned with ensuring that the project can be completed within that time span. Unfortunately, the duration of most of the activities is not known with any degree of certainty. We will now see how uncertainty can be dealt with in project planning.

Activity Time Estimates

Variability of activity times is often acknowledged by considering three time estimates for the duration of an activity. The shortest possible completion time for an activity is called the *optimistic time,* the longest possible activity time is referred to as the *pessimistic time,* and the time with the highest likelihood of occurrence is called the *most likely time.* The relationship among these estimates is shown in Figure 16-7.

As we will show shortly, these three time estimates can be used to calculate an *expected activity duration* for each activity t_e and an *activity variance* $\sigma^2(t_e)$. The expected activity durations can then be used to find the length of the critical path and the critical activities in the usual manner. The activity variances are used to provide an estimate of the variance of the length of the project.

The expected duration t_e and variance $\sigma^2(t_e)$ for each activity can be calculated from the most likely (m), optimistic (a), and pessimistic (b) estimates as follows:

$$t_e = \frac{a + 4m + b}{6} \tag{16-1}$$

$$\sigma^2(t_e) = \left(\frac{b-a}{6}\right)^2 \qquad (16\text{-}2)$$

These equations assume that the activity duration follows what is called the beta distribution. Although we don't need to know much about this distribution, it is useful to point out that the beta distribution has several properties that make it particularly useful for modeling activity durations. The beta has a single peak, or mode, which corresponds to our most likely time estimate. The beta also has lower and upper limits (values beyond those limits have a zero probability of occurring) which correspond to our optimistic and pessimistic time limits. In addition, the peak value can fall anywhere between these limits. This provides great flexibility in modeling activities.

Note that the denominator of 6 in the equation defining the expected duration t_e is equal to the sum of the coefficients of a, b, and m in the numerator. Thus the expected time is equivalent to a weighted average of the three time estimates, with the most likely time given four times the weight of the other two estimates. The variance or variability is equivalent to the square of one-sixth of the range from optimistic to pessimistic and is not affected at all by the most likely time.

To demonstrate the use of these relationships, refer again to our Harkness research problem (see Figure 16-6). The optimistic, pessimistic, and most likely time estimates for each activity are shown in Figure 16-8. The expected times and variances, which are calculated using equations (16-1) and (16-2), are also shown in Figure 16-8. For instance, activity A has a pessimistic time of 2, an optimistic time of 14, and a most likely time of 5. Thus,

$$t_e = \frac{2 + 4(5) + 14}{6} = \frac{36}{6} = 6$$

$$\sigma^2(t_e) = \left(\frac{14 - 2}{6}\right)^2 = \left(\frac{12}{6}\right)^2 = 4$$

The expected times and variances for the other activities are calculated in a similar manner.

Estimating Completion Times and Variances for Paths

Once the expected times have been calculated, the critical path is found exactly as before. In this case it is convenient to enumerate the paths since there are only two:

FIGURE 16-7 Relationship of three time estimates for activity duration.

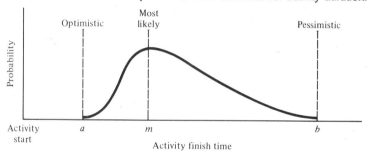

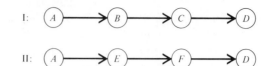

The completion time for each path T_e is found by adding the expected durations for the activities on that path. Thus, for path I we add together the expected durations for activities A, B, C, and D:

$$T_e = 6 + 7 + 9 + 13 = 35$$

and for path II we use the times for activities A, E, F, and D:

$$T_e = 6 + 6 + 12 + 13 = 37$$

Similarly, the variance of the sum of the activity times, $\sigma^2(T_e)$, can be found by adding together the individual activity variances. For path I,

$$\sigma^2(T_e) = \sigma^2(t_A) + \sigma^2(t_B) + \sigma^2(t_C) + \sigma^2(t_D)$$
$$= \quad 4 \quad + \quad 16 \quad + \quad 1 \quad + \quad 4 \quad = 25$$

and for path II,

$$\sigma^2(T_e) = \sigma^2(t_A) + \sigma^2(t_E) + \sigma^2(t_F) + \sigma^2(t_D)$$
$$= \quad 4 \quad + \quad 0 \quad + \quad 1 \quad + \quad 4 \quad = 9$$

These expected completion times and variances can be used to obtain

FIGURE 16-8 Optimistic (a), pessimistic (b), most likely (m), expected (t_e), and variance [$\sigma^2(t_e)$] of activity durations for Harkness Research Company project.

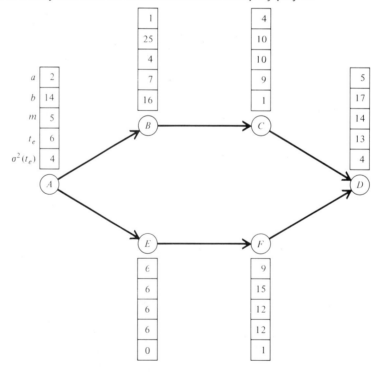

probabilities of completing each path by particular dates and can then be combined to determine the probability of completing the entire project by a specific date, as will be shown below.

Implications of Variability   A comparison of the expected completion times and variances for the two paths for the Harkness Research Company problem indicates that although path II is longer than path I (37 to 35), path I has a much higher variance (25 to 9). What are the implications of these relations? Based on expected times alone, path II is the critical path, containing activities A, E, F, and D, and activities B and C are not critical since they don't lie on the critical path. However, that doesn't mean that activities B and C should be ignored. For one thing, the path they lie on is very close in length to the critical path, thus making B and C near-critical activities. For another, the higher variance, largely due to activity B, increases the likelihood that path I, and hence activities B and C, can turn out to be critical, since only a slight increase in the actual duration of either activity B or C will cause the length of path I to be larger than for path II. The high variance of path I, relative to the small difference in the expected lengths of the two paths, contributes to the possibility that path I and thus activities B and C can become critical. Thus management must indeed pay attention to these activities and, in particular, must closely monitor the progress of activity B, since it seems the most volatile, with a variance of 16.

   In addition to these basic management concerns, we can be more precise about the likelihood that a particular path will be completed by a specific date. In order to do this, we rely on the *central limit theorem* from statistics.

Central Limit Theorem   The central limit theorem states, essentially, that the distribution of the sum of a large number of random variables will be approximately normal, regardless of the type of distributions for the independent random variables. Recall that the expected completion time for any path was the sum of the individual activity durations. Even though the individual activity times were assumed to follow the beta distribution, the central limit theorem

FIGURE 16-9   Normal curve for length of path through a network.

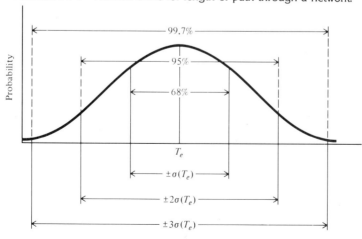

Length of path

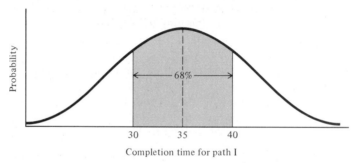

FIGURE 16-10   68 percent confidence limits for path I of the Harkness Research Company problem.

tells us that the expected completion time for any path is approximately normally distributed.

A typical *normal*, or bell-shaped, *curve* is illustrated in Figure 16-9. It is useful to review several characteristics about the normal distribution. The standard deviation of the normal distribution is equal to the square root of the variance. Because the expected completion time for a project path is normally distributed, we can calculate a standard deviation for the completion time of that path, $\sigma(T_e)$, by taking the square root of its variance, $\sigma^2(T_e)$:

$$\sigma(T_e) = \sqrt{\sigma^2(T_e)}$$

Furthermore, 68 percent of the distribution lies within one standard deviation of the mean. This means that there is a 68 percent chance that a given path will have an actual time duration within 1 standard deviation on either side of its expected duration. For path I we know that $T_e = 35$, $\sigma^2(T_e) = 25$ and hence $\sigma(T_e) = \sqrt{25} = 5$. Thus we are 68 percent sure that the length of path I is within 35 ± 5, or between 30 and 40, as shown in Figure 16-10.

Other probability measures are readily available. For instance, approximately 95 percent of the area of the curve lies within ± 2 standard deviations and 99.7 percent within ± 3 standard deviations. Tables are available for calculating other probabilities; the Appendix to this chapter provides such a table.

Finding Probability of Path Completion by Target Date

How can we make use of this information? To illustrate the application of the normal curve, recall that the Harkness Research Company project has a contract that calls for completion in 40 days. Therefore, management is likely to be interested in the probability that the project can be completed in that length of time. Figure 16-11 represents the probability graphically for path I. We wish to find the shaded area under the curve, which corresponds to the probability that path I takes no more than 40 days to complete. To find this area, we must first determine by how many standard deviations the target completion time of 40 lies to the right of the expected or mean duration of 35 days. This is found by dividing the distance from the mean by the standard deviation:

$$\frac{40 - 35}{5} = 1 \text{ standard deviation}$$

In general, we refer to this as a Z-score and would calculate it as

$$\text{Z-score} = \frac{\text{(due date)} - \text{(mean)}}{\text{standard deviation}}$$

Using the Appendix, we find that a Z-score of 1 represents an area under the curve of .3413. This is the area falling between the mean of 35 and the due date of 40. To this would have to be added .5, which is the area to the left of the mean (the normal distribution is symmetrical and $\frac{1}{2}$ lies on either side of the mean). Thus the probability that path I is completed in 40 days or less is .5 + .3413 = .8413. Management must decide if this is sufficiently large to accept the .1587 risk of not meeting the target date, with possible penalties for being late.

INSTANT REPLAY What is the probability that path I is completed within 45 days?

CHECK This yields a Z-score of

$$Z = \frac{45 - 35}{5} = \frac{10}{5} = 2$$

The Appendix shows that the area between the mean and 2 standard deviations to the right of the mean is .4772. Thus the probability of completing path I in 45 days is .5 + .4772 = .9772.

Next consider path II. Path II has a mean of 37, a variance of 9, and hence a standard deviation of 3. The Z-score for 40 days in the case of path II is

$$Z = \frac{40 - 37}{3} = 1$$

Hence the probability of completing path II by that date is the same as for path I, or .8413. This will not always be the case, as illustrated by our next example.

Suppose that the contract called for a bonus to be paid if the project could be completed in 32 days. What are the probabilities of completing the two paths in 32 days?

For path I we calculate the Z-score as

$$Z = \frac{32 - 35}{5} = -.6$$

This Z-score is negative because the due date of 32 lies to the left of the

FIGURE 16-11 Probability that path I of Harkness Research Company project takes no more than 40 days to complete.

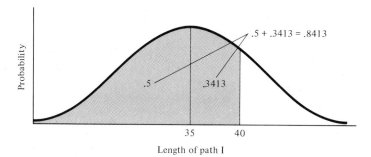

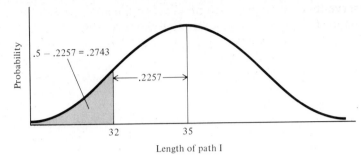

FIGURE 16-12 Probability that path I of Harkness Research Company project will be completed in 32 days or less.

mean. However, this creates no analytic problem because the distribution is symmetric and therefore the area under the curve .6 standard deviations to the left of the mean is the same as that for .6 standard deviations to the right of the mean. Thus the area between 32 and 35 is .2257, as found from the Appendix. This represents the probability that path I will be completed sometime between 32 and 35 days. We wish to know the probability that it is completed in 32 days or less. To obtain this, we note that the probability of completing in 35 days or less is .5. Since the probability of 32 to 35 days is .2257, the probability of completing in 32 days or less must be .5 − .2257 = .2743, as shown in Figure 16-12.

Similarly, for path II we find

$$Z = \frac{32 - 37}{3} = -1.67$$

Using the Appendix we determine that the area between 32 and 37 is .4525. Thus the probability that path II takes 32 days or less to complete is .5 − .4525 = .0475. This is shown in Figure 16-13.

INSTANT REPLAY What is the probability that path I will be completed no earlier than 32 days but no later than 40 days?

CHECK This requires adding the area between the mean and 32 days to that between the mean and 40 days. This adds to .2257 + .3413 = .5670.

FIGURE 16-13 Probability that path II of Harkness Research Company project will be completed in 32 days or less.

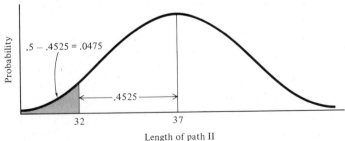

Observe that although paths I and II have the same probability (.8413) of completion in 40 days, path II has a much smaller probability, .0475, than does path I, .2743, of being completed in 32 days. This difference is due to the fact that the completion probabilities are related to the number of standard deviations that the target completion times lie from the mean completion times; 40 days is 5 days to the right of the mean for path I but only 3 days to the right of the mean for path II. In both cases, however, the deviations from the mean were exactly equal to 1 standard deviation, 5 for path I and 3 for path II. On the other hand, 32 days is 3 days to the left of the mean for path I and 5 days for path II. Since these values represent less than 1 standard deviation for path I and more than 1 standard deviation for path II, the resulting completion probabilities must be different.

Finding Probability of Project Completion by Target Date

We have been dealing with *path* probabilities in the examples discussed above. As useful as these probabilities may be, management would also like to know what the probability is of completing the *project* by a particular date.

Observe that the probability of completing the critical path (II) in 40 days or less was .8413. If we only consider path II, we can say that the probability of completing the project in 40 days or less is equivalent to the probability of completing path II in 40 days or less, or .8413. However, path I is nearly as long as path II, and we found earlier that it also has a .8413 probability of being completed in 40 days or less. Since *both* paths must be completed in 40 days or less if the project is to be completed within that time, the probabilities must be multiplied together to obtain the probability that the project is completed on time (assuming that the two paths are independent of each other). Thus, $(.8413) \times (.8413) = .7078$ is the probability that the project is completed in 40 days or less.

Similarly, we could estimate the probability of earning the bonus for completing the project in 32 days or less by multiplying the probability that path I is completed in 32 days or less by the equivalent probability for path II. The probability of earning the bonus is thus $(.2743) \times (.0475) = .0130$, which is not high. Management may decide to expedite some activities to increase the chance of earning the bonus.

INSTANT REPLAY   What is the probability that the project is completed in no more than 36 days?

CHECK   The probability is .2147.

This probability of completion can be used in conjunction with the cost, or penalty, associated with being late to determine the acceptability of the current situation. Since there is a .7078 probability that the project will be completed in 40 days, there must be a $1 - .7078$ probability that the project will not be completed on time. If some penalty, say $10,000, is incurred for failure to complete the project on time, the expected penalty can be calculated as

$$.2922 (\$10,000) = \$2,922$$

Similarly, suppose that Harkness will earn a $5,000 bonus for finishing the project in 32 days or less. The expected bonus is equivalent to

$$.0130 (\$5,000) = \$65$$

These expected penalties and bonuses can then be used to determine whether or not it is desirable to assign additional resources to one or more of the activities in order to reduce the expected penalty cost and increase the expected bonus.

INSTANT REPLAY Suppose Harkness can reduce the expected length of paths I and II by 1 day for a cost of $500. If the variance (and standard deviations) for those paths remain unchanged, is this expenditure justifiable in terms of the $10,000 penalty for failing to complete the project in 40 days or less and the $5,000 bonus for finishing in 32 days or less?

CHECK The revised probabilities of path completion times are .8849 that path I is 40 days or less, .9082 that path II is 40 days or less, .3446 that path I is 32 days or less, and .0918 that path II is 32 days or less. The revised project completion probabilities are thus .8849 (.9082) = .8037 that the project will be completed in 40 days or less and .3446 (.0918) = .0316 that the project takes 32 days or less. The expected penalty is thus (1 − .8037)($10,000) = $1,963 and the expected bonus is .0316 ($5,000) = $158. The expected penalty dropped by $2,922 − $1,963 = $959 and the expected bonus increased by $158 − $65 = $93. Thus, allowing for the $500 additional cost to gain the 1-day reduction, the net expected benefits are $959 + $93 − $500 = $552. Thus the expenditure can be justified.

Project Methods with Resource Limitations

The next issue to be considered is determination of the proper utilization of resources to complete the project. Every project manager has limited quantities of these various resources, such as people, materials, equipment, and money. Certain decisions relative to the utilization of these resources that the manager needs to make include:

1. Is it economical to assign additional resources to selected activities, thereby reducing the length of the project?
2. Can the activities be scheduled to reduce peak resource requirements and still meet a constraint on project duration?
3. If the resources available for the project are not sufficient to permit its completion in the shortest possible time, how can these resources be assigned to activities so as to find the shortest possible project duration consistent with these resource limitations?

The types of approaches that can be used to answer these questions will be illustrated by focusing on the first question. This will be done by next examining what are called *time/cost tradeoffs*.

The expected duration for an activity can almost always be affected in some manner by the allocation of resources to the activity. For example, a particular activity might take 10 days to complete with 2 people assigned to it and only 6 days with 4 people assigned. Of course, as additional personnel are assigned to an activity, the cost of performing that task normally increases. Note that in the example described, the cost of completing the activity with 2 people assigned was 20 person days while with 4 people assigned it took 24 person days to complete.

This illustrates a basic tradeoff available with most projects: activities can be completed in less time, but only up to a point and at additional cost. The minimum cost time to complete an activity is often called *normal time,* implying a normal or reasonable allocation of resources. Adding resources to reduce an activity is called *crashing,* and the minimum time is appropriately called *crash time.* If it is desirable to reduce the time required to complete the project, additional resources can be assigned to activities on the critical path. Often the cost of the additional resources assigned is more than offset by a reduction in costs associated with the length of the project. As an example, if the project is under contract which calls for a penalty to be assessed for each day the project takes beyond the target due date, the cost of assigning additional resources may be more than compensated for by the reduction or elimination of such penalties.

A distinction is made here between two kinds of costs, direct costs which are related to the resources assigned to a specific activity and indirect costs which are determined by the length of the project.

As the activity time decreases with the addition of resources, the direct costs associated with the project increase. On the other hand, the indirect costs will normally decrease if the activity to which additional resources are assigned is on the critical path. These costs for a typical project are shown in Figure 16-14. Note the two end points of the total cost curve. The left end of the curve represents the cost of completing the project in the shortest possible time, regardless of the resources assigned. The other end of the curve corresponds to the maximum completion time associated with the assignment of the minimum direct cost resources required to complete the project.

FIGURE 16-14   Effects of project duration on costs.

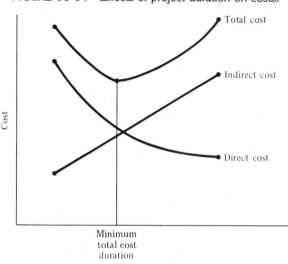

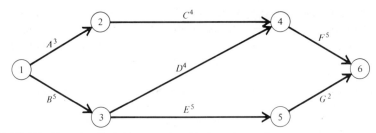

FIGURE 16-15 Brandon Park Racetrack odds board installation project in AOA format with minimum direct cost activity times.

Observe that the minimum total cost point does not occur at either extreme but at some point in between. Thus management would like to know how to assign additional resources on a selective basis so as to achieve the minimum total cost project duration, trading off additional direct costs to reduce the indirect cost.

To illustrate, consider the situation faced by management at Brandon Park Racetrack. Figure 16-15 shows the activities, expected durations (in days), and precedence relationships for the installation of a new electronic board to display betting odds and other information. This board will replace an existing, older board. The times shown are the minimum direct (not total) cost times for each activity.

The network has three paths *ACF*, *BDF*, and *BEG* with lengths of 12, 14, and 12 days, respectively. Thus the project can be completed in 14 days if no additional resources are assigned. Table 16-3 provides additional information for the Brandon Park project, including the maximum number of days each activity can be shortened and the cost per each day of reduction. We are assuming here that the direct activity costs are linearly related to activity duration, which permits us to use a fixed cost per day of reduction for our calculations. For example, activity *C*, rewiring, can be shortened 1 day for $50, 2 days for $100, etc. Similarly, we will assume that the indirect costs (supervisory and technical help required for the installation project) can be expressed as a fixed cost per day, in this case $150 for each day of project duration.

Note that if each activity is reduced to its minimum duration (crash time), the project length is decreased from 14 days to 8 days. (Path lengths are *ACF* 7, *BDF* 8, and *BEG* 6.)

TABLE 16-3
Cost of Reduction in Activity Times and Maximum Reductions
for Brandon Park Racetrack Odds Board Installation Project

Activity	Minimum cost time	Cost per day of reduction	Maximum number of days saved
A. Remove old board	3		0
B. Assemble new board	5	$150	2
C. Rewiring	4	$ 50	2
D. Install new board	4	$ 50	1
E. Hire maintenance personnel	5	$ 25	3
F. Final hookup and testing	5	$130	3
G. Train maintenance personnel	2	$100	1

One approach that can be followed is to consider the possible tradeoffs available at each step as we continue to reduce the project duration by assigning additional resources to critical activities until it is no longer economical to make any further reductions. We are trading off additional direct costs to reduce indirect costs. As long as the increase in direct cost is less than the savings in indirect cost, we continue. Once such tradeoffs are no longer economical, we stop.

To illustrate, refer again to the Brandon Park example of Figure 16-15 and Table 16-3. Before any resources are assigned, the three paths had lengths of:

$$ACF: \quad 3 + 4 + 5 = 12$$

$$BDF: \quad 5 + 4 + 5 = 14$$

$$BEG: \quad 5 + 5 + 2 = 12$$

If we are to reduce the length of the project, we must reduce the duration of one or more activities on the critical path. Activity B (assembling the new board) costs $150 per day of reduction, activity D (installing the new board) $50 per day, and activity F (training maintenance personnel) $130. Because activity D is the cheapest to reduce, we first assign additional resources to it. We can, however, reduce D at most 1 day according to Table 16-3. Thus we save $150 (the 1-day reduction in indirect costs saved by reducing the length of the project) at a cost of $50 (the increase in direct costs caused by assigning additional resources to activity D). At this point our three paths have lengths of

$$ACF: \quad 3 + 4 + 5 = 12$$

$$BDF: \quad 5 + 3 + 5 = 13$$

$$BEG: \quad 5 + 5 + 2 = 12$$

Again we must reduce one of the three critical activities $B, D,$ or F in order to reduce the length of the project. Since D cannot be reduced any further, our choice is between B at $150 per day and F at $130. Since F is cheaper, we select it for our second allocation of resources. This reduction is beneficial, since we gain $150 per day of reduction at a cost of $130. Activity F can be reduced up to 3 days. However, reducing it more than 1 day will not gain anything at this point, since path BEG will become critical. To illustrate, after activity F is reduced 1 day, the paths are

$$ACF: \quad 3 + 4 + 4 = 11$$

$$BDF: \quad 5 + 3 + 4 = 12$$

$$BEG: \quad 5 + 5 + 2 = 12$$

Note that the reduction of F by 1 day caused the ACF path to be shortened by 1 day as well as the reduction in BDF. Observe also that paths BDF and BEG are now both critical. Any further reductions in the length of the project can be achieved only by reductions in both paths.

Since activity B is shared by both critical paths, a reduction in activity B's time duration will cause both critical paths to decrease; this costs $150 per day. Two other options exist, both involving two activities. Activity F, on path BDF, can be reduced in conjunction with either activity E or G. The FE combination costs $130 + 25 = $155 per day, while the FG grouping costs $130 + 100 = $230 per day.

TABLE 16-4
Identifying the Least Total Cost Assignment of Resources to the Brandon Park Racetrack Project

Step	Length of path			Potential reduc-tions	Cost per day reduced	Activity reduced	Days reduced	Direct cost	Indirect cost	Total cost
	ACF	BDF	BEG							
1	12	14	12	B	150	D	1	50	1,950	2,000
				D	50					
				F	130					
2	12	13	12	B	150	F	1	180	1,800	1,980
				F	130					
3	11	12	12	B	150	B	1	330	1,650	1,980
				FE	155					
				FG	230					
4	11	11	11	FB	280	FE	2	640	1,350	1,990
				FE	155					
				FG	230					
				CBE	225					
				CBG	300					
5	9	9	9	CB	200	CB	1	840	1,200	2,040
6	8	8	8	Further reductions not feasible						

The first option, reducing activity B, is the least costly, but observe that its cost exactly equals the savings generated by the reduction of the project length. Thus a decision as to whether or not to assign the additional resources to B would probably have to be based on considerations other than cost. For example, the additional resources might be assigned if early completion was considered important in establishing an on-time record.

Normally we would stop at this point if we were interested only in the minimum total cost solution. Table 16-4 displays the results we would obtain if we were to continue to trace through the other options until no further reductions in the project duration are possible. This allows us to observe the total cost pattern over the full range of project durations. Note that the lowest-cost solution is completion in either 11 or 12 days at a cost of $1,980.

INSTANT REPLAY If the indirect costs in the Brandon Park project were $190 per day, what would be the least total cost project length?

CHECK 9 days at a total cost of $2,350 (vs. a cost of $2,660 with no additional resources).

Observe that in the process of obtaining the least total cost solution, a number of solutions were found. Examining Table 16-4 we find (step 1) a solution with project duration of 13 days and a total cost of $2,000, (step 2) a duration of 12 days and a cost of $1,980, (step 3) a duration of 11 days and a cost of $1,980, (step 4) a duration of 9 days and a $1,990 cost, (step 5) a duration of 8 days and a cost of $2,040. These solutions provide management alternatives to choose from that will allow them to consider factors other than cost. Thus they might decide to choose the 8-day $2,040 cost alternative instead of the least-cost option, concluding that the savings in time is worth the extra cost.

Computer Implementation

The success of project planning and control methods is evidenced by the growing number of commercially available computer packages capable of performing sophisticated PERT/CPM analysis. The development of fast, large-capacity computers has aided this growth, permitting more complex but realistic approaches to be used on very large problems.

Table 16-5 provides a brief summary of the features and characteristics of five such computer packages designed to handle the resource allocation problem. As can be seen, these packages offer a variety of features, including the capability to schedule multiple projects simultaneously (thus treating the allocation of scarce resources among these projects as well as within a project), to consider projects with the number of activities in the thousands, to deal with dozens of different resource types (e.g., carpenters, plumbers, electricians), to provide cost information and specially tailored reports, and to permit flexibility with respect to the choice of scheduling procedures.

TABLE 16-5
Sample Features of Some Commercially Available Computer Packages for PERT/CPM with Constrained Resource Scheduling Capabilities

Package name and supplier	Features and characteristics
CPM-RPSM (Resource Planning and Scheduling Method), CEIR, Inc.	2,000–8,000 activities per project, 4 resource types per project, 26 resource limits, job splitting allowed, job start/finish constraints allowed. Uses fixed scheduling heuristic
MSCS (Management Scheduling and Control System), McDonnel Automation Co.	Multiproject capability (25 projects), 18,000 tasks, 12 resource types, flexible job conditions, easy updating, project costing capability, report generation. Scheduling heuristics based on complex priority function, controllable by user
PMS/360 (Project Management System), IBM Corp.	Multiproject capability (225 projects), 32,000 activities, 250 resource types, many costing and updating features with report options and choice of scheduling heuristics. Complex management information system
PPS IV (Project Planning System), Control Data Corp.	2,000 jobs per project, 20 resource types, multiple project capability, permits overlapping tasks, resource costing and progress reporting. Will do resource leveling with fixed project duration. Resource priorities may be specified and multishift work is allowed. Uses a fixed heuristic for scheduling
PROJECT/2, Project Software, Inc.	Multiproject capability (50), 32,000 activities, several hundred resource types. Handles AOA or AON input. Includes automatic network generation for repetitive sequences of activities, easy updating and many cost analysis features. Choice of scheduling heuristics, specified by user

Source: Edward W. Davis, "Network Resource Allocation," *Journal of Industrial Engineering,* April 1974.

Final Comments

In this chapter we have examined several models that treat project planning and control problems. The importance of this area is derived from the universal existence of projects that need management in organizations of all kinds. Frequently these projects involve large numbers of people and substantial amounts of other resources, and they may require quick reactions as problems develop. All these factors argue for the use of effective planning and control procedures.

Each of the models described here can be represented as a network. The arcs that form the interconnections of this network correspond to the precedence relationships that exist for the various project activities. We observed that the nodes could correspond to activities in the AON approach or the arcs could be used for the activities in the AOA approach. The AOA method requires the use of dummy activities, while AON does not.

We paid particular attention to what was called the critical path, which consisted of a set of critical activities. The use of the word "critical" implied that any delay in these activities would delay the entire project. It was pointed out that near-critical activities also need watching as the inevitable changes that occur in a project could cause these activities to become critical. Noncritical activities have slack time which represents potential noncritical delays. Total slack for any activity consists of free slack, which can be used without affecting any other activity, and interruptive slack, which if used would cause delays in other noncritical activities.

We considered also the effect of variation in each activity's duration. Estimates of an activity's most likely, optimistic, and pessimistic completion times were used to calculate an expected time and variance. The critical path and critical activities are determined using expected durations. The activity variances were used to determine probabilistic estimates of the project duration.

The impact of resource limitations on project scheduling situations was also discussed. We saw how the option of assigning additional personnel could be used to lower the total cost of completing a project. This was done by comparing the tradeoff between direct and indirect project costs.

In the final section we briefly considered a few of the many competing computerized packages available for project planning and control. As was shown, these procedures are capable of handling problems with thousands of tasks and with a variety of other characteristics.

Key Words

Activities on arcs **550**

Activities on nodes **550**

Activity **548**

Activity time **551**

Activity variance **562**

AOA **550**

AON **550**

Arc **549**

Beta distribution **563**

Central limit theorem **565**

CPM **548**

Crashing **571**

Crash time **571**

Critical activity **551**

Critical path **551**

Critial path method **548**

Direct cost **571**

Dummy activities **550**

Problems

16-1. Tranquillity Studios has just purchased the movie rights for the latest disaster book, *Flood*, and is now developing plans to convert the book into a movie.

The activities involved in the production and distribution of the film have been summarized below with their estimated completion times in days and precedence requirements.

Activity	Description	Immediate predecessors	Expected duration, days
A	Produce script		30
B	Prepare budgets		10
C	Develop special effects	A	60
D	Cast the parts	B	20
E	Develop advertising plans	B	15
F	Shoot exterior scenes	A, D	35
G	Shoot disaster scene	C, F	10
H	Shoot interior scenes	F	15
I	Edit the film	G, H	10
J	Previews	I	5
K	Prepare promotional materials	E, I	8
L	Revise editing	J	5
M	Distribute	L	10

Determine for this project:
 a. The critical activities and length of the critical path.
 b. The early start and finish times for each activity.
 c. The late start and finish times for each activity.
 d. The total and free slack for each activity.
 e. Suppose that activities *A* through *E* were completed on time but that bad weather has caused the shooting of exterior scenes to be completed in 50 days rather

than 35 days as planned. What is the revised project duration? What activities yet to be completed are the best candidates for reducing the length of the project?

16-2. The Franklin Shoe Company has decided to modernize its manufacturing process by removing much of its existing equipment and replacing it with the latest and most productive equipment available. Although this change-over will occur during a slack seasonal period for Franklin Shoe, the firm wishes to minimize the effects of this transformation as much as possible. Thus it recognizes the need to invest a great deal of time in planning and controlling the change-over.

The figure below illustrates the precedence relationships assumed to exist for the various conversion project activities.

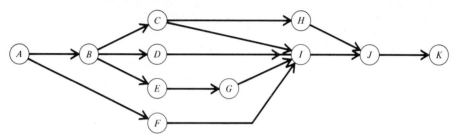

Estimated durations for each activity have been obtained and this information together with the activity descriptions is shown in the table below. The estimated times are assumed to be accurate and are based on experience with similar change-overs.

Activity	Description	Estimated duration, weeks
A	Prepare plans	3
B	Review available equipment and select desired units	4
C	Redesign production process	10
D	Order and receive equipment	13
E	Train shift 2 operators	6
F	Hire technicians	8
G	Train shift 1 operators	6
H	Prepare operating procedures	4
I	Install and test equipment	6
J	Switch production from old to new	2
K	Remove old equipment	2

a. Enumerate the five paths in the network.
b. Determine the length of the critical path.
c. Identify the critical activities.

16-3. For the Franklin Shoe Company problem (16-2), complete a summary table similar to Table 16-2 showing early and late start and finish times and total slack.

16-4. For the Franklin Shoe Company problem (16-2), the most disruptive period of the transition occurs during the completion of activities I, J, and K. If it is desired that these activities take place during the last 10 weeks of the year:
a. During what week does the project have to begin?
b. What would be the latest date that the company would have to begin hiring technicians?

16-5. Management of the Franklin Shoe Company (problem 16-2) is concerned about the length of the equipment conversion project. It is estimated that it will cost the company $1,200 per week to complete the project because of the various overhead expenses connected with the project. Department heads have been asked to suggest ways in which the project can be shortened. Three such proposals were presented.

1. Process redesign (activity C), expected to take 10 weeks to complete, could be shortened 2 weeks by hiring an additional planner. This would cost about $1,600.
2. Ordering and receiving the equipment (activity D) can be reduced from 13 weeks to 11 weeks by expediting the shipping. This is expected to cost the company an additional $2,000.
3. The installation and testing phase could be reduced from 6 weeks to 3 weeks by hiring a consulting organization that specializes in installation and testing of similar equipment. These consultants charge $2,500 for their services.

Which of the above suggestions should be adopted and why?

16-6. Consider the Franklin Shoe Company problem (16-2).
    a. Redraw the network diagram in the AOA format.
    b. Identify any dummy activities that were added.
    c. What reason motivates a change from AON to AOA?
    d. Are there any managerial considerations regarding the format of the network (AON to AOA) to be used?

16-7. Calculate free and interruptive slack for the activities in the Franklin Shoe Company problem (16-2).

16-8. The Riscuit Baking Company is planning a special promotion for their packaged doughnuts sold through food stores. The company plans to produce and sell a special package containing a baker's dozen, or 13 doughnuts instead of the normal 12 to the box.
    The AOA network shown below presents the various activities, events, and precedence relationships.

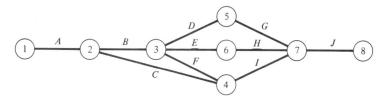

The estimated times and a description of the various activities are shown below.

Initial event	Ending event	Activity	Description	Expected time, weeks
1	2	A	Determine budget	2
2	3	B	Select advertising theme	2
2	4	C	Produce special packages	12
3	5	D	Buy radio time	3
3	6	E	Schedule magazine ads	3
3	4	F	Alert salespeople	1
5	7	G	Prepare copy for radio	4
6	7	H	Prepare magazine copy	6
4	7	I	Distribute packages	2
7	8	J	Run special	3

a. What is the earliest that the special can be finished if all preparations begin now?

b. Which of the above activities are most critical?

c. Determine the earliest and latest activity start and finish times.

d. Which of these activities has the most slack?

16–9. Determine the mean and the variance for each of the activities shown below, based on the estimated pessimistic, optimistic, and most likely times as shown.

Activity	Optimistic time	Most likely time	Pessimistic time
A	2	8	14
B	3	5	9
C	8	8	8
D	0	2	4
E	5	20	23
F	7	15	19

16–10. Suppose that the following network accurately represents the tasks and relationships for a major overhaul of a U.S. Navy destroyer, the *U.S.S. Duarte.*

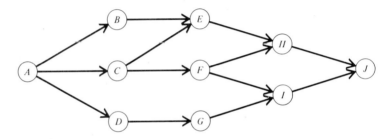

The mean time and variance in days for each activity have been calculated based on estimates provided by the preoverhaul inspection team and are provided in the table below.

Activity	Mean time	Variance	Activity	Mean time	Variance
A	3	0	F	12	5
B	3	1	G	5	3
C	4	3	H	4	0
D	2	3	I	5	7
E	3	2	J	3	1

a. Identify the critical path.

b. What are the expected length and variance for the critical path?

c. What is the probability that the critical path can be completed in 31 days or less? In 22 days or less? In no fewer than 22 days but no more than 32 days?

d. How many days should the shipyard crew set aside for the overhaul if they desire a 95 percent chance that the critical path is completed in that period?

e. What is the expected length of the other four paths in the network? What are the variances?

f. What is the probability that the second most critical path will be finished in 31
days or less?

g. What are the probabilities that the other three paths are completed in 31 days or less?

h. What is the probability that the project will be completed in 31 days or less?

i. Suppose that a penalty of $20,000 is incurred if the overhaul is not completed within 31 days and that a bonus of $25,000 will be earned if the overhaul can be accomplished in 22 days or less. What are the expected penalty and bonus for this project?

16-11. The Lackatracka Railroad is about to construct a new section of track to provide a more direct connection between two existing sections of its rail network. The project activity relationships are defined as shown here:

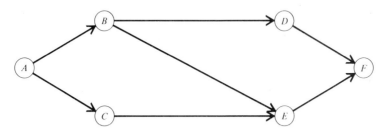

The activities, times, and appropriate cost information are given in the table below.

Activity	Description	Normal time, weeks	Cost per week of reduction	Maximum number of weeks of reduction
A	Acquire right of way	6	$2,100	1
B	Prepare access roadbed	6	400	2
C	Excavate tunnel	11	1,000	5
D	Lay access track	5	1,200	1
E	Lay tunnel track	3	1,500	1
F	Test track	5	800	1

Construction of the new track is expected to generate approximately $2,400 per week in revenue that is now lost to competing interstate truckers.

a. What is the expected project length based on the minimum cost activity times (normal times) as shown above?

b. What is the minimum project length achievable by reducing all activities to the full extent allowed above? How much would this cost in additional direct costs? How much would this earn in additional revenue?

c. Prepare a table similar to Table 16-4 showing the net revenue of the various project length options between that of parts *a* and *b* above.

d. What project length is associated with the highest net revenue? What activities should be shortened to achieve this maximum net revenue, and how many weeks should each be shortened?

Appendix

Areas under the Normal Curve between the Mean and Various Z-Scores

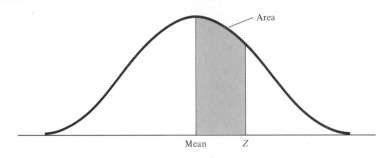

Z	.00	.01	.02	.03	.04	.05	.06	.07	.08	.09
.0	.0000	.0004	.0080	.0120	.0160	.0199	.0239	.0279	.0319	.0359
.1	.0398	.0438	.0478	.0517	.0557	.0596	.0636	.0675	.0714	.0753
.2	.0793	.0832	.0871	.0910	.0948	.0987	.1026	.1064	.1103	.1141
.3	.1179	.1217	.1255	.1293	.1331	.1368	.1406	.1443	.1480	.1517
.4	.1554	.1591	.1628	.1664	.1700	.1736	.1772	.1808	.1844	.1879
.5	.1915	.1950	.1985	.2019	.2054	.2088	.2123	.2157	.2190	.2224
.6	.2257	.2291	.2324	.2357	.2389	.2422	.2454	.2486	.2517	.2549
.7	.2580	.2611	.2642	.2673	.2704	.2734	.2764	.2794	.2823	.2852
.8	.2881	.2910	.2939	.2967	.2995	.3023	.3051	.3078	.3106	.3133
.9	.3159	.3186	.3212	.3238	.3264	.3289	.3315	.3340	.3365	.3389
1.0	.3413	.3438	.3461	.3485	.3508	.3531	.3554	.3577	.3599	.3621
1.1	.3643	.3665	.3686	.3708	.3729	.3749	.3770	.3790	.3810	.3830
1.2	.3849	.3869	.3888	.3907	.3925	.3944	.3962	.3980	.3997	.4015
1.3	.4032	.4049	.4066	.4082	.4099	.4115	.4131	.4147	.4162	.4177
1.4	.4192	.4207	.4222	.4236	.4251	.4265	.4279	.4292	.4306	.4319
1.5	.4332	.4345	.4357	.4370	.4382	.4394	.4406	.4418	.4429	.4441
1.6	.4452	.4463	.4474	.4484	.4495	.4505	.4515	.4525	.4535	.4545
1.7	.4554	.4564	.4573	.4582	.4591	.4599	.4608	.4616	.4625	.4633
1.8	.4641	.4649	.4656	.4664	.4671	.4678	.4686	.4693	.4699	.4706
1.9	.4713	.4719	.4726	.4732	.4738	.4744	.4750	.4756	.4761	.4767
2.0	.4772	.4778	.4783	.4788	.4793	.4798	.4803	.4808	.4812	.4817
2.1	.4821	.4826	.4830	.4834	.4838	.4842	.4846	.4850	.4854	.4857
2.2	.4861	.4864	.4868	.4871	.4875	.4878	.4881	.4884	.4887	.4890
2.3	.4893	.4896	.4898	.4901	.4904	.4906	.4909	.4911	.4913	.4916
2.4	.4918	.4920	.4922	.4924	.4927	.4929	.4930	.4932	.4934	.4936
2.5	.4938	.4940	.4941	.4943	.4945	.4946	.4948	.4949	.4951	.4952
2.6	.4953	.4955	.4956	.4957	.4958	.4960	.4961	.4962	.4963	.4964
2.7	.4965	.4966	.4967	.4968	.4969	.4970	.4971	.4972	.4973	.4974
2.8	.4974	.4975	.4976	.4977	.4977	.4978	.4979	.4979	.4980	.4981
2.9	.4981	.4982	.4982	.4983	.4984	.4984	.4985	.4985	.4986	.4986
3.0	.4987	.4987	.4987	.4988	.4988	.4989	.4989	.4989	.4990	.4990

17

Waiting Line Models: An Analysis of Service Systems

One of the most frequently encountered decision situations involves the design and operation of a *service system*. A service system consists of a *service facility*, containing one or more *servers*, which provides a specific type of service to *customers* arriving at the facility. Because of limited capacity at the service facility, it is common for some of the customers to have to wait before being served. This chapter will study a number of models, called *waiting line* or *queuing models*, that examine the design and operation of sevice systems. These models are largely of a descriptive nature. That is, the models predict what is expected to happen, given certain specific characteristics for the system. These characteristics include the rate and pattern of customer arrivals, the waiting behavior and capacity to accommodate those waiting, and the number, arrangement, and service pattern of the servers. These models can be used to predict several performance measures for a service system, including the expected size of the waiting line, length of waiting time, utilization of the servers, and costs of operating the system.

The pervasiveness of service systems should be readily apparent after a moment's reflection on the variety of waiting lines we have all participated in. Table 17-1 lists a few examples of the many types of customers and servers. Observe that "customer" can refer to people, such as patients, production workers, and purchasers, or to objects, such as automobiles, documents, and airplanes. In a similar way, we see that "server" can also be defined as a person, such as a teller, a doctor, or a barber, or as an object, such as an emergency room, a gas pump, or a tennis court.

Because of the diverse characteristics associated with customers and servers, including their waiting and service behavior, there are many types of **583**

TABLE 17-1
Common Examples of Customers and Servers

Customers or units arriving for service	Servers or service facilities
Automobile	Tollbooth, drive-in teller, car wash, parking garage, auto repair shop, state inspection facility
Patient	Emergency room, hospital, clinic, dentist, doctor, x-ray unit
Production worker	Parts storeroom, shared machine, lunchroom
Purchaser of goods	Supermarket checkout, hot dog vendor, department store clerk, gas pump
Purchaser of services	Barber, hairdresser, tax return preparer, welfare caseworker, motel room
Recreationer	Tennis court, amusement park ride, theater box office attendant, season ticket for professional sports
Document	Office worker, typist, mail room clerk, keypuncher, photocopying machine
Airplane	Airport runway, engine maintenance facility
Financial transaction	Teller, posting clerk, loan officer, bond trader, stockbroker
Production material	Inspector, storage facility, production equipment
Transport unit	Loading crew, docking space, repair crew, tugboat, waterway pilot
Traveler	Elevator, subway train, bus, taxi, aircraft seat
Criminal	Jail cell, lawyer, judge, parole officer

waiting line models. The first section of this chapter will discuss these characteristics, pointing out some of the more important differences. Then we will examine several of the more common types of models. There we will see that these models can be used to predict system performance measures. The final section will examine how we can evaluate the costs of various service facility design alternatives.

Components and Characteristics of Service Systems

Despite the great variety of ways in which customers and servers can be specified, a number of general components and characteristics are common to most service systems. A graphic representation of a typical service system is illustrated in Figure 17-1.

A general interpretation of the terms used in Figure 17-1 can be obtained by considering an example. Suppose we are modeling a bank teller service facility. The *source population* in this case represents current and potential bank customers. The service system, denoted by a dotted line in Figure 17-1, could in this instance refer to the physical facilities of the bank itself. Thus a customer enters the system upon physically entering the bank and is considered an *arrival*. The customer then enters a waiting line and waits for an available teller. There are many designs for grouping waiting lines (e.g., separate lines for

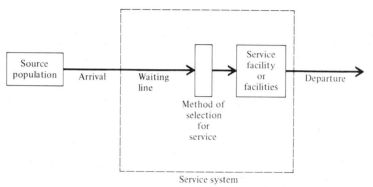

FIGURE 17-1 Graphic representation of typical service system.

each teller, one single line feeding all tellers). The *selection for service* step refers to the mechanism by which the next customer from among those waiting is selected when a teller or server becomes available. In the example, it is likely that a first-in-line, first-served selection process is used. Once "selected," the customer engages the available server, or teller. When the service is completed, the customer departs from the bank, or system. For many systems the arrow marking departure from the system could be extended back to the source population. This is because the customer just served is now a potential arrival for future service.

The following sections will review in more detail these common elements, suggesting a number of options available in characterizing the many types of service systems.

Source Population

The source population, or collection of potential arrivals, is usually identified as either *finite*, meaning a limited number of potential customers, or *infinite*, meaning an unlimited source of customers. Although almost any service system actually has a finite limit on the source of potential arrivals, those with a large number of potential customers are treated as if they were infinite. Only those systems whose source population is strictly limited to a relatively small finite number are defined as having finite populations. As a rule of thumb, those systems with source population in excess of 100 can be treated as infinite.

Thus systems such as banks, tollbooths, and department stores are treated as having infinite populations. Systems such as a machine repair facility in a factory or a computer terminal shared by a small number of office employees are considered as having finite populations. The reason for this distinction, and a basis for judging whether a population should be classified as finite or infinite, is that for a small finite population the rate at which customers arrive is affected by the number of customers already in the system.

For example, suppose we are studying a repair facility in a factory with 10 machines. An arrival in this case occurs when one of these machines breaks down or needs repair. The probability of an arrival during, say, the next minute is definitely affected by how many machines have already broken down, i.e., arrived for service. This probability would be zero if all 10 machines are already out of commission. On the other hand, the probability would be at its maximum if all 10 machines were operating.

By now you may see why large finite populations can be treated as infinite. With a large finite source population, the probability of an arrival is affected by the number of customers already in the system. However, this effect is so negligible that it can be disregarded. As we shall see, considering large finite populations as infinite greatly simplifies the analysis required.

Arrival Characteristics

There are a number of dimensions on which we can distinguish between the arrival characteristics of units requiring service. One of the most important is the *arrival rate*. This identifies an average number of arrivals per unit of time and is usually designated as λ. Thus we might model a system in which, on average, 12 customers arrive per hour. The arrival rate would be specified as $\lambda = 12$ per hour, or $\lambda = 96$ per 8-hour shift, or $\lambda = 0.2$ per minute.

In addition to the arrival rate it is important to identify the *distribution of arrivals*. The arrival distribution specifies the spacing, or interval, between arrivals. For example, if arrivals are strictly controlled, such as with fixed-cycle machine output, the system would be said to have a constant arrival pattern, or distribution, with zero variance. That is, the arrivals are all evenly spaced with a constant time interval between arrivals.

Another type of arrival pattern that occurs in practice is that in which customers arrive in *batches* rather than individually. For example, if the system of interest is a baggage handling facility for an airport, we find that arrivals for the unloading portion of the system arrive in batches corresponding to the arrival of each flight.

A frequent distribution encountered is one in which arrivals appear to follow a *random pattern*. This would be the case when the probability of arrival in the next increment of time is unaffected by whether or not an arrival occurred during the last increment of time. In such a case, we say that the system has a *Poisson arrival pattern*, because the distribution of arrivals for a fixed time length would follow the Poisson distribution, with mean $= \lambda$.

It is also useful to note that the time between arrivals for a system with a Poisson arrival pattern follows the *exponential distribution*, with mean $1/\lambda$. Thus, if we have a system with an arrival rate $\lambda = 12$ units per hour which follows a Poisson distribution, we know that the interarrival times follow an exponential distribution with a mean time of 5 minutes ($1/\lambda = \frac{1}{12}$ hour = 5 minutes) between arrivals. The models that we will examine in this chapter will assume a Poisson arrival pattern, or exponential interarrival times.

Another component of arrival characteristics is the influence sometimes exerted by management on the timing and rate of arrivals. In this regard, we may wish to classify arrivals as being either *controllable* or *uncontrollable*. For example, the arrival times of patients arriving for emergency medical service are usually uncontrollable. Service systems satisfying highly variable demand often attempt to smooth this demand (and consequent capacity needs) through scheduling or pricing mechanisms. To illustrate, patient demand for nonemergency services at a medical clinic is often smoothed by use of an appointment scheduling system.

Theaters often use differential pricing to shift demand from peak periods, such as weekends, to off-peak periods during the week. Airlines use a combination of scheduling (flight reservation system) and pricing (off-peak rates) to control demand or arrivals for service.

In other cases, management policies may be used to increase the rate of arrivals. Advertising and discount coupons are examples of such policies.

Waiting Line Accommodations and Behavior

The manner in which waiting for service is accomplished also has a number of interesting dimensions. One distinction that can be made is whether waiting is accomplished on-site or not. Most systems that we associate with waiting lines are those where the customers or units awaiting service do so in some common area or *waiting facility*. This would be true for situations in which actual lines develop, such as for a supermarket checkout counter, and for those in which a waiting area is used but customers do not actually physically wait in a line, such as a waiting room for a doctor.

There are other situations, however, in which the waiting is not done in a common waiting area. For example, customers on a waiting list for a particular airline flight may spend most, if not all, of their waiting at home or going about their normal daily tasks. Library patrons who have requested the loan of a particular book do not physically remain waiting at the library for a copy of the book to be returned but hold their "position in line" by virtue of the relative order of their name on the waiting list for the book. It is usually advantageous if management of a service system can shift waiting time from on-premises to off-premises. This usually reduces the cost of the wait for both the customer and the service system.

An important factor in determining the performance of a service system as well as a potential system design consideration is the size or *capacity of the waiting area*. Some systems, such as waiting space at a tollbooth on a major toll road, are characterized by an infinite (or nearly so) waiting line capacity. On the other hand, other systems because of either space limitations or customer behavior patterns, have only limited waiting capacity, which in some cases may be zero. For example, the waiting room in a doctor's office or a barbershop has some finite capacity which limits the number of waiting customers. In other cases the capacity may be severely limited such that, in effect, no waiting space is available. For instance, a motel can be treated as a system with no waiting capacity. Once all rooms are taken, arriving customers do not normally wait but instead seek accommodations elsewhere.

An important consideration in situations with limited (or finite) waiting capacity is what happens to an arrival when the waiting line is filled to capacity. In some instances, such as the motel, the arrival does not return but seeks some alternative system. This results in an *opportunity cost* because the facility loses any revenue or benefits that could have been earned from such customers if the facility had been larger. In other cases, such as a barbershop, the customer may return at a later time hoping to find an available space. Although the revenue from this customer is not lost, some *frustration cost* is certainly incurred by the customer which may impact on the arrival pattern in future periods.

In still other cases, an arrival at a facility with waiting capacity filled may *block* some other service facility. Consider an automated production line consisting of two processes, A followed by B, with a buffer inventory between them of limited capacity. This buffer inventory is used to adjust for differences in production rates and to allow either process to continue working even if the other breaks down. When that buffer inventory reaches capacity, any further output from process A is blocked from entering the buffer area. This, in turn, will shut down process *A*, possibly leading to other blocking conditions for processes that precede *A*. This blockage will affect the output rate of the system.

In any of these finite capacity situations, it is important to realize that the system output rate is definitely affected when the available waiting capacity is filled. Thus, when the waiting system is at capacity, potential arrivals are turned away and the effective arrival rate is zero. No arrivals can occur because the system is filled.

Another characteristic of the waiting process is the *number of waiting lines* used and the way in which customers are placed in these lines. In some systems even though more than one server is available, a single waiting line is used to preserve the order of arrival. This can occur literally, where customers stand in line, or figuratively, where they may take a number and wait until their number is called.

In other systems with multiple servers a separate waiting line is allowed to develop for each server. Lines of cars backed up at toolbooths or shoppers at checkout counters are examples of this waiting pattern. In these cases the customer is permitted to select which line to wait in. In other cases the customers may be assigned to specific lines or to wait for specific servers. This is particularly true where the service needs of the customers or the skills of the servers can be differentiated. Examples include assignment to doctors in a clinic on the basis of the patient ailment, establishment of express checkout facilities in a supermarket for those with few purchases, or exact change lanes at tollbooths.

Customer waiting behavior may also be important in system modeling. *Line switching behavior* (jockeying) often exists in systems with multiple waiting lines. Here customers may switch lines if it appears that the expected wait in some other line is less than in their current line. Although switching may help balance the length of the waiting lines, it can also lead to frustration when the actual waiting time turns out to be greater than had been anticipated. Note that if some customers are adept at jockeying and others are not, the customers tend not to be served in a first-come, first-served order. This increases the waiting time variability for the system, since the average time for adept jockeyers will be less than the average time for those not adept.

Another behavioral aspect occurs when customers who have joined a waiting line tire of waiting and depart before being served. These *defections* affect the arrival pattern and carry opportunity costs due to lost revenues, disgruntled customers, etc.

In other instances the arriving customer does not actually enter the waiting line even though space is available because the expected waiting time is greater than some personal limit for that customer. These *deflections* carry penalties similar to those for defections but create additional problems in judging system performance, since we may not be able to measure their magnitude. A lighted no-vacancy sign for a motel will cause potential customers to drive on by without management's being aware of the size of potential demand lost because of capacity limits.

Selection Process

Another important aspect of service system design that can significantly impact on performance is the process or mechanism used to select customers from the waiting area for service. The most frequently used system is the first-come, first-served procedure, although, as discussed earlier, the number of waiting lines and the waiting behavior of customers can serve to disrupt this order.

In some instances, where the establishment of waiting lines may be difficult or impossible, the selection process may approach a purely random choice. Department store service by a clerk during peak periods is a good example of this pattern. To avoid ill will, many systems for which it would be difficult to use waiting lines to maintain first-come, first-served order use a take-a-number system to accomplish the same thing. Bakeries and ice cream shops are good examples. As mentioned earlier, some systems use reservation systems to schedule service selection, which maintains some elements of the first-come, first-served process while reducing on-site waiting. This may be important to such service facilities as restaurants where space not used for waiting customers could be used to increase the service capacity.

Where the length of the waiting time has a differential effect on the quality of the service, a priority scheme may be used for selection. For instance, in a medical system, emergency patients are usually given *priority* over non-emergency cases. Also note that certain priority classes (emergencies) may require that service be interrupted on some lower-priority customer (nonemergency) to process the high-priority customer. This is referred to as *preemptive priority*.

In cases where the customers are objects rather than people, the question of preserving first-come, first-served order as the "fairest" selection process is less important. This permits the use of selection procedures that are based on improving some aspect of system performance. Suppose, for example, the customers are jobs to be completed in a manufacturing facility. If we always select the customer with the shortest expected service time, we will be able to serve more customers than if we select them in the order that they arrive. Alternatively, we might decide to select the customer, or job, that represents the greatest profit. This reduces the waiting time for high-profit jobs, although it increases waiting time for low-profit jobs. In any event, the choice of a selection rule is an important managerial consideration.

Service Facility Characteristics

A number of options exist for specifying the design of the service facility, some of which may be at least partly dictated by the nature of the process itself. Important options are the *number and arrangement of service facilities*. The simplest case is that where a single facility exists. A traffic light, one-chair barbershop, or hot dog vendor in the park are examples.

In some cases the service operation consists of more than one stage. This creates difficulties in balancing the service rates and waiting lines that develop in the system. In the simplest situation all service facilities are in *tandem,* one after the other. An example would be a cafeteria line or a car wash facility. Other situations may have multiple service facilities in *parallel,* offering essentially the same service, such as tellers in a bank or tollbooths on a highway. Still others involve more complex combinations of facilities, some in parallel, some in tandem, with a multitude of alternate routings. Patient routings in a hospital and registration processing for a university are examples of more complex situations.

At any point in the system where an individual service operation takes place, we are concerned with the *service rate* and the *distribution of service times*. Some operations, particularly those that are machine-paced, may have constant service rates. That is, each unit produced or served takes exactly the same amount of time. On the other hand, frequently it is assumed that service time can be described by the exponential distribution. As we saw with interarrival times, the times between serivce completions are of random length if an exponential service time distribution is assumed. This means that the likelihood of a service completion is independent of how long the service has already taken. Studies have shown that service times for many activities follow the exponential distribution.

A. K. Erlang, a Danish pioneer in the field of telephone waiting line systems, developed a whole family of service distributions (containing the exponential and the constant service rate distributions as special cases), which are today referred to as the *Erlang distributions* (in his honor).

The service rate, usually represented as μ, defines the average rate at which customers can be served by a single server. Thus, if a server takes 10 minutes, on average, to serve a customer, we would say that the service rate is 6 customers per hour, or $\mu = 6$. For the models that we will consider here, service times are assumed to be exponential with mean μ.

Departure

In some systems it is important to consider the disposition of customers upon departure from the system. This is particularly the case for finite source systems. The key issue is whether or not the departing units return to the source population as potential new arrivals or whether such units enter some other population with a low or zero probability of ever requiring service again.

For example, a person who has contracted yellow fever once will never require treatment for that disease again. A yellow fever victim either dies or survives with a permanent immunity. On the other hand, a person who contracts a common cold develops no immunity and a surviving patient can contract the disease again and again.

Performance Measures

Since waiting line models are largely descriptive, we need some way of evaluating different system designs in order to select some "best" design. In general, the two performance measures of major importance are the *cost of providing the service* and the *cost of waiting customers*. Unfortunately, these two costs react differently to changes in the level of service provided, leading to the cost tradeoff decision as pictured in Figure 17-2. As the level of service is increased (e.g., providing more servers), the cost of providing service increases while the cost of waiting customers decreases. A decrease in the level of service provided will decrease the cost of providing service but increase the cost of waiting customers. We want to find the appropriate level of service that minimizes the sum of these costs.

Unfortunately, several factors complicate any direct analysis of these cost tradeoff factors. One is the difficulty in determining the actual cost of a waiting customer. Although in some cases we can measure the costs of providing waiting facility capacity, the cost of ill will or frustration on the part of the

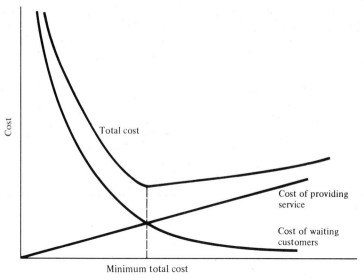

FIGURE 17-2 Cost tradeoffs for design of service system (assuming linear continuous service facility cost).

customer is extremely difficult to measure accurately. As we shall see, this frequently leads to the use of surrogate measures such as the average number of customers in the system or in the waiting line, the average time spent in the system or in the waiting line by each customer, or the probability that the waiting line will exceed some fixed size.

The cost of providing service also presents some difficulties. This cost does not normally follow a continuous linear pattern, as is indicated in Figure 17-2. This is because the level of service provided cannot be changed in continuous fashion. Instead, the level of service is normally changed by varying the number of servers used. This leads to a *discontinuous function* for service cost as shown in Figure 17-3. The function is discontinuous because levels of service can be defined only for an integer number of servers. That is, we cannot use, say, 3.46 servers, but could use either 3 or 4. Note that the cost of waiting is also shown as a discontinuous function (for the same reason). Thus the two costs behave similarly in response to changes in the number of servers. Cost discontinuities such as these restrict the use of classical optimization techniques and normally require us to search for the appropriate cost tradeoff point.

In addition to service costs, the average *utilization of the service facility* may also be of importance. Utilization is defined as the proportion of time that the server is actually engaged in serving customers. *Idle Time,* or time not spent serving the customer, is thus equivalent to 1 minus the average utilization. When utilization is low, idle time will be high and a large opportunity cost will be incurred. If during idle periods the servers can be used for other purposes, the overall operating cost for the system can be reduced. Unfortunately, one of the difficulties in managing service systems is that the system capacity may have to be set at a level sufficient to meet peak demands, thereby incurring considerable idle time during nonpeak periods. Although the use of part-time help and efficient scheduling of the work force may help compensate, there are

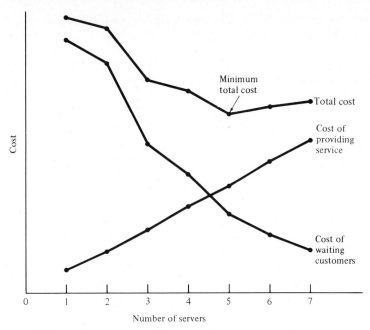

FIGURE 17-3   Cost tradeoff patterns for discontinuous cost functions.

many systems where capacity cannot easily be varied to match demand. As an example, the number of telephone lines between New York and Chicago must be adequate to handle peak demand, such as at 11:00 A.M. on weekdays, thereby incurring considerable idle time in off-peak periods.

Waiting Line Models

The sections that follow will examine several of the more frequently encountered waiting line or service system models. We will begin with the simple, single-server model. Then we will consider some special modifications to this model and will finish with the multiple-server situation. In some cases, an intuitive derivation of the equations used to measure system performance is presented.

General Relationships of Performance Measures

Several of the performance measures and their relationships are general enough to be discussed outside the context of a specific model. The results presented below are based on the assumption that the service system is operating under equilibrium, or *steady-state,* conditions. For many systems the operating day begins with no customers in the system. It will take some initial time interval for enough customers to arrive such that an equilibrium, or steady-state, balance is reached.

A steady state does not mean that the system will reach a point where the number of customers in the system never changes. Even when the system reaches equilibrium, fluctuations will occur. What a steady-state condition implies is that the various system performance measures, such as the *average* number of customers in the system, reach stable values. Thus, at equilibrium we would expect the average number of units in the system to stabilize at some equilibrium value.

It is useful to characterize the state of the system by the number of units or customers in the system, which includes those waiting as well as those actually being served. For example, if there were 20 customers in a bank, 3 being served and 17 waiting, we would say that there are 20 customers in the system, or $n = 20$. The proportion of time that there are n units in the system or the probability of n units in the system is referred to symbolically as P_n. Thus P_o would refer to the probability of an idle system, P_4 the probability of 4 customers in the system, etc.

Figure 17-4 shows the manner in which the number of units in the system changes from $n - 1$ to n or vice versa. A change from $n - 1$ to n units in the system can happen only if an arrival occurs. To change from n to $n - 1$ units in the system, a service must be completed. In other words, the number of customers in the bank can change from 19 to 20 only if a customer arrives. To change from 20 customers in the bank to 19, one of the customers must complete service and depart. In order for the system to be in equilibrium, the rates of change between these two states must be equal. This leads to the *fundamental balance equation:*

$$\begin{pmatrix} \text{Rate} \\ \text{of} \\ \text{arrivals} \end{pmatrix} \times \begin{pmatrix} \text{probability} \\ \text{of } n - 1 \text{ units} \\ \text{in the system} \end{pmatrix} = \begin{pmatrix} \text{rate} \\ \text{of} \\ \text{service} \end{pmatrix} \times \begin{pmatrix} \text{probability} \\ \text{of } n \text{ units} \\ \text{in the system} \end{pmatrix}$$

If, as defined earlier, λ is the arrival rate and μ the service rate (both expressed for an equivalent time interval, such as customers per hour), we can then define

$$\lambda P_{n-1} = \mu P_n \tag{17-1}$$

which can be rewritten as

$$P_n = \frac{\lambda}{\mu} P_{n-1} \tag{17-2}$$

This simple balance equation can be used to derive most of the interesting performance measures.

Two other performance measures of interest, the *average number of customers in the system* L_s or *in the waiting line* L_q and the *average time spent in the system* W_s or *in the waiting line* W_q have a relationship that can also be intuitively derived. We will assume that customers are served in the order in which they arrive and that the source population and waiting capacity are infinite.

Consider first the average number of units in the system L_s and the aver-

FIGURE 17-4   Steady-state balance for service system models.

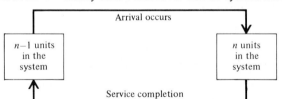

age time spent in the system W_s. Observe that at the time a unit completes service, on average, there will be L_s units in the system, all of which will have arrived during the time that this unit spent in the system, which, as defined above, is on average W_s. The number of units arriving during the time W_s is equivalent to λW_s, since λ represents the arrival rate per unit of time and W_s is the time that the finishing unit spent in the system. Therefore, the average number in the system is equal to the arrival rate times the average time spent in the system, or

$$L_s = \lambda W_s$$

A similar argument can be used to deduce logically a relationship between the average number in the waiting line L_q and the average waiting time in the line W_q, which is

$$L_q = \lambda W_q$$

Also note that a simple relationship exists between waiting time in the line and time in the system. This is because any time spent in the system that was not spent waiting must have been the actual service time itself. Since μ is the service rate or customers per unit time, $1/\mu$ must be the average service time. Thus

$$W_s = W_q + \frac{1}{\mu}$$

It should be noted that these relationships may have to be modified for those cases in which the rate at which customers enter the system is not the same as λ, because of a finite source population or finite waiting capacity. This will be shown in a later section.

Basic Single-Server Model

The simplest model to consider is that with a single service facility and consequently a single waiting line. We shall assume an infinite source population from which arrivals occur with a mean rate of λ per unit of time and whose interarrival times are exponentially distributed. The service facility processes customers on a first-come, first-served basis at the rate of μ per unit of time, such service times being exponentially distributed.

Table 17-2 shows a number of equations for determining the system performance measures. Note that determination of L_s allows us to derive W_s, W_q, and L_q easily using the general relationship described previously.

To illustrate, equation I-2 in Table 17-2 shows that

$$L_s = \frac{\lambda}{\mu - \lambda}$$

From the relationship that $L_s = \lambda W_s$ we can derive W_s, the average time spent in the system (equation I-4):

$$\lambda W_s = L_s = \frac{\lambda}{\mu - \lambda}$$

$$W_s = \frac{1}{\lambda} \frac{\lambda}{\mu - \lambda} = \frac{1}{\mu - \lambda}$$

Knowledge of W_s allows us to determine W_q (equation I-5) since the time

TABLE 17-2
Formulas for Calculating Various Performance
Measures for the Basic Single-Server Model

Performance measure	Equation	Equation No.
Utilization of server	$\rho = \dfrac{\lambda}{\mu}$	I-1
Average number in system	$L_s = \dfrac{\lambda}{\mu - \lambda}$	I-2
Average number waiting	$L_q = \dfrac{\lambda^2}{\mu(\mu - \lambda)}$	I-3
Average time in system	$W_s = \dfrac{1}{\mu - \lambda}$	I-4
Average time waiting	$W_q = \dfrac{\lambda}{\mu(\mu - \lambda)}$	I-5
Probability of n in system	$P_n = \left(\dfrac{\lambda}{\mu}\right)^n \left(1 - \dfrac{\lambda}{\mu}\right)$	I-6
Probability of more than k in system	$P_{n>k} = \left(\dfrac{\lambda}{\mu}\right)^{k+1}$	I-7
Average length of nonempty lines	$L_a = \dfrac{\mu}{\mu - \lambda}$	I-8
Average waiting time of an arrival who waits	$W_a = \dfrac{1}{\mu - \lambda}$	I-9

λ = mean arrival rate (Poisson)
μ = mean service rate (exponential service time)

spent in the system is equal to the time spent in the line plus the service time or $W_s = W_q + 1/\mu$:

$$W_s = W_q + \frac{1}{\mu} = \frac{1}{\mu - \lambda}$$

$$W_q = \frac{1}{\mu - \lambda} - \frac{1}{\mu} = \frac{\mu - (\mu - \lambda)}{\mu(\mu - \lambda)} = \frac{\lambda}{\mu(\mu - \lambda)}$$

Finally, we can determine L_q (equation I-3) from the relationship that $L_q = \lambda W_q$:

$$L_q = \lambda W_q = \lambda \left[\frac{\lambda}{\mu(\mu - \lambda)}\right] = \frac{\lambda^2}{\mu(\mu - \lambda)}$$

To illustrate the use of these equations, consider the problem faced by the Oglethorpe Typewriter Repair Shop. Tom Oglethorpe is the sole proprietor and employee of this firm, which repairs and services typewriters. Typewriters are brought to Tom's shop at an average rate of 10 per 8-hour day. Although the time to service each typewriter is quite variable, Tom averages 30 minutes per typewriter. The interarrival and service times are thought to be exponential. Tom is concerned that he will lose customers if the average time each typewriter remains in the shop is too long.

Tom's situation seems to fit the basic single-server model quite well. The arrival rate is given as 10 per day and the service rate (assuming an 8-hour day) is found by

$$\mu = \frac{(8 \text{ hours per day})(60 \text{ minutes per hour})}{30 \text{ minutes per unit}} = 16 \text{ units per day}$$

Referring to Table 17-2, we can now calculate the various performance measures for Tom's operations. The system utilization, from equation I-1, is

$$\rho = \frac{\lambda}{\mu} = \frac{10}{16} = .625$$

Thus, on average, Tom is busy 62.5 percent of the time or idle 37.5 percent.

The average number of typewriters in the shop is given by equation I-2, or

$$L_s = \frac{\lambda}{\mu - \lambda} = \frac{10}{16 - 10} = \frac{10}{6} = 1.67$$

The average number waiting for service is (from equation I-3)

$$L_q = \frac{\lambda^2}{\mu(\mu - \lambda)} = \frac{10^2}{16(16 - 10)} = \frac{100}{96} = 1.04$$

The average time each typewriter spends in the shop is (equation I-4)

$$W_s = \frac{1}{\mu - \lambda} = \frac{1}{16 - 10} = \frac{1}{6} = .17$$

Note that since λ and μ were expressed in units per day, all time measures such as W_s will also be in days. Thus each typewriter will spend $\frac{1}{6}$ day or $1\frac{1}{3}$ hours or 80 minutes in the shop.

Similarly we can calculate the average waiting time

$$W_q = \frac{\lambda}{\mu(\mu - \lambda)} = \frac{10}{16(16 - 10)} = \frac{10}{96} = .104$$

or approximately $\frac{1}{10}$ day. This is equivalent to .83 hour or 50 minutes.

The probability of a specific number of units in the system can be calculated using equation I-6 in Table 17-2:

$$P_n = \left(\frac{\lambda}{\mu}\right)^n \left(1 - \frac{\lambda}{\mu}\right)$$

For example, the probability that no typewriters will be in the shop is

$$P_0 = \left(\frac{10}{16}\right)^0 \left(1 - \frac{10}{16}\right) = 1\left(\frac{6}{16}\right) = .375$$

Note that an empty shop is equivalent to an idle Tom and a P_0 of .375 is equivalent to the idle proportion found earlier.

Similarly the probability of four typewriters in the shop is

$$P_4 = \left(\frac{10}{16}\right)^4 \left(1 - \frac{10}{16}\right) = .1526(.375) = .0572$$

Of more interest may be the probability of more than a given number of typewriters in the shop ($P_n > k$). This might be important in determining how much room to allocate for waiting typewriters, for instance. The formula to use is equation I-7 or

$$P_{n>k} = \left(\frac{\lambda}{\mu}\right)^{k+1}$$

where k is the cutoff point. For instance, Tom may wish to know the likelihood that he will need room for more than 9 waiting typewriters (more than 10 in the system). This is found as

$$P_{n>10} = \left(\frac{10}{16}\right)^{10+1} = (.625)^{11} = .006$$

which is an extremely low probability (6 days out of 1,000).

The last two equations in Table 17-2 (I-8 and I-9) require some additional explanation. Observe that the average length of the waiting line L_q includes cases in which no line actually exists. This occurs when there is no more than one in the system. It may be useful, therefore, to determine the average line length during those periods in which a line actually exists. This is accomplished when L_q is divided by the probability that a line exists.

As stated, a line exists whenever more than one person is in the system. Thus we need to find $P_{n>1}$, which can easily be calculated using equation I-7 from Table 17-2:

$$P_{n>1} = \left(\frac{\lambda}{\mu}\right)^{1+1} = \left(\frac{10}{16}\right)^2 = .39$$

Letting L_a represent the average length of the waiting line when a line exists, we find

$$L_a = \frac{L_q}{P_{n>1}} = \frac{1.04}{.39} = 2.67$$

which is a larger number than found before. This is because no line forms nearly 61 percent of the time ($P_0 + P_1 = .375 + .234 = .609$) and the average line size during the other 39 percent of the time must be large in order for the overall average to be 1.04.

For a single server, the average length of the waiting line during those periods when a line exists is found from

$$L_a = \frac{L_q}{P_{n>1}} = \frac{\lambda^2/[\mu(\mu - \lambda)]}{(\lambda/\mu)^2} = \frac{\mu}{\mu - \lambda}$$

Thus we could have solved directly for L_a as

$$L_a = \frac{\mu}{\mu - \lambda} = \frac{16}{16 - 10} = 2.67$$

In a similar manner we can define W_a as the average waiting time for those arrivals that wait. This excludes those units that arrive while the server is idle. Consider a unit that has just arrived and that must wait since the server is busy. The expected length of the waiting line given that a line exists was found above to be L_a. The expected waiting time for our recent arrival is equal to the expected number in the line times the expected or average service time. Thus

$$W_a = L_a \frac{1}{\mu} = \frac{\mu}{\mu - \lambda} \frac{1}{\mu} = \frac{1}{\mu - \lambda}$$

For our example problem, the expected waiting time for those typewriters that must wait is found then from

$$W_a = \frac{1}{\lambda - \mu} = \frac{1}{16 - 10} = \tfrac{1}{6} \text{ day}$$

or $1\tfrac{1}{3}$ hours or 80 minutes.

Arguments similar to those above for determining the average number and time *in the waiting line* can be used to derive corresponding measures for average number and time *in the system*.

INSTANT REPLAY Recalculate each of the performance measures for Tom assuming that he spends only 6 hours in the shop rather than 8. The arrival rate is now 10 typewriters per 6-hour day and the service rate is 12 typewriters per 6-hour day.

CHECK $\lambda = 10$, $\mu = 12$, $\rho = \tfrac{5}{6}$, $L_s = 5$, $L_q = 4.17$, $W_s = .5$, $W_q = .42$, $P_0 = \tfrac{1}{6}$, $P_4 = .08$, $P_{n>10} = .13$, $L_a = 6$, $W_a = .5$

Finite Source Model

One major variant of the basic single-facility model is that in which the source population is finite. As described previously, the arrival rate for this model is affected by the current state of the system, i.e., the number of units currently in the system. It is convenient in this case to define λ as the arrival rate for a single unit in the source population. Thus, $1/\lambda$ represents the average time each unit spends as part of the source population or, equivalently, the time between a service completion and the next need for service. Thus if we are modeling a health care system for a small group of people, $1/\lambda$ would represent the average time a person remains healthy.

Table 17-3 contains a summary of the relevant equations for determining system performance for this class of models. As with many of the more complex models, derivation of most of the performance equations requires knowledge of P_0, the probability of no units in the system. Unfortunately, this model has a somewhat unwieldy equation for P_0, which normally is solved by means of a computer program or reference to appropriate tables. We can best illustrate the calculations required by means of an example.

The Selectron Power Company provides electrical power for a small regional area of the country, supplied mainly by three large generators. These generators are subject to occasional breakdowns which past data show occur on average once every 12 months for each generator. Selectron employs a repair crew whose responsibility is to repair the generators as quickly as possible. At present it takes an average of 2 months to repair a generator and get it back in service. Although the current repair crew has been adequate to handle the existing set of generators, Selectron will soon be installing a fourth generator, and there is concern that the current repair crew may not be adequate, thereby limiting the overall generating capacity.

In order to study this situation, let us first determine the performance measures for the current system of three generators. We begin by calculating P_0, which corresponds to the proportion of time in which all three generators are operating.

The individual generator breakdown rate λ is 1 per year, since the time between breakdowns averages 1 year. The service rate μ is 6 per year, since the

TABLE 17-3
599

WAITING LINE
MODELS: AN
ANALYSIS OF
SERVICE SYSTEMS

Formulas for Calculating Various Performance Measures for Finite Source Models

Performance measure	Equation	Equation No.
Probability of no units in system	$P_0 = \dfrac{1}{\displaystyle\sum_{k=0}^{C} \left(\dfrac{\lambda}{\mu}\right)^k \dfrac{C!}{(C-k)!}}$	II-1
Probability of n in the system	$P_n = \dfrac{C!}{(C-n)!} \left(\dfrac{\lambda}{\mu}\right)^n P_0$	II-2
Average number waiting	$L_q = C - \dfrac{\lambda + \mu}{\lambda}(1 - P_0)$	II-3
Average number in system	$L_s = L_q + (1 - P_0)$	II-4
Average waiting time	$W_q = \dfrac{L_q}{\lambda(C - L_s)}$	II-5
Average time in system	$W_s = W_q + \dfrac{1}{\mu}$	II-6

λ = mean arrival rate, where $1/\lambda$ is the average time between arrivals per unit in the source population (Poisson)

μ = mean service rate (exponential service time)

C = size of source population

average service time is 2 months. The size of the source population C is 3, corresponding to the number of generators.

The formula for P_0 is (equation II-1)

$$P_0 = \frac{1}{\displaystyle\sum_{k=0}^{C} \left(\frac{\lambda}{\mu}\right)^k \frac{C!}{(C-k)!}} = \frac{1}{\displaystyle\sum_{k=0}^{3} \left(\frac{1}{6}\right)^k \frac{3!}{(3-k)!}}$$

$$= \frac{1}{1 + \frac{1}{6}\left(\frac{3!}{2!}\right) + \left(\frac{1}{6}\right)^2 \left(\frac{3!}{1!}\right) + \left(\frac{1}{6}\right)^3 \left(\frac{3!}{0!}\right)}$$

$$= \frac{1}{1 + \frac{1}{2} + \frac{1}{6} + \frac{1}{36}} = \frac{1}{1.694} = .59$$

P_0 represents the proportion of time that the repair crew is idle. This is equivalent to the proportion of time that all three generators are in service (operating). Selectron is also likely to be interested in the proportion of time that one or more generators are out of commission. The probability of $n - 1$ units waiting and one receiving service, i.e., n units in the system, is obtained from equation II-2 in Table 17-3:

$$P_n = \frac{C!}{(C-n)!} \left(\frac{\lambda}{\mu}\right)^n P_0$$

$$P_1 = \frac{3!}{2!}\left(\frac{1}{6}\right)^1 (.59) = .29$$

$$P_2 = \frac{3!}{1!}\left(\frac{1}{6}\right)^2 (.59) = .10$$

$$P_3 = \frac{3!}{0!}\left(\frac{1}{6}\right)^3 (.59) = .02$$

Thus our model predicts that 59 percent of the time all three generators will be operating, 29 percent with 2 generators, 10 percent with one, and 2 percent with none.

The average number of generators waiting for repair to begin L_q is defined in equation II-3 as

$$L_q = C - \frac{\lambda + \mu}{\lambda}(1 - P_0)$$

$$= 3 - \frac{1 + 6}{1}(1 - .59) = .13$$

The average number of generators out of service is given by L_s in equation II-4:

$$L_s = L_q + (1 - P_0)$$

$$= .13 + (1 - .59) = .13 + .41 = .54$$

The average time spent by a generator waiting for repair to begin is equivalent to W_q, which is defined in equation II-5:

$$W_q = \frac{L_q}{\lambda(C - L_s)}$$

$$= \frac{.13}{1(3 - .54)} = .053 \text{ year}$$

or .636 month.

The average downtime per generator is equivalent to W_s, defined in equation II-6 as

$$W_s = W_q + \frac{1}{\mu}$$

$$= .053 + \tfrac{1}{6} = .22 \text{ year}$$

or 2.64 months.

INSTANT REPLAY What impact on these performance measures will the addition of the fourth generator have?

CHECK $P_0 = .47, P_1 = .31, P_2 = .16, P_3 = .05, P_4 = .01, L_q = .29, L_s = .82,$ $W_q = .09,$ and $W_s = .26.$

Note that with three generators the average number of operating generators is $3 - .54 = 2.46$. An increase of one generator raises this average to $4 - .82 = 3.18$ generators, an effective increase of only .72. Selectron may wish to consider an expansion of the repair crew to reduce repair time or possibly adding a second crew.

TABLE 17-4
Formulas for Calculating Various Performance Measures for Limited Waiting Capacity Models

Performance measure	Equation	Equation No.
Probability of none in the system	$P_0 = \dfrac{1 - (\lambda/\mu)}{1 - (\lambda/\mu)^{M+1}}$	III-1
Probability of n in the system $(n \leq M)$	$P_n = \left(\dfrac{\lambda}{\mu}\right)^n P_0$	III-2
Average number in the system	$L_s = \dfrac{M(\lambda/\mu)^{M+2} - (M + 1)(\lambda/\mu)^{M+1} + \lambda/\mu}{[1 - (\lambda/\mu)^{M+1}](1 - \lambda/\mu)}$	III-3
Average number waiting	$L_q = L_s - \dfrac{\lambda(1 - P_M)}{\mu}$	III-4
Average time in system	$W_s = \dfrac{L_s}{\lambda(1 - P_M)}$	III-5
Average waiting time	$W_q = W_s - \dfrac{1}{\mu}$	III-6
Proportion of arrivals lost	$P_M = \left(\dfrac{\lambda}{\mu}\right)^M P_0$	III-7

λ = mean arrival rate (Poisson)

μ = mean service rate (exponential service time)

M = system capacity (maximum number including those waiting as well as those in service)

Limited Waiting Capacity Model

Another variant of the single-facility model, which occurs frequently in practice, is that caused by the existence of limited waiting space. This is referred to as the *limited waiting capacity model*. Table 17-4 provides a summary of the relevant equations for this model. Again we can illustrate by means of an example.

The Newcoat Painting Company has for some time been experiencing high demand for their automobile repainting service. Management is concerned that the limited space available to store cars awaiting painting has cost them revenue, since they have had to turn away business. A small vacant lot next to their painting facility has recently been made available for rental on a long-term basis at a cost of $10 per day. Management estimates that each lost customer costs them $20 in profit. They wish to know whether or not the vacant lot should be leased.

Current demand is estimated to be 21 cars per day with exponential interarrival times (including those turned away), and their facility can service 24 cars per day, service times also exponentially distributed. Cars are processed in first-come, first-served order. Waiting space is now limited to 9 cars but can be increased to 20 cars with the lease of the vacant lot.

We begin by analyzing the current situation using the performance equations in Table 17-4. The probability of no units in the system is given by equation III-1:

$$P_0 = \frac{1 - \lambda/\mu}{1 - (\lambda/\mu)^{M+1}}$$

$$= \frac{1 - \frac{21}{24}}{1 - (\frac{21}{24})^{10+1}} = \frac{.125}{.770} = .162$$

The average number of cars on the premises is equivalent to L_s (equation III-3):

$$L_s = \frac{M(\lambda/\mu)^{M+2} - (M+1)(\lambda/\mu)^{M+1} + \lambda/\mu}{[1 - (\lambda/\mu)^{M+1}](1 - \lambda/\mu)}$$

$$= \frac{10(\frac{21}{24})^{12} - (10+1)(\frac{21}{24})^{11} + \frac{21}{24}}{[1 - (\frac{21}{24})^{11}](1 - \frac{21}{24})}$$

$$= \frac{2.014 - 2.532 + .875}{(.770)(.125)} = \frac{.357}{.096} = 3.72$$

The average number of waiting cars is L_q (equation III-4):

$$L_q = L_s - \frac{\lambda(1 - P_M)}{\mu}$$

where P_M is defined by equation III-7:

$$P_M = \left(\frac{\lambda}{\mu}\right)^M P_0$$

$$P_{10} = \left(\frac{21}{24}\right)^{10} (.162) = .043$$

Observe that P_M is the proportion of customers turned away due to no waiting space, since that is the proportion of time that the system is filled to capacity. Continuing, we find from equation III-4:

$$L_q = 3.72 - \frac{21(1 - .043)}{24} = 3.72 - .84 = 2.88$$

The average time each car spends on the premises is given by W_s (equation III-5):

$$W_s = \frac{L_s}{\lambda(1 - P_M)}$$

$$= \frac{3.72}{21(1 - .043)} = \frac{3.72}{20.097} = .185 \text{ day}$$

The average waiting time per car is found from equation III-6:

$$W_q = W_s - \frac{1}{\mu}$$

$$= .185 - \tfrac{1}{24} = .143 \text{ day}$$

At present, since 4.3 percent of Newcoat's customers are being turned away, they are losing

$$(.043)(21) = .903$$

customers per day. At a profit potential of $20 per customer, this is costing Newcoat $20(.903) = \$18.06$ per day in lost profit. Since this cost exceeds the daily leasing cost of $10 for the additional facility, it appears to be profitable to enter into a lease agreement. This must be confirmed by determining the cost of turned away customers for the increased system size.

INSTANT REPLAY   If the lease agreement is signed, what will be the daily lost profit due to turned away customers? (Note that $M = 21$.)

CHECK $P_0 = .132$, $P_M = .008$, and lost profit equals $3.36 per day.

As shown in the Instant Replay, the lost profit due to turned away customers did not completely disappear with the increased facilities. Nevertheless it was reduced from $18.06 to $3.36 per day, a net daily savings of $14.70, which exceeds the $10 daily cost of renting by $4.70. Assuming a 6-day work week this amounts to an increase in annual profits of $1,466.40.

Multiple-Server Model

The final category of models we consider introduces the option of using more than one server to satisfy service demands and is referred to as the *multiple-server model*. A key issue with this model is the number of servers to use. A summary of the performance measures appears in Table 17-5.

TABLE 17-5
Formulas for Calculating Various Performance Measures for Multiple-Server Models

Performance measure	Equation	Equation No.
Probability of none in the system*	$P_0 = \dfrac{1}{\sum\limits_{k=0}^{s-1} (\lambda/\mu)^k/k! + \dfrac{(\lambda/\mu)^s}{(s - \lambda/\mu)(s - 1)!}}$	IV-1
Probability of n in the system where n is no greater than the number of service units ($n \leq s$)	$P_n = \dfrac{P_0(\lambda/\mu)^n}{n!}$	IV-2
Probability of n in the system where n is greater than the number of service units ($n > s$)	$P_n = \dfrac{P_0(\lambda/\mu)^n}{s!(s^{n-s})}$	IV-3
Average number in system	$L_s = \dfrac{\lambda\mu(\lambda/\mu)^s}{(s - 1)!(s\mu - \lambda)^2}\,P_0 + \dfrac{\lambda}{\mu}$	IV-4
Average number waiting	$L_q = L_s - \dfrac{\lambda}{\mu}$	IV-5
Average waiting time	$W_q = \dfrac{L_q}{\lambda}$	IV-6
Average time in system	$W_s = W_q + \dfrac{1}{\mu}$	IV-7

λ = mean arrival rate (Poisson arrivals)

μ = mean service rate for each server (exponential service time)

s = number of service facilities

*Also see the Appendix.

603

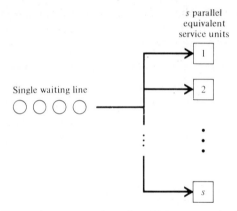

FIGURE 17-5   Pictorial representation of multiple-server, single waiting line model.

It should be noted that the only assumption here that is different from the basic single-facility model is the number of service facilities s. In particular note that a single waiting line is assumed, as shown in Figure 17-5, and each server has an identical service rate μ. A system with s servers would have a *system service rate* of $s\mu$.

As with some of the other models, most of the performance equations are stated in terms of P_0, the probability of no units in the system. Because of the messy calculation required to obtain a specific value for P_0, a computer-generated table is provided in the Appendix of this chapter. This table presents P_0 values for various ratios of the arrival rate to the system service rate $\lambda/s\mu$, which is sometimes called the *system utilization ratio*.

For example, if the arrival rate is 30 and the individual service rate is 10, the system utilization ratio for 4 servers would be

$$\frac{\lambda}{s\mu} = \frac{30}{4(10)} = .75$$

Referring to the Appendix (page 618), we find the row with the appropriate system utilization ratio, in this case .75, and the column with the appropriate number of servers, here 4, to find the table element corresponding to the correct value for P_0, which is in this instance .0377.

The savings in calculation time provided by this can be demonstrated by computing P_0 according to equation IV-1 in Table 17-5:

$$P_0 = \frac{1}{\left[\displaystyle\sum_{k=0}^{s-1}(\lambda/\mu)^k/k!\right] + \dfrac{(\lambda/\mu)^s}{(s - \lambda/\mu)(s - 1)!}}$$

$$= \frac{1}{\left[\displaystyle\sum_{k=0}^{3}\left(\frac{30}{10}\right)^k/k!\right] + \dfrac{(\frac{30}{10})^4}{(4 - \frac{30}{10})(3!)}}$$

$$= \frac{1}{1 + 3 + (3)^2/2 + (3)^3/6 + (3)^4/6}$$

$$= \frac{1}{1 + 3 + 4.5 + 4.5 + 13.5} = \frac{1}{26.5} = .0377$$

which is the same value as found in the table.

One final point concerning use of the table is worth noting. For values of $\lambda/s\mu$ that are not shown directly in the table it is best to interpolate between the two closest values. For example, suppose $\lambda = 23$, $\mu = 7$, and $s = 4$. The system utilization ratio is

$$\frac{\lambda}{s\mu} = \frac{23}{4(7)} = \frac{23}{28} = .82$$

The closest two utilization ratios in the table are .80 and .85 with P_0 values of .0273 and .0186, respectively. We can approximate the value of P_0 for a system utilization ratio of .82 by making a *linear interpolation* using the known values of P_0 for these two closest utilization ratios. Letting ρ_L and ρ_S represent the largest and smallest, respectively, of the two closest known utilization ratios, and letting L and S be the corresponding table values for P_0, and Δ be the difference between the utilization ratio of interest and the smallest utilization ratio ρ_S, we can estimate the desired P_0 from

$$P_0 = S + \Delta\frac{(L - S)}{(\rho_L - \rho_S)}$$

$$= .0273 + .02\left(\frac{.0186 - .0273}{.85 - .80}\right)$$

$$= .0273 + .02\left(\frac{-.0087}{.05}\right) = .0273 - .0035 = .0238$$

To illustrate the application of the multiple-service facility model, consider the following example. The Milltown Post Office normally operates with two clerks to handle customer transactions. Recently, long lines have developed and the Milltown postmaster has decided to request that an additional clerk position be authorized for Milltown. He would like some supporting data to substantiate this claim.

The post office is currently open 8 hours per day for customer transactions. Recent data show that customers arrive during the day at an average rate of 60 per hour and that either clerk averages about $1\frac{1}{2}$ minutes per customer transaction.

As before, we begin our analysis by examining the current system. The data above show that $\lambda = 60$ per hour, $\mu = 60/1.5 = 40$ per hour, and $s = 2$. This leads to a system utilization ratio of

$$\frac{\lambda}{s/\mu} = \frac{60}{2(40)} = .75$$

Referring to the Appendix (page 618), we find that a .75 utilization ratio for 2 servers yields a .1429 value for P_0.

Note that two equations, IV-2 and IV-3, are shown in Table 17-5 for calculating the probability of n units being in the system. Equation IV-2 applies to those cases where n is no greater than the number of servers, in this case two. Thus the probability of 1 in the system would be calculated as

$$P_1 = \frac{P_0(\lambda/\mu)^1}{1!}$$

$$= .1429\left(\tfrac{60}{40}\right) = .2144$$

Equation IV-3 is used for those cases where the number of units in the system exceeds the number of servers (therefore, a waiting line exists). If we wish to know the probability of 5 customers being in the system, we would compute

$$P_5 = \frac{P_0(\lambda/\mu)^5}{s\,!(s^{5-2})}$$

$$= \frac{.1429(\frac{60}{40})^5}{2(2^3)} = \frac{1.085}{16} = .0678$$

The average number of customers in the post office, called L_s, is found from equation IV-4:

$$L_s = \frac{\lambda\mu(\lambda/\mu)^s}{(s-1)!(s\mu - \lambda)^2}\,(P_0) + \frac{\lambda}{\mu}$$

$$= \frac{60(40)(\frac{60}{40})^2}{(2-1)!(2(40)-60)^2}\,(.1429) + \frac{60}{40}$$

$$= \frac{5,400(.1429)}{400} + 1.5 = 3.43 \text{ customers}$$

The average number of customers waiting to be served L_q is given by equation IV-5:

$$L_q = L_s - \frac{\lambda}{\mu}$$

$$= 3.43 - \frac{60}{40} = 1.93 \text{ customers}$$

The average waiting time per customer, or W_q, is calculated from equation IV-6:

$$W_q = \frac{L_q}{\lambda}$$

$$= \frac{1.93}{60} = .032 \text{ hour}$$

or 1.92 minutes.

The average time each customer spends in the post office W_s is given by equation IV-7:

$$W_s = W_q + \frac{1}{\mu}$$

$$= .032 + \tfrac{1}{40} = .057 \text{ hour or } 3.42 \text{ minutes}$$

INSTANT REPLAY   What values for these performance measures would you find if the third clerk was authorized?

CHECK   System utilization ratio $= .5$, $P_0 = .2105$, $P_1 = .3158$, $P_5 = .0296$, $L_s = 1.74$, $L_q = .24$, $W_q = .004$ hour, and $W_s = .029$ hour.

What information can be drawn from the performance measures calculated above that might support the postmaster's request for a third clerk? Observe that the average number of customers in the post office L_s declined from 3.43 with two clerks to 1.74 with three clerks. This is a decrease of (3.43 −

1.74)/3.43 = 49.3 percent. Likewise, the average time spent in the post office by each customer W_s also decreased, in this case from 3.42 minutes to 1.74 minutes, a drop of 49.1 percent. If we consider the average length of the waiting line L_q or the average time spent in the line W_q, we find a decrease of 87.5 percent. Although these percentage differences are impressive, the absolute change in either customers waiting or waiting time are so small as to make it difficult for the postmaster to support his case.

Considering Costs

With the exception of an earlier general discussion and the Newcoat example, preceding sections of the chapter have failed to include cost considerations when evaluating alternative system designs. In the remainder of this chapter we will see how costs can be applied to waiting line models.

One difficulty mentioned earlier in using cost data was the problem of attaching a cost to waiting customers. In some instances, however, where the customers are themselves employees of the organization operating the service system, it is possible to estimate the customer waiting cost.

Consider, for example, the Wextall Automotive Repair Shop. Wextall employs a large number of auto mechanics to repair vehicles brought in for service. A mechanic needing parts to repair a vehicle walks to a central parts storeroom and requests the parts from the stock clerk. The clerk then selects the required parts from the shelves and turns these over to the mechanic, who returns to the vehicle being repaired.

Mechanics are paid $10 per hour and the clerk receives $4 per hour. Management is concerned about the lost time spent by mechanics waiting in line and is considering adding more stock clerks to reduce mechanic waiting time.

Mechanics arrive at the central parts storeroom at an average rate of 18 per hour. The stock clerk takes 3 minutes, on average, to serve each mechanic. We assume that interarrival times and service times are exponentially distributed.

In this case we can determine precisely the cost of mechanic waiting time because Wextall is paying each mechanic $10 per hour (whether working or waiting). The cost of adding additional stock clerks may be more than offset by a reduction in the cost of mechanic waiting time. Any reduction in waiting time for mechanics can be used to service additional vehicles, or presumably, Wextall could service the same number of vehicles as at present with fewer mechanics.

The total costs from Wextall's viewpoint consist of

$$\begin{pmatrix} \text{Total} \\ \text{cost} \end{pmatrix} = \begin{pmatrix} \text{cost of mechanic} \\ \text{waiting time} \end{pmatrix} + \begin{pmatrix} \text{cost of} \\ \text{stock clerks} \end{pmatrix}$$

It is convenient to consider the hourly costs. During any given hour the average number of mechanics waiting is L_q. Since each mechanic is paid $10 per hour, the hourly cost is

$$\text{Hourly cost of mechanic waiting time} = \$10L_q$$

As an alternative way of determining the mechanic waiting cost, note that λ mechanics arrive each hour, on average, and that each mechanic waits W_q time units. Thus the total waiting time for mechanics arriving during any hour is

λW_q. As derived earlier, λW_q is equal to L_q, which leads to the same conclusion with respect to waiting cost:

$$\text{Hourly cost of mechanic waiting time} = \$10\lambda W_q = \$10 L_q$$

The stock clerks are paid $4 per hour, and s represents the number of clerks being used. This stock clerk hourly cost is

$$\text{Hourly cost of stock clerks} = \$4s$$

Total costs are therefore defined as

$$\text{Hourly total cost} = \$10 L_q + \$4s$$

As discussed earlier, this cost function is discontinuous because we can hire only an integer number of stock clerks. To solve for the lowest total cost requires an enumeration and evaluation of each potential level of service, starting with the present system of one clerk. Note that with one stock clerk we can use the basic single-facility model. The equation for L_q can therefore be found in Table 17-2:

$$L_q = \frac{\lambda^2}{\mu(\mu - \lambda)}$$

Based on the data for the problem, $\lambda = 18$ mechanics per hour and $\mu = 20$ per hour (since each service takes 3 minutes on average). Thus,

$$L_q = \frac{(18)^2}{20(20 - 18)} = \frac{324}{40} = 8.1 \text{ mechanics}$$

Total costs for 1 stock clerk are therefore

$$\text{Hourly total costs} = \$10(8.1) + \$4(1) = \$81 + \$4 = \$85$$

Clearly the mechanic waiting cost far exceeds the stock clerk cost, and it appears highly likely that total costs can be reduced by hiring additional clerks.

Next consider a system with two clerks. In this instance we must use the multiple-server model with $\lambda = 18$, $\mu = 20$, and $s = 2$. The formula for L_q in Table 17-5 requires first determining P_0. Using the Appendix, we note that P_0 for a system utilization ratio of

$$\frac{\lambda}{s\mu} = \frac{18}{2(20)} = \frac{18}{40} = .45$$

and 2 servers is .3793.

Observe that since $L_q = L_s - \lambda/\mu$, as shown in equation IV-5, by subtracting λ/μ from L_s as defined in equation IV-4 we find directly that

$$L_q = \frac{\lambda\mu(\lambda/\mu)^2}{(s - 1)!(s\mu - \lambda)^2} P_0$$

Substituting our parameters, we find

$$L_q = \frac{18(20)(\tfrac{18}{20})^2}{(2 - 1)!(2(20) - 18)^2} (.3793) = \frac{110.60388}{484} = .229$$

Total costs for two clerks are thus

$$\text{Hourly total costs} = \$10(.229) + \$4(2)$$
$$= \$2.29 + \$8 = \$10.29$$

The hourly costs for two clerks are substantially below that for one clerk.

Should we consider three clerks? Note that adding a third clerk will increase stock clerk costs by exactly $4. This will have to be offset by a reduction in mechanic waiting costs of at least $4. However, hourly mechanic waiting cost with two clerks is only $2.29. It would be impossible to obtain a savings of more than $2.29 even if waiting went to zero. Therefore, we can conclude that Wextall should use two stock clerks and they will save $85.00 − $10.29 = $74.71 per hour.

INSTANT REPLAY Suppose that because of an expected increase in auto repair demand over the next 6 months, the arrival rate of mechanics at the stockroom is expected to increase to 30 per hour. Would this change cause you to choose the three-clerk option? Would four clerks be appropriate?

CHECK Hourly costs with 2 clerks becomes $27.29. Hourly costs with 3 clerks would be $14.37. Because the mechanic waiting cost with 3 clerks is only $2.37, a change to 4 clerks is clearly not justified.

As another example of how costs can be incorporated, consider the Last National Bank. Each night armored trucks arrived at the central bank with cash proceeds from the day's transactions at outlying branch offices. These trucks arrive randomly throughout the evening at a rate of 10 per hour. The central facility uses a single crew of 6 to unload each truck and sign for the funds transferred. This crew can process trucks at the rate of 12 per hour.

If a waiting line develops, the armored trucks must wait and the driver/guard crew is paid at a rate of $25 per hour. The bank is thinking of increasing the size of the unloading crew to reduce the waiting costs of the armored trucks. The unloading crew members are paid $5 per hour, and any increase in crew size is expected to increase the service rate μ proportionately. Since a 6-member crew can service 12 trucks, a 7-member crew can handle 14 trucks per hour, etc. Thus we see that if k is the crew size, $\mu = 2k$ or $k = \mu/2$.

Total hourly costs are thus

$$\begin{array}{l} \text{Total} \\ \text{hourly costs} \end{array} = \left(\begin{array}{c} \text{hourly armored truck} \\ \text{waiting costs} \end{array} \right) + \left(\begin{array}{c} \text{hourly unloading} \\ \text{crew costs} \end{array} \right)$$

$$= \$25L_s + \$5k = \$25L_s + \$5\left(\frac{\mu}{2}\right) = \$25L_s + \$2.50\mu$$

Note that in this case the single-facility model applies no matter what unloading crew size is used. Additional unloading crew members serve to increase the facility service rate μ rather than increasing the number of facilities. Also note that we have used the time in the system L_s rather than waiting time L_q, as was done previously, to measure waiting time for the armored truck crew. This is because in the Wextall example adding additional clerks reduced waiting time but did not reduce service time. In the Last National Bank example, however, service time, as well as waiting time, is reduced by adding extra crew members. Thus, we must consider both waiting time and service time as measured by L_s.

The calculations necessary to evaluate the options are, in this case, quite simple, since the formula for L_s is given by equation I-2 in Table 17-2:

$$L_s = \frac{\lambda}{\mu - \lambda}$$

Thus for the present crew of 6 with $\mu = 12$ we find

$$L_s = \frac{10}{12 - 10} = 5$$

and total hourly costs (THC) are

$$\text{THC} = \$25(5) + \$2.50(12) = \$125 + \$30 = \$155$$

Similar analysis for other crew sizes would lead to the results shown in Table 17-6. Note that as the crew size is increased, the total costs first fall, reach a minimum of $75 at a crew size of 10, and then start to rise.

Actually for this example it is possible to derive an equation for determining the optimal service rate μ^* and from that an optimal crew size. Letting C_w be the cost of customer time spent in the system and C_μ be the cost per unit of service, the general expression for total hourly costs is

$$\text{THC} = C_w L_s + C_\mu \mu$$

We know from Table 17-2 that L_s is equivalent to

$$L_s = \frac{\lambda}{\mu - \lambda}$$

Making this substitution in the total cost equation leads to

$$\text{THC} = C_w \frac{\lambda}{\mu - \lambda} + C_\mu \mu$$

Although it is not shown here, an expression can be derived for the value of μ that will minimize this total cost. This requires that

$$\mu^* = \lambda + \sqrt{\frac{C_w \lambda}{C_\mu}}$$

For the Last National Bank example we have $\lambda = 10$ and $C_w = \$25$. C_μ is obtained by recalling that the hourly cost per crew member is $5 and that each crew member causes the service rate to increase by 2 ($\mu = 2k$). Thus each unit increase in μ requires $\frac{1}{2}$ crew member or $C_\mu = \$5/2 = \$2.50$. Substituting these values, we find

$$\mu^* = 10 + \sqrt{\frac{\$25(10)}{\$2.50}} = 20$$

Note that this is the service rate that had the lowest cost in Table 17-6. Be careful to note that we are fortunate that μ^* turned out to be an integer value and one that could be achieved. If μ^* was fractional, say 10.43, we would have to consider the cost of the closest achievable μ on either side of the calculated μ^*. For a μ^* of 10.43 we would look at the costs for $\mu_1 = 10$ and $\mu_2 = 12$, corresponding to crew sizes of 5 and 6, respectively.

INSTANT REPLAY   Suppose that for the Last National Bank example, $\lambda = 15$, and all other facts were the same. What would be the optimal crew size?

CHECK $\mu^* = 27.247$; so we must look at $\mu_1 = 26$ and $\mu_2 = 28$ (crews of 13 and 14, respectively). These have costs of $99.09 and $98.85, respectively. Thus the optimal crew size is 14.

TABLE 17-6
Cost Summary for Various Unloading Crew Sizes for Last National Bank

Unloading crew size	Service rate	Number of armored trucks in system L_s	Armored truck cost	Unloading crew cost	Total cost
6	12	5.000	125.00	30	155.00
7	14	2.500	62.50	35	97.50
8	16	1.667	41.67	40	81.67
9	18	1.250	31.25	45	76.25
10	20	1.000	25.00	50	75.00
11	22	.833	20.83	55	75.83

Final Comments

This chapter has considered several waiting line models that can be applied to service systems. These models have broad applicability because of the large number of real-world situations involving waiting lines.

In the beginning of the chapter the many variations that exist for the basic elements of a service system were discussed. These elements include the source population of arriving customers, the arrival characteristics, the waiting line accommodations and waiting behavior of customers, the process by which the next customer to be served is selected, the characteristics of the service facility, and the nature of system departures. These elements were emphasized for two reasons. One is to examine various design and operational alternatives for these systems, many of which cannot be easily treated with waiting line models. The second reason is to develop familiarity with the service system characteristics that will dictate which waiting line model is appropriate to use.

Four models were considered. These were the single-server model, the finite source model, the limited waiting capacity model, and the multiple-server model. In each case a number of equations were presented that can be used to predict various system performance results. These included server utilization, number of customers waiting or in the system, time spent waiting or in the system, and the probability of a specific number of customers in the system.

We also saw how cost information could be used to evaluate various system design alternatives. The difficulties in obtaining costs related to customer waiting were emphasized as well as the problems caused by cost discontinuities. Although the use of cost information can be important, in many cases management will be interested in other performance measures, such as line length and waiting time, when choosing among design alternatives.

Key Words

Arrival **584**
Arrival rate **586**
Batch arrivals **586**
Blocking condition **587**
Controllable arrivals **586**
Cost of providing service **590**

Cost of waiting customers **590**
Customer **583**
Defections **588**
Deflections **588**
Departure **590**
Discontinuous function **591**

Problems

17-1. The *Metropolis Daily Bugle* operates a popular sports wire service, which allows people to call the special number requesting scores of national and local sports events. The newspaper has assigned one clerk to answer the questions of those who call in. On average, calls arrive at the rate of 45 per hour and are assumed to follow the Poisson distribution. It takes (on average) 1 minute to handle each call and the service time is assumed to be exponential. If the clerk is busy when a call arrives, the caller is placed on hold until the clerk is free.

    a. What proportion of the time does the clerk actually spend handling these calls?

    b. How many callers, on average, are waiting for the clerk?

    c. How many callers, on average, are being served or waiting for service?

    d. What is the average time, in minutes, each caller waits for the clerk?

    e. What is the average time, in minutes, that each caller spends waiting and having his or her question answered?

    f. What is the probability that exactly four callers are waiting or being served?

    g. What is the probability that more than six callers are waiting or being served?

    h. If a caller has to wait, what is the average time spent waiting?

    i. What is the average number of callers waiting during those periods that a waiting line exists?

17-2. The Cleansweep Car Wash operates a single washing facility which can complete all operations in 5 minutes, on average, with service times exponentially distributed. Cars arrive for service at the rate of 10 per hour in an approximately random (Poisson) pattern.

    a. What proportion of the time is the facility idle?

    b. On average, how many cars are at the facility being washed or waiting for service at one time?

c. How many cars are waiting, on average?

d. What is the average time each car spends waiting to be washed?

e. What is the average time each customer spends at the car wash?

f. What is the probability that 10 or more cars will be on the premises?

g. A customer has just arrived and found the facility busy. How long can she expect to wait and how long was the waiting line when she arrived?

17-3. A photocopying machine is shared by five accountants in an office. On average, each accountant uses the machine once every hour and takes on average 10 minutes of machine time to complete photocopying. Assume exponential interarrival and service times.

a. What proportion of time is the machine actually in use?

b. What is the probability that all five accountants will be using or waiting for the machine?

c. What is the average number of accountants waiting for the machine?

d. On average, how many accountants are using or waiting for the machine?

e. What is the average time spent waiting for the machine?

f. What is the average time spent using or waiting for the machine?

g. On average, what proportion of the accountant's time is spent on tasks other than photocopying?

17-4. The Metropolis Airport Facility is concerned with maintenance of air traffic control monitoring equipment. The facility has on hand at present three consoles. These consoles break down, on average, once every 20 days. It takes, on average, 2 days for the single maintenance crew to repair a console so that it can go back into service. Assume exponential interarrival and service times.

a. Under the present system, what is the average number of consoles in operation?

b. When a console breaks down, how long, on average, does it stay out of service?

c. What is the likelihood that only one console will be operating?

d. What is the likelihood that none of the consoles will be operating?

e. To improve the operating performance of the air traffic control system, the facility is considering two options. One is to purchase an additional console and the other is to expand the repair crew so that the average repair time is reduced to 1 day. If these options are considered independently, which appears to offer the best improvement in system operating performance?

17-5. Refer again to the sports wire service offered by the *Metropolis Daily Bugle*, as described in problem 17-1. Suppose that as calls arrive at the switchboard, only five lines are available for incoming calls to the sports wire clerk. One of these is actually connected to the clerk and the other four, if necessary, are used for calls put on hold. If all five lines are in use, any incoming call will receive a busy signal and will be, in effect, turned away. Assume that such callers will then turn to a rival newspaper with their request.

a. What proportion of the time does the clerk actually spend answering questions?

b. What proportion of calls are turned away by the busy signal?

c. What is the average number of phone lines tied up by the sports wire?

d. How long on average do the callers spend waiting for the clerk?

e. How long does it take from the time a caller is put on hold until the question has been answered?

f. A follow-up study has been done that shows that 1 percent of customers who use the sports wire service eventually become subscribers to the newspaper. An annual subscription to the paper is estimated to contribute $10 to profit. The cost of leasing additional phone lines is known to be $300 per year. How many additional phone lines, if any, should the newspaper lease for the sports wire?

17-6. McWhamburger is a rapidly expanding chain of fast food hamburger outlets. In response to competition, they are thinking of adding a drive-in window facility. They anticipate that during peak hours drive-in window customers will arrive at a Poisson rate of 20 per hour. Time study analysis has shown that the service from receipt of order to receipt of payment can be accomplished, on average, in 160 seconds, distributed exponentially.

The major concern of McWhamburger is the proper positioning of the window so as to provide enough waiting space for cars and also hold down the costs of modifying existing facilities. Two designs are currently under consideration. The first is based on minimizing the conversion cost of existing facilities. This approach will provide room for 6 cars, 5 waiting and 1 being served, and is estimated to increase fixed costs by $2.50 per hour. The second is based on maximizing the available waiting space for cars and provides room for a total of 10 cars (9 waiting and 1 being served). This second option is more costly from a conversion viewpoint, adding approximately $5 per hour to fixed costs.

Based on market survey data, they estimate that the average drive-in customer will yield $2.10 in profit. If all waiting spaces are filled, it is assumed that 80 percent of customers turned away will go to a competitor, the other 20 percent parking at McWhamburger and obtaining their order at the counter inside the facility.

Which of the options should McWhamburger choose?

17-7. The Last National Bank is considering a restructuring of their teller waiting facilities. At present during peak periods the bank has 5 tellers on duty, each with a separate waiting line. Customers arrive, on average, at a Poisson rate of 100 customers per hour, selecting what appears to be the shortest waiting line at the time of their arrival. In effect, on average, each teller handles one-fifth of all customers. Because of the physical layout of the bank, once a customer enters a waiting line, switching lines is difficult. Thus we can assume that switching does not take place. Each teller transaction requires on average 2 minutes, distributed exponentially.

a. On average, how long does each customer spend in the bank? How long waiting in line?

b. What is the average length of the waiting line for any one teller? How many customers are waiting, on average, in the bank as a whole?

c. What is the average teller utilization?

One option the bank is considering is designating one teller as a quick-serve teller for customers with a single transaction such as a deposit or a withdrawal. A survey showed that 32 percent of all customers would be eligible for this category of services, with a reduced service time of .5 minute. The service time for the remaining customers would, of course, be greater and is expected to average 2.7 minutes per customer. The non-quick-serve customers would select one of the other four lines on the same basis as present.

d. How long, on average, would each quick-serve customer spend in the bank? How long waiting in line?

e. How long, on average, would each non-quick-serve customer spend in the bank? How long waiting in line?

f. What is the average length of the waiting lines for the two types of customers? On average, how many bank customers are waiting?

g. Are there differences in average teller utilization between quick-serve and non-quick-serve tellers?

Another option being considered by the bank is to have all customers, regardless of type, form into a single waiting line. As soon as any teller is free, the first person in line would be dispatched to that teller. Arrival rates and service times are expected to be unchanged with this option.

h. On average, how long would each customer spend in the bank? How long waiting in line?

i. What is the average length of the waiting line?

j. What is the average teller utilization?

k. How can you explain any differences between performance measures for the three waiting line options?

l. Which system do you think the bank should adopt?

17-8. Ships arrive at a port facility at the average rate of 2 every 3 days. On average it takes a single crew 1 day to unload or load a ship. Assume interarrival and service times are exponential. The shipping company owns the port facility as well as the ships using that facility. It is estimated to cost the company $1,000 per day that each ship spends in port. The crew used to service the ships consists of 100 workers paid an average wage of $30 per day.

a. How many ships on average are waiting for the crew?

b. What is the expected time in port that each ship spends waiting?

c. What is the average daily waiting cost for the company?

The company estimates that by hiring an additional 25 workers they can reduce the crew's service time by 20 percent.

d. What would this do to the average number of ships waiting and the expected waiting time in port?

e. Is it profitable for the company to do this?

Another option suggested is to hire an additional 40 workers and split the employees into two equal-sized crews of 70 each. This would give each crew an unloading or loading time of $1\frac{1}{2}$ days on average.

f. What effects would this change have in the number of waiting ships and the expected waiting time?

g. Would it be profitable for the company to pursue this option?

h. Which crew arrangement would you recommend to the company?

17-9. The Metropolis Police Department, among other duties, is responsible for removal of abandoned cars from the streets of Metropolis. In addition to the unsightliness of the abandoned cars, their presence creates problems for the street sweeping crews of the sanitation department.

Past data indicate that cars are abandoned at the rate of 50 per day (Poisson). A police tow truck operating 24 hours a day can remove an average of 20 cars per day (exponential owing to varying towing distances) at an estimated daily cost of $300 per truck per 24-hour day. The city at present assigns three tow trucks to the abandoned car removal operation.

a. On average, how many abandoned cars grace the streets of Metropolis?

b. How busy on average are the trucks?

c. How long, on average, does an abandoned car remain on the streets before it is removed?

d. What proportion of the time are the city's streets empty of abandoned cars? (Assume that cars being removed are no longer abandoned.)

e. The mayor on a recent inspection tour became incensed at the number of abandoned cars that he saw. What is the probability that there were more than two abandoned cars not being removed by the police?

f. In response to the mayor's anger, the police department has assigned an additional truck to car removal duty. By how much will this additional truck reduce the average number of abandoned cars on the streets of Metropolis?

g. Compare the cost per car removed for the 4-truck system with that under the 3-truck system.

17–10. Video Television normally stocks one unit of a deluxe video home recorder. This item is replenished whenever the one unit stocked is sold and the replenishment time averages 1 week (exponential). Customers arrive to purchase this unit, on average, once every 5 weeks (exponential). It is assumed that if Video is out of stock, the customer does not wait but goes elsewhere. Profit per unit sold is estimated at $200.

    a. What is the likelihood that a customer will find the unit in stock?

    b. What is the weekly cost of lost customers?

Application: Management Science and the Gas Shortage*

It is probably safe to assume that no one is unaware of the recent gasoline shortage. The debates still go on regarding whether or not the shortage was "real" but one thing is sure: The lines at the gas pumps were real. This report focuses on the problem as seen by the average driver. The key issue is: "What can be done to shorten ridiculously long lines at the pumps?"

    For this analysis let us consider a single gas station. Assume that the customer set is fixed in size and no one goes elsewhere for gas. Also assume that the station has only one pump and that service times are exponential. As you may have guessed, arrival times are Poisson. This simple model is sufficient to explore the general dynamics of the situation. We want to determine whether suggested solutions to the problem will tend to increase or decrease the customer waiting time, not predict the exact size of the waiting line.

    The average time in the system is thus defined to be (see Table 17-2)

$$W_s = \frac{1}{\mu - \lambda}$$

    Suppose that for our analysis we assume the normal (i.e., preshortage) situation to yield an average service rate of $\frac{1}{5}$ customer per minute (5-minute average service time) and an average arrival rate of $\frac{1}{20}$ customer per minute (3 customers per hour). This would result in an average time in the system of $6\frac{2}{3}$ minutes. Although these data are arbitrary, they define a situation that corresponds to many individuals' experience of relatively insignificant (a minute or so) average waiting time for service.

    Is it possible to have long lines at the pumps even if there is no real shortage (supply adequate to meet normal demand)? It turns out that it is possible if, for some reason, consumers believe that there is going to be a shortage and respond by filling up their tanks earlier than they would have ordinarily. The major effect of this behavioral change is an increased arrival rate of customers at stations.

    If the average customer filled up when empty under normal conditions and now fills up when half empty, the customer will be arriving for service twice as often as normal. Thus $\lambda = 2(.05) = .10$ and $W_s = 10$ minutes. The lines would grow without limit if the average customer filled up when the tank registers one-fourth empty. So the first thing noticed by customers is longer lines.

    Furthermore if we assume that the average tank holds about 20 gallons and there are about 100 million cars in the country, a shift from filling up when empty to filling up when only half empty represents a one-time increase in consumption of half a billion gallons. Now even if weekly demand and supply remain unchanged, the shift of half a billion gallons from dealer tanks to customer tanks will probably result in occasional temporary outages. Thus the consumer sees longer lines and occasional stations out of gas. All evidence points to a shortage, when the only real change was a panic reaction by the consumers.

*Adapted from Warren J. Erikson, "Management Science and the Gas Shortage," *Interfaces*, vol. 4, no. 4 (August 1974), pp. 47–51.

How can a relatively small cut in gasoline supply result in such long lines? To answer this question, assume that our station receives 90 percent of its normal allotment of gasoline and that the station will pump gas until they run out. In the first period (day, week, or whatever) they will satisfy 90 percent of their customers and then shut down 10 percent early.

In the next period, everyone adjusts. All the customers know that the station is only open 90 percent as long as before; so they attempt to arrive during this restricted period. However, in addition to the regular collection of customers, we will have the 10 percent who missed out last time.

In any period i, the time taken to exhaust the gas supply E_i can be defined as $E_i = G_i S_i / D_i$, where G_i is the time scheduled to sell gas in period i, S_i is the gas supply in period i, and D_i is the gas demand in period i. The station operating policy of closing when the supply is used up means that $G_{i+1} = E_i$.

With no controls, customer demand remaining constant, and stations selling only 90 percent of normal volume each day, we find a rapid decline in station operating hours E_i as a natural result. By the fifth period, the station can stay open only 38 percent as long as it did before the shortage, the average waiting time exceeds 1 hour, and only 50 percent of potential customers actually receive gas.

What can be done to alleviate the problem? Consider the following suggestions and whether or not they really help:

Price increases. This is the favorite solution of the economists, and they are right as far as the effect is concerned. To the degree that price increases actually lower demand, the arrival rate will decrease and the line lengths, etc., will improve.

Less customer attention. Many gas station operators eliminate services other than pumping gas (i.e., washing windows, checking oil, etc.). This too is beneficial, since it reduces the service time.

Maximum gallon or dollar limits. Imposing purchase limits does have the effect of increasing the number of customers served and the number of hours the station is open. However, these limits also tend to increase the customer arrival rate.

Minimum purchase limits. These involve variations of "no gas unless your tank is at least half empty." These are clearly beneficial, since they tend to lower the customer arrival rate.

Odd/even license plate system. The effects of this system are more difficult to estimate. The so-called California system which couples odd/even with an additional requirement that the tank be half empty appears to work best. It reduces the early fill-up possibility, at least temporarily lowers the arrival rate, and has the effect of shortening lines to a greater degree than having the half-empty tank requirement alone.

I would like to write more, but it's my turn at the pump next.

Discussion Questions

1. What type of waiting line model was used for the gas pump? What assumptions were necessary in order that this model could be used? Which of these assumptions seem unrealistic? Does the fact that unrealistic assumptions were used leave any of the conclusions in doubt? If so, which ones?
2. Using the service system components and characteristics discussed in the text, describe a typical gas pumping service system. Are there other service systems connected with a gas station? If so, what are they?
3. Demand for gas at a typical gas station is not likely to be evenly distributed throughout the day. Because of fluctuations in the arrival rate, there are peak and off-peak periods. How does the typical gas station manage its labor force so as to minimize the cost of meeting peak demands?
4. Can you think of any other suggestions for dealing with gasoline shortages? Evaluate these in terms of their effect on the waiting line model.

Appendix

Probability of No Units in the System (P_0) for Multiple-Server Facilities

System utilization ratio $\rho = \lambda/s\mu$	Number of servers s								
	2	3	4	5	6	7	8	9	10
.05	.9048	.8607	.8187	.7788	.7408	.7047	.6703	.6376	.6065
.10	.8182	.7407	.6703	.6065	.5488	.4966	.4493	.4066	.3679
.15	.7391	.6373	.5487	.4724	.4066	.3499	.3012	.2592	.2231
.20	.6667	.5479	.4491	.3678	.3012	.2466	.2019	.1653	.1353
.25	.6000	.4706	.3673	.2863	.2231	.1738	.1353	.1054	.0821
.30	.5385	.4035	.3002	.2228	.1652	.1224	.0907	.0672	.0498
.35	.4815	.3451	.2449	.1731	.1222	.0862	.0608	.0428	.0302
.40	.4286	.2941	.1993	.1343	.0903	.0606	.0407	.0273	.0183
.45	.3793	.2496	.1616	.1039	.0666	.0426	.0272	.0174	.0111
.50	.3333	.2105	.1304	.0801	.0490	.0298	.0182	.0110	.0067
.55	.2903	.1762	.1046	.0614	.0358	.0208	.0121	.0070	.0040
.60	.2500	.1460	.0831	.0466	.0260	.0144	.0080	.0044	.0024
.65	.2121	.1193	.0651	.0350	.0187	.0099	.0052	.0028	.0015
.70	.1765	.0957	.0502	.0259	.0132	.0067	.0034	.0017	.0009
.75	.1429	.0748	.0377	.0187	.0091	.0044	.0021	.0010	.0005
.80	.1111	.0562	.0273	.0130	.0061	.0028	.0013	.0006	.0003
.85	.0811	.0396	.0186	.0085	.0038	.0017	.0008	.0003	.0001
.90	.0526	.0249	.0113	.0050	.0021	.0009	.0004	.0002	.0001
.95	.0256	.0118	.0051	.0022	.0009	.0004	.0002	.0001	.0000

λ = arrival rate (Poisson)
s = number of servers
μ = service rate (per individual server and exponential service time)

18

Extrapolation Forecasting Models

Management decisions almost always require some knowledge of the future. This knowledge often takes the form of a *forecast* of future events or conditions. For example, the decision making under risk models that we considered in Chapters 2 through 4 required specifying the relative likelihood or probabilities of the future uncontrollable events. Similarly, the inventory models that we considered in Chapters 14 and 15 all required an estimate of future demand.

The next two chapters will consider a number of models that can be used to provide these forecasts. The importance of forecasting should not be underestimated. The forecasts obtained will be used to provide information for other decision models. If errors are made in these forecasts, they can lead to incorrect decisions throughout the organization, which could result in costly and unprofitable outcomes. For example, many decisions require estimation of future demand. These demand estimates may be used in making decisions concerning the level of advertising expenditures, quantities to be produced, size of the work force, the level of purchase commitments for raw materials and supplies, capacity expansion, the level of external financing, etc. Incorrect forecasts of demand (too high, too low, wrong product mix, etc.) can therefore lead to the wrong decisions being made and if the errors are large enough could lead to disastrous results.

This chapter will begin with a discussion of general considerations that will be useful in developing and successfully implementing forecasting models. Many different types of forecasting models exist. Choosing the right model and knowing how to use it properly is not always easy. The first section of this chapter will touch on some of the factors to be considered in selecting and using   **619** forecasting models. We will then briefly examine the steps involved in developing, implementing, and evaluating the effectiveness of forecasting models. Because of their importance, several methods that can be used to measure forecasting effectiveness will then be discussed in more detail.

The treatment of forecasting models has been divided into two major sections. The first class of models is called *extrapolation models*. These models examine past observations to identify patterns that can be extended, or extrapolated, to the future. Thus an extrapolation model would use past sales patterns to forecast future sales. The second class of models is called *explanatory models*. These models identify relationships between the variable being forecast and other so-called explanatory variables. These relationships are then used to provide forecasts. Thus an explanatory model might use future levels of advertising expenditures to forecast sales. Extrapolation models will be covered in this chapter. Explanatory models will be treated in Chapter 19.

Nature of Forecasts

Our discussion of forecasting models begins by considering the general nature of forecasts. Several factors will be discussed including the forecast horizon, or time period for which the forecast is made, the forecasting environment, which relates to the difficulties in making good forecasts, and the distinction between forecasts and predictions, which deals with behavioral considerations in using forecasts.

Forecast Horizon

It is important to recognize that forecasts are made with different lead times, or *forecast horizons*—from short-range to medium-range to long-range. Although a precise definition will differ from organization to organization, we can loosely classify long-range forecasts as those dealing with periods more than 2 years in the future, medium-range forecasts involving periods from 1 month to 2 years, and short-range forecasts applying to periods of no more than 1 month. The informational requirements of each decision problem are an important factor in choosing an appropriate forecasting model. If long-range forecasts are needed for a particular decision, it would make little sense to use a forecasting model that was developed to provide short-run forecasts.

Long-range forecasts are used to determine what resources are needed to meet long-run goals and requirements. For instance, the decision about whether or not a firm should move into a new product line area is often quite sensitive to long-run forecasts of potential demand as well as the cost and availability of materials and labor. As another example, the bed capacity of a new community hospital will depend upon long-range forecasts of patient demand, construction costs, and other pertinent factors. As you can see from these examples, long-run decisions often involve sizable resource commitments. Furthermore, decisions made on the basis of long-range forecasts normally restrict the options or choices available for medium-range or short-range decisions.

Medium-range decisions are usually involved with the acquisition or release of medium-range resources. These decisions typically require medium-range forecasts ranging from, say, 1 month to 2 years in length. As an example, a product with seasonal demand frequently requires year-ahead demand forecasts so that production and work force schedules can be established that anticipate the seasonal demand fluctuations. In the case of the community hospital, determining appropriate staffing levels is normally a medium-range decision. The time is necessary to permit effective and timely hiring and layoff actions to be implemented. Although the size of resources committed by medium-range decisions is not as large as in long-run situations, the impact of these decisions on the organization remains high. This is because these medium-range decisions are made more frequently than long-range decisions. Note also that medium-range decisions impose further constraints on actions available for short-range decisions. That is, the resources made available through medium-range decisions cannot easily be changed in the short run.

Short-run decisions normally are focused on the scheduling of resources that were made available through long- and medium-range decisions. Here we might be concerned with the use of overtime or subcontracting to meet short-run demand fluctuations. Referring again to the hospital example, the short-run decision may be to schedule usage of the available operating rooms, given medical requirements, available staff, etc.

Forecasting Environment

Although forecasting models have existed for many years, there has been a major increase in sophistication and accuracy in recent years. Three major reasons for this are the growth of computer capabilities, the increase in data availability, and the development of better, more accurate forecasting methods. The recent widespread growth in the utilization and application of computers in organizations of all sizes has been an important factor in the development of forecasting techniques. Calculations that would have been laborious and time-consuming if done manually can now be done quickly and efficiently on the computer.

This jump in computational capability has also permitted an expansion of the type and quantity of information, or data, that can be utilized in forecasting. All forecasting methods require data on past history. In many cases, data which simply would not have been available before computers are now frequently available as a by-product of an information system serving some other function. For instance, detailed demand data may be easily obtained from a firm's customer order processing system. In addition, a number of firms exist today whose business is the collection, organization, and dissemination (for a price) of data. Thus a firm can purchase additional data, as a supplement to its own internally generated data, which may help it to generate more accurate forecasts.

Just as important has been the development of better and more accurate forecasting techniques. Management science has, to a large extent, been responsible for these new methods, although their application would not have been possible without the concurrent growth in computers and data availability.

At the same time, certain other developments have made the forecasting problem a more difficult one. The rapid growth in technology required to compete in today's world has tended to increase the length of the forecast horizon. The implementation of decisions requiring high-technology resources requires longer periods of time than previously, which means that forecasts must now be made further into the future. This lengthening of the implementation lead time has also reduced the time available for making a decision.

The higher resource cost associated with sophisticated technology has also increased the cost of forecast errors. Long-range forecasts are more susceptible to error, because of greater uncertainty and more opportunity for unforeseen events to occur. The combination of lengthening forecast horizons and greater penalties for error has therefore increased both the risk and the importance of forecasting.

A further problem that accompanies the lengthening forecast horizon is increased difficulty in knowing what should be forecast. For example, a decision today as to whether or not to bring out a new product frequently involves consideration of environmental impact, energy requirements, and product safety, none of which were given much weight 10 or 20 years ago.

Forecasting and Prediction

It is important to note the distinction between a forecast and a prediction, two terms which commonly are given the same interpretation. Forecasting involves specifying *probabilities or likelihoods for potential* outcomes. Predicting requires the *choice or identification of one particular outcome*. To illustrate, the odds attached to horses in a race reflect the probability or likelihood of each horse's winning that race. The placing of a bet on one particular horse corresponds to a prediction. As another example, a weather forecast may state that there is a 70 percent chance of rain. Whether or not you take your umbrella with you when you leave home in the morning is dependent on your prediction.

The manner in which a particular decision maker reaches a prediction often reflects behavioral consideratons which have little to do with the forecast. To illustrate, consider the short-range demand forecast shown in Table 18-1, which we use to represent a baker's forecast of the number of customers asking for birthday cakes the next day. The baker needs to decide today how many birthday cakes to bake in advance of these forecasted needs. Leaving aside profit considerations, if asked to make a prediction of demand for birthday cakes, he has several likely alternatives. He might choose the average demand, which in this case is 2.75, or 3 cakes when rounded. On the other hand, he might choose the most likely outcome, which is 2 cakes, because that demand has the highest probability.

If he is a pessimist, he might predict 0 demand, because this is the worst outcome. Alternatively, an optimist might select the best outcome, 5 cakes. His

TABLE 18-1
Daily Demand Forecast for Birthday Cakes

Level of demand (1)	Probability (2)	(1) × (2)
0	.05	.00
1	.10	.10
2 *Most likely*	.30	.60
3 *level of demand*	.25	.75
4	.20	.80
5	.10	.50 *Average*
		2.75 *demand*

prediction also might reflect considerations other than probabilities. If he enjoys making birthday cakes, he might hope that demand will be greater than 5, even though the forecast attaches a probability of 0 to that outcome, to justify his desire to work on birthday cakes. You can probably think of other behavioral mechanisms for making predictions.

Most of the models that we will consider in this chapter provide predictions based on the expected outcome. Statistical analysis can then be used to determine the likelihood of that outcome or any others actually occurring.

This does not mean that these other approaches are useless or irrational. For example, suppose we are forecasting demand for hospital beds in order to determine the appropriate bed capacity for a new community hospital. It is not likely that we would design a hospital with sufficient size to meet average expected demand. This would mean turning away patients when demand exceeds the average. Instead, the size of the hospital is likely to be based on some higher demand level, striking a balance between the cost of higher capacity and the cost of insufficient capacity. This is similar to the reorder point problem considered in Chapter 15. The reorder point was not set equal to expected demand during the replenishment period but was based on some level of "maximum reasonable demand," where what was reasonable was based on the costs involved.

Types of Forecasting Models

It is useful to classify forecasting models broadly as either *quantitative* or *qualitative* models. Quantitative models are used to develop precise estimates for short- to medium-range horizons using quantitative data. Qualitative models usually provide less precise forecasts for medium- to long-range decisions relying on subjective or intuitive data. These two categories can be further subdivided as discussed below.

Quantitative Models

Quantitative models, as the name implies, require data about the past that can be measured quantitatively. All such models assume that whatever patterns exist in the past data will continue to exist in the future. In fact, the quantitative forecasting model can be thought of as a filter that separates patterns usable for forecasting from purely random fluctuations, or "noise." This is shown graphically in Figure 18-1.

There are two basic categories of quantitative models, which we shall refer to as *extrapolation* and *explanatory*. Extrapolation models use historical data for the variable to be forecast and possibly past forecast errors to project or extrapolate to the future. These models are also called time-series models.

FIGURE 18-1 Concept of a quantitative forecasting model as a filtering device.

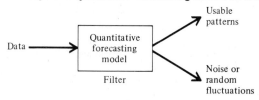

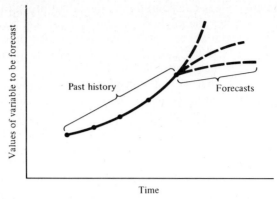

FIGURE 18-2   Conceptual view of extrapolation forecasting model.

They identify historical patterns (simple and complex) and then project or extrapolate these patterns into the future, as shown in Figure 18-2. For example, an extrapolation, or time-series model, would provide forecasts of future demand on the basis of observed patterns in past demand.

Explanatory models attempt to identify relationships between the variable to be forecast and a set of explanatory variables which are thought to influence changes in the forecasted variable. For instance, we may feel that changes in market share are largely a function of the level of advertising.[1] This suggests an explanatory model of the general form:

$$\text{Market share} = f(\text{advertising})$$

which states that market share is some function of advertising. The exact mathematical form of this function would be determined on the basis of historically observed patterns. Figure 18-3 portrays a linear relationship between an explanatory variable and the variable to be forecast.

On a comparative basis, extrapolation models are usually easier to use for forecasting and are normally more parsimonious in terms of data requirements than are explanatory models. On the other hand, since explanatory models attempt to get at the underlying structure of what causes changes to occur in the variable to be forecast, they are usually more appropriate for policy and decision making than are extrapolation models; but they are potentially more dangerous because of the difficulties in correctly identifying such underlying structure. Extrapolation models are most frequently used for short- to medium-range forecasting, while explanatory models are more likely to be used in medium- and long-range forecasting situations.

Qualitative Models

Qualitative models differ from quantitative models largely in the type of data used for forecasting purposes. Although both types of models may use numbers, qualitative models frequently rely on subjective or intuitive estimates,

---

[1]The reverse is often true because of managerial heuristics or policies. In other words, advertising levels may be determined on the basis of market share. This could confuse results by making it appear that sales are a function of advertising when at least part of the observed relationship is really reversed.

often of a highly specialized nature, and are more concerned with ranges of numbers or relative relationships (e.g., greater, less, etc.) than with precise estimates.

The unprecise nature of the data used by qualitative models usually derives from the fact that these models were developed to provide long-range forecasts. Recall that quantitative models are built on the assumption that historical patterns will continue in the future. While this may be true for short- to medium-range forecasts, it is much less likely that these historical patterns will hold in the longer run. This fact necessitates greater reliance on subjective or speculative information. Nevertheless, past and current data may prove a useful starting point in qualitative forecasting.

There are two categories of qualitative models, *exploratory* and *normative*. Exploratory forecasting begins with current and past data and then explores, in a logical but subjective manner, a variety of potential future patterns.

As an example, the governor of one of the so-called sun belt states was concerned with the state's relatively low ranking with regard to the average hourly wage in manufacturing, considerably below the national average. Although the state had been aggressively seeking continued industrial development, the governor was concerned that little relative improvement had occurred in the average manufacturing wage in the past 10 years.

The governor directed that the state undertake a long-range study with the objective of anticipating what changes in manufacturing and economic environment were likely to occur in the next 20 years and how these changes would impact on the relative wage rate. This exploratory study began by examining the factors in the past that had affected the relative wage rate and then developed a range of future relative wage growth based on subjective estimates of the likelihood, strength, and influence of potential future environments.

Normative forecasting models begin by defining some desired objectives or states in the future and then work backward to see how these can be achieved. As an example, a company might develop a long-range goal of being the market leader in some relatively new technology. Given this long-range goal or objective, they might then use normative forecasting to work backward from that target, developing intermediate goals and alternative paths to reach these goals.

Our attention will be focused on some of the more frequently used quantitative forecasting models, since management science has had a greater

FIGURE 18-3 Conceptual view of explanatory forecasting model.

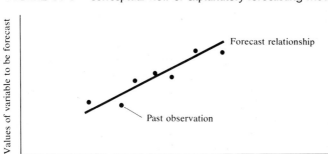

impact in this area than in qualitative forecasting. Selected extrapolation models will be examined later in this chapter. Explanatory models will be covered in the next chapter.

Selecting, Implementing, and Monitoring a Forecasting Model

The process of selecting a forecast model, tailoring the model to the problem, implementing the model, and monitoring its success consists of a number of common steps, as shown in Figure 18-4. The objectives for which the forecast will be used must be identified. Then the variable or variables to be forecast should be identified. Next we need to choose a set of alternative forecasting models to be tested. Necessary data are then obtained for these models and the models are tailored to fit the problem by specifying the values of the parameters. The alternative models are then tested using past data, their performance is measured, and a "best" model is selected for implementation. After the model has been implemented, its performance is monitored to detect the need for changes, such as the parameters the model used, the variable to be forecast, or forecast objectives. The sections below will briefly examine each of these steps.

Determining Forecast Objectives

If the model is to be successful, it must be designed with explicit knowledge of the forecasting objectives. If, for example, we are building a model to forecast

FIGURE 18-4   Steps in selecting, implementing, and monitoring a forecasting model.

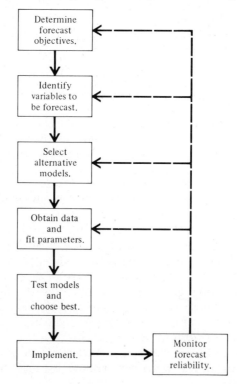

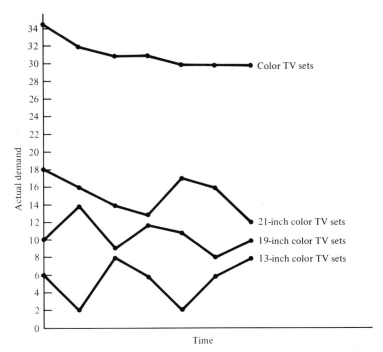

FIGURE 18-5   Comparison of aggregate actual demand pattern variability with individual item variability of color TV sets for a large retail store.

product demand, we need to know whether this model is to be used in planning marketing strategies or whether the demand forecasts are to be used in an inventory control system. This information will guide our choice of the appropriate model to use by determining the forecast horizon, computation cost limitations, types of data to include, what type of model to use, etc.

Identifying Variables to Forecast

A second major decision concerns the choice of variables to forecast. This may seem trivially obvious but in fact can be a quite difficult decision. A frequent question concerns the proper level of aggregation, or how detailed the forecast is to be. If we are forecasting product demand, is it sufficient to forecast demand for product classes (e.g., middle-sized cars) or do we need to forecast for individual products (e.g., specific brands and models) or even for specific product options (e.g., those with AM radio, AM/FM radio, or no radio)?

It should be noted here that, in general, it is easier to accurately forecast *aggregated variables* than the individual items that make up that aggregate. For example, Figure 18-5 shows the individual daily demand for 21-, 19-, and 13-inch color TV sets as well as total demand for color TV sets for a large retailer. As Figure 18-5 shows, unique variations in actual demand for individual sizes tend to cancel each other out when aggregated. Thus the demand for the different sizes of color sets is much more variable and harder to predict than that for the aggregate total demand for color sets.

In cases where the item being forecast is related to another variable, we may find it easier to forecast this other variable and use the relationship between the two to derive a forecast for the item of interest. For instance, if we forecast demand for a tire manufacturer, we are likely to find that tire sales are directly related to sales of new automobiles, past and present. We then may be able to base our tire demand forecast on the estimated or forecasted new car sales.

Selecting Alternative Models

Many models exist for providing forecasts. It is often difficult to know in advance which model will be best for a particular forecasting situation. Thus it is usually wise to select a set of alternative models for testing purposes. These models should be selected so that their characteristics match the objectives of the forecasting problem. Here we must frequently rely on ingenuity, knowledge of the range of existing models, and past experience with forecasting problems and models. Future sections of this and the following chapter will discuss some of the more frequently used forecasting models. Knowledge of the model characteristics is an important first step in the model identification phase.

Obtaining Data and Fitting Parameters

Once the models to be tested have been chosen, the data necessary to drive these models must be obtained and then used to fit parameters. Although Figure 18-4 shows that data collection occurs after the alternative models have been identified, knowledge of what data are available may be important in narrowing the list of potential models. It would be unrealistic to choose a model that requires data known to be unavailable.

The values of the model parameters are normally chosen so as to minimize forecasting error. Parameter estimation is often a complicated process but an important one. We may have chosen the correct forecasting model, but if we fit the wrong parameters the forecasting accuracy can be inadequate.

Testing Models and Choosing Best

Once the best-fitting parameters have been identified, the alternative models can be tested and the results evaluated so that the best model can be chosen for implementation. Tests are normally conducted using some set of past data. One problem that frequently arises concerns use of the same data for parameter estimation as for testing of the fitted model.

Model parameters define the specific relationship between the variable to be forecast and the data used to make that forecast. Suppose, for example, we are developing a model to forecast sales demand as a function of advertising. One possible model is $F = a + bX$, where F is sales demand, X is advertising expenditures, and a and b are the model's parameters.

Since the model, if implemented, will of necessity be basing its parameter estimates on past data, it is normally argued that if the same data on which the model is to be tested are also used to fit parameters, the test results are likely to show greater accuracy than will be true in a working environment. Therefore, what is normally done is to divide the data into two subsets, the earliest subset used to fit parameters, and the later subset for testing purposes. The choice of where to divide the data is frequently arbitrary (a 50/50 split is often used), although the number of observations required to obtain parameter estimates may dictate the point of division.

Implementing and Monitoring Selected Model

Once the best model has been selected, it can be implemented or used for forecasting. The model building process should not end with implementation. It is always wise to monitor the accuracy of the model's predictions either automatically, such as by use of a *tracking signal*, or manually on a periodic basis. If the forecast accuracy is less than expected, all aspects of the model may have to be reevaluated. Perhaps the parameters need to be recalculated. Perhaps the model being used is no longer the best choice and some alternative model should now be used instead. Alternatively, the problem situation being forecast may have changed sufficiently that we need to redefine the variables being forecast. Less frequently we may need to reconsider the forecast objectives, on the premise that these need to be modified. If the wrong problem is being addressed, this can be the most grievous penalty situation. The impact of the monitoring process is shown in Figure 18-4 by means of the dotted line feedback loops to the earlier model building stages.

Measuring the Effectiveness of Forecasting Models

Measuring forecasting effectiveness is an important step in the successful use of forecasting models. As we saw above, it is important in selecting the best forecasting model and in monitoring the performance of that model to detect necessary changes. Therefore, just how forecasting effectiveness can be measured will next be considered in detail. A number of such measures can be used. In general, each approach is concerned with how close the predictions made by the model are to the actual observations for the item being forecast.

The effectiveness of a forecasting model can be measured by considering the *bias* of the forecast, the *consistency* of the forecast, and the *correlation* of the forecast to the actual data. Bias is concerned with whether the forecasts are, on average, too high or too low. Consistency is concerned with the variability of the forecast error. Correlation is concerned with how strong the relationship is between the forecast and the actual data. Each of these three measures is useful both in selecting a forecast model to implement and in monitoring its performance. A fourth measure of forecast effectiveness is called the *tracking signal*. The tracking signal is primarily used to monitor the performance of an implemented forecasting model. It is useful in detecting when the model provides forecast errors that differ significantly from past performance. Each of these performance measures will be demonstrated in the following sections.

Forecast Error

Forecast error is defined as the numerical difference between the predicted and actual outcomes, or

Forecast error = (predicted outcome) − (actual outcome)

Thus, if we define e as the forecast error, F as the forecast, and A as the actual outcome, we have

$$e = F - A$$

Clearly we would prefer to use a forecast model that keeps forecast error as low as possible. Since evaluation of a forecasting model is usually conducted over a series of observations, we need to determine a way to average the forecast errors for all observations. We must be careful how this is done in order to reach the proper conclusions, for reasons that will soon be apparent.

Bias and Consistency

Consider Figure 18-6, which compares the distribution of forecast errors for three hypothetical forecasting models, called A, B, and C. The average or expected forecast error for models B and C is clearly somewhere near zero, while Model A's average error is biased in a negative direction. On the other hand, the variability of the forecast error for model B is considerably greater than that for models A and C.

If one had to choose one of these three models, it seems likely that model C would be chosen, since it is both unbiased (average error approximately zero) and consistent (high likelihood of small error). Nonetheless, an argument can be made for model A, as well, since it is a simple matter to correct for the bias of model A. In this case the negative average error for model A implies that the forecast is on the average too low by this amount. If the forecast were adjusted upward by the amount of this average error, the forecast error distribution would shift to the right, with the result that there would be little, if any, difference between models A and C.

Forecast Bias Let F_i be the forecast, A_i the actual outcome, and e_i the forecast error for the ith observation. Then for n observations we can define bias, or the average forecast error, as

$$\text{Bias} = \frac{\sum_{i=1}^{n} e_i}{n} = \frac{\sum_{i=1}^{n} (F_i - A_i)}{n}$$

Forecast Consistency Although it is relatively easy to correct for forecast bias, lack of consistency of forecast errors presents a tougher problem. As we saw in Figure 18-6, a forecasting model with very poor consistency or high variability can have a zero average forecasting error; this was the case for model B. This is

FIGURE 18-6 Comparison of forecasting errors for three hypothetical forecasting models.

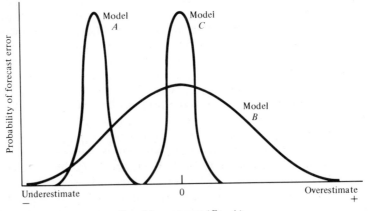

Probability of forecast error

Model A

Model C

Model B

Underestimate −   0   Overestimate +

Size of forecast error $(F_i - A_i)$

because positive and negative errors tend to cancel each other out in the computation of average forecast error. We therefore need some measure other than average forecast error to detect the presence or absence of consistency. Several such measures exist.

Mean Absolute Deviation   In Chapter 15, one method used for measuring demand variability (i.e., consistency) was the mean absolute deviation, or MAD. This measure can be used to evaluate forecasting consistency, where it is defined as

$$\text{MAD} = \frac{\sum_{i=1}^{n} |e_i|}{n} = \frac{\sum_{i=1}^{n} |F_i - A_i|}{n}$$

As defined previously, the bars indicate that the absolute value (without regard to sign) should be used. In essence, MAD is equivalent to the average absolute error. Note that by eliminating the direction or sign of the error, positive and negative errors accumulate, no longer canceling each other out. Therefore, inconsistent forecasting models will tend to have high values of MAD.

Mean Squared Error   Another convenient measure of forecast consistency is called the mean squared error, or MSE. As the name implies, MSE is the average of the squares of the forecast errors:

$$\text{MSE} = \frac{\sum_{i=1}^{n} e_i^2}{n} = \frac{\sum_{i=1}^{n} (F_i - A_i)^2}{n}$$

Note that by squaring the error term we have eliminated the direction of the error, since both negative and positive errors will yield a positive squared error.

The difference between MAD and MSE is the relative weighting given to different sizes of errors. MAD essentially weights errors on a linear or constant proportional basis; an error of 200 will have twice the weight of an error of 100 in computing MAD. MSE, on the other hand, assigns quadratic or nonproportional weights, with larger errors given significantly more relative weight; an error of 200 would be given four times the weight of 100 in calculating MSE, because 200 squared (40,000) is four times 100 squared (10,000).

MSE is often preferred over MAD in developing and evaluating forecasting models for several reasons. Many models choose parameter values such that these parameters minimize MSE. Suppose, for example, we are developing a forecast model which assumes that demand is a linear function of gross national product. In other words, if F is the demand forecast and G is gross national product, our model might appear to be $F = a + b\,G$, where a and b are parameters to be determined that define that precise relationship between demand and GNP. Many values could be chosen for these parameters. How do we decide which is best? We can easily determine values for a and b that would have provided the smallest MSE for our model's forecasts of these past data. Although one could choose parameters to minimize MAD, it is more difficult computationally to do so, which is one reason that MSE is used instead.

Another reason that MSE is used rather than MAD relates to the cost of forecasting errors. Many decision models that require forecast data as input

TABLE 18-2
Calculating Bias, MAD, and MSE for Forecasts of Monthly Bicycle Demand

Period i	Predicted demand F_i	Actual demand A_i	Forecast error e_i	Absolute forecast error $|e_i|$	Squared forecast error e_i^2
1	5,647	5,541	106	106	11,236
2	6,150	5,756	394	394	155,236
3	6,359	6,873	−514	514	264,196
4	6,316	5,913	403	403	162,409
5	6,208	6,436	−228	228	51,984
6	5,799	5,950	−151	151	22,801
7	6,199	5,227	972	972	944,784
8	6,634	6,590	44	44	1,936
9	6,218	6,577	−359	359	128,881
10	6,420	6,529	−109	109	11,881
Totals			558	3,280	1,755,344

$$\text{Bias} = \frac{\Sigma e_i}{n} = \frac{558}{10} = 55.8$$

$$\text{MAD} = \frac{\Sigma |e_i|}{n} = \frac{3,280}{10} = 328$$

$$\text{MSE} = \frac{\Sigma e_i^2}{n} = \frac{1,755,344}{10} = 175,534$$

have cost functions that are essentially quadratic or nonlinear. The inventory models of Chapters 14 and 15 are good examples. You may recall that a plot of the total relevant cost curve for the EOQ model had an approximate U shape, reflecting the quadratic nature of the cost function. Thus using MSE to evaluate forecasting models is consistent with the nonlinear costs that result from forecast errors; i.e., bigger errors should be given proportionately larger penalties.

Let us now see how bias, MSE, and MAD are calculated. Suppose we are attempting to evaluate the performance of a model for forecasting monthly demand for a bicycle manufacturer. The model is to be tested using demands for 10 recent months, as shown in the third column of Table 18-2. The forecasts provided by the model are shown in the second column. Subtracting the actual demand from the predicted demand yields the actual forecast error, as shown in the fourth column. The sum of these errors divided by the number of observations, 10, provides the bias of 55.8. Dropping the sign of each error leads to the absolute forecast errors shown in the fifth column. These values are summed and then divided by 10 to produce a MAD of 328. Finally, we square each error term, as shown in the sixth column, add these squared errors, and divide by 10 again to calculate MSE of 175,534.

INSTANT REPLAY Suppose another forecasting model has provided the following predictions for bicycle demands corresponding to the 10 periods shown in Table 18-2:

Period	Predicted demand	Period	Predicted demand
1	5,613	6	5,858
2	6,040	7	6,132
3	6,250	8	6,418
4	6,338	9	6,295
5	6,200	10	6,318

Calculate the bias, MAD, and MSE for this new set of forecasts. Which of the two sets of forecasts would you consider better?

CHECK Bias = 7.0, MAD = 330.2, and MSE = 169,140.8. This second model produces forecasts with lower bias and MSE and only slightly higher MAD. Thus it is slightly better, on balance.

Correlation

Another method for evaluating forecasting models is based on the fact that if the forecast is close to the actual data the relationship between these two items should be statistically significant. You may recall from statistics that the measure used to describe how two variables vary in relation to each other is called *covariance*. The formula for calculating the covariance (cov) between two variables x and y is

$$\text{cov}(x,y) = \frac{\sum_{i=1}^{n} (x_i - \bar{x})(y_i - \bar{y})}{n - 1}$$

where $\bar{x}$ and $\bar{y}$ are the means of the two variables and n is the number of observations. Clearly the covariance measure will be a high positive number when both x and y consistently deviate from the mean in the same direction, either positively or negatively. Alternatively, if y is consistently below the mean when x is above the mean, the covariance will be a high negative measure. But when the relationship between the two is weak, positive and negative deviations will tend to cancel each other out and the covariance will be close to zero.

Table 18-3 illustrates how the covariance would be calculated for the actual and forecasted bicycle demand of Table 18-2. The mean for each variable is determined and then subtracted from each observation to find the deviation from the mean. The deviations are then multiplied together and the resulting product is summed and then divided by 9, one less than the number of observations. This leads to a covariance of 89,871.

Such a high covariance as this suggests that a strong relationship exists between the two variables. It is difficult, however, to know exactly *how* strong the relationship is without standardizing the covariance. This is done by dividing the covariance by the product of the *standard deviations* of the two variables. This standardized measure is normally referred to as the *correlation coefficient r*.

$$r = \frac{\text{cov}(x, y)}{s_x s_y}$$

TABLE 18-3
Calculation of Covariance and Correlation between Actual and Predicted Monthly Bicycle Demand

Period	Predicted demand F_i	Mean predicted demand $\bar{F}$	Predicted deviation $F_i - \bar{F}$	Actual demand A_i	Mean actual demand $\bar{A}$	Actual deviation $A_i - \bar{A}$	Predicted deviation multiplied by actual deviaton $(F_i - \bar{F})(A_i - \bar{A})$
1	5,647	6,195	−548	5,541	6,139.2	−598.2	327,813.6
2	6,150	6,195	− 45	5,756	6,139.2	−383.2	17,244.0
3	6,359	6,195	164	6,873	6,139.2	733.8	120,343.2
4	6,316	6,195	121	5,913	6,139.2	−226.2	− 27,370.2
5	6,208	6,195	13	6,436	6,139.2	296.8	3,858.4
6	5,799	6,195	−396	5,950	6,139.2	− 189.2	74,923.2
7	6,199	6,195	4	5,227	6,139.2	−912.2	− 3,648.8
8	6,634	6,195	439	6,590	6,139.2	450.8	197,901.2
9	6,218	6,195	23	6,577	6,139.2	437.8	10,069.4
10	6,420	6,195	225	6,529	6,139.2	389.8	87,705.0
Totals	61,950	61,950	0	61,392	61,392	0	808,839

$$\bar{F} = \frac{61,950}{10} = 6,195 \qquad \bar{A} = \frac{61,392}{10} = 6,139.2$$

$$\text{cov} = \frac{808,839}{9} - 89,871$$

$$S_F = \sqrt{\frac{\Sigma(F_i - \bar{F})^2}{n - 1}} = \sqrt{\frac{744,742}{9}} = 287.7 \qquad S_A = \sqrt{\frac{\Sigma(A_i - \bar{A})^2}{n - 1}} = \sqrt{\frac{2,597,143.6}{9}} = 537.2$$

$$r = \frac{\text{cov}}{S_F S_A} = \frac{89,871}{(287.7)(537.2)} = .581$$

The correlation coefficient is probably not unfamiliar to you. You may recall that it has several nice properties. The value of this coefficient must always fall between +1.0 and −1.0. If the two variables are perfectly correlated (if you know the value of one of them you can always exactly predict the value of the other), the correlation coefficient will be either +1 or −1, the sign determined by whether both move in the same direction (+1) or in the opposite direction (−1). Values near zero for r would indicate that there is little or no relation between these variables.

If r is used to measure the strength of the relationship between forecast and actual values, we would expect r to be positive, and if the forecast is perfect, r would be +1.0.

Since any comparison of forecast with actual values is based on a sample of observations, we must be careful to use a divisor of $n - 1$ when calculating the standard deviations for the two variables to use in computing r. Thus

$$r = \frac{\text{cov}(F, A)}{S_F S_A}$$

where $\quad S_F = \sqrt{\dfrac{\displaystyle\sum_{i=1}^{n} (F_i - \bar{F})^2}{n - 1}} \quad$ and $\quad S_A = \sqrt{\dfrac{\displaystyle\sum_{i=1}^{n} (A_i - \bar{A})^2}{n - 1}}$

Table 18-3 shows the calculations necessary to compute r for the forecast and actual data of Table 18-2. The individual squared deviations (not shown) for each variable are summed and divided by $n - 1 = 9$, and the square roots are taken to determine the sample standard deviations. The product of these is then divided into the covariance to compute r as .581. This value indicates a lack of high correlation although some relationship exists.

INSTANT REPLAY   Refer to the preceding Instant Replay in which a second set of forecasts was provided for the 10-period bicycle demand data. Calculate the covariance and correlation coefficient appropriate for the relationship between this second set of forecasts and the actual demand data.

CHECK   cov $= 81,169.7$, $S_F = 248.3$, $S_A = 537.2$, and $r = .609$.

Tracking Signal

Although the measures we have examined (MSE, MAD, correlation) for evaluating forecasting models are quite useful for developing a model and determining the appropriate parameters, they are somewhat computationally cumbersome to use for monitoring a forecasting model that has been implemented and is in use, even with computer assistance.

One can, however, use a measure called the tracking signal to monitor and control forecast errors for an implemented forecast model. There are a number of ways in which a tracking signal can be defined. A simple tracking signal method will be examined in this section to illustrate its usefulness. Later, another definition will be considered.

Consider for a moment the ratio of bias to MAD over some set of observations, say n. Call that ratio TS_n, where

$$ TS_n = \frac{\sum_{i=1}^{n} e_i/n}{\sum_{i=1}^{n} |e_i|/n} = \frac{\sum_{i=1}^{n} e_i}{\sum_{i=1}^{n} |e_i|} $$

If the forecast model is tracking or predicting the actual data in an unbiased manner, we would expect this ratio to be approximately zero, since the numerator will average out to zero. However, if the forecast is biased, this ratio is likely to grow in either a positive or negative direction, depending upon the nature of the bias. If the forecast is consistently biased in, say, a positive direction, TS_n will equal $+1.0$; alternatively, perfect negative bias will yield -1.0 for TS_n.

TS_n thus represents a tracking signal. The further away from zero the tracking signal is, the more bias exists in the forecasting model. Management can select a *tracking signal upper limit TS* which can then be used to detect situations that require restudying. As long as $TS_n \leq TS$, we assume that forecasts are unbiased and continue to use the model unchanged. If $TS_n > TS$ for one or more periods, the model or its parameters may need to be changed to correct for the apparent bias. The tracking signal limit TS is usually set at a value of $\pm .5$, although it can be raised or lowered depending on whether or not the costs of forecast errors are lower or higher than normal, respectively.

TABLE 18-4
Illustration of Use of Tracking Signal

Period	Forecast	Actual	e_i	$|e_i|$	Σe_i	$\Sigma |e_i|$	TS_n
1	11	10	1	1	1	1	1.00
2	19	20	−1	1	0	2	.00
3	31	30	1	1	1	3	.33
4	41	50	−9	9	− 8	12	− .67
5	52	60	−8	8	−16	20	− .80

$$TS_n = \frac{\sum\limits_{i=1}^{n} e_i}{\sum\limits_{i=1}^{n} |e_i|}$$

To illustrate the use of the tracking signal, refer to Table 18-4. The cumulative sums of the actual (Σe_i) and absolute ($\Sigma |e_i|$) forecast errors are calculated after each period. Then the ratio of the cumulative actual error to the cumulative absolute error is computed to find the tracking signal. The initial tracking signal will always be +1 or −1; so we can disregard it.

The forecast was close to the actual value for the first three periods, and the tracking signal was found to be zero in period 2 and .33 in period 3. Suppose we have established a critical value for the tracking signal at, say, ± .5. Since the computed tracking signal is less than .5 for periods 2 and 3, we can assume that the forecasting model is in control.

Actual demand takes a jump in period 4 and the forecast model does not correct for this jump, causing the forecast error also to increase markedly in periods 4 and 5. This jump is immediately reflected in the tracking signal, changing to −.67 in period 4 and then to −.80 in period 5. Both these values exceed the critical tracking signal value, which suggests that the forecasting model needs to be reexamined.

INSTANT REPLAY What would be the tracking signal value for period 6 if the forecast was 64 and the actual observation was 62?

CHECK $TS_6 = -.64$.

Extrapolation Models

Now that we have examined the steps followed in selecting, implementing, and monitoring forecast models, we next examine specific forecasting models. This section will consider the category of forecasting models referred to earlier as extrapolation models. Extrapolation models use past observations of the variable to be forecast to extrapolate into the future. These models generally rely on some means of averaging the past data. The method by which the average is computed largely differentiates the various extrapolation models. If our previous notation is modified by adding a time subscript, where F_t is the forecast for period t and A_{t-k} is the actual observation k periods prior to period t, the general extrapolation model is of the form

$$F_t = f(A_{t-1}, A_{t-2}, \ldots)$$

The following sections will examine several ways in which the precise nature of the functional relationship can be defined. These include (1) *moving average models* and (2) *exponential smoothing models*.

Moving Average Models

A frequently used class of extrapolation models includes what are called moving average models. A forecast is provided by averaging past observations. The averaging is usually accomplished by assigning a weight W_{t-k} to each past observation included in the average. With this model the number of past observations is always fixed at n, where n is a parameter to be selected. It is referred to as a "moving" average because, as each new observation becomes available, the average is recalculated by substituting the newest observation in place of the oldest.

If we let n represent the number of past observations to be used, we can define a general moving average model as

$$F_t = \frac{\sum\limits_{k=1}^{n} W_{t-k} A_{t-k}}{\sum\limits_{k=1}^{n} W_{t-k}}$$

Thus the moving average forecast is based on the sum of the weighted past observations divided by the sum of the weights.

Equal-Weighted Moving Average   The simplest version of the general moving average model assigns equal weights of 1 to all n observations. Since each weight is 1, the sum of these weights for n past periods will be simply n. Thus the forecast equation simplifies to

$$F_t = \frac{\sum\limits_{k=1}^{n} A_{t-k}}{n}$$

and F_t is simply the average of the previous n observations.

For example, suppose we are using a six-period moving average ($n = 6$) and the actual demand observations for the last six periods were as shown below:

Jan	10	Apr	9
Feb	12	May	10
Mar	8	June	11

Our forecast for July would be

$$F_{\text{July}} = \frac{10 + 12 + 8 + 9 + 10 + 11}{6} = 10$$

Suppose further that the actual observation for July demand was 13. In calculating the forecast for August we would delete the value for January and substitute the value of July. Thus,

$$F_{\text{August}} = \frac{12 + 8 + 9 + 10 + 11 + 13}{6} = 10.5$$

INSTANT REPLAY   Suppose the actual observation for August is 10. What would be the 6-period moving average forecast for September?

CHECK $F_{\text{September}} = 10.2$.

The choice of the number of observations to be used in the average, the parameter n, is influenced by the nature of the variable being forecast. Frequently, the number of periods is chosen so that the average is based on the past year's data. Thus, if we used monthly data we would set $n = 12$; on the other hand, if quarterly data were used, we would set $n = 4$. The use of 1 year's worth of data in the moving average eliminates the influence of any seasonality that may be in the data, which is generally not desirable for forecasting purposes, although it can be useful for detecting trends and other nonseasonal patterns. If seasonal effects are present, the forecast derived in this manner would normally have to be adjusted to account for the seasonal impact.

The size of n also has an impact on the speed with which the forecast responds to a change in the pattern of the variable being forecast. This can be seen by rewriting our formula for calculating the moving average as

$$F_t = \sum_{k=1}^{n} \left(\frac{1}{n}\right) A_{t-k}$$

Observe that the weight given to each individual observation is inversely proportional to the size of n. When n is smaller a larger weight is given to each observation than when n is large. Thus, when a change in pattern occurs, the model with the smaller n will react quickly to this change, since it assigns a greater weight to newer observations than does the model with a larger n. This is illustrated in Table 18-5, where a moving average model with $n = 6$ is compared with one with $n = 3$.

Beginning with period 7, the actual observations show a sudden step increase in the average level of demand which continues through period 12. This change is picked up much more slowly with the $n = 6$ model than with the $n = 3$ model. Observe that Table 18-5 shows the MAD for both approaches as a measure of forecast accuracy. The MAD for the three-period moving average model is consistently lower than for the six-period model.

As is generally true with other forecasting procedures, a model that responds quickly to real changes in the pattern also tends to overreact to random influences. Table 18-6 illustrates the case in which a random impulse occurs only in period 7. The model with $n = 3$ reacts quickly to this new observation and consequently does not perform as well as that with $n = 6$, as indicated by the higher MAD for the three-period model.

A comparison of these two examples (Tables 18-5 and 18-6) illustrates a major problem faced in forecasting. We would prefer to have a forecasting model that responds quickly to real pattern changes but does not react to random influences. The $n = 3$ model reacted more quickly to the real change (Ta-

TABLE 18-5
Comparison of Forecast Accuracy for Moving Average Method with Different
Parameter Settings for a Demand Pattern with a Step Increase

Period	Actual observation	Moving average forecast		MAD	
		$n = 6$	$n = 3$	$n = 6$	$n = 3$
1	10				
2	12				
3	8				
4	11				
5	9				
6	10				
7	15	10.0	10.0	5.0	5.0
8	14	10.8	11.3	4.1	3.9
9	16	11.2	13.0	4.3	3.6
10	15	12.5	15.0	3.9	2.7
11	14	13.2	15.0	3.3	2.3
12	15	14.0	15.0	2.9	1.9

$$\frac{84}{6} = 14.0 \qquad \frac{45}{3} = 15.0 \qquad \frac{5(2.3) + (15 - 15)}{6} = 1.9$$

$$\frac{5(3.3) + (15 - 14)}{6} = 2.9$$

ble 18-5) but also overreacted to the random impulse. The $n = 6$ model did not react as much to the random impulse but also did not react as quickly to the real change. In order to deal with both objectives, a tradeoff of one against the other must be made. Quicker response to real changes in pattern (setting n small) is achieved at the cost of less dampening or smoothing of random changes. Larger n values provide more smoothing of random influences but are less quick to respond to real changes. The best tradeoff may call for some intermediate n.

TABLE 18-6
Comparison of Forecast Accuracy for Moving Average Method with Different
Parameter Settings for a Demand Pattern with a Random Impulse

Period	Actual observation	Moving average forecast		MAD	
		$n = 6$	$n = 3$	$n = 6$	$n = 3$
1	10				
2	12				
3	8				
4	11				
5	9				
6	10				
7	15	10.0	10.0	5.0	5.0
8	9	10.8	11.3	3.4	3.7
9	10	10.3	11.3	2.4	2.9
10	11	10.7	11.3	1.9	2.2
11	8	10.7	10.0	2.0	2.2
12	10	10.5	9.7	1.8	1.0

Unequal-Weighted Moving Average   Note that regardless of the number of periods included in calculating an equal-weighted moving average forecast, each observation that is included receives a weight of $1/n$. This implies that the most recent observation carries as much weight as the oldest observation. While this may be reasonable for situations that remain quite stable over time, in practice such iron-cast stability does not often exist and the assignment of equal weights is not justified. This problem can be overcome by use of what we refer to as the *unequal-weighted moving average model.*

The use of unequal weights increases the complexity of the parameter estimation problem, since the model builder now needs to determine a precise set of weights to use as well as the number of periods to be included. Although any set of weights can be chosen, it is computationally convenient to use fractional weights whose sum equals 1, since the formula

$$F_t = \frac{\sum\limits_{k=1}^{n} W_{t-k} A_{t-k}}{\sum\limits_{k=1}^{n} W_{t-k}}$$

reduces to

$$F_t = \sum_{k=1}^{n} W_{t-k} A_{t-k}$$

when the weights are so chosen.

To illustrate how the procedure is applied, suppose we have chosen to set $n = 4$ with the most recent period receiving a weight of .40, the next most recent period of weight of .30, and the two oldest periods weights of .20 and .10, respectively. The forecast for period t would then be easily calculated from

$$F_t = .40A_{t-1} + .30A_{t-2} + .20A_{t-3} + .10A_{t-4}$$

If the most recent 4 observations were 40 (newest), 37, 38, and 36 (oldest) our forecast would be

$$F_t = .40(40) + .30(37) + .20(38) + .10(36)$$

$$= 16 + 11.1 + 7.6 + 3.6 = 38.3$$

Note that the weights assigned to the observed values will change as each subsequent observation is included. For instance, if the next observation received for the example above is 42, our new forecast, for period $t + 1$, would be calculated as

$$F_{t+1} = .40(42) + .30(40) + .20(37) + .10(38) = 40.0$$

INSTANT REPLAY   If the weights selected for the example above had been .50 (latest observation), .25, .15, and .10 (oldest observation), what would your forecasts have been for periods t and $t + 1$?

CHECK $F_t = 38.55$ and $F_{t+1} = 40.35$.

Exponential Smoothing Models

One of the biggest disadvantages in using either the equal- or unequal-weighted moving average method is the requirement to keep track of past observations. For instance, if $n = 12$ and we are using an unequal-weighted moving average, we need to retain the most recent 12 observations plus the 12 weights to be used in calculating the forecast. Although keeping track of 24 values may not seem to be much of a drawback, if we are using this method to forecast demand for use in a large inventory control system, the data storage requirements may be very costly. It is not uncommon to find a system with as many as 50,000 inventory items which would require that 1,200,000 (24 × 50,000) data elements be maintained. Of course, this could be reduced if some or all of the items used the same set of weights.

There is, however, a special form of the weighted moving average method which has minimal data storage requirements and yet consists of a weighted average of all past observations. This method, referred to as exponential smoothing, has received wide application. Several exponential smoothing models exist, and as we shall see, the choice of model depends on the assumed pattern of the data.

Simple Exponential Smoothing   Our discussion begins by considering what is frequently called *simple exponential smoothing*. The forecast is based on a weighted average of past observations, called the *smoothed average S_t*.

In the simple smoothing case the forecast for period $t + 1$ is simply the current smoothed average, or

$$F_{t+1} = S_t$$

The current smoothed average is calculated by taking a weighted average of the most recent observation and the old smoothed average. Letting α represent the weight given to the most recent observation, we define

$$S_t = \alpha A_t + (1 - \alpha) S_{t-1}$$

It may not be obvious at this point that S_t is in fact a weighted average of past observations. This can be seen by expanding our formula for S_t. Since

$$S_{t-1} = \alpha A_{t-1} + (1 - \alpha) S_{t-2}$$

we find through substitution that

$$S_t = \alpha A_t + (1 - \alpha) [\alpha A_{t-1} + (1 - \alpha) S_{t-2}]$$
$$= \alpha A_t + \alpha(1 - \alpha) A_{t-1} + (1 - \alpha)^2 S_{t-2}$$

In a similar manner we can substitute for S_{t-2} to derive

$$S_t = \alpha A_t + \alpha(1 - \alpha) A_{t-1} + (1 - \alpha)^2 [\alpha A_{t-2} + (1 - \alpha) S_{t-3}]$$
$$= \alpha A_t + \alpha(1 - \alpha) A_{t-1} + \alpha(1 - \alpha)^2 A_{t-2} + (1 - \alpha)^3 S_{t-3}$$

Continued substitution leads to the relationship

$$S_t = \alpha A_t + \alpha(1 - \alpha) A_{t-1} + \cdots + \alpha(1 - \alpha)^k A_{t-k} + \cdots$$

Thus we see that the current smoothed average is really a weighted average of past observations, the weight assigned to observation $t - k$ being $\alpha(1 - \alpha)^k$.

Parameter Specification   The value of α can range from 0 to 1. In general the higher the value of α used, the more weight is given to recent observations and the less weight is given to older observations. This is illustrated by the graph

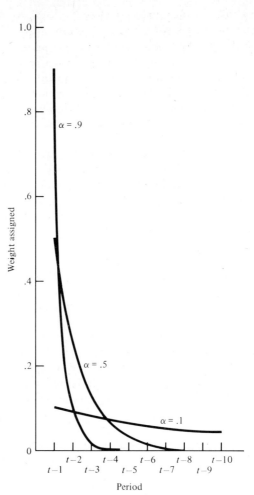

FIGURE 18-7 Comparison of weights given to past observations in exponential smoothing for various α values.

shown in Figure 18-7. With $\alpha = .1$ the weights decline at a much slower rate than they do with $\alpha = .9$. The fact that the weights decline exponentially accounts for the term "exponential" in the name of this procedure.

By rearranging the terms in the smoothing equation we can gain additional understanding of the exponential smoothing model.

$$S_t = \alpha A_t + (1 - \alpha) S_{t-1}$$
$$= \alpha(A_t - S_{t-1}) + S_{t-1}$$

Since the forecast for period t is equal to the smoothed average for period $t - 1$, we can substitute F_t for S_{t-1} in our equation, which leads to

$$F_{t+1} = \alpha(A_t - F_t) + F_t$$

Note that $A_t - F_t$ is by definition the difference between the forecast and the actual observation at time T. This is equivalent to the forecast error for period t, or

$$F_{t+1} = F_t + \alpha e_t$$

Interpreting this formula, we see that the forecast for period $t + 1$ is

equivalent to the forecast for the previous period adjusted by some portion of the previous period's forecast error. Note that if the forecast was less than the actual observation, e_t will be positive and our new forecast will be higher than the old forecast. Likewise, if the old forecast was too high, the new forecast will be adjusted downward. This ability to self-correct on the basis of the most recent error is sometimes referred to as negative feedback. The degree to which the forecast is adjusted by the error is dependent on the size of α, large α causing a larger adjustment than small α.

A simple exponential smoothing model requires selection of an appropriate α value as well as an initial forecast or smoothed average. In practice the value for α is normally chosen by experimenting on a set of past observations. Several likely α values can be tested, and the one which proves most accurate on the test data can then be used in practice. It is convenient to use the earliest observation as the initial forecast value for test purposes.

Illustration of Calculations To illustrate the use of the simple exponential smoothing model, consider Table 18-7, which shows the forecasts that would result for two smoothing models, one with $\alpha = .1$ and the other with $\alpha = .7$, applied to the demand data of Table 18-5, which reflects a step increase from period 7 on.

In each case the initial smoothed average is assumed to be $10(S_0 = 10)$. The remaining calculations proceed iteratively as follows (the $\alpha = .1$ model will be used, although the calculations are handled identically for $\alpha = .7$). The forecast for period 1 is set equal to the initial smoothed average, $F_1 = S_0 = 10$. Once the demand for period 1 is known (10), the smoothed average is updated:

$$S_1 = \alpha A_1 + (1 - \alpha)S_0$$
$$= .1(10) + .9(10) = 10$$

TABLE 18-7
Comparison of Exponential Smoothing Models with α Values of .1 and .7
for a Demand Pattern with a Step Increase

Period	Actual demand	$\alpha = .1$			$\alpha = .7$		
		F_t	S_t	e_t	F_t	S_t	e_t
0			10.00			10.00	
1	10	10.00	10.00	.00	10.00	10.00	.00
2	12	10.00	10.20	2.00	10.00	11.40	2.00
3	8	10.20	9.98	−2.20	11.40	9.02	−3.40
4	11	9.98	10.08	1.02	9.02	10.41	1.98
5	9	10.08	9.97	−1.08	10.41	9.42	−1.41
6	10	9.97	9.97	.03	9.42	9.83	.58
7	15	9.97	10.47	5.03	9.83	13.45	5.17
8	14	10.47	10.82	3.53	13.45	13.84	.55
9	16	10.82	11.34	5.18	13.84	15.35	2.16
10	15	11.34	11.71	3.66	15.35	15.11	− .35
11	14	11.71	11.94	2.29	15.11	14.33	−1.11
12	15	11.94	12.25	3.06	14.33	14.80	.67
			MAD = 2.42			MAD = 1.62	

This updated smoothed average becomes the forecast for period 2. That is, $F_2 = S_1 = 10$.

The demand in period 2 turned out to be 12, which results in an increase in the smoothed average:

$$S_2 = .1(12) + .9(10) = 10.2$$

This in turn becomes the forecast for period 3, $F_3 = S_2 = 10.2$. The actual demand in period 3 is 8, which leads to

$$S_3 = .1(8) + .9(10.2) = 9.98$$

The calculations for the other periods shown in Table 18-7 follow in a similar manner.

INSTANT REPLAY   What would be the forecast for period 14 if the actual demand in period 13 is 16? (Use $\alpha = .1$.)

CHECK $F_{14} = S_{13} = 12.63$.

Because of the way in which α determines the weight assigned to past observations, the degree to which the model responds to changes in observed data can be controlled by the choice of α. Thus a low α will not react quickly to random fluctuations but will also tend to react slowly to real changes in pattern; using a high α level leads to opposite results. Thus a low α is said to provide more smoothing than a high α. In practice, α values between .1 and .3 are frequently used, reflecting the relative stability of the system being forecast.

Note that exponential smoothing is very parsimonious in its data storage requirements, needing only to keep track of the smoothing constant α, the latest observation A_t, and the current smoothed average S_t.

Trend-Adjusted Exponential Smoothing   When the variable being forecast by simple exponential smoothing has a trend present, the forecast tends to lag behind the observed data, the degree of the lag being dependent upon the smoothing constant used. This is illustrated in Figure 18-8, in which the forecasts for two smoothing models, one with $\alpha = .1$ and the other with $\alpha = .7$, are shown in comparison with the observed data for a time series with a linear deterministic trend having a positive slope, or per-period incease, of 10.

Although, eventually, both forecast models begin to reflect the same upward slope as that for the series being forecast, the forecasts never quite catch up to the actual observations but lag by a specified amount that depends upon the size of α. If the per-period trend is b, the size of the lag is given by b/α. For $\alpha = .1$ and $b = 10$, this lag is $10/.1 = 100$, and for $\alpha = .7$ the lag is $10/.7 = 14.3$. Thus, although high α values will react more quickly to a trend, they will never catch up to the trend without external adjustment. Neither will low α, and the size of the lag will be much greater.

Of course, simple smoothing models were not developed to deal with trend patterns and are more appropriate for time series that are statistically stable around some horizontal mean. Several other exponential smoothing models were designed with trend patterns specifically in mind. This class of models will

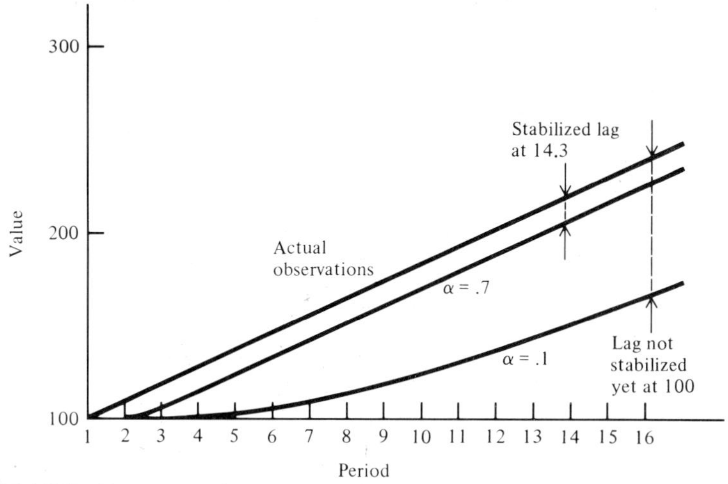

FIGURE 18-8 Response of simple exponential smoothing models to a time series with deterministic trend.

be called trend-adjusted exponential smoothing. To avoid confusion, coverage will be limited to one of these models, that developed by Holt.[1]

The model we shall consider has two smoothing constants: α is used to smooth the mean or base of the series S_t and β is used to smooth the trend T_t. Because of the lag evidenced by the simple model when tracking a trend, we need to modify the formula for calculating the smoothed average. This is done by adding the trend to the old smoothed average. Thus

$$S_t = \alpha A_t + (1 - \alpha)(S_{t-1} + T_{t-1})$$

To calculate a new smoothed trend, we need to average the latest *apparent trend* with the old smoothed trend. The latest apparent trend is given by the difference between the new and old smoothed averages:

$$\text{Apparent trend} = S_t - S_{t-1}$$

Thus the formula for new smoothed trend is

$$T_t = \beta(S_t - S_{t-1}) + (1 - \beta) T_{t-1}$$

Finally, the forecast for period $t + 1$ is formed by adding the new smoothed trend to the new smoothed average:

$$F_{t+1} = S_t + T_t$$

which eliminates the lag effect.

Illustration of Calculations Table 18-8 illustrates the response of the model with two different parameter settings. The actual observations, as shown in column 2, follow a precise trend, increasing by 10 in each period. The forecasts, smoothed averages, and smoothed trend values are shown to the right for the two parameter settings ($\alpha = .1/\beta = .5$ and $\alpha = .5/\beta = .3$). In both cases we be-

---

[1] C. C. Holt, "Forecasting Seasonal and Trends by Exponentially Weighted Moving Averages," Office of Naval Research, Memorandum 52, 1957.

TABLE 18-8
Comparison of Trend-Adjusted Models with Different Parameter Settings
on a Time Series with Deterministic Trend

Period	Actual observation	$\alpha = .1, \beta = .5$			$\alpha = .5, \beta = .3$		
		F_t	S_t	T_t	F_t	S_t	T_t
1	100		100	5		100	5
2	110	105	105.5	5.3	105	107.5	5.8
3	120	110.8	111.7	5.8	113.3	116.7	6.8
4	130	117.5	118.8	6.5	123.5	126.8	7.8
5	140	125.3	126.8	7.3	134.6	137.3	8.6
6	150	134.1	135.7	8.1	145.9	148.0	9.2
7	160	143.7	145.3	8.9	157.2	158.6	9.6
8	170	154.2	155.8	9.7	168.2	169.1	9.9
9	180	165.5	167.0	10.5	179.0	179.5	10.1
10	190	177.5	178.8	11.2	189.6	189.8	10.2
11	200	190	191	11.7	200	200	10.2
12	210	202.7	203.4	12.1	210.2	210.1	10.1
13	220	215.5	216	12.4	220.2	220.1	10.0
14	230	228.4	228.6	12.5	230.1	230	10.0
15	240	241.1	241	12.4	240	240	10.0
16	250	253.4	253.1	12.2	250	250	10.0
17	260	265.3	264.8	12.0	260	260	10.0
18	270	276.8	276.1	11.7	270	270	10.0
19	280	287.8	287.0	11.3	280	280	10.0
20	290	298.3	297.5	10.9	290	290	10.0
		MAD = 8.6			MAD = 1.7		

gan with initial estimates of 100 for the smoothed average and 5 for the smoothed trend.

To illustrate how the calculations were performed for Table 18-8, consider the $\alpha = .5$ $\beta = .3$ model. The initial forecast, for period 2, was calculated from

$$F_2 = S_1 + T_1 = 100 + 5 = 105$$

Since $A_2 = 110$, we need first to calculate a new smoothed average

$$S_2 = \alpha A_2 + (1 - \alpha)(S_1 + T_1)$$
$$= .5(110) + .5(100 + 5) = 107.5$$

Then we revise the smoothed trend:

$$T_2 = \beta(S_2 - S_1) + (1 - \beta) T_1$$
$$= .3(107.5 - 100) + .7(5) = 5.8$$

Then the forecast for period 3 is calculated:

$$F_3 = S_2 + T_2$$
$$= 107.5 + 5.8 = 113.3$$

The other values shown in Table 18-8 were calculated in a similar manner.

Parameter Specification In this case the model with $\alpha = .5$ and $\beta = .3$ performed much better than that with $\alpha = .1$ and $\beta = .5$. In both cases, in their haste to catch up, the models tend to overshoot before locking correctly onto the true pattern, although the $\alpha = .1, \beta = .5$ model takes a much longer time to adjust. The forecast errors for the model with $\alpha = .1$ and $\beta = .5$ parameters are quite small.

The Holt trend-adjusted exponential smoothing model presents a more difficult parameter estimation problem, since two parameters need to be selected. If historical data are available, the model builder can experiment with different combinations of the two parameters to determine the best set. This can be quite simple to do when a computer is available to carry out the tests. Most exponential smoothing packages will include the Holt model or one of the other trend-adjusted models. In any event these methods are fairly simple to program.

Trend- and Seasonally Adjusted Exponential Smoothing Models When the data contain a seasonal as well as a trend pattern, two approaches are possible. With one approach, the seasonal pattern can be estimated independently and a trend-adjusted model, as described above, can be applied to the seasonally adjusted data. The forecast obtained from the exponential smoothing model would then have to be adjusted to reflect any seasonality. This approach is illustrated in Table 18-9, for quarterly data, in which the seasonality factors have been determined previously to be 90, 115, 120, and 75 percent. These factors can be interpreted to mean that the first quarter is typically 90 percent of an average quarter, the second 115 percent of average, the third 120 percent, and the fourth 75 percent. Values of $\alpha = .3$ and $\beta = .2$ were used for this illustration.

As shown in Table 18-9, the actual observations are divided by the seasonality factors to yield the deseasonalized data. The smoothing model is applied to the deseasonalized data and the forecast obtained is then multiplied by the appropriate seasonal factor to derive a seasonally adjusted forecast.

An initial smoothed average of 90 and smoothed trend of 10 were assumed. The smoothed forecast for period 1 was thus

$$F_1 = 90 + 10 = 100$$

The adjusted forecast F_1' is calculated by multiplying by the appropriate seasonal factor Q_i, which for quarter 1 is $Q_1 = .90$.

$$F_1' = Q_1 F_1 = .9(100) = 90$$

The actual observation for period 1 turned out to be 90. This figure must be deseasonalized to arrive at an adjusted observed value for period 1, A_1':

$$A_1' = \frac{A_1}{Q_1} = \frac{90}{.9} = 100$$

TABLE 18-9
Use of Deseasonalized Data with Trend-Adjusted Model ($\alpha = .3$, $\beta = .2$)

Period	Actual observation A_t	Seasonality factor Q_t	Deseasonalized observation A'_t	F_t	S_t	T_t	Seasonally adjusted forecast F'_t
0					90	10	
1	90	.90	100.0	100	100	10	90
2	128	1.15	111.3	110	110.4	10.1	126.5
3	144	1.20	120.0	120.5	120.4	10.1	144.6
4	97	.75	129.3	130.5	130.1	10.0	97.9
5	128	.90	142.2	140.1	140.7	10.1	126.1
6	171	1.15	148.7	150.8	150.2	10.0	173.4
7	181	1.20	150.8	160.2	157.4	9.4	192.2
8	122	.75	162.7	166.8	165.6	9.2	125.1

Then the smoothing model is applied:

$$S_1 = \alpha A'_1 + (1 - \alpha)(S_0 + T_0)$$
$$= .3(100) + .7(90 + 10) = 100$$
$$T_1 = \beta(S_1 - S_0) + (1 - \beta) T_0$$
$$= .2(100 - 90) + .8(10) = 10$$
$$F_2 = S_1 + T_1 = 100 + 10 = 110$$
$$F'_2 = Q_2 F_2 = 1.15(110) = 126.5$$

INSTANT REPLAY If the actual observation turns out to be 140 in period 9, what would be the forecast for period 10 (refer to Table 18-9)?

CHECK $S_9 = 169.0$, $T_9 = 8.0$, and $F_{10} = 203.6$.

Winters' Model The approach described above is convenient to use as long as the seasonality pattern remains stable. When there is some reason to believe that this is not the case, a seasonally and trend-adjusted model such as that developed by Winters can be used.[1] Instead of using externally determined and fixed seasonality factors, the Winters model actually smooths the seasonal factors as well. The number of seasonal factors maintained L is determined by the length of the seasonal pattern and the length of the period being forecast. Normally L would equal 4 for quarterly data, 12 for monthly data, etc.

The formula for calculating the new smoothed average is similar to that for the trend-adjusted model, with the exception that the actual observation must be divided by the appropriate seasonal factor, which was calculated L periods ago. Thus,

$$S_t = \alpha \frac{A_t}{Q_{t-L}} + (1 - \alpha)(S_{t-1} + T_{t-1})$$

[1]P. R. Winters, "Forecasting Sales by Exponentially Weighted Moving Averages," *Management Science*, vol. 6, no. 3 (1960), pp. 324–342.

The equation for calculating the new smoothed trend is unchanged:

$$T_t = \beta(S_t - S_{t-1}) + (1 - \beta) T_{t-1}$$

The seasonality is estimated by dividing the actual observed value by the new smoothed average, or A_t/S_t. This new estimate of seasonality is then averaged with the old seasonality factor, using a third smoothing constant γ:

$$Q_t = \gamma \frac{A_t}{S_t} + (1 - \gamma) Q_{t-L}$$

The forecast for period $t + 1$ is similar to that for the trend-adjusted model except that the seasonality factor appropriate for period $t + 1$ is multiplied by the sum of the new smoothed average and trend:

$$T_{t+1} = (S_t + T_t) Q_{t-L+1}$$

It is important to note that the seasonality factor used in calculating the forecast for period $t + 1$ is not the new smoothed seasonality factor Q_t just calculated. Actually the forecast uses a seasonality factor calculated $L - 1$ periods ago. For example, if $t = 12$ represents December, the forecast for January, $t + 1 = 13$, would use the seasonal factor for the previous January, $Q_1(t - L + 1 = 12 - 12 + 1 = 1)$. The seasonality factor just calculated for December will be used the next time we attempt to forecast for December.

Illustration of Calculations Table 18-10 illustrates the calculations required to use the Winters model for the data in Table 18-9. We have assumed the initial smoothed quarterly factors are the same as the fixed seasonality factors used in the previous example. Parameter values of $\alpha = .3$, $\beta = .2$, and $\gamma = .9$ were used.

The forecast for period 1 will use the quarterly factor $Q_{1-l} = Q_{1-4} = Q_{-3}$ and is found by

$$F_1 = (S_0 + T_0) Q_{-3}$$
$$= (90 + 10) .9 = 90$$

Then we update the smoothed values using the actual observation of 90 for period 1

$$S_1 = .3\left(\frac{A_1}{Q_{-3}}\right) + .7 (S_0 + T_0)$$

$$= .3\left(\frac{90}{.9}\right) + .7 (90 + 10) = 100$$

$$T_1 = .2 (S_1 - S_0) + .8 T_0$$
$$= .2 (100 - 90) + .8(10) = 10$$

$$Q_1 = .9\left(\frac{A_1}{S_1}\right) + .1 (Q_{-3})$$

$$= .9\left(\frac{90}{100}\right) + .1 (.9) = .9$$

The remaining calculations are performed in a similar manner.

TABLE 18-10
Use of Trend- and Seasonally Adjusted Exponential Smoothing Model
($\alpha = .3$, $\beta = .2$, and $\gamma = .9$)

Period	Actual observation	F_t	Q_{t-L}	S_t	T_t	Q_t	Q_{t-L+1}
−3						.9	
−2						1.15	
−1						1.20	
0				90	10	.75	.9
1	90	90	.9	100	10	.9	1.15
2	128	126.5	1.15	110.4	10.1	1.16	1.20
3	144	144.6	1.20	120.4	10.1	1.20	.75
4	97	97.9	.75	130.2	10.0	.75	.9
5	128	126.2	.9	140.8	10.1	.91	1.16
6	171	175.0	1.16	149.9	9.9	1.14	1.20
7	181	191.8	1.20	157.1	9.4	1.16	.75
8	122	124.9	.75	165.4	9.2	.74	.91

INSTANT REPLAY Suppose we are using a trend- and seasonally adjusted exponential smoothing model with $\alpha = .1$, $\beta = .2$, and $\gamma = .5$ and monthly seasonality factors that include Dec = 1.10, Jan = 1.12, and Feb = 1.20. After the actual observation for November was known, the model was used to derive $S_{\text{Nov}} = 30.7$, $T_{\text{Nov}} = 6.1$, and $Q_{\text{Nov}} = 1.05$. What would be your forecast for December? If the actual observation for December is 45.7, what would be your forecast for January?

CHECK $F_{\text{Dec}} = 1.1(30.7 + 6.1) = 40.5$, $S_{\text{Dec}} = .1(45.7/1.1) + .9(30.7 + 6.1) = 37.3$, $T_{\text{Dec}} = .2(37.3 - 30.7) + .8(6.1) = 6.2$, and $F_{\text{Jan}} = 1.12(37.3 + 6.2) = 48.7$.

Drift in Seasonal Factors One of the difficulties of the Winters model is that as the seasonal factors are smoothed to reflect new observations, the average seasonal factor tends to drift away from 1.0. To illustrate this seasonal drift, the average of the *initial* seasonal factors is seen to be 1.0 for the example problem:

$$\frac{.9 + 1.15 + 1.20 + .75}{4} = 1.0$$

After eight periods of updating and smoothing, although none of the seasonality factors had evidenced much change, their average is now less than 1.0:

$$\frac{.91 + 1.14 + 1.16 + .74}{4} = \frac{3.95}{4} = .9875$$

The degree of such drift is influenced by changes in the trend or seasonal patterns as well as random fluctuations, and if left unchecked can be rather substantial. To avoid forecasting errors due to this drift, it is normally advisable to renormalize the seasonal factors periodically by dividing each by the current average seasonal factor. Thus, for our example (above) the revised seasonal factors would be

$$\frac{.91}{.9875} = .92 \qquad \frac{1.14}{.9875} = 1.15 \qquad \frac{1.16}{.9875} = 1.18 \qquad \frac{.74}{.9875} = .75$$

These adjusted seasonal factors now average to 1.0:

$$\frac{.92 + 1.15 + 1.18 + .75}{4} = 1.0$$

Adaptive Exponential Smoothing   As pointed out previously, one of the critical problems for a forecasting method is to enable it to react quickly to real changes in pattern and yet not react to, but to smooth, random fluctuations. We saw that low values of α did a good job of smoothing, while higher values of α did a better job reacting to pattern changes.

Although all the models we have heretofore considered have required a specific choice of fixed smoothing constants, there is another class of exponential smoothing models which offers the advantage of variable smoothing constants. These models are referred to as adaptive exponential smoothing models in that the smoothing constants are adapted or changed as conditions suggest.

By adapting the smoothing constant the models can use low values for α until the strength and direction of the forecast errors suggest that the smoothing constants need to be increased, at least temporarily, to correct for an apparent pattern change. Some adaptive models use a continually changing smoothing constant while others change periodically or after one or more forecast errors have exceeded prespecified control limits.

Our coverage will be limited to one of the continuous change models in which the α or *smoothing constant is based on the tracking signal,* a concept introduced earlier in this chapter. Although we will concern ourselves only with a simple adaptive model, the approach followed can be applied to trend- and seasonally adjusted models as well.

The basic smoothing equations are similar to those for the nonadaptive case. The key difference is that the smoothing constant now carries a subscript to indicate that it is recalculated each period. Thus our basic equations are

$$S_t = \alpha_t A_t + (1 - \alpha_t) S_{t-1}$$

$$F_{t+1} = S_t$$

The smoothing constant α_t is set equal to the current tracking signal, although the tracking signal is defined somewhat differently than before. Previously we defined the tracking signal, based on n observations to be

$$TS_n = \frac{\sum\limits_{i=1}^{n} e_i}{\sum\limits_{i=1}^{n} |e_i|}$$

Rather than use a sum of the errors for the numerator and a sum of the absolute errors for the denominator, we can define a new tracking signal in which the numerator is *smoothed average error* and the denominator is *smoothed average absolute error* (smoothed MAD). If E_t is smoothed error at time t,

$$E_t = \beta e_t + (1 - \beta) E_{t-1}$$

and if M_t is the smoothed absolute error at time t, it is similarly defined as

$$M_t = \beta\,|e_t| + (1 - \beta)\,M_{t-1}$$

The value of α to be used in updating the smoothed average S_t is equal to the absolute value of this adjusted tracking signal, or

$$\alpha_t = \left|\frac{E_t}{M_t}\right|$$

Table 18-11 summarizes the calculations required for this model for eight periods of hypothetical data. The initial value of .2 was used for α as well as the fixed value for β, and S_0 was assumed to be 100. Thus the initial forecast is $F_1 = 100$ and the forecast error for period 1 is

$$e_1 = 102 - 100 = 2$$

Smoothed error and smoothed absolute error are then calculated:

$$E_1 = .2e_1 + .8E_0$$

$$= .2(2.0) + .8(0) = .4$$

$$M_1 = .2\,|e_1| + .8\,M_0$$

$$= .2(2.0) + .8(0) = .4$$

Since the first smoothed error will always equal the first smoothed absolute error (assuming both are initialized at zero), we do not use the tracking signal value (which will be 1.0) but instead use some initially specified α value, which was defined above to be .2. This value, which is used simply to get things started, will be used only until $|E_t/M_t| < 1.0$. Therefore, we find

$$S_1 = .2(102) + .8(100) = 100.4$$

$$F_2 = S_1 = 100.4$$

The observed value for period 2 was 99; so we can update our smoothed error factors:

TABLE 18-11
Illustration of Adaptive Simple Exponential Smoothing Model ($\beta = .2$)

Period	Actual observation	Forecast F_t	Error e_t	Smoothed error E_t	Smoothed absolute error M_t	α_t	S_t
0						.2*	100
1	102	100	2.0	.40	.40	.2*	100.4
2	99	100.4	−1.4	.04	.60	.07	100.3
3	115	100.3	14.7	2.97	3.42	.87	113.1
4	114	113.1	.9	2.56	2.92	.88	113.9
5	113	113.9	− .9	1.87	2.52	.75	113.2
6	111	113.2	−2.2	1.06	2.46	.44	112.2
7	109	112.2	−3.2	.27	2.61	.08	111.9
8	114	111.9	2.1	.59	2.51	.24	112.4

*Initial α set at .2 and not changed until $|E_t/M_t| < 1.0$.

$$e_2 = 99 - 100.4 = -1.4$$

$$E_2 = .2(-1.4) + .8(.4) = .04$$

$$M_2 = .2|-1.4| + .8(.4) = .60$$

$$\alpha_2 = \left|\frac{.04}{.60}\right| = .07$$

Therefore, $F_3 = S_2 = .07(99) + .93(100.4) = 100.3$

Until now the forecast errors have been rather small, resulting in a low value for α. However, in period 3 the pattern in the observed series appears to shift up suddenly. This is immediately reflected in the error factors resulting in a high α value:

$$e_3 = 115 - 100.3 = 14.7$$

$$E_3 = .2(14.7) + .8(.04) = 2.97$$

$$M_3 = .2(14.7) + .8(.60) = 3.42$$

$$\alpha_3 = \left|\frac{2.97}{3.42}\right| = .87$$

The high α results in the new forecast being based much more heavily on the most recent actual observation and less on past values in an attempt to correct for the high error.

$$F_4 = S_3 = .87(115) + .13(100.3) = 113.1$$

As will be seen from Table 18-11, the high α value remains for one more period before starting to drift slowly back toward lower values. Also note that the forecast reacted very quickly to the apparent change in pattern. Therefore, this is an effective method when significant changes are likely to occur in the time series being forecast.

INSTANT REPLAY   If the next observed value for the series in Table 18-11 is 111 (period 9), what will be the new α value and forecast for period 10?

CHECK $e_9 = -1.4$, $E_9 = .19$, $M_9 = 2.29$, $\alpha_9 = .08$, and $F_{10} = 112.3$.

Final Comments

Forecasting is an important problem that touches all types of organizations and managers. Forecasts provide the central framework upon which organizational plans are built, analyzed, and changed. Many decisions, short-range as well as long-range, must necessarily be based on one or more forecasts. It should be clear that better plans and better decisions can be made if the forecasts and predictions on which they are based can be made more accurate.

Two chapters have been devoted to demonstrating how management science models can be used to improve the forecasting process. This first chapter has examined the role of forecasting, the steps to be followed in developing good forecasting models, the means by which forecasting models can be evaluated, and a class of forecasting models called extrapolation models.

Extrapolation models are normally quite easy to use. This is because the only data required are a set of past history for the variable to be forecast. Each extrapolation model assumes that the past data, and also the future data, follow a specific pattern. For instance, the simple exponential smoothing model assumes that the data are stable and require only a smoothing of random fluctuations. Trend-adjusted models assume that the data are following a trend. Trend- and seasonally adjusted models assume that both trend and seasonal factors are present. It is important for the manager to realize that the appropriate model must be chosen to fit the characteristics of the variable being forecast. The simple exponential smoothing model, for example, will not perform well if the data have trend or seasonal influences.

Two types of extrapolation models were considered: moving average models and exponential smoothing models. Moving average models base the forecast on an equal- or unequal-weighted average of past observations. Exponential smoothing models use an exponentially weighted average. Several variations of exponential smoothing models can be used, depending on whether the data are stable, have a trend, are seasonally influenced, or are subject to pattern shifts.

The choice of extrapolation model depends to a great extent on the type of data being forecast. If frequent forecasts of numerous items are required, such as would be the case for a large inventory system, exponential smoothing models are often used. This is because exponential smoothing is computationally economical and, once initialized, self-perpetuating. Many inventory systems incorporate exponential smoothing models to provide forecasts automatically. Where the forecasting requirements are less frequent or numerous, the choice is not as clear. It may be necessary, in this case, to experiment with a variety of approaches to see which is more accurate.

Chapter 19 considers explanatory forecasting models. These models are not as easy to use as extrapolation models because they require the identification of relationships between the variable to be forecast and other, explanatory, variables. This also increases the data-gathering costs. Nevertheless, explanatory models offer policy testing capabilities in addition to providing forecasts. That is, an explanatory model, because it assumes an explanatory relationship, can be used to test the effects of changes in policy variables (e.g., advertising expenditures) on the variable to be forecast (e.g., sales).

Key Words

Problems

18-1. Two forecasting models, A and B, have been used to provide forecasts for a particular time series as shown below.

Actual observation	Forecast (model A)	Forecast (model B)
100	99.5	100
104	104.3	105
111	109.2	110
118	114.3	115
119	119.8	120
125	124.6	125
130	129.2	130
134	133.9	135

Compare the effectiveness of the two models using the following evaluation measures: (a) bias, (b) MAD, (c) MSE, (d) correlation.

18-2. For the demand and forecast data shown below, compute the tracking signal for each period. Assuming that the tracking signal control limits are $\pm .50$, at what point does the tracking signal indicate the model is out of control?

Period	1	2	3	4	5
Demand	10	11	10	15	16
Forecast	11	10	10	10	13

18-3. The Knit-wit Textile Company wishes to forecast demand for a new fabric that they recently introduced. Demand for the first 8 weeks is shown below. One forecasting model that they are considering is the equal-weighted moving average method. Compare the forecast effectiveness of a two-period moving average with that of a three-period model.

Period	1	2	3	4	5	6	7	8
Demand	10.4	13.3	14.1	16.2	18.1	20.2	20.3	19.1

18-4. The Knit-wit Textile Company (problem 18-3) is also considering using an un-equal-weighted moving average model. Compare the performance of a two-period weighted moving average model with weights of .7 (most recent) and .3 (oldest) with that of the equal-weighted models in problem 18-3.

18-5. Another model under consideration by the Knit-wit Textile Company is simple exponential smoothing. Using the data of problem 18-3, compare the forecasting effectiveness of simple exponential smoothing models with αs of .2 and .6. Assume an initial smoothed average of 10 in each case.

18-6. One official of the Knit-wit Textile Company has observed an apparent trend in the data for the new fabric (problem 18-3) and suggests that a trend-adjusted exponential smoothing model be tested. Using $\alpha = .3$, $\beta = .2$, an initial smoothed average of 8, and an initial smoothed trend of 2, determine the forecasts for a trend-adjusted exponential smoothing model using the data shown in problem 18-3. Compare this model's effectiveness with that for the simple models of problem 18-5.

18-7. Because of the uncertainty of the demand pattern experienced by a new product, the Knit-wit Textile Company (problem 18-3) is also considering the use of an adaptive simple exponential smoothing model. Assuming an initial smoothed average of 10, smoothing constants of .3 for smoothed error and smoothed MAD, initial smoothed error of 0, and initial smoothed MAD of 0, determine the adaptive forecasts for the 8 periods of data shown in problem 18-3. Use $\alpha = .2$ until $\alpha_t < 1.0$.

18-8. The management of *Starburst,* a quarterly science fiction magazine, is concerned with the problem of determining the best size for the press run of *Starburst.* If more copies are produced than can be sold, the cost of the excess copies must be absorbed by *Starburst.* On the other hand, too few copies produced represents lost sales and hence lost profits. The management of *Starburst* hopes that exponential smoothing can be used to forecast demand accurately so that the correct press run size can be determined. Because of the seasonal nature of newsstand sales and the annual growth in demand experienced, the company wishes to use the Winters seasonally and trend-adjusted model. Determine the forecasts that would have resulted for the past 2 years (actual sales in thousands, shown below), assuming an initial smoothed average of 6.3, initial smoothed trend of .2, initial smoothed seasonal factors of .80 (Q1), 1.00, 1.05, and 1.15 (Q4), and smoothing constants of $\alpha = .2$, $\beta = .2$, and $\gamma = .4$. What would your quarterly forecasts be for the coming year using this model?

Year	Q1	Q2	Q3	Q4
1978	5.3	6.2	6.6	7.4
1979	6.1	7.3	7.9	8.6

18-9. Suppose that the management of *Starburst* (problem 18-8) had felt that the seasonal factors were likely to remain stable at .80 (Q1), 1.00, 1.05, and 1.15 (Q4). In this event they could use a trend-adjusted exponential smoothing model with deseasonalized data. What would the forecasts have been for this model using the data of problem 18-8 and the quarterly factors stated above? Assume an initial smoothed average of 6.3, an initial trend of .2, and smoothing constants of $\alpha = .3$ and $\beta = .1$. Contrast the results of this model with those found in problem 18-8 for the Winters model.

19

Explanatory Forecasting Models

The emphasis with extrapolation models, as discussed in Chapter 18, was the development of good forecasts of future events based on past observations. The models developed provide very little explanatory power in that they do not explain why a particular forecast is valid or why a particular result is expected. On the other hand, *explanatory forecasting models,* to be considered in this chapter, attempt to develop logical relationships that not only provide useful forecasts but identify the causes and factors that determine why a particular forecast value is expected.

This chapter will begin with a brief discussion of how we can identify explanatory factors, or variables, for use in explanatory forecasting models. Then it will examine a major class of explanatory models called *regression models.* A regression model specifies that the variable to be forecast is a function of one or more explanatory variables. Regression models are quite general and can be applied in a wide variety of situations. For instance, we might develop a sales forecasting regression model that uses knowledge of product price and advertising expenditure to determine or predict the expected sales volume. Alternatively, we might develop a regression model based on the fact that production volume has a direct impact on production costs. This relationship could be exploited to project production costs for the following year based on planned production volume.

The chapter concludes with a more specific category of explanatory models called *Markovian models.* These models have been applied most frequently to predicting market shares for competing products. Given knowledge of the current market share for each competing brand and certain assumptions about the brand switching behavior of customers, a Markovian model can be used to forecast future market shares.

Each explanatory model uses information concerning other factors to predict the variable in question. One of the critical decisions to be made with an explanatory model is the selection or identification of those factors that are likely to have an effect on the variable being forecast. For example, suppose we are developing an explanatory model to predict demand for a product. This requires identification of those factors that will have a material effect on demand. Many factors, such as the price, advertising, and number of salespeople, for a product and for its competitors can be included in the model. Determining which of these should be included is not always easy.

For one thing, there is a tendency to include too many *explanatory variables* in a model of this sort. The rationale for this approach is that a variable should be included in the model if it has any possible relationship with the variable to be forecast. Although this may be acceptable for forecasting purposes, inclusion of all variables that might improve the forecast results in a model without much real explanatory power.

Not only must we be concerned with the choice of explanatory variables but we also must determine the timing of the effects of the explanatory variables on the variable being forecast. The effect of advertising on sales is not usually an immediate impact. Advertising expenditures in one period often have a delayed impact on sales in future periods. In other words, to forecast sales for the coming period, we may need to include, as explanatory variables, not only projected advertising expenditures for the coming period but also the expenditures in recent periods as well. Thus we often speak of *lagged effects* of explanatory variables. Estimating the size of the lag adds another level of complication to the development of explanatory models.

Nevertheless, the existence of lagged effects does have positive benefits. For example, we might determine that some explanatory variable will affect the size of the variable we are trying to forecast after a 2-month delay (e.g., sales in March are affected by advertising expenditures in January). We can use this lagged relationship to forecast sales 2 months ahead. In this sense, we often refer to such explanatory variables as *leading indicators*.

As may already be apparent, the major advantage of an explanatory model is that it can be used to set policy in order to push the variable being forecast in some desired direction. To illustrate, if we have a model that allows us to forecast sales on the basis of price and advertising, it can be used for more than simply forecasting sales. The model in effect tells us what the expected impact on sales would be for selective changes in advertising or pricing policy.

Although we refer to the forecasting models examined in this chapter as explanatory models, we must caution the reader that the explanation provided by these models should not be construed as implying that the explanatory variables cause or explain why changes occur in the variable to be forecast. Indeed, all that should be implied is that there is an apparent relationship. The direction of this relationship, what causes what, can only be hypothesized. In other words, if a relationship can be found between two variables x and y, the reason for the observed relationship could be that x causes y or y causes x or that x and y are both influenced by some third variable z. Thus an increase in advertising could cause an increase in sales, or an increase in sales could lead to higher levels of advertising, or a lower price could have led to higher sales and higher advertising expenditures (to let customers know of the lower price). Therefore, any explanations provided by explanatory forecasting models are those provided by the model builder or user to explain the measured relationship.

Regression Models

In this section we examine a class of models called regression models. These models assume that a *linear relationship* exists between one variable called the *dependent variable* and one or more other variables called *independent variables*. The dependent variable is the variable to be forecast and the independent variables are the explanatory variables. The first model we will examine assumes there is only one explanatory, or independent, variable. This type of model will be referred to as a *simple regression model*. This section will conclude by examining regression models with more than one independent variable. Such models are called *multiple regression models*.

Simple Regression Model

As described above, a simple regression model consists of one dependent and one independent variable which are assumed to be linearly related. Recall that a linear, or straight-line, relationship has the equation form

$$A = a + bX$$

In our terminology A represents the dependent variable, or variable to be forecast, and X is the independent, or explanatory, variable. Parameters a and b are used to define the specific relationship between A and X.

To illustrate, suppose the management of the Wright Can Opener Company is developing a model for forecasting production cost on the basis of projected production volume for its electric can opener. In this case, production cost would be the dependent variable and production volume would be the independent variable. The simple regression model defining the relationship between volume and cost would thus be

$$\text{Production cost} = a + b \text{ (production volume)}$$

If this model is to provide a good forecast of production cost, the relationship between volume and costs must be approximately linear. To test this relationship, production volume and cost data have been gathered for the past 10 months, as shown in Table 19-1.

The next step in testing the linear hypothesis is to plot the data, as shown in Figure 19-1. If the points, corresponding to the cost-volume relationship, do not fall approximately on a straight line, the linear hypothesis is not appropriate. In a later section we will examine certain steps that can be taken to transform a nonlinear relationship into a linear one. For our example, however, we note that the relationship is approximately linear with all the points lying close to the line shown.

Specifying Parameters Once the validity of the linear hypothesis has been confirmed, the next step is to identify the precise form of the relationship. This is done by specifying values for parameters a and b, which, in turn, identify a specific straight line. It should be obvious that any number of straight lines can be hypothetically selected to describe the relationship between A and X. We need to establish a means by which one straight line can be judged better than

TABLE 19-1
Historical Production Volume and Cost Data
for the Wright Can Opener Company

Month	Actual production cost (A)	Actual production volume (X)
1	$48,600	4,400
2	51,700	4,800
3	51,800	5,000
4	46,900	4,200
5	49,100	4,600
6	54,200	5,300
7	59,500	5,800
8	49,700	4,700
9	56,400	5,500
10	54,800	5,200

all others. Although many criteria exist, the one almost universally used is to select the straight line that minimizes MSE (the mean squared error). An error, in this case, is defined as the distance between any observed value of the dependent variable and the value forecast by the straight line. Figure 19-2 illustrates this measurement for a simple example with five observations. For each

FIGURE 19-1 Plot of relationship between production volume and cost for Wright Can Opener Company.

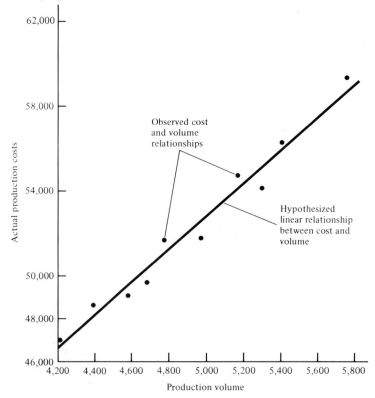

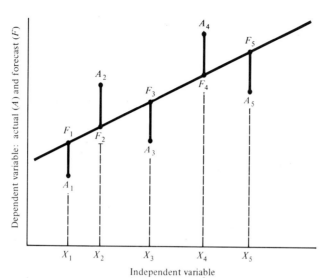

FIGURE 19-2 Forecast errors as measured for simple linear regression.

of the five observations A_i, there is a corresponding forecast value F_i. The difference between A_i and F_i is the forecast error. We wish to choose parameters a and b for our straight line to minimize the average squared forecast error. Based on this criterion, it is not difficult to see why this method is known as the *method of least squares*.

This method uses two equations for calculating the values of a and b that minimize the MSE. They are

$$b = \frac{n \sum_{i=1}^{n} X_i A_i - \sum_{i=1}^{n} X_i \sum_{i=1}^{n} A_i}{n \sum_{i=1}^{n} X_i^2 - \left(\sum_{i=1}^{n} X_i \right)^2}$$

$$a = \overline{A} - b\overline{X}$$

where $\overline{A}$ and $\overline{X}$ are the mean values for A and X, respectively.

To illustrate, we return to the Wright Can Opener example of Table 19-1. From our equations for finding a and b we note that we need to find the sum of the products of X and A ($\Sigma X_i A_i$), the sum of the Xs (ΣX_i), the sum of the As (ΣA_i), and the sum of the squares of the Xs (ΣX_i^2). These calculations are shown in Table 19-2, where X refers to the production volume and A to production cost. Parameter b can then be found from

$$b = \frac{n \Sigma X_i A_i - \Sigma X_i \Sigma A_i}{n \Sigma X_i^2 - (\Sigma X_i)^2}$$

$$= \frac{10(2,604,950,000) - (49,500)(522,700)}{10(247,310,000) - (49,500)^2}$$

$$= \frac{175,850,000}{22,850,000} = 7.6958 \approx 7.7$$

Having found b, we can now determine parameter a:

$$a = \overline{A} - b\overline{X}$$

$$= 52,270 - 7.7(4,950) = 14,155$$

The linear equation that minimizes MSE for our example problem is

$$F = 14{,}155 + 7.7X$$

Forecasting The regression equation says, in effect, that monthly production cost for the Wright Can Opener Company is equivalent to $14,155 plus $7.70 for each can opener produced. This equation can be used to predict production costs for any projected production volume. Suppose, for example, that Wright management is planning on a production volume of 5,500 can openers during the coming month. Production costs can be forecast by substituting the 5,500 volume for X in the regression equation:

$$\text{Production cost} = F = \$14{,}155 + \$7.70X$$

$$= \$14{,}155 + \$7.70\,(5{,}500) = \$56{,}505$$

INSTANT REPLAY The owner of the Babcock Plumbing Supply Company feels that sales are strongly related to the number of new construction permits issued. To test this hypothesis, the following set of observations were obtained for the most recent 6 months:

Plumbing sales, thousands of dollars	New construction permits
30	100
38	121
42	130
40	118
28	94
25	90

Determine the least-squares equation with plumbing sales as the dependent variable and construction permits as the independent variable. Suppose that a total of 1,500 new construction permits are projected for the coming year. What level of plumbing sales would your model forecast?

CHECK $\Sigma A = 203$, $\Sigma X = 653$, $\Sigma AX = 22{,}660$, $\Sigma X^2 = 72{,}401$. The least squares equation is $F = -12.421 + .425X$. Plumbing sales are projected at $625,079 for 1,500 new construction permits.

Interpreting Parameters At this point it is beneficial to consider the interpretation of the two parameters a and b. The linear relationship assumes that the dependent variable (here production cost) is determined solely by the independent variable (production volume). If production volume is zero, the forecast equation predicts that production costs will be $14,155. In economic terms, the $14,155 is equivalent to fixed production costs, or those costs that are unaffected by volume. Parameter b is directly multiplied by the production volume and is thus equivalent to the per-unit variable production costs.

For the Wright Can Opener Company problem there is a definite eco-

TABLE 19-2
Derivation of Simple Linear Regression Parameters for Wright Can Opener Problem
Using the Method of Least Squares

Dependent variable (production cost) A_i	Independent variable (production volume) X_i	A_iX_i	X_i^2
48,600	4,400	213,840,000	19,360,000
51,700	4,800	248,160,000	23,040,000
51,800	5,000	259,000,000	25,000,000
46,900	4,200	196,980,000	17,640,000
49,100	4,600	225,860,000	21,160,000
54,200	5,300	287,260,000	28,090,000
59,500	5,800	345,100,000	33,640,000
49,700	4,700	233,590,000	22,090,000
56,400	5,500	310,200,000	30,250,000
54,800	5,200	284,960,000	27,040,000
522,700	49,500	2,604,950,000	247,310,000
↑	↑	↑	↑
ΣA_i	ΣX_i	ΣA_iX_i	ΣX_i^2

$$\bar{A} = \frac{522,700}{10} = 52,270 \qquad \bar{X} = \frac{49,500}{10} = 4,950$$

nomic interpretation of parameter a that makes sense. In other cases, however, the use of parameter a is unjustifiable in any realistic form. For example, suppose we were attempting to specify a relationship between the number of customers served (dependent variable) and the number of tellers on duty (independent variable) for a bank. If our model included parameter a, its value would represent the number of customers that could be served with no tellers on duty. This interpretation is, of course, inconsistent with reality. When situations such as this present themselves, the model should be modified to omit the a parameter:

$$A = bX$$

The optimal value for b is computed using

$$b = \frac{\sum_{i=1}^{n} X_iA_i}{\sum_{i=1}^{n} X_i^2}$$

Note that the relationships assumed for the two forecasting situations discussed above, between production cost and production volume, on the one hand, and customers served and tellers on duty, on the other hand, are intuitively obvious. Using regression to determine the precise form of these relationships makes sense because the implied relationship is easily seen. However, regression can provide ridiculous results when it is used for relationships with unknown or nonobvious links. This topic will be discussed further in a later section, where we examine more closely the assumptions and problems related to the use of linear regression.

Previously we have examined situations in which the dependent variable was assumed to be predictable in terms of a single independent variable. Frequently one independent variable is not enough, and several independent variables are found to influence the dependent variable. This section will extend our analysis to include regression models with more than one independent variable, or multiple regression models.

If A is the variable to be forecast and $X_1, X_2, \ldots$ are the independent or explanatory variables, the multiple regression forecasting model assumes the relationship between these variables is of the general form

$$A = a + b_1 X_1 + b_2 X_2 + \cdots$$

where $a, b_1, b_2, \ldots$ are the model parameters.

The caution raised earlier concerning the explanatory ability of regression models must be particularly emphasized when dealing with multiple regression models. Multiple regression models assume that the effect of each explanatory variable is independent of the others and that the combined effect is the sum of the independent effects. Because of these assumptions, we need to use restraint in attributing causation with such models.

To illustrate the development of a multiple regression model, suppose the product manager for Glowteeth toothpaste is interested in determining the effects of promotional effort on sales. Data have been gathered for sales, magazine advertising, and television advertising for each of the last 12 months, as shown in Table 19-3.

The use of multiple regression to explain the relationship of sales to promotional spending is defined by the following model:

$$S = a + bM + cT$$

where S is monthly sales in units, M is magazine advertising in thousands of dollars, T is television advertising in thousands of dollars, and a, b, and c are

TABLE 19-3
Sales and Advertising Expenditure Data for Glowteeth Toothpaste

Month	*Dependent variable* *Observed sales, thousands of units*	*Independent variables* *Magazine advertising, thousands of dollars*	*Television advertising, thousands of dollars*
January	540	100	190
February	600	110	170
March	630	140	150
April	700	160	140
May	750	200	130
June	720	170	130
July	690	130	150
August	670	120	180
September	630	100	210
October	720	120	240
November	850	150	220
December	1,020	180	250

ROW	SALES	MAGADS	TVADS	
* 1 *	540.	100.	190.	
* 2 *	600.	110.	170.	
* 3 *	630.	140.	150.	
* 4 *	700.	160.	140.	
* 5 *	750.	200.	130.	
* 6 *	720.	170.	130.	Summary of input data
* 7 *	690.	130.	150.	
* 8 *	670.	120.	180.	
* 9 *	630.	100.	210.	
* 10 *	720.	120.	240.	
* 11 *	850.	150.	220.	
* 12 *	1020.	180.	250.	

	SALES	MAGADS	TVADS	
SALES	1.000			Table of simple correlation coefficients
MAGADS	0.678	1.000		
TVADS	0.443	−0.285	1.000	

MULTIPLE R	R—SQUARE	
0.948	0.900	Multiple correlation coefficient R and coefficient of determination R^2

FIGURE 19-3   Selected output for computerized multiple regression analysis of Glowteeth toothpaste sales and advertising data.

the parameters to be estimated that define the relationship between sales and advertising.

Specifying Parameters   The least-squares method is used to determine the values of the parameters, as it was for simple regression, regardless of the number of independent variables. Unfortunately, the mathematics becomes much more complex as more variables are added and normally requires the use of a computer. Figure 19-3 is typical of the output for a computerized multiple regression program. The data used by the program are those reported in Table 19-3 for Glowteeth toothpaste.

   In order to gain an understanding of the basics involved, the example problem will be solved without the aid of a computer. Although the specific procedures followed by the computer may vary from those shown here, the principles involved are the same and apply to 20 independent variables just as much as they do to 2 independent variables.

   For multiple regression problems, the method of least squares uses a set of *basic balance equations* to solve for the optimal (minimum MSE) parameters for multiple variables. The equations to be solved, in terms of our model, using variables S, M, and T as previously defined, are

$$\Sigma S = na + b\Sigma M + c\Sigma T$$

$$\Sigma SM = a\Sigma M + b\Sigma M^2 + c\Sigma MT$$

$$\Sigma ST = a\Sigma T + b\Sigma MT + c\Sigma T^2$$

Note that for each of the variables, sales S, magazine advertising M, and television advertising T, we require the sum of the values (ΣS, ΣM, and ΣT), the sum of the squares for the independent variables (ΣM^2 and ΣT^2), and the sum of the products of each pair of variables (ΣMT, ΣSM, and ΣST). Table 19-4 shows the calculations necessary to provide these sums. As shown, we find $\Sigma S = 8,520$, $\Sigma M = 1,680$, $\Sigma T = 2,160$, $\Sigma M^2 = 246,800$, $\Sigma T^2 = 408,400$, $\Sigma MT = 298,100$, $\Sigma SM = 1,223,200$, and $\Sigma ST = 1,559,400$. Substituting these values leads to

$$8,520 = \quad 12a + \quad 1,680b + \quad 2,160c$$
$$1,223,200 = 1,680a + 246,800b + 298,100c$$
$$1,559,400 = 2,160a + 298,100b + 408,400c$$

This yields three equations and three unknowns (a, b, and c). The three unknowns can be found by solving these equations simultaneously. Although sophisticated computer techniques exist for solving simultaneous equations, one method that can be used manually is to eliminate variables successively by multiplying one equation by a constant and then adding that equation to or subtracting it from another. For instance, note that the coefficient for a in the second equation (1,680) is $1,680/12 = 140$ times as large as the coefficient for a in the first equation (12). We can therefore eliminate variable a by multiplying the first equation by 140 and subtracting it from the second:

$$1,223,200 = 1,680a + 246,800b + 298,100c$$
$$-[1,192,800 = 1,680a + 235,200b + 302,400c]$$
$$30,400 = \qquad\qquad 11,600b - \quad 4,300c$$

Next we can combine the first and third equations. The coefficient of a in the third equation is 2,160 and in the first equation is 12. Dividing 2,160 by 12, we

TABLE 19-4
Calculations Necessary to Determine Parameters for Multiple Regression for Glowteeth Toothpaste

	Sales	Magazine advertising		Television advertising				
	S	M	M^2	T	T^2	MT	SM	ST
1	540	100	10,000	190	36,100	19,000	54,000	102,600
2	600	110	12,100	170	28,900	18,700	66,000	102,000
3	630	140	19,600	150	22,500	21,000	88,200	94,500
4	700	160	25,600	140	19,600	22,400	112,000	98,000
5	750	200	40,000	130	16,900	26,000	150,000	97,500
6	720	170	28,900	130	16,900	22,100	122,400	93,600
7	690	130	16,900	150	22,500	19,500	89,700	103,500
8	670	120	14,400	180	32,400	21,600	80,400	120,600
9	630	100	10,000	210	44,100	21,000	63,000	132,300
10	720	120	14,400	240	57,600	28,800	86,400	172,800
11	850	150	22,500	220	48,400	33,000	127,500	187,000
12	1,020	180	32,400	250	62,500	45,000	183,600	255,000
	8,520	1,680	246,800	2,160	408,400	298,100	1,223,200	1,559,400
	ΣS	ΣM	ΣM^2	ΣT	ΣT^2	ΣMT	ΣSM	ΣST

see that multiplying the first equation by 180 will give identical coefficients for a so that subtracting the first from the third will eliminate a.

$$1,559,400 = 2,160a + 298,100b + 408,400c$$
$$-[1,533,600 = 2,160a + 302,400b + 388,800c]$$
$$25,800 = \qquad -4,300b + 19,600c$$

We now have two equations with two unknowns b and c. This time suppose we choose to eliminate variable c. The coefficient of c is $-4,300$ in one equation and $19,600$ in the other. If we multiply the first of these by $-19,600/4,300$, both equations will have a coefficient for c of $19,600$. Subtracting one from the other will thus eliminate variable c:

$$25,800 = -4,300 \; b + 19,600c$$
$$-[-138,567.4 = -52,874.4b + 19,600c]$$
$$164,367.4 = 48,574.4b$$

We now have an equation with one unknown which can easily be solved:

$$b = \frac{164,367.4}{48,574.4} = 3.384$$

Having found one variable, we can now retrace our steps to obtain the values of the remaining parameters. We can use either of our two-parameter equations to solve for b. Thus, using the first,

$$4,300c = 11,600b - 30,400$$
$$c = \frac{11,600(3.384) - 30,400}{4,300} = 2.059$$

Finally, we can substitute the values for b and c in any of the original three-parameter equations to solve for a. Using the first,

$$12a = 8,520 - 1,680b - 2,160c$$
$$a = \frac{8,520 - 1,680(3.384) - 2,160(2.059)}{12} = -134.38$$

Thus all three parameters have been found and the multiple regression equation is

$$S = -134.38 + 3.384M + 2.059T$$

INSTANT REPLAY   What would have been the least-squares equation if we had used only the first four observations in Table 19-4 to fit the parameters?

CHECK   The least-squares equation is

$$S = 785.078 + .939M - 1.768T$$

Forecasting   To use this model for forecasting purposes, we need only substitute the appropriate values for magazine and television advertising and then calculate the predicted value for sales. To illustrate, suppose the Glowteeth toothpaste product manager is considering an advertising plan that calls for magazine advertising of $170,000 and television advertising of $200,000. The sales forecast for this plan can be found by substituting the appropriate advertising expenditures in the multiple regression model:

$$S = -134.38 + 3.384(170) + 2.059(200)$$

$$= -134.38 + 575.28 + 411.80 = 852.70$$

This is equivalent to a predicted sales volume of 852,700 units. (Sales data were expressed in thousands.)

INSTANT REPLAY What would the projected sales volume be if the magazine and television advertising figures were reversed? In other words, $200,000 spent on magazine advertising and $170,000 on television advertising.

CHECK 892,450 units are projected.

We need to emphasize again that in practice one would use one of the many computer packages available to determine these parameters rather than relying on the manual approach followed here. Normally the computer packages provide many supplementary statistical measures that are useful in determining the significance and reliability of the relationship identified by regression. The next sections will examine these measures and their interpretation.

Interpreting Regression Results

Strength of Relationships

The least-squares method of determining parameters guarantees that no better-fitting set of parameters can be found (none with a lower MSE). However, it should be noted that a regression equation can be fitted to any set of data, whether or not a true relationship exists between the variables. What is needed, then, is some way of determining the strength of these relationships. Chapter 18 discussed a measure called *correlation,* which it was suggested could be used to determine how close a forecast fits actual observations. The same measure can be used to identify the strength of the relationship between any two variables. In this way, we can determine the correlation, or strength of the relationship, between the dependent variable and each independent variable.

Coefficients for Simple Regression Models The *correlation coefficient* for two variables x and y was defined in Chapter 18 as

$$r = \frac{\sum_{i=1}^{n} (x_i - \bar{x})(y_i - \bar{y}) \Big/ [n - 1]}{S_x S_y}$$

where S_x and S_y were defined as

$$S_x = \sqrt{\frac{\sum_{i=1}^{n} (x_i - \bar{x})^2}{n - 1}} \qquad S_y = \sqrt{\frac{\sum_{i=1}^{n} (y_i - \bar{y})^2}{n - 1}}$$

This is equivalent to dividing the *covariance* for the two variables by the product of their *standard deviations*. When used with regression, it is normally easier to calculate the correlation coefficient r based on the following formula, where A is the dependent variable and X is the independent variable:

$$r = \frac{n\Sigma XA - \Sigma X \Sigma A}{\sqrt{[n\Sigma X^2 - (\Sigma X)^2][n\Sigma A^2 - (\Sigma A)^2]}}$$

The factors included in this formulation are easily obtainable from the calculations required to determine the parameters (with the exception of the ΣA^2).

To illustrate, we previously determined that the regression equation for the Wright Can Opener Company production cost and volume data (Table 19-1) was

$$\text{Cost} = 14,155 + 7.7 \text{ (volume)}$$

In determining the parameters for this equation (Table 19-2), we found (letting X represent volume and A cost)

$$\Sigma X = 49,500 \qquad \Sigma X^2 = 247,310,000$$

$$\Sigma A = 522,700 \qquad \Sigma XA = 2,604,950,000$$

In order to calculate the correlation coefficient, we also need ΣA^2, which we provide here without detail as

$$\Sigma A^2 = 27,460,490,000$$

The correlation coefficient is then found by substitution:

$$r = \frac{n\Sigma XA - \Sigma X \Sigma A}{\sqrt{[n\Sigma X^2 - (\Sigma X)^2][n\Sigma A^2 - (\Sigma A)^2]}}$$

$$= \frac{10(2,604,950,000) - (49,500)(522,700)}{\sqrt{[10(247,310,000) - (49,500)^2][10(27,460,490,000) - (522,700)^2]}}$$

$$= \frac{175,850,000}{178,192,560.2} = .987$$

This high value for r (close to 1.0) implies that a very strong positive relationship exists between production cost and volume.

A similar measure, r^2, called the *coefficient of determination,* is calculated by squaring the correlation coefficient. This factor can also be calculated directly from

$$r^2 = \frac{\Sigma(F_i - \bar{A})^2}{\Sigma(A_i - \bar{A})^2}$$

where F_i is the forecast value based on a simple linear regression equation ($F_i = a + bX_i$), A_i is the observed value of the dependent variable corresponding to the independent variable X_i, and $\bar{A}$ is the observed mean for the dependent variable.

It is called the coefficient of determination because it represents the ratio of *explained variation* to *total variation* of the dependent variable, or the proportion of total variation that has been explained or determined by the model. Note that the total variation from the mean for a particular observation of the dependent variable is ($A_i - \bar{A}$). The variation not explained by the regression model is equivalent to $A_i - F_i$, the forecast error. The explained variation is the difference between total variation and the *unexplained variation* or

$$(A_i - \overline{A}) - (A_i - F_i) = A_i - \overline{A} - A_i + F_i = F_i - \overline{A}$$

Since our objective is to minimize the squared errors, or deviations, we square the individual variations and then sum them so that the ratio of explained to total variation can be determined.

The coefficient of determination r^2 can be easily found for the Wright Can Opener data by squaring the value for r that we found previously (.987). Thus,

$$r^2 = (.987)^2 = .974$$

This says that the linear regression model has explained 97.4 percent of the variation in the data, leaving only 2.6 percent unexplained.

INSTANT REPLAY In a preceding Instant Replay we found a regression equation relating plumbing sales to new construction permits. For convenience, the original data are repeated here:

Plumbing sales, thousands of dollars	New construction permits
30	100
38	121
42	130
40	118
28	94
25	90

Calculate the correlation coefficient and coefficient of determination for this model.

CHECK $r = .984$ and $r^2 = .968$.

Coefficients for Multiple Regression Models The correlation coefficient, as we have so far used it, is sometimes called the *simple correlation coefficient* because it refers to a simple linear regression model involving two variables. When we are dealing with a multiple linear regression model, by definition we are interested in the relationship among more than two variables. Nevertheless, we can still calculate simple correlation coefficients between any two variables in a multiple-variable model. To identify the simple correlation coefficients for any two variables correctly from among all those possible, we add a pair of subscripts to the correlation coefficient. Thus the simple correlation between variables x and y would be referred to as r_{xy}. If we had three variables of interest, one dependent and two independent, we could define three simple correlation coefficients. If these three variables are labeled w, x, and y, we can identify r_{wx}, r_{wy}, and r_{xy}. These would, respectively, measure the correlation between variables w and x, w and y, and x and y.

In addition to these simple correlation coefficients, we can define a combined correlation coefficient, called the *multiple correlation coefficient R*, which measures how well the multiple regression equation explains variation in the dependent variable. If y is the dependent variable and w and x are the independent variables, the multiple correlation coefficient would be computed using

$$R = \sqrt{\frac{r_{xy}^2 + r_{wy}^2 - 2r_{xy}\,r_{wy}\,r_{wx}}{1 - r_{wx}^2}}$$

The *coefficient of multiple determination* R^2, or the ratio of explained variation to total variation for the dependent variable, is found by squaring the multiple correlation coefficient.

To illustrate, refer again to the multiple regression model developed for Glowteeth toothpaste (Table 19-3) relating sales to expenditures for magazine and television advertising. To the calculations given in Table 19-4 we add the value for ΣS^2, which leads us to the following summary of information needed to calculate simple and multiple correlation coefficients:

$$\Sigma S = 8{,}520 \qquad \Sigma S^2 = 6{,}222{,}600$$

$$\Sigma M = 1{,}680 \qquad \Sigma M^2 = 246{,}800$$

$$\Sigma T = 2{,}160 \qquad \Sigma T^2 = 408{,}400$$

$$\Sigma MT = 298{,}100 \qquad \Sigma ST = 1{,}559{,}400$$

$$\Sigma SM = 1{,}223{,}200$$

The simple correlation coefficients would be calculated using the formula shown previously. For instance,

$$\begin{aligned}
r_{SM} &= \frac{n\Sigma SM - \Sigma M \Sigma S}{\sqrt{n[\Sigma S^2 - (\Sigma S)^2][n\Sigma M^2 - (\Sigma M)^2]}} \\[2mm]
&= \frac{12(1{,}223{,}200) - (1{,}680)(8{,}520)}{\sqrt{[12(6{,}222{,}600) - (8{,}520)^2][12(246{,}800) - (1{,}680)^2]}} \\[2mm]
&= \frac{364{,}800}{\sqrt{(2{,}080{,}800)(139{,}200)}} = .678
\end{aligned}$$

The others would be found in a similar manner.

$$r_{ST} = \frac{12(1{,}559{,}400) - (8{,}520)(2{,}160)}{\sqrt{[12(6{,}222{,}600) - (8{,}520)^2][12(408{,}400) - (2{,}160)^2]}} = .443$$

$$r_{MT} = \frac{12(298{,}100) - (1{,}680)(2{,}160)}{\sqrt{[12(246{,}800) - (1{,}680)^2][12(408{,}400) - (2{,}160)^2]}} = -.285$$

Finally, the multiple correlation coefficient R and the coefficient of determination would be calculated from

$$\begin{aligned}
R &= \sqrt{\frac{r_{SM}^2 + r_{ST}^2 - 2r_{SM}r_{ST}r_{MT}}{1 - r_{MT}^2}} \\[2mm]
&= \sqrt{\frac{(.678)^2 + (.443)^2 - 2(.678)(.443)(-.285)}{1 - (-.285)^2}} \\[2mm]
&= \sqrt{\frac{.827}{.919}} = \sqrt{.8999} = .949
\end{aligned}$$

and

$$R^2 = (.949)^2 = .901$$

Note that the combined effects of including both magazine and television advertising have a higher correlation to sales (.949) than does advertising for magazines (.678) or television (.443) taken individually. The low correlation $(-.285)$ between magazine and television advertising indicates that they are relatively independent. Furthermore, we note that the multiple regression model has explained 90 percent of the total variation.

INSTANT REPLAY   In an earlier Instant Replay we found a regression equation based only on the first four observations in Table 19-4. For convenience, we provide summary information related to those four observations here:

$$\Sigma S = \quad 2,470 \qquad \Sigma S^2 = 1,538,500$$

$$\Sigma M = \quad 510 \qquad \Sigma MT = \quad 81,100$$

$$\Sigma T = \quad 650 \qquad \Sigma SM = \quad 320,200$$

$$\Sigma M^2 = \quad 67,300 \qquad \Sigma ST = \quad 397,100$$

$$\Sigma T^2 = 107,100$$

Based on this information, determine each of the simple correlation coefficients, the multiple correlation coefficient, and the coefficient of determination.

CHECK $r_{SM} = .960, r_{ST} = -.966, r_{MT} = -.969, R = .975,$ and $R^2 = .951.$

Statistical Significance of Correlation   Regression analysis is a statistical approach in which we use a sample (the observed data) to estimate the true relationship among variables. The smaller the sample size the greater the likelihood that the measured correlation could be due to sampling error rather than a true relationship.

Fortunately, we have available a test of significance called the F test. This can be used to distinguish between statistically significant correlations and those due to sampling error. The F test consists of calculating an F statistic based on the coefficient of determination and the sample size and comparing this value with a critical value. Only if the F statistic exceeds the critical value can we conclude that the observed correlation is high enough to be called statistically significant.

The F *statistic* is calculated from

$$F = \frac{R^2/(k-1)}{(1-R^2)/(n-k)}$$

where R^2 is the coefficient of determination, k is the number of variables, and n is the number of observations or sample points. This calculated F statistic is then compared with the appropriate critical F value found in the Appendix of this chapter. If the calculated F statistic is less than the critical F value found in the table, we conclude that the observed correlation could have been entirely due to chance or sampling error, no matter how high the value of R or R^2. On the other hand, if the calculated F statistic exceeds the critical F value, we conclude that it is unlikely that the correlation coefficient we calculated is the result of chance. We therefore conclude that the regression result is believable, or significant.

Returning to our simple regression model relating Wright can opener production costs to volume, we note that we had 10 observations ($n = 10$), there were 2 variables ($k = 2$), and we found $R^2 = .974$. Thus the calculated F statistic would be

$$F = \frac{R^2/(k-1)}{(1-R^2)/(n-k)}$$

$$= \frac{.974/1}{(1-.974)/(10-2)} = 299.69$$

The critical F value to be used depends upon what are called the number of *degrees of freedom* for the numerator and the denominator (of the F statistic). These are simply $k - 1$ for the numerator and $n - k$ for the denominator. Thus, for the Wright can opener problem we find

$$\text{Degrees of freedom for numerator} = k - 1 = 2 - 1 = 1$$

$$\text{Degrees of freedom for denominator} = n - k = 10 - 2 = 8$$

Refer to the Appendix at the end of this chapter. Note that the columns correspond to degrees of freedom for the numerator and the rows represent the degrees of freedom for the denominator. Thus the *critical F value* for the Wright can opener situation is the table entry shown in column 1 and row 8. This tabular value is 5.32. Since our calculated F value (299.69) was considerably greater than the critical value, we conclude that the regression is significant (explained below).

Note that the table entries are based on a 95 percent confidence level. This can be interpreted as saying that for every 100 samples, we would expect the F statistic not to exceed the value shown approximately 95 times if in fact no true relationship exists ($R^2 = 0$). Thus when we obtain a calculated value that exceeds the critical value we are 95 percent confident that the regression is *significant*. There is a 5 percent chance that the tabulated correlation could have been due to chance. The more the calculated F statistic exceeds in size the table value, the greater is our confidence that the result is statistically significant.

For the Teethglow toothpaste multiple regression model we found $R^2 = .901$ with 12 observations ($n = 12$) and 3 variables ($k = 3$). This leads to a calculated F statistic of

$$F = \frac{.901/(3-1)}{(1-.901)/(12-3)} = 41.0$$

The critical F value obtained from the Appendix for $3 - 1 = 2$ and $12 - 3 = 9$ degrees of freedom in the numerator and denominator, respectively, is 4.26. Since the calculated value of 41.0 is considerably greater than the critical value, we conclude, in this case as previously, that we are 95 percent confident that the regression is significant.

The reader should be cautioned against attaching special meaning to a regression model solely on the basis of a high R or R^2. It is possible to have a high R^2 when the sample size is small even though there is no true relationship between variables. For instance, suppose for a two-variable model we found $R^2 = 0.70$ using four observations. The calculated F would be 4.67 while the critical F is 18.51. Clearly the calculated F is well below the critical F and any observed correlation could easily have been due to chance.

If regression is to be accurately and fairly used, it is important to understand some of the assumptions on which it is based. These assumptions include (1) the relationship between the dependent and independent variables is linear, (2) the variance of forecast errors is constant, (3) the forecast errors are independent of each other, and (4) the forecast errors are normally distributed. In addition it is useful to consider the problems of *multicollinearity* and *spurious correlation*. Each of these will be briefly examined below.

Linearity   We emphasized earlier the importance of checking for a linear relationship between dependent and independent variables by plotting the data. An attempt to fit a linear model to a relationship that is nonlinear or does not exist will yield a low and insignificant coefficient of determination. An observed nonlinear relationship can be handled by transforming one or more of the variables, such as by using the logarithms or square roots of the observations.

Homoscedasticity   When the forecast errors have a constant variance, this condition is referred to as *homoscedasticity*. When not true, we say that the data are *heteroscedastic*. If heteroscedasticity exists, it is highly likely that we will obtain a low and insignificant coefficient of determination. The existence of homo- or heteroscedasticity can often be found by examining a plot of the data. For example, Figure 19-4 shows a case in which the variance is not constant, i.e., it is heteroscedastic. The deviation of the dependent variable around the regression line increases as the independent variable gets larger.

Heteroscedasticity can sometimes be eliminated by introducing other independent variables which are assumed to be the cause of the heteroscedasticity. For example, the plot in Figure 19-4 might represent sales (dependent variable) versus advertising expenditures (independent variable). The increased variability in sales for higher levels of advertising may represent the impact of special advertising campaigns, some of which did lead to increased sales and

FIGURE 19-4   Graphic evidence of heteroscedasticity in simple linear regression.

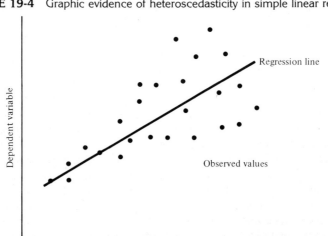

some of which had very little impact on sales. This would suggest that total advertising expenditures be broken down into several categories, each of which can be treated as a separate independent variable. This in turn may eliminate the heteroscedasticity.

Independence of Forecast Errors   It is always wise to examine the forecast errors ($F_i - A_i$), or *residuals,* which are normally provided by computer regression routines. This can be done by graphing the residuals or examining their signs. The purpose of doing this is to detect patterns in the residuals (e.g., a number of consecutive negative residuals). When patterns appear in the residuals, indicating lack of independence, the model being used has not taken full advantage of the explanatory potential in the data. This can be corrected for by adding other variables to the model or by transforming one or more existing ones.

Normally Distributed Residuals   Regression assumes that the residuals or errors are normally distributed with a mean of zero. Although this assumption is not usually one to worry about, it is important because it underlies the various tests of significance and the confidence limit determination. As a rough guide if the number of observations is 30 or more, we can assume that the residuals are normally distributed. A spot check of the residuals can also be made to ensure that they cluster near zero with large values occurring only infrequently (i.e., approximately normal). The best way to correct for nonnormality is to increase the sample size. The existence of a nonzero mean for the residuals indicates bias and suggests that the forecasting model or parameters need to be reexamined.

Multicollinearity   Multicollinearity exists when two or more independent variables are themselves highly correlated. When this occurs, the apparent significance and accuracy of the results can be affected. The simple correlation coefficients should be examined to determine whether any independent variables are substantially correlated with each other. If they are, one or more of these should be eliminated and the model redetermined. As a general rule, you should eliminate one of a pair of independent variables whose simple correlation is .7 or greater. In the Glowteeth toothpaste example we found that the correlation between the two independent variables, television and magazine advertising, was −.285. This value is sufficiently low to assume that multicollinearity does not exist and no correction is necessary.

Spurious Correlation   As a final comment on the use of regression, we consider the problem of spurious correlation. This occurs when two variables appear to be highly correlated when in fact they are not. This happens frequently with business and economic data because many of the factors are increasing or decreasing over time. For instance, over a 10-year period in the life of almost any firm one is likely to find a positive correlation between sales and expenditures on, say, postage. This apparent correlation is due not to any interdependence between these factors but to the fact that both have grown, stabilized, or declined at approximately the same rate throughout the 10-year period. We should not conclude that an increase in postage expenditures will bring about or cause an increase in sales.

In this section we will consider a forecasting model quite different from that of regression. This class of models is referred to as *Markovian models* or sometimes *Markov chains*. They are named in honor of the Russian mathematician, A. A. Markov, who first developed this line of analysis.

A Markov model is most often used in marketing to model consumer buying behavior. Consumers are assigned to classes depending on which brand of a particular product, such as toothpaste, they last purchased. *Transition probabilities* are determined that represent the aggregate purchase behavior for each class. These probabilities correspond to the proportions of consumers in a class that will next purchase each of the competing brands. Suppose, for example, we have two competing brands, *A* and *B*. Those consumers who last purchased brand *A* will be assigned to one class and those who last purchased brand *B* will be assigned to the other class. Transition probabilities would be determined for each class. Thus we might find that of those who last purchased brand *A*, 80 percent will purchase brand *A* and 20 percent will purchase brand *B* when they make their next purchase. Similar probabilities will be established for those who last purchased brand *B*. If we know how many customers are in each class and that the transition probabilities are stable, we can predict future purchase patterns in this competitive market.

Markovian models are not limited to marketing situations. For example, they can also be used to model consumer payment patterns for accounts receivable, changes in the personnel structure of an organization, or car rental pickup and delivery patterns.

Basic Assumptions

Several characteristics or assumptions of Markov models are worth considering at this point. An important one is to recognize that the transition probabilities represent aggregate behavior rather than individual behavior. That is, when we define a 20 percent transition probability from purchasing brand *A* to purchasing brand *B*, the probability does not mean that each individual who last purchased *A* has a 20 percent chance of next purchasing *B*. Rather, we mean that 20 percent of those customers who last purchased *A* will next purchase *B*. A second assumption is that this aggregate behavior is stable in a statistical sense. By this we mean that the transition probabilities are not expected to change. A third and important assumption is that these transition probabilities are dependent only on the most recent purchase and are not affected by prior purchase behavior. Thus, if we specify that 20 percent of the individuals who last purchased brand *A* will next purchase brand *B*, this proportion is assumed not to be affected by purchases made prior to the most recent purchase of brand *A*. This characteristic allows us to refer to a Markov model as a *memoryless process*. Predicting future behavior does not require any more information than the way in which the most recent purchase conditions the probabilities of the next brand to be purchased.

Determining Transition Probabilities

Consider for a moment a simple two-brand model as shown in Figure 19-5, representing consumer purchases of brand *A* and brand *B*. Note that after a

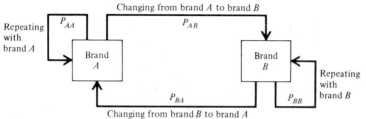

FIGURE 19-5 Transition flows and probabilities for a two-brand Markov model.

specific purchase, two actions are possible. The consumer either purchases the same brand as before or switches to the alternate brand. As stated above, we assume that we can measure the probability, or likelihood, of each of these actions. The symbol p is used to represent the transition probabilities for these purchase actions. p_{AA} and p_{BB} represent the probabilities that the consumers will continue purchasing the same brands, A and B, respectively. p_{AB} and p_{BA} represent the probabilities that they will switch brands (from A to B in the first case and from B to A in the latter case).

For a consumer purchase model, these probabilities are often called *brand switching probabilities*. As we shall see, it is convenient to write these probabilities in tabular form as

	To	
From	*Brand A*	*Brand B*
Brand A	p_{AA}	p_{AB}
Brand B	p_{BA}	p_{BB}

Given knowledge of the most recent purchase actions and these transition probabilities it is easy to predict aggregate purchase patterns in the future.

Forecasting Short-Range Effects

To illustrate, consider the situation faced by the Trenton Company. They produce and sell a natural breakfast food cereal, called Crunch. This product directly competes with two other brands of natural cereal. Trenton is concerned about recent sales patterns for Crunch. Their market share has steadily declined and is now at 30 percent. The other two brands, Applin and Brano, have 40 and 30 percent of the market, respectively. Based on market research data, Trenton management has determined the current brand switching probabilities. These are shown below, where we let A represent Applin, B represent Brano, and C represent Trenton's brand, Crunch.

	To		
From	*A*	*B*	*C*
A	.7	.2	.1
B	.2	.6	.2
C	.3	.2	.5

The table entries can be interpreted as the proportion of customers switching from the row brand to the column brand. Thus 30 percent of those who last purchased brand C will next purchase brand A and 10 percent of those who last purchased brand A will switch to brand C on their next purchase. Note that the probabilities in each row sum to 1 because the columns represent the only three possible brand purchase options.

Given the switching possibilities available, it is not likely that the current market shares will continue in the future. Assume that the average consumer will make a purchase once every 3 months. What will the market shares be in 3 months (that is, in the next quarter)?

Consider first the purchasers of brand A. According to the transition probabilities, 70 percent of those who last bought brand A, 20 percent of those who bought brand B, and 30 percent of those who bought C will next purchase brand A. Therefore, brand A's new market share will consist of

$$\text{Brand } A\text{'s new share} = .7\left(\begin{array}{c}\text{brand } A\text{'s} \\ \text{current share}\end{array}\right) + .2\left(\begin{array}{c}\text{brand } B\text{'s} \\ \text{current share}\end{array}\right) + .3\left(\begin{array}{c}\text{brand } C\text{'s} \\ \text{current share}\end{array}\right)$$

$$= .7(.4) + .2(.3) + .3(.3) = .43$$

Thus our projection for next quarter shows brand A's market share increasing to 43 percent. In a similar manner we can calculate the new shares for products B and C.

Brand B's new share $= .2(.4) + .6(.3) + .2(.3) = .32$

Brand C's new share $= .1(.4) + .2(.3) + .5(.3) = .25$

Note that the new shares sum to $1(.43 + .32 + .25 = 1)$. Clearly, brands A and B are projected to increase their share of the market at the expense of brand C. A question of interest to Trenton's management is whether or not this trend in market share for Crunch will continue in the future.

One approach to answering that question is to repeat the calculations using the new market shares. This would yield projected market shares two quarters in the future. Then these shares could be used to determine shares three quarters ahead. Repeated application of this method would yield forecasts of market shares as many periods ahead as desired.

For instance, the shares for two quarters ahead would be calculated as

Brand $A = .7(.43) + .2(.32) + .3(.25) = .440$

Brand $B = .2(.43) + .6(.32) + .2(.25) = .328$

Brand $C = .1(.43) + .2(.32) + .5(.25) = .232$

As you can see, the trend of brands A and B gaining market share and brand C losing is expected to continue but at a slower rate of change.

INSTANT REPLAY   What would be the new shares three periods ahead?

CHECK $A = .4432$, $B = .3312$, and $C = .2256$

Continued application of these calculations will eventually lead to the market share change pattern shown in Figure 19-6. Observe that after some initial adjustments, the market shares stabilize at equilibrium values of 44.5 percent for brand A, 33.3 percent for brand B, and 22.2 percent for brand C.

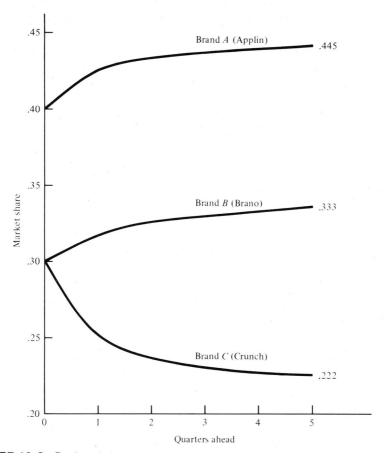

FIGURE 19-6 Predicted changes in market share for Applin, Brano, and Crunch natural cereals.

For most sets of transition probabilities such an equilibrium will be reached after an initial adjustment period. A rather remarkable property of such Markov models is that no matter what the initial market shares are, the final *equilibrium shares* will always be the same for a given set of transition probabilities.

To illustrate this property, suppose we took an extreme initial case wherein brand C had 100 percent of the market. Using the same transition probabilities as before, after one period brand A would have 30 percent, B 20 percent, and C 50 percent. After two periods, A has 40 percent, B 28 percent, and C 32 percent, and after three periods the shares would reach 43 percent for A, 31 percent for B, and 26 percent for C. Repeated projections will very soon reach equilibrium conditions identical to that for the first example.

Calculating Equilibrial Shares

Actually there exists a more direct method of calculating the equilibrial, or steady-state, market shares. If we let A_t, B_t, and C_t represent the market shares for the respective brands at time t, our previous calculations were of the form

$$A_t = .7A_{t-1} + .2B_{t-1} + .3C_{t-1}$$

$$B_t = .2A_{t-1} + .6B_{t-1} + .2C_{t-1}$$

$$C_t = .1A_{t-1} + .2B_{t-1} + .5C_{t-1}$$

But observe that when the shares have reached equilibrium they remain unchanged from period to period, so that $A_t = A_{t-1}$, $B_t = B_{t-1}$, and $C_t = C_{t-1}$. Therefore, letting A^*, B^*, and C^* represent the equilibrium, or steady-state, shares we find that the following equations must be satisfied:

$$A^* = .7A^* + .2B^* + .3C^*$$

$$B^* = .2A^* + .6B^* + .2C^*$$

$$C^* = .1A^* + .2B^* + .5C^*$$

$$A^* + B^* + C^* = 1$$

The first three equations derive from our share calculation formulas and the last represents the condition that the equilibrium shares must sum to 1.

We have, in effect, four equations and three unknowns. Since only three equations are necessary to solve for the three unknowns, one of the equations is redundant and can be dropped. Any of the first three equations can be eliminated but not the last. Suppose we drop the third. After rearranging and grouping like terms, we find

$$-.3A^* + .2B^* + .3C^* = 0$$

$$.2A^* - .4B^* + .2C^* = 0$$

$$A^* = 1 - B^* - C^*$$

Substituting the last equation for A^* in each of the first two will eliminate A^* from both. Thus the first equation becomes

$$-.3(1 - B^* - C^*) + .2B^* + .3C^* = 0$$

$$-.3 + .3B^* + .3C^* + .2B^* + .3C^* = 0$$

$$.5B^* + .6C^* = .3$$

and the second

$$.2(1 - B^* - C^*) - .4B^* + .2C^* = 0$$

$$.2 - .2B^* - .2C^* - .4B^* + .2C^* = 0$$

$$-.6B^* = -.2$$

$$B^* = .333$$

We were quite fortunate with this second equation in that not only did A drop out but C as well. Normally this would not occur. Instead, we would be left with two equations and two unknowns. At that point we would solve for one of the unknowns in terms of the other using either equation, substitute this relation in the other equation, and solve for the remaining unknown.

Once the equilibrial value for one of the unknowns has been found, such as B^* above, we can substitute its value in any two-unknown equation obtaining a second equilibrial value. This process is repeated until all steady-state market shares have been found.

Thus we can substitute .333 for B^* in the equation containing only B^* and C^* to find C^*:

$$.5B^* + .6C^* = .3$$
$$.5(.333) + .6C^* = .3$$
$$.6C^* = .3 - .167$$
$$C^* = .222$$

Finally, we can substitute the values of B^* and C^* into any of three-unknown equations. The easiest to use is the last equation. Thus

$$A^* = 1 - B^* - C^*$$
$$= 1 - .333 - .222 = .445$$

We have now found the steady-state, or equilibrium, market shares. To check our computational results we can substitute the values found in each of the four original equations to ensure that the values satisfy these equations.

$$A^* = .7A^* + .2B^* + .3C^*$$
$$.445 = .7(.445) + .2(.333) + .3(.222)$$
$$.445 = .445$$
$$B^* = .2A^* + .6B^* + .2C^*$$
$$.333 = .2(.445) + .6(.333) + .2(.222)$$
$$.333 = .333$$
$$C^* = .1A^* + .2B^* + .5C^*$$
$$.222 = .1(.445) + .2(.333) + .5(.222)$$
$$.222 = .222$$
$$A^* + B^* + C^* = 1$$
$$.445 + .333 + .222 = 1$$
$$1 = 1$$

In this case all four equations were satisfied, verifying that we have indeed found the steady-state shares. (Because of rounding errors, you may have to observe some leeway with this method of proving the correctness of the figures.)

INSTANT REPLAY   What would be the steady-state shares for a two-brand model with the following transition probabilites:

	To	
From	X	Y
X	.6	.4
Y	.2	.8

CHECK   Shares would be $X = 33$ percent and $Y = 67$ percent.

Note that the steady-state or equilibrium shares were found using only the transition probabilities. This supports the previous statement that the initial market share conditions have no effect on the final equilibrium conditions.

Using Markovian Models for Decision Making

Several caveats need to be stated with respect to the use of Markov models. Although equilibrium shares may be quite useful information in predicting market trends, it is not usually likely that the equilibrium will ever be reached. This is because the transition probabilities, although stable in the short run, are subject to change in the long run. Promotional expenditures, price changes, and economic conditions are some of the many factors that can impact on the consumer buying behavior leading to adjustments in these transition probabilities.

On the other hand, analysis of the impact of proposed marketing strategies on these transition probabilities can be useful in evaluating various alternatives. As we saw, the market share for Trenton's Crunch cereal (brand C) is expected to drop from the current level of 30 percent to the equilibrium level of 22.3 percent. This expected trend is not likely to be viewed favorably by Trenton management. Suppose, in response to this unfavorable forecast, management is considering two promotional strategies, one an advertising campaign aimed at purchasers of brands A and B to get them to switch to brand C, and the other a discount coupon to be included with each box of Crunch to encourage current purchasers to stay with Crunch next time. If these two strategies could be applied to small test markets, it would be possible to estimate the changes, or adjustments, that would occur in the transition probabilities as a result.

Suppose this was done and that the advertising strategy did attract more brand A and B users to brand C as reflected in the following transition probabilities:

		To	
From	*A*	*B*	*C*
A	.65	.15	.2
B	.15	.55	.3
C	.3	.2	.5

In a manner similar to that followed above, we can derive adjusted steady-state shares. These as computed would be 39.8 percent for brand A, 27.7 percent for brand B, and 32.5 percent for brand C.

Alternatively, suppose that the test market results for the coupon strategy led to the following revised transition probabilities:

		To	
From	*A*	*B*	*C*
A	.7	.2	.1
B	.2	.6	.2
C	.25	.15	.6

Solving for the steady-state shares would yield 42.7 percent for brand A, 31.1 percent for B, and 26.2 percent for C.

Clearly, brand C can pick up a larger market share through the advertising strategy than is possible with the coupon strategy, based on the test market results. Which strategy should in fact be selected by Trenton management cannot be answered on the basis of the projected steady-state shares alone. The costs associated with each strategy must also be considered as well as the response of the competing brands to Trenton's strategy choice.

Final Comments

This chapter completes the treatment of forecasting models. We examined here what are called explanatory models. Extrapolation models, covered in Chapter 18, were based on historical patterns for the variable to be forecast. They provide no explanation of why these patterns exist but attempt only to project them to the future. Explanatory models, on the other hand, are based on assumptions concerning the relationship of the variable to be forecast with other variables thought to influence it.

The major advantage of an explanatory model is that it can be used not only to forecast but also to analyze policy changes. The disadvantage is that it is much more difficult to build and use explanatory models. As we discussed, spurious correlation may be measured between two variables even though no real cause and effect relationship exists. Thus extreme caution must be exercised when basing policy decisions on the relationships hypothesized in an explanatory model.

The major portion of this chapter was devoted to regression models. Our treatment included simple linear models (one independent variable) and multiple regression models (more than one independent variable). Much of the discussion centered around the process by which the model parameters are determined. The process used is called the method of least squares because it identifies parameters which will minimize the sum of the squares of the forecast errors. Considerable attention was also devoted to the procedures used to determine the significance of the model. These procedures are necessary because the data used to develop the model and fit the parameters are samples, which makes the results subject to sampling error.

The final segment of the chapter dealt with a more specific explanatory model called a Markovian model. This model can be used to project future market shares on the basis of current shares and consumer transition probabilities. Equilibrium shares can be determined solely on the basis of the transition probabilites. These can be used to evaluate alternative marketing policies.

Key Words

Basic balance equations **665**
Brand switching probability **677**
Coefficient of determination **669**
Coefficient of multiple
   determination **671**

Confidence level **673**
Correlation **668**
Correlation coefficient **668**
Covariance **669**
Critical F value **672**

Problems

19-1. The Metropolis Health Care Planning Committee has been concerned with planning for a major new hospital facility to be built in the near future. One of the issues they have been concerned with is the projection of future hospital-related health care demands so that they can determine an appropriate capacity for the new hospital facility. Data for population growth and hospital admissions for the past 10 years are shown below:

Year	Metropolitan area population, thousands	Hospital admission, thousands
1969	1,240	130
1970	1,302	128
1971	1,415	145
1972	1,480	147
1973	1,500	153
1974	1,560	165
1975	1,633	170
1976	1,699	177
1977	1,780	180
1978	1,850	192

a. Develop a simple linear regression model which uses area population to predict the number of hospital admissions.

b. What percent of the total variability in hospital admissions can be attributed to population growth?

c. Is the regression significant at the 95 percent level?

d. If the total population for the metropolitan area is expected to reach 2,400,000 by the year 1985, what does your model predict will be the level of hospital admission that year?

e. Assuming that existing hospital capacity in the area is measured at 2,500 beds and the average stay per admission is 4 days, what capacity, in number of beds, should the new hospital facility have, such that it, together with existing facilities, can be expected to handle the projected 1985 hospital admissions?

19-2. The Benton Manufacturing Company is concerned with manufacturing cost measurement for its large color television manufacturing facility. Quarterly production volume and total cost data are shown below for the past 2 years.

Quarterly production volume, units	Total manufacturing costs, thousands
4,200	$1,114
3,800	1,153
3,600	1,170
3,500	1,110
3,900	1,170
4,400	1,330
4,700	1,390
5,200	1,470

a. Using simple linear regression determine the relationship between manufacturing costs (dependent variable) and production volume (independent variable).

b. What percent of the variability in manufacturing costs can be attributed to production volume?

c. Is the regression significant at the 95 percent level?

d. What would you estimate to be the quarterly fixed manufacturing costs?

e. What would you estimate to be the per-unit variable manufacturing costs?

f. If the color television unit sells at a manufacturing net price of $300, what quarterly sales volume must the company achieve in order to break even?

19-3. The SiphonJet Company, a major manufacturer of washing machines, has experienced some difficulties in training and employing competent customer service people. The firm maintains its own training school but has found that a significant number of people who complete the training program do not perform at a level of competence sufficient to maintain the quality image of the product. A study of the training program has convinced the personnel manager that the problem is not due to the training program but instead is due to the lack of an effective screening mechanism to select those individuals with the necessary skills. To correct this deficiency, an aptitude test was developed and tested on a sample of 50 individuals and then compared with the on-the-job performance of these individuals. A simple linear regression model was used to test the correspondence between aptitude test results and actual performance. Various statistics are summarized below:

$$n = 50, T = \text{test score}, P = \text{performance rating} (100 = \text{best})$$

$$\Sigma T = 3,600 \qquad \Sigma TP = 304,440$$

$$\Sigma P = 4,180 \qquad \Sigma T^2 = 262,750$$

$$\Sigma P^2 = 353,300$$

a. Determine the linear regression equation to predict performance rating on the basis of test score.

b. Can you conclude that the aptitude test score is a good predictor of on-the-job performance?

c. What statistical information can you provide to substantitate your conclusion?

d. What test score would you recommend as a cutoff point for selection in the training program if the minimum acceptable performance rating is 85?

19-4. The Atlantis Airline Company had conducted a study of the relationship between income levels of a sample of passengers and the average number of flights these passengers took per year. Statistical information obtained from this study is summarized below:

$n = 20$, I = annual income (thousands of dollars), F = number of flights per year

$$\Sigma I = 408 \qquad \Sigma IF = 3{,}583$$

$$\Sigma F = 145 \qquad \Sigma I^2 = 10{,}264$$

$$\Sigma F^2 = 1{,}343$$

a. Determine the linear regression equation that could be used to predict the number of flights per year on the basis of annual income.

b. What interpretation can you give to the slope or regression coefficient b?

c. How strong is the relationship between income and demand for air travel?

d. Is the relationship significant at the 95 percent level?

19-5. The Zenota Computer Company has recently implemented a data monitoring system to enable it to determine the impact of different marketing strategies on sales of its home computer unit. Data for 8 months of sales volume and selected marketing expenditures are shown below.

Sales volume, units	Television advertising, thousands	Direct mail, thousands
240	$ 5	$ 2
315	8	4
300	10	5
290	10	9
400	12	10
420	20	15
450	22	15
480	25	18

a. Develop a multiple linear regression model to predict sales volume based on television advertising and direct mail expenditures.

b. Is the total regression significant at the 95 percent level?

c. Determine the simple correlation between sales and each of the independent variables.

d. Determine the simple correlation between the two independent variables.

e. Do the data show evidence of multicollinearity?

19-6. The Hardrock School of Business is concerned with the improvement of the quality of students that they admit to their M.B.A. program. The program director has selected the records of 10 recent graduates of the program in an attempt to determine the relationship between program performance and two predictive measures, admissions test scores and undergraduate grade point averages. The data for these 10 students are shown below.

M.B.A. grade point average	Standardized admissions test score	Undergraduate grade point average
2.0	465	2.7
3.8	620	4.0
3.2	570	3.6
3.1	580	3.0
2.9	550	3.2
2.4	510	2.6
3.8	590	3.5
3.6	620	3.4
3.3	604	3.5
2.7	500	3.0

a. Determine the multiple linear regression equation, including both admission test scores and undergraduate grade point average as independent variables.

b. Suppose that it is desirable to admit only those students whose undergraduate grade point average and admission test scores project or predict an M.B.A. grade point average of 2.8 or higher. How would the regression equation from part *a* be used in making admissions decisions?

c. How reliable do you expect this model (parts *a* and *b*) to be? What statistical information supports your analysis?

19-7. The Baldwin Pharmaceutical Company has been studying the impact of advertising on sales for NoStuff, a nonprescription nasal decongestant. NoStuff has a highly seasonal demand pattern which peaks during the height of the cold-flu season, with a smaller peak during the summer allergy season. Because of this exaggerated seasonal demand pattern the company wishes to time its advertising expenditures so as to reap the maximum benefits during the seasonal peaks. Ads placed too early or too late will not be as effective.

To assist it in its analysis of this problem, it has gathered data showing deseasonalized demand and actual advertising expenditures for a recent 12-month period, as shown below.

Month	Deseasonalized demand, thousands	Actual advertising expenditures, thousands
July	103	95
August	92	98
September	99	95
October	94	96
November	98	106
December	108	110
January	107	85
February	80	95
March	100	102
April	105	110
May	110	104
June	104	100

a. Develop a simple linear regression model for predicting monthly deseasonalized demand on the basis of advertising expenditures in the *same* month.

b. Develop a simple linear regression model for predicting monthly deseasonalized demand on the basis of advertising expenditures in the *previous* month.

c. Based on the results found for the two models in parts *a* and *b*, would you estimate that advertising expenditures in the current month or the previous month have the greatest impact on demand?

d. Develop a multiple linear regression model that predicts monthly demand where current month's advertising and the previous month's advertising are both included as independent variables.

e. Compare the performance of the model in part *d* with that of the models from parts *a* and *b*.

f. Does multicollinearity exist in the model in part *d*?

g. Does a plot of the residuals suggest that some other factor may be an important determinant of demand?

19-8. Sudsglow, a light beer sold on a regional basis, currently holds 20 percent of the market, and the other 80 percent is divided among a number of competing brands. Market analysis has shown that from one month to the next Sudsglow has managed to retain 80 percent of its customers while picking up 15 percent of the customers of competing brands.

a. What share of the market will Sudsglow have after 1 month?

b. What share of the market will Sudsglow have after 2 months?

c. If the current switching behavior continues, what will be Sudsglow's equilibrium, or steady-state, share of the market?

19-9. El Cheapo Rental Car Agency maintains three rental facilities, at locations *W*, *X*, and *Y*, in Texas. A car picked up at one location can be returned at any of three El Cheapo facilities. Historical data have shown the following pattern of pickups and returns:

Cars picked up at:	Were returned to:			Total
	W	*X*	*Y*	
W	84	30	36	150
X	30	96	24	150
Y	15	45	90	150

a. At the moment, each of the three facilities has 100 cars available for rental. How will these 300 cars be distributed among the three facilities after they are returned from their next rental?

b. If this pickup and return pattern were to continue, what would be the long-run or steady-state distribution of these cars?

c. At which location should a service or repair facility be located? (*Hint:* Which location will have the most cars?)

d. Suppose that the demand for rental cars is approximately 100 per week at each location and that the average length of rental is 1 week. Because of the imbalance in the pickup and delivery patterns some cars will have to be transported from the location(s) with excess cars to those with deficiencies. On average how many cars will have to be transported each week among the three facilities?

19-10. The Battle Creek Breakfast Food Company currently holds a 30 percent share of the raisin bran market, with 40 percent held by its biggest competitor Toast Posties, and the remaining 30 percent is divided among a number of smaller competitors. Assume that the brand purchase behavior for consumers of the competing products in this market is currently

From	Battle Creek	To Toast Posties	Other brands
Battle Creek	.7	.2	.1
Toast Posties	.15	.8	.05
Other brands	.3	.2	.5

The Battle Creek product currently sells for $.80 a box and costs the company $.35 to produce and distribute. In an attempt to increase its market share, Battle Creek test-marketed a discount coupon which was intended to gain a larger share of repeat purchasers and offered a 10-cent reduction in the purchase price.

The results of the test market experiment showed that repeat purchasers increased to 80 percent, those switching to Toast Posties dropped to 15 percent, and those switching to other brands declined to 5 percent. Based on the number of discount coupons returned to Battle Creek, it is estimated that 20 percent of all purchasers of the Battle Creek brand actually used the coupons.

a. What would Battle Creek's long-run market share have been if the discount strategy had not been followed?

b. What change in the long-run market shares would result from the use of the discount coupon?

c. What impact on the contribution of the Battle Creek brand raisin bran product would the discount coupon have?

d. Would you recommend that the discount option be employed?

e. Suppose there is a 30 percent probability that Toast Posties would respond to Battle Creek's discount coupon by offering one of its own, thereby retaining 85 percent of its customers and losing 12 percent to Battle Creek and 3 percent to other brands. What would Battle Creek's long-run share be if both companies offered discount coupons?

f. What would Battle Creek's *expected* long-run share be? Would this change your answer to part *d*?

Application: Forecasting Teller Window Demand*

Increasing labor costs are causing many banks to pay more attention to the problem of scheduling laborpower efficiently. Because of the number of personnel involved, the teller window operation is frequently the first to be considered for improvement in productivity. This paper focuses on the problem of predicting the total daily demand for teller window services. Its objective is to demonstrate how a relatively simple forecasting technique, exponential smoothing, can be used to provide good-quality forecasts of daily teller demand, using data provided by the Purdue National Bank of Lafayette, Indiana. This technique was selected for two reasons. First, it provides a routine procedure for projecting systematic variations in historical demand, e.g., from paydays and holidays, which are frequently observed in the demand for teller window services. Second, the computational requirements are minimal for this technique.

*Adapted from William L. Berry, Vincent A. Mabert, and Myles Marcus, "Forecasting Teller Window Demand with Exponential Smoothing," Institute for Research in the Behavioral, Economics, and Management Sciences, Paper 536, November 1975, Krannert Graduate School of Industrial Administration, Purdue University, West Lafayette, Indiana.

During the fall of 1974, PNB's management decided to collect information on actual customer traffic patterns for use in forecasting teller window demand. A review of their reporting procedures indicated that an exact count of customer traffic at the teller windows was not currently being recorded. Their processing system collected information only on the number of transaction items processed. A 9-week traffic survey was conducted at each branch to determine the actual number of customers. Since actual customer arrival data are expensive to collect on a continuous basis, it was felt that it might be possible to relate teller window demand to one of the transaction items (cash slips) which is routinely collected for other purposes.

A regression analysis was performed on the relationship between customer arrivals and the corresponding cash slip data. The least-squares equation developed was

$$\text{Number of customers} = 64.725 + 1.465 \text{ (cash tickets)}$$

and produced a coefficient of determination of $R^2 = .71$, indicating a high degree of correlation.

The use of cash tickets in forecasting demand and determining teller requirements involves two steps: (1) determining the relationship between teller window service time and cash slip transactions, and (2) analyzing the cash slip data to determine the causes of systematic fluctuations in the demand for teller service.

A sample of 3,000 customer transactions indicated that a teller spent an average 1.5 minutes with each customer. This estimate of the average service time per customer was used with the regression equation above to determine the number of tellers required to service the cash slip forecast for a given day:

$$\text{Tellers required} = [64.725 + 1.465 \text{ (cash slip forecast)}] \left(\frac{T}{L}\right)$$

where T is the average service time per customer (in minutes) and L is the length of time the teller windows are open for service during the day (in minutes).

The cash slip data were next analyzed to determine whether systematic variations could be detected in the demand for teller window services at the eight branches. Substantial differences in the demand level were noted both (1) between the days of a week, and (2) between the different weeks of a month for a particular day, e.g., a Monday.

Part of this variation is due to unpredictable causes such as the weather and an individual's own financial needs. However, a large portion of this variation can be predicted in terms of the weekly, biweekly, and monthly pay periods that most organizations follow. Likewise, social security checks typically arrive around the first part of each month. Each of these events causes a predictable increase in traffic at a branch.

Analysis of past data showed that it was necessary to distinguish eight types of days: (1) regular day, (2) academic payday, (3) the day after an academic payday, (4) fiscal year payday, (5) the day after a fiscal year payday, (6) biweekly payday, (7) the day after a biweekly payday, (8) day on which *both* academic and fiscal paydays occurred.

In this study, a modified version of the seasonally adjusted exponential smoothing model described by Winters was used to forecast teller window demand. There are two major modifications. First, no appreciable trend was observed in the 56 weeks of data studied. Therefore, a trend factor was not included. Second, special day factors corresponding to the eight types of days listed above were used in place of the usual seasonal factors. For example, the special day factor for an academic payday might have a value near 1.5, reflecting the substantial increase in teller window demand on those days.

Since each day of the week exhibited a different demand pattern, a separate forecasting model was developed for each day.

Experiments were conducted to evaluate the performance of these models, using the standard deviation of the forecast errors as the performance criterion. The degree of improvement provided by the addition of the different special day factors is indicated by comparison with a simple exponential smoothing model. The introduction of the special day factors produced a marked decrease in standard error, averaging 48.4 percent less error than for the simpler model.

This application of exponential smoothing demonstrates that systematic causes of teller window demand can be identified and exploited to improve forecasting performance. Often these sources of variation are well known to bank officers. For example, four of PNB's eight branch offices are located near large and dominant employers in the Lafayette area. Thus, knowing their payday schedules allows management to anticipate teller window demand changes. Also, the remaining four branches tend to follow regular patterns, because of the similarity in payroll policies for local employers, businesses, and residents. These common pay periods occur at mid-month and month-end, and also involve the distribution of social security checks around the third day of the month. Management is generally aware of the impact of these events on teller window demand and has in the past used this information in an intuitive manner in making staffing decisions.

Discussion Questions

1. What type of regression model was used to forecast the daily number of bank customers? What interpretation can you provide for the *a* parameter (64.725)? What interpretation can you provide for the *b* parameter (1.465)? Does the model appear reasonable?
2. How many tellers would be required for a particular day if each teller is open for service a total of 6 hours and the bank expects a total of 1,000 cash slips to be processed that day?
3. Why was exponential smoothing used to handle the systematic variation in teller window demand due to the type of day? Could these variations be incorporated in a regression model? What other forecasting approach might be appropriate?
4. Determine the modifications necessary to the equations for Winters' model to omit the trend factor. Is there any danger to leaving out the trend factor? Is there any danger in leaving the trend factor in even though no trend has been apparent in the past?
5. Is the modified exponential smoothing model described an extrapolation or an explanatory model? Why?
6. Can you identify other situations in which the seasonal factor can represent special situations such as those used here?

Appendix

Critical Values for the F Distribution (.95 Level)*

$k-1$ / $n-k$	1	2	3	4	5	6	7	8
1	161.4	199.5	215.7	224.6	230.2	234.0	236.8	238.9
2	18.51	19.00	19.16	19.25	19.30	19.33	19.35	19.37
3	10.13	9.55	9.28	9.12	9.01	8.94	8.89	8.85
4	7.71	6.94	6.59	6.39	6.26	6.16	6.09	6.04
5	6.61	5.79	5.41	5.19	5.05	4.95	4.88	4.82
6	5.99	5.14	4.76	4.53	4.39	4.28	4.21	4.15
7	5.59	4.74	4.35	4.12	3.97	3.87	3.79	3.73
8	5.32	4.46	4.07	3.84	3.69	3.58	3.50	3.44
9	5.12	4.26	3.86	3.63	3.48	3.37	3.29	3.23
10	4.96	4.10	3.71	3.48	3.33	3.22	3.14	3.07
11	4.84	3.98	3.59	3.36	3.20	3.09	3.01	2.95
12	4.75	3.89	3.49	3.26	3.11	3.00	2.91	2.85
15	4.54	3.68	3.29	3.06	2.90	2.79	2.71	2.64
20	4.35	3.49	3.10	2.87	2.71	2.60	2.51	2.45
25	4.24	3.39	2.99	2.76	2.60	2.49	2.40	2.34
30	4.17	3.32	2.92	2.69	2.53	2.42	2.33	2.27
40	4.08	3.23	2.84	2.61	2.45	2.34	2.25	2.18
60	4.00	3.15	2.76	2.53	2.37	2.25	2.18	2.12
120	3.92	3.07	2.68	2.45	2.29	2.17	2.09	2.02
∞	3.84	3.00	2.60	2.37	2.21	2.10	2.01	1.94

n = number of observations
k = number of variables
*This table is abridged from Samuel M. Selby, (eds.), *Standard Mathematical Tables,* 15th ed., The Chemical Rubber Company, Cleveland, Ohio, 1967.

20

Simulation Analysis of Complex Decisions

In this chapter we treat *simulation*, a method of analyzing complex decision situations that has seen widespread application. The term simulation has many meanings but as used here it is intended to mean experimentation with a model of some real system, usually performed with a computer. Laboratory tests of, say, some chemical effect are not what we mean by simulation. Generally, a simulation involves abstract rather than physical experimentation. Of course, there are different types of abstract simulations. For example, the testing of an airfoil in a wind tunnel is a type of simulation involving physical abstraction. The type of simulation we will be dealing with here involves *mathematical or computer abstractions of managerial decision situations*.

Experiments performed with simulation models can have many objectives, including evaluating design alternatives for some new operating system, examining the effects on an existing system of changes in that system's environment, or exploring alternative modifications to an existing system. Simulation has seen rapid adoption in recent years at higher management levels where it is often used as a strategic planning tool.

It should be pointed out that a simulation model is almost always a *descriptive model* rather than an optimization model. That is, the simulation model provides answers to "what if" questions in which the experimenter uses the model to predict the consequences of strategic and tactical alternatives. For instance, the model of a bank's teller operations may provide details of what impact a particular work force scheduling rule will have on customer waiting, teller utilization, and payroll costs, but the model cannot be used in a direct fashion to specify the best scheduling rule. We can, however, test the performance of one rule under different conditions, or we can experiment with a number of scheduling rules by using the simulation model to predict the impact of these rules on the system's performance. In this latter case, although we could then choose the scheduling rule which gave the best results for implementation, we have no guarantee that we have not overlooked some other, better rule.

Simulation can also search for an optimal solution by systematically exploring the potential solutions, focusing on those areas that appear to be the most promising, and eventually identifying some best solution.

Our coverage of simulation modeling will begin with an overview of the steps involved in the design and use of simulation models. This will be followed by a discussion of how probabilistic behavior is treated in simulation models. The practice of simulation will be illustrated by detailed examination of three example situations. The remaining sections of the chapter will examine in more detail some of the approaches that can be used to improve the validity, accuracy, and usefulness of simulation models.

Simulation Methodology

The methodology followed in designing and using a simulation model follows the general pattern shown in Figure 20-1. The six steps to be followed consist of (1) defining the problem and the objectives, (2) designing and building the simulation model, (3) testing and validating the model, (4) designing the simulation experiments, (5) running the model, and (6) evaluating the results. In the sections below each of these steps will be briefly described.

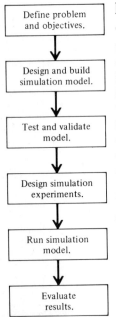

FIGURE 20-1
Steps in design
and use of
simulation models.

Problem Definition

The first step shown in Figure 20-1 identifies the *problem definition phase*. Here the problems or reasons that make the simulation model necessary must be clearly spelled out. The objectives of the system to be modeled must be identified and appropriate operational means of measuring these objectives must be selected. For example, suppose we are developing a model of an inventory system and an objective of the study is to examine the effects of alternative inventory policies on customer service. We must be careful to clearly establish how the model is to measure customer service, because a number of different measures are possible (time out of stock, number of shortages, value of shortages, etc.).

This phase also includes a specification of just what is to be included in the model of the system. This decision has two aspects: *system boundary* and *level of detail*. The system boundary problem refers primarily to the breadth or scope of the system. That is, it concerns choosing the elements that should be included in the model, from among the potential alternatives. Thus, in building a simulation model of a hospital, the question may arise as to whether the model should be limited to inpatient care or should include outpatient care as well. Or alternatively, should the model be of a single hospital or should all hospitals serving a community be included?

The level of detail decision concerns how far we go in disaggregating the system, or distinguishing between similar system elements. For example, if we have decided to include the hospital's emergency room in our model, we can treat all emergency patients similarly or we can distinguish between patients on the basis of the nature of the emergency or care needed. Other breakdowns might include distinguishing patients on the basis of income level, how far their residences are from the hospital, or whether or not they are covered by medical insurance.

Building the Model

The second step in the modeling process is the design and construction of the simulation model itself. Normally this consists of first developing the structure of the model and then writing a computer program of the model for the purposes of conducting experiments. Although the programming can be done in one of the standard algorithmic languages, such as FORTRAN or PL/1, many models are written in one of the specialized simulation languages, such as GPSS, SIMSCRIPT, or DYNAMO.[1]

This phase also involves the gathering of data necessary for the model to be representative of the real system. The types of data required are a function of the scope and level of detail of the simulation model and might include customer arrival rates, service times, departmental routing or flow patterns, etc. The greater the detail of the model, or the larger its scope, the more difficult the data collection problem.

Another important factor to be considered when the model is being constructed is the type of decision alternatives to be tested with the model. If, for example, detailed scheduling rules are to be tested, the model must incorporate the data and level of detail necessary to form the basis for such scheduling decisions. Thus, if a scheduling rule requires job due dates in order to schedule a set of jobs, the model must be capable of providing the due dates. Otherwise, the scheduling rule cannot be used.

Validating the Model

Once the model has been developed, it is important to test and validate the model, as shown as the third step in Figure 20-1. There are several kinds of validity checks that can be made. One involves checking the computer program to ensure that it works as the model builder intended. By running the model with historical data and existing management policies we can determine whether or not the model performs as the real system did during that historical period.

A second type of validity check should be conducted that examines the reasonableness of the model. When parameters are changed does the model respond as we would expect the real world system being modelled? Reasonableness, as used here, refers more to the *direction* of the model's response to such changes than to the actual *magnitude* of the response. After all, if the exact response of the real system is already known, there is little need to develop a simulation model. As an example of such a reasonableness check, we might examine the response of a marketing model to a decrease in price for one of the products included in the model. Clearly, if demand falls in response to a price cut, we would likely conclude that the model's response is unreasonable. De-

[1]For a detailed discussion of these languages, the interested reader is referred to T. J. Schriber, *Simulation Using GPSS*, Wiley, New York, 1974; P. J. Kiviat, R. Villanueva, and H. M. Markowitz, *SIMSCRIPT II.5 Programming Language*, Consolidated Analysis Center, Inc., 1973; A. L. Pugh III, *DYNAMO II User's Manual*, M.I.T. Press, 1970.

spite the disclaimer above, we can usually perform a rough check on the magnitude of the model's responses to changes. For example, if a price cut of 1 percent leads to an increase in demand of 50 percent, we would again probably judge that response as unreasonable.

In addition, we need to verify that the assumptions, model structure, and parameter values are acceptable to those who will use this model, if implemented, or to those knowledgeable of the system being modeled. Verification of the reasonableness of these factors must involve those people who will eventually be responsible for its use. If they are not convinced of the soundness of the model, they will never be convinced of the usefulness of the model's results.

Designing Simulation Experiments

Once the model has been developed, tested, and validated, the experiments that are to be performed with the model must be carefully designed. This is the fourth step of the simulation process outlined in Figure 20-1. The essence of the design problem is to find the least-cost way of solving the decision problem that prompted the simulation approach. Most simulation experiments are explorations in which the controllable elements of the system—the decision points—are varied in some systematic fashion while the effects of these changes on the performance measures are observed. The type of experimentation required will depend on the type of decision variables. The cost problem arises because of the large number of options normally available. This often prevents us from trying every possible combination. Thus, some form of intelligent search must usually be substituted for total enumeration.

In addition to the combinatorial nature of decision options, there are certain tactical questions that must be considered as well. Since simulation usually involves observing system performance over a specified time interval, the values obtained for the various performance measures are equivalent to the results of taking statistical samples. As with other statistics, the degree of correspondence between the values observed in the sample and the population parameter we are trying to estimate is affected by the size of the sample. In a simulation, sample size is often identical to the time period covered by the simulation.

Thus, if we are using a simulation model to estimate the costs of alternative distribution system structures, we need to specify the length of time over which these costs are to be measured. Should the costs be based on performance for 1 week, 1 month, 1 year, etc.? Shorter time periods are less expensive but longer time periods provide better estimates of the true distribution system cost.

Another tactical problem relates to the *start-up behavior* of the model. If, for example, we are modeling a hospital, it may be computationally convenient to begin the simulation with an empty hospital. After running the model for, say, several months (of simulated time), we would expect the occupancy pattern of the hospital model to closely match that of an operating hospital. Clearly, the performance statistics for the initial period (the first few months) would only be appropriate for a newly opened hospital and would not reflect those of an existing, operating hospital. Thus, the initial statistics should be disregarded in evaluating the effect of various decision alternatives on operating performance. Throwing away these initial or transient performance figures increases the cost of the simulation, and we would like to restrict this transient period to as small a period as possible. Unfortunately, it is not always possible, on an *a priori* basis, to define the length of time necessary to get past this transient state. One option is to perform preliminary tests with the model to empirically estimate the length of this transient period.

Another option sometimes used is to start the model from a prespecified, (supposedly) nontransient state. Thus, we might begin the hospital simulation by assuming that a certain number of patients, with prespecified illnesses, already occupy hospital beds. This eliminates the cost of the starting-up period but introduces the possibility of bias. Bias can result because the steady-state or nontransient conditions that are appropriate will often be different depending on the decision alternatives being tested. As an example, suppose we are considering how many drive-in windows should be operated by a bank. The size of the waiting line in the steady state will be different for the case of one drive-in window as compared with a few or several windows.

Evaluating Results

The final stage in the simulation process involves the analysis and interpretation of the simulation results. Much of the groundwork for this step would have been laid when the experiments were designed. To increase the statistical significance of confidence in the model's results requires keeping the variance of that output as small as possible. This is particularly important if we are trying to carefully distinguish between the performance resulting from two decision alternatives. It is not sufficient to say that option A did better than option B. We would like to say that the observed difference is statistically significant and not simply a result of sampling error. The size of the sampling error is related both to the size of the sample and the variance of the performance measure. Variance reduction techniques are used to provide smaller variances for a given sample size than would be possible otherwise. We will examine these methods later in this chapter. With this background in mind, let us now consider in more detail the steps involved in developing simulation models.

Modeling Probabilistic Variables

Frequently, simulation models require the periodic specification of values for a variable based on some *probability distribution*, empirical or theoretical. For instance, we may be building a model that requires the daily demand for a product to vary according to the probability distribution shown in Table 20-1. Thus, we need some way of generating these demands so that the frequency with which they occur in the simulation model matches the probability distribution.

For a manual simulation (not using a computer), we could generate these demands directly by writing the demands on slips of paper and then drawing one of the slips from a hat. We would need to ensure that the distribution of slips exactly matched the demand distribution. Thus 10 percent of the slips would have a demand of 10 written on them, 20 percent a demand of 20, 20 percent a demand of 30, etc. A computer cannot draw slips of paper from a hat, of course, which is why with computer simulations we rely on other approaches, such as the Monte Carlo method.

TABLE 20-1
Probability Distribution for Demand of a Hypothetical Item

Demand	Probability	Random numbers assigned
10	.1	0
20	.2	1, 2
30	.2	3, 4
40	.3	5, 6, 7
50	.2	8, 9

Monte Carlo Method

The *Monte Carlo* method generates random variables from a uniform distribution and transforms these variables to ones which correspond to the distribution of interest. A *uniform distribution* exists whenever the values of a variable are limited to a specific range and are equally likely, or have identical probabilities. Frequently these uniform random variables are referred to as *random numbers*. They satisfy two important conditions: (1) all of the values are equally likely; (2) each new value is independent of any previous values generated. In other words, if we are generating single random digits, each of the digits 0, 1, . . . , 9 is equally likely to be generated regardless of which digits have been generated in the past. Thus the digit 3 has the same 10 percent chance of being generated that every other digit in the range from 0 to 9 has.

The transformation of random uniform numbers to the random variables we need for the simulation model can be carried out in a variety of ways. The simplest is to assign a subset of digits to specific events so that the combined probability of the digits in the subset exactly matches the probability of the event being modeled.

For example, if we were simulating a coin toss with a fair coin, we would assign one-half the digits to the event "head" and one half to the event "tail"; thus, we might interpret the digits 0–4 as a head and the digits 5–9 as a tail. Since the digits 0–4 should occur one half the time, the corresponding simulation event "head" would also occur one-half the time.

INSTANT REPLAY How frequently would the event "head" occur if the digits 1, 3, 5, 7, and 9 were assigned to that event and 0, 2, 4, 6, and 8 to the event "tail"?

CHECK Each event would be expected to occur half the time. Which specific digits are assigned is not important; the combined probability of the assigned subset of digits determines the relative frequency of the simulated event.

As another example, suppose we wished to simulate an unfair coin, one whose probability of a head is .6. Since each digit has a probability of .1, we would need to assign six digits to the event head and four to the event tail to achieve the correct probability distribution for the simulated event.

Returning to the demand distribution of Table 20-1, observe the random number assignments shown in the last column. The event "demand of 10" has been assigned the digit zero whose probability of .1 exactly matches that event's probability. Since a demand of 20 occurs with probability of .2, we assigned two digits to that event. Demand of 40 has a probability of .3, so three digits were assigned to that event.

INSTANT REPLAY What event in Table 20-1 corresponds to the random number 5?

CHECK Demand of 40.

As the precision of the required event probabilities increases, the number of digits required to determine a simulation event also increases. For example, suppose we wish to simulate the effect of the length of a baseball playoff series on the probability that the better team wins. Specifically, suppose that we have determined that the Los Angeles Dodgers have a .63 probability of beating the Philadelphia Phillies in any single game and we wish to compare the probability of either team winning a best two-out-of-three series with that for a best three-out-of-five series.

If we try to assign single random digits to the events "Los Angeles wins" or "Philadelphia wins," the closest we can get to the desired probability is .6 by assigning six digits to Los Angeles winning and four to Philadelphia. This problem can be easily overcome by using pairs of digits. Since successive random digits are independent of each other, it follows that the pair 35 is no more likely to occur than the pair 64; each of these pairs would have a probability of .01 of occurring. Therefore, by assigning 63 pairs of digits to the event "Los Angeles wins" and the remaining 37 pairs of digits to Philadelphia winning we can exactly match the desired event probabilities for our model. Thus, if we assign 00–62 to Los Angeles and 63–99 to Philadelphia, the pair 35, for example, would correspond to a Los Angeles win and the pair 64 to a Philadelphia win.

INSTANT REPLAY Suppose you are developing a simulation model of a toll booth service system for a bridge. Based on actual observation of 1,000 cars arriving at the toll booth, you found that 354 cars entered the exact change lines, while the remaining 646 entered the lines for booths with attendants. How would you assign random digits to the events "exact change line" and "attendant line" so as to reproduce your empirical observations?

CHECK You would need to use three-digit random numbers. These should be split so that 354 of the 1,000 possible three-digit numbers are assigned to the event "exact change line." Thus, you might have assigned the numbers 000–353 to "exact change line" and 354–999 to "attendant line."

For manual (noncomputer) simulations, we can use a table of random digits, as provided in Appendix A for this chapter, to model stochastic variates. In using this table it does not matter where you start, but you should be consistent by moving across a row or down a column. Haphazard selections (such as closing your eyes and pointing) tend to be biased in that the probability of selection is not equally likely for each of the digits.

Computer generation of random numbers by table lookup is fairly inefficient, which is why computers use other methods. An early method used is called the *midsquare method*. Although this procedure is no longer used, examining how it works and why it fell out of favor is instructive. In this approach, the numbers are generated in sets and each set just generated is used to generate the next set. To illustrate, suppose that we use a four-digit set and that the last set generated was 1325. This set is treated as a four-digit number and squared:

$$(1325)^2 = 01755625$$

The middle four digits of this result become the next set of random digits. In this case the digits 7556 are the chosen digits (the first two digits, 01, and the last two digits, 25, are discarded). They would then be used to determine the next set:

$$(7556)^2 = 5709\underbrace{3136}_{\text{Next set}}$$

The reason that the midsquare method is no longer used is that the sets generated tend to repeat themselves, or cycle, rather quickly. For the example above, as soon as the set 1325 is generated a second time, the subsequent sets will also repeat. This cycling tends to violate the independence assumption described earlier. That is, the probability of one random digit following another is no longer .1, but is biased and therefore higher or lower than it should be.

The most popular methods used today are the *congruential methods*, of which there are several. The *multiplicative congruential method* bases the next random number x_{i+1} on the last random number x_i by calculating

$$x_{i+1} = ax_i(\text{modulo } m)$$

This requires that the old random number x_i be multiplied by some constant a and divided by another constant m using what is called modulo division. In *modulo division* the integer portion of the answer is discarded and only the remainder is retained. Thus the new random number is the remainder after dividing the product of ax_i by m. Note that the largest value for the random number is $m - 1$ since that is the largest remainder that can occur with a divisor of m.

For an illustration, suppose we use values of $a = 1473$ and $m = 32,000$. If the last random number generated (x_i) was 21438, the next random number would be calculated from

$$x_{i+1} = 1473(21438)(\text{modulo } 32,000)$$

Thus, we would first multiply 1473 by 21438, which yields 31578174. This would then be divided by 32,000, which results in 986 with a remainder of 26,174. The new random number would be this remainder, or 26174.

Modeling Theoretical Distributions

In the examples used previously we applied the Monte Carlo method to empirical probability distributions for the simulated events that we desired to model. In many cases we may wish to assume a *standard theoretical distribution* for our simulation model, such as the *Poisson*, *exponential*, or *normal distri-*

butions. There are several ways in which these theoretical distributions can be modelled.

Tabular Approach   One approach, used in the GPSS computer simulation language, is to construct a table of probabilities that approximates the nature of one of these standard distributions. We then assign random numbers to the tabulated events as we did with empirical distributions (such as in Table 20-1).

Using the Inverse of the Cumulative Probability Distribution   Another approach uses the *inverse of the cumulative probability distribution*. To illustrate, suppose we are interested in generating events according to the *negative exponential distribution*. You will recall from the chapter on waiting lines that this distribution is often used to describe the time between arrivals or the service time. The cumulative probability distribution for the negative exponential distribution is given by

$$F(t) = 1 - e^{-\lambda t}$$

where λ is the mean arrival rate and $F(t)$ is the probability that the next, say, arrival will occur before time t. A plot of this relationship is shown in Figure 20-2. The function shown above allows us to determine the cumulative probability given a specific t. For simulation modeling purposes it is necessary to determine a value for t, given a cumulative probability. This requires solution of the above equation for t, which is equivalent to finding the inverse of the cumulative probability distribution. To do this we first rearrange the equation:

$$1 - F(t) = e^{-\lambda t}$$

Then we take logs of both sides:

$$\log_e[1 - F(t)] = \log_e(e^{-\lambda t})$$
$$\log_e[1 - F(t)] = -\lambda t$$

Then we solve for t:

$$t = \frac{\log_e[1 - F(t)]}{-\lambda}$$

We can now use this formula to generate random exponentially distri-

FIGURE 20-2   Cumulative negative exponential probability distribution.

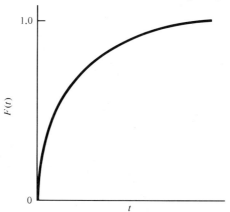

buted values for t. The cumulative distribution $F(t)$ for the exponential distribution is assigned corresponding values from the cumulative uniform distribution. This is easily done, since both cover the range 0 to 1.0 and we would expect, say, 15 percent, of the values of both distributions to fall between 0 and .15. Thus if we can generate uniform random variables we can transform these to exponential random variables by finding the specific exponential values t whose cumulative probability $F(t)$ is the same as the cumulative probability $F(x)$ for some randomly generated uniform variable x. This is equivalent to calculating

$$t = \frac{\log_e[1 - F(x)]}{-\lambda}$$

and is represented pictorially in Figure 20-3. In Figure 20-3 we assume that the random digit 6 has been generated as shown on the left side of the graph. Note that this has a cumulative probability of .6, since the probability of a value less than or equal to 6 includes the digits 1, 2, 3, 4, 5, and 6, each with probability .1, for a total cumulative probability of .6. This cumulative probability of .6 has been assigned to a cumulative probability of .6 for the exponential distribution on the right side of the graph in Figure 20-3 which is seen as equivalent to a value of $.916/\lambda$ for the exponential variable t:

$$t = \frac{\log_e(1 - .6)}{-\lambda} = \frac{\log_e(.4)}{-\lambda} = \frac{-.916}{-\lambda} = \frac{.916}{\lambda}$$

Actually, in practice, we would not limit the uniform random variable to single digits, since this does not provide sufficient precision to accurately model a continuous distribution such as the exponential. In fact, we would likely use three or more random digits and convert these to the cumulative uniform distribution by placing a decimal point in front. Thus, the digits 367 would be consid-

FIGURE 20-3 Use of the uniform distribution to obtain randomly generated exponential values.

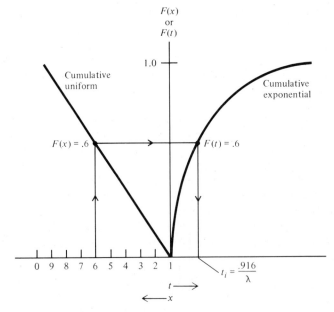

ered as the cumulative uniform probability of .367. Furthermore, since the **703**

cumulative probability .367 will occur as often as the cumulative probability

$1 - .367$, it is convenient to use the following modified formula to generate exponential variables:

IMULATION
ANALYSIS OF
COMPLEX
DECISIONS

$$t = \frac{\log_e F(x)}{-\lambda}$$

Thus, the cumulative probability of .367 would be converted directly to an exponential value as

$$t = \frac{\log_e(.367)}{-\lambda} = \frac{-1.002}{-\lambda} = \frac{1.002}{\lambda}$$

As an example, if the mean number of arrivals per hour is 5, the exponential interarrival time associated with the random digits 367 would be

$$t = \frac{1.002}{5} = .2004 \text{ hour or } 12.024 \text{ minutes}$$

INSTANT REPLAY What would be the exponential interarrival time corresponding to the random digits 743 if the mean arrival rate is 10 per hour? [*Hint*: $\log_e(.743) = -.297$.]

CHECK The desired time is found from:

$$t = \frac{\log_e(.743)}{-10} = \frac{-.297}{-10} = .0297 \text{ hour or } 1.78 \text{ minutes}$$

Generating Normally Distributed Numbers Although a number of theoretical distributions can be modeled through the use of similar inverse transformations, not all distributions have an easily calculated inverse. A case in point is the normal distribution, which has a complex cumulative probability equation, making it difficult to solve explicitly for the normally distributed value.

Instead, normally distributed random variables can be generated by a method based on the central limit theorem (see Chapter 16 for a more detailed discussion of the central limit theorem). In essence, the central limit theorem states that the mean of samples of size n (based on the sum of n independent variables) follows the normal distribution regardless of the distribution from which the n variables are derived. This is true even for relatively small values of n.

To illustrate, Table 20-2 shows the distribution of the sum of 5 uniform random digits, for 100 samples drawn from the Table of Random Digits in Appendix A. Even though the digits are uniformly distributed, the distribution of the sums is certainly not uniform and approaches the normal distribution. The convergence to normal could be made more dramatic by taking larger samples.

A common way of generating normal random variables is to generate 12 uniform variables between 0 and 1 (whose expected sum is 6) and subtract 6 from the sum. If x_i is a uniform random variable between 0 and 1, R is an approximately normal random variable with mean 0 and standard deviation 1, where

$$R = \sum_{i=1}^{12} (x_i - 6)$$

TABLE 20-2
Distribution of the Sum of Five Uniform Digits Drawn from
the Table of Random Digits (100 Samples)

Sum	Frequency	Sum	Frequency	Sum	Frequency
10–11	2	20–21	11	30–31	4
12–13	4	22–23	12	32–33	5
14–15	8	24–25	8	34–35	4
16–17	8	26–27	10	36–37	1
18–19	11	28–29	11	38–39	1

Note that since the x_is have a mean of .5, the mean of a sum of 12 x_is will be 6 (12 × .5). Subtracting 6 from the sum leads to a mean of 0 for R. Similar reasoning can be used to show that R has a standard deviation of 1.0.

If we wished to include a normally distributed variable, say Z, with mean 18 and standard deviation 3 in our simulation model, we would need to transform R (with mean 0 and standard deviation 1) to Z as follows:

$$Z = 18 + 3R$$

Suppose, for instance, we generated 12 uniform random variables and summed them as shown below:

.548 + .971 + .170 + .854 + .892 + .647 + .012 + .495 +
.006 + .248 + .702 + .823 = 6.368

We then would subtract 6 from that sum to get R:

$$R = 6.368 - 6 = 0.368$$

and substitute for R to get Z:

$$Z = 18 + 3(.368) = 19.104$$

We have provided in Appendix B a table of normally distributed random variables, with mean 0 and standard deviation 1. This is in effect a table of Rs and the values therein would need to be multiplied by the true standard deviation and added to the mean to obtain a normally distributed random variable with given mean and standard deviation.

INSTANT REPLAY   The first value of the Table of Random Normal Numbers is −.36. What simulated normal value would this correspond to for a normal distribution with mean 20 and standard deviation 5?

CHECK   20 + (−.36)(5) = 18.2.

Simulation Examples

We have now examined the process by which random variables of both empirical and theoretical distributions can be incorporated in a simulation model. Next we turn our attention to the process of developing simulation models, using them to compare decision alternatives and analyze simulation results. To do this we will take you through three example situations. In each case we will describe the problem, discuss how the model was developed, show the results obtained, and provide some discussion of managerial considerations.

Each of the examples presented will cover a slightly different aspect of simulation modeling. The first will present a simple situation with a single decision variable and empirical probability distributions. The model developed uses a *constant time increment*. That is, the time increment used in the model is of fixed, constant duration, in this case, a single day. Thus, the model determines the aggregate results for 1 day, then proceeds to the next day, and so on.

The second simulation model uses a *variable time increment* approach. This model is event-oriented and is less aggregated than the first model. That is, the model traces the flow of individual customer arrivals, waiting, and service. The time increment is variable because the time interval between customer arrivals is not fixed but variable. This model will also demonstrate the use of theoretical probability distributions in a simulation model. As with the first model, a single decision variable is relevant.

The third example presented involves two interacting decision variables. When we say that the two variables interact, we mean that they influence the performance measure of interest, both individually and collectively. That is, the best value of one decision variable is influenced by the value of the other decision variable. As such, the experimental design and analysis of simulation output is more difficult than in the first two cases.

Constant Time Increment Model

Our first model deals with an overbooking problem for an airline. The problem as described below concerns a single decision variable, determining the number of passengers to take reservations for in excess of the seat capacity for a flight. These excess reservations represent the level of overbooking. The model to be described uses a constant time increment of one day. Thus, the model will determine the costs per day of specific overbooking options. Let us now examine this problem in more detail.

Problem Description The Wings Airline Company is faced with an important decision because of frequent capacity problems on many of the company's routes. At present, the company offers only as many confirmed reservations for a flight as it has seats. Although this seems a logical policy, the company frequently flies with empty seats on flights that were 100 percent booked. This is because each flight has a number of passengers with confirmed reservations who do not show up. Because of CAB regulations, these "no-shows" are not assessed a penalty and can obtain a full refund, even though they caused the company to lose the revenue it could have earned by selling that seat to some other passengers.

Wings has for some time considered overbooking its flights by confirming reservations in excess of the actual available seats. Thus, 104 reservations might be confirmed for a flight with only 100 seats. This runs the risk that all 104 passengers will show up for the flight. However, if four or more passengers are no-shows, the company will earn revenue on four more seats than it would have if it had not overbooked. To avoid angering passengers who are "bumped" because there are fewer no-shows then expected and to comply with CAB requirements, the company will notify each passenger confirmed above capacity that they are in a special status and subject to being bumped off the flight. If this

TABLE 20-3
Probability of Seat Demand for Wings Airline Simulation

Demand	Probability	Random numbers assigned
No more than 100	.28	00–27
101	.18	28–45
102	.15	46–60
103	.12	61–72
104	.10	73–82
105	.07	83–89
106	.05	90–94
107	.03	95–97
108	.02	98–99

occurs Wings will refund the cost of the flight and fly the bumped passenger on the next available flight.

The company is not sure of the economic consequences of the proposed overbooking plan. Even if the plan is adopted, there is the question of how many travelers to confirm as special status passengers. To help answer this problem, Wings management has decided to simulate the overbooking/no-show problem. Toward this aim they have gathered probability data for demand and no-shows for a particular flight where they have been experiencing capacity problems. A single flight is used to avoid differences in the patterns of demand and no-shows that would exist for different times of the day, day of the week, or routes. The data are shown in Tables 20-3 and 20-4 with the random number assignments to be associated with each event. Note that capacity for this flight is 100 seats. The probability for no-shows is assumed to be independent of the demand for seats.

In terms of performance we wish to determine the number of empty seats flown that could have been filled through overbooking as well as the number of special-status passengers that get bumped. For instance, suppose demand is 102 and 3 no-shows occur. If we do not allow overbooking, 100 passengers

TABLE 20-4
Probability of No-Shows for Wings Airline Simulation

Number of no-shows	Probability	Random numbers assigned
0	.10	00–09
1	.13	10–22
2	.17	23–39
3	.15	40–54
4	.12	55–66
5	.10	67–76
6	.08	77–84
7	.06	85–90
8	.04	91–94
9	.03	95–97
10	.02	98–99

would have been confirmed but the flight would have had 3 empty seats because of the no-shows. If we had allowed overbooking and 102 passengers had been confirmed, the 3 no-shows would leave 1 empty seat ($102 - 3 = 99$). However, this seat could not have been filled no matter what overbooking policy had been used. Thus the cost of not overbooking would have been two empty seats since demand existed to fill those seats.

On the other hand, if we had confirmed 102 and only 1 no-show resulted, we would have to bump 1 passenger. A policy of no overbooking would have prevented this cost but also would have lost the one extra passenger carried to cover the one no-show.

Simulation Description   As shown in Table 20-5, a detailed simulation was performed to cover 30 days in which the results for the no-overbooking policy were compared with those for overbooking up to a maximum of four passen-

TABLE 20-5
Wings Airline Simulation Results for 30-Day Period

Day	RN 1	Initial demand	RN 2	No-shows	Loss due to capacity	Policy A, no overbooking		Policy B, overbook max. of 4	
						Passengers lost	Passengers bumped	Passengers lost	Passengers bumped
1	32	101	40	3	0	1	0	0	0
2	14	100	08	0	0	0	0	0	0
3	30	101	14	1	0	1	0	0	0
4	24	100	60	4	0	0	0	0	0
5	87	105	52	3	2	3	0	0	1
6	94	106	92	8	0	6	0	2	0
7	59	102	60	4	0	2	0	0	0
8	86	105	35	2	3	2	0	0	2
9	23	100	74	5	0	0	0	0	0
10	68	103	55	4	0	3	0	0	0
11	76	104	55	4	0	4	0	0	0
12	80	104	97	9	0	4	0	0	0
13	31	101	08	0	0	1	0	0	1
14	88	105	56	4	1	4	0	0	0
15	02	100	20	1	0	0	0	0	0
16	40	101	45	3	0	1	0	0	0
17	03	100	73	5	0	0	0	0	0
18	32	101.	19	1	0	1	0	0	0
19	56	102	62	4	0	2	0	0	0
20	13	100	38	2	0	0	0	0	0
21	32	101	71	5	0	1	0	0	0
22	64	103	94	8	0	3	0	0	0
23	82	104	68	5	0	4	0	0	0
24	37	101	47	3	0	1	0	0	0
25	73	103	45	3	0	3	0	0	0
26	86	105	23	2	3	2	0	0	2
27	66	103	66	4	0	3	0	0	0
28	46	102	37	2	0	2	0	0	0
29	47	102	08	0	2	0	0	0	2
30	78	104	77	6	0	4	0	0	0
					11	58	0	2	8

gers. For each day a pair of random two-digit numbers were selected from the table of random digits. One of these was then converted to an equivalent flight demand. The other was used to determine the number of no-shows for that flight. The appropriate conversions were based on the random number assignments of Tables 20-3 and 20-4. The demand and no-show information was then examined in light of each policy alternative to determine the number of passengers lost or bumped.

To illustrate, consider day 8. Random numbers of 86 and 35 led to flight demand of 105 and no-shows of 2. The policy not allowing overbooking would have booked 100 passengers but flown with 2 empty seats because of the no-shows. This accounts for the 2 shown in the "passengers lost" column of Table 20-5. No passengers were bumped by this policy as shown. Furthermore, note that the net demand for this flight is equal to the original demand (105) less the number of no-shows (2) or 103. Since the capacity of the flight is 100, 3 passengers would be turned away irrespective of the overbooking policy employed. Thus, we show 3 for that day in the column labeled "loss due to capacity." Although this loss is not due to the overbooking policy it is nonetheless a cost (of turnaways) from not having a larger plane, or not having more flights, or not charging a higher fare.

Policy B, which allows as many as 4 passengers to be overbooked would have confirmed 104 passengers given demand of 105. When only 2 no-shows resulted, policy B would have forced Wings to bump 2 passengers. Since the flight went full, no passengers were lost with this policy, except the 3 that were lost because of the plane's capacity limitations.

INSTANT REPLAY   What would have been the results for day 31 if RN1 was 85 and RN2 was 60?

CHECK   Demand of 105 and 4 no-shows. Thus, the no-overbooking policy would have resulted in 4 passengers lost. The policy of overbooking 4 passengers would have resulted in no passengers lost or bumped. One passenger was lost due to capacity.

Analysis of Results   Clearly, based on this 30-day simulation, the overbooking policy would drastically reduce the number of empty seats flown, but at a cost of more bumped passengers. In Table 20-6 we show the results that would have been achieved by other levels of overbooking for the same pattern of demand and no-shows. The total cost column assumes that the lost revenue due to an empty seat or due to a refund of the fare to a bumped passenger is $100 in either case.

Obviously the company can save money by using overbooking and it appears that the best level to overbook is approximately 4. To be more precise a longer simulation run would be necessary.

INSTANT REPLAY   Suppose this model is to be used by Wings for other flights. What additional data would be needed?

CHECK   Other flights are likely to have different demand patterns, seat capacities, and no-show probabilities. These would have to be obtained in order to use the model. In addition, the revenue figures for lost and bumped passengers would also have to be changed.

General Characteristics   Several characteristics of this simulation are worth noting. One is that we needed to change only one decision variable, the number of passengers permitted to be overbooked. This greatly reduced the number of simulation runs required. In fact the same set of random numbers was used to simulate all the overbooking policies. The use of the same set of random numbers for each of the overbooking policies ensures that any differences observed in total cost are a result of policy differences and not a result of a different set of demands and no-shows. In contrast, our third example simulation will be a situation in which the interactions between two decision variables must be considered.

A second characteristic is that the model used a constant time increment of one day. Other models, particularly waiting line problems, use a variable time increment approach in which the time of the next event is itself a random variable. The modeling properties of a variable time increment model are somewhat more subtle than they are with a constant time increment model. Our second simulation example is of the variable time increment type and is introduced in the next section.

Variable Time Increment Model

Our second simulation example, like the first, treats a single decision variable. In this case, we are concerned about the size of a rental car fleet. The model we will use is a variable time increment model. We use that approach here because we are interested in the behavior of individual customers. Since individual customers will not arrive at constant time intervals, we require a model that can simulate variable interarrival times. We also demonstrate with this model the use of theoretical probability distributions.

Problem Description   The Lemon Auto Rental Agency has been experiencing capacity problems similar to those of Wings Airline. In certain locations they

TABLE 20-6
Comparison of Alternative Overbooking Policies for Wings Airline

| Number overbooked | Passengers lost | | Passengers bumped | Total monthly cost* |
	Due to capacity limit	Due to overbooking policy		
0	11	58	0	$6,900
1	11	34	2	$4,700
2	11	19	3	$3,300
3	11	8	5	$2,400
4	11	2	8	$2,100
5	11	1	12	$2,400
6 or more	11	0	12	$2,300

*Assumes $100 cost for each passenger lost or bumped.

seem to be frequently running out of cars to rent and, therefore, have to turn away customers. Since capacity expansion is relatively expensive, the company wishes to study the problem closely before purchasing additional cars. They have decided to simulate the rental car flow for one particular location to aid in their decision.

A preliminary study has found that the time between customers is exponentially distributed with a mean time between customers of 4 hours or an average of $\frac{1}{4}$ arrival per hour. The rental time, or time the car is kept by the customer, has been found to be approximately normal with a mean of 20 hours and a standard deviation of 5 hours.

Simulation Description The optimal number of cars or fleet size is believed to be 10 or fewer cars. Therefore, the simulation will be limited to fleet sizes of 10 or less. We will illustrate the flow of cars for a 1-week period or 168 hours (7 days × 24 hours per day). As you will see, it is convenient to show the flow for the maximum complement of 10 cars, since the results for smaller complements can be easily read directly from the results for the full complement.

The simulation proceeds by drawing exponentially distributed random numbers corresponding to the time between arrivals for each customer and normal random numbers for the length of time each customer keeps a rental car. We start with a clock time of zero and continue generating customer arrivals until the next arrival exceeds the end-of-week clock time of 168.

Table 20-7 provides the details of the week's simulation. Observe that the forty-sixth customer of the week is scheduled to arrive exactly at time 168.0. We assumed that the forty-sixth customer counts for the week being simulated, while the forty-seventh customer, not due to arrive until time 174.75, is not included in this week's business.

Note that the expected number of customers arriving in a 168-hour period is 168/4 = 42 customers. Thus our simulation represents a period that is somewhat busier than average. This may tend to bias the results toward selecting a larger fleet size than necessary. Such a bias could be reduced by simulating for a longer time interval than done here.

For purposes of simplification, we have rounded each interarrival time and each rental time to the nearest quarter hour. For example, for customer number 1 we select a two-digit random number, 94, and treat it as .94. Thus, the first interarrival time is calculated as

$$t = \frac{\log_e F(x)}{-\lambda} = \frac{\log_e(.94)}{-.25}$$

$$= \frac{-.062}{-.25} = .248$$

This is rounded to the nearest quarter hour, or .25.

From the table of normal random numbers in Appendix B we select the first such number, which is −0.36. The length of the rental time is calculated from

$$\mu - 0.36(\sigma) = 20 - .36(5) = 18.2$$

This is also rounded to the nearest quarter-hour, or 18.25. Therefore, the first customer is due to arrive at time 0 + .25 = 0.25 and will not return the rental car until clock time 0.25 + 18.25 = 18.50. A similar pattern was followed for other customers.

TABLE 20-7
Lemon Auto Rental Simulation Results for 1 Week

Customer number	RN 1	Inter- arrival time	Arrival clock time	Cars available for rental	Car assigned to customer	RN 2	Hours rented	Time returned
1	.94	0.25	0.25	1–10	1	−0.36	18.25	18.50
2	.37	4.00	4.25	2–10	2	.06	20.25	24.50
3	.74	1.25	5.50	3–10	3	.24	21.25	26.75
4	.98	.25	5.75	4–10	4	1.52	27.50	33.25
5	.13	8.25	14.00	5–10	5	1.84	29.25	43.25
6	.44	3.25	17.25	6–10	6	−1.21	14.00	31.25
7	.35	4.25	21.50	1, 7–10	1	−.72	16.50	38.00
8	.42	3.50	25.00	2, 7–10	2	.73	23.75	48.75
9	.89	0.50	25.50	7–10	7	−.72	16.50	42.00
10	.65	1.75	27.25	3, 8–10	3	.63	23.25	50.50
11	.35	4.25	31.50	6, 8–10	6	−.79	16.00	47.50
12	.29	5.00	36.50	4, 8–10	4	−.67	16.75	53.25
13	.43	3.50	40.00	1, 8–10	1	−1.34	13.25	53.25
14	.76	1.25	41.25	8–10	8	.50	22.50	63.75
15	.32	4.50	45.75	5, 7, 9–10	5	−.46	17.75	63.50
16	.95	.25	46.00	7, 9–10	7	−1.24	13.75	59.75
17	.79	1.00	47.00	9–10	9	−.35	18.25	65.25
18	.55	2.50	49.50	2, 6, 10	2	−1.00	15.00	64.50
19	.35	4.25	53.75	1, 3, 4, 6, 10	1	.57	22.75	76.50
20	.20	6.50	60.25	3, 4, 6, 7, 10	3	.29	21.50	81.75
21	.06	11.25	71.50	2, 4–10	2	.03	20.25	91.75
22	.87	.50	72.00	4–10	4	.36	21.75	93.75
23	.52	2.50	74.50	5–10	5	−1.60	12.00	86.50
24	.49	2.75	77.25	1, 6–10	1	−1.41	13.00	90.25
25	.75	1.25	78.50	6–10	6	.93	24.75	103.25
26	.21	6.25	84.75	3, 7–10	3	−.61	17.00	101.75
27	.92	0.50	85.25	7–10	7	−.33	18.25	103.50
28	.32	4.50	89.75	5, 8–10	5	2.05	30.25	120.00
29	.70	1.50	91.25	1, 8–10	1	−1.44	12.75	104.00
30	.02	15.75	107.00	1–4, 6–10	1	.79	24.00	131.00
31	.92	.50	107.50	2–4, 6–10	2	−.79	16.00	123.50
32	.36	4.00	111.50	3, 4, 6–10	3	−1.55	12.25	123.75
33	.44	3.25	114.75	4, 6–10	4	−.57	17.25	132.00
34	.10	9.25	124.00	2, 3, 5–10	2	.44	22.25	146.25
35	.81	0.75	124.75	3, 5–10	3	−1.36	13.25	138.00
36	.16	7.25	132.00	1, 4–10	1	−.38	18.00	150.00
37	.29	5.00	137.00	4–10	4	1.62	28.00	165.00
38	.07	10.75	147.75	2, 3, 5–10	2	−.17	19.25	167.00
39	.85	0.75	148.50	3, 5–10	3	.34	21.75	170.25
40	.63	1.75	150.25	1, 5–10	1	1.23	26.25	176.50
41	.73	1.25	151.50	5–10	5	−.25	18.75	170.25
42	.69	1.50	153.00	6–10	6	−1.08	14.50	167.50
43	.70	1.50	154.50	7–10	7	.97	24.75	179.25
44	.48	3.00	157.50	8–10	8	.05	20.25	177.75
45	.29	5.00	162.50	9–10	9	−.62	17.00	179.50
46	.26	5.50	168.00	2, 4, 6, 10	2	−0.76	16.25	184.25
47	.18	6.75	174.75				888.75	

INSTANT REPLAY Suppose RN1 is .56 and RN2 is .72 for customer number 48. When will that customer arrive and how long will the car be rented for? [*Hint*: $\log_e(.56) = -.5798$.]

CHECK Interarrival time is found from

$$t = \frac{\log_e(.56)}{-.25} = \frac{.5798}{.25} = 2.319$$

which is rounded to 2.25 (nearest quarter-hour). Customer 47 arrived at 174.75. Therefore, customer 48 will arrive at $174.75 + 2.25 = 177.00$. The rental time is found from:

$$20 + .72(5) = 23.6$$

which is rounded to 23.5. Thus, customer 48 will keep the car for 23.5 hours.

The most difficult part of this simulation is keeping track of the cars in service and those available for rental so that appropriate statistics can be gathered for different rental fleet sizes. This can be accomplished by keeping track of those cars available for rental as shown in the fifth column of Table 20-7. Thus, all 10 cars are available for rental when the first customer arrives and the first car does not again become available until the seventh customer arrives. This is because customers 2 through 6 arrive during the interval .25 to 17.25 and car number 1 is not due back until 18.50, as shown in the last column of the table.

Thus, when customer 11 arrives, only four cars are available—numbers 6, 8, 9, and 10—since all other cars are in use.

Note that the lowest-numbered available car is always assigned to the customer. This facilitates interpretation of the simulation results since the rentals made with each car then correspond to the marginal revenue obtained by adding that car to the fleet. For example, note that car 10 was always available, never rented, and therefore offers zero marginal revenue. Car 9 was rented twice for a total of 35.25 hours and would contribute marginal revenue for those hours.

INSTANT REPLAY What cars will be available for rental for customer 47? Which car will be assigned?

CHECK Customer 47 arrives at 174.75. Cars 1, 2, 7, 8, and 9 will not be returned until after that time. Cars 3, 4, 5, 6, and 10 are available and car 3 will be assigned.

Analysis of Results Table 20-8 summarizes the performance results based on different fleet sizes. Revenue is assumed to be $1 per rental hour and costs are assumed to be $.34 per hour whether or not the car is actually in operation (all costs are amortized over the expected rental life of the car). From Table 20-7 we see that the 46 customers of that week will keep the cars for a total of 888.75 hours, thus generating revenue of $888.75 for a 10-car fleet. Since the tenth car was never needed, the rental revenue is the same for a nine-car fleet. As noted earlier, the ninth car was needed only twice for a total of 35.25 hours. There-

TABLE 20-8

713

SIMULATION
ANALYSIS OF
COMPLEX
DECISIONS

Performance Results for Lemon Auto Rental Agency Simulation

Number of cars available for rental	Average utilization	Rental revenue*	Operating costs†	Net weekly revenue
10	.529	$888.75	$571.20	$317.55
9	.588	888.75	514.08	374.67
8	.635	853.50	456.96	396.54
7	.689	810.75	399.84	410.91
6	.732	737.50	342.72	394.78
5	.796	668.25	285.60	382.65
4	.834	560.25	228.48	331.77
3	.891	449.00	171.36	277.64
2	.949	318.75	114.24	204.51
1	.987	165.75	57.12	108.63

*Based on $1 per rental hour.
†Based on $.34 per car per hour whether rented or not.

fore, the revenue for an eight-car fleet would be $853.50, or $35.25 less than for a nine-car fleet. The other revenue figures were calculated in a simlar manner.

The weekly operating costs (defined to include fixed cost amortization) are easy to calculate according to

$$\begin{pmatrix} \text{Weekly} \\ \text{operating} \\ \text{costs} \end{pmatrix} = \begin{pmatrix} \text{number} \\ \text{of} \\ \text{cars} \end{pmatrix} \times \begin{pmatrix} \text{hours} \\ \text{per} \\ \text{week} \end{pmatrix} \times \begin{pmatrix} \text{cost} \\ \text{per} \\ \text{hour} \end{pmatrix}$$

$$= \quad n \quad \times \quad 168 \quad \times \quad \$.34 \quad = \$57.12n$$

where n is the fleet size. Thus a 10-car fleet will cost $571.20 per week, a 2-car fleet $114.24, etc.

The net weekly revenue was derived by subtracting operating costs from revenue. In addition, we may be interested in the fleet utilization. We have chosen to approximate the utilization rate from

$$\text{Utilization} = \frac{\text{rental hours for fleet size } n}{n \times 168}$$

Actually, for the week simulated, the utilization would be somewhat lower than that shown in Table 20-8 since some of the rental hours included in the numerator do not occur until the second week. For example, the forty-sixth customer picks a car up at time 168 and all 16.25 of that customer's rental hours will not occur until next week. For longer simulation periods, the allocation of rental hours between periods will stabilize, eliminating the bias shown here.

However, since we started the simulation with no cars in use, or a full fleet, we have biased the utilization on the low side. Therefore, we have partially corrected for this bias by considering total rental hours for the 46 customers without regard to within which week those hours occur.

For this simulation, the best fleet size appears to be seven cars, since net weekly revenue was highest for this level. Note that the added cost of $57.12 for increasing the fleet to eight cars exceeds the $42.75 in additional revenue generated, which is why the net revenue declines for that option.

Some caution is necessary in interpreting these results because the initial conditions assumed that all cars were available for rental at the start of the simulation. Observe that when the simulation ended only 3 of the 10 cars were available. Thus it is possible that results reported here may underestimate the need for larger fleet sizes. In practice we would certainly want to simulate for longer periods and discard the statistics for the early transient period.

General Characteristics With this example we have illustrated the generation of both exponential and normal random variables. We have also dealt with a variable time increment model in which the events "customer arrives" and "car returned" occur at varying intervals. As shown, this requires careful record-keeping to ensure, for example, that we do not assign to a customer a car that is already in service with another customer. In this problem, as with our first example, a single decision variable, the fleet size, was used as the basis for experimentation. In the example that follows we consider a situation in which two interacting decision variables are used for experimentation.

Two-Variable Simulation Model

Our last example illustrates the simulation of an inventory problem in which two decision variables are involved. As we will show, the performance of the system depends on the setting of both these variables. The experimental design, running of the simulation, and analysis of results are more complicated with two decision variables. Therefore, they will receive greater attention than earlier.

Problem Description The Winter Cigar Company is concerned with the costs of stocking and maintaining inventory for the various brands the company carries. Management knows that stockouts occur frequently for some brands, despite the fact that they feel the overall inventory investment is too high.

To study the situation more fully, the managers want to develop a simulation model that will allow them to determine an appropriate inventory policy. They have chosen their Palma brand panatella cigar for first study. The Palma

TABLE 20-9
Demand and Lead-Time Distributions for Palma Cigars
with Monte Carlo Assignment of Random Numbers

Daily demand	Probability	Random numbers
2	.1	00–09
3	.25	10–34
4	.3	35–64
5	.25	65–89
6	.1	90–99

Lead time, days	Probability	Random numbers
3	.1	00–09
4	.1	10–19
5	.5	20–69
6	.3	70–99

panatella is felt by management to be a typical inventory item with regard to demand pattern, lead time, etc. The daily demand distribution for Palmas is shown in Table 20-9 along with the lead-time distribution for stock replenishment.

The company has estimated that inventory-related costs for this item include a $25 cost per replenishment order, holding costs of $.10 per unit per day, and a stockout cost of $10 per unit per day.

The inventory system used by the company has two policy variables, the reorder point R and the order-up-to level Q. At the end of each day, the stock records are examined and if the on-hand inventory balance is equal to or below the reorder point, an order is placed equal to the difference between the current inventory balance and the specified order-up-to level Q.

The replenishment orders are received at the end of the day, before a new replenishment decision is made. Stockouts are assumed to be back-ordered and then shipped when the replenishment order is received.

Simulation Description   An example of how this simulation could be accomplished is shown in Table 20-10 for one 25-day period. We have assumed an initial inventory of 40 units and are testing an inventory policy with a reorder point of 20 and an order-up-to level of 40. Thus, when the inventory drops to 20 or

TABLE 20-10
Winter Cigar Company Simulation with Reorder Point Equal
to 20 and Order-up-to Level Equal to 40

Day	RN 1	Demand	Ending inventory	RN 2	Lead time	Date due in	Quantity ordered	Unit day stockouts
1	81	5	35					0
2	99	6	29					0
3	90	6	23					0
4	52	4	19	22	5	9	21	0
5	76	5	14					0
6	26	3	11					0
7	75	5	6					0
8	55	4	2					0
9	15	3	20	67	5	14	20	1
10	61	4	16					0
11	73	5	11					0
12	52	4	7					0
13	90	2	5					0
14	60	4	21					0
15	10	3	18	70	6	21	22	0
16	68	5	13					0
17	41	4	9					0
18	42	4	5					0
19	67	5	0					0
20	75	5	−5					5
21	97	6	11	55	5	26	29	11
22	79	5	6					0
23	12	3	3					0
24	15	3	0					0
25	79	5	−5					5

less, we order the difference between 40 and the current balance (e.g., when the on-hand balance is 18 we order $40 - 18 = 22$ units).

For our example, as shown in Table 20-10, no action is necessary until day 4, at which point the inventory drops below the reorder point. The two-digit random number, 22, corresponds to a lead time of 5 days and therefore the order will not be received until the end of day 9. The order size is set equal to $40 - 19 = 21$ units.

On day 9 our demand of 3 units exceeds the inventory balance of 2 and we therefore incur a 1 unit stockout for that day, as shown in the last column. At the end of that same day, the replenishment order placed at the conclusion of day 4 is received. The 20-unit ending balance is calculated from

$$\underset{\text{balance}}{\text{Ending}} = \begin{pmatrix} \text{beginning} \\ \text{balance} \end{pmatrix} - \begin{pmatrix} \text{day's} \\ \text{demand} \end{pmatrix} + \begin{pmatrix} \text{order} \\ \text{received} \end{pmatrix} - \begin{pmatrix} \text{previous day's} \\ \text{backorders} \end{pmatrix}$$

$$20 \quad = \quad 2 \quad - \quad 3 \quad + \quad 21 \quad - \quad 0$$

The ending balance of 20 is equal to the reorder point, causing another order to be released, for 20 units $(40 - 20)$. The lead time is found to be 5 days for this order, so it is due at the end of day 14.

This new order arrives in time to avoid further stockouts; however, on day 15 the on-hand balance drops from 21 to 18, triggering a new order for, in this case, $40 - 18 = 22$ units. The random numbers call for a lead time of 6 days.

Before that order arrives we stock out by 5 units on day 20 and 6 more units on day 21. The ending balance of 11 units on day 21 is found by subtracting the 11 units back-ordered from the 22 units received that day. Since this new balance is below the reorder point, a new order is placed which will not arrive until day 26. On day 25 we run short by 5 units.

INSTANT REPLAY   Suppose the demands for the next four days are 4, 5, 3, and 4. When will the next order be placed and for what quantity? Refer to Table 20-10.

CHECK   On day 26 the order of 29 is received. Of these units, 5 are needed to staisfy back orders and 4 are needed for demand that day. This leaves a balance of 20 on hand. Since this equals the reorder point, a new order will be issued for $40 - 20 = 20$ units.

Analysis of Preliminary Results   To evaluate the performance of the policy simulated, we need to know the number of orders placed, the average inventory, and the number of units short. From Table 20-10 we note that four orders were placed during the course of the simulation. The average inventory can be calculated by adding the daily ending inventory balances (ignoring negative balances) and dividing by the number of days. Thus,

$$\text{Average inventory} = \frac{284}{25} = 11.36 \text{ units per day}$$

The last column of Table 20-10 contains the daily shortages. The total number of daily shortages is thus found to be 22. Total daily cost can then be calculated from

$$\text{Daily} \atop \text{cost} = \begin{pmatrix} \text{ordering} \\ \text{cost} \end{pmatrix} + \begin{pmatrix} \text{inventory} \\ \text{holding cost} \end{pmatrix} + \begin{pmatrix} \text{stockout} \\ \text{cost} \end{pmatrix}$$

$$= \frac{(\$25)(4)}{25} + 11.36(\$.10) + \frac{(22)(\$10)}{25}$$

$$= \$4.00 + \$1.14 + \$8.80 = \$13.94$$

In this case the average daily stockout cost is high relative to the other two costs, particularly in relation to the inventory holding cost. This suggests that costs can be improved by increasing the reorder point, which should reduce stockout costs although holding costs will increase.

Experimental Design   Note, however, that there are two decision variables, order-up-to level and reorder point, and that they interact with each other in influencing the three cost elements. For example, an increase in the order-up-to level reduces ordering costs, increases holding costs, and reduces stockout costs by decreasing the number of exposures to stockout. This in turn may suggest a decrease in the reorder point, since the safety stock required to achieve a particular service level is lower with the reduced risk of stockout.

In other words, the best choice of a reorder point is at least partially dependent on the order-up-to level. Alternatively, a similar line of reasoning will show that the best order-up-to level is dependent on the reorder point. This suggests that the experiments conducted with the simulation model should be designed so that various combinations of both decision variables are tested. Since many values of each variable are possible, the complexity of the search problem is greatly compounded.

One approach frequently followed for this problem is to first search over rather broad ranges for the decision variables to determine the approximate zone of good combinations, and then search more precisely within that zone.

For our example problem we note that the average lead time is 5 days and the average demand per day is 4 units. Thus, the average demand during lead time is 20. On the other hand, maximum lead time is 6 days and maximum daily demand is 6 units. Thus maximum demand during lead time is 36 units. This suggests that the best reorder point irrespective of the order-up-to level should be somewhere in the range of 20 to 36. We might then decide to test five reorder point values of, say, 20, 25, 30, 35, and 40.

The experimental range for order-up-to levels is more difficult to determine. Because of the greater uncertainty involved in identifying a search range for the order-up-to level, a larger range is called for. As a first guess, we might select a range of 40–120, in increments of 20. Thus, we might decide to simulate with order-up-to levels of 40, 60, 80, 100, and 120. This gives us five levels for each decision variable, or a total of 25 combinations to be simulated.

Analysis of Broad Search Results   The results of such an experiment are shown in Table 20-11. Each combination was simulated for 1,000 days with a computer version of the model simulated manually in Table 20-10. The best combination found was a reorder point of 25 and an order-up-to level of 80 for an average daily cost of $5.18. The results of this search suggest that if a more precise specification of the best reorder point and order-up-to level values is desired, the search should be concentrated in the range of 20 to 30 for reorder point and 60 to 100 for order-up-to level. We will not report the results of such a search

TABLE 20-11
Average Daily Cost Performance for Various Combinations of Reorder Point
and Order-up-to Level for the Winter Cigar Company Simulation

Reorder point	Order-up-to level				
	40	*60*	*80*	*100*	*120*
20	8.67	6.05	5.72	6.12	6.81
25	8.15	5.25	5.18*	5.70	6.43
30	8.96	5.80	5.54	5.94	6.58
35	8.67	6.58	5.98	6.27	6.94
40	8.78	7.59	6.47	6.71	7.26

*Lowest-cost combination found.

here but typical values examined might have included varying the reorder point by units of 2 from 20 to 30 and the order-up-to level by units of 5 from 60 to 100. This leads to 54 additional combinations for a total of 79 for the two-step search. Contrast this with the 187 combinations that would have been required had we tested at the eventual level of detail over the original range.

It is interesting to examine the effects that the decision variables have on costs. Note that for any given order-up-to level, the costs first decline and then increase as the reorder point is increased. This is because the stockout costs are at first decreasing at a faster rate than the ordering and holding costs are increasing, though eventually the change in ordering and holding costs surpasses the change in stockout costs.

On the other hand, for a given reorder point, as the order-up-to level is increased the costs decline and then rise. This is because the combined decrease in the stockout and ordering costs at first exceeds and later falls below the increase in holding costs.

Now that we have examined several examples of simulation models, we turn, in the next sections, to a more detailed look at the validation, experimental design, and output analysis phases of simulation modeling.

Validation of Simulation Models

Checking the validity of a simulation model is important if the manager is to have any confidence in conclusions reached on the basis of the model. In this respect, simulation modeling is at a disadvantage over optimization models. The validity of using an optimization model, such as linear programming, is dependent on whether the generally known assumptions of linear programming do not violate the realities of the problem being solved. Simulation is such a broad flexible tool that its assumptions are really problem specific and in many cases are implicit in the model and never explicitly spelled out. The assumptions required for simulation models are on a very detailed level. For example, in the Wings Airline simulation we assumed that the number of no-shows was independent of the demand level. We did this for convenience, not because it was something required by simulation. In practice, this assumption needs to be addressed and changed if it is not correct. Since each simulation model is unique, the assumptions themselves are specific to the problem being modeled and do not, therefore, follow some standard pattern.

Internal Validity

There are several types of validity checks that can be made with a simulation model. The *internal validity* of the model relates to the stability of the model's outputs. For instance, refer to the Winter Cigar Company model. In Table 20-11 we found that a reorder point of 25 and an order-up-to level of 80 had a lower average daily cost ($5.18) than did the combination of reorder point of 30 and order-up-to level of 80 ($5.54). Based on this run we might conclude that the 25–80 combination is preferred to the 30–80 combination.

Suppose that we ran the model five times (with five different sets of random numbers) for each of these two parameter settings and found the following cost results:

Combination	Run 1	Run 2	Run 3	Run 4	Run 5
25–80	$5.18	$5.91	$7.29	$5.01	$4.80
30–80	$5.54	$4.65	$4.47	$5.84	$4.67

It is no longer clear which of these two policy settings is preferred because the cost variability among runs for each policy overwhelms the cost differential between the two policies. This lack of internal validity makes it difficult to reach any significant conclusions concerning which policy combination is best with the model. Nonetheless, the model can be used to determine a distribution of average costs for each policy combination and these distributions, in turn, can be used to estimate the probability that one policy combination is better than another.

Face Validity

Another kind of validity, called *face validity*, refers to the degree of realism for the simulation model. An evaluation of face validity requires an examination of the model by those familiar with the real system that the model purports to represent. For example, if a simulation model of patient flows in a hospital were developed, the model's face validity should be examined by the hospital management to ensure that all relevant elements have been included. Such an examination might include checking that all real flow patterns are possible in the model, that policies that can affect the flow patterns are incorporated, that patient delays are faithfully represented, etc.

Interrelationship Validity

A third type of validity refers to the interrelationships assumed by the model and could be called *interrelationship validity*. This normally requires some form of sensitivity testing of the model, to determine whether the model reacts to hypothetical changes as we would expect the real system to respond. For instance, in the Lemon Auto Rental Agency model, if we increase the rate at which customers arrive, does the model show an increase in fleet utilization?

Alternatively, we may run the model with the existing fleet size to determine whether the utilization rate and revenues correspond to those currently in existence.

It is useful to note that a distinction can be made between models that accurately portray distributions of events and those that accurately predict the timing of events. For instance, all three simulation examples we considered involved stockouts of one kind or another, whether seats on a flight, cars available for rental, or items in inventory. Because of the uses to which these models were intended, we were not concerned as to the precise timing of these stockouts but were trying to identify their distribution over time. If, on the other hand, the cost of a stockout varied, depending on when it occurred, then we would be concerned that the model accurately represented the timing of these stockouts as well as their number.

Performance Validity

As a final point, remember that whether a model is valid or not depends, in the design phase, on whether the user of the model believes it to be so, irrespective of its true validity. Furthermore, although a comparison of actual system performance with that predicted by the model can serve as a test of validity, we can make such a comparison only for one decision variable combination—that which has been used in the real system. Although the model may pass that test, this *performance validity* is not a complete test of validity. This is because we have no way of validating the model for those policies that were not implemented. The ability to check the model's validity through observation of the performance of the real system is further clouded by unforeseen changes in the system's environment. An unexpected price drop by a competitor will have measurable impact on the system's performance that may overshadow any improvements achieved by policy decisions based on the use of the simulation model.

Despite the difficulties mentioned above in carrying out validation of the model, its importance as a management concern must be emphasized. Management has to examine carefully whether the model is a good fit to reality and does what it is supposed to do. Otherwise, there is a high likelihood that the model will bring disappointment.

Design of Simulation Experiments

The major objective of the experimental design phase of simulation modeling is to ensure that the options or alternatives tested include those potentially optimal. In other words, with reference again to the Lemon Auto Rental Agency, if the best fleet size is in fact seven and we limit the options tested to fleet sizes of, say, two to six, we have unnecessarily limited the usefulness of the model by excluding the best alternative.

Another objective of the experimental design is to find the "best" alternative with the least computation cost. The interaction of these two goals should ultimately lead to intelligent design tradeoffs. This is the essence of the experimental design problem.

With integer decision variables there is normally some limited set of feasible levels or options that need be considered. Nevertheless, as the number of decision variables or the number of options that each may have increases, the number of feasible combinations grows rapidly.

For example, in the Winter Cigar Simulation we tested two variables each with 5 levels. This represented 5×5 or $5^2 = 25$ combinations. Suppose we had 6 variables, 2 of which had 5 levels, 3 of which had 6 levels and one of which had 10 levels. The number of combinations in this case is

$$(5)^2(6)^3(10)^1 = 54,000$$

Even if each of these took only 1 minute of computer time to simulate, it would take 900 hours to examine all of them.

In the case of continuous variables, there are, effectively, an infinite number of potential combinations. Clearly what are needed are procedures that systematically reduce the area to be searched without unnecessarily eliminating potentially good areas.

With continuous variables the search problem is similar to finding the peak of a hill, as shown in Figure 20-4. In some cases we find that the performance measure has only one hill (unimodal) and our job is to find its peak. In other cases, however, we find the situation depicted in Figure 20-4, where several hills exist and the task is to find the highest peak. The problem is compounded in simulation since the performance measure achievable for a particular setting of the decision variable is a sample statistic and subject to probabilistic variation. A common approach in this case is to average the performance measure values achieved for common settings of the decision variable and then find the highest peak. In Figure 20-4, the curve drawn represents an averaging of the individual observations plotted.

The problem becomes more difficult when more than one decision variable exists. We saw this compounding effect with the Winter Cigar simulation where the performance measure, total inventory cost, was affected by both the reorder point and the order-up-to level. The best value for either of these decision variables could not be determined without consideration of the other.

FIGURE 20-4 Search for best value of a decision variable when the performance measure to be maximized is a probabilistic function of the decision variable.

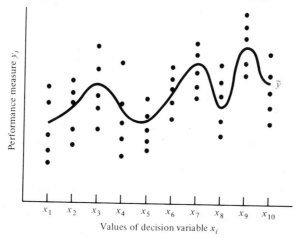

Performance measure y_i

x_1 x_2 x_3 x_4 x_5 x_6 x_7 x_8 x_9 x_{10}

Values of decision variable x_i

In Figure 20-1, the last step in the design and use of a simulation model is the evaluation of results. As we shall see shortly, preparation for this step actually begins in the experimental design stage. Preparation is important in that well-designed experiments can significantly reduce computation costs, increase confidence in the results, or both. Because of this importance we have chosen to include certain design elements in this section.

The basic unit for gathering statistical data is the *simulation run*, which represents an uninterrupted block of simulation time during which all controllable decision variables remain unchanged. Each run can be broken into segments or *blocks* representing computational subsets, such as days, weeks, months, etc. At the completion of each block, statistics can be gathered for the values of various performance measures. For example, with the Lemon Auto Rental Agency problem, we might decide to limit each run for a particular fleet size to 1 year with weekly blocks or segments. Thus we would obtain separate measures of net weekly revenue and fleet utilization for each of the 52 weeks in a run. If we were testing four different fleet sizes, we would obtain 52 samples of both performance measures for each of the four settings of the decision variable (fleet size).

Steady-State and Transient Conditions

It is important to distinguish between two performance conditions under which a simulation model may operate. A model is said to be operating under steady-state conditions when successive observations of the model's performance measures are statistically stable. This means that the effects of start-up or initializing behavior have passed and the model is operating under "normal" conditions. The second condition is generally referred to as transient behavior and is circuitously defined by saying that any model not in a steady-state condition is in a transient state.

Most models will experience transient behavior in the initial stages of a simulation run as a result of the transition from starting conditions to normal conditions. For example, in the Lemon Auto Agency problem we began the simulation with a full fleet of 10 cars available for rental. This clearly biases such statistics as fleet utilization until a more normal "in-use/available" pattern develops during the course of the run.

Other simulation models may include perturbation effects or unusual events that periodically push the model from a steady-state condition to a temporary transient state. These effects may take the form of low-probability events, such as a technological breakthrough, fire damage, or a product liability law suit, or they may be of a more periodic variety such as a plant shutdown for 1 week to take inventory, periodic preventative maintenance of equipment, or unusual orders from special customers.

Some models experience only transient behavior and never reach what we defined as steady-state behavior. A model that includes a steady growth in sales will always be in a transient state since the performance measures such as profit will never be statistically stable. For these models, it is the transient behavior that is of interest. Other systems exhibit oscillatory behavior in which the performance measures are in a continual, but sometimes predictable, state of flux. For example, inventory levels will oscillate in a seasonal pattern if a level production plan is followed in the face of seasonal demand. Inventories increase when demand is less than production and decrease when demand exceeds production.

If the steady-state behavior of the model is of interest, it is important to eliminate the effects of the transient conditions from the statistics gathered for the relevant performance measures. Several methods have been suggested for accomplishing this. One method is to choose starting conditions for the model that as closely as possible match those we would expect to represent steady-state conditions. For example, suppose we have constructed a simulation model of an aircraft maintenance shop in which we wish to test various work scheduling rules. The easiest way to begin the simulation would be with an empty shop (no jobs in process). However, it may take a considerable length of time before the simulation conditions reach a steady-state condition. This transient period can be shortened by initially providing the shop with an average number of in-process jobs rather than allowing the shop to slowly fill.

As promising as this approach may appear, it suffers from one major defect: it may be difficult to estimate in advance an unbiased set of starting conditions. What we perceive to be a starting condition that closely approximates normal or steady-state conditions may, in fact, not be very close at all. Unless this unanticipated transient behavior is eliminated, the performance results will be biased.

Even if we can successfully choose approximately steady-state initial conditions for a given set of decison variable values, the problem is compounded when we consider that the decision values will affect the steady-state conditions which in turn will affect what constitutes an unbiased starting condition. For example, in the aircraft maintenance case we may be comparing a "shortest processing time" scheduling rule (when two or more jobs compete for a worker or machine, first do the job with shortest processing time) with an "earliest due date" rule (first do the job which has the earliest due date). The steady-state behavior of the simulation model is likely to vary, depending upon the scheduling rule in use.

The question then arises as to whether the model should be started at an approximate steady-state point appropriate to each scheduling rule or at some intermediate compromise point. The individually chosen points promise quicker convergence to the steady state but at the risk of introducing bias. A common compromise starting point may be easier to use (only a single, common starting point need be identified), but an unbiased starting point is not easy to choose and is more costly in computation time, since it will take longer to reach the steady state for each option if custom-picked starting points had been chosen.

Regardless of which method is used, some transient effects will be present in the model. These effects are normally removed by running the model until we are reasonably assured that steady-state conditions exist and throwing away any statistics gathered during the preliminary stage. Note that although the statistics are discarded, the state of the model is left unchanged. For the aircraft maintenance example, the jobs in process at the end of the initial period become the starting conditions for gathering performance statistics in the later periods of the run.

The major difficulty is determining how long this initial nonrecording period should be. It must be long enough to remove transient effects but not so long as to waste good results. Unfortunately there is no easy solution to this

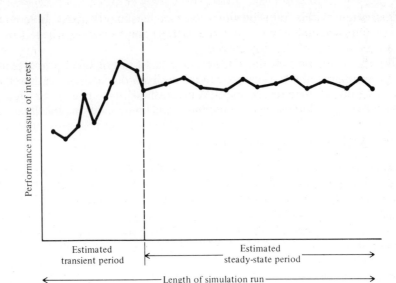

FIGURE 20-5   Estimating the length of the transient period for a simulation run.

problem. Frequently the model builder must resort to experimentation. A plot of periodic statistics during this experimentation stage, such as shown in Figure 20-5, is often useful.

As mentioned earlier we may not always be interested in eliminating transient behavior in a model but may actually be primarily concerned with observing and measuring that transient behavior. Suppose, for example, that a company which had been using a perpetual EOQ inventory system desired to switch to an MRP system (see Chapter 15). A normal transient phenomenon that occurs with a major change in an inventory control system is for the inventory to increase dramatically for a while before declining to a new steady-state level. This is because a comparison of existing, on-hand stock levels with those desired by the new system will find some items in an overstock situation and others understocked. The understocked items can be corrected rather quickly by ordering additional stock. The overstocked items, on the other hand, can usually be reduced only gradually as demand reduces the excess quantities. The net impact is for total inventory to increase in the short run before dropping down to more normal levels.

Although the ultimate steady-state inventory levels may be of great interest, the transient behavior is also important. We are likely to be concerned with the maximum inventory investment required during this transient period as well as the length of time before normal levels are reached.

Note that statistics gathered for transient periods are of a different form than for steady-state conditions. We are normally interested in extreme conditions, such as maximum inventory investment, rather than averages, such as average inventory investment. Furthermore, to obtain greater statistical significance when studying steady-state behavior we can increase the run length. When transient behavior is of concern, we can normally obtain statistical significance by performing multiple runs or replications. For the inventory example, each run represents a sample point for one possible transition brought about by the change in inventory system.

Also observe that since the worst extreme conditions are likely to have a low probability we may have to generate a large number of replications to obtain a good estimate of the true extreme.

For the remaining portions of this section we will concentrate on the statistical problems involved in estimating the mean or average performance level for a given set of values of decision variables. We assume in what follows that any transient behavior has been eliminated by methods discussed earlier.

Increasing Significance of Observed Results

For most simulations we are not concerned with one specific mean but are interested in comparing means obtained for two or more settings of the decision variables. For an illustration, suppose the average daily profit in the aircraft maintenance shop was $150 for scheduling rule A (shortest processing time) and $160 for scheduling rule B (earliest due date). Although rule B had a higher average daily profit, we need to know whether the profit differential was statistically significant or could have occurred by chance.

In order to answer this question we need to know the variance of the daily profit for each rule. If the variances are small enough we can conclude that the difference is significant and that rule B will generate higher profits for the shop than rule A. With large variances we are unable to reach any definite conclusions. Therefore it is useful to design simulation experiments in a way that reduces the variance as much as possible.

Consider for the moment that we wish to estimate as closely as possible the true steady-state average daily profit for scheduling rule A. According to standard statistical inference methods, the unbiased estimate of the true profit $\hat{u}$ is defined as

$$\hat{u} = \frac{\sum\limits_{i=1}^{n} x_i}{n}$$

where x_i is the ith daily profit in a sample of n.

The standard error of this estimate, σ_u, if the daily profits are independent of each other, is given by

$$\sigma_u = \frac{\sigma}{\sqrt{n}}$$

where σ is the true standard deviation of the daily profit.

Observe that the error in estimating the true mean can be reduced by increasing the sample size. This, of course, increases the computation costs.

Introducing Negative Correlation between Runs   Fortunately, a cheaper alternative exists for reducing estimation error that makes use of what are called *antithetic variates*. Suppose we make two runs or replicates with $n/2$ observations in each such that observations from one run are *negatively correlated* with the observations from the other. (How this negative correlation is to be achieved will be described below.) The mean is now estimated from

$$\hat{u} = \frac{\sum\limits_{i=1}^{n/2} x_i + y_i}{n}$$

where the x_is are the observations from the one run and the y_is are from the other run.

When correlation exists between the pairs of observations, the standard error of the estimate is defined as

$$\sigma_{\hat{u}} = \frac{\sigma}{\sqrt{n}}(\sqrt{1 + \rho_{xy}})$$

where ρ_{xy} is the coefficient of correlation (see Chapter 18). If there is no correlation ($\rho_{xy} = 0$), the formula for the standard error is the same as defined previously. However, when the correlation is *negative*, the standard error of the estimate is less than it would be for one continuous run of n observations.

Thus the use of negatively correlated runs will yield tighter estimates of the true profit than would a single uncorrelated run of the same size. It is actually quite easy to produce negatively correlated simulation runs. If, for example, we are using single-digit random numbers to generate processing times of jobs that arrive in the aircraft maintenance shop, we convert the string of random numbers used in the first run to a negatively correlated string for the second run. If RN_i is the random digit used to determine the processing time for the ith job in the first run, $9 - RN_i$ would be the random digit for the ith processing time in the second run.

INSTANT REPLAY   If the first five random numbers used for processing times in the first run were 3, 7, 0, 1, and 6, what would be the corresponding digits for the second run?

CHECK   6, 2, 9, 8, and 3.

Introducing Positive Correlation   A different form of correlation is useful in comparing performance for two or more settings of decision variables. Under normal circumstances if the means and standard errors for two policies A and B were $\hat{u}_A$, σ_A and $\hat{u}_B$, σ_B, respectively, the mean of the difference between the means would be

$$\hat{u}_{A-B} = \hat{u}_A - \hat{u}_B$$

and the standard error of the difference is

$$\sigma_{A-B} = \sqrt{\sigma_A^2 + \sigma_B^2}$$

Whether the observed difference in means is significantly large enough to conclude that the true means are different depends to a large extent on how small σ_{A-B} is. As before, larger runs will reduce σ_{A-B} but at the cost of greater computational expense. Another means of reducing the standard error of the difference is to introduce *positive correlation* between the runs for the two policies. In this case the standard error is redefined as

$$\sigma_{A-B} = \sqrt{\sigma_A^2 + \sigma_B^2 - 2\rho_{AB}\sigma_A\sigma_B}$$

where ρ_{AB} is the correlation between the two runs. Any positive correlation will lead to a lower standard error than if no correlation existed. Note that the reduction in the standard error is accomplished by removal of variance due to differences in the random numbers while variance due to policy differences is retained. This improves our ability to detect true differences in performance for these policies.

Positive correlation can be introduced by ensuring that the *same random numbers are used in both runs*. In this way, each policy is exposed to the same experimental conditions, such as the pattern and rate of arrival of customers, service times, etc. This was done in all three simulation examples presented in this chapter. Thus, in the Wings Airline simulation, all overbooking policies were tested on a common set of demands and no-shows; in the Lemon Auto Rental Agency problem we used a single set of customer arrivals and rental times to test all fleet sizes; in the Winter Cigar situation we used a common set of demands and replenishment lead times to measure performance under the various reorder point and order-up-to levels tested.

Note that both kinds of correlation can be used in the same simulation experiment. Negative correlation is used for replication of runs for any one policy and positive correlation is used between runs for different policies.

INSTANT REPLAY   The first three random numbers used for run 1 for policy A are 2, 5, and 6. What would be the first three random numbers for run 2 of policy A? For run 1 of policy B? For run 2 of policy B?

CHECK   7, 4, and 3 for run 2 of policy A; 2, 5, and 6 for run 1 of policy B; 7, 4, and 3 for run 2 of policy B.

Ensuring Independence of Observations   Note that throughout this discussion we have been assuming that the individual observations in any run are independent of each other. For example, we have assumed that the profit earned on day 10 is independent of the profit earned on day 9. This is not likely to be true for our example, since conditions in the shop on day 10 are likely to be heavily influenced by conditions on day 9.

A common method of overcoming this problem is to group the individual (e.g., daily) observations and consider the average for each group as a sample point. Thus, rather than use n successive daily profits as the n sample points, we might run the simulation for n months and use the average daily profit for each month as a sample point. Even grouping by weeks or pairs of days will help in keeping the observations independent.

The difficulty is in choosing a group size large enough to ensure independence but small enough to avoid excessive computation time. Independence of observations can be tested by calculating correlation coefficients for successive observations (called autocorrelation) and checking these for significance.

Sensitivity Analysis   One of the real values of using simulation models is the ability they provide to perform sensitivity testing. We have assumed previously that the analysis of output concerned measuring differences between two or more decision options or policies for a given specification of system environment. Since many aspects of that assumed environment (demand rates and patterns, no-show probabilities, revenues, costs, etc.) may be estimates of the true environment, it is useful to test the effects of changes in these factors on the system's performance. This sensitivity testing can be an important part of simulation applications.

For instance, in the Lemon Auto Rental Agency problem, we may be interested in knowing how sensitive the optimal fleet size is to changes in the demand rate. This can be accomplished by changing the assumed demand rate and rerunning the model. This can be done as often as desired, in each case testing the impact of these new demand levels on net revenues for best fleet size. We may find, for example, that as long as average demand is no less than three cars per hour or no more than five per hour, a fleet size of seven will yield the highest net revenue. Beyond these limits, some other fleet size will be best (most likely six cars if demand is less than three per hour or eight cars if demand is greater than five per hour).

Similar tests can be performed for other environmental assumptions, such as a change in the average rental time. The results of these tests provide a set of best decisions that are conditional on the true state of the environment. Sensitivity testing can also be used to anticipate the effects of future environments on existing or alternative policies. Management can ask "what if" questions of the model, choosing whatever environmental conditions they wish. This issue will be explored in more detail in the next chapter.

Final Comments

Most of the models we have discussed prior to this chapter apply to specific kinds of problems (linear programming problems, dynamic programming problems, etc.). These problems are defined by a set of precise assumptions. If we have a real-world problem to solve and it fits the assumptions of, say, the linear programming model, we can apply that model to the problem with reasonable assurance of success. If, however, one or more of the linear programming assumptions is not satisfied, the application of the model may not be wise.

Fortunately, we are not so restricted with simulation. A simulation model has no inherent assumptions concerning the problem characteristics necessary for its application. Thus, simulation is an extremely flexible and powerful management science tool. However, in gaining this flexibility, we create other problems. Since there is no natural structure to a simulation model, the process of developing the model takes on added significance and is no easy matter. If we use one of the specialized simulation computer languages, such as GPSS, SIMSCRIPT, or DYNAMO, this process can be simplified to some extent. This is because these languages have built-in capabilities for modeling certain common, real-world phenomena, gathering statistical information, and controlling the simulation run.

Another difficulty with simulation concerns the need to check the validity of the model. Validation checks are important whether we use simulation or some other technique. It is more difficult to accomplish with simulation because of the lack of natural structure or assumptions. For this same reason, however, it is also more important.

Interpreting the results of simulations is also complicated. This is because these results are sample observations and, as such, subject to sampling error. Simulation models are descriptive rather than prescriptive. That is, they enable us to predict what will happen if a certain course of action is followed but cannot be used to directly identify which course of action is best. We can attempt to do this, indirectly, by trying out various alternatives. However, we have no way of knowing that we have not overlooked some better option.

Despite these difficulties, simulation is one of the most widely used management science approaches. Because of its flexibility, simulation is often the only approach available that can handle complex decision situations. The ability to try out many alternatives and compare the consequences makes simulation an attractive managerial decision aid.

Key Words

Antithetic variate **725**
Autocorrelation **727**
Block **722**
Central limit theorem **703**
Congruential method **700**
Constant time increment **705**
Correlation **725**
Cumulative probability
   distribution **701**
Descriptive model **693**
DYNAMO **695**
Empirical probability
   distribution **704**
Experimental design **696**
Exponential distribution **700**
Face validity **719**
FORTRAN **695**
GPSS **695**
Internal validity **719**
Interrelationship validity **719**
Inverse **701**
Level of detail **694**
Midsquare method **700**
Modulo division **700**
Monte Carlo method **698**
Multiplicative congruential
   method **700**
Negative exponential
   distribution **701**
Normal distribution **700**

Optimization model **693**
Order-up-to level **715**
Overbooking **705**
Performance validity **720**
PL/1 **695**
Poisson distribution **700**
Probability distribution **697**
Random number **698**
Random variable **698**
Reorder point **715**
Sample **696**
Sampling error **697**
Sensitivity analysis **727**
SIMSCRIPT **695**
Simulation **693**
Simulation model **693**
Simulation run **722**
Standard error **726**
Start-up behavior **696**
Steady state **722**
System boundary **694**
Theoretical probability
   distribution **700**
Transient **697**
Uniform distribution **698**
Unimodal **721**
Validation **718**
Variable time increment **705**
Variance reduction **725**
What-if question **693**

Problems

20-1. Determine an assignment of random numbers that will accurately model the following probability distributions:
   a. The number of heads in three tosses of a fair coin.
   b. Daily demands for tennis courts which have the following probabilities:

Courts demanded	Probability
0	.05
1	.12
2	.23
3	.34
4	.20
5	.04
6	.02

c. Number of fires occurring per day which has the following set of probabilities.

Fires per day	Probability
0	.596
1	.214
2	.106
3	.059
4	.025

d. Number of batches of defective output per day based on the following frequencies for a 250-day period:

Defective batches	Frequency
0	143
1	62
2	21
3	13
4	7
5	4

20-2. Write out the equations that would be used to generate the following types of stochastic variables:

    a. Exponential distribution with mean of 100.

    b. Normal distribution with a mean of 50 and standard deviation of 10, where a table of random normal numbers will be used.

    c. Normal distribution with a mean of 240 and standard deviation of 30, where a table of uniform random numbers will be used.

20-3. Repeat the Wings Airline simulation described in the text, assuming that seat demand is normally distributed with mean of 102 and standard deviation of 3 (rounded to the nearest passenger). Run the simulation for 10 days and compare a strategy of no overbooking with one where up to three passengers may be overbooked. Assume that the no-show distribution is as given in Table 20-4.

20-4. Repeat the Wings Airline simulation described in the text, assuming that seat demand is defined as given in Table 20-3. Run the simulation for 10 days and compare a strategy of no overbooking with one where up to five passengers may be overbooked. Assume that the no-show distribution is as defined below:

Number of no-shows	Probability
0	.30
1	.15
2	.05
3	.05
4	.10
5	.15
6	.20

20-5. The First National Bank of Metropolis is designing a new branch bank to be operated in one of the suburbs. The bank is undecided as to whether one or two drive-in window facilities are to be established.

Demand for the drive-in window facilities is expected to arrive at intervals determined by the exponential distribution with mean of 4 minutes. However, because of limited waiting space, if as many as four cars are backed up in line (not counting the one being served), the arriving customers do not enter the line but drive elsewhere.

The service time necessary to complete each customer's banking transaction is exponential with mean of 3 minutes.

Simulate the operation of the drive-in window (assuming a single teller) for a period of 2 hours. If the bank is willing to pay $10 to avoid a lost customer (one unable to enter the waiting line), how much would it be willing to spend per day to operate with two tellers, assuming that no lost customers will result?

20-6. Repeat the First National Bank of Metropolis simulation (problem 20-5), assuming first that arrivals occur at the rate of 20 per hour (exponential interarrival time) and then that arrivals occur at the rate of 12 per hour (also exponential). How sensitive is the performance of the system to the customer arrival rate?

20-7. The following diagram illustrates the precedence relationships among the six activities for a project.

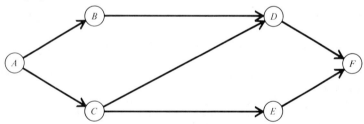

The time that each activity is expected to take is forecast by the following probability distributions (in days):

Time	A	B	C	D	E	F
			Probability for activity			
1				.1	.3	
2	.1	.1	.2	.2	.1	
3	.2	.6	.3	.3	.1	.3
4	.4	.2	.4	.4	.3	.4
5	.2	.1	.1		.2	.3
6	.1					

a. Using the probabilities shown, calculate the expected activity times and determine the length of the critical path. Identify the critical activities (see Chapter 16).

b. Simulate the completion of this project 10 times.

c. What was the expected project length based on your simulation? How do you account for any differences between the simulated expected project length and the calculated length from part *a*?

d. On the basis of your simulation results, what probability would you attach to each activity to represent the likelihood of actually being on the critical path? (*Hint*: How often was each activity on a critical path?)

20-8. Special tanker ships are used to transport liquid natural gas (LNG) between a Middle Eastern port and a storage facility located on the East Coast of the United States.

Loading time at the Middle Eastern port and unloading time at the U.S. facility follow the distributions shown below:

Loading time, days	Probability	Unloading time, days	Probability
1	.3	1	.2
2	.4	2	.5
3	.3	3	.3

Travel time between ports can be described by the same distribution regardless of which direction the tanker travels:

Travel time, days	Probability
7	.1
8	.2
9	.3
10	.3
11	.1

Each ship can transport 1 billion cubic feet of LNG per trip. Port facilities are such that only one ship at a time can be loaded or unloaded. The current contract calls for supplying 20 billion cubic feet to meet peak winter demands; the East Coast storage facility has a capacity of 20 billion cubic feet.

Five tankers have been leased, at a cost of $12,000 per day, and are scheduled to arrive for initial loading at the Middle East port at 2-day intervals. The leasing cost does not begin until the ships reach the Middle Eastern port.

Simulate the delivery of the 20 billion cubic feet of LNG, providing answers to the following questions:

a. How long does the delivery process take?

b. What was the total leasing cost for the tankers, if costs end as soon as each ship has unloaded after its fourth trip.

c. What proportion of the cost was spent by ships waiting to be loaded or unloaded?

20-9. Jobs arrive at a computer center with interarrival times that follow an exponential distribution with mean of 2 hours. The computer time required to process each job can be estimated accurately in advance and follows a normal distribution with mean $1\frac{1}{2}$ hours and standard deviation of $\frac{1}{4}$ hour. The computer can work on only one job at a time.

At present the jobs are scheduled on a first-in, first-out (FIFO), or a first-come, first-served, basis but one analyst has recommended that a shortest processing time (SPT) rule (process the job with the smallest processing time first) might provide faster turnaround.

Simulate the operation of the computer system until 20 jobs have been processed using both scheduling rules (FIFO and SPT).

a. What were the utilization rates for the computer during the time of the simulation?

b. How long on average did the 20 jobs that were processed spend in the computer center?

c. Do you feel the relative performance of the two scheduling rules would have been different if the simulation had continued until the *first 20 jobs to arrive* had completed processing and statistics had been measured on those 20 jobs only?

20–10. The Metropolis Sanitation Department is studying the relative efficiency of their refuse collection operations. At present they use a three-worker crew for each truck, which has a capacity of 3.5 tons of refuse. The crew proceeds along a fixed route loading the truck until capacity is reached, at which time the truck travels to a dumping area, unloads, and returns to the route.

The amount of refuse per block follows the distribution shown below:

Tons of refuse per block	Probability
.09	.10
.12	.15
.15	.20
.18	.35
.21	.15
.24	.05

The time to complete a round trip to the dumping site is given by the following distribution:

Time per round trip, minutes	Probability
30	.2
40	.3
45	.3
50	.2

The time to collect the refuse from one block is normally distributed with mean equal to 24 minutes times the number of tons collected and standard deviation of 3 minutes per ton collected.

a. Assuming that each crew puts in 6 hours per shift collecting and transporting refuse, determine the productivity in tons per shift using simulation. Assume that partial truck loads at the end of the shift are left in the truck and not dumped until the truck is filled on the next shift. Trips started to the dump before the end of the shift are completed even though the trip time extends beyond the end of the shift. Also assume that the truck is not sent to the dump site until it has completed the block which pushes the cumulative refuse over the 3.5-ton (approximate) capacity of the truck. Simulate for one truck for one shift of 6 hours.

b. The department is contemplating the purchase of a new-type truck which has a capacity of 5 tons and requires a crew of two. The required time to collect the refuse for one block with this truck crew setup is 36 minutes times the number of tons collected and standard deviation is 10 minutes per ton collected (normal distribution). What is the productivity of tons per shift simulated for one truck for one shift.

    c. For the following operating costs compare the per-shift costs of a fleet of new trucks (two-worker crews) with those for a fleet of old trucks (three-worker crews), assuming that the average amount of refuse to be collected per shift is 38 tons.

Shift labor cost per crew member	$40
Shift operating cost (3.5-ton truck)	$100
Shift operating cost (5-ton truck)	$130

20–11. The Maybridge Movie Company has at present 12 scripts under contract which they wish to film and release for distribution. From past experience the time it takes to complete the filming fits the following distribution:

Time to film, months	Probability
6	.05
7	.10
8	.15
9	.25
10	.30
11	.10
12	.05

    The cash expenses related to filming vary according to the following distributions:

Monthly cash production costs	Probability
$300,000	.15
$400,000	.20
$500,000	.25
$600,000	.20
$700,000	.15
$800,000	.05

    Once the film is released, the length of time it can be shown in movie theaters fits the following distribution:

Length of run in theaters, months	Probability
1	.05
2	.10
3	.15
4	.20
5	.25
6	.15
7	.07
8	.03

The revenue received for films while they are shown in theaters varies according to this distribution:

Monthly revenue	Probability
$500,000	.30
$750,000	.15
$1,000,000	.25
$1,500,000	.15
$2,500,000	.10
$5,000,000	.05

Suppose the company decides to go into production with each of the 12 scripts scheduled at 3-month intervals, releasing the films to the theaters as soon as production is completed.

a. Perform one simulation of the production and showing of these 12 films.

b. Calculate cash flow on a month-by-month basis for your simulation in part *a*.

c. What estimate can you give as to the amount of cash the company will need to obtain from outside sources to finance its production/release plan?

20–12. The Zander Medical Clinic is concerned about maintaining a balance between patient waiting time and utilization of doctors. Under the present system two types of patients are served by the clinic: those with scheduled appointments and "walk-in" patients (those arriving without appointments). A block appointment system is currently used in which six patients are given a scheduled appointment on the hour; for example six would be scheduled for 9 A.M., 6 for 10 A.M., etc.. These scheduled patients would then be seen during the hour following their appointment, in order of their arrival. Frequently, however, patients with appointments fail to arrive. At present 20 percent, on average, of block appointment patients are no-shows.

Walk-in patients arrive throughout the day at a rate of about four per hour (exponential interarrival time). Walk-ins are allowed to see the doctor whenever all scheduled patients during a block have been seen and at least 5 minutes remain before the next block begins. Otherwise they can wait until all scheduled appointments for that day have been seen, as described below. Service time for the doctor to see one of the patients, regardless of type, is exponential with a mean of 8 minutes.

The clinic is considering going to a staggered appointment system in which each patient is given an individual unique appointment time spaced at 10-minute intervals. This individual unique appointment system has been used at other clinics and the no-show rate is expected to be reduced to 10 percent. The new system is expected to have no effect on patient service time or the walk-in patient demand. Walk-ins will be allowed to see the doctor whenever at least 5 minutes remain before the next scheduled patient is due to arrive or in place of a no-show.

The clinic currently schedules patients from 9:00 A.M. until 3:00 A.M. (last block arrives at 2:00 P.M.). Walk-ins that arrive before 3:00 P.M. that were not seen by a doctor prior to 3:00 P.M. are seen after the last scheduled patient for that day. Walk-ins arriving after 3:00 P.M. are given an appointment or told to return tomorrow.

a. Compare these two systems by simulation of a typical day's operation. Assume that scheduled patients arrive on time unless they are no-shows.

b. What differences did you observe in the average waiting time for scheduled patients? For walk-in patients? For all patients?

c. What differences did you observe in the utilization of the doctor?

d. What other measures might you use to make a comparison between the two systems?

20-13. A simulation experiment was run in which the weekly profits generated for one policy of the model were:

Week	Profit	Week	Profit
1	$975	6	$1,043
2	$958	7	$1,091
3	$1,106	8	$1,123
4	$943	9	$1,131
5	$1,041	10	$1,116

a. Plot the data shown above and estimate the length of the transient period.

b. What is your best estimate of the average daily profit for the policy tested?

20-14. The data shown below represent the number of defective parts caught per day by a given inspection policy, as found by two runs of a simulation model. An attempt was made to introduce negative correlation between the runs by using antithetic variates.

Run 1: 10   15   18   15   21   13   16   11   16   10
Run 2: 20   12   9   14   8   17   12   17   11   15

a. Treating each run separately, calculate a mean and a standard error of the estimate.

b. Calculate the degree of correlation between the runs.

c. Use the correlation found in part *b* to find the standard error of the estimate of the mean for the combined runs.

20-15. The simulation model described in problem 20-14 was rerun with a different inspection policy. The two runs for this second policy were positively correlated with those for the first policy (shown in problem 20-14) and an attempt was made to use negative correlation between the two runs for the second policy.

Run 1: 11   17   8   21   14   19   9   15   20   10
Run 2: 17   11   19   6   11   10   17   15   9   20

a. Using both runs for the second policy, estimate the mean number of daily defects. What is the adjusted standard error for that estimate?

b. What is the mean difference between the policies and what is the standard error of that estimate?

Appendix A

Table of Random Digits

32401	40830	14246	08752	94925	96086	35237	46855	76558
09731	08885	60220	40450	37321	95662	13383	27164	94826
83747	73458	62366	66463	74708	78773	52429	26594	22809
67137	95522	86260	70028	98027	71461	16046	45275	88972
95773	05709	97664	93758	13929	94348	10355	32845	79749
13844	79660	71124	42641	44368	53247	77693	71811	36458
47565	37306	02406	47071	35449	63564	39518	62144	61311
18165	30675	14805	95632	42107	47284	56234	12155	81420
45751	03186	23684	16532	89810	45083	00257	56977	99078
91189	69779	26006	77556	65161	77167	86884	63533	38061
81999	05276	26755	15617	35290	60106	84142	67759	77912
15795	40504	23807	59882	29071	62651	58724	27660	30907
60363	58117	94830	48602	43856	87326	20482	93968	37925
58066	00725	09020	30999	76634	57690	03585	47171	29745
57885	79641	74665	02132	32738	91602	03739	54365	98932
60756	23725	59307	49084	95695	23735	56725	18046	07684
35793	23872	73484	55266	79706	95673	15740	10521	33084
22677	05593	20006	08199	55482	45030	64291	88969	34247
33411	60078	62924	18063	35291	33671	25871	44615	34885
94000	69875	88590	96892	20265	17928	35123	08059	71325
17990	09915	47822	29061	06075	53158	42164	59413	11673
83498	37258	98547	28526	87287	34239	32115	47854	97573
60301	76244	44852	54800	52367	27623	01178	23326	11954
58260	60782	51336	99012	49500	62487	02823	26546	96545
54897	17085	48926	47621	75135	35425	71769	30397	83780
38368	80486	00875	00532	21040	17097	10176	00100	51598
71622	30436	94100	64259	26043	83965	68711	31710	65040
52890	60588	47356	03363	77245	49128	13677	16095	16016

Appendix B

Table of Random Normal Numbers

−.36	.79	−.25	1.57	.07
.06	−.79	.99	−.23	−1.06
.24	−1.55	−.20	.75	−.25
1.52	−.57	.72	−.08	.37
1.84	.44	.08	1.20	−.71
−1.21	−1.36	−.82	1.20	.64
−.72	−.38	−.26	2.29	−1.08
.73	1.62	.46	−.60	1.26
−.72	−.17	.41	.02	.28
.63	.34	−.41	.03	−.39
−.79	1.23	.09	.67	−1.24
−.67	−.25	.35	−.57	−.25
−1.34	−1.08	−1.01	−.41	−.40
.50	.97	−1.87	.17	.53
−.46	.05	1.37	.35	−1.54
−1.24	−.62	.35	−1.50	.29
−.35	−.76	2.11	−2.09	−.28
−1.00	.37	−.56	1.42	−.14
.57	−2.00	1.00	−1.54	1.08
.29	−1.89	−.53	−.60	.72
.03	3.29	−.18	1.02	−.68
.36	−.79	.91	−.58	−.79
−1.60	1.38	1.65	−1.06	.57
−1.41	−.87	−.48	.59	−.71
.93	2.61	.40	.65	−1.59
−.61	−1.09	1.31	.68	−.15
−.33	−.11	−1.02	−2.05	.56
2.05	1.13	.95	.27	−.14
−1.44	.53	1.21	.73	.03

21

Management Science and Management Information Systems

Today's managers are faced with decision problems of growing complexity and challenge. As we move into the final decades of the twentieth century, the number of factors affecting managerial decisions will continue to increase. The increasing demands of international competition, rapid technological change, the ever-changing role of government in the marketplace and in other business activities, the effects of reduced availability of natural resources on production cost and capacity, and escalating interest rates are only a few of the factors that will have to be accounted for. Compounding the problem is the fact that simple solutions will no longer work. The interrelationships between the factors call for a more integrated approach.

This increase in decision-making complexity has led to demands for better information to provide the basis for deciding about such interacting factors. The need for more sophisticated procedures for making interrelated decisions has increased. The major purpose of this text has been to examine the role that management science can play in helping managers deal with complex decision situations. In preceding chapters we consider a number of decision models and solution approaches appropriate for multifactor situations. In this chapter we examine, in general terms, the relationship of management science models and *management information systems* (*MIS*). In recent years it has become common to refer to management information systems that contain management science models and solution capabilities as *management decision support systems*.

The purpose of this chapter is to explore the joint role that management science models and management information systems play in aiding and augmenting management decision making capabilities. To accomplish this objective, we will begin by discussing the nature of management information systems. This will involve a description of the major elements of an information system and the role each plays in the acquisition, processing, and use of information, or data. A major focus in this discussion will be on the decision-making utilization of management information systems. We conclude the chapter with an overview of the interaction between management science models and management information systems.

Structure of Management Information Systems

Figure 21-1 provides a simplified, abstract view of a management information system. Note the central portion occupied by the data base. The other portions of the system either provide new information to the data base or draw on information that already exists in the data base. These include data collection or acquisition, standard processing, report writing, and decision support functions. Each of these will be considered in more detail in the sections that follow.

Data Base

The data base normally consists of data files, which contain sets of records, each record containing individual data elements. The *data elements* correspond to numeric and descriptive data, such as inventory balances, customers' names, employee mailing addresses, etc. A *data record* contains a set of related data elements. Thus, an inventory record will contain information (in the form of data elements) related to a specific inventory item, a customer record will contain information related to a specific customer, and an employee record will contain information related to a specific employee. A *data file* contains a set of related data records. For instance, the inventory file will contain all the inventory records, the customer file will consist of all customer records, and the personnel file will include all the individual employee records.

A data base is illustrated in Figure 21-2, where we show an accounts re-

FIGURE 21-1   Abstract view of management information system.

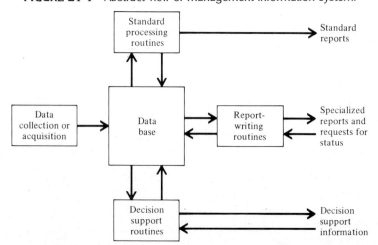

741

MANAGEMENT
SCIENCE AND
MANAGEMENT
INFORMATION
SYSTEMS

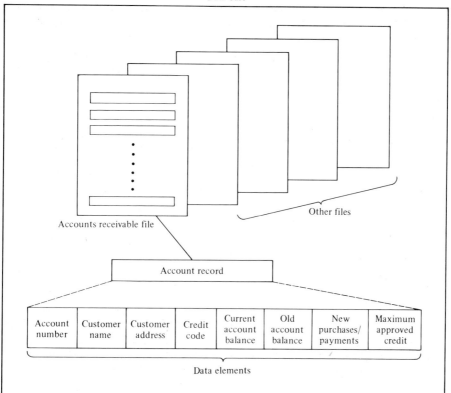

FIGURE 21-2 Relationship of data elements to records and files in a company's data base.

ceivable file, which contains individual account records for all charge customers, typical of that for a retail store. Each individual account record for a customer contains all information relevant to that account, including account number, customer's name and address, current balance, maximum approved credit, balance at time of last billing, new purchases and payments made since date of last billing, and so on.

A typical data base will have many files similar to that described here. The files usually also include sales data, inventory status files, accounts payable files, purchasing files, and so on.

Data Collection

To the left of Figure 21-1 we show that data or information that makes up the data base must somehow be collected and added to the data base. We have referred to this portion of the management information system as *data collection or acquisition*. This is frequently one of the most expensive portions of the system. Most systems typically require the collection of a large volume of information. Furthermore, a computer stores and processes data electronically. This requires that the data be recorded in a form that can be automatically converted to electronic impulses. This can be done by preparing punched cards, punched paper tapes, magnetic tapes, etc. Unfortunately, this preparation step is quite labor-intensive, which adds greatly to the data acquisition cost.

Many technological changes have occurred in this area in recent years that have lowered the data acquisition cost. In particular, the widespread use of *point-of-transaction input devices* has had a significant impact. These devices permit direct capture of information related to each transaction at the time it occurs and in a form that can be read directly by the computer without any intermediate keypunching or machine coding. Their use has lowered the cost of data collection to the point where data gathering that was previously uneconomical can now be done.

For example, a major retail book chain is able to maintain up-to-date inventory status of all titles stocked by its hundreds of retail stores through point-of-sale capture of sales information. Each book has attached to it a computer-generated stock number. When a book is sold, the cashier enters this code number on the cash register, and the number is then recorded by the register. At the close of each business day, the company's central computer phones each store and the sales information captured by the register is then transmitted directly to the central computer. Once all stores have been contacted and the day's sales recorded, the central computer processes the data to update the current inventory status for each item as well as to provide item-by-item sales information for the system of stores. This information can be analyzed for management to detect important trends and adjust purchase patterns accordingly. The availability of store-by-store inventory status allows the company to meet stockouts in one store by shipments from a nearby store which has the item in stock.

Point-of-transaction capture of data is not limited to retail sales. Many manufacturing companies use similar systems to capture information concerning work performed and job status. This is done in a timely manner via input terminals distributed throughout the manufacturing plant. For example, if an employee completed work on a particular job, transferring it to some other department, the information, such as employee number, employee's department, type of work performed, time to complete the work, and so on, would be entered by the employee at one of these terminals. This information would be sent directly to the computer so that such information could be used to update the data base reflecting the job's current status, as well as updating payroll and other related files.

Preparation of Standard Reports

At the top of Figure 21-1 is shown another segment of management information systems, the performance of standardized, *routine information processing* and the generation of standardized reports. This segment, because of the volume of such standardized processing, represents the bulk of the computer's work in any management information system. Much of this work is routine, involving the updating of files, records, and data elements contained in the data base. The updating of item-by-item inventory status for our retail bookstore chain and the changes reflected in job status and payroll records for our manufacturing firm are examples of such routine data-base maintenance operations. Despite the routine nature of such processing, it is of considerable importance. Unless the data base reflects the current status of the firm's operations, with accuracy and timeliness, any decision based on information contained in the data base may be made incorrectly.

As you will note in Figure 21-1, the output of the standardized processing segment are the numerous standardized, periodic reports. These reports reflect the need for periodic status information used for routine decision making or various external or internal reporting requirements. The preparation of balance sheets, income statements, stock status reports, customer billings, payroll checks, payments to suppliers, and so on, are examples of this category of report preparation.

743

MANAGEMENT
SCIENCE AND
MANAGEMENT
INFORMATION
SYSTEMS

For the retail bookstore chain, the previously mentioned current sales information and out-of-stock reports would be examples of standard output. For the manufacturing firm a variety of reports can be generated routinely. These might include a job status report (showing the current location and status of each job), a labor efficiency report (comparing hours worked in each work center with workload completed), a quality control report (showing defects detected by work center), etc.

One difficulty with standard, automatic routines that should be recognized is the need for careful audits. Because much of the processing carried out with an information system is done by a computer, the opportunity exists for fraudulent and unauthorized manipulation. The growing evidence of such so-called computer crime is warning enough that management can no longer rely on the computer's reputation for accuracy. A computer will accurately and faithfully carry out what it is programmed to do. A clever person with fraudulent intent can easily use the computer for unlawful purposes. Thus, management must build information systems with careful safeguards and auditing capabilities designed to protect against and detect such fraud.

Exception Reports

An important capability of any management information system is the preparation of what are called *exception reports*. Exception reporting is a means of providing selective status information, and frequently suggests a need for action. Exception reports are often used to identify situations requiring specific action or investigation. For example, the accounts receivable or inventory status files for many companies contain thousands of records detailing the current status of customer accounts and inventory positions. At any point in time, only a small number of these records require any action or decision making, such as sending payment reminder notices to delinquent accounts or preparing purchase orders for inventory items in need of replenishment. It would be senseless to ask for a list of all customer account records and then search through that list manually to determine which accounts need payment reminder notices. Similarly, a search through a list of all inventory records to find those items needing replenishment would also be unnecessary. In both of these examples it is much easier to request the computer to do the search and prepare a list of *only* those accounts behind in payments or those inventory items requiring replenishment. Such exception-reporting capability is a standard feature with most management information systems.

We should point out that management review and intervention is normally a requisite part of exception-reporting schemes. That is, although the computer reports the *need* to take action (customers behind in payments or inventory items with on-hand balances below the reorder point), such action is usually not taken automatically without management review. Thus, management might decide to exclude payment reminder notices to customers in the New York area because equipment failure at the New York regional post office may have delayed the receipt and recording of payments from customers in that area. Similarly, management may decide not to prepare replenishment orders for a group of inventory items because these items are used exclusively in a product now being phased out. Thus, management must take responsibility for exceptions that are difficult to handle automatically.

Management science models are frequently built into some of the standard or exception-reporting schemes in management information systems. Two prime examples are the use of forecasting models and inventory models. Forecasting models can be used for many purposes, such as providing demand projections for budgeting purposes, production and distribution planning, inventory analysis, and so on. In Chapter 15 we discussed several types of inventory systems, including perpetual, periodic, and material requirements planning. Exception reports are often used with these systems. An example would be the identification of inventory items whose current balance exceeds projected needs for, say, the next 6 months. Our retail bookstore chain might use an exception-reporting approach to identify all books that have not sold during, say, the last 6 months. These items might then be recalled from the stores for return to the publisher for credit against future purchases.

Obtaining Nonstandard Information

On the right side of Figure 21-1 appears another major use of management information systems—the generation of nonstandard information for decision making. Generally, this use can be divided into two categories: preparing specialized, nonperiodic reports and furnishing status information on demand. In both cases the information required is drawn from the data base and organized as necessary to satisfy a management request. Frequently, however, the two types of requests require different types of processing, as discussed below.

Specialized Nonperiodic Reports   Preparing *nonstandard reports* is usually accomplished through the use of a special report-generator program. This program allows the user to define what information is to be included in the report, how it is to be organized, and the form in which it is to be presented. The definition of what information is to be included is usually accomplished by reference to predefined key words, which identify the nature of the information, the level of detail, and the time period to be covered.

For example, suppose a publisher is offering a special discount for orders placed in the coming month. The purchasing manager for our retail bookstore chain would like to take advantage of this discount by ordering books from the publisher that have good sales records. To help the manager decide which titles to order, a special report could be prepared showing sales for each book sold by this publisher. This might be done using a report generator by entering a simple command with the appropriate key words, such as

LIST SALES.P14.JAN-MAR.1980 BY TITLE

For this example, P14 is a code identifying the publisher and the other key words are self-explanatory. The report asked for will show sales for each title by this publisher for the period January through March, 1980. The coding shown above is hypothetical; the exact form and coding required would depend on the report generator being used and the coding scheme defined for that data base.

745

MANAGEMENT
SCIENCE AND
MANAGEMENT
INFORMATION
SYSTEMS

Providing Status Information on Demand   Providing *status information on demand* is one information system function that should be familiar to all. Airline reservation systems are an example. These systems provide the ability to determine current operational status information about a company that can be used in guiding employees' actions or in decision making. For example, an airline reservations clerk can determine, in response to a request for a seat reservation on a specific flight, whether seats are available. If seats are available, the clerk can then enter information concerning that passenger into the data base, thereby reserving a seat on the desired flight. This information can then be accessed later for purposes of issuing a ticket, canceling the reservation, informing the passenger of a delay, etc.

Similar systems can be used in other situations. For example, a request for inventory status information can be made by a salesperson to determine whether or not a particular order can be shipped directly from stock. A bank teller can check a customer's account balance before allowing that customer to make a withdrawal. In some situations, even the customer has access to status information. Many banks now use computer-controlled, 24-hour machine tellers. The customer, using a machine-readable bank card, can obtain personal status information concerning checking and savings account balances or even change the status by withdrawing or transferring funds.

Management science models can also be used in helping with decisions based on this status information. The airline reservations situation is an example. In Chapter 20 we considered the Wings Airline overbooking decision problem. A simulation model was used to establish the appropriate level of overbooking to be used. A second example relates to computerized seat assignment. For safety reasons it is important that seats be assigned to passengers in a balanced pattern. This ensures that passenger weight is approximately evenly balanced. Management science models can be used to dynamically balance the weight distribution while meeting the passengers' smoking/nonsmoking and window/aisle preferences.

Decision Support Routines

At the bottom of Figure 21-1 appears a segment that provides *decision support information*. We should note that both the standard processing and report-writing routines furnish information that is used in making decisions. In general, however, the type of information provided by these routines is limited to past and current status or short-run projections. We show a separate decision support segment to highlight the use of the information system in dealing with medium- to long-run decisions and the information necessary to make them. These routines will make use of information about past or current status. However, they tend to be more forward-looking and therefore frequently require detailed information describing expected or hypothetical future situations.

A management support system, or decision support system, generally includes a model, a data base, and a solution procedure. Such a system is used to provide information that supports or is useful in making managerial decisions and almost always is computer-based. The *model* as it is used here can be similar to many of the management science models described in this text or it can be more complex. Such models are intended to be a description of the process to be managed, such as the manufacturing and distribution system for a firm. The data base contains the relevant information necessary to describe the parameters of the system of interest. Such information might include demand patterns (i.e., seasonality, trend, etc.), cost information, manufacturing lead times, etc. Frequently the data required is provided from two sources. Past historical data and current status information is normally drawn from the company's data base. Future, projected or hypothetical information is usually provided by the users of the decision support system or by forecasting procedures, as discussed in Chapters 18 and 19.

The solution procedure used to determine the consequences of possible actions can take many forms. The procedure may be nothing more than a descriptive exploration, similar to those provided by a simulation model. In other cases an optimization routine, such as linear programming, may be used to optimize some designated performance measure. In still other cases, systematic search routines can be used to determine a set of policies necessary to achieve a prespecified target level for a designated performance measure. For instance, management might be interested in determining the annual sales volume necessary for a specific product in order to achieve a target profit of, say, 10 percent on sales.

For an illustration, recall that in Chapter 13 we discussed the warehouse location problem. That problem required a decision about the number and location of distribution warehouses in order to minimize distribution costs. The rapid growth in transportation costs in recent years has increased the significance of this decision problem for many firms. The warehouse location decision can be made more effectively if the cost, capacity, and demand data are representative of future expected patterns, rather than limited to past or current patterns.

Management science can play an important role in these decision support routines in several ways. Forecasting models can be used to project future environments. Thus, in the warehouse location case, we might use exponential smoothing or linear regression to project future product demand. Many of the various management science decision-making approaches can be used to determine the effectiveness of potential alternatives for these future environments. For example, the add and drop heuristics discussed in Chapter 13 might be used to determine low-cost warehouse location alternatives for anticipated or projected transportation costs, warehouse operating costs, factory capacities, and product demands.

Alternatively a simulation approach might be used to explore the impact of hypothesized future environments on available decision alternatives. A simulation model might be developed in the warehouse location situation that would permit the use of various future demand patterns, cost behavior options, and so on.

Corporate Planning Models   The model component of a management information system can be fairly simple and focused on a specific decision problem or it can be complex and directed at more general decision situations. The warehouse location situation is an example of a simpler, specific type of model.

Many companies have developed or are now developing more complex models, which are called *corporate planning models*, or some variation on that theme. These models attempt to describe the overall operation of a firm, including marketing, production, distribution, and finance functions.

747

MANAGEMENT
SCIENCE AND
MANAGEMENT
INFORMATION
SYSTEMS

A number of firms have reported successful use of corporate planning models. United Air Lines, for example, employs such a model to evaluate the financial impact on the firm of such actions as modifications to air fares, changes in the fleet of aircraft, increases in the price of jet fuel, and so on. The *New York Times* uses a planning model to forecast future advertising demand and circulation levels. A Swedish shipbuilder uses a planning model to determine which currencies to use when buying raw materials and which to use when selling the ships. Others such as Monsanto, Pennzoil, and Mobil use planning models to forecast cash requirements.[1]

Although corporate planning models are designed to fit specific organizations, we can obtain a general view of the structure and use of these models by examining one of the general-purpose planning systems.

Typically these systems contain three main elements: (1) data base, (2) modeling system, and (3) report writer. The data base for the corporate planning system is usually independent of the firm's principal data base maintained as part of the information system. This is because much of the data used by the corporate planning model is hypothetical future data, either entered by the user of the model or generated by the model itself. Historical data can, of course, also be used.

The modeling system is the heart of the corporate planning model. It is this system that describes the elements and relationships of the corporate model. The model typically contains both definitional and behavioral relationships. Thus, we might include a definition of total assets for the firm as the sum of cash, inventory value, accounts receivable, and fixed assets. Behavioral relationships reflect the assumed behavioral response of one or more elements in the firm to changes in other factors. These might reflect automatic decisions such as assuming that advertising expenditures will be equal to 5 percent of sales revenue. Or they might reflect external factors, such as assuming that 60 percent of sales in any month will be for cash and the remaining 40 percent will be an addition to accounts receivable.

In many cases the corporate planning models will focus on modeling the financial behavior of the firm. These models center around the items found in the firm's balance sheet and income statement and measure hypothetical financial flows. Marketing and production segments are included, but they typically provide projected sales revenues and marketing and production costs.

A typical model might require demand projections for, say, a 5-year period. These projections would be used for the marketing segment of the model to determine sales revenues and marketing expenditures for each of these 5 years. Next, the production segment of the model would calculate the production costs and inventory projections for this same period. The financial segment would use the marketing and production projections to prepare pro-forma, or projected, balance sheets and income statements for these periods.

The report-writing segment of a corporate planning system allows the user to define specific reports to be generated by the system. Thus, the user can

---

[1]Thomas H. Naylor, "Why Corporate Planning Models," *Interfaces*, vol. 8, no. 1 (November 1977), pp. 87–94.

select those items of interest that are to be reported, the time periods to be covered by the report, and the printing format to be used for the reports to be produced.

Corporate planning systems often offer a variety of ways in which the models can be used. The most frequent option is the ability to answer "what if" questions. In this case, the user can specify alternative future environments and use the model to project the firm's performance, assuming these environments. For example, the user might ask "what will our net profit after taxes be if demand increases at a rate of 5 percent per year for the next 5 years?" In practice, the user may wish to examine much more complex hypothetical situations than indicated above. In addition to demand growth patterns, the user may wish to specify alternatives for labor cost, material cost, financing plans, depreciation methods, and so on. Using multiple alternatives, or options, such as these is often facilitated by the use of an *option menu*. The "menu" shows a variety of options from which the user may select those desired. The speed of the computer in incorporating these options and carrying out the required calculations allows the user to explore many more alternatives than could be done manually.

Incorporating Management Science Models   Decision support systems can be developed internally, by a company's management science personnel, or they can be obtained from outside services, in the form of standardized or tailor-made systems. The degree to which internal and external sources are relied on depends upon the nature of the company and the problem being dealt with. Larger companies are much more likely to have their own management science professionals and to rely less on outside sources. Nevertheless, even large firms will make use of commercially available models, systems, and data. This is particularly true in the area of data which would be too costly or impractical to gather for use by one company alone but is economical when the cost is shared by a number of companies.

For example, Lever Brothers used internal and external sources to develop a complex system for determining low-cost shipment patterns. Each night the system examines that day's incoming customer orders and determines shipment routings for each order using a commercially available automatic routing system. Then the system considers alternative ways of combining these orders to cut costs. The customer orders are transmitted to the appropriate warehouse together with recommendations for combining or pooling orders for shipment. The warehouse manager can then accept or reject these recommendations.[1]

General-purpose management science models, such as linear programming, inventory control, and forecasting models, are also frequently obtained from outside sources. Some of these models, such as inventory control and forecasting, are incorporated directly into a firm's management information system. In this way they are used to update the data base and provide standard and nonstandard reports. Other approaches, such as linear programming, project planning and control procedures, simulation, and so on are mainly segregated from the company's information system for use on an as-needed basis in providing decision support information. In some cases the computer package

[1]"Saving Money When Freight Rates are Computerized," *Business Week*, Feb. 25, 1980, pp. 111, 114.

for implementing these procedures is developed internally by the firm's own management science personnel. This is particularly true of large companies and where the application would require significant modification to the commercially available packages.

749

MANAGEMENT
SCIENCE AND
MANAGEMENT
INFORMATION
SYSTEMS

Interaction between Management Science and Management Information Systems

It is important to understand the relationship between management science models and management information systems. The design and implementation of one influences the other. This influence or interaction occurs in several ways. One of the most important dependencies concerns the data base. As should now be evident, any management science model requires that a specific set of data be provided. For instance, a typical inventory control model would need data concerning anticipated demand, ordering costs, holding cost, lead time, and so on. To implement this model requires a data base capable of providing this information.

Such shared data requirements can influence the design of both the information system and the management science model. If the current data base does not provide the data necessary for implementing the management science model (a more common situation than you might think), either the information system will have to be modified to include the needed data or the model will have to be redesigned to use what information is available. The best choice will depend on the relevant costs of modifying the data base and of using an adjusted model.

Data-base modification costs include the cost of modifying the information system itself, the cost of obtaining the needed data, and the cost of updating the data. The cost of using a modified management science model is more difficult to estimate. The costs depend upon the type of modification used. These modifications include using a heuristic decision-making procedure instead of an optimizing method, applying the model using aggregate rather than detailed data, subdividing an interrelated decision problem into several subproblems that are solved independently, using the model for a subset of the potentially applicable situations, etc. Frequently, a simulation or other controlled sample model can be developed that will help analyze the impact of using an adjusted management science model.

For an illustration, suppose a company is considering using an EOQ inventory ordering policy. The company at present uses a fixed ordering policy requiring that each item be ordered four times per year. The implementation costs, including costs of the data base and of processing system redesign, are expected to include a one-time cost of $100,000 as well as an extra $70,000 per year if the EOQ system is adopted. The key issue is whether these costs will be offset by savings in inventory cost.

To answer this question, suppose the company took a sample of five inventory items that it felt were representative of the company's inventory. Table 21-1 shows a comparison of ordering policies, inventory levels, and costs for both the current system and the proposed EOQ system. Total inventory costs for the five items are estimated to drop from $1,985 to $880 per year if the present system is replaced by an EOQ system. To project these savings for the en-

TABLE 21-1
Estimating Annual Savings in Inventory Costs for Proposed EOQ System*

| Item | Annual demand | Present system | | Proposed EOQ system | |
		Orders per year	Average inventory	Orders per year	Average inventory
1	$40,000	4	$5,000	25.0	$800
2	$10,000	4	$1,250	12.5	$400
3	$6,400	4	$800	10.0	$320
4	$1,600	4	$200	5.0	$160
5	$400	4	$50	2.5	$80
	$58,400	20	7,300	55.0	$1,760

Estimated annual costs
for present system $= 20(\$8) + .25(7,300) = 160 + 1,825 = \$1,985$

Estimated annual costs
for proposed system $= 55(\$8) + .25(1,760) = 440 + 440 = \$880$

*Assumes $8 cost per order and 25 percent holding cost rate per year.

tire system, the firm needs to know the proportion of all inventory items that these five items represent. Suppose these five items are equivalent to 1 percent of the total inventory. Then the EOQ approach should yield savings equal to 100 times those obtained for the five-item sample, or

Projected annual savings
for EOQ system $= 100 \, (\$1,985 - \$880) = \$110,500$

In this case the annual savings for the EOQ model of $110,500 are expected to exceed the costs of modifying and operating the information system ($70,000). Management must decide whether these annual savings are sufficient to justify the $100,000 one-time cost of system conversion. If they decide that the savings are not sufficient, the EOQ model might have to be abandoned or modified. One modification that might be considered, for example, is to continue using the current ordering policy for all items except those with high annual usage. A modified EOQ system could be implemented for the high-dollar-volume items at a lower information system cost and might thus be economical.

Another interaction that occurs between management science models and information systems relates to decision-making requirements. If the management information system is to be used to aid the decision-making process for a particular problem, a number of options usually exist. These options can be examined by considering the roles to be played in the decision-making process by the decision maker, the management science model, and the management information system. The potential roles to be filled include the provider of the data, the generator of the alternatives, the analyzer of the alternatives, the selector of a decision, and the implementer of the decision.

Table 21-2 illustrates six possible role assignments, ranging from a completely unsupported system to one that is completely automated. At the top of the figure we show a situation, category 1, in which all the steps from data gathering to decision implementation are carried out by the decision maker. Since no support is provided by the information system or a management science model we refer to this role assignment as completely unsupported.

751

MANAGEMENT
SCIENCE AND
MANAGEMENT
INFORMATION
SYSTEMS

Category 2 shows that the decision maker draws information from the data base maintained by the information system. This information could be obtained in a variety of ways, such as from standard reports or from specialized nonperiodic reports.

Category 3 uses a management science model to provide automatic analysis of the alternatives selected by the decision maker. In this case the model is used in a descriptive, or what-if, mode to provide quick and accurate analyses for use by the decision maker in selecting and implementing a decision.

The role of the management science model is expanded in category 4 to include automatic generation of alternatives. The alternatives can be generated exhaustively (e.g., by complete enumeration) or selectively (e.g., by the use of heuristics). The burden of decision selection and implementation rests with the decision maker. Such an approach is particularly useful for problems with multiple objectives or with an explosively large number of alternatives.

The role of the management science model is expanded again for category 5, allowing the model to select the best decision. This category would include the use of optimizing approaches such as linear programming. The decision maker's role has been reduced to that of implementation, although the decision maker often has the authority to overrule the model.

Category 6 represents those situations in which automatic decision rules are used for decision making. Thus, the management science model, using data

TABLE 21-2
Optional Roles Played by Decision Maker, Management Science Model (MS Model), and Management Information System (MIS) in General Decision-Making Process

Category	Data provided by	Alternatives analyzed by	Alternatives generated by	Decision selected by	Decision implemented by	Type of system
1	←———————————— Decision maker ————————————→					Completely unsupported
2	MIS	←———————— Decision maker ————————→				Information support
3	MIS	MS model	←———— Decision maker ————→			Automatic analysis of alternatives
4	MIS	←——MS model——→		←—Decision maker—→		Automatic generation and analysis of alternatives
5	MIS	←————MS model————→			Decision maker	Systematized decision making with decision maker override
6	MIS	←———— MS model ————→			MIS	Automatic decision rule

provided by the information system, generates and evaluates alternatives and selects a decision which is automatically implemented by the information system. This category requires no external intervention by the decision maker. An example of such a system would be an automated inventory system. Once a reordering situation has been recognized, the order quantity would be determined by an appropriate management science model. The information system could then implement the decision by preparing a purchase order for that item.

The situations we have described above are typical of the approaches followed by many firms. However, you should recognize that there are many variations that can be made to these categories. The automatic implementation described for the sixth category can be overridden, for example. This is often accomplished through the use of exception reports. These reports identify those decisions which violate one or more guidelines and therefore call for management intervention. For example, a company may have established an inventory policy that only in exceptional cases will an order be placed for more than 1 year's supply of an item. Thus, orders for any items that exceed this guideline will not be carried out automatically but will be listed on an exception report for review by management.

The roles of the decision maker and the management science model are somewhat understated by the categorization of Table 21-2. Management plays a major role in the design and development of both the information system and the management science model. Furthermore, management science models can be used in nonautomatic situations. Recall that the first category (completely unsupported) assigns the decision maker all tasks from data gathering to implementation. In practice, the decision maker may rely on manual use of management science models to help in the analysis or decision selection process. An example here would be the use of decision trees to assist in an otherwise unsupported decision situation.

We should note that there are two trends related to the relative roles of management science, management information systems, and management. One is the use of more automation in the decision-making process as represented by the lower categories in Table 21-2. A second is the substitution of more complex and sophisticated management models at all levels.

There are three factors accounting for these trends. The continuing improvements in computers and information systems has played an obvious part. Phenomenal increases in speed and memory capacity continue to be accompanied by a rapid decline in cost.

The second factor is the continued development of management science methodology. This includes the development of new models to meet new decision situations, better models to meet old situations, and more efficient procedures for finding solutions.

The third factor is the recognition by management of the advantages that can be obtained by the use of computerized management science models. This recognition has come about because managerial receptivity to computer-based technology has increased and because of the ineffectiveness of traditional decision-making approaches in dealing with the increasing complexity of decision problems. The objective of this text has been to provide you with the knowledge needed to exploit the valuable contributions that management science can provide.

Key Words

Audit **743**
Corporate planning model **746**
Data base **740**
Data collection **741**
Data element **740**
Data file **740**
Data record **740**
Decision support information **745**
Exception report **743**
Information **739**
Intervention **743**
Key word **744**
Management decision support
  system **739**

Management information system
  (MIS) **739**
MIS **739**
Nonstandard report **744**
Option menu **748**
Point-of-transaction input device **742**
Routine information processing **742**
Specialized nonperiodic report **744**
Standard report **742**
Status information on demand **745**
What-if question **748**

Index

(*Continued from inside front cover*)

Management science model An abstract representation of a managerial decision problem, usually expressed mathematically or symbolically.

Managerial decision problem A situation requiring the selection of a decision alternative that best meets a decision objective in a managerial setting.

Marginal resource value The improvement in the objective function for a linear programming problem that would result if one additional unit of a constrained resource is made available.

Markovian model A forecasting model in which the steady-state behavior can be determined solely from the prior-state transition probabilities.

Material requirements planning system An inventory control system which calculates requirements for individual item replenishment on the basis of a master assembly schedule for end items and bills of material.

Mean absolute deviation (MAD) The average absolute difference in value between a set of observations and the mean or average of those observations.

Mean squared error (MSE) The average squared difference between a set of observations and the mean or average of those observations.

Method of least squares A procedure for obtaining parameters for a forecasting model in which the parameters are chosen so as to minimize the sum of the squared forecast errors.

Minimal spanning tree problem The least-cost set of joined routes that provide a path from any one activity in a network to every other activity.

Monte Carlo method A procedure used to generate random variables from a uniform probability distribution which transforms these variables to ones that correspond to some other probability distribution.

Moving average model A forecasting model that bases forecasts on either a weighted or unweighted average of a limited set of past observations.

Multiple-objective decision problem A decision problem with more than one (often conflicting) objective.

Multiple-server model A descriptive model of a service system which includes more than one server, generally with identical service rates.

Net-change value The difference between entering gain and entering cost for a nonbasic variable as used with the linear programming simplex method. It is equivalent to the change in the objective function resulting from a one-unit increase in that nonbasic variable.

Network flow problem A class of problems that can be graphically represented as a network.

Nonbasic variable A variable with a zero value for a feasible solution to a linear programming problem.

Normative forecasting model A qualitative forecasting model which is used to identify desired objectives or potential states in the future and which then works backward to show how these can be achieved.

Northwest-corner method A procedure for finding an initial feasible solution to a transportation problem. The procedure begins by allocating the maximum amount to the transportation route appearing in the northwest (upper left) corner from which it derives its name.

Objective function An equation that specifies the dependent relationship between the decision objective and the decision variables.

Opportunity cost The difference between the outcome value earned by a decision alternative and that which could be earned by the best alternative.

Outcome The result achieved by selecting a specific decision alternative when a particular uncontrollable event occurs. This result is usually measured in terms of the decision objective.

Parameter An element in a management science model that, when given a precise value, fits that model to a specific real-world problem. Parameters include such factors as costs, resource utilization rates, capacities, arrival rates, and trends.

Perfect information Information that allows a decision maker to know exactly which uncontrollable event is to occur.

Pivot element Used with the simplex method for solving linear programming problems, the pivot element corresponds to the rate at which the departing variable will decline in value for a one-unit increase in the value of the entering variable.

Precedence relationship A requirement that one activity (predecessor activity) must precede or be accomplished prior to another activity (successor activity). In graphical terms, where activities are represented by nodes in a network, a precedence relationship is indicated by an arrow, or directed arc, from the predecessor activity to the successor activity.

Project activities Basic elements, tasks, or jobs that are required to be completed as part of a project.